SOUTH-WESTERN
CENGAGE Learning

Transportation: A Supply Chain Perspective, Seventh edition

John J. Coyle, Robert A. Novack, Brian J. Gibson and Edward J. Bardi

Executive Vice President and Publisher, Business & Computers: Jonathan Hulbert

Vice President of Editorial, Business: Jack W. Calhoun

Editor-in-Chief: Joe Sabatino

Senior Acquisitions Editor: Charles E. McCormick, Jr.

Developmental Editor: Julie Klooster

Vice President of Marketing, Business & Computers: Bill Hendee

Marketing Coordinator: Suellen Ruttkay

Editorial Assistant: Nora Heink

Content Project Manager: Melena Fenn

Production Manager: Jennifer Ziegler

Media Editor: Chris Valentine

Frontlist Buyer, Manufacturing: Miranda Klapper

Senior Art Director: Stacy Jenkins Shirley

Production Service: Pre-PressPMG

Cover Designer: Lou Ann Thesing

Internal Designer: Patti Hudepohl

Cover Images: iStock Photo/Getty Images

Printer: RR Donnelley/Von Hoffmann

Sr. Text Rights Acquisitions Account Manager: Mardell Glinski Schultz

Text Permissions Researcher: Sarah D'Stair

...ur families. John Coyle would like ... and their grandchildren Lauren, ...ary. Bob Novack would like ...h, and Alex. Brian Gibson ...ardi would like to thank ... grandchildren Maggie, ...atherine.

Printed in the United States of America

1 2 3 4 5 6 7 14 13 12 11 10

Brief Contents

Contents

Part II

Part III

Preface

Transportation has continued to gain importance in firms and in our economy since the last edition of this book in 2006. The United States has seen an increased importance placed on transportation security both within and outside its borders. The dramatic volatility in worldwide fuel prices has put a strain on transportation costs and capacity. All of these events have shown that transportation might be the most critical, and yet the most vulnerable, component of global supply chains.

In the 7th edition we have tried to capture, as best as possible, the new transportation environment in both the domestic and global arenas. The addition of a new author—Brian Gibson—has allowed us to bring new insights to transportation and highlight some of the emerging trends in the field.

In keeping with these changes, we have organized the 14 chapters of this book into three parts. Part I offers an overview of transportation to the reader. Chapters 1 (micro) and 2 (macro) offers insights into the importance of transportation to the firm and to our economy, respectively. Chapter 3 provides a discussion of the regulatory and public policy framework that helped shape and continues to influence transportation in the United States. Chapter 4 offers a basic discussion of the economics of transportation costing and pricing in a free market economy.

Providers of transportation service are the focus of Part II. The five basic modes of transportation are covered in Chapter 5 (motor carriers), Chapter 6 (railroads), Chapter 7 (airlines), and Chapter 8 (bulk carriers—water and pipeline). Each modal chapter offers an in-depth view of the industry, its competitors, its advantages, and its challenges. The purpose of this part is to provide the reader with a thorough understanding of the diversity and similarities of the basic modes of transportation.

The chapters in Part III are new and represent emerging transportation management issues. Chapter 9 addresses the concept of transportation risk management with a focus on transportation and national security. Chapters 10 and 11 explain global transportation planning and global transportation execution, respectively. Chapter 12 explains the roles and industry composition of third-party logistics providers. Chapter 13, which was included in early editions of this text, has been brought back because of the growing importance of private transportation and fleet management. Finally, Chapter 14 provides insights into issues and challenges facing global supply chains.

Features

1. Learning objectives in the beginning of each chapter provide students with an overall perspective of chapter material and also serve to establish a baseline for a working knowledge of the topics that follow.

2. Transportation Profile boxes are the opening vignettes at the beginning of each chapter that introduce students to the chapter's topics through familiar, real-world examples.

3. On the Line features are applied, concrete examples that provide students with hands-on managerial experience of the chapter topics.

4. Transportation Technology boxes help students relate technological developments to transportation management concepts.

5. Global Perspectives boxes highlight the activities and importance of transportation outside of the United States.

6. End-of-chapter Summaries and Study Questions reinforce material presented in each chapter.

7. Short cases at the end of each chapter build on what students have learned. Questions that follow the cases sharpen critical thinking skills.

Ancillaries

The *Instructor's Resource CD* (ISBN 1-439-08006-2) contains three essential resources:

1. The *Instructor's Manual* includes chapter outlines, answers to end-of-chapter study questions, commentary on end-of-chapter short cases, and teaching tips.

2. A convenient *Test Bank* offers a variety of multiple-choice, short-answer, and essay questions for each chapter.

3. *PowerPoint slides* cover the main chapter topics and contain figures from the main text.

4. The book companion site (www.cengage.com/decisionsciences/coyle) provides additional resources for students and instructors. Appendix A, Selected Transportation Publications, and Appendix B, Transportation-Related Associations, can be found on the companion site. The Instructor's Manual and PowerPoint files are downloadable from the site for instructors.

Acknowledgements

The authors are indebted to many individuals at our respective academic institutions as well as other individuals with whom we have had contact in a variety of venues. Our university students and our executive program students have provided an important sounding board for the many concepts, techniques, metrics, and strategies presented in the book. Our faculty and corporate colleagues have provided invaluable insights and appropriate criticism of our ideas. Some individuals deserve special consideration: Danielle Gallagher (Penn State), Ms. Jean Beierlein (Penn State), Ms. Tracie Shannon (Penn State), and Kusumal Ruamsook (Penn State). The authors would also like to thank the following fellow faculty members for their insightful contributions to several chapters in this text: John C. Spychalski, Professor Emeritus of Supply Chain Management (Penn State), Joe Hanna, Professor of Supply Chain Management (Auburn), and Wesley Randall, Assistant Professor of Supply Chain Management (Auburn).

We extend our appreciation to the members of our Cengage Learning team, who are very professional: Charles McCormick, Jr., Senior Acquisitions Editor, and Julie Klooster, Developmental Editor; Melena Fenn, Senior Project Manager and Stacy Shirley, Senior Art Director.

Special thanks should be given to the following reviewers who provided meaningful input for our seventh edition:

Michael W. Babcock	*Kansas State University*
Kent N. Gourdin	*College of Charleston*
George E. Hoffer	*Virginia Commonwealth University*
Walter E. Martin	*Lenoir Community College*

James Sisk   *Gaston College, North Carolina*
Lee J. Van Scyoc   *University of Wisconsin Oshkosh*
Bill Waxman   *Edison Community College*
Rick Yokeley   *Forsyth Tech Community College*
Angela K. Hansen   *Northwestern Transportation Center*
S. Scott Nadler   *East Carolina University*
John R. Grabner   *University of North Texas*
Matthew J. Drake   *Duquesne University*
A. Michael Knemeyer   *The Ohio State University*
Jerry W. Wilson   *Georgia Southern University*
Kathryn Dobie   *North Carolina A&T State University*
Daniel L. Rust   *University of Missouri-Saint Louis*
Zachary Williams   *Central Michigan University*
Donald R. Bechtel   *University of Arkansas*

Special thanks go to Dr. Gary Gittings (Penn State) for developing the Powerpoint slides for this edition, and to Dr. Wesley Randall (Auburn) for writing the questions for the test bank. Finally, the authors would like to thank Michael Levans, editor of Logistics Management magazine, for his support on this textbook.

About the Authors

John J. Coyle is currently Director of Corporate Relations for the Center for Supply Chain Research and Professor Emeritus of Supply Chain and Information Systems at Penn State University. He holds a bachelor's degree and master's degree from Penn State, and he earned his doctorate at Indiana University, Bloomington, Indiana, where he was a U.S. Steel Fellow. Professor Coyle has written more than 100 publications in the areas of transportation and logistics. He has presented papers on these same topics at professional meetings, including the Council of Supply Chain Management Professionals, the American Marketing Association, the National Academy of Sciences, the Transportation Research Forum, and the Southern Marketing Association. He is the co-author of two best-selling books, *Supply Chain Management: A Logistics Perspective* (8e) and *Transportation*. He was the editor of the *Journal of Business Logistics* from 1990 to 1996. He served on the editorial review board of the *Journal of Business Logistics*, the *Supply Chain Review*, and the *International Journal of Physical Distribution and Logistics Management*. Dr. Coyle's current research is focused upon supply chain transformation and effectively measuring improved supply chain performance at the "C" level in an organization. A closely related topic that he is pursuing is reverse channels of distribution and their special logistics problems. In 1991, Dr. Coyle received the Council for Supply Chain Management Professionals' top honor – the Distinguished Service Award. This accolade is emblematic of an individual who has made a significant contribution to the art and science of logistics. In 2003, the Philadelphia Traffic Club named him its "Person of the Year" and in 2004, he received the Eccles Medal from the International Society of Logistics and the Lions Paw Medal from Penn State. Dr. Coyle serves on the Board of three logistics companies.

Robert A. Novack is currently an Associate Professor of Supply Chain Management and Associate Director in the Center for Supply Chain Research at Penn State. Dr. Novack worked in operations management and planning for the Yellow Freight Corporation and in planning and operations for the Drackett Company. He received his bachelor's and MBA degrees from Penn State and a Ph.D. from the University of Tennessee in Knoxville. Dr. Novack has numerous articles published in the *Journal of Business Logistics,* the *Transportation Journal*, and the *International Journal of Physical Distribution and Logistics Management*. He is also the co-author of three textbooks: *Creating Logistics Value: Themes for the Future, Supply Chain Management: A Logistics Perspective* (8e), and *Transportation*. He is on the editorial review board for the *Journal of Business Logistics* and is an area editor for the *Journal of supply Chain Management*. Dr. Novack is very active in the Council for Supply Chain Management Professionals, having served as overall program chair for the annual conference, as a track chair, and as a session speaker. In addition, he has served on numerous committees with this organization. Dr. Novack holds the CTL designation from the American Society of Transportation and Logistics. His current research interest is on the development and use of metrics in managing supply chains. In 2009, he received the Atherton Teaching Award from Penn State, the highest award given for teaching at that university.

Brian Gibson is a professor of Supply Chain Management and program coordinator for the Department of Aviation and Supply Chain Management at Auburn University. Previously, he served for five years on the faculty of Georgia Southern University as director of the Southern Center for Logistics and Intermodal Transportation. Dr. Gibson also has 10 years of experience as a logistics manager for two major retailers. He is an accomplished faculty member who has received multiple awards for outstanding teaching, research, and outreach, most notably the Auburn University Alumni Association Undergraduate Teaching Excellence Award in 2006. Dr. Gibson has coauthored more than 50 refereed and invited articles in the *Journal of Business Logistics, Supply Chain Management Review, International Journal of Logistics Management, International Journal of Physical Distribution and Logistics Management,* and other leading publications. He is actively engaged in executive education, seminar development, and consulting with leading organizations. Dr. Gibson currently serves in leadership roles for the Council for Supply Chain Management Professionals, the Distribution Business Management Association, and the Retail Industry Leaders Association. Dr. Gibson earned a B.S.B.A from Central Michigan University, an MBA from Wayne State University, and a Ph.D. in logistics and transportation from the University of Tennessee.

Edward J. Bardi is principal of Bardi Consulting and professor emeritus of Business Logistics at the University of Toledo. He received his Ph.D., M.S., and B.S. from Penn State University, majoring in Business Logistics/Transportation Economics. Dr. Bardi has held faculty positions at the University of Toledo and Iowa State University. In addition, he was acting dean and associate dean of the College of Business Administration at the University of Toledo. Dr. Bardi is co-author of two textbooks: *Supply Chain Management: A Logistics Perspective* (8e) and *Transportation*. He has published numerous articles dealing with business logistics, transportation management, carrier selection, economic development, and employee household goods movement in various journals including *Transportation Journal, Journal of Business Logistics, Handling and Shipping, Baylor Business Review, International Journal of Physical Distribution and Logistics Management, Logistics & Transportation Review,* and *Personnel Journal*. Dr. Bardi has served as a consultant to numerous business and public agencies in the areas of business logistics, marketing, and economic development. He is a popular seminar leader of domestic and global business logistics management development programs.

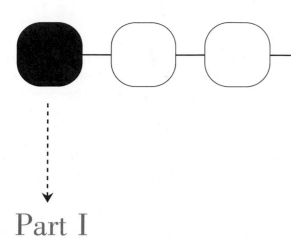

Part I

Competitive transportation rates during most of the 1990s and the early years of the 21st century, coupled with excess capacity particularly in the motor carrier sector of the industry, allowed many companies and other organizations to develop demand-driven or demand-pull supply chains. The low transport rates extended to global water carriers which, when coupled with low labor rates in some foreign countries, led to increased outsourcing of manufacturing and other related activities. Transportation both global and domestic, played a key role in the global supply chains that developed with the increased outsourcing, but transportation was not always fully appreciated.

Times have changed, however, with consequent implications for supply chains and especially transportation service providers. Fuel prices have escalated; transport capacity is tighter; labor costs have increased for many global locations; there is more concern about the environment and sustainability; and there are growing infrastructure problems with ports, highways, bridges, terminals, rail right-of-ways, rivers, and canals. The net impact is that transportation can no longer be taken for granted and its importance to efficient and effective supply chains is significant and increasing.

In Part I, we will provide a framework and foundation for the role of transportation from a micro and macro perspective in supply chains. The discussion will include both the theoretical and managerial dimensions of transportation in supply chains, including regulation and public policy.

Chapter 1 explores the role of transportation from a micro perspective and focuses upon transportation as a critical link in supply chain management. An examination of the external forces impacting supply chains is discussed in the Transportation Profile. The chapter will examine the special nature of transportation demand and how transportation services can add value to products. The final section of the chapter discusses the development and importance of supply chain management with special emphasis upon the criticality of transportation to effective and efficient supply chains.

Chapter 2 examines the role of transportation from a macro perspective with special emphasis upon transportation's effect upon the development of global economies. The political, social, and economic impact of transportation is discussed and historical and current perspectives are provided in the discussion. The effect of improved transportation upon land values and the prices of goods and services is also examined.

Chapter 3 discusses regulation and public policy as it applies to transportation. Federal, state, and local regulation has been an important dimension of the history and development of transportation in the United States and in other countries. There has been significant deregulation of transportation at the federal level in particular. However, regulation is still an important aspect of the role of transportation in our economy and globally.

Chapter 4 examines costing and pricing in transportation, which was introduced in Chapter 1. Given the importance of transportation to the cost and value of goods and services, the topic of costing and pricing deserves the detailed examination it is given in this chapter. Transportation rates and prices have some unique features that are important to understand. The economic and managerial dimensions of pricing are covered to provide an explanation of the theory and practice of transport pricing.

Chapter 1

TRANSPORTATION: CRITICAL LINK IN THE SUPPLY CHAIN

Learning Objectives

After reading this chapter, you should be able to do the following:

- Discuss the changing global landscape for businesses and other organizations and the external forces that are driving change in the global economy

- Understand the special nature of transportation demand and the influence of transportation on companies and their supply chains operating in a global economy

- Appreciate the role of transportation in the movement of people and the influence such movement has on population centers and businesses

- Gain insight into the challenge of developing appropriate metrics for transportation output

- Discuss the economic concept of price elasticity as it relates to transportation demand

- Explain the concept of derived demand as it applies to transportation movements

- Discuss how transportation service adds value to a product

- Explain the importance of the components of transportation service that relate to the movement of freight and their impact upon supply chain costs

- Appreciate how transportation affects the development of economic activity for companies and other organizations

- Understand the development of supply chain management and the importance of transportation to supply chains

Transportation Profile

The Changing Economic Landscape: Driving Forces

Most sections of the U.S. economy and other global economies are operating in an environment which is much more complex and competitive than it was in the 1990s. The situation is exacerbated by a rapid rate of change which is being driven by external forces that have changed the economic landscape. Businesses and other organizations are striving to be more efficient (reducing their cost of doing business) and more effective (improving customer service) to survive in the new environment. A critical element for achieving these two objectives simultaneously is the supply chain organizations, and transportation is a critical ingredient for overall supply chain performance. It can be argued that transportation is the glue that holds the supply chain together. The external forces driving the change include globalization, technology, supply chain integration and consolidation, consumer empowerment, and government regulation and policy. Each of these five forces deserves some additional consideration in the present context.

While there is some disagreement about which of these factors is the most important, **globalization** is usually at the top of the list for most companies and other organizations. Some individuals have described globalization as "the good, the bad, and ugly." That is, we have experienced all three aspects, with the "ugly" being the global recession of 2009-10; the "bad" being the loss of manufacturing and service jobs that we have experienced in our economy over the last several decades; and the "good" being the lower prices, wider availability of goods, and new employment opportunities that we have enjoyed during this same period. Over-all in our economy, we have more complexity and global interdependence, shorter product life-cycles, and new business models, often with a significant amount of outsourcing involved in the organization. Globalization increases the importance of transportation because of the longer shipping distances and transit times, as well as increasing risk.

Technology can be viewed as an internal change factor since it can enhance the efficiency and effectiveness of an organization's operations. However, technology can also be viewed as an external driver of change in most organizations since the rapid development of technology (hardware and software) and its application by individuals forces companies to change and adapt; otherwise, they may perish. The Internet, for example, makes information available in real time to a large segment of the population via their personal computers. It also makes information available to individuals working in organizations—managers and others—in real time. The development and sharing of so much information has had a major impact upon many businesses and other organizations. For example, individuals can make their own arrangements for air travel, lodging, restaurants, and so on, which has minimized the role of and the need for travel agents. Companies have been able to outsource call centers to other countries with advancements in technology. Technology has also afforded individuals in small organizations the opportunity to participate in the global economy from distant locations via the technology that they have at their disposal. Individuals and small organizations can provide a variety of services, such as financial auditing, computer-assisted design, or mathematical modeling from global locations. Overall, technology can help to create a dynamic and increasingly competitive environment that promotes the development of new businesses and different approaches to business in industries including transportation and related supply chain services.

The third factor is the power shifts that have occurred along supply chains with **consolidation and integration** among retailers, wholesalers, and other members of channels of distribution. The emergence of such retail giants as Walmart, McDonalds, Target, and others has transformed many supply chains. These giant organizations have sufficient economic power and leverage to influence business practices among their suppliers and their customers. Consider the fact that if Walmart were a country, it would be China's eighth-largest trading partner. Retailers have come to recognize the importance of efficient (read low cost) and effective supply chains for delivering the best value-price combinations for consumers. The other members of their supply chains, including transportation companies, have had to respond to their requests for scheduled deliveries, special packaging (such as shrink wrap and rainbow pallets), advanced shipment notices (ASNs), and other related services. It can be argued that retailers and wholesalers have influenced more innovation and change in supply chains in the last two decades than manufacturers did in the previous five decades.

The fourth factor is today's **enlightened consumer**, who is empowered by education, income, and especially by information from the Internet and from other media. Consumers' access to distant supply sources has expanded dramatically on a national and global basis. Their ability to garner information about products and services has enabled them to obtain the best price-value propositions for their situation. Consumers want and demand quicker response times, more comprehensive and convenient offerings of products and services, and more customization of the products they buy. The five-day service week of eight to nine hours per day is frequently not acceptable in this fast-paced world with two working spouses and long hours of work and commuting. So whether it is 24/7 operations, one-stop shopping, Internet search and buy, or customization of products, retailing operations have dramatically changed and have also changed the way that supply chains must function.

Consumers are demanding competitive prices, high quality, flexibility of operations and service, and responsiveness to their special needs. This consumer revolution has dramatically impacted not only retailers but also the other organizations in the supply chain, such as the transportation companies and logistics services companies that provide service along the supply chain. For example, smaller, more frequent deliveries on a time-sensitive basis are often expected. In and of themselves, these particular requirements will result in higher overall logistics and supply chain costs. Consequently, retailers, transportation companies, logistics service providers, and others have had to search for ways to lower the costs of the new levels of service by developing different strategic approaches. Collaboration has frequently become a key ingredient in the success of such changes.

The final factor is **government policy and regulation**. The **deregulation** of interstate transportation services, communication companies, and financial institutions which occurred primarily during the 1980s created a more competitive environment in these industry sectors, which has had a significant impact on how they position and sell their services. In more recent years, a major push by various government agencies toward sustainability and green supply chains has caused companies to reexamine their business practices, business models, supply chains, and so forth. Transportation can have a significant impact on the environment, and some sectors (such as the motor carrier industry) are frequently cited for their carbon footprint. Other areas such as safety, security, trade relations, and taxes are also important issues for businesses and their supply chains. These areas are all impacted by government policy and regulation. Government regulation and policy is continually being reexamined to see what is best in the current economic and global environment. They continually change, which means that logistics and transportation services and overall supply chains have to adjust to the new requirements. The new administration elected in 2008 ushered in many changes that will continue to impact supply chains.

The net consequence of the external forces discussed is a rapidly changing economic, political, and social environment in which competitive advantage can quickly diminish if an organization becomes too complacent and does not adjust its business practices and/or business model to changes in the marketplace. For example, during the 1990s and the early part of the 21st century, many organizations developed demand-driven supply chains which could rapidly respond to change. They adopted business practices which reflected that approach, such as rapid delivery, smaller and more frequent shipments, and cycle time reductions. The increase in fuel charges and concern for sustainability has caused businesses to put more focus upon fuel efficiency and overall transportation efficiency. Consequently, supply chains may become more transport-driven, as opposed to demand-driven, than they were during the 1990s and early 21st century.[1]

Introduction

As indicated in the transportation profile box previously, the external environment is causing organizations to give more attention to the integration of their supply chains. The focus of this chapter is to discuss and explain the critical role that transportation plays in helping organizations to improve their supply chain integration and to be more efficient and effective overall. It is the view of the authors that transportation's role in the supply chain is growing in importance and becoming critical to success. Transportation can be viewed as the glue that holds the supply chain together. Initially a conceptual and theoretical discussion of the dimensions of transportation will be presented to establish an appropriate appreciation of the fundamentals of transportation economics. Then the focus will switch to the basics of supply chain management. The final section of the chapter will examine more closely the role of transportation in the supply chain.

Economics of Transportation

In the 21st century, transportation systems will face significant challenges and problems because of global competition, government budget constraints, increased demand from special interest groups such as senior citizens, infrastructure challenges, sustainability issues, and energy costs. The pattern of trade that helps to drive transportation requirements is changing more quickly and becoming more complex because of the dynamic global environment and the changing economic base in the United States.

Transportation touches the lives of all U.S. citizens and citizens in other areas of the world. It affects their economic wellbeing, their safety, their access to other people and places, and the quality of their environment. When the transportation system does not function well, it is a source of great personal frustration and perhaps economic loss. But when the transportation system performs well it provides opportunities and rewards for everyone. Understanding the fundamentals of transportation economics will provide important insights into the role of transportation in the economic viability of a country, and also the businesses and other organizations that provide the output, revenue, and income that really drive an economy.

Demand for Transportation

Transportation is an important and pervasive element in our society that affects every person either directly or indirectly. The goods we consume, our economic livelihoods, our mobility, and our entertainment are impacted by transportation. The growth of the

U.S. economy, as well as the economies of most industrialized countries, is attributable in part to the benefits derived from mass production and the associated division or specialization of labor that enables mass production to occur. This specialization of labor and production can result in an oversupply of goods at one location and demand for these goods in another area. For example, a large food processing plant in Hanover, Pennsylvania will produce far more product than can be consumed in the immediate market area, and will need to sell its output in distant markets to take advantage of the scale of their plant operations. Transportation plays an important role in helping to bridge the supply and demand gap inherent in the mass-production approach.

The interrelationship between transportation and mass production points out the dependency of our global economy upon transportation. As geographical areas begin to specialize in the production of particular goods and/or services, they are relying more upon the other regions to produce the additional goods and services that they need or desire. We depend upon transportation to move these goods and provide these services to different locations in an efficient and effective manner. Like the citizens of most industrialized countries, U.S. citizens, as individuals, are not self-sufficient. On a global scale, countries recognize their international interdependencies. The United States supplies many countries with a variety of agricultural products, manufactured products, and services, while other countries provide the United States with raw materials, agricultural products, and additional manufactured products. For example, the United States is dependent upon the Middle East, South America, and Canada for energy production even though the United States produces some itself; the amount that we produce is not sufficient for our needs. The other countries usually rely on the United States to provide a variety of manufactured goods such as aircraft, clothing, computers, and so forth to meet their needs. Again, transportation plays a key role in this international or global dependency by providing the ability to match supply and demand requirements on a global basis. The ability of countries to trade among themselves and to efficiently move goods is a key element in the success of global development.

Similarly, people move from areas where they are currently situated to areas where they desire to be on a daily, weekly, or permanent basis. Within the supply-demand context, the origin of a passenger may be in the area of "oversupply" and the destination may be an area of "undersupply." Transportation also provides the bridging function between supply and demand for people to move from their current places of residence to new locations. As with freight, people depend on transportation for mobility. The more mobile a society, the more critical an efficient, economical passenger system is to its citizens. With today's technology, an executive in Chicago can leave home early on a Monday morning, catch a flight to Los Angeles, and attend an early afternoon meeting. At the end of the afternoon that same executive can board a flight to Australia with a continuation to London later in the week. This global workweek is possible because of the speed and effectiveness of air transportation, and such travel has become commonplace in the global economy.

Transportation has a definite, identifiable effect upon a person's lifestyle. An individual's decisions about where to work, live, and play are influenced by transportation. Cultural differences among geographic regions in the United States, as well as among countries and regions of the world, are mitigated or diffused by the ability of residents to travel outside the confines of their region or area of residence. This mobility also has an effect on the development of tactics and strategy to improve global supply chains and transport systems. It allows the exchange of ideas and the development of new approaches in the interchanges that can occur among people in different parts of the world.

The automobile has been a form of transportation that affects most people's lifestyle, particularly in the United States. The convenience, flexibility, and relatively low cost of automobile travel permits individuals to live in locations distant from where they work. The growth of suburban areas is usually attributable largely to the automobile and the appropriate roadway infrastructure, although in some areas efficient mass transportation is also important. It is not unusual in some areas of the United States for people to travel 20 or more miles one way to go to work. The automobile also enables people to seek medical, dental, and recreational services at various locations throughout their region, their country, or even in other global locations.

A prime ingredient for increased passenger travel is an economical transportation system. The rising costs of automobile and air travel occurring as a result of escalating energy, labor, and equipment costs are beginning to cause some change in lifestyles. Instead of traveling long distances for vacations, some people now stay closer to home or do not travel at all. Areas of the country that are highly dependent on tourists have experienced some economic difficulties and a need to change their economic base. This same set of factors is affecting the movement of freight and causing companies to source for their supply chains in more contiguous locations. The combination of low labor costs in some global locations and relatively low transportation costs in the past have made some distant sources of supply more attractive, but this may change with the rising costs of energy and labor mentioned previously. Consequently some companies are reevaluating their logistics and transportation networks to determine more optimal locations.

Transport Measurement Units

Transportation demand is essentially a request to move a given weight or amount of cargo a specific distance between two specific points. The demand for transportation is usually measured in weight-distance units for freight and passenger-distance units for people. For freight, the usual demand unit or metric is the **ton-mile** and for people the appropriate unit is the **passenger-mile**. Both of these measurements are two-dimensional, which can present some challenges for intermodal comparisons. The ton-mile, for example, is not homogeneous for comparison purposes. The demand for 200 ton-miles of freight transportation could be a movement of 200 tons for one mile, 100 tons for two miles, or one ton for 200 miles. In fact, any combination of weight and distance that equals 200 ton-miles would be regarded as the same or equal. In addition, the unique requirements for transportation, equipment, and services may vary among customers for a 200 ton-mile movement. For example, demand for 200 ton-miles of ice cream from Pittsburgh may require movement to multiple destinations in a refrigerated vehicle with same-day delivery, whereas the demand for 200 ton-miles of gasoline from Philadelphia may be a movement to one destination in a tank car vehicle with two-day delivery.

These examples are aimed at describing the heterogeneous nature of the transportation demand unit. The same unit of demand could have different costs for producing it and different user requirements. Measuring only the miles moved or the weight moved also does not adequately reflect the components of freight transport demand for comparison purposes. The relative importance of transportation movements can best be measured using the ton-mile concept.

Similarly, the passenger-mile is a heterogeneous unit. Five hundred passenger-miles could be one passenger moving 500 miles or 500 passengers moving one mile. The demand for 500 passenger-miles could be via automobile, railroad, or airplane. It could be first class or coach. It could be fast or slow. The demand attributes of the passenger-mile vary from passenger to passenger. However, the passenger-mile is still the single best measure of the relative importance of transportation alternatives. While neither the ton-mile nor the passenger-mile is perfect, they are still the best unit of measure that we have. As long as we recognize the challenges inherent in the units when comparisons are made, both are useful.

The demand for transportation can also be examined at different levels of aggregation. Aggregate demand for transportation is the sum of the individual demands for freight or for passengers. In addition, aggregate demand can mean the sum of the demand for transportation via different modes or the aggregate demand for a particular mode. Table 1-1 shows the allocation of aggregate passenger-miles and Table 1-2 shows the allocation of aggregate ton-miles via different modes of transportation. The dominance of the private automobile for passengers is clearly demonstrated in Table 1-1, but note the decline in 2006, which is probably indicative of a downward trend as individuals react to higher fuel prices. Table 1-2 is interesting in light of the previous discussion about the ton-mile measurement unit. Motor carriers account for 75 to 80 percent of the individual shipments, but their shorter hauls and lower shipment weights place them second to rail in terms of ton-miles. Surprisingly, pipelines are relatively close in terms of ton-miles to the motor carriers, even though they carry

Table 1-1	Modal Split of For-Hire Passenger Miles and Private Auto (millions)			
YEAR	AIR	BUS	RAIL	AUTO
1990	345,873	121,398	25,185	2,281,391
2000	516,129	160,919	30,100	2,544,457
2005	583,758	147,992	30,972	2,699,305
2006	590,633	148,285	31,441	2,658,621

Source: U.S. Department of Transportation, Bureau of Transportation Statistics, *Pocket Guide to Transportation, 2009,* Washington, DC.

Table 1-2	U.S. Domestic Freight Ton-Miles by Mode (Billions)			
YEAR	AIR	TRUCK	RAIL	WATER	PIPELINE
1990	10.4	848.8	1,064.4	833.5	864.8
2000	15.8	1,192.8	1,546.3	645.8	927.9
2005	15.7	1,291.5	1,733.8	591.3	942.2
2006	15.4	1,294.5	1,852.8	561.6	913.2

Source: U.S. Department Transportation, Bureau of Transportation Statistics, *Pocket Guide to Transportation, 2009,* Washington, DC.

| Transportation Technology | *Asset Visibility* |

Hidden assets can be a challenge to individuals and to business organizations, giving rise to loss and damage, theft, or miscalculation of important data for business decisions. **Enterprise asset management** is recognized in both the private and military sectors as being a powerful approach not only to increasing efficiency (lowering cost) but also to improving effectiveness in executing strategies to improve competitiveness. Historically, the challenge has been having a practical method for collecting the data to gain necessary visibility without on-site inspection and measurement. Periodic on-site visits and/or sampling methods have been used, but cost and effectiveness are often issues.

The development of new technologies has helped to solve the real-time visibility problem of assets, including inventory and equipment. New technology allows the implementation of enterprise asset management systems to be applied in a practical manner. Technologies such as radio frequency identification (RFID) tags and global positioning systems (GPS) have enabled companies to accurately pinpoint the exact location of equipment and materials. Such visibility allows decisions to be made more quickly and accurately to solve problems and reduce uncertainty.

There are numerous possible applications of this technology in the transportation industry and related supply chain operations. For example, the oil and chemical industry has been using a device in their storage tanks to track the level and amount of product in the tank on a real-time basis, which allows them to prevent stock outs and to schedule deliveries on a more cost-efficient basis. In the long-haul motor carrier industry, keeping track of drivers and their equipment had traditionally been a challenge. But now, with GPS and wireless computers for drivers and RFID tags on trailers, keeping track of the assets has become much less challenging. Instructions can also be relayed to drivers to help them solve problems or address other issues such as finding specific locations. The tags can also store valuable information about the maintenance and use history of the equipment for preventing breakdowns and for general records. The railroad industry has also been using these technologies for the same purposes. Keeping track of their rolling stock has been a long-standing challenge since the stock can be off-loaded at numerous locations along the way.

The hardware and software continues to improve, which bodes well for the future as transportation companies face the challenge of improving their operational costs and minimizing their carbon footprint. The costs of the new technologies can be a barrier to adoption, along with the personnel training necessary to use the technology effectively. Over time, the costs have come down and individuals are receiving training in a variety of places. There is no question that this technology can help organizations with visibility on an enterprise-wide basis.

a very limited array of products. Again, the ton-mile unit increases their importance in this comparison.

Demand Elasticity

Demand elasticity refers to the sensitivity of customers to changes in price. If customers are sensitive to price, a price reduction will increase the demand for the item and the total revenue will also usually increase. An increase in price will have the opposite effect—less revenue and a reduction in sales. If customers are not sensitive to a change in price we consider demand to be **inelastic**, because a price reduction will result in a small relative increase in the quantity demanded and the total revenues will decrease. In mathematical terms, demand elasticity is the ratio of the percentage change in the quantity demanded to the percentage change in price; or, elasticity equals percentage change in quantity divided by percentage change in price. If demand is elastic, the quantity demanded changes more than the change in price and the elasticity coefficient is greater than one. Conversely, a product or service is said to be price inelastic or insensitive to price changes if the quantity demanded changes less than the change in price or, in other words, the coefficient is less than one.

Elasticity = % change in quantity/% change in price

In general, aggregate demand for transportation is inelastic. Freight rate reductions will not dramatically increase the demand for freight transportation because transportation costs generally represent, in the aggregate, less than 4 percent of a product's landed cost, and the demand is a derived demand (to be discussed later). Substantial rate reductions would be required for a meaningful increase in the demand for the product and, consequently, the demand for transportation of that product. On the other hand, if we consider specific modes of transportation or specific carriers, the demand is generally elastic or price sensitive. The modal share of the aggregate demand is, in part, determined by the rates charged. Reductions in rates charged by a particular mode will usually result in increases in the volume of freight by that mode, other things being equal. This assumes that the mode that reduced the rate is physically capable of transporting the freight.

For example, long-haul transportation of new automobiles was dominated by motor carriers in the 1960s and into the 1970s. The railroads developed a new rail car specifically designed to transport new automobiles. This new rail car enabled the railroads to improve efficiency and reduce the rates that they charged for hauling automobiles and also improved some of the service characteristics of the movements. The percentage of new automobiles hauled by railroads increased with the introduction of the new rail car and the lower rates, and the share of intercity ton-miles of new automobiles transported by motor carriers decreased. Today, motor carriers are usually used primarily to transport new automobiles shorter distances from rail yards to dealerships. Also, when plant locations are close to the points where new cars are needed or where dealers are located, motor transportation is frequently used. So for shorter distances and for movements from the rail freight yard to the dealer the motor carrier is dominant; for the longer hauls, railroads are hauling a larger share of the traffic than previously.

For modal shipments or for a specific carrier within that mode, demand may also be service elastic. Assuming no price changes, the mode or specific carrier demand is often sensitive to changes in service levels provided by competing carriers. For example, many air passengers monitor the on-time service levels of the various air carriers and when possible select the air carrier that provides the best on-time transportation service. Transit time and service reliability have become much more important to freight movement during the last several decades, as shippers have become increasingly aware of the impact of carrier service on inventory levels and customer service. Consequently, higher-cost service providers such as UPS and Federal Express now move larger-size shipments because of their superior direct service and some of the ancillary logistics services that they provide.

Freight Transportation

The demand for freight transportation is usually dependent upon the demand for a product in another location. As indicated previously, specialization and mass production create a need for market expansion at more distant locations, which gives rise to increased demand for freight transportation. In this section, attention is given to the characteristics of that freight transportation demand.

Derived Demand The demand for transporting a product from a given location depends on the existence of demand to consume or use that product in the distant location. Freight is not usually transported to another location unless there is a need for the product. Thus, the demand for transportation is generally referred to as a **derived demand**, as opposed to customer demand for a product. Sometimes it is also referred to as a secondary demand as opposed to a primary demand. Derived demand is not unique to transportation since the demand for many raw materials is dependent upon the demand for the finished products that are produced from these raw materials. Figure 1-1 illustrates the derived demand nature of freight transportation. An oversupply of widgets is available at the production site, City A, but widgets will not be moved or transported to City C because there is no demand for widgets at City C. However, there is a demand for widgets at City B. Because of the demand for 100 widgets in City B, there is a demand for the transportation of 100 widgets from City A to City B.

The derived demand characteristics imply that freight transportation would not be effected by transport carrier actions. As noted previously, this assumption is true for the demand for transportation at the aggregate level. For example, if a freight carrier lowers the rate to zero for moving high-tech personal computers from the United States to a developing nation, this free transportation may not materially change the demand for personal computers in the developing nation since it is a derived demand. The demand for personal computers is dependent on the educational level of the citizens, electrical availability, and the price of the computer itself. However, at the disaggregate level (a single mode, carrier, or specific traffic lane) the rates charged for the service level provided can influence the demand for the product and the demand to transport the product. This impact on product demand considers the value of the service provided to the user of the product. This concept is discussed in the next section.

Value of Service Value of service considers the impact of transportation costs and service on the demand for the product. Lower transportation costs can cause a shift in demand for transportation among the modes and the specific carriers. It can also affect the demand to transport freight over a specific traffic lane where several carriers are

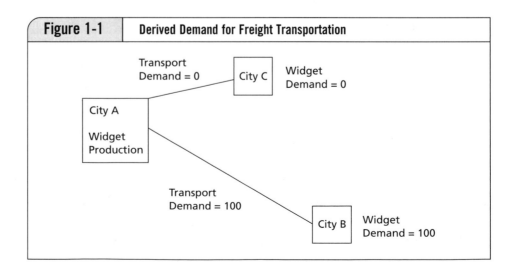

| **Figure 1-1** | **Derived Demand for Freight Transportation** |

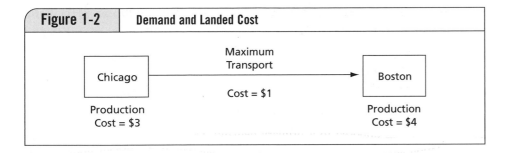

Figure 1-2 | **Demand and Landed Cost**

Chicago

Maximum Transport Cost = $1

Boston

Production Cost = $3

Production Cost = $4

competing for the traffic. The impact of transportation costs on the demand for a product at a given location usually focuses on what we call the landed cost of the product. The **landed cost** of the product includes the cost of the product at the source, the cost to transport the product to its destination, plus any ancillary expenses such as insurance or loading costs. If the landed cost of the product is lower than that of other sources, there will usually be a demand for that product and also for the transportation of that product from its origin point.[2]

For example, in Figure 1-2, a manufacturer of bicycle tires located in Chicago is competing in Boston with local producers. For the Chicago bicycle tire manufacturer to be competitive, the landed costs of the tire must be lower than the cost of the local manufacturer's tire prices. The Boston manufacturers have a cost of $4 per tire, whereas the Chicago manufacturer can produce the same tire for $3 because of its inherent advantages in labor productivity. As long as the transportation costs per tire from Chicago to Boston are less than $1, the Chicago tire maker will have a landed cost advantage and a demand for the Chicago tire will exist in Boston (assuming the quality is equal to that of the locally produced tires). Conversely, if transportation costs exceed $1 per tire, Boston consumers will not purchase tires from the distant source but rather they will purchase the tire from the local manufacturer. Consequently, there will be no demand for the product, as well as no demand to transport the product that was produced in Chicago.

The landed cost also determines the extent of the market for business. The greater the distance the product is shipped, usually the higher the landed cost. At some distance from the product's source, the landed cost usually becomes prohibitive to the buyer and there will be no demand for that product at that point. Also, the landed cost usually determines the extent of the market between two competing companies. To illustrate this concept, Figure 1-3 presents an example of two producers located 200 miles apart. Producer P has a production cost of $50 per unit and transportation cost of $0.60 per unit per mile. Producer S also has a production cost of $50 per unit

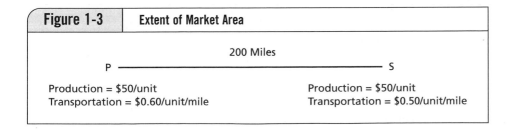

Figure 1-3 | **Extent of Market Area**

200 Miles

P ——————————————————————— S

Production = $50/unit
Transportation = $0.60/unit/mile

Production = $50/unit
Transportation = $0.50/unit/mile

but a transportation cost of $0.50 per unit per mile. The extent of the market between the two producers is the point at which their landed costs are equal:

$$LC\ (P) = LC\ (S)$$

Production Cost (P) + Transportation Cost (P)

$$= \text{Production Cost (S)} + \text{Transportation Cost (S)}$$

$$\$50 + \$0.60(x) = \$50 + \$0.50(200 - x)$$

$$\$0.60(x) + \$0.50(x) = \$50 + \$100 - \$50$$

$$\$1.10(x) = \$100$$

$$x = 90.9 \text{ miles from P}$$

Solving the equation for x shows that P has a market area that extends 90.9 miles from its plant and S has a market area that extends 109 miles from its facility. The company with the lower landed cost will have a greater market area than the firm with the higher transportation costs. Just looking at the numbers, one would conclude that the company located at S with the transportation costs of $0.50 per unit would have an advantage in the extent of the market, but this formula will allow you to calculate exactly what the distance between those two companies would be in terms of their market area.

Service Components of Freight Demand

Shippers of freight have varying service requirements for their transportation providers as indicated previously. These service requirements range from specific pickup times to communication requirements. The service demands are related to the costs implications of the transportation service provided. The transportation service characteristics of freight include transit time, reliability, accessibility, capability, and security.[3]

Transit time can affect the level of inventory held by both the shipper and the receiver as well as the associated carrying cost of holding that inventory. The longer the transit time, the higher the inventory levels required and the higher the carrying costs. Also, transit times impact the inventory costs in the overall supply chain. For example, the supply of clothing produced in the Pacific Rim might require 45 days transit time from manufacturer's shipping point to a specific retail store. While the clothes are in transit, either a buyer or a seller incurs the cost of financing the inventory for the 45 days. If the transit time is reduced to 15 days by use of air transportation, the in-transit inventory financing costs will be reduced by two-thirds. Also, longer transit time increases the potential cost for stockouts. Using the Pacific Rim example previously, a stock out of clothing at the retail store could mean a maximum of 45 days without inventory with sales and related profits lost during this period. Shorter transit times reduce the potential losses from stockouts.

Reliability refers to the consistency of transit times. Meeting pickup and delivery schedules enables shippers and receivers to optimize service levels and minimize stockout costs. Unreliable transit time requires the freight receiver to either increase inventory levels to guard against stockout conditions or incur stockout-related costs. Reliable service directly affects the level of modal and specific carrier demand; that is, a shipper may shift from an unreliable carrier to one that is more reliable and provides more consistent service. The customer may switch from a supplier who provides unreliable delivery service to one that is reliable, thereby impacting the transportation demand for specific carriers or specific traffic lanes.

Global Perspectives

Stay Cool

Given all the attention paid to world hunger, global warming, and energy shortages, it's little wonder that the focus on improving best practices in controlled atmosphere shipping is being sharpened. Mega- and medium-sized shippers alike are telling us that a seamless controlled atmosphere network is an absolute must if their businesses are to thrive in the coming years. And by all indications, the carrier community is beginning to measure up.

"Because there's a growing demand for perishables, this is by far the most exciting time in the history of our nation to be involved in refrigeration," says Bill Hudson, president of the International Refrigerated Transportation Association (IRTA). "But a lot depends on how well we work with our global partners to ensure long term success with this kind of shipping."

Indeed, a convergence of international issues is making a profound impact on the direction controlled atmosphere transport will be taking in the coming years. According to Hudson, IRTA and the three logistics associations comprising the Global Cold Chain Alliance (GCCA) (the International Association of Refrigerated Warehouses, the World Food Logistics Organization, and the International Association for Cold Storage Construction) are confronting challenges associated with much broader environmental and economic concerns beyond the movement of goods.

"We realized a few years ago that a greater level of cooperation was necessary in the supply chain," Hudson said. "As a consequence, our members are now sharing intelligence and research that helps us stay on top of accelerated demands."

Launched as an umbrella organization in April 2007, the GCCA has identified three strong influences changing the cold chain industry. Chief among them is the fact that refrigerated warehouse operators have invested in trucking assets, and continue to explore various arrangements and structures with their customers both domestically and overseas. "One of the most notable examples of this has been Walmart's recent move in Mumbai, India, with a huge capital outlay," says Hudson.

The second trend comes as an immediate consequence, he adds, noting that Walmart and other "mega" retailers operate all aspects from food production to food delivery, and have even created 3PLs to expedite the process.

"The third thing we discovered was the need for carriers to concentrate on core competencies—maintaining proper temperatures and instilling best practices. The cold chain had to take on the development of all links from post-harvest handling, to processing, to retail," says Hudson.

Source: Burnson, Patrick, "Stay Cool," *Logistics Management,* September 2008, p. 33. Reprinted by permission.

Accessibility is the ability of the transportation provider to move the freight between a specific origin and destination. The inability of a carrier to provide direct service between an origin and destination results in added costs and transit time for the shipper. For example, an air carrier does not move freight from Toledo, Ohio directly to Angers, France. First the freight is moved by motor carrier from Toledo to Detroit, Michigan, and then flown to Paris where it will be moved to Angers by either motor or rail. When a carrier cannot provide direct service between the shipping and receiving points, it usually requires additional transportation service by motor carrier, which adds to the transit time and the total cost. Motor carriers have a distinct advantage over other carriers in terms of accessibility in most countries.

Table 1-3	Service Components of Freight Demand
SERVICE COMPONENT	**USER IMPLICATION**
Transit Time	Inventory, Stockout Costs
Reliability	Inventory, Stockout Costs
Accessibility	Transit Time, Transportation Cost
Capability	Meets Products' Unique Physical and Marketing Requirements
Security	Inventory, Stockout Costs

The ability of the carrier to provide special service requirements is the essence of **capability**. Based on the physical and marketing characteristics of the freight, shippers might have unique demands for transportation, facilities, and communication—for example, products requiring controlled temperature that necessitate the use of a refrigerated vehicle; time sensitive shipments which need state-of-the-art communications systems to monitor their exact location and arrival times; or even the cubic capacity for a large piece of equipment. Marketing considerations might dictate that the carriers provide freight consolidation and break-bulk facilities to lower freight costs and transit time. These are just a few of the many and varied demands placed on transportation service providers. Their capability to provide these required services are often instrumental in getting the business.

Finally, **security** is concerned with the safety of the goods in transit. Shipments that are damaged or lost in transit can cause increased cost in the areas of inventory and/or stockouts. A damaged shipment will usually not be accepted and the buyer faces the possibility of losing a sale or stopping the production process. Increasing inventory levels to protect against stockout costs resulting from a damaged shipment causes increased inventory carrying costs. Table 1-3 provides a summary to the transportation service components of freight demand. As indicated previously, the focus upon supply chain management has raised the awareness of shippers to the importance of carrier service characteristics to total cost and to customer service.

Location of Economic Activity

Transportation has been a determinant in the location of industrial facilities since the industrial revolution. The cost of transporting raw materials to a production facility and the cost of transporting finished goods to the appropriate markets directly affects the profitability of the business. In addition, the quality of the transportation services, such as time required to traverse the spatial gap between sources of supply, the plants, the warehouses, and the markets, affects inventory cost, stockout costs, and other costs as identified in Table 1-3.

Water transportation played an important role in the location of many major cities around the world. For example, early settlers in the United States relied on water transportation (via the ocean) to link European markets and supply sources to the new, developing colonies. Thus, cities that are major population centers such as New York, Philadelphia, and Baltimore are frequently port cities. As the frontier in the United States was settled, it became tied to these port cities that provided a source of supply and markets for the western region. Other cities, such as Pittsburgh, Cincinnati, Chicago, Minneapolis, and St. Louis developed along the rivers. As rail transportation developed, however, cities and industrial facilities grew along the railroads even though they were not always adjacent to the waterways. Later, the motor carriers enabled the development of cities and industrial facilities at virtually any location where there was a highway.[4]

As the U.S. markets grew, firms had to decide where new facilities should be located. Today, many companies are again faced with the question of where to locate plants and warehouses in light of changing markets and supply points given the global nature of their supply chains. As distances and transit times increased, firms began to experience higher costs for transportation and also for inventory and warehousing in many instances. Companies must consider these increases in terms of their prices.[5]

As the location of economic activity changes so does the demand for transportation. For example, the aging of the U.S. population has seen the shifting of the population to areas of the country such as Florida and North and South Carolina as well as Arizona. This shift in the population requires businesses that supply consumer products to demand more transportation services to these states. Some companies have responded to this population shift by locating production facilities in these states. The same types of changes are occurring with the new global economy. For example, Mexico has seen an increase in production facilities because of its combination of lower labor costs and their proximity to the United States. In the next section, we are going to shift our discussion to a look at transportation within the supply chain since transportation is a critical part of all supply chains.

Supply Chain Concept

While references to supply chain management can be traced to the 1980s, it is safe to say that it was not until the 1990s that supply chains captured the attention of senior level management in numerous organizations. They began to recognize the power and the potential impact of supply chain management to make organizations more globally competitive and to increase their market share with consequent improvement in share-holder value.

Development of the Concept

It can be argued that supply chain management is not a new concept. Rather, supply chain management represents the third phase of an evolution that started in 1960s with the development of the physical distribution concept, which focused on finished goods or the outbound side of a firm's logistic system—in other words, the distribution-related activities that occurred after a product was produced. In the 1980s the concept of business logistics or integrated logistics began to be recognized, which added the inbound side to the production point to the outbound side. This was really the second phase of development for the supply chain concept. As indicated previously, the supply chain management concept was developed primarily in the 1990s and represented the third phase of development.

A number of studies done during the 1950s and 1960s indicated the potential of the **systems concept** if it were applied in business-related situations. The focus of **physical distribution management** was on the system costs and analyzing trade-off scenarios to arrive at the best or lowest physical distribution system cost. The system relationships that exist among transportation, inventory levels, warehousing, exterior packaging, materials handling, and customer service cost centers were analyzed and evaluated. For example, the selection and use of a carrier such as rail service impacts inventory, warehousing, packaging, customer service, and materials handling costs, whereas motor carriers would have a different impact on the same cost centers. While rail service would usually have the lowest transportation rate, there could be higher costs for inventory, warehousing, packaging, and so forth, which would result in higher total costs. The type of product, volume of movement, distances, and other factors would influence which mode of transportation would have the lower total cost.

The initial focus on physical distribution or outbound logistics was logical since finished goods were usually higher in value, which meant that their inventory, warehousing, materials handling, and packaging costs were relatively higher than for inbound raw materials. The impact of transportation selection was, therefore, usually more significant for total physical distribution costs. Managers in certain industries, such as consumer package or grocery products, high-tech companies, and other consumer product companies, as well as some academicians, became very interested in physical distribution management. A national organization called the National Council of Physical Distribution Management (NCPDM) was organized to focus the leadership, education, research, and interest in the area of physical distribution management.

The 1980s were a decade of change with the deregulation of transportation, financial institutions, and the communication industry. The technology revolution was also well underway. During the 1980s, the **business logistics** or **integrated logistics management** concept developed in a growing number of organizations. Logistics in its simplest form added the inbound side to the outbound logistics of physical distribution management. See Figures 1-4 and 1-5. This was a logical addition since deregulation of transportation provided an opportunity to coordinate the inbound and outbound transportation movements of large shippers, which could positively impact a carrier's outbound costs by minimizing empty backhauls, which with deregulation could lead to lower rates for the shipper. Also, international or global sourcing of materials and

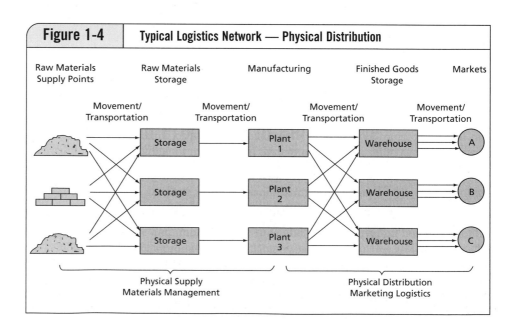

Figure 1-4 | **Typical Logistics Network — Physical Distribution**

Figure 1-5	Typical Logistics Network—Materials Management

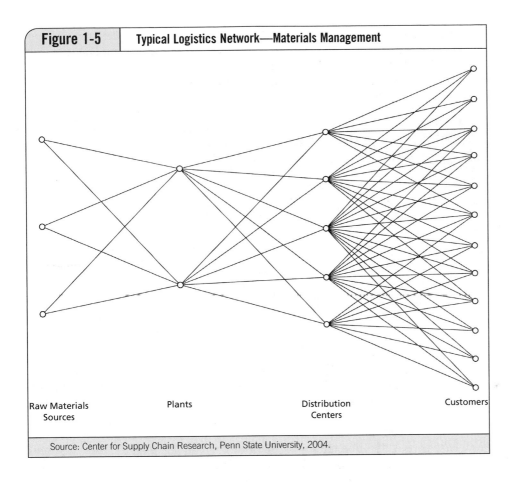

Raw Materials Sources   Plants   Distribution Centers   Customers

Source: Center for Supply Chain Research, Penn State University, 2004.

supplies was growing in importance. As will be discussed subsequently in more detail, global transportation presents some special challenges for production and scheduling. Therefore, it became increasingly apparent that coordination between the outbound and the inbound dimensions of logistics systems provided an opportunity for increased efficiency and also better levels of customer service.

The underlying logic of the systems concept was also the rationale for the development of the logistics management concept, because in addition to analyzing trade-offs for total cost it could also include the value or demand aspects of customer service effectiveness. Logistics authors usually include procurement as an element in a logistics system. The rationale for the inclusion is the opportunity for a trade-off analysis between procurement quantity discounts, transportation discounts, inventory and warehousing costs, and other related costs to obtain the lowest cost.[6]

Supply chain management came into vogue during the 1990s and continues to be a focal point for making organizations more competitive in the global marketplace. Supply chain management can be viewed as a pipeline or conduit for the efficient and effective flow of products and materials, services, information, and financials (usually cash) from the supplier's supplier through the various immediate organizations out to the customer's customer (see Figure 1-6). In essence, it is a system of connected networks between the original vendor and the ultimate final consumer. The extended enterprise or boundary spanning perspective of supply chain management represents a logical extension of the logistics concept, providing an opportunity to view the total system of

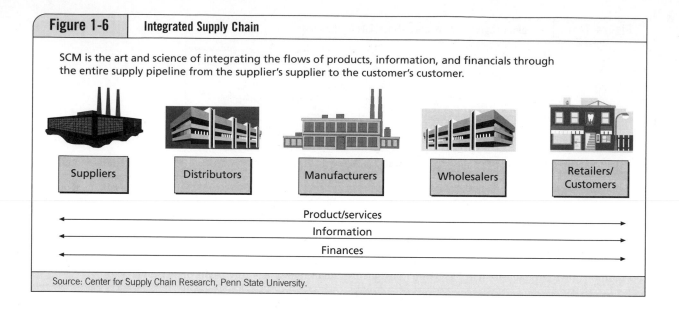

| Figure 1-6 | Integrated Supply Chain |

SCM is the art and science of integrating the flows of products, information, and financials through the entire supply pipeline from the supplier's supplier to the customer's customer.

Suppliers   Distributors   Manufacturers   Wholesalers   Retailers/Customers

Product/services
Information
Finances

Source: Center for Supply Chain Research, Penn State University.

interrelated companies and their impact for the final product in the marketplace in terms of its price-value relationship.

At this point, a more detailed discussion of the supply chain is appropriate. Figure 1-6 presents a simplified, linear example of a hypothetical supply chain. A real-world supply chain would usually be more complex than this example because supply chains are often nonlinear and have more supply chain participants. Also, Figure 1-6 does not adequately portray the importance of transportation in the supply chain. As indicated previously, transportation can be viewed as the glue which holds the supply chain together to allow the member organizations to operate efficiently and effectively as a system. It should be noted that some companies may be a part of several supply chains. For example, chemical companies may provide ingredients for manufacturers of different products that will be distributed by many different retail and wholesale establishments.

Figure 1-6 does illustrate the basic characteristics of a supply chain that are important to this discussion. The definition, which is a part of the illustration, indicates several important points. A supply chain is an **extended enterprise** that crosses the boundaries of the individual firms to span their related activities involved in the total supply chain. This extended enterprise should attempt to execute a coordinated or integrated two-way flow of goods, information, and financials (especially cash). The three flows illustrated in the figure are very important to the competitive success of the organizations. Integration across the boundaries of the several organizations in essence means that the supply chain needs to function like one organization in satisfying the ultimate customer by delivering an appropriate price-value relationship for products in the marketplace.

The top flow, products and related services, has traditionally been an important focus of logistics and transportation and is an important element in supply chain management. This particular flow is directly dependent upon effective transportation, which is the focus of this text. Customers expect their orders to be delivered in a timely, reliable, and damage-free manner; and transportation is critical to this outcome. Figure 1-6 also indicates that product flow is a two-way flow in the environment of the

On the Line

Transportation's Impact on Global Supply Chains

Many global supply chains are characterized by outsourcing production to low labor cost countries such as China and India. These global supply chains often evolved as a consequence of trade agreements and aggressive government incentives, along with cheap fuel prices, which gave rise to low transportation rates. New technology, especially the Internet, has allowed the development of collaborative relationships on a real-time basis across globally extended enterprise systems. Consequently, world trade has flourished between and among developed and underdeveloped economies. For example, U.S. imports have grown at an accelerated rate, increasing from 10 percent of its aggregate demand in the late 1980s to approximately 20 percent by 2008.

The transportation landscape, which is a key factor or link in the success of global supply chains, is facing some major challenges. The rapid growth that has occurred in global trade in the United States has placed much pressure on the ports, which are the gateways for about 80 percent by weight of the international freight moving in and out of the U.S. Congestion has become a problem, especially on the West Coast during peak periods. This is mainly attributable to the tremendous growth in the trade between the United States and the Asia-Pacific countries. Congestion has also become a widely acknowledged problem on highways and at major rail gateways, which increases the West Coast port congestion problem. A further challenge is the potential for a shortage of over-the-road drivers, especially in the long-haul sector. The average driver age is such that retirements by 2015 could cause a shortage of over 110,000 drivers.

A concern of major proportions is escalating energy costs. While fuel prices did decline toward the end of the first decade of the 21st century, the expectation is that they will increase again to the $4.00 or higher level for a gallon of fuel. Motor carriers and airlines are affected the most by these higher fuel prices because they are relatively inefficient in fuel consumption compared to the other three major modes of transportation—rail, water, and pipeline. When you consider the fact that about 75 to 80 percent of the freight shipments in the United States move via motor carrier for at least part of the distance, the higher fuel costs have major implications for the transportation system and the economy.

Sustainability is also an issue for the 21st century as individuals, organizations, and the government are showing a growing concern for the environment. **Green supply chains** have become a part of our vernacular. Organizations discuss their carbon footprint in the context of sustainability, and evaluate methods to reduce their carbon footprint. Transportation is an area that receives much attention in such discussions because the modes of transportation vary in terms of their impact. As pointed out previously, rail, water, and pipelines are more fuel efficient than motor and air carriers. Fuel consumption relative to ton-miles moved is important to the size of the carbon footprint. Consequently, shippers will be placing more emphasis in this area in making modal choices and will place more emphasis on network efficiency, that is, on reducing trip miles, eliminating empty moves, and using cargo capacity. The implications for transportation are significant. There has been much discussion over the last two decades of demand-driven supply chains. The supply chain of the future maybe transport-driven.

21st century because a growing number of organizations are involved in **reverse logistics systems** for returning products that were unacceptable to the buyer for some reason—damage, maintenance, obsolescence, and so forth. Note also that networks for reverse systems usually have to be designed somewhat differently than for forward systems. The location, size, and layout of facilities are frequently different. The transportation carriers that need to be utilized may be different. Consequently, there are growing number of logistics companies (including transportation companies) that specialize in managing reverse flow systems for retailers and manufacturers. They can provide a valuable service in appropriate situations.

The second flow indicated is the **information flow**, which has become a very important factor for success in supply chain management. Figuratively, information is the trigger or signal for the logistics or supply chain system to respond to a customer order. Traditionally, we have viewed information as flowing back from the marketplace as customers purchased products and wholesalers and retailers replenished their inventory. The information was primarily demand or sales data, which triggered replenishment and was also the basis for forecasting future sales or orders. Note that in addition to the retailer or final seller, the other members of the supply chain traditionally reacted to replenishment orders. If there were long time intervals between orders, the members of the supply chain were faced with uncertainty about the level and the potential pattern of demand, which usually resulted in higher inventory (safety stock) or stockout costs. The uncertainty contributed to a phenomenon known as the **bull whip effect** in the supply chain. One of the objectives of supply chain management is to mitigate the bull whip effect by reducing the level of uncertainty. In traditional supply chains with independent organizations, the level or magnitude of uncertainty increased with the "distance" from the market or customer. Therefore, the level of safety stock increased to cover the degree of uncertainty as you moved back through the supply chain.

One of the realizable outcomes of supply chain management is the sharing of sales information on a more real-time basis to reduce uncertainty, which reduces the need for safety stock. In this sense, the supply chain is compressed through timely information flows from the marketplace. In other words, inventory can be reduced in the supply chain by timely, accurate information about demand. If point of sale (POS) data were available from the retail level on a real-time basis, it would help to mitigate the bull whip effect associated with supply chain inventories and would reduce costs. It should also be noted that transportation plays an important role in the level of supply chain inventory. One of the components of transportation service as discussed was reliability of delivery. It was noted that if service was unreliable, companies carried more inventory or safety stock, which would be true along the whole supply chain. It was also noted that transit time had an effect upon inventory, namely, longer transit times could contribute to higher inventory levels. Longer transit times combined with unreliable service exacerbate the need for safety stock in the supply chain. Consequently, transportation is an important cog in the whole supply chain in terms of efficiency and effectiveness.

Note the illustration also indicates a two-way flow of information. In a supply chain environment information flowing forward in the supply chain has taken on increased significance and importance. Forward information can take many forms, such as **advanced shipment notices** (ASNs), order status information, inventory availability information, and so on. The overall impact of good forward information has been to reduce uncertainty with respect to order replenishment. A related aspect of forward information flow has been the increased utilization of bar codes and radio frequency tags, which can increase inventory visibility and help reduce uncertainty in the safety stock. The improved visibility of pipeline inventory, including transportation equipment, also makes possible many opportunities for improved efficiency such as transportation consolidation and merging in transit strategies. These latter two have contributed to some shift in modal selection because of the opportunity for consolidation of larger shipments and the opportunity to use merging in transit strategies to eliminate warehousing. The combined two-way flow of timely, accurate information lowers supply chain related costs (including transportation), which also improves effectiveness or customer service.

The third and final flow indicated is financials, or usually and more specifically, cash. Traditionally, financial flows have been viewed as one-directional—backward in the supply chain. In other words, this flow is payment for goods, services, and orders received. A major impact of supply chain compression and faster cycle order times has been faster cash flow. Customers receive orders faster, they are billed sooner, and companies can collect sooner. The faster cash-to-cash or order-to-cash cycle has been very important for companies because it reduces the amount of working capital they need in their system. If cash flow is slow, a company needs more working capital to finance the processes until they collect from the customers. There are some companies that have negative working capital or what financial organizations refer to as **"free" cash flow**. They collect from their customers before they have to pay their vendors or suppliers. In such companies as Dell and Hewlett Packard, the period between collection and payment may be as much as 30 or more days. This cash can be used for financial investment purposes or another source of funding for product development or other improvements. Cash flow measures have become an important metric of the financial community to gauge the viability of companies. Frequently, one will see in the financial analysis of an organization references to their cash flow situation. Supply chain management provides organizations with an opportunity to improve customer service and cash flow, and transportation sevice is an important part of this equation.

As indicated previously, it is important to be aware of the significant role that transportation provides in the supply chain framework. At the end of the day, the customer expects to have the right product delivered at the right place in the right quantity in the right condition at the right cost, and transportation plays a very critical role in these attributes for a good system.

SUMMARY

- The dynamics of the changing environment for business are being driven by a set of external factors that include globalization, technology, supply chain integration, consolidation, consumer empowerment, and government regulation and policy.

- Globalization is usually considered to be one of the most important external factors impacting organizations and how they have to compete, as well as their associated supply chains.

- Technology has revolutionized how organizations go to market with their products and opens up the door for different business models. It has also had a major impact on how supply chains are organized and the distances over which supply chains have to operate in connecting the global points in the supply chain.

- During the latter part of the 20th century, there was a noticeable shift in economic power in many supply chains where large consolidated retailers and some wholesalers were able to exert major influence on how supply chains operated. Those large retailers that accounted for a major proportion of manufacturing companies' business were able to influence them particularly in the area of their supply chains. The retailers recognize the impact of the supply chain in enabling them to reduce their cost and improve their effectiveness in serving their customers.

- Today's consumers can be considered as being enlightened and empowered by their education and the information that they have at their disposal from the Internet and other media sources. This power allows them to access supply chain sources on an expanded market basis and apply pressure to the supply chain to deliver the value-price relationship they expect. The most effective supply chains are the ones that have responded to these empowered consumers and deliver products in a way that meets their particular needs.

- The various levels of government—local, state, and federal—also have a major impact on supply chains. This has been most notable in the last decade in the area of sustainability and the emphasis upon green supply chains. Companies have responded in a variety of ways and have found opportunities to meet sustainability objectives at the same time as lowering some of their costs.

- Transportation is an important and pervasive element in our economy, and it affects almost every person directly and/or indirectly. The goods we consume, our economic livelihoods, our mobility, and our environment are in some way impacted by transportation.

- Transportation bridges the supply and demand gap inherent in specialization by region or area and the related mass production. The interrelationship between transportation and large-scale production points out the dependency of our global economy upon effective and efficient transportation.

- As with freight transportation, people depend on transportation for their mobility and access to areas where they need to work, shop, or live. The more mobile a society, the more critical efficient and economical transportation is to its citizens.

- One of the challenges in evaluating transportation is the need for a simple, comprehensive, but comparable unit of measurement. The unit which is most frequently used for freight is the ton-mile, and for passengers, the passenger-mile. Both metrics are two-dimensional because they look at both weight and distance. This complicates the measurement process, but if you recognize the shortcomings, it is a very usable way to compare the transportation modes.

- Demand elasticity is an important economic concept, especially in the area of pricing, and it is very important for transportation pricing. Generally speaking, it is indicated that demand elasticity for overall freight movements between regions is relatively inelastic for transportation because transportation is often a relatively small percentage of the final selling price. There are exceptions but in general this is true.

However, for a particular mode of transportation operating between two points, the demand is relatively elastic because of the competition that may exist between the modes operating those two points.

- An important point to recognize about freight transportation is that it is a derived demand or secondary demand because demand for transportation is dependent upon the need or demand for a good in a distant location, requiring transportation to transport it to that distant location. In other words, the demand for freight transportation is derived from the customer demand for the product.

- When transportation cost is added to the manufactured cost of a product at a particular point, we develop what is called the landed cost of the product in the actual market. The landed cost helps determine the extent of the market for business and its ability to compete against other producers or similar products manufactured in other locations.

- Transportation service is very frequently important for the selection of a particular mode operating between two points. The dimensions of service would include reliability, accessibility, and security. These factors are looked at in terms of their cost impact as well as the actual transportation cost itself in selecting a particular model.

- Transportation is a critical link in the overall supply chain, which has become an important concept for organizations in the 21st century. Transportation can be viewed as the glue that helps to hold the supply chain together.

- The concept of supply chain management has evolved from the 1960s when organizations looked at the outbound side of logistics, physical distribution management, through the 1980s for the second phase where integrated logistics management became an important focus. The latter added inbound logistics to outbound logistics. Finally, supply chain management in the 1990s became the focal point, looking at an extended organization of all of the companies in the supply chain from the original vendor to the ultimate consumer.

STUDY QUESTIONS

1. What are the major forces or external factors that have impacted our economy during the latter part of the 20th and early part of the 21st centuries? How have each of these factors influenced companies as well as their respective supply chains? Which of these factors do you feel is the most important for a computer company? Why?

2. What is the actual nature of transportation demand? How does transportation demand influence individual companies in the economy?

3. Measuring transport output can be challenging to individuals trying to make a comparison among modes of transportation. Why is this measurement so challenging or difficult? Is there a better measure? Why or why not?

4. What is meant by the concept of derived demand? Why is it so important in the area of transportation for shippers and carriers? Does this concept have application in other areas? Give some examples.

5. Explain the difference between elastic and inelastic demand. Why are the two concepts important to transportation demand?

6. The aggregate demand for transportation service is said to be inelastic while the demand for an individual mode or carrier is often elastic. Explain why this is important to carriers and shippers.

7. Explain the concept of total landed cost as it relates to transportation. How does it influence market boundaries?

8. Discuss the various dimensions of transportation service and their impact upon costs for a company.

9. What is the role of transportation in a supply chain? Why is this role so important in today's environment?

10. Provide a brief overview of the three phases of development for supply chain management.

NOTES

1. Coyle, J. J., C. J. Langley, B. J. Gibson, R. A. Novack, and E. J. Bardi, *Supply Chain Management,* (Mason, OH: South-Western Cengage Learning, 2009), 14–20.

2. *Ibid.,* 425–429.

3. *Ibid.,* 423–425.

4. Donald Harper, *Transportation in America,* (Englewood Cliffs, NJ: Prentice Hall), 8–9.

5. *Ibid.*

6. *Op. cit.,*

CASE 1-1

Red Ball Express

George Harry, CEO of Red Ball Express, was frustrated and upset with the latest quarterly report on profit margins and overall level of profit for the company. Increased fuel prices were a concern for several of the previous quarters during the current year, but George thought that this quarter would be better since fuel prices had declined somewhat. However, Red Ball's operational costs were approximately the same this quarter as the previous three quarters. Just then, Dave Smith, one of his newest hires, came into his office without knocking, which was unusual. George could tell that Dave was excited and then Dave exclaimed, "Wow, George, did you see the latest issue of *Motor Carrier News*?" George indicated that he had not had the opportunity to review the magazine, and asked, "What is so darn exciting about it?" "Well, our biggest competitor, Roadway Carriers, was featured in an article for their cost-saving initiatives. They are expected to make a significant improvement in their profit for the last quarter. Our shareholders are really going to be upset when they see our quarterly results." George wondered how Roadway did it and immediately asked Dave that question. Dave indicated that the article discussed some new technology that they were using to improve equipment and driver productivity. Specifically, he mentioned RFID tags and GPS systems. George was not familiar with the new technologies and asked Dave to prepare a report on technology that Red Ball could employ to help them address their challenges with equipment management.

CASE QUESTIONS

1. Help Dave prepare this report by providing some information on the benefits of RFID tags and GPS systems in the transportation industry.

2. Are there additional technologies that Red Ball could implement to help them improve efficiency? Explain.

CASE 1-2

Clearfield Cheese Company Case

Andy Reisinger, CIO, and Sandy Knight, CSCO, of the Clearfield Cheese Company in central Pennsylvania had just returned from a meeting with Tom Powers, who was the CEO of the company. Andy and Sandy were both feeling the pressure of the competitive problems that Tom had presented in their weekly senior staff meeting. It was clear that Clearfield Cheese Company faced challenging market conditions.

Background

Clearfield Cheese Company was established in 1931 by two brothers, Ted and Terry Edwards, in Clearfield, which is located in an agricultural area in central Pennsylvania. At the time, the U.S. economy was in the throes of a severe economic depression. The local dairy farmers were experiencing financial duress because they could not sell their milk at a price which would cover their costs. Part of the problem was transporting the milk to Pittsburgh and other larger cities at a landed cost that was competitive with farmers in Ohio. The Edwards brothers owned several tank trucks for transporting milk, but saw an opportunity to purchase milk and process it into cheese. With meager savings and some borrowed capital they managed to set up a processing facility in Clearfield (hence the name of the company). Their grandfather, who had emigrated to the United States from Switzerland, was familiar with Swiss cheese processing techniques and helped them establish their operation. The company was a success and the Edwards brothers became legends to the local farmers and the employees of the company. The longer shelf life of the cheese allowed sales to expand into eastern Pennsylvania and Ohio.

Current Situation

Canada is the problem at the present time. Several cheese processing companies had been established near Toronto in the 1980s. For many years, the Canadian companies were not a problem, but with government subsidies to improve their manufacturing facilities and a much more favorable currency exchange rate, they were now encroaching into the established market areas of Clearfield Cheese Company with a quality product that had a competitive landed cost in central Pennsylvania.

Andy and Sandy were given the charge by Tom Powers to come back to the next staff meeting with some suggestions to help improve their competitive situation. They all felt that their product processing and the quality of their product were not the issue, but that their supply chain was not as efficient and effective as it needed to be to compete with the Canadian producers. Their inventory levels were high and their transportation costs were increasing.

CASE QUESTION

1. What strategies would you suggest for them to explore to improve their competitive situation?

Chapter 2

TRANSPORTATION: CRITICAL LINK IN THE ECONOMY

Learning Objectives

After reading this chapter, you should be able to do the following:

- Understand the importance of transportation to the economic vitality of countries or regions
- Appreciate the role and contributions of transportation systems to the economic development of countries or regions
- Understand how transportation impacts the social and political dimensions of an economy or region
- Appreciate the historical role of transportation from an economic, social, and political perspective
- Discuss the impact that improved transportation has upon land values
- Understand how transportation affects the price of goods and services
- Appreciate the function and scope of transportation in advanced and developed economies

Transportation Profile

Investing in Transportation Infrastructure

The meeting room was relatively quiet as the chairman of the newly established Joint Transportation Task Force entered, which was probably indicative of the serious nature of the issues that the task force members faced. To some members, their challenge probably seemed daunting, while to others the task force presented a great opportunity. But to all, their task was a complex set of interrelated issues. There was a sense of urgency, but at the same time, a recognition that careful consideration of the various proposals was critical for the long-term success of the objectives that they hoped to achieve.

Chairman Gary Gittings began: "Ladies and gentlemen, I'm sure that I don't have to waste your time with an extended statement of the rationale for this meeting. In my opinion, it's obvious that our task is important and critical to our country and the economy. The 21st century has presented us with some expected challenges, for example, global competitiveness for our various industries, but also some unexpected challenges such as a global recession."

"Our immediate task is to address the current shortcomings and future needs of our transportation system. Specifically, we need to investigate the infrastructure which supports the flow of commerce within our country and the global flow of goods and services into and out of our country. However challenging this task may seem, we have to recognize any investment in transportation-related infrastructure will also impact the overall economy in terms of employment opportunities, wages and income, capital investment opportunities, and so on. If we accomplish our task judiciously and as expeditiously as possible, it has the potential to have a tremendous 'ripple' effect in our economy that will help us to increase and sustain the economic growth that we so desperately need. Contrary to the opinion of some of our colleagues, I do not view this as a government giveaway program or 'pork barrel legislation,' but rather as a potential capital investment for our future growth and development."

"Even Adam Smith, the famed economist of the 18th century who developed the underlying tenets of a capitalistic market economy, recognized the need for government investment in capital projects such as **transportation infrastructure**. Over the course of our history, our government saw fit to make such investments and our economy was the beneficiary of these actions. One of the best examples was the National System of Interstate and Defense Highways Bill that was prepared during the Eisenhower Administration. The enabling legislation was actually passed in 1954 to build a system of limited access, modern highways to connect the various states and their respective areas of economic opportunity. Everyone in this room has been the beneficiary of this highway system on a personal level with respect to travel, but also we have benefited on an economic level with the tremendous growth that was spawned by this system."

"We have with the opportunity to recommend a spending program that could have a comparable economic, political, and social impact. However, caution is necessary to mitigate the potential for waste. We need to take a holistic approach and not fall victim to a spending plan which focuses upon local, vocal constituencies whose proposed projects, or should we say pet projects, will have limited or even negligible impact on our economic growth now or in future. Let's not build any 'bridges—or roads—to nowhere.'"

"As a first step, we need to identify our most critical infrastructure needs on a general level, not a project-specific level. We also need to present an overview of the benefits that we can expect to accrue from judicious and timely expenditures on improvements in our transportation infrastructure. Any insights into the possible sources of funding would also be useful."

Chairman Gittings looked around the room and noted that there appeared to be more interest and enthusiasm than when he began his comments. He was not naïve enough to believe that there was overall agreement among the members of the task force, or that some ideas and proposals would not be resisted. He found himself looking forward to the challenge ahead. After this reflective pause, he added several additional suggestions. "As a first step in this process, I recommend that we develop a white paper on the economic benefits that we could expect for our country and its various regions from the investment in transportation infrastructure, whether new projects or maintenance of old systems."

"We are at a crossroad which is very similar to what existed after World War II in terms of our potential. We have tasted the fruit of increased global interaction and the benefits which accrue in terms of an increased amount of goods being available at reasonable prices, and also some of the benefits which accrue from the expansion which has occurred in our economy. We have stalled at the present time and we need to restart the engine, so to speak. A potential way to achieve this objective is to invest in transportation infrastructure—highways, ports, airports, railways, and related facilities."

As you read this chapter, you will be presented with the benefits and rationale for investing public monies in transportation infrastructure. You will be provided with sufficient information to respond in depth to the first study question at the end of the chapter, which asks you to explicate the benefits and rationale for public investment in transportation infrastructure.

Introduction

The case statement outlined above provides some insights into why governments (federal, state, or local) invest in transportation infrastructure and systems and why they continue to maintain and sustain such systems and infrastructure. At a certain level, we accept and expect such action. For example, when it snows, we expect the roadway to be cleared so that we may gain access to our destination points. When a roadway becomes congested and traffic moves rather slowly, we expect highway improvements that will accommodate the greater flow of traffic. However, the benefits of improved transportation are much greater when we view them from a macro perspective, which is one of the objectives of this chapter. We will more fully appreciate the overall significance and impact of improved transport if we take this more holistic view.

Transportation is a pervasive and vital function in all industrialized economies. Transportation systems provide the necessary critical links between producers and consumers both domestically and globally. The citizens of industrialized countries are dependent upon transportation systems to move products from distant locations where they are produced to markets where they are needed and can be sold and consumed. An efficient and effective transportation system is essential for businesses to produce and sell products and services. It has long been recognized that one of the critical ingredients for underdeveloped countries to improve economically is the need to invest in transportation infrastructure. This investment is frequently referred to as social capital; that is, society as a whole is the beneficiary of such investment because of the economic benefits associated with new businesses, higher wages, more jobs, and so forth.

Transportation is one of the requirements of a developed economy because it can bring order out of chaos. It reaches in and touches every phase and facet of our well-being. Viewed in its totality from a historical, economic, social, and political perspective,

On the Line   *Transportation Infrastructure*

The state of the U.S. transportation-related infrastructure and capacity is of growing concern because the Federal Highway Administration has estimated that total freight volume moved in the United States is expected to triple by 2035. The growth in volume includes domestic shipments as well as global imports and exports that are moving to or from global gateways. This rapid growth in global trade is placing much pressure on the water gateways (ports), particularly on the West Coast of the United States with the rapid growth in trade with Asian countries. In fact, about 80 percent of the U.S. global freight (by weight) moves through port gateways. The rail and highway carriers providing service to and from the ports are also feeling the impact of the growth in terms of infrastructure capacity. At peak times, the congestion causes delays in loading and unloading as well as in movement into and out of the port areas. The net result is longer transit times, higher inventory costs, and stockouts.

The obvious solution to the capacity problem is new investment in transportation infrastructure—ports, highways, and railroads. Historically, the investment in port and highway infrastructure has been with public funds including user charges (tolls, gas tax, license fees, and so forth), but the rail investment has been privately funded to a large extent. In regard to needed infrastructure for railroads, it is estimated that there will be a $53 billion shortfall by 2025. The Highway Trust Fund (fuel taxes) is expected to have a $3.5 billion shortfall in needed funds for highway maintenance and expansion by 2010.

The U.S. recession of 2009–10 provided some relief from the infrastructure congestion, but as the economy fully recovers, we are very likely to experience congestion problems again.

Source: Dawn Russell and Kusumal Raumsook, "Emerging Conditions in Transport" [White paper], The Pennsylvania State University, Center for Supply Chain Research, January 2009, p. 2. Reprinted by permission of the authors.

it is unquestionably the most important industry in the world. Without transportation, you could not operate a grocery store or win a war. The more complex life becomes and the more developed the economy, the more indispensable are the elements of transportation.

Unfortunately, our transportation system is frequently taken for granted, and we do not consider the benefits that accrue to us. Therefore, it is appropriate at this point to discuss the societal benefits of improved transportation. This chapter will investigate the historical, economic, environmental, social, and political effects of a well-designed and improved transportation system.

Historical Significance

The importance of transportation becomes more apparent when one understands its history-making role. The growth of civilizations is directly associated with the development of transportation systems. For example, the strengths of ancient Egypt demonstrated how one form of transportation, water, could become the foundation for a great society. The Nile River held Egypt together. It provided a means to transport Egyptian goods, a way to communicate, and a method for Egyptian soldiers to move to defend their country. The Nile River, like all transportation systems, also affected the society's political and cultural development as people traveled and communicated.

A transportation system can help create a social structure. People traveling or living within the bounds of a particular transportation network share ideas and experiences. Eventually, a society develops with somewhat unified political opinions, cultural ideals, and educational methods. However, methods of transportation can also tear societies apart. People may become alienated from the common government system. For example, America's secession from Great Britain can be partly attributable to localized systems developing in the 13 colonies. Transportation to and from Britain was slow and inefficient, and American families could economically lead better lives trading among themselves without having to pay duties (taxes) to the government of King George III. As the colonies grew into a separate economic nation, political and cultural attitudes that were unique to America took hold. This led to an alienation with Great Britain and eventually to the Revolutionary War.

The United States continued to grow in tandem with its transportation networks in the 19th century. Few families thought to move west without first knowing that explorers had blazed trails and found rivers suitable for travel. The **Erie Canal**, steamboats, early turnpikes, and the early rail system were developed to meet the economic and social needs of the growing nation. See Table 2-1 for an overview of transport developments in the United States. This table illustrates important developments and implies how they impacted the growth in the United States.[1]

Transportation also plays a major role in **national defense**. This role has long been recognized by governments. The Roman Empire built its great system of roads primarily for military purposes, but they had an overall economic impact. Sir Winston Churchill once wrote that transport was the underlying basis for all that could be accomplished in effectively fighting a war. In other words, transportation was a critical ingredient to success on the battlefield. United States requirements for national defense have been a major reason for a number of important transportation projects. As indicated

Table 2-1	U.S. Transport Developments		
YEAR	**DEVELOPMENT**	**YEAR**	**DEVELOPMENT**
1774	Lancaster Turnpike: first toll road—Pennsylvania	1927	Lindbergh solo flight—New York to Paris
1804	Fulton's steamboat—Hudson River, New York	1961	Manned space flights begin
1825	Erie Canal: first canal—New York	1970	Amtrak established
1830	Baltimore and Ohio Railroad begins service	1976	Contrail established
1838	Steamship service—Atlantic Ocean	1978	Act to deregulate airlines passed
1865	First pipeline—Pennsylvania	1980	Act to deregulate motor carriers and Staggers Rail act
1866	Completion of transcontinental rail link	1982	Double Stack Rail container service initiated
1869	Bicycles introduced—United States	1986	Conrail profitable and sold by government
1887	First daily rail service coast to coast	1986	Norfolk Southern initiates roadrailer service
1887	Federal regulation of transportation begins	1990	National Transportation Policy Statement
1903	First successful airplane flight—Wright Brothers	1995	ICC Abolished
1904	Panama Canal opens	1998	Internet applications widely used in transportation
1919	Transcontinental airmail service by U.S. Post Office begins	2002	Airline industry suffers after 9/11 terrorist attacks
1925	Kelly Act: Airmail contract to private companies		

previously, under the Eisenhower Administration enabling legislation was passed for "National System of Interstate and Defense Highways." This highway system was envisioned as being a system of superhighways connecting the states and the major centers within the states, which could enhance our ability to defend against enemy attack. The economic and social benefits of the interstate highway system have thus far exceeded the defense contribution. Generally, the expenditures on air transport infrastructure are based primarily on military and political considerations as opposed to economic benefits, but the economic benefits usually outweigh the political and military benefits over the longer run.[2]

Economic Significance

Transportation systems have a major impact upon population patterns and urban economic development. Consider Table 2-2, which shows per capital consumption of major food commodities in the United States. The total of the top six items is about 1300 pounds per capita per year, or 25 pounds per week. For a city of 3 million individuals, this would be 75 million pounds per week or over 10 million pounds per day. If all the items on this list were included along with all the other consumer and industrial items that are needed on a daily or weekly basis in this hypothetical city, the numbers would be staggering. The transportation services of a city are the life support system of the citizens. The city would not be able to survive without its transportation system. Even the suburban areas surrounding the city are dependent on the transportation systems. Needless to say, the transportation service adds value to the goods shipped and this topic deserves consideration.

Value of Goods

Transportation systems help determine the economic value of products. A simple model will serve to illustrate this point. Consider a certain commodity that is desired in one location, provided it is offered below a certain price. In Figure 2-1, this commodity is produced at point A and costs OC at the point of production. The community that needs the commodity, located at point B, is the distance AB from A. The maximum price that people will pay for the commodity is shown on the vertical axis as OE, at community B.

If the original, inefficient transport system is used, moving the commodity from A to B will cost CH. The CD portion of the cost line is known as the fixed cost, and the DH portion of the line is the cost per mile (a variable cost) or slope of the line. With the inefficient system, the total cost at B is OH, a price greater than the maximum cost or price limit (OE) in community B.

Assume the transport system is improved, and the cost per mile or slope is reduced, and the transportation variable cost line becomes DJ. Now the cost at community B becomes OJ, which is below the maximum cost or price limit of OE. The market for the commodity produced at A will be expanded to community B. The efficiency of the new system enables the producer located at Point A to expand their market area to include B, which is a value-added service.

Place Utility The reduction in transportation costs between points A and B, illustrated above, gives the commodity **place utility** or **place value**. In the less efficient system, the goods will have no value at B because they could not be sold at the market

Table 2-2	2006 U.S. Per Capita Consumption of Major Food Commodities
PRODUCT	**QUANTITY (POUNDS)**
Red meats	109.9
Poultry	74.8
Fish and shellfish	16.5
Eggs	32.4
Cheese (excluding cottage)	32.4
Beverages and milk products	181.6
Fluid cream products	12.9
Yogurt (excluding frozen)	11.0
Ice cream	14.4
Low-fat ice cream	6.8
Frozen yogurt	1.4
Butter and margarine (product weight)	9.3
Fruit	269.6
Vegetables	406.40
Peanuts (shelled)	6.5
Tree nuts (shelled)	3.4
Flour and cereal products	192.5
Caloric sweeteners (dry weight equivalent)	138.6
Coffee (green bean equivalent)	9.5
Cocoa (chocolate liquor equivalent)	5.2

Source: U.S. Department of Agriculture, Economic Research Service (2008), *Agricultural Outlook: Statistical Indicators,* Washington, DC, p. 37.

price. The more efficient method of transportation creates place utility; since the goods can now be sold at point B for a competitive price.

Reductions in transportation costs permit market areas to purchase products from distant suppliers that might otherwise only be produced locally at a higher price. The reduction in transportation cost is actually greater for longer distances than for short ones because of the fixed charges indicated in Figure 2-1. If a supplier can cover the transportation cost in his or her price range, an increase in the distance over which this given amount will cover the transport of goods will increase the market area of the product in an even greater ratio.

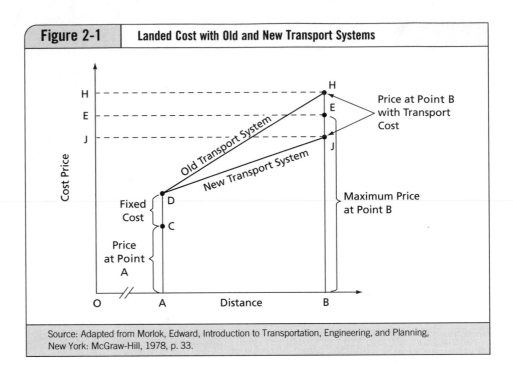

Figure 2-1 | **Landed Cost with Old and New Transport Systems**

Source: Adapted from Morlok, Edward, Introduction to Transportation, Engineering, and Planning, New York: McGraw-Hill, 1978, p. 33.

Dionysius Lardner, an early transportation economist, referred to this phenomenon as the **Law of Squares** in transportation and trade (also known as **Lardner's Law**). As shown in Figure 2-2, a producer at Point A can afford to transport a product 100 miles and meet competitive laid-down or landed costs. The boundary of the relevant market area is shown by the circumference of the smaller circle. If transportation cost is cut in half, the same sum will now transport the supplier goods for twice the distance, that is, 200 miles. Now the market boundary is shown by the circumference of the larger circle. The relevant market area increased four times in size when the radius doubled from 100 to 200 miles.

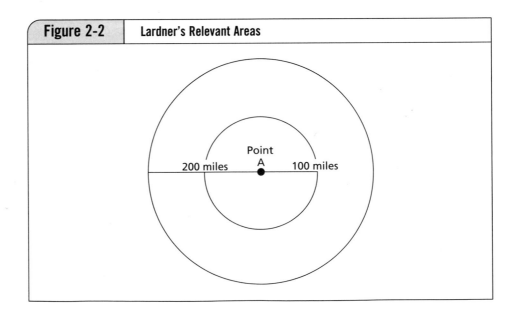

Figure 2-2 | **Lardner's Relevant Areas**

Time Utility The concept of **time utility** is closely aligned to that of place utility. The demand for a particular commodity may exist only during certain periods of time. If a product arrives in a market at a time when there is no demand for it, then it possesses no value. For example, the demand for Halloween costumes exists during a specific time of the year. After Halloween passes, these goods cannot be sold because they have little or no value in the market. Effective transportation can create time utility by ensuring that products are at the proper locations when needed. For example, raw materials for production, fruit, and Christmas toys all need to arrive at certain locations during specific times or their value will be diminished. The increased emphasis upon just-in-time and scheduled deliveries as well as lean inventories has heightened the importance of time utility, especially for high-value products and emergency shipments. Air freight shipments are particularly affected by the importance of time utility.

Lardner's Law can also be related to time utility. For example, the speed of transportation might be a governing factor for the transportation of certain perishable products that have a limited shelf life. Assume the small circle in Figure 2-2 represents the current market area based on a specific transportation speed. If the speed were doubled, the potential service area would quadruple.

Quantity Utility In addition, transportation gives goods **quantity utility** through the assurance that the goods will arrive without damage in the right quantity. This helps assure that the quantity demanded is the same as that delivered. This utility has increased in importance in recent years with the high level of importance placed on minimizing safety stock inventories for both shippers and receivers. Shippers might alter the form of the product to ensure safe transportation or change carriers with

Global Perspectives

Supply Chain Manager as Economist: Think Like a Global Economist

How can a supply chain manager use these broad economic trends to their advantage? By applying global economic logic to supply chain design and operation. Change creates not only pain but also opportunity—and today's tectonic shifts in the global economic landscape offer many intriguing openings. Enterprising supply chain managers can use practical economics to benefit their companies in four ways:

- **Pricing**: Reflecting updated cost-to-serve economics in product prices for specific customer segments and locations.
- **Sourcing**: Buying closer to point of use, partially reversing past globalization norms to reduce freight intensity.
- **Making**: Exploring efficient ways to manufacture and export more from the United States, leveraging the currently weak dollar.
- **Moving**: Downshifting transportation modes and adding distribution locations to save fuel and reduce cost.

These strategies form the core of a supply chain playbook that will set your company apart from the competition. Rather than merely responding to tough times, the supply chain leader can build strategic advantage through differentiated services and performance. This is a goal truly worth pursuing.

Source: David Bevet, "Global Logistics: The supply chain manager as global economist," *Logistics Management,* November 2008, p. 38. Reprinted by permission.

repeated failures. Carriers can use special bracing, blocking, and/or strapping, along with temperature control, to help ensure damage-free delivery. Time and quantity utility generally increase in importance as the value of goods increases because of related inventory-carrying costs and stock-out costs. For example, if the sale of a product is dependent upon its delivery on Tuesday afternoon and it arrives on Wednesday, the potential buyer may reject delivery. If the product had a profit margin of $100.00, the late delivery would cost the seller $100.00 in lost sales.

Utility of Goods

Transportation adds utility to goods because efficient transportation systems promote geographic specialization, large-scale production, increased competition, increased market areas, and increased land values. These outcomes usually result in lower consumer prices and more profit for producers as indicated below.

Geographic Specialization The concept of **geographic specialization** assumes that each nation, state, or city produces products and services for its citizens with its capital, labor, and raw materials. Since most areas cannot produce all of the needed products for their citizens, transportation is necessary to exchange (buy and sell) the goods that can be produced more efficiently at another location in return for different goods produced locally. The concept is closely aligned to the principle of **absolute** or **comparative advantage**. This principle assumes that an area will specialize in the production of goods for which it has the greatest advantage or the least comparative disadvantage. Gain from the specialization of goods will be mutually advantageous when the cost ratios of producing two commodities are different in different areas. Hence, Pennsylvania can concentrate on the production of coal or steel, Arizona on citrus fruit, and the Greek islands on olives. The development of specialization usually leads to lower prices, an increased availability of goods, and a higher standard of living.

Large-Scale Production Geographic specialization is complemented by large-scale production or **economies of scale**, which are the result of more efficient operations. However, without the use of efficient transportation networks, the advantages of scale economies, production efficiencies, and specialization could be lost. The raw materials for production need to be transported to a manufacturing facility, and the finished products must be transported out of an area at reasonable costs to markets and consumers at acceptable prices. Otherwise, the goods have no value. Geographic specialization assumes that the large-scale production of goods is demanded at distances away from the production site. Obviously, one area cannot rely upon its comparative advantage and large-scale production without the use of efficient transportation systems. The more efficient the transportation, the larger the potential market area and the possibility of increased scale economies. Time value can also be important in these situations, especially with perishable and/or seasonal products.

Increased Competition Efficient transportation can also provide the consumer with the benefit of increased market competition. Without transportation, local entrepreneurs could produce goods inefficiently and charge high prices for their consumption. Transportation can increase the market area for a product; thus, goods must be produced in the most efficient fashion, or distant competitors will enter the market and capture market share. The synergism among economies of scale, specialization, and efficient transportation is the basis for economic development and global trade.

Land Values Transportation improvements, which enhance an area's economy, can also increase the value of land that is adjacent to or served by the transport improvements because the land becomes more accessible and potentially more useful. Today, the suburban centers provide excellent examples of land areas that have increased in value due to the accessibility that results from efficient transportation systems or infrastructure. Suburbanites can take advantage of nearby city life for work and pleasure and then retire to rural areas via public transportation networks or highways to avoid crowded living conditions. Commuters from Greenwich, Connecticut, to New York City and from Cherry Hill, New Jersey, to Philadelphia all reap both city and suburban benefits as the result of reliable public transportation systems. Consequently, the value of the land in these areas has increased to reflect the advantageous lifestyles that the new or improved transportation systems have made possible. The land values within the city are also obviously enhanced by the economic development.

It is important to note that transportation may not always have a positive impact on land values. Noise and air pollution accompanying some networks can decrease adjacent land values. The homeowners who have to bear the burden of pollution also suffer from over-accessibility. Like most system changes, there are always advantages and disadvantages when transportation improvements are made. Consequently, it is important that a thorough analysis be made of costs (including social costs) and potential benefits before an investment in transportation infrastructure is made. Such cost-benefit analyses are not an exact science, but careful analysis can help preclude a bad investment decision.[3]

Transportation Patterns

Transportation patterns reflect the flow of people and commerce. Transportation has a catalytic effect on a society in that it stimulates commerce and movement. The reverse is also true. That is, the demand for commerce and movement will cause transportation to be developed.

The world's major water routes for transporting merchandise are shown in Figure 2-3. The merchandise includes finished and semifinished goods but does not

| Figure 2-3 | Major World Water Routes—Merchandise Traffic |

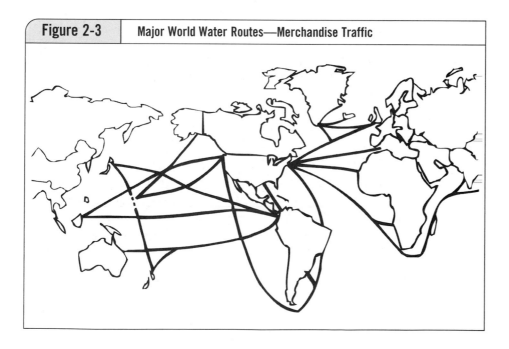

include heavy bulk goods such as ores and petroleum. These routes traditionally go to and from Europe, the United States, and the Far East (Japan, Korea, Hong Kong, and Taiwan). These routes have an east–west pattern between the developed nations and a north–south pattern between the developed nations primarily in the Northern Hemisphere and developing nations in Africa and South America. These routes closely approximate major air cargo and passenger routes of the world.

Major North American routes of commerce are shown in Figure 2-4. In the United States, these routes link the major metropolitan areas and represent the existing rail trunk line, interstate highway, and inland waterway patterns. The Canadian pattern links the major cities that are in a narrow population band along its border with the United States. These links connect Halifax, Montreal, Toronto, and the industrial sectors of southern Ontario, Edmonton, Calgary, and Vancouver. The route follows the

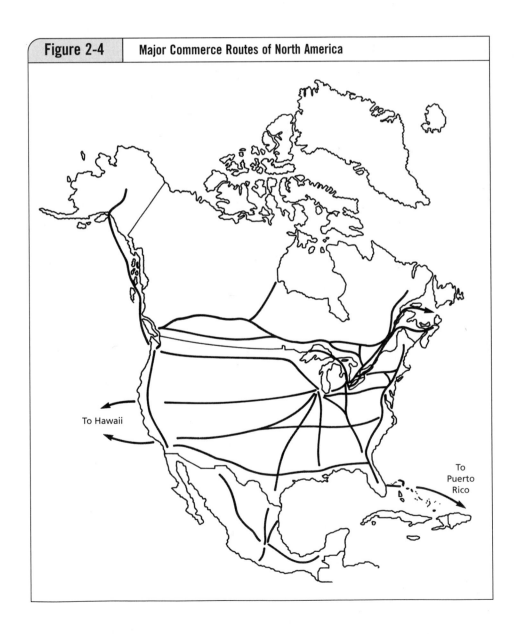

Figure 2-4 | **Major Commerce Routes of North America**

To Hawaii

To Puerto Rico

Trans-Canada Highway as well as the mainlines of the Canadian Pacific and the Canadian National Railroads. The Great Lakes and St. Lawrence River water system is also important because it is an outlet for exported grain and other products from Canada to the rest of the world.

Mexico's major commerce routes are strongly tied to its economic center, represented by Mexico City. Here again, the railroad mainlines and early highway development created an economic and social orientation to this pattern. During the last two decades, a significant band of economic development has occurred along the Mexico-U.S. border as U.S. companies established facilities to manufacture parts and finished products to take advantage of lower labor and operating cost in Mexico and the benefits of the North American Free Trade Agreement (NAFTA). The Mexico-based facilities have frequently been referred to as *maqueladora* operations, and they have contributed to the cross-border flow of commerce between Mexico and the United States. There are still cross-border challenges to the flow of goods, especially since the 9/11 attacks in 2001, but the amount of commerce has continued to increase between the United States and Mexico.

Gross Domestic Product (GDP)

Transportation plays a major role in the overall economy of the United States (see Table 2-3). On average, transportation accounts for about 10.5 percent of gross domestic product in the United States, compared to housing (24.3 percent), health care (17.4 percent), food (11.6 percent), and education (7.6 percent). It is safe to say that transportation is a major component of total expenditures in the U.S. economy. If we examine transportation as a component of household expenditures (Table 2-4), it accounts for 18 percent of household expenditures. Transportation expenditures are exceeded only by housing (24.3 percent). This is another indication of its importance not only in the economy but also to individual households.

Passenger transportation has been growing in relation to the GDP until recently. Much of this increase is due to the greater use of automobiles and the energy costs

Table 2-3	U.S. Gross Domestic Product by Major Societal Function, 2007
FUNCTION	PERCENT OF GDP
Housing	24.3
Health care	17.4
Food	11.6
Transportation	10.5
Education	7.6
Recreation	7.0
Other	21.5

Source: U.S. Department of Transportation, Bureau of Transportation Statistics, *Pocket Guide to Transportation—2007*, Washington, DC, p. 32.

Table 2-4	Average Household Expenditures, 2007
CATEGORY	PERCENT OF HOUSEHOLD EXPENDITURES
Housing	34
Transportation	18
Food	12
Personal Insurance and Pensions	11
Health Care	6
Other	22

Source: U.S. Department of Transportation, Bureau of Transport Statistics, *Pocket Guide to Transportation—2009*, Washington, DC, p. 33.

associated with operating them. Air travel also accounts for a major part of transportation expenditures in the economy. The U.S. Department of Transportation (DOT) reports that in 2006 airlines accounted for about 10.6 percent of the total passenger miles. Travel for business, personal, and vacation purposes is an important activity in the economy. With fuel prices fluctuating but expected to spiral upward again, it is anticipated that private vehicle travel will decrease with a move to public transportation and increased joint ridership.

Freight transportation, which traditionally accounted for between eight and nine percent of GDP, has decreased due to the more efficient use of transportation equipment and better network scheduling. Although the economy has been expanding, productivity increases in, and better use of, existing transportation systems have enabled this growth to take place without proportionate increases in total freight expenditures. It is interesting to note that overall transport expenditures as a percentage of GDP are slightly less than food expenditures and more than education expenditures. (See Table 2-3.)

Modal split is a useful analytical tool for the study of transportation because it divides the total transportation market for passenger and freight movements according to use or volume by the major modes of transportation. As indicated in Chapter 1 (see Table 1-1), highway transportation (public and private) dominates the movement of people in the United States and represents more than 77 percent of passenger-miles traveled in the United States. The proportion of highway travel decreased slightly over the past two decades due to growth in airline travel. Deregulation of airline service in the late 1970s brought about an increase in travel options and services for the traveling public. During this period, the relative level of airfares did not keep pace with the overall inflation level. As a result, air travel became more convenient and relatively cheaper for long-distance travel.

The freight intercity modal split is dominated by railroads, with about 40 percent of the ton-miles in 2006 (see Table 1-2 in Chapter 1). Railroads have declined in relative share since World War II, but have increased in share since 1990 because of fuel prices and other factors. Motor carriers have also increased their relative share of the total ton-mile market since 1980, but their share has remained relatively stable since 2000.

Railroads typically move bulk, low-value commodities such as grain, coal, ore, and chemicals for longer distances, which impacts their ton-miles share. In recent years, rail traffic by container, which transports relatively higher-value finished goods, has increased. The air mode, while highly visible, still handles less than one percent of the total ton-miles in the United States. Each of these modes will be accorded more detailed analysis in subsequent chapters (Chapters 5 through 8).

The total ton-miles of freight have increased between 1980 and 2006, as shown in Table 1-2, but the economy has expanded at a faster rate than the demand for freight transportation. The increase in global trade is one of the reasons for this phenomenon. For example, in the past, a domestic steel firm usually purchased transportation service for inbound raw materials (ore, lime, and coal) and the movement of the outbound finished goods to the customer. At the very minimum, this involved four different movements. Today the steel may be imported, requiring one domestic movement between

Transportation Technology   *Automated Gate Systems*

Intermodal transportation has been lauded for many years as a means to improve transport efficiency (read lower cost) and perhaps, transport effectiveness (read better service). A frequent stumbling block to achieving the desired objectives of lower cost and better service has been the interchange point where the intermodal exchange of equipment takes place. For example, if we were discussing rail-truck intermodal service, it would be at the point where the truck trailer is dropped by the truck tractor to be placed on a rail flat car.

Traditionally, a manual inspection was made with a checksheet, which was completed by the inspector looking for damage and other relevant information. The inspection was relatively slow, often with missing and sometimes inaccurate data. The terminal worker-inspector typically had to walk around the container, crawl under it, and maybe even climb up on top—causing time delays and safety concerns.

The actual development of the automated gate system began in 1992 as a joint project of a major railroad and a large consulting company. Over the course of several years, the technology went through several iterations. The net benefits of the automated gates are that they improve data integrity, process efficiency, and damage inspection procedures. A synergistic impact has been an environmental improvement. Because of the speed of the process, trucks do not sit near the interchange points as long with their engines idling.

The new technology eliminates disputes about damage since digital photo images are shot from several angles as the truck enters the exchange area. Any damage can be assigned to the appropriate party with no arguments. The process takes about 30 seconds unless there is some unusual problem.

These regional facilities are very important economically to the geographic area in which they are located. The efficiency of the technology contributes to continued viability for the area. The reduction in pollution mentioned above is also very positive given the emphasis upon sustainability and green supply chains. This is a good example of how a regional infrastructure facility is adding economic benefit and mitigating social cost through technology.

Source: Adapted from "AGS Offers Benefits at Intermodal Gates," *Intermodal Insights,* January 2009, pp. 3, 6. Copyright (c) 2009 Intermodal Association of North America. Reprinted by permission.

the port and the customer. Thus, steel is being used in the economy, but fewer transportation moves are involved in making it available to the customer.

As stated previously, good transportation spurs economic development by giving mobility and lower landed cost to production factors, which permits scale economies and increased efficiency. Good transportation enlarges the area that consumers and industries can draw on for resources and products. It expands the area to which a given plant or warehouse can distribute its products economically, and the resulting specialization and scale economies provide a wider choice of products for consumers at a lower cost. The overall economic importance and significance of improved transportation systems need to be understood and appreciated.

Environmental Significance

Although transportation provides the economy with numerous benefits, these positive aspects are not without some associated social costs. As indicated previously, transportation sometimes pollutes the environment and exploits natural resources, although many citizens feel that the overall benefits provided by transportation exceed these costs. The environmental challenge of the future will be to accurately assess the relationship between industrial and consumer benefits compared to the external societal costs associated with transportation improvements.

The Environment

There has been growing concern over the impact of transportation on the environment in recent years, with particular emphasis on air quality (pollution), noise, and water quality. The synergy between the transportation system and the environment is increasingly being investigated by both environmentalists and transportation planners at all governmental levels. In fact, increasing pressure from the environmentalists has resulted in legal restrictions that help govern the balance between a sound and efficient transportation system and a safe and clean environment. The term **green supply chains** has become a part of our vocabulary. Transportation is an important part of all supply chains and will receive increasing attention in environmental analyses and discussions. The major change that has occurred since the previous edition of this book was published is the growing acceptance by businesses and other organizations that they have an important role to play in helping to make improvements in this area. Perhaps even more important is a growing recognition that environmental issues do not have to be a zero-sum game. In other words, reductions in an organization's carbon footprint, for example, can be accomplished along with reductions in the cost of transportation operations with careful planning. Many companies are looking at their transportation operations from this "win-win" perspective.

There is already a growing challenge in the 21st century to ensure efficient transportation facilities and mobility by maintaining the present system and developing alternatives to meet the growing needs of individuals and organizations. There will probably be even more trade-offs between competing objectives. Highway and air planners will be particularly challenged to develop innovative design solutions because of the large number of federal statutes and executive orders governing the environment. From a user perspective, these constraints may be viewed as burdensome bureaucracy that slows down the completion of the project, but they are, for the most part, a necessary "filter" to screen changes in our transportation infrastructure.

Air Quality and Acid Rain Pollution is an external side effect of transportation because of the widespread use of internal combustion engines. In fact, the internal combustion engine emissions are a concern not only for their effect on urban air quality (pollution) but also for their involvement in producing acid rain and potential global climate changes. Transportation is a major contributor to air pollution. Reductions have taken place in motor vehicle emission rates because of governmental requirements, but economic and population growth makes it a persistent problem especially on a global basis.

Essentially, **acid rain** is a pollution-related phenomenon that causes falling rain to be much more acidic than normal. The addition of sulfur dioxide, nitrogen oxides, and volatile organic compounds to the atmosphere causes acid rain. The pollutants result from industrial and commercial processes and combustion, as well as vehicle emissions. The acid deposits have an adverse impact on aquatic systems, crops, forests, human health, and visibility. It is difficult to reliably measure transportation's contribution to acid rain, but it is likely that this area will be a source of growing concern and increased regulation on transportation emissions in the future.

An important issue facing the United States and the rest of the world is the so-called greenhouse effect and the related climate changes. Basically, the greenhouse effect is the physical process by which energy from the sun passes through the atmosphere relatively freely, while heat radiating from the earth is partially blocked or absorbed by particular gases in the atmosphere released by human activities such as transportation.

Ozone reduction in the stratosphere is a big concern because ozone reduces the amount of ultraviolet radiation reaching the earth's surface from the sun. The hole in the ozone layer has been the focus of much concern and investigation because of health-related problems and increased risk of skin cancer. A particular concern in this area is the chlorofluorocarbon (CFC) compounds used as the refrigerant for recharging and servicing air conditioning units in homes and vehicles. Again, we can expect worldwide concern and the development of protocols to reduce the risks in this area.

Maritime and Water Quality The protection of the marine environment from the adverse effects of oil spills, garbage dumping from ships, hazardous material losses, and so on, is a growing concern shared by many federal and state agencies. One of the largest oil spills occurred in 1989 near Prince William Sound, Alaska, from a tanker ship, The *Exxon Valdez*, which was carrying crude oil from Alaska for the Exxon Oil Company. Almost 11 million gallons of crude oil were spilled; this environmental disaster raised awareness for controls and better contingency preparedness to respond to such accidents. But there have been a continuing number of spills on various waterways and in the oceans. The increased size of vessels has heightened the concern and increased the potential for significant damage.

In recent years, there has been a growing concern about the damage that plastic items and other ship-generated garbage can cause to the marine environment. Birds, marine mammals, and sea turtles are susceptible to this type of refuse because they can ingest the materials and die as a result. It is estimated that more than one million birds die each year from ingesting these materials. It is very difficult to control or regulate this form of pollution.

Water quality, both for surface water and for drinking water sources, is an area of risk and concern. Both surface water and drinking water sources are highly susceptible to many types of potential pollutants. Again, there will be continuing pressure to protect water quality by governmental controls and standards.

Noise Another type of pollution is noise, which can be emitted from many sources, including transportation. There is an annoyance factor, but also a health concern involved. Airplanes and motor vehicles are the major causes of noise. The U.S. DOT and the Federal Aviation Administration have been particularly active in this area, helping to guide land-use planning for compatibility with transportation facilities and conducting research to help solve the problem. Noise emissions are governed by the Noise Control Act of 1972, which allows the setting of operational standards for aircraft and trucks and even rail equipment operated by interstate carriers.

Safety

One of the more disturbing by-products of transportation is injury and loss of life. In 2006, a total of 44,912 persons lost their lives in the United States while engaged in transport. Approximately 95 percent of those fatalities occurred in highway vehicles. However, the number of deaths has remained relatively stable in relation to the ever-growing demand for transportation. This positive statistic is the result of increased licensing regulations and more reliable vehicle designs. Unfortunately, trends in the area of safety for freight transportation are not as promising. Train accidents, oil spills, and the threat of gaseous explosions while in transit have increased. With an increasing variety of products being shipped and an increasing volume of transportation, these problems require greater attention. We can hope that safety in freight transportation will soon parallel the progress made in passenger transportation; however, much work remains to be done.

The nation's increasing demand for transportation services has imposed social costs in addition to monetary costs. Over the past 25 years, great strides have been made, particularly at the national level, in mitigating those negative social costs. Overall, the benefits far outweigh the costs to society, but vigilance is necessary.

Recent studies have shown that less than one percent of drivers tested were positive for alcohol and less than two percent tested positive for drugs. Much has been achieved by joint industry–carrier partnerships that changed attitudes from adversarial to cooperative. The federal government has also played a significant role by drafting regulations that focus not only on detection but on assistance as well.

Social Significance

A good transportation system can also enhance the health and welfare of a population. One of the major problems that has faced the famine relief efforts in the various region of Africa is the lack of sufficient and effective transportation networks to move needed food and farm supplies from the ports inland to the population centers. Insufficient railroads, roads, vehicles, storage, and related distribution facilities hampered effective delivery of the needed food and supplies. In addition, one of the problems facing the region in normal times is insufficient transportation, which hinders inbound and outbound product flows.

A well-developed transportation also contributes improved health and education delivery systems and effective communications among regions of a country. Overall, transportation plays a major social role in our economy that is not always fully appreciated nor understood by the citizenry.

Political Significance

The origin and the maintenance of transportation systems are dependent on the government. Government intervention is needed to design feasible routes, cover the expense of building public highways, and develop harbors and waterways. Adequate transportation is needed to create national unity; the transportation network permits the leaders of government to travel rapidly to and communicate with the people they govern.

The government is responsible for aiding all passenger and freight transportation systems in which the costs cannot be covered reasonably by a central group of users. The government has also created regulations that offer consumers the opportunity to transact in a competitive free-market environment.

One outgrowth of regulation is the **common carrier**. The common carrier has a duty to render service without discrimination based upon set rates for specific commodities.

The government's role as a regulator of transportation services may entail certain drawbacks for the public. For example, the right of **eminent domain** may require individuals to move and sell their land, even though they might not wish to do so. The government's power of eminent domain gives it the right to acquire land for public use. Hence, the construction of many highways displaces families because governmental intervention has opened the right-of-way for certain transportation routes. Although families might be displaced, the government's role is to act in the best interest of the public by designing routes that help the citizens of the nation efficiently conduct their business and meet their social needs.

Closely connected with transportation's political role is its function as a provider for national defense. Today our transportation system enhances our lifestyles and protects us from outsiders. The ability to transport troops acts as both a weapon and a deterrent in this age of energy shortages and global conflicts. The conflicts in Central America, Africa, and the Middle East place even greater emphasis on the importance of transportation in protecting our distant vital interests.

Although it is accurate to say that the American transportation system has been shaped by economic factors, political and military developments have also played important roles. Transportation policy incorporates more than economics—the expected benefits of the system extend beyond the economic realm.

Overview of Modern Transportation

As indicated previously, the transportation system influences many aspects of our life. For example, the location of transportation facilities has effects on the surrounding communities. Railroads and superhighways can divide towns and neighborhoods, and the location of highway interchanges can determine the location of manufacturing, retailing, and distribution operations. The character of a neighborhood or a city may be determined by its ability to act as a transportation center. The port city of New Orleans, the rail city of Altoona, Pennsylvania, and St. Louis's role as the "Gateway to the West" are examples of towns that have become known for their ability to provide transportation services.

Factors can be identified correlating network changes to changes in neighborhood characteristics. Transportation factors can be synergistic with a whole series of other factors that cause sociological change and extend beyond transportation factors alone. For example, regional shopping centers; higher-income commuter enclaves; and resort, vacation, and amusement districts can grow as the result of available transportation networks and the appropriate combination of economic and social factors.

The consumer makes decisions based on transportation services, availability, cost, and adequacy. Product decisions (what products or product to produce or distribute) are closely related to this availability of transportation and adequacy of the transporter to move the goods. Market area decisions are dominated by the ability of the transporter to get the product to market at a low cost. Decisions about whether to purchase parts, raw materials, supplies, or finished goods for resale must reflect transport costs. Location decisions, too, are influenced by many transportation factors. The decisions about where plants, warehouses, offices, and stores should be located all take transportation requirements into consideration. Last but not least, pricing decisions are strongly affected by the transportation system. The logistics area of the firm, which includes transportation, is often considered a cost center; therefore, changes in the price of transportation will often have an impact on the price of products in general.

Overall, transportation interacts with three groups of our society: users, providers, and the government. Thus, transportation decision makers are expected to consider all aspects of society in one form or another.

The role of the user is to make decisions that will maximize the relevant consumer-oriented goals. The power of the user lies in the ability to demand and pay (or not pay if the wrong service is offered) for certain forms of transportation. The next chapter will explore in some detail the role of the government in enabling efficient and effective transportation through regulation and public policy.

The providers, both public and private, including agencies such as freight forwarders and brokers, must determine the demands of the system and services to be offered. These decisions are made in light of total modal use, the importance of each mode to the economy, profits, and the way in which each company views itself in relation to its competitors. Chapters 5 through 8 discuss the role of the transportation providers.

Overview of Transportation Trends

The transportation industry is in a continuing state of change. It is intertwined with the social, political, and economic forces in a society and economy. The industry as a whole has undergone a tremendous change since deregulation in the late 1970s and early 1980s. This has affected how carriers have organized, priced, sold their services, and managed operations. Table 2-5 presents many of the key forces in transportation during the 1990s and the first decade of the 21st century, and the impact they might have in the future. These points set the stage for the remaining chapters of this book, which deal with individual modes of transportation, cost and rate making, the buying and selling of transportation service, government regulation and policies, and carrier management.

Table 2-5	Transportation Trends

THE TRANSPORTATION MARKET

Customized services and equipment to meet specific shipper/receiver needs

Increased concern about equipment utilization

Increased global commerce with longer shipping distances

International transactions made faster and easier with improved information technology

Shift from heavy industrial production-oriented transportation to fast, service-demanding finished goods transportation

Transportation becoming more integrated with production, sourcing, labor, distribution, and marketing factors in a supply chain context.

Greater marketing orientation by carriers

Higher fuel charges causing shifts in modal split

More international transportation

TRANSPORTATION SUPPLY

Increased use of third-party services

Consolidation in air, rail, and motor modes

Increased use of public transportation in urban and suburban areas

Integration of modes via joint ownership or special arrangements

Continued technological advances in most modes

Less private carriage use for reasons of cost savings; still present where special services are involved

More international alliances of carrier

More concern with security and terrorism

OPERATIONS AND MANAGEMENT

Operations in closer link with marketing and sales of the carrier

Leasing of containers, aircraft, terminal facilities, and other assets on increase

Information-driven organization and structures

Decision making and accountability being pushed lower in the organization

GOVERNMENT POLICIES AND REGULATION

Increased noneconomic regulation (environmental, substance abuse, safety and security)

Government funding not keeping up with the deterioration of transportation infrastructure

Increased concern about the financial viability of some modes of transportation, for example, air transport.

In the 21st century, our transportation system faces significant challenges and problems because of global competition, governmental budget constraints, increased demands from special interest groups such as senior citizens, and especially, the threat of terrorism. The patterns of trade that help to drive transportation are changing more quickly and becoming more complex because of the dynamic global environment that we now live in, the changing economic base in the United States, and the increased competitiveness of previously undeveloped countries such as China.

SUMMARY

- Transportation is a pervasive and very important part of all developed economies and is a key ingredient for underdeveloped countries to progress to economic independence.

- The history of the United States is replete with evidence of the close correlation of advances in transportation technology with advancing economic development, from the Erie Canal to our modern highways and air systems.

- Transportation systems are the lifelines of our cities and the surrounding suburbs. Tons of products are moved into our cities every day to promote the health and welfare of its citizens. Also, products that are produced in the cities are moved out for shipment elsewhere.

- Transportation contributes to the value of goods by providing time and place utility. That is, effective and efficient transportation moves products to points where there is a demand for the product and at a time when it is needed.

- Geographic and labor specialization are important cornerstones of industrialized countries, and transportation provides one of the necessary ingredients for this to occur.

- The more efficient the transportation system, the greater the possibility of scale economies and increased market areas.

- Improved transportation in an area will usually increase land values because of the improved accessibility to raw materials and markets.

- The flow and patterns of commerce influence transportation infrastructure patterns of developing countries.

- Transportation expenditures for freight and passengers are an important part of the gross domestic product in the United States.

- While transportation provides many benefits, it can also contribute to environmental problems including pollution, poor air quality, acid rain, and global climate changes.

STUDY QUESTIONS

1. Help the Chairman of the Joint Transportation Task Force (discussed in the beginning of this chapter) by providing a rationale for spending money from the stimulus package to improve and maintain the transportation infrastructure. In other words, why should the investment be made in improved transport systems?

2. "Transportation is the most important factor for economic development." Defend this statement.

3. Why were the opening of the Erie Canal, the building of the transcontinental railroads, and the building of the National System of Interstate and Defense Highways after World War II so important to the United States?

4. Why are highways serving major metropolitan areas sometimes described as their lifelines?

5. Explain the nature and importance of time and place utility, and how they contribute to the value of a product.

6. Adam Smith stated that the specialization of labor was limited by the extent of the market and that transportation helps to expand the market. Explain this statement.

7. What is the relationship between improved transportation and land values?

8. "Transportation patterns reflect the flow of people and commerce." Explain this statement and its significance for transportation systems.

9. While improved transportation systems provide economic benefits, there may be some associated environmental costs. What are the major environmental costs associated with transportation, and what are their potential negative impacts?

10. "Improved transportation systems can also have social and political significance." Explain.

NOTES

1. D. Philip Locklin, *Economics of Transportation* (7th ed.), Richard D. Irwin, Inc.: Homewood, Illinois, 1972, 28–33.

2. Ibid., 34–37.

3. Ibid., 38–40.

CASE 2-1

Opportunity Knocks

Terry Edwards, vice president of HOG, Inc., a highway construction company in central Pennsylvania, has just returned from a meeting of the senior management team of the company. At the meeting, Harry O. Growbaker, president of HOG, Inc., had reported on his recent trip to Washington, D.C., and Harrisburg, Pennsylvania. The focus of the presentation and discussion was a new federal legislative package that would provide funding for new regional highway projects in the various states. Harry O. Growbaker felt that HOG, Inc., could participate but that they needed to be proactive to demonstrate the economic impact of such stimulus spending in central Pennsylvania. Harry asked Terry to give this matter some thought and provide some discussion points for the next meeting of the senior management team.

Terry decided to meet with two of his staff members, Sandy Knight and Tom Collins, to help with his assignment. During the course of their discussion, Tom pointed out the lack of good connections between two major interstate highways that traversed central Pennsylvania, namely Interstates 80 and 78. Both were major arteries for truck traffic with mostly an east-west flow in Pennsylvania. The economic growthin Central Pennsylvania, Tom said, was creating a need for an effective north-south link between I-80 and I-78. Tom felt that a proposed highway link would be attractive to the state and federal government.

Sandy, who had worked for Penn State University for a number of years, pointed out the possible synergism with the University Park campus of Penn State and perhaps some of their satellite locations such as Harrisburg. She noted the development of the research park at Penn State's University Park Campus and its active role in encouraging new companies based upon applied research at the university. She felt that there was a lot of opportunity to encourage and enhance this development with improved transportation. She also pointed out that the state was giving away land that had been part of a prison that could be used for economic development.

Terry Edwards became excited as he listened to this discussion. He felt that he could develop a list of discussion points for the next senior management meeting that could then be developed into a white paper for the State and Federal Departments of Transportation.

CASE QUESTIONS

1. You have recently been hired by HOG, Inc., and Mr. Edwards has asked you to develop a set of discussion points that would point out the economic and perhaps social benefits from a new highway link in central Pennsylvania.

CASE 2-2
The Green Team

Yourway Subs, of Naperville, Illinois, like other quick-serve restaurants, is often cited as an example of a business organization that contributes to the growing environmental challenges of the 21st century. They have daily deliveries to their many relatively small and dispersed retail locations to ensure the freshness of their products. Their customers usually carry out their food purchases in plastic containers and bags. They purchase their food-related products from large producers and distributors who are often located relatively long distances from the retail stores of Yourway Subs. Their store distribution network is based upon assured supply at the stores, that is, "never stock-out of an item."

Jean Beierlein, CEO of Yourway Subs, is very cognizant of the emphasis or pressure from the federal government, especially under the new president, to reward eco-friendly companies with tax credits. This is particularly true for city operations where environmental pollution was a great concern. Ms. Beierlein has decided to start a pilot program in the Midwest. She has appointed Lauren Weber, director of sustainability, to lead what she calls her "Green Team." Lauren has a degree with a major in Supply Chain Management and has worked as a consultant for a number of years. Lauren's Green Team consists of Tracy Shannon, principal with CSCR, LLC, and Emily Heuer, director of produce and social responsibility for Yourway Subs.

The Green Team has decided to meet the Green Standard for Fast Food Chains and not just pay lip service to their sustainability action program. They have identified a number of key initiatives to get the ball rolling:

- Procure produce locally
- Bake bread on site
- Reduce miles the inbound products are shipped
- Collaborate with suppliers to reduce packaging and transport miles
- Re-evaluate inventory strategies

CASE QUESTIONS

1. You have been asked by the Green Team to critique their pilot program, pointing out strengths and weaknesses as well as the addition of new initiatives for them to consider.

Chapter 3

TRANSPORTATION REGULATION AND PUBLIC POLICY

Learning Objectives

After reading this chapter, you should be able to do the following:

- Understand the bases for the regulation of transportation in the United States
- Appreciate the roles of regulatory agencies and the courts in regulating transportation
- Obtain a knowledge of previous and current regulations affecting transportation
- Understand the need for a national transportation policy
- Identify and assess the need and roles of public promotion in transportation
- Appreciate the role of user charges
- Obtain a knowledge of transportation safety and security regulations in the United States

Transportation Profile

Reregulating the Railroads

The railroads in the United were the first major industry to be economically regulated by the federal government. The driving factor in this decision was the railroads' tendency to be monopolistic in nature. Because of the high level of fixed investment in track and equipment, the railroads faced little, if any, competition during the developmental period of the United States in the late 1880s. Because of this, many shippers complained that rail prices were excessive and service was poor. This was especially true for small and captive shippers. As a result, the United States federal government regulated the railroad industry with the passage of the Act to Regulate Commerce of 1887.

From 1887 to 1979, the federal government strengthened the regulation of the railroads and brought motor carriers, water carriers, airlines, and pipelines under federal regulatory control. The intent of this regulation was to provide shippers with a level of competition within and between modes that would result in reasonable rates and adequate service. The theory behind this was that a sound, efficient, and effective transportation system would benefit not only freight shippers but also the general public as well.

In 1980, however, the federal government deregulated the railroad industry with the passage of the Staggers Rail Act. The intent of the Act was to allow railroads more freedom in how they set prices and served markets. With this freedom, the railroads were supposed to be able to attract private capital for infrastructure investments. The ability to set differential prices (that is, prices that reflected not only the cost to provide the service but also the shipper's willingness to pay) by the railroads was intended to help grow railroad revenue to allow railroads to be selective in the freight they carried. Some opponents of this legislation argued that small and captive shippers would now be without adequate rail service, which would harm them and the general public. Proponents countered that now the railroads could operate as firms normally do in a free-market economy.

The deregulation of the railroad industry culminated with the passage of the ICC Termination Act of 1995. The Surface Transportation Board (STB) replaced the Interstate Commerce Commission as the regulatory body for the railroad industry. This Act increased the freedoms enjoyed by the railroad industry in setting prices, entering or leaving markets, and determining service levels. The deregulatory environment seemed to work as the railroads have enjoyed substantial profitability since the Act passed in 1995.

However, new legislation proposed in 2007 by both the House of Representatives and the Senate seeks to reregulate the railroad industry. This legislation, the Railroad Competition and Service Act (H.R. 2125, S. 953), proposes to: (1) ensure competition in the railroad industry; (2) enable rail customers to obtain reliable rail service; and (3) provide customers (shippers) with a reasonable process for challenging rate and service disputes. The proposed legislation would empower the STB to determine rate reasonableness, allow the STB to define areas of inadequate rail competition, and establish an Office of Rail Customer Advocacy. The rationale behind this proposed legislation is to limit the ability of the railroads to set differential prices because they discriminate against small and captive shippers. Many industry and trade groups oppose this proposed legislation on the grounds that reregulating the railroad industry would cause much needed capital for infrastructure projects to disappear because industry revenues would decline. This lack of funds for improvements would cause a severe deficiency in rail capacity to meet increasing railroad freight demand.

The role of transportation in our economy cannot be overstated. It provides a means for commerce and our national defense. Because of its impact on the general public, the federal government has an obligation to ensure a sound, efficient, and effective transportation network. However, the question remains as to how this type of transportation network should be achieved. Does government regulation or the free-market economy provide the best transportation network that satisfies the demands of the transportation providers, customers, and the general public? This chapter will examine the role of government in transportation, the role of regulation in transportation, and the benefits of transportation to the general public.

Introduction

Transportation has long been a critical component of every world economy. From the development of the Egyptian empire because of the Nile River to the establishment of colonies on the east and west coasts of the U.S. because of ocean transportation, transportation has allowed civilizations to expand through trade with other countries. Because of its impact on a nation's economy, many countries have developed policies and regulations for transportation to assure a safe, reliable, and fair transportation network for their citizens.

When the United States was an agricultural society, it relied on wagons and railroads to move products from points of surplus to points of demand. As the United States evolved into a manufacturing economy, it utilized railroads, motor carriers, water carriers, pipelines, and air carriers to create time and place utilities. Today, while the United States is mainly an Internet-based society, it still relies on transportation to add value to products not only for domestic movements but also for global movements. All through this history, the United States has attempted to set policies and establish regulations, at both the state and federal levels, to govern its transportation network so it is fair and equitable to transportation providers, shippers, and citizens. However, because of the boundary-spanning nature of transportation and its multiple constituents, developing a fair and equitable transportation network for all parties has been and continues to be a challenge for U.S. government agencies.

This chapter will examine the basis of this regulation, along with the roles of the regulatory commissions and the courts. A discussion of the development of transportation regulation from its inception at the federal level in 1887 to its role today will be presented, along with the national transportation policies directing and promoting transportation and national security.

Regulation of Transportation

Nature of Regulation

In the United States, the government influences the activities of industries in many different ways. The amount of influence in industry activity varies from providing the legal foundation and framework in which industries operate to government ownership and control of firms in some industries. The degree of government regulation in some industries has sometimes met with stiff opposition from firms in those industries. However, because of the impact some industries have on the economy of the United States, some level of government intervention is necessary.

The amount of government control and regulation has increased as the United States has grown and prospered. If the amount of government controls in existence 150 years ago was compared to that in place today, the former would seem insignificant. The expansion of government influence, however, has been necessitated by the increase in the scope of activity, complexity, and size of individual firms.

In the United States, our economic activity is usually viewed as one of private enterprise. Competition is a necessary requirement for a free-market economy. A competitive market can decide the allocation of scarce resources. Economists have soundly developed the concepts of competition and free markets for years.

The definitions of *pure competition* and *free market* involve several conditions that might not exist in reality. Products are justified only by the market's willingness to buy them. A product should not be sold at a price below the marginal cost of making the last unit. The free market theory also assumes that producers and consumers are able to assess whether or not a given economic act will provide them with a positive return.

Although pure competition provides a marketplace that is desirable to consumers, a **monopoly** does not. In a monopoly, only one seller exists and can control the price of each individual unit of output. Consumers have no opportunity to switch suppliers. If all market structures took the form of either pure competition or monopoly, the solution would be simple. Most individuals would not disagree with government regulation of a monopoly, and a valid case could be made for no government intervention in an economy characterized by pure competition. However, the prevailing situation is not that simple. Market structures usually take some form between the extremes of pure competition and monopoly.

The imperfections in the marketplace in a free-enterprise economy provide the rationale for government controls. The controls exercised by the government can take one of several forms. One form is that of maintaining or enforcing competition—for example, the antitrust laws set forth by the government. Second, the government can substitute economic regulation for competition, as it has done in the transportation industry. Third, the government can assume ownership and direct control, as it has done with the U.S. Post Office.

The basic challenge of regulation in our society is that of establishing or maintaining the conditions necessary for the economical use of resources under a system of private enterprise. Regulation should seek to maintain a competitive framework and rely on competitive forces whenever possible. The institutional framework for regulating transportation is provided by federal statute. A perspective on the overall legal basis for regulation is important to the student of transportation, and will be examined in the next section.

Common Law

The legal system in the United States is based upon **common law** and civil or statutory law. The former is a system basic to most English-speaking countries because it was developed in England. Common law relies on judicial precedent, or principles of law developed from former court decisions. When a court decision establishes a rule for a situation, then that rule becomes part of the law. As conditions change, the law sometimes needs further interpretation. Therefore, an important feature of the common law system is that it changes and evolves as society changes. There are many examples of such change in the interpretation of the areas of federal and state control or responsibility for regulation of transportation.[1]

The common law approach fits well with a free market economy because the individual is the focus of attention and can engage in any business that is not prohibited. Each individual is regarded as possessing equal power and responsibility before the law.[2] The early regulation of transportation developed under common law. The obvious connection is with the concept of *common carriage*, in which transportation providers were required to serve all shippers and charge reasonable rates without discrimination.

Statutory law or civil law is based upon the Roman legal system and is characteristic of continental Europe and the parts of the world colonized by European countries. Statutory law is enacted by legislative bodies, but it is a specific enactment. A large part of the laws pertaining to business in general and to transportation are based upon statutory law. However, two points are important to note in this regard. First, common law rules are still very important in the transportation industry because many statutes were, in effect, copied from common law principles. Second, statutes are usually general in nature and need to be interpreted by the courts. Thus, in the United States, there is a very close relationship between common law and statutory law.

The regulation of transportation in the United States began at the state level under the common law system when a number of important regulations, as well as the basic issue of whether a business could even be regulated at all, were developed. In the latter regard, a concept of "business affected with the public interest" was developed under common law. **State regulation** also included the use of charters for some of the early turnpike companies and canal operations. The development of the railroad industry necessitated a move to statutory regulation, which was in effect by 1870 with the passage of **granger laws** in several states. Granger laws were the product of the granger movement, which began about 1867 in states such as Illinois, Iowa, Minnesota, and Wisconsin. Granges were organizations formed by farmers in various states and functioned as political action groups where farmers could discuss problems. Farmers joined the granger movement because of their dissatisfaction with railroad rates and service. The development of state laws, and later federal laws, also gave rise to independent regulatory commissions, which are the topic of the next section.

Role of the Independent Regulatory Commissions

The U.S. federal government is subject to a system of checks and balances in three separate branches—executive, judicial, and legislative. An independent regulatory commission is an administrative body created by legislative authority operating within the framework of the U.S. Constitution. The members of these commissions are appointed by the president and approved by the Senate for a fixed term in office.

The **Interstate Commerce Commission** (ICC) was the first federal independent regulatory commission established in the United States under the Act to Regulate Commerce of 1887. This Act gave the ICC the power to regulate the U.S. railroad industry. Originally, the ICC had limited powers, partially because of the inexperience of the U.S. government in regulating an entire industry. However, over several years many additional pieces of legislation were passed to strengthen the powers of the ICC over the railroad industry. The Motor Carrier Act of 1935, the Transportation Act of 1940, and the Freight Forwarder Act of 1942 gave similar powers to the ICC over the motor carrier, domestic water carrier, and freight forwarding industries, respectively.

The ICC served as an expert body, providing continuity to regulation that neither the courts nor the legislature could provide. The ICC exercised legislative, judicial, and executive powers. As a result, it was often labeled a quasi-legislative, quasi-judicial, and quasi-executive body. Regulatory agencies can be regarded as a fourth branch of the government. When the ICC enforced statutes, it served in its executive capacity. When it ruled upon the reasonableness of a rate, it served in its judicial capacity. When it expanded legislation by promulgating rules or prescribing rules or rates, it exercised its legislative powers.

On December 31, 1995, the ICC was abolished. The ICC Termination Act of 1995 (ICCTA) ended the 108-year-old ICC and replaced it with the **Surface Transportation Board** (STB), which today is focused only on the railroad industry. The STB is housed in the **U.S. Department of Transportation** (DOT), but it is still considered to be an independent regulatory agency. The president appoints members of the STB with the approval of the Senate.

The role of the STB in the economic operations of the railroads has been greatly reduced from that of the ICC. Congress intended for the marketplace, not the STB, to be the primary control mechanism for rates and service. (See "Current Economic Regulations," later in this chapter, for more details on the ICCTA regulations).

In addition to the ICC and STB, other independent regulatory commissions were established for transportation. In 1938, the **Civil Aeronautics Board** (CAB) was established to administer the economic regulations imposed upon airlines. The CAB was abolished in 1985 by the Civil Aeronautics Board Sunset Act and the remaining regulatory jurisdictions (safety issues) were transferred to the DOT.

The **Federal Maritime Commission** (FMC) was created in 1961 to administer the regulations imposed on international water carriers. The FMC exercises control over the rates, practices, agreements, and services of common carriers operating in international trade and domestic trade to points beyond the continental United States. The Ocean Shipping Reform Act of 1998 relaxed some of the economic powers of the FMC by allowing shippers and ocean carriers to enter into confidential contracts. This will be discussed more in Chapter 8.

The **Federal Energy Regulatory Commission** (FERC) was created to administer the regulations governing rates and practices of oil and natural gas pipelines. However, the FERC is not an independent regulatory commission that reports to Congress, as is the STB or FMC. Rather, it is a semi-independent regulatory commission that reports to the Department of Energy.

Our regulatory laws are often stated in vague terms, such as *reasonable rates, inherent advantages*, and *unjust discrimination*. The roles of the regulatory commissions are to interpret the meaning of these terms as they are stated in the law and to develop regulations that define their intent. These regulations, then, are codified and serve as the basis for decisions made by the regulatory commissions. However, these decisions are still subject to the intent of the law and to decisions made by the courts.

Role of the Courts

Even though the regulatory commissions play a powerful role in regulating transportation, they are still subject to judicial review. The courts are the sole determinants of the intent of the law, and only court decisions can serve as legal precedent under common law. The courts make the final ruling on the constitutionality of regulatory statutes and the interpretation of the regulation. The review of the courts act as a check on arbitrary or capricious actions, on actions that do not conform to statutory standards or authority, or on actions that are not in accordance with fair procedure or substantial evidence. The parties involved in a commission decision have the right, therefore, to appeal the decision to the courts.

Over the years, the courts had come to recognize the ICC as an expert body on policy and the authority on matters of fact. This recognition has now been given to the STB. The courts limited their restrictions on ICC and STB authority. The courts would not substitute their judgment for that of the ICC or STB on matters such as what constitutes a reasonable rate or whether discrimination is unjust because such judgments would usurp the administrative function of the commission.

Safety Regulations

Various federal agencies administer transportation safety regulations. Some of these regulations are enacted into law by Congress, whereas others are promulgated by the respective agencies. A thorough discussion of the specific regulations pertaining to each type of transportation is beyond the scope of this book, but a general description of safety regulations is warranted.

Safety regulations have been established to control operations, personnel qualifications, vehicles, equipment, hours of service for vehicle operators, and so forth. The **Federal Aviation Administration** (FAA) enforces and promulgates safety regulations governing the operations of air carriers and airports. The **Federal Motor Carrier Safety Administration** (FMCSA) administers motor carrier safety regulations, and the **National Highway Traffic Safety Administration** (NHTSA) has jurisdiction over safety features and the performance of motor vehicles and motor vehicle equipment. The **Federal Railroad Administration** (FRA) has authority over railroad safety regulations while the **Coast Guard** is responsible for marine safety standards for vessels and ports. The newly created **Pipeline and Hazardous Material Safety Administration** (PHMSA) contains a Pipeline Safety Office that is responsible for hazardous materials standards for oil and natural gas pipelines and a Hazardous Materials Safety Office that manages hazardous materials regulations for all other modes of transportation. The **National Transportation Safety Board** (NTSB) is charged with investigating and reporting the causes, facts, and circumstances relating to transportation accidents.

In addition, the states, through the **police powers** contained in the Constitution, exercise various controls over the safe operation of vehicles. These safety regulations set standards for speed, vehicle size, operating practices, operator licensing, and so forth. The purpose of the state safety regulations is to protect the health and welfare of the citizens of that state.

Often, federal and state safety regulations conflict. For example, the federal government restricted the automobile speed limit to 55 miles per hour on the highway system during the energy crisis of the 1970s. Some states did not agree with the mandate but followed the requirement to qualify for federal money to construct and maintain the highway system. In 1982, the Surface Transportation Act established federal standards for vehicle weight and length of tractor-trailers operating on the interstate highway system. The states complied with the standards for the interstate highways but many maintained different standards for state highways.

After the September 11, 2001 terrorist attack on the United States, transportation security has taken on a new dimension. Securing the nation's transportation system from terrorism became a major governmental focus because of the massive geographic expanse of the U.S. border and the millions of tons of freight and millions of passengers entering and leaving the United States. The Aviation and Transportation Security Act, enacted in November of 2001, created the Transportation Security Agency (TSA) which is responsible for securing the safety of the U.S. air transportation network. In 2002, Congress passed the Maritime Transportation Security Act, which governs the security of U.S. ports. Also, the Homeland Security Act of 2002 was passed to provide a central coordinating mechanism, along with the DOT, for all security issues dealing with transportation of passengers and freight within the United States and flowing into and out of the United States.

State Regulations

The states establish various transportation safety regulations to protect the health and welfare of their citizens. In addition, the states exercise limited economic regulations over the transportation of commodities and passengers wholly within the state. These powers were given to the states by the Commerce Clause of the U.S. Constitution. The states' powers were greatly limited under various federal laws. States generally cannot impose stricter regulation than imposed on a given mode at the federal level. States can still regulate safety, provided these regulations do not impose an undue burden on interstate commerce. This type of transportation is known as **intrastate commerce**, and most states had a regulatory commission that was charged with enforcing these intrastate controls. These agencies might still exist to regulate utilities, such as telephone or electric companies.

Intrastate economic regulations vary from state to state, but they are generally patterned after federal economic regulations. In 1994, the federal government eliminated the intrastate economic regulation of motor carriers with the passage of the FAA Authorization Act. The law, which applies to all motor carriers of property except household goods carriers, prohibits the states from requiring operating authority or regulating intrastate motor carrier rates, routes, and services. The states have the option to regulate the uniform business practices, cargo liability, and credit rules of intrastate motor carriers.

The determination as to what constitutes commerce subject to state economic regulations is generally based on whether the shipment crosses a state boundary. If the shipment has an origin in one state and a destination in another state, it is an interstate shipment and is subject to federal regulations, if any exist. However, for shipments that are moved into a distribution center from a point outside the state and then moved from the distribution center to a destination in the same state, the distinction is not that clear. The move within the state from the distribution center to the final destination can be considered interstate commerce and subject to federal regulations.

Development of Regulation

As has been seen in this chapter, transportation does not operate in a completely free-market environment. Government has controlled the economic operations of transportation since the 1860s. The driving force behind this regulation was the recognition in the 1800s of the importance of the railroad industry to the development of our country and its inherently monopolistic nature. The role of economic regulation by the government is to transform a monopolistic industry into a competitive one. Under economic regulation, the government can: (1) determine if a firm can enter an industry; (2) determine which market(s) a firm can serve in that industry; and (3) determine the prices that firm can charge customers in the markets it serves. By enforcing these three regulatory practices, the government can provide the basis for competition in a monopolistic industry.

Table 3-1 provides a chronology of transportation regulation. The regulatory history is broken down into four eras. First, the Initiation Era from 1887 to 1920 saw the establishment of federal transportation regulation and the ICC. Second, the Era of Positive Regulation from 1920 to 1935 was oriented toward promoting transportation. Third, the Intermodal Era from 1935 to 1976 witnessed the expansion of regulation to motor

Table 3-1	Chronology of Major Transportation Regulation	
DATE	**ACT**	**NATURE OF REGULATION**
Initiation Era		
1887	Act to Regulate Commerce	Regulated railroads and established ICC; required rates to be reasonable; discrimination prohibited
1903	Elkins Act	Prohibited rebates and filed rate doctrine
1096	Hepburn Act	Established maximum and joint rate controls
1910	Mann-Elkins Act	Gave shipper right to route shipment
1912	Panama Canal Act	Prohibited railroads from owning water carriers
Positive Era		
1920	Transportation Act of 1920	Established a rule of rate-making; pooling and joint use of terminals permitted; began recapture clause
1933	Emergency Transportation Act	Granted financial assistance to railroads
Intermodal Era		
1935	Motor Carrier Act	Federal regulation of trucking, similar to rail
1938	Civil Aeronautics Act	Federal regulation of air carriers; established Civil Aeronautics Board (CAB)
1940	Transportation Act	Provided for federal regulation of water carriers; declaration of national transportation policy
1942	Freight Forwarder Act	Federal Reregulation of surface freight forwarders
1948	Reed-Bulwinkle Act	Established antitrust immunity for joint rate making
1958	Transportation Act	Eliminated umbrella (protective) rate making and provided financial aid to railroads
1966	Department of Transportation Act	Established the U.S. Department of Transportation
1970	Rail Passenger Service Act	Established Amtrak
1973	Regional Rail Reorganization Act	Established Consolidation Rail Corporation (Conrail)
New Economic Era		
1976	Railroad Revitalization and Regulatory Reform Act	Granted rate freedom; allowed ICC to exempt rail operations; began abandonment and merger controls
1977	Airline Deregulation Act	Deregulated air transportation, sunset CAB (1985)
1980	Motor Carrier Act	Eased entry restrictions and permitted rate negotiation
1980	Rail Staggers Act	Permitted railroads to negotiate contracts, allowed rate flexibility, and defined maximum rates
1993	Negotiated Rate Act	Provided for settlement options for motor carrier undercharges
1994	Trucking Industry Regulatory Reform Act	Eliminated motor carrier filing of individual tariffs; ICC given power to deregulate categories of traffic

(continued)

Table 3-1	Continued	
DATE	**ACT**	**NATURE OF REGULATION**
1994	FAA Reauthorization Act	Prohibited states from regulating (economic) intrastate trucking
1995	ICC Termination Act	Abolished ICC; established STB; eliminated most truck economic regulation
1996	Maritime Security Act	Authorized a program to assist an active, privately owned U.S.-flagged and U.S.-crewed merchant shipping fleet
1998	Transportation Equity Act for the 21st Century	Allocated $216 + billion for the maintenance and safety of surface transportation
2001	Aviation and Transportation Security Act	Established the Transportation Security Administration
2002	Homeland Security Act	Moved Coast Guard and TSA into Department of Homeland Security

carriers, air carriers, water carriers, and freight forwarders. Finally, the New Economic Era from 1976 to the present was the period of gradual lessening and eventual elimination of economic regulation, culminating in the elimination of the ICC. This era also saw the development and strengthening of transportation safety and security regulations.

The next section will provide a summary of current regulations as they pertain to railroads and motor carriers.

Current Economic Regulations

As previously stated, the air carrier industry is free from economic regulation. Cargo and passenger rates are not controlled by the government and domestic air carriers are permitted to serve any market as long as the carrier meets safety regulation and landing slots are available.

The majority of the economic regulation of pipelines has been transferred to the Federal Energy Regulatory Commission. Because most water carrier operations are exempt from economic regulation, domestic water carrier economic regulation is a moot issue.

Effective January 1, 1996, the ICC Termination Act of 1995 abolished the Interstate Commerce Commission, further deregulated transportation, and transferred the remaining ICC functions to the **Surface Transportation Board** (STB) located within the DOT. The STB now administers the remaining economic regulations exercised over railroads, motor carriers, freight forwarders, freight brokers, water carriers, and pipelines. However, the majority of the remaining economic regulations pertain to railroad transportation. The key provisions of the ICCTA are summarized below:

Railroad Regulations
- Rail economic regulation is basically unchanged by the ICCTA.
- The STB has jurisdiction over rates, classifications, rules, practices, routes, services, facilities, acquisitions, and abandonments.
- Railroads continue to be subject to the common carrier obligations (to serve, not discriminate, charge reasonable rates, and deliver).

- Rail tariff filing is eliminated; railroads must provide 20 days advance notice before changing a rate.
- Rail contract filing is eliminated except for agricultural products.

Motor Carriers

- All tariff filing and rate regulation is eliminated, except for household goods and noncontiguous trade (trade between the continental United States and Hawaii, for example).
- Motor carriers are required to provide tariffs to shippers upon request.
- Motor carriers are held liable for damage according to the conditions of the Carmack Amendment, (that is, the full value of the product at destination). However, motor carriers can use released value rates that set limits on liability.
- The Negotiated Rates Act undercharge resolution procedures are retained and the unreasonable practices defense is extended indefinitely for pending undercharge cases.
- Undercharge/overcharge claims must be filed within 180 days from receipt of the freight bill.
- The STB has broad powers to exempt operations from economic regulation with the existing exemptions remaining.
- Antitrust immunity for collective rate making (publishing the national motor freight classification, for example) is retained.
- The motor carrier is required to disclose to the person directly paying the freight bill whether and to whom discounts or allowances are given.
- The concepts of common and contract authorities are eliminated; all regulated carriers can contract with shippers.

Freight Forwarders and Brokers

- Both are required to register with the STB.
- The freight forwarder is regulated as a carrier and is liable for freight damage.
- The broker is not a carrier and is not held liable for freight damage.
- The STB can impose insurance requirements for both.

The Surface Transportation Board Reauthorization Act of 1999 removed most of the remaining economic regulations imposed by the STB on motor carriers. The STB would no longer consider competitive issues and would eliminate references to federal regulatory approval requirements for collective motor carrier activities submitted to it for approval. The STB would no longer be able to grant antitrust immunity for motor carriers for collective activities such as rate bureaus and national freight classification. The motor carrier industry would be subject to competitive regulations as in other industries.

In summary, the ICCTA brought the economic regulation of transportation back to its beginning in 1887 by retaining regulatory powers over the railroads, while allowing the other modes to operate in a free-market economy. While all of the modes, except rail, operate in this environment, they are subject to antitrust and other regulations that govern all other industries. Because of the decreasing cost nature of the railroad industry and its tendency towards monopoly, the STB maintains comprehensive guidelines to assure that railroads operate without discrimination or undue or unjust prejudice towards shippers.

Antitrust Laws in Transportation

The deregulatory movement has exposed many practices to be in violation of antitrust laws. Antitrust regulations were first established in 1890 with passage of the **Sherman Antitrust Act**. The key points of this act are as follows:

Section 1: Trusts, etc., in restraint of trade illegal; penalty.

Every contract, combination in the form of trust or otherwise, or conspiracy, in restraint of trade or commerce among the several States, or with foreign nations, is declared to be illegal. Every person who shall make any contract or engage in any combination or conspiracy declared by Section 1 to 7 of this title to be illegal shall be deemed guilty of a felony, and, on conviction thereof, shall be punished by fine not exceeding one million dollars if a corporation, or if any other person, one hundred thousand dollars, or by imprisonment not exceeding three years, or both said punishments, in the discretion of the court.

Section 2: Monopolizing trade a felony; penalty.

Every person who shall monopolize, or attempt to monopolize, or combine or conspire with any other person or persons, to monopolize any part of the trade or commerce among the several States, or with foreign nations, shall be deemed guilty of a felony...[3]

The thrust of the Sherman Act was intended to outlaw price fixing among competing firms, eliminate business practices that tended toward monopolization, and prevent any firm or combination of firms from refusing to sell or deal with certain firms or avoiding geographic market allocations.

The law was strengthened in 1914 by the **Clayton Act**. This act specifically described some other practices that would be interpreted as attempts to monopolize, or as actual monopolization. These practices include exclusive dealing arrangements whereby a buyer and/or seller agree to deal only with the other party for a period of time. Another prohibited practice is a tying contract. This is where a seller agrees to sell goods to a buyer only if the buyer also buys another product from the seller.

Also in 1914 legislation was passed that created the **Federal Trade Commission** (FTC). This agency was the primary overseer and enforcement agency in antitrust situations.

Collective rate making by transportation carriers was made exempt from antitrust laws by the passage of the **Reed-Bulwinkle Act of 1948**, which empowered the ICC to oversee carrier rate making. As such, it limited traditional jurisdiction by the FTC and the Department of Justice in this area. Today, carriers are not immune from antitrust regulations as they pertain to rate bureaus and freight classification.

Another major law that might apply to the deregulation of transportation is the **Robinson-Patman Act of 1936**. This law prohibits sellers from practicing price discrimination among buyers unless the difference in price can be justified by true differences in the costs of servicing these buyers (this will be discussed further in Chapter 4, Costing and Pricing in Transportation). Defenses against such a practice are: (1) differences in cost, (2) the need to meet competition, and (3) changing market conditions. Although this law was created for application to the buying and selling of goods, it may be applicable to contracts for transportation services. Whether this law applies in carrier pricing is only determined by the courts as suspected violations occur.

In the selling and purchase of transportation services, two types of antitrust violations can occur. The first is called a **per se violation**. This type of violation is illegal regardless of whether any economic harm is done to competitors or other parties. Types of per se violations include price fixing, division of markets, boycotts, and tying agreements. If economic harm has been caused to any party because of this violation, the damages are tripled as compensation to the harmed parties.

The second type of antitrust violation is called **rule of reason**. In this type of violation, economic harm must be shown to have been caused to competitors or other parties because these activities can be undertaken by firms with no antitrust implications. Rule of reason violations include exclusive deals, requirements contracts, joint bargaining, and joint action among affiliates.

Carriers, in the selling of transportation services, are normally thought to be the party to which antitrust regulations apply. However, in buying these services, shippers are also subject to the same laws and are at an equal risk of committing an antitrust violation. Because transportation has been subject to antitrust laws for a short period of time, these laws as they pertain to transportation have not yet been fully tested in the courts.

Transportation Policy

The federal government has played an important role in molding the transportation system that exists in the United States today. The federal government's role has been defined through various laws, rules, and funding programs directed toward protecting and promoting the different modes of transportation. The federal government's policy toward transportation is a composite of these federal laws, rules, funding programs, and regulatory agencies. However, there is no unified federal transportation policy statement or goal that guides the federal government's actions.

In addition to the Congress and the president, more than 60 federal agencies and 30 congressional committees are involved in setting transportation policy. Independent regulatory agencies interpret transportation law, establish operating rules, and set policy. Lastly, the Justice Department interprets statutes involving transportation and reconciles differences between the carriers and the public.

The purpose of this section is to examine the national transportation policy, both explicit and implicit, that has molded the current U.S. transportation system. Although the national transportation policy is constantly evolving, there are some major underpinnings upon which the policy is built. These basic policy issues will be examined, as well as the declared statement of national transportation policy contained in the ICC Termination Act of 1995.

Why Do We Need A Transportation Policy?

A good starting point for examining the nature of our national transportation policy is the consideration of our need for such a policy. The answer to the question of need lies in the significance of transportation to the very life of the country. Transportation permeates every aspect of a community and touches the life of every member. The transportation system ties together the various communities of a country, making possible the movement of people, goods, and services. The physical connection that transportation gives to spatially separated communities permits a sense of unity to exist.

In addition, transportation is fundamental to the economic activity of a country. Transportation furthers economic activity—the exchange of goods that are mass-produced in one location to locations deficient in these goods. The secondary benefits of economic activity—jobs, improved goods and services, and so on—would not be enjoyed by a country's citizens without a good transportation system.

An efficient transportation system is also fundamental to national defense. In times of emergencies, people and materials must be deployed quickly to various trouble spots within the United States or throughout the world to protect American interests. Without an efficient transportation system, more resources would have to be dedicated to defense purposes in many more locations. Thus, an efficient transportation system reduces the amount of resources consumed for national defense.

Many of our transportation facilities could not be developed by private enterprise. For example, the capital required to build a transcontinental highway would very likely be beyond the resources of the private sector. Efficient rail and highway routes require government assistance in securing land from private owners; if the government did not assert its power of eminent domain, routes would be quite circuitous and inefficient. Furthermore, public ownership and the operation of certain transportation facilities, such as highways or waterways, are necessary to ensure access to all who desire to use the facilities.

The purpose of transportation policy is to provide direction for determining the amount of national resources that will be dedicated to transportation and for determining the quality of service that is essential for economic activity and national defense. National policy provides guidelines to the many agencies that exercise transportation decision-making powers and to Congress, the president, and the courts that make and interpret the laws affecting transportation. Thus, transportation policy provides the framework for the allocation of resources to the transportation modes.

The federal government has been a major factor in the development of transportation facilities—highways, waterways, ports, and airports. It also has assumed the responsibility to:

- Ensure the safety of travelers;
- Protect the public from the abuse of monopoly power;
- Promote fair competition;

- Develop or continue vital transportation services; balance environmental, energy, and social requirements in transportation; and,
- Plan and make decisions.[4]

The statement of the federal government's transportation responsibility indicates the diversity of public need that transportation policy must serve. The conflicts inherent in such a diverse set of responsibilities will be discussed in a later section.

Declaration of National Transportation Policy

The ICC Termination Act of 1995 included statements of national transportation policy. Congress made these statements to provide direction to the STB in administering transportation regulation over railroads, motor carriers, water carriers, and pipelines.

The declaration of national transportation policy is stated in Public Law 104-88:

In regulating the railroad industry, it is the policy of the United States Government:

1. to allow, to the maximum extent possible, competition and the demand for services to establish reasonable rates for transportation by rail;
2. to minimize the need for Federal regulatory control over the rail transportation system and to require fair and expeditious regulatory decisions when regulation is required;
3. to promote a safe and efficient rail transportation system by allowing rail carriers to earn adequate revenues, as determined by the Board;
4. to ensure the development and continuation of a sound rail transportation system with effective competition among rail carriers and with other modes, to meet the needs of the public and the national defense;
5. to foster sound economic conditions in transportation and to ensure effective competition and coordination between rail carriers and other modes;
6. to maintain reasonable rates where there is an absence of effective competition and where rail rates provide revenues which exceed the amount necessary to maintain the rail system and to attract capital;
7. to reduce regulatory barriers to entry into and exit from the industry;
8. to operate transportation facilities and equipment without detriment to the public health and safety;
9. to encourage honest and efficient management of railroads;
10. to require rail carriers, to the maximum extent practicable, to rely on individual rate increases, and to limit the use of increases of general applicability;
11. to encourage fair wages and safe and suitable working conditions in the railroad industry;
12. to prohibit predatory pricing and practices, to avoid undue concentrations of market power, and to prohibit unlawful discrimination;
13. to ensure the availability of accurate cost information in regulatory proceedings, while minimizing the burden on the rail carriers of developing and maintaining the capability of providing such information;

14. to encourage and promote energy conservation; and

15. to provide for the expeditious handling and resolution of all proceedings required or permitted to be brought to this part.

The declaration of national transportation policy for motor carriers, water carriers, brokers, and freight forwarders is stated in the same document:

In General. To ensure the development, coordination, and preservation of a transportation system that meets the transportation needs of the United States Postal Service and national defense, it is the policy of the United States government to oversee the modes of transportation and:

1. in overseeing these modes:

    A. to recognize and preserve the inherent advantage of each mode of transportation;

    B. to promote safe, adequate, economical, and efficient transportation;

    C. to encourage sound economic conditions in transportation, including sound economic conditions among carriers;

    D. to encourage the establishment and maintenance of reasonable rates of transportation, without unreasonable discrimination or unfair or destructive competitive practices;

    E. to cooperate with each State and the officials of each State on transportation matters; and

    F. to encourage fair wages and working conditions in the transportation industry;

2. in overseeing transportation by motor carrier, to promote competitive and efficient transportation in order to:

    A. encourage fair competition, and reasonable rates for transportation by motor carriers of property;

    B. promote efficiency in the motor carrier transportation system and to require fair and expeditious decisions when required;

    C. meet the needs of shippers, receivers, passengers, and consumers;

    D. allow a variety of quality and price options to meet changing market demands and the diverse requirements of the shipping and traveling public;

    E. allow the most productive use of equipment and energy resources;

    F. enable efficient and well-managed carriers to earn adequate profits, attract capital and maintain fair wages and working conditions;

    G. provide and maintain service to small communities and small shippers and intrastate bus services;

    H. provide and maintain commuter bus operations;

    I. improve and maintain a sound, safe, and competitive privately owned motor carrier system;

    J. promote greater participation by minorities in the motor carrier system;

    K. promote intermodal transportation;

3. in overseeing transportation by motor carriers of passengers:

   A. to cooperate with the States on transportation matters for the purpose of encouraging the States to exercise intrastate regulatory jurisdiction in accordance with the objectives of this part;

   B. to provide Federal procedures which ensure the intrastate regulation is exercised in accordance with this part; and

   C. to ensure that Federal reform initiatives enacted by section 31138 and the Bus Regulatory Reform Act of 1982 are not nullified by State regulatory actions; and

4. in overseeing transportation by water carrier, to encourage and promote service and price competition in the noncontiguous domestic trade.

The declaration of pipeline national transportation policy is as follows:

In General. To ensure the development, coordination, and preservation of a transportation system that meets the transportation needs of the United States, including the national defense, it is the policy of the United States Government to oversee the modes of transportation and in overseeing these modes:

1. to recognize and preserve the inherent advantage of each mode of transportation;

2. to promote safe, adequate, economical, and efficient transportation;

3. to encourage sound economic conditions in transportation; including sound economic conditions among carriers;

4. to encourage the establishment and maintenance of reasonable rates for transportation without unreasonable discrimination or unfair or destructive competitive practices;

5. to cooperate with each State and the officials of each State on transportation matters; and

6. to encourage fair wages and working conditions in the transportation industry.

Policy Interpretations

Although the declarations of national transportation policy are general and somewhat vague, they do provide a guide to the factors that should be considered in transportation decision making. However, the statements contain numerous conflicting provisions. This section analyzes the incompatibility of the various provisions.

Provisions The declarations are statements of policy for those modes regulated by the STB. Therefore, only railroads, oil pipelines, motor carriers, and water carriers are considered. **Air carriers** are excluded from consideration.

The requirement of "fair and impartial regulation" also overlooks **exempt carriers** in motor and water transportation. The exempt carriers are eliminated from the economic controls administered by the STB and therefore are not included in the stated policy provisions.

Congress requested the STB to administer transportation regulation in such a manner as to recognize and preserve the inherent advantage of each mode. An inherent advantage is the innate superiority one mode possesses in the form of cost or service characteristics when compared to the other modes. Such modal characteristics change over time as technology and infrastructure change.

It has been recognized that railroads have an inherent advantage of lower cost in transporting freight long distances and that motor carriers have the advantage for moving freight short distances—less than 800 miles. If the preservation of inherent advantage were the only concern, the STB would not permit motor carriers to haul freight long distances (more than 800 miles) nor railroads to haul freight short distances. However, shippers demand long-distance moves from motor carriers and short-distance moves from railroads, and the STB permits these services to be provided.

Safe, adequate, economical, and efficient service is not totally attainable. An emphasis on safety might mean an uneconomical or inefficient service. Added safety features on equipment and added safety procedures for employees will increase total costs and cost per unit of output and might reduce the productivity of employees. However, when lives are involved, safety takes precedence over economical and efficient service.

Providing adequate service has been construed to mean meeting normal demand. If carriers were forced to have capacity that is sufficient to meet peak demand, considerable excess capacity would exist, resulting in uneconomical and inefficient operations. Fostering sound economic conditions among the carriers does not mean ensuring an acceptable profit for all carriers. Nor does it imply that the STB should guarantee the survival of all carriers. The STB must consider the economic condition of carriers in rate rulings so as to foster stability of transportation supply.

The policy statement regarding reasonable charges, unjust discrimination, undue preference, and unfair competitive practices is merely a reiteration of the **common carrier** obligations. Congress made no attempt to define these concepts. The STB was given the task of interpreting them as it hears and decides individual cases.

A number of laws provide some degree of definition for these common carrier policy statements. For example, the Staggers Rail Act of 1980 defined a reasonable rail rate as one that is not more than 160 percent of variable costs. The Motor Carrier Act of 1980 defined a zone of rate freedom in which a rate change of 10 percent either up or down in one year is presumed to be reasonable. Both acts defined the normal business entertainment of shippers as acceptable practice and not an instance of undue preference.

The cooperative efforts between the federal and state governments have not always been amicable. The very foundation for federal regulation of transportation was the judicial decision that only the federal government could regulate interstate transportation. Through police powers, the states have the right to establish laws regarding transportation safety. Thus, for example, states have enacted laws governing the height, length, weight, and speed of motor carrier vehicles. However, the federal government has standardized weight and speed laws on interstate highways. One approach the federal government has taken has been to threaten to withhold federal highway money from states that do not comply with federal regulations.

Finally, the STB was charged with the responsibility of encouraging fair wages and working conditions in transportation. No attempt was made to interpret the terms **fair wage** and **working conditions**. A wage that is deemed fair by an employee might be unfair to an employer. This might also conflict with the policy statement regarding the promotion of economical and efficient service.

The stated goals of the national transportation policy are to provide a system of transportation that meets the needs of commerce, the U.S. Postal Service, *and* national defense. A possibility exists that a system that meets the needs of commerce might be insufficient to meet the needs of national defense during an emergency situation. In addition, a system that has the capacity to meet national defense needs will have excess capacity for commerce and postal service needs during peace times. For example, the United States maintains a merchant marine fleet that can be called into service to transport defense material during a national defense emergency. However, this fleet might be twice the size of that needed for commerce. Many government critics claim a fleet with such excess capacity is a waste of resources. Defense advocates argue that national defense needs dictate that such a fleet be operated to preclude dependency on a foreign country for water transportation during defense emergencies. From these two viewpoints it is easy to see how conflicts can occur in the national transportation goals.

The ICCTA provides specific direction to the STB regarding the railroads and motor carriers. For the railroads, the STB is directed to minimize the need for federal regulatory control, reduce regulatory barriers to entry and exit, prohibit predatory pricing, and promote energy conservation. For motor carriers, the STB is to allow pricing variety, to promote greater participation by minorities, and to promote transportation.

Who Establishes Policy?

National transportation policies are developed at various levels of government and by many different agencies. The specifics of a particular policy might reflect the persuasion of a group of individuals (for example, a consumer group) or of a single individual (for example, an elected official). The purpose of this section is to examine the basic institutional framework that aids in the development of national transportation policy.

Executive Branch[5] Many departments within the executive branch of government influence (establish) transportation policy. Leading these departments is the office of the president. The president has authority over international air transportation and foreign air carriers operating in the United States. The president also appoints individuals to lead the various agencies that influence transportation and to lead the two regulatory agencies—the STB and the Federal Maritime Commission (FMC).

The Department of State is directly involved in developing policy regarding international transportation by air and water. The policies and programs designed to encourage foreign visitors to the United States are implemented by the U.S. Travel Service. The Maritime Administration is involved with ocean (international) transportation policy. It determines ship requirements, service, and routes essential to foreign commerce. In addition, international transportation policies and programs are shaped by the Military Sealift Command, Military Airlift Command, and Military Traffic Management Command—agencies responsible for the movement of military goods and personnel.

On the domestic level, the Department of Energy develops policies regarding energy availability and distribution (fuel and rationing). The U.S. Postal Service contracts for transportation of the mail; such contracts have been used to promote air transportation as well as motor and rail transportation. The Department of Housing and Urban Development (HUD) consults with the DOT regarding the compatibility of urban transportation systems within the HUD-administered housing and community development programs. The Army Corps of Engineers is responsible for constructing and maintaining rivers, harbors, locks, and dams for the protection of navigable waterways.

The DOT, however, is the most pervasive influence of transportation policy at the domestic level. The Secretary of Transportation is responsible for assisting the president in all transportation matters, including public investment, safety, and research. (See Appendix A at the end of this chapter for a list of agencies within the DOT).

Congressional Committees The laws formulated by Congress are the formal method by which Congress influences national transportation. The congressional committee structure is the forum in which Congress develops policies, programs, and funding for transportation.

Within the Senate, the two committees that influence transportation are the Committee on Commerce, Science, and Transportation and the Committee on Environment and Public Works. Within the Committee on Commerce, Science, and Transportation is the Subcommittee on Surface Transportation and Merchant Marine Infrastructure, Safety, and Security. This subcommittee is concerned with bus safety, supply chain security, motor carrier driver hours of service, the STB, railroad safety, hazardous material transportation by motor carriers, the Maritime Administration, and the Coast Guard. Another subcommittee is concerned with Aviation Operations, Safety, and Security. This subcommittee focuses on air traffic congestion, aviation safety, the Federal Aviation Administration (FAA), and the National Transportation Safety Board (NTSB). The Environment and Public Works Committee deals with internal waterway and harbor projects, highway construction and maintenance projects, and air and water pollution regulations.

The House of Representatives has restructured its committees regarding transportation. The two main House committees on transportation are the Transportation and Infrastructure Committee and the Energy and Commerce Committee. The Transportation and Infrastructure Committee is concerned with the FAA, rail infrastructure projects, the STB, pipeline safety, hazardous material transportation, the NTSB, and the Coast Guard. The other House committee is the Energy and Commerce Committee. Its basic responsibility is interstate and foreign commerce.

In addition to the above committees, numerous other congressional committees have an impact on transportation. Federal funding can be decided in the Appropriations Committee, Senate Banking Committee, Housing and Urban Affairs Committee, House Ways and Means Committee, or the Senate Finance Committee.

Regulatory Agencies The STB and FMC are independent agencies charged with implementing the laws regulating transportation. The agencies have quasi-judicial, quasi-executive, and quasi-legislative powers. They can establish policy when they interpret law, can decide on cases (such as the reasonableness of rates), and can enforce their decisions with the help of the court system.

Judicial System The courts have been called upon to interpret laws or reconcile conflicts. In doing so, the courts have an impact on transportation policies. Carriers, shippers, and the general public can call upon the courts to change existing policy through interpretation of statutes. As the regulatory agencies exercise quasi-legislative, quasi-judicial, and quasi-executive powers, the affected parties seek recourse to the courts to determine the legality of the decisions. The role of the courts is basically to interpret the meaning of policy as stated in laws, regulations, and executive orders.

Transportation Technology   *Survival of the Fittest*

The air cargo industry must ramp up its investment in information technology if it is to survive the current fuel crisis, at least that was the bold declaration made last month by Giovanni Bisignani, director general and CEO of the International Air Transport Association (IATA). Speaking at the SITA Air Transport IT Summit, Bisignani said everything has changed in the wake of rising fuel: "With fuel accounting for 34 percent of industry costs, airlines are feeling the impact more than most." He added that cost savings are crucial in every corner of the business, but there is not much "low hanging fruit left." Critical decisions on everything from aircraft allocation based on cost, capacity, and demand, to making best use of new labor opportunities are needed. "Those with state-of-the-art route planning systems fed with the best available market data will have a clear advantage," he added. Stay tuned.

Source: *Logistics Management*, July 2008, p. 2. Reprinted by permission.

Industry Associations   One facet of national policy development that is often overlooked in the study of transportation is the role of industry associations in shaping national, state, and local promotion, regulation, and policy. These associations exist in most industries and their focus is to lobby Congress and other influential groups in the government to pass laws that will help their members.

These associations are nonprofit entities that derive their powers and resources from member firms. They act on the charges given to them by their members. In transportation, the railroads in the Association of American railroads (AAR) and the motor carriers in the American Trucking Associations (ATA) often meet to resolve matters of equipment uniformity and loss and damage prevention. On the policy side, these associations develop legislative and administrative ruling concepts that favor the collective membership, or they serve as a united front against proposals that are perceived to be harmful to the group.

The major industry associations in the transportation industry have evolved from specific modes. The AAR represents the large railroads in the United States; it was instrumental in the passage of the Staggers Rail Act of 1980. The ATA is divided into sub-conferences including agriculture and food transporters, automobile carriers, and intermodal motor carriers. The Air Transport Association represents the airline industry in the United States. The American Waterways Operators (AWO) consists of barge operators on the inland waterway network. The American Bus Association represents common and charter bus firms.

Two major associations exist for the interests of large shippers. One is the National Industrial Transportation League (NITL), and the other is the National Shippers Strategic Transportation Council (NASSTRAC). Both are active before congressional bodies, regulatory agencies, and carrier groups.

The Transportation Association of America (TAA), which ceased operation in 1982, had as its concern the health and vitality of the entire U.S. transportation system. It became involved in policy issues relating to two or more modes, or between modes and shippers, as well as investors. The TAA was largely instrumental in the passage of the act that created the DOT, as well as the passage of the Uniform Time Standards Act, which caused all areas of the United States electing to recognize daylight savings time to do so at the same time in April. Previously, each state did so on different dates, which caused major confusion in railroad and airline scheduling systems and timetable publication. At one point, United Airlines had to publish 27 different timetables during the spring as various states recognized daylight savings time on different dates. Since it was enacted in 1967, the Uniform Time Standards Act has simplified these facets of transportation management.

Other groups and associations are involved in transportation policy, including non-transportation special interest groups such as the grange and labor unions. Various government agencies such as the Department of Agriculture and the Department of Defense influence existing and proposed transportation legislation on their behalf, or on the behalf of groups within them.

One of the most important government policy issues has been the public promotion of transportation. All of the above groups and associations have been involved over the years in this important area. The topic is of such importance as a policy issue that it is considered in detail in the next section.

Public Promotion

This section presents an overview of the major transportation planning and promotion activities conducted in the U.S. public sector. Promotion connotes encouragement or provision of aid or assistance so transportation can grow or survive. *Planning* and *promotion* are general terms used to refer to programs, policies, and actual planning. Programs involve actual public cash investments into or funding for transportation activities both privately and publicly owned. Agencies make policies to encourage beneficial actions or impacts for transportation. Planning determines future transportation needs and then establishes policies or programs to bring about certain goals through the public or private sector. All three activities promote transportation and cause it to grow or survive in instances in which pure market forces could not have done so.

Transportation Planning and the Public Sector

Transportation project planning is the process whereby federal, state, or local groups review the movement needs or demands of a region or population segment, develop transportation alternatives, and usually propose and implement an alternative. This process enables the development of new movement processes or allows existing ones to continue in an environment of change.

Transportation project planning is a public activity; purely financial returns and other concerns are not the overriding benefits sought. It is a major part of the public activity in the U.S. economy for several reasons. First, public transportation processes can facilitate trade or movement where private actions have not or would not have been enticed to do so for financial gain alone. Second, various cultural and political benefits often come from projects and programs provided publicly. Third, transportation planning also lowers the cost of living or reduces the social costs of delay or congestion. Finally, transportation planning provides services that are not remunerative but are deemed socially necessary or desirable.

Transportation planning has been a critical factor in the beginning of the 21st century. There are many areas of transportation investment from which private firms have withdrawn. Many forms of transportation today are no longer economically profitable or compensatory. Urban bus systems, commuter railroads, rail and urban research and development, and many rail services are examples of transportation forms that would not exist without public sector involvement.

Many forms of transportation require large capital investments that would normally discourage or basically prohibit private investment. Port dredging and development, as well as airport and highway construction, are examples of capital items that are not affordable by the carriers using them. Instead, the ability of a public authority to attract capital enables the asset to be built; cost is recovered through user charges.

Public planning of transportation is generally found in situations where environmental or social needs override financial ones. A major argument used in modern subway construction is that, although the system might not recover its full costs from passenger fares, the city as a whole will benefit by increased access to already existing downtown facilities, including buildings, offices, stores, and water utility systems. Constructing other facilities in developing suburban areas will not be necessary. Also, commuters save money because the subway eliminates the need for a second family auto, long driving times, excess fuel consumption, costly parking in downtown areas, and so on. Public planning of transportation involves a different viewpoint and set of objectives than does capital investment analysis in private firms.

An Approach to Public Project Planning Analysis

While a private firm seeks a financial return to the firm itself, public planning agencies compare the initial costs of a project to the financial, environmental, and measurable social benefits to everyone affected by the project. Thus, it compares total societal cost to total societal benefits, whether they be monetary or nonmonetary in nature.

The specific analytical tool typically used in public planning is the **benefit/cost ratio** (BCR). In essence, the BCR is a measure of total measurable benefits to society divided by the initial capital cost. The formula in its basic form is as follows:

$$\text{BCR} = \frac{\text{Sum of yearly benefits to society}}{\text{Sum of costs to agencies and those in society initially impacted}}$$

$$= \frac{\text{Sum of benefits}}{\text{Sum of initial costs}} = \frac{\text{Year 1 benefit} + \text{Year 2 benefit} + \dots}{\text{Sum of all initial costs}}$$

If the resulting answer is greater than one, the project is said to produce a "profit" for society. A BCR of one indicates the break-even point; less than one indicates that the agency will spend more on the project than society will reap in long-term benefits.

The major costs of a project include those expenses typically involved in private projects. Planning, engineering, construction, and financing costs are critical to the decision. Other costs include delay or congestion measured in terms of dollars per hour and in terms of everyone in society who will be inconvenienced during the construction phase of a transportation project. Project costs can also include a cost of lost sales to businesses; for example, stores are more difficult to access during several years of subway construction. The costs of bond financing incurred to construct the system are also pertinent. All costs are measured or translated into monetary terms and listed according to the year in which they will occur. Typically, the major expenses arise in the initial years of construction; financing is a major cost carried through the project's life.

The benefits of a project include any measurable benefit to the agency, other agencies, and the public. Benefits include increased employment, decreased prices for products, lowered costs of commuting or freight transport, reduced maintenance, improved health due to lessened pollution, and so on. Many benefits are easily quantified, though others pose analytical difficulties in the form of forecasting volumes and cost relationships in future periods.

The timing and **time value of funds** are important parts of any capital project analysis. Political controversy exists about the choice of the specific discount rate and its application. Several analytical points can be examined that will shed light on this task. First, the discount rate should reflect the interest cost and impact to the public agency that borrows the initial funds. Second, the rate should become higher in later years to reflect increasing risk, inflation, uncertainty, and forecasting difficulties. This is a conservative practice of private project financial managers, and the logic of it can be applied soundly in a public setting. Third, the counting of benefits should cease in some future period, even though the project might last longer. This is another practice that is an implicit way of conservatively considering only those benefits within the intermediate term, unless a logical case can be made for an extended period of time. These points are made as to ensure that benefit overcounting is minimized.

An example of a benefit/cost ratio application to a proposed subway line will show how public planning processes are employed. Costs include those of organization development, design, engineering, initial financing, land purchases, relocation, and disruption to the public. Costs projected into the future include operations, lost property taxes, interest costs, and any other costs directly tied to the project. Benefits to the agencies include lowered operational costs of city buses; alternative application of funds released from the bus operation (reduced street and highway requirements); decreased need to expand highways or downtown parking; increased property, sales, and wage taxes from higher economic activity downtown; avoidance of federal penalties for not reducing city-wide auto emissions; and many others. Benefits to society include the income multiplier effect from the initial project investment in the form of employment and flow of dollars from the construction itself. The system will improve society in the form of saved time, lower pollution levels, and reduced commuting stress. The subway will generally cause the downtown to become more fully utilized resulting in a steady or increasing tax base.

From the above discussion it can be concluded that public planning involves many of the basic concepts inherent in private planning, but the application is different. The public agency is concerned about costs and benefits to all parties affected by the project. Thus, costs, benefits, and "profits" are measured for society as a whole in tangible and intangible ways. The following discussion presents those forms of modal promotion found in the United States.

Air

The domestic air system receives the benefits of several government programs. Foremost is the Federal Aviation Administration's (FAA) **air traffic control system**. This system provides navigation and safety for every aircraft in flight within the United States. The system assesses no direct fee to the airlines for its use and captures its operating expenses from airlines and passengers through user charges.

Another direct airline benefit is the subsidy program. These subsidies generally apply to short and medium non-jet flights to cities that are unable to support high traffic volumes. The subsidy has been a significant support mechanism for regional airlines. In recent years, the growth of commuter airlines has enabled regional airlines to discontinue service to small cities. The Air Deregulation Act of 1978 accelerated this trend, which resulted in a lessened need for regional airline subsidies.

The U.S. Postal Service also provides substantial support to airlines. The prime source of income for airlines during their early years came from this subsidy program. In recent years, mail income has not been as significant, but this subsidy is a major revenue source for the industry.

State and local agencies help promote the airline industry through air terminal development and construction. Terminals represent substantial capital investments and would be difficult for the industry to finance and construct. State and local agencies are able to raise the necessary construction funds at reasonable municipal bond interest rates, often backed by the taxing power of the community. The airlines then rent terminal and hangar facilities and pay landing fees for each flight.

Many aircraft safety matters are handled by the federal government. The FAA provides aircraft construction and safety rules as well as pilot certification. In another capacity, the National Transportation Safety Board (NTSB) investigates accidents so that others might be avoided or reduced through aircraft specifications or flight procedures.

Another indirect form of promotion to the airline industry comes from the military. Defense contracts for military aircraft development often provide direct benefits to commercial aviation in the form of mechanical or navigational aircraft improvements. Without military-related research and development activity, advancements in this area would take place at a slower pace and at a higher cost to the private sector.

A last form of airline promotion, which is not found in the U.S. system, is direct government ownership, operation, or subsidy of air service. This is common with foreign airlines that serve the United States. In these instances, African, Asian, Latin American, and many European airlines are subsidized so the countries can operate their airlines for purposes of national defense, have some degree of control over traffic to and from their nations, and gain balance-of-payment benefits and hard currencies through ticket revenues.

A related form of such **home-flag airline** promotion exists in the United States and in most foreign nations. In the United States, there is a requirement that only United States flag carriers with domestically owned aircraft and domestic crews may originate and terminate domestic passengers and freight. Many foreign lines serve both New York and Los Angeles, for example, with a flight originating abroad, but these flights are limited to international passengers. The only way in which a foreign line can originate and terminate a passenger in two U.S. cities is when that passenger is exercising stopover privileges as part of a tour or through movement. This home-flag requirement serves to protect U.S. airlines.

Several forms of **user charges** are designed, in whole or part, to have the modes pay for many of the public benefits they receive. As mentioned before, landing fees are charged to repay investments or generate revenue for specific airports. A major user charge is levied against passenger movements through ticket taxes. An international per-head tax is also part of this user tax, as are some aircraft registration fees. Many of these funds go into the **Airport and Airway Trust Fund**, which is used for airport facility projects on a shared basis with local agencies.

Motor and Highway

With regard to public promotion, the highway system and motor carrier firms have a joint relationship. There is no direct promotion to the motor carriers themselves, but indirect benefit comes to the industry through **highway development** because most highway projects are completed with government funds.

The Federal Highway Administration (FHWA) branch of the DOT is responsible for federal highway construction and safety. A predecessor agency, the Bureau of Public Roads, carried out the mandate to build the Interstate Highway System, which was paid for on a 90 percent/10 percent federal/state sharing basis. Today the FHWA is largely devoted to highway research, development, and safety. It also is charged with certain repair projects on critical parts of the federal and interstate highway system. Motor carriers benefit from the increased access, speed, and safety of this system because without it they would have to travel more congested routes, presenting safety hazards.

The National Highway Traffic Safety Administration (NHTSA) is responsible for highway and auto safety. It also conducts major research into vehicle safety, accidents, and highway design related to safety. This agency provides administrative regulations for certain minimum automobile safety features.

The Federal Motor Carrier Safety Administration (FMCSA) is a non-economic regulatory body whose main purpose is motor carrier vehicle safety. Though this agency imposes strict standards on motor carrier vehicle safety, the long-term benefit is increased safety for everyone on the highways.

Highway development also comes from states and various regional planning commissions. One example is the Appalachian Regional Commission, which is charged with improving the infrastructure and economy of that region. Many highway and improvement projects are funded by this agency.

User charges are present in the highway systems in several forms. A major form is the fuel tax. States look to this per-gallon tax as a major revenue source for highway construction and maintenance. The federal government's fuel taxes go to the **Federal Highway Trust Fund**, which is the financing source for the Interstate Highway System. Some states have switched from a per-gallon to a percent of sales price method of fuel-based taxation because, in recent years, the number of gallons of fuel sold has decreased, leaving state agencies with less revenue in times that demand greater highway maintenance. The percent of sales price approach can avoid much of this decline. Another public revenue source is the federal excise tax on vehicle tires. States also obtain revenues through vehicle registration fees. These mostly are assessed on a vehicle weight basis so as to recoup, somewhat, a proportionate share of construction costs related to heavier versus lighter vehicles. Further, some states (such as Oregon) assess a ton-mile tax. Finally, tolls are a form of user taxes on turnpikes and many bridges.

Two major controversies are taking place with regard to highway user charges. One concerns the Federal Highway Trust Fund. The tax money that goes into this fund is collected primarily for interstate highway construction. Approximately 96 percent of the interstate system has been built, but doubt exists over whether the remaining portions, mostly very costly urban sections, will ever be built. Meanwhile, the fuel tax continues to be collected and accumulated in the fund.

A second problem with user taxes is on the state level. Most states collecting vehicle fees and vehicle taxes only return a portion of them for highway purposes. Some states have earmarked some of these funds for education and other uses. In addition, industry groups continue to seek a greater share of these funds for highway development and improvement.

Rail

The railroads currently can avail themselves of direct assistance from the Regional Railroad Reorganization Act of 1973, the Railroad Revitalization and Regulatory Reform Act of 1976, and the Staggers Rail Act of 1980. Most of the assistance is in the form of track repair and motive power acquisition financing. These provisions are attempts to overcome the problem of poor equipment and facilities, which lead to ineffective service and severe financial conditions.

Another form of funding has been available as a subsidy to lines that are abandoned by railroads but that states and other groups continue to operate. This assistance was designed to make rail line abandonment easier for railroads while still allowing service to continue.

The Consolidated Rail Corporation (Conrail) had been the subject of special federal funding and promotion. It had received special appropriations for operations capital improvements, mainly through provisions of the Regional Railroad Reorganization Act of 1973. Recently, after a successful transformation, Conrail was purchased by the Norfolk Southern and CSX Railroads. Conrail's routes were integrated into these two companies.

Research and development in this mode essentially disappeared in the late 1950s. Financial problems in most railroads caused reductions in the research and development area, thereby stagnating the technology. In response to this situation, the Federal Railroad Administration (FRA) was created as part of the DOT in 1966. The FRA has become a major source of gains in railroad technology as well as in safety. A test facility located near Pueblo, Colorado, originally owned by the FRA, is used to test improvements in existing motive power and rolling equipment and to develop advanced high-speed rail technologies for the future. This facility, now known as the Transportation Technology Center, has been privatized and is managed by the Association of American Railroads (AAR).

Another form of assistance to the railroad industry is **Amtrak**. In 1969, the industry's intercity passenger deficit reached more than $500 million. Because the ICC, the DOT, and the public deemed many of these services essential to the public need, the railroads could only discontinue them slowly after major procedural steps were taken. Amtrak was created to relieve this burden from the railroads, while at the same time providing some of the needed services to the public. Thus, much of the passenger train deficit was shifted from the railroads and their customers and stockholders to the federal taxpayer.

Domestic Waterway Operations

The inland barge industry receives two major forms of federal promotion. The first is from the **Army Corps of Engineers**, which is responsible for river and port channel dredging and clearances, as well as lock and dam construction. Operation and maintenance of these facilities rest with the Corps as well. The second is provided by the **U.S. Coast Guard**, which is responsible for navigation aids and systems on the inland waterway system.

Historically, the barge industry paid no user charges except what could be interpreted as a very indirect form through general income taxes. A major controversy over a critical lock and dam on the upper Mississippi River in Alton, Illinois, brought the free-use issue to a decision. The competing railroad industry lobbied to prevent this lock from being improved and enlarged. The resulting legislation and appropriation provided for improvement of that lock and initiated a fuel tax user charge for the barge industry.

International Water Carriage

The American flag overseas steamship industry receives major assistance from the federal government through the Maritime Administration (**MARAD**). The Merchant Marine Act of 1936 was designed to prevent economic decline of the U.S. steamship industry. One major portion of this act is construction differential subsidies (CDS). These are paid by MARAD to U.S. steamship yards that are constructing subsidized lines' ships. A ship that might only cost $20 million to build in Asia might cost $30 million to build in a U.S. yard. A CDS of $10 million is given to the U.S. shipyard so it can charge the U.S. steamship company $20 million, rather than $30 million, to build its ship. Without CDS, U.S. lines would build their ships abroad and American ship-building capacity would cease to exist. The survival of the U.S. shipyard is also viewed as essential to U.S. military capability. The Merchant Marine Act of 1936 also provides for operating differential subsidies (ODS), which cover the higher cost increment resulting from having higher-paid American crews on ships, rather than less costly foreign labor.

Several **indirect** forms of **promotion** exist in this industry as well. The U.S. cabotage laws state that freight or passengers originating or terminating in two U.S. points can only be transported in ships constructed in the United States and owned and managed by U.S. citizens. The United States also has a **cargo preference** law that assists the U.S. fleet. Enacted in 1954, it stipulates that at least 50 percent of the gross tonnage of certain U.S. government-owned and -sponsored cargoes must be carried by U.S. flag ships. This law extends to Department of Defense military goods, foreign aid by the State Department, surplus food movements by the Department of Agriculture, and products whose financing is sponsored by the Export-Import Bank. To be granted a U.S. flag registry, all of a ship's officers and pilots, as well as 75 percent of its other onboard personnel, must be U.S. citizens or residents. The ship must also be owned by U.S. citizens and constructed in a U.S. shipyard.

Several planning and facilitating promotional efforts also assist the American flag ocean fleet. MARAD continually studies and develops plans for port improvements and ways in which export-import movements can be made more efficient. The Department of Commerce has a subagency (the International Trade Administration) whose prime purpose is to stimulate export sales that also benefit the U.S. fleet.

Two points should be mentioned with regard to the major funding and support roles played by MARAD. One deals with the control MARAD has over the lines it subsidizes. The agency exercises decision powers over the design and construction of each ship. It also plays a major role in the routes taken by each one. In this manner, the agency makes certain decisions that are normally within the discretion of carrier managements. This form of control is unique to the transportation industry in the United States.

The other point relates to the rationale for such extensive assistance to this one industry. A strong U.S. shipping fleet is a vital part of national defense sealift capacity in the event of war. Also, existence of the fleet tends to exert some influence on services and rates on various trade routes to the benefit of the United States and its interests.

The **Shipping Act of 1984** (now replaced with the Shipping Act of 1998) is a further example of the U.S. policy toward supporting a strong U.S. ocean fleet. The act was designed to reduce the regulation on foreign ocean shipping with the following goals:

- Establishing a nondiscriminatory regulatory process for common ocean carriers with a minimum of government intervention and regulatory costs;

- Providing an efficient and economic transportation system in the ocean commerce of the United States that is in harmony and responsive to international shipping practices; and,
- Encouraging the development of an economically sound and efficient U.S. flag fleet capable of meeting national security needs.

The St. Lawrence Seaway Development Corporation within the DOT functions as the U.S. financing and operating arm of the joint United States/Canada venture to upgrade the Great Lakes waterway and lock system to accommodate ocean-going ships. This waterway opened a fourth seacoast for the United States, enabling ocean-going ships to call at Buffalo, Cleveland, Toledo, Chicago, Duluth, and other inland ports.

A final, and major, positive role in the water carrier industry is played by various port authorities. These agencies provide financing, major construction, and leasing of facilities in much the same way that the airport authorities provides facilities to the air industry.

Pipeline

The pipeline industry receives no public financial support, but it has benefited in a legal sense from the right of eminent domain permitted to oil, gas, and petroleum product lines. Typically, a pipeline will negotiate for land acquisition or rental. If the landowner will not negotiate at all or in good faith, the law of eminent domain will uphold the use of the land for a pipeline right-of-way in a court of law.

Miscellaneous Forms of Promotion

Various other activities directly or indirectly benefit the transportation industry. The DOT conducts planning and research activities in several ways. First, the Office of Assistant Secretary for Policy and International Affairs is involved with improving international goods flow and conducting studies about the transportation system and data coordination. Second, other research and development studies of benefit to transportation are conducted by the Transportation Research Board and the National Science Foundation. Third, a small but effective group within the Department of Agriculture is concerned with improving loading, unloading, packaging and carriage methods of food products on all modes of transportation. Many of these efforts result in equipment design changes that make transportation equipment more efficient for food movements. Finally, the Department of Defense continually examines methods to improve shipping, and many improvements carry over to the commercial sector.

Transportation Promotion in Perspective

Two major concepts override the entire topic of transportation promotion: user charges and nationalization. User charges often are created and assessed to pay for some or all of the services used by the carrier or mode. Nationalization represents an extreme form of public assistance or provision of transportation.

User Charges

User charges are assessments or fees charged by public bodies against carriers. They are created for a variety of reasons. One is to compensate the public for assistance during modal conception and encouragement. Some user charges are assessed to finance construction. The federal fuel tax on gasoline and diesel is an example, as is the barge fuel tax. Coverage of operating costs is often a reason for the origin of user charges. Examples here are airport landing fees, road tolls, and state fuel tax when it is applied to road maintenance. In addition, a user charge can also serve to equalize intermodal competitive conditions. The barge fuel tax, while paying for some lock construction, also makes barge operators bear some of the full cost of providing their service. This lessens, to a degree, some of the advantage that existed when right-of-way costs were borne by the public and not by the barge firm.

Forms User charges are present in three basic forms. The first is an **existence charge**, a charge related to the existence of some tangible item. This is similar to driver's license and auto registration fees. A charge is made against the person or unit regardless of the extent of use made of the services.

A second user charge is a **unit charge**. This is a fee assessed for use of a facility or resource. This fee is variable according to use, but it does not distinguish between passengers or freight within each unit. Tolls and fuel mileage taxes are examples. Thus, a bus with two passengers pays the same as does a bus with 40 passengers. An empty tractor-trailer or one that is full is charged the same. This form of fee assessment does not take into account the economic value of the service being performed.

A third user fee is based upon **relative use**. This form assesses fees according to the investment of cost incurred by the agency to provide the service. An increased vehicle registration fee for heavier tractor-trailers is an example. Deeper road bases are required for heavier vehicles. Road and bridge wear and damage are believed to be experienced on the basis of vehicle weight. Another example of relative use charge is a commuter route bridge toll. In the San Francisco area, bridge tolls are assessed for each vehicle. However, cars and vans having more than four passengers can cross the bridge toll-free. In this instance, the user charge becomes a behavior inducement. A form of *non-user fee* has arisen in recent years. Atlanta and San Francisco and area counties are partially paying for their shares of rapid transit development through a one-cent additional sales tax on all retail transactions within those areas. Here, many persons do not, or might not, ever use the rapid transit system, but they do bear some of its costs. A major rationale behind this non-user charge is that all persons in a community benefit at least indirectly from the improved infrastructure provided by the system.

Nationalization

Nationalization is an extreme form of public promotion. It basically consists of public ownership, financing, and operation of a business entity. No true forms of nationalization exist in the U.S. transportation system except the Alaska Railroad, which was owned by the DOT and is now owned by the state of Alaska. Nationalization is a method of providing transportation service where financing, ownership, or operations are not possible by private sources. Railroads and airlines in foreign countries are examples of nationalization, but many countries, such as Mexico, New Zealand, and Great Britain, are privatizing their railroads. Transportation service in many lands probably would not exist in a desirable form, or at all, without such government intervention. Advantages of nationalization that are often cited are that services can be provided that would not exist under private ownership, and that capital can be attracted at favorable rates. But nationalized organizations have been criticized as being slow to innovate, unresponsive to the general public, dependent on large management staffs, and subject to political influence.

Transportation Safety

As noted earlier, the federal government has assumed the responsibility of ensuring the safety of travelers. It has promulgated numerous safety regulations for all modes and has centralized safety enforcement in the DOT. Protection of the traveler and the general public is an increasing government concern in light of the reduced economic regulation of transportation and the resultant concerns that carriers will sacrifice safety matters for profitability or economic viability.

Since **economic deregulation**, greater attention has been given to the establishment and enforcement of safety regulation to ensure that the transportation providers do not defer required vehicle and operating safety requirements in lieu of competition. Critics of economic deregulation cite the market pressures on carriers to increase productivity and improve efficiency at the expense of safety. The deregulation experience in the airline and motor carrier industries has resulted in economic pressures on the carriers and a deleterious effect on safety, whereas the opposite is true for the railroads, which have been able to increase profitability and safety.[6]

Federal safety regulations cover all aspects of transportation operations from labor qualifications and operating procedures to equipment specifications. The primary objective of the safety regulations is to establish a **minimum level of safety** for transportation providers to maintain. Many transportation companies establish higher safety levels than those required by law, and these companies have their own enforcement personnel to ensure compliance.

Labor safety regulations have established minimum qualifications for operating personnel, including such factors as age, health, training, licensing, and experience. Minimum age requirements were established for driving a tractor-trailer in interstate commerce, and a nationwide commercial driver-licensing program was initiated in 1988. Airline pilots are required to pass a physical exam, to have training and experience on specific types of aircraft, and to be certified for various types of flying conditions. Similar regulations govern rail engineers and ship captains.

The policy of safe transportation has been extended to the specification of **standards** for transportation vehicles. These standards range from design specifications for aircraft to required safety equipment for automobiles. The vehicle manufacturer is obligated to adhere to the safety specifications, and the vehicle operator is required to maintain the vehicle and equipment in good operating condition and to use the safety equipment. For example, the automobile manufacturer must equip each vehicle with seat belts, a minimum number of headlights and taillights, a horn, and so forth. The auto owner then is required by state law to use the seat belts and to ensure proper functioning of the lights, horn, and other features.

Of all the commodities moved within the boundaries of the United States, **hazardous materials** pose the greatest threat to public safety. Consequently, the movement of hazardous materials and hazardous wastes has been subjected to considerable regulations. A hazardous material is a substance that poses more than a reasonable risk to the health and safety of individuals and includes products such as explosives, flammables, corrosives, oxidizers, and radioactive materials. Regulations regarding the transportation of hazardous materials can be found in the Code of Federal Regulations, Title 49. The safety regulations govern the movement of hazardous wastes as well, and can be found in the Code of Federal Regulations, Title 40.

Many hazardous material and hazardous waste safety regulations have been imposed upon their transportation. The regulations govern loading and unloading practices, packaging, routing, commodity identification, and documentation. Transportation personnel must be trained to properly handle hazardous cargoes and to respond to emergencies.

These regulations overlap somewhat because of the overlapping jurisdiction of the regulatory agencies originating and enforcing the rules. For example, the DOT promulgates and enforces hazardous materials regulation, while the Environmental Protection Agency regulates the movement of hazardous wastes. In addition, the various states and municipalities within the states establish laws affecting the movement of hazardous commodities through their jurisdiction.

As indicated above, the states are involved in regulating the safe operation of transportation vehicles. The police powers of the Constitution grant the states the right to protect the health and welfare of their citizens. The states have used this power to establish safety regulations governing the safe operations of trains through a state, and to limit the maximum speed, height, length, and weight of tractor-trailers. These regulations are not standard from state to state because of the differing political, economic, sociological, and geographic conditions. However, the common denominator in state safety regulations is that all states regulate transportation safety matters.

Transportation safety matters have been extended to include environmental safety. Auto emission standards are designed to protect air quality; flight take-off procedures and patterns are designed to reduce noise levels for the citizens living near airports; and tanker loading and unloading procedures for petroleum products are designed to protect animals, sea life, and the landscape from the devastating effects from an oil spill.

One effect of the myriad safety regulations is an increase in the cost of transporting people and goods. The safety controls exercised by government usually add a direct cost to a transportation operation, making its service more costly to consumers. However, when the indirect social costs are considered, society feels that the benefits of safety regulations, including fewer deaths and injuries and a cleaner environment, more than offset the direct cost. In the future, the number and scope of safety regulations will increase as government expands its safety regulating authority into additional transportation areas.

Transportation Security

After the September 11, 2001 terrorist attack on the United States, the Department of Homeland Security (DHS) was established with the goal of mobilizing and organizing the nation to secure the homeland from terrorist attacks. Its mission is to lead a unified national effort to secure America; to prevent and deter terrorist attacks and protect against and respond to threats and hazards to the nation; and to ensure and secure borders, welcome lawful immigrants and visitors, and promote the free flow of commerce.

DHS is charged with protecting the security of the transportation system, encompassing approximately 742 million air passengers (domestic and international), 11 million imported containers, and 11.5 million motor crossings among the United States, Canada, and Mexico.[7] The DHS transportation security programs and regulations are administered through the Coast Guard (CG), Customs Service (CS), and Transportation Security Administration (TSA).

On the Line

GAO Cites Challenges for 100 Percent Scanning of U.S.-Bound Cargo Containers

WASHINGTON — A report released by the Government Accountability Office (GAO) last month on supply chain security found that there are various ongoing challenges concerning the inspection of U.S.-bound cargo containers from foreign ports.

Data and information for this report was based on mandates from H.R. 1, Implementing Recommendations of the 9/11 Commission Act, which requires 100 percent scanning of U.S.-bound containers by 2012. As part of this bill, the U.S. Customs and Border Protection group was charged with establishing the Secure Freight Initiative (SFI), a pilot program at seven foreign seaports.

The GAO's report cited nine major challenges to continuing the SFI pilot and the 100 percent cargo container scanning requirement: workforce planning; a lack of information about host government cargo examination practices; measuring performance outcomes; undefined resource responsibilities for the cost and labor for implementation; logistical feasibility for scanning equipment and processes; technology and infrastructure issues; use and ownership of scanning data; consistency with risk management; and reciprocity and trade concerns from foreign governments.

Supply chain security experts told *Logistics Management* that the concept of 100 percent cargo scanning remains flawed.

"One hundred percent scanning is far from being a reality…. I do not believe it ever was or will be realistic," said Albert Saphir, president of international trade consultants ABS Consulting in Marietta, Ga. "It looks good on paper, but once you add up the cost and the impact on the supply chain and then contrast it to the fact that we are still not 100 percent secure, it becomes clear that this may not be such a good idea."

Saphir's comments were in line with those from Senator Susan M. Collins (R-Maine) who said in a statement that several challenges would have to be overcome before 100 percent cargo scanning becomes a reality.

"Until X-ray scanning technology is proven effective at detecting radiological material and not disruptive of trade, requiring the scanning of all U.S.-bound cargo, regardless of risk, at every foreign port is misguided and provides a false sense of security," said Collins.

It is not just politicians and security experts that are leery of the viability of 100 percent cargo scanning efforts. The World Customs Organization, the World Shipping Council, the European Commission, and the American Chamber of Commerce to the European Union have all been vocal in their opposition of 100 percent scanning, saying that it is unlikely, unreasonable, and doesn't provide a level of security commensurate with their costs.

When asked about the viability of 100 percent scanning, King Rogers, executive vice president of SC-integrity, a provider of security technology and information services, put it this way: "Can all of these organizations consisting of trade partners, logistics experts, and security practitioners be wrong?"

Source: Jeff Berman, *Logistics Management,* July 2008, p. 18. Reprinted by permission.

The Coast Guard patrols the U.S. coastline and internal navigable waterways implementing the various security measures set forth by the DHS. The Coast Guard can stop a vessel from entering a U.S. port, board the vessel, and prevent any undesirable freight from being off-loaded from a vessel.

The TSA administers the air passenger security screening process at U.S. airports. TSA hires and manages the airport screeners and sets forth items that are prohibited from being carried on board commercial passenger aircraft. TSA is testing various security devices and procedures to ensure the safety of passengers as well as reduce delays resulting from the security-screening process.

TSA has conducted a transit and rail inspection program with the goal of implementing rail passenger and luggage screening similar to that in the air passenger industry. In conjunction with Amtrak and the DOT, TSA is implementing Phase III of a first-time rail security technology study to evaluate the use of emerging technologies to screen checked and unclaimed baggage as well as temporarily stored personal items and cargo for explosives. TSA has also outlines guidelines for freight railroads on the handling of Toxic Inhalation Hazard (TIH) materials when they are being transported near heavily populated areas.

The U.S. Customs and Border Protection Agency (CBP) has been focusing on implementing security measures for cargo entering the United States. CBP has established the 24-hour rule that requires shippers to electronically transmit a description of the cargo to CBP 24 hours before loading. CBP can block any prohibited cargo items from being unloaded at any U.S. port or airport. CBP is working in partnership with shippers to streamline the security paperwork in an attempt to reduce the negative consequences on global commerce entering the United States.

Transportation security has been increased to protect the public against future terrorist attacks. President Bush signed into law the Implementing Recommendations of the 9/11 Commission Act of 2007 (public law 110-53). This law has four major sections: (1) transportation security planning and information sharing; (2) transportation security enhancements; (3) public transportation security; and (4) surface transportation security. As the security measures increase, the impact on the transportation system and transportation users is increased transit time and cost. The transportation security agencies are aware of the commercial impact and are taking steps to reduce the shipping and traveling delays while at the same time maintaining the needed level of security.

SUMMARY

- Imperfections in the marketplace in a free-enterprise economy provide the rationale for government intervention in business operations.
- Potential monopolistic abuses in transportation motivated the federal government to create the Interstate Commerce Commission (ICC) to regulate the transportation industry. The Surface Transportation Board (STB) replaced the ICC.
- The U.S. court system, through decisions under a common law system, also influences transportation regulation.
- All modes are subject to safety regulations administered by both federal and state agencies.
- The Department of Transportation (DOT) is the federal agency responsible for developing and implementing the overall transportation policy for the United States.
- Transportation regulation has progressed through four phases: Initiation Era, Positive Era, Intermodal Era, and the New Economic Era.
- In today's transportation environment, the federal government is a proponent of less economic regulation, preferring to allow market forces to regulate carrier prices and availability of supply.
- Increasing regulations for safety and security are placing a higher burden on carriers but lessening the risk to the public at large.

STUDY QUESTIONS

1. Discuss the rationale for the economic regulation of transportation.
2. How has common law provided a basis for the government's regulation of transportation in the United States?
3. Discuss the role of antitrust laws in transportation during the regulated versus deregulated eras.
4. How do the police powers of the Constitution affect transportation?
5. Why does the United States need a national transportation policy? What purpose does it serve?
6. Analyze the major issues addressed by the ICC Termination Act national transportation policy statements.
7. Unlike may industrialized nations, the United States has fostered private ownership of transportation companies. What is the rationale for private ownership?
8. What is the rationale for the public promotion of transportation?
9. What are transportation user charges? What is the purpose of such charges?
10. Discuss the advantages and disadvantages of increasing regulations relating to transportation safety and security. Be sure to include both transportation providers and transportation users in your discussion.

NOTES

1. Dudley F. Pegrum, *Public Regulation of Business,* Homewood, IL: Richard D. Irwin, 1959, pp. 21–24.

2. Ibid.

3. Sherman Antitrust Act of 1890, Sections 1 and 2.

4. U.S. Department of Transportation, *A Statement of National Transportation Policy,* Washington, D.C., 1975, p. 1.

5. The material in this section is adapted from: Transportation Policy Associates, *Transportation In America,* 4th ed., Washington, D.C., 1986, pp. 28–31.

6. Paul Stephen Dempsey, "The Empirical Results of Deregulation: A Decade Later, and the Band Played On," *Transportation Law Journal,* vol. 17, 1988, pp. 69–81.

7. http://www.bts.gov

CASE 3-1

Who Pays the Price?

Over the last ten years the federal government has dramatically increased the number of regulations pertaining to transportation security and the effects of transportation on the environment. After the terrorist attack on the United States on September 11, 2001, the Department of Homeland Security (DHS) was established. Within the DHS is the Transportation Security Administration, which is responsible for implementing regulations to protect the safety of passengers using the U.S. airline industry. These regulations require passengers to be screened for illegal items before they enplane, limit the size and nature of items in carry-on luggage, and provide guidelines for more intense scrutiny of randomly selected passengers. Critics of these policies complain that these policies delay passengers, increase time through airports, cause delays, and increase costs for the airlines. Proponents of these policies argue that the safety of air passengers is more important that these delays and increased costs.

The federal government passed legislation requiring all motor carrier tractors purchased after 2007 to meet more stringent EPA guidelines for engine emissions of particulate matter. These new guidelines require new engine technology that has increased the cost of these engines by over $10,000. Motor carriers are critical of these guidelines, arguing that the increased engine cost and resulting increase in maintenance costs are prohibitive and are difficult to pass on to customers in the form of higher prices. Proponents of these guidelines argue that cleaner engine exhaust is better for the environment and, therefore, a benefit to the general public.

Legislation is being considered to dramatically increase the number of inspections on containers entering U.S. ports from foreign origins. The purpose of the inspection is to reduce the likelihood of terrorist activity that could occur by using a container to hold weapons or explosives that are meant to harm U.S. citizens. The inspection would require physically unloading the container at the port and inspecting its contents. The rationale behind increasing the number of containers inspected is the resulting reduction in the probability of a terrorist attack on U.S. soil. Critics of this legislation argue that with the thousands of containers entering U.S. ports every, increased inspection activity would increase congestion at the ports, slow down the movement of goods into the United States, and add costs to carriers and shippers.

CASE QUESTIONS

1. In each of the three scenarios presented in the case, opponents and proponents have divergent views of government regulations. One view is on the public benefit, the other is on the cost to private industry. How can you decide which view to accept?

2. In each of the scenarios above, identify the benefits versus the costs for both viewpoints.

3. Should the government intervene in setting regulations to increase security and help the environment? Or should private industry take on this role? Discuss.

CASE 3-2

The U.S. Airline Industry Public Support

After the September 11 terrorist attack in 2001, the U.S. airline industry was grounded by the federal government for security reasons. During this forced grounding, the air carriers faced ongoing expenses, but no income. After the grounding order was lifted, the airlines began to restore flights, but the flying public was not flying. Planes were virtually empty, so the air carriers reduced the number of flights and placed planes in mothball storage.

The financial plight caused by the grounding and subsequent reduction of demand was tremendous. Congress passed emergency legislation to provide operating funds for the air carriers to assure that U.S. citizens would have a viable air carrier system. These public monies helped sustain the industry while the flying public overcame its fear of flying.

In 2008, after some airline mergers and proposed mergers, the airline industry is still in financial trouble. There is again a call for federal money to help support the vital air carrier industry. There are opponents who claim the air carrier plight is a result of mismanagement, overly aggressive flight scheduling that caused overcapacity, and an overall reduction in demand. On top of this, customer service ratings for most of the major U.S. airlines are suffering.

CASE QUESTIONS

1. What are the arguments in favor of the federal government providing financial support to the U.S. airlines?

2. What are the arguments against the federal government providing financial support to the U.S. airlines?

3. If federal financial assistance is provided, should the air carriers and/or the flying public be expected to repay the government? If so, what form of repayment would you suggest? Why?

APPENDIX 3A

Department of Transportation

The United States Department of Transportation (DOT) was established in 1966 to co-ordinate the administration of government transportation programs and to establish overall transportation policy that enables the provision of fast, safe, efficient, and convenient transportation at the lowest cost. As indicated in Figure 3A-1, the DOT consists of 12 different agencies with the Secretary of Transportation having the responsibility of coordinating the activities of these agencies as each administers the programs under its respective jurisdiction. The centralization of federal transportation activities under the auspices of one department in the executive branch focuses attention on the critical nature of transportation in the economy.

The operating programs of most of the individual agencies are basically organized by mode. The secretary and deputy secretary are responsible for the overall planning, direction, and and control of departmental activities but do not exercise direct operating control over the agencies. Rather, the secretary's office is concerned with policy development, resource allocation, program evaluation, agency coordination, and intermodal matters.

The secretary is the principal advisor to the president on matters relating to federal transportation. The responsibility for domestic and international transportation policy development and review is delegated to the assistant secretary for policy and international affairs. On the domestic level, this policy formulation is directed toward assessing the economic impact of government regulations and programs on the industry and the economy. Such policy issues as public trust funds, user charges, energy and environmental concerns, subsidy levels for subsidized carriers, international mail rates, aviation and maritime concerns in multilateral and bilateral negotiations, and coordination of

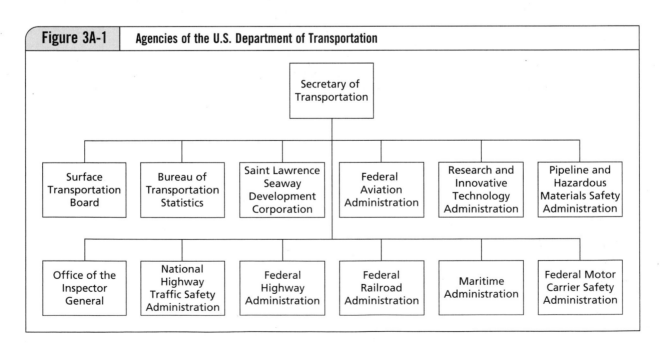

Figure 3A-1   Agencies of the U.S. Department of Transportation

efforts to combat transportation-related terrorist acts and drug smuggling are representative of the wide range of policy responsibilities of the Secretary of Transportation.

Through its various agencies and departments, the DOT has responsibility and control over transportation safety, promotion, and research. The individual agency programs provide insight into the overall role of government in transportation matters other than economic regulation. A brief description of some of the activities included in the DOT can be found on the following pages.

Federal Aviation Administration

The Federal Aviation Administration (FAA) is responsible for regulating air safety, promoting development of air commerce, and controlling navigable air space in the interest of safety and efficiency. The FAA is most noted for its air safety regulations governing the manufacture, operation, and maintenance of aircraft, the certification pilots and navigators, and the operation of air traffic control facilities. It conducts research and development of procedures, systems, and facilities to achieve safe and efficient air navigation and air traffic control.

The FAA administers a grant program for planning and developing public airports and provides technical guidance on airport planning, design, and safety operations. The agency maintains registration and records of aircraft, aircraft engines, propellers, and parts. It promotes international aviation safety by exchanging aeronautical information with foreign authorities, certifying foreign repair facilities and mechanics, and providing technical assistance in aviation safety training.

Federal Highway Administration

The Federal Highway Administration (FHWA) is concerned with the overall operation and environment of the highway system, including the coordination of research and development activities aimed at improving the quality and durability of highways. In this capacity, the FHWA administers the federal-aid highway program, which provides financial assistance to the states for the construction and improvement of highways and traffic operations. For example, the interstate system is a 46,876 mile network financed on a 90 percent federal/10 percent state basis. Improvements for other federal-aid highways are financed on the 75 percent federal/25 percent state basis. The monies are generated from special highway use taxes, which are deposited into the Highway Trust Fund. Congress authorizes disbursement of money from the trust fund for payment of the federal government's portion of the highway expenditures.

Federal Railroad Administration

The promulgation and enforcement of railroad safety regulations are major responsibilities of the Federal Railroad Administration (FRA). The safety regulations cover maintenance, inspection, and equipment standards and operating practices. It administers research and development of railroad safety improvements and operates the Transportation Test Center near Pueblo, Colorado, which tests advanced and conventional systems that improve ground transportation.

The FRA administers the federal assistance program for national, regional, and local rail services. The assistance is designed to support continuation of rail freight and passenger service and state rail planning. In addition, the FRA administers programs designed to improve rail transportation in the northeast corridor of the United States.

National Highway Traffic Safety Administration

Motor vehicle safety performance is the major jurisdiction of the National Highway Traffic Safety Administration (NHTSA). In this capacity, the NHTSA issues prescribed safety features and safety-related performance standards for vehicles and motor vehicle equipment. The agency reports to Congress and to the public the damage susceptibility, crashworthiness, ease of repair, and theft prevention of motor vehicles. It is charged with the mandate of reducing the number of deaths, injuries, and economic losses resulting from traffic accidents. Finally, the NHTSA establishes fuel economy standards for automobiles and light trucks.

Federal Transit Administration

The Federal Transit Administration (FTA) is charged with improving mass transportation facilities, equipment, techniques, and methods; encouraging the planning and establishment of urban mass transportation systems; and providing financial assistance to state and local governments in operating mass transportation companies. Capital grants or loans of up to 75 percent of the project cost are made available to communities to purchase equipment and facilities, Formula grants are available in amounts of up to 80 percent of the project cost for capital and planning activities and 50 percent for operating subsidies. In addition, the FTA makes funding available for research and training programs.

Maritime Administration

The Maritime Administration (MARAD) oversees programs designed to develop, promote, and operate the U.S. Merchant Marine fleet and to organize and direct emergency merchant ship operations. MARAD maintains a national defense reserve fleet of government-owned ships that are to be operated in times of national defense emergencies. It also operates the U.S. Merchant Marine Academy, which operates training for future Merchant Marine officers.

MARAD administers maritime subsidy programs through the Maritime Subsidy Board. The operating subsidy program provides U.S. flag ships with an operating subsidy that represents the difference between the costs of operating a U.S. flag ship and a foreign competitive flag ship. A construction subsidy program provides funds for the difference between the costs of constructing ships in U.S. shipyards and in foreign shipyards. It also provides financing guarantees for construction or reconditioning of ships.

St. Lawrence Seaway Development Corporation

The St. Lawrence Seaway Development Corporation (SLSDC) is a government-owned operation that is responsible for the development, maintenance, and operation of the U.S. portion of the St. Lawrence Seaway. The SLSDC charges tolls to ship operators who use the seaway. These tolls are negotiated with the St. Lawrence Seaway Authority of Canada. The U.S. and Canadian seaway agencies coordinate activities involving seaway operations, traffic control, navigation aids, safety, and length of shipping season.

Research and Innovative Technology Administration

Established in 2005 through the Norman Y. Mineta Research and Special Programs Improvement Act, the Research and Innovative Technology Administration (RITA) coordinates the DOT's research programs and is charged with advancing the deployment of cross-cutting technologies to improve our nation's transportation system. RITA is charged with: (1) coordinating, facilitating, and reviewing the DOT's research and development programs and activities; (2) advancing innovative technologies, including intelligent transportation systems; (3) performing comprehensive transportation statistical research, analysis, and reporting; and (4) providing education and training in transportation and transportation-related fields.

The specific agencies that report to RITA are: (1) the Bureau of Transportation Statistics; (2) the Transportation Safety Institute; (3) Intelligent Transportation Systems; (4) the National Transportation Library; (5) Research, Development, and Technology; (6) the University Transportation Centers; and (7) the Volpe National Transportation System Centers.

Pipeline and Hazardous Materials Safety Administration

The Pipeline and Hazardous Materials Safety Administration (PHMSA) was also established through the Norman Y. Mineta Research and Special Programs and Improvement Act of 2005. It replaced the Research and Special Programs Administration. The mission of the PHMSA is to protect people and the environment from the risks inherent in transportation of hazardous materials by pipeline and other modes of transportation. It regulates the safe, reliable, and environmentally sound operation of the nation's 2.3 million miles of pipeline and nearly 1 million daily shipments of hazardous materials by land, sea, and air.

PHMSA has four goals. First, PHMSA is charged to reduce the risk of harm to people due to the transportation of hazardous materials by pipelines and other modes. Second, it needs to reduce the risk of harm to the environment due to the transportation of oil and hazardous materials by pipeline and other modes. Third, it strives to harmonize and standardize the requirements for pipeline and hazardous materials internationally and to facilitate the efficient and safe transportation through ports of entry and through the supply chain. Finally, PHMSA is charged to reduce the consequences (harm to people, environment, and economy) after a pipeline or hazardous material failure has occurred.

Federal Motor Carrier Safety Administration

The Federal Motor Carrier Safety Administration (FMCSA) was established as a separate administration within the DOT on January 1, 2000, pursuant to the Motor Carrier Safety Improvement Act of 1999. The primary mission is to reduce crashes, injuries, and fatalities involving large tractor-trailers and buses. In carrying out its safety mandate, FMCSA:

- Develops and enforces data-driven regulations that balance motor carrier (motor carrier and bus companies) safety with industry efficiency;
- Harnesses safety information systems to focus on higher-risk carriers in enforcing the safety regulations;

- Targets educational messages to carriers, commercial drivers, and the public; and
- Partners with stakeholders including federal, state, and local enforcement agencies, the motor carrier industry, safety groups, and organized labor on efforts to reduce bus and motor carrier-related crashes.

FMCSA develops, maintains, and enforces Federal Motor Carrier Safety Regulations (FMCSRs), Hazardous Materials Regulations (HMRs), and the Commercial Driver's License (CDL) Program, among others.

Office of the Inspector General

The Office of the Inspector General (OIG) is committed to fulfilling its statutory mission and assisting members of Congress, the secretary, and senior department officials in achieving a safe, efficient, and effective transportation system that meets vital national interests and enhances the quality of life of the American people, today and into the future.

The OIG works within the DOT to promote effectiveness and to stop waste, fraud, and abuse in departmental programs. This is accomplished through audits and investigations. OIG also consults with Congress about programs in progress and proposed new laws and regulations.

Surface Transportation Board

The Surface Transportation Board (STB) was created by the Interstate Commerce Commission Termination Act of 1995 and is the successor agency to the Interstate Commerce Commission. The STB is an economic regulatory agency that Congress charged with the fundamental missions of resolving railroad rate and service disputes and reviewing proposed railroad mergers. The STB is an independent agency, although it is administratively affiliated with the DOT.

The STB serves as both an adjudicatory and a regulatory body. The agency has jurisdiction over railroad rate and service issues and rail restructuring transactions (mergers, line sales, line construction, and line abandonments). Although the STB does have regulatory authority over a few matters regarding other modes, its primary focus is on the railroad industry.

SUMMARY

- The agencies that make up the DOT administer federal programs covering all modes of transportation.
- DOT establishes national transportation policy, enforces safety regulations, provides funding for transportation programs, and coordinates transportation research efforts.
- The Secretary of Transportation is the principal advisor to the president on transportation matters.

Chapter 4

COSTING AND PRICING FOR TRANSPORTATION

Learning Objectives

After reading this chapter, you should be able to do the following:

- Understand the relationship between a rate and a price
- Be familiar with the various types of market structures found in the transportation industry
- Gain knowledge of the impact of transportation prices on the relevant market area for a product
- Be able to explain the differences between cost of service and value of service pricing
- Understand the different forms of rates used in transportation
- Appreciate how transportation rates have changed under deregulation
- Determine the strategic role of pricing for transportation firms
- Calculate the costs of both truckload and less-than-truckload freight moves

Transportation Profile

What Are We Shipping?

In the course of any year, hundreds of thousands of different types of products are transported throughout the United States, with new products constantly being developed that also require transportation. When transportation carriers need to decide what to charge these products, they use three criteria: the weight of the shipment, the distance it is going, and the nature of the commodity. Combining all of the different weights a shipment can take with all of the possible origins and destinations and with all of the types of products can result in trillions of possible rates. Carriers have simplified this process by developing weight breaks, establishing rate basis zones (for distance), and constructing a classification tariff that groups similar commodities into common product classifications.

Determining the weight of a shipment and the distance it is going is a relatively easy process since it can be measured quantitatively. This is not the case with determining what a product is for transportation purposes. The National Motor Freight Classification Committee (NMFCC) has identified four criteria that are used to group similar products together in a particular classification: product density (pounds per cubic foot), stowability, handling, and liability. All of these criteria influence the cost to the carrier of transporting a product and thus have an impact on the rate that should be charged. If a new product is developed and needs a freight rate for it to be transported, the Committee uses these four criteria to determine, for transportation purposes, what classification group is applicable to this new product. A good example is paint in cans. There are many sizes of paint cans in numerous colors. Determining a different rate for every size of paint can in every color would be tedious and unnecessary. So a general classification for *paint, NOI* (not otherwise indexed) would include all size cans for all colors since the density, stowability, handling, and liability would be the same for all variations.

However, classifying some products is not easy. When recycling aluminum cans in the United States became the rage, railroads began charging the same freight rates on recycled cans moving to a recycling center as it did on new cans moving to bottlers. The rationale was that the density, stowability, handling, and liability for the recycled cans were the same as for new cans. Can recycling companies countered that recycled cans had a lower value and could not bear the higher freight rates of new cans. In fact, these companies argued to the Interstate Commerce Commission (ICC) that the higher freight rates would prohibit the profitable recycling of aluminum cans.

Another example can be found in a case brought by IBM against motor carriers in the United States. When IBM was still in the personal computer business in the 1990s, it would import computer monitors from overseas and transport them domestically to distribution centers to be merged with the computer towers. Domestic motor carriers, using the four criteria for classification, determined that these monitors had the same transportation characteristics as television sets. The logic of the motor carriers was sound. From a transportation perspective, a computer monitor was the same as a television set. However, IBM argued to the ICC that these monitors were not television sets, but were computer peripherals, which would result in a different classification and a lower freight rate than for television sets. The ICC ruled in favor of IBM and declared that, in fact, computer monitors were computer peripherals.

Currently, the NMFCC has cases pending classification involving basketball nets, hay, clothing, charged fire extinguishers, and tortillas. What historical cases have shown is that cost-driven classification works well for most products. However, the classification for certain products must examine market value and potential use. Similar products from a cost perspective (computer monitors and television sets) will have a different market value and potential use, thereby having different elasticities of demand based on freight prices. So before tendering a newly developed product to a carrier for transportation, a shipper needs to ask, "What am I shipping?"

Introduction

Federal regulation of transportation business practices was initiated in the United States in 1887 when Congress passed the Act to Regulate Commerce (later named the Interstate Commerce Act). This legislation established a framework of control over interstate rail transportation and created the Interstate Commerce Commission (ICC) to administer it. Between 1906 and 1940, oil pipelines, motor carriers, and domestic water carriers were also subjected to ICC control. Air transportation came under federal economic regulation in 1938, with the passage of the Civil Aeronautics Act.

Reduction of federal economic regulation of the various modes began with partial curtailment of rail regulation in 1976 (Railroad Revitalization and Regulatory Reform Act), air cargo in 1977, and air passenger transportation in 1978 (Airline Deregulation Act). Two years later, interstate motor carriage was almost completely deregulated (Motor Carrier Act of 1980), and extensive additional reductions in railroad regulation were enacted (Staggers Rail Act of 1980). In the 1980s, legislative moves to further curtail transportation regulation continued. Intercity bus service was deregulated in 1982, followed by surface domestic freight forwarders in 1986.

A federal political climate favorable to deregulation continued in the 1990s. Passage of the Trucking Industry Regulatory Reform Act of 1992 removed the power of the states to regulate intrastate motor freight transportation. Three years later, passage of the ICC Termination Act of 1995 (ICCTA) eliminated almost all remaining elements of motor carrier regulation, further reduced rail regulation, and replaced the 108-year-old ICC with the Surface Transportation Board (STB). The STB holds responsibility for administering the remnants of economic rail regulation that remain law within the ICCTA.

A prime objective of deregulation was market-driven pricing of transportation services free from regulatory intervention. Thus, motor carriers are free to charge whatever rates they can to generate revenue. Deregulation also freed motor carriers to operate wherever they choose, geographically. Rail carriers are also free to charge rates based exclusively on market conditions, except in situations where the STB might find a rail firm's market power strong enough to subject rail customers to economic abuse or injury.

Before deregulation, all interstate rail freight traffic and much motor freight traffic was moved on published (tariff) rates. Both motor and rail carriers still offer tariff rates. However, under freedom from economic regulation, the use of rates set in confidential contracts between carriers and shippers has become prominent, particularly for traffic tendered by large-volume shippers.

The use of contracts, if managed well, ensures that both the carrier and the shipper have a clear understanding of each other's requirements (for instance, profitability of service rendered for the carrier, and value derived from freight movement for the shipper) when they enter into a binding agreement. However, if a shipper or carrier negotiates terms that are unwise, no federal agency will be available to offer a remedy.

Individuals studying transportation should understand the theoretical underpinnings of the rates and prices of transportation agencies. A key point to master at the outset is the idea that a difference exists between the terms *rate* and *price*.

In the past, when transportation regulation was at its peak, it was more appropriate to use the term *rate* than *price*. A rate is an amount that can be found in a rate tariff book, as payment to a carrier for performing a given transportation service. This rate is the *lawful* charge that a carrier can impose on a given commodity movement;

therefore, a rate has the full force of the law behind it for its timely payment. A rate is determined primarily by considering a carrier's costs only and not by assessing the overall market situation at that moment in time and how these market forces influence supply and demand. A discussion of cost concepts can be found in Appendix 4A.

A price, however, involves a much clearer notion of how post-deregulation transportation firms determine and impose charges for their services. A price implies a value or level that is determined based on prevailing market forces. Clearly, the notion of *price* implies a dynamic economic environment, one that is receptive to changes in customer demand and carrier supply.

Although the transportation industry is not completely unique compared to other industries, there are enough differences to justify a thorough discussion of transportation pricing. The first part of this chapter on transport prices will explore the market structure of the transportation industry. The section on market structure will be followed by an analysis of cost-of-service pricing. This analysis will provide the basis for a discussion on value-of-service pricing. The final part of the chapter will address rate systems and pricing in transportation.

Market Considerations

Before discussing the characteristics of the transportation market, a brief review of basic market structure models is appropriate. Such a discussion will provide some insights into the unique nature of transportation market situations.

Market Structure Models

The necessary conditions for **pure competition** are generally stated as follows:

- There are a large number of sellers.
- All sellers and buyers are of such a small size that no one can influence prices or supply.
- There is a homogeneous product or service.
- There is unrestricted entry.

The demand curve facing the individual firm is one of perfect elasticity, which means the producer can sell all output at the one market price, but none above that price. Although pure competition is not a predominant market structure, it is frequently used as a standard to judge optimal allocation of resources.

If pure competition is one type of market structure, the other extreme is a perfectly monopolistic market with only one seller of a product or service for which there is no close competitor or substitute. In such a situation, the single seller is able to set the price for the service offered and should adjust the price to its advantage, given the demand curve. To remain in this situation, the single seller must be able to restrict entry. The single seller maximizes profits by equating marginal cost and marginal revenue and might make excess profit.

A third type of market structure is **oligopoly**. Oligopoly can be defined as competition between a few large sellers of a relatively homogeneous product that has enough cross-elasticity of demand (substitutability) that each seller must take into account competitors' reactions in making pricing decisions. In other words, oligopoly is characterized by mutual interdependence among the various sellers. The individual seller is aware that in changing price, output, sales promotion activities, or the quality of the product, the reactions of competitors must be taken into account. All modes encounter some form of oligopolistic competition.

The fourth type of market structure is **monopolistic competition**. In this type of market structure there are many small sellers but there is some differentiation of products. The number of sellers is great enough and the largest seller small enough that no one controls a significant portion of the market. No recognized interdependence of the related sellers' prices or price policies is usually present. Therefore, any seller can lower price to increase sales volume without necessarily eliciting a retaliatory reaction from competitors.

This brief description of the four basic market models is by no means complete. The interested student can obtain additional perspectives from any standard microeconomics text. For our purposes, the above discussion provides enough background to focus more closely on transportation markets.

Theory of Contestable Markets[1]

The relevant market structure faced by each mode of transportation provided the basis for arguments made by proponents of deregulation. This was especially the case with airline deregulation. For deregulation to work for a mode, its market structure must closely resemble pure competition. On the surface, it appeared that the passenger airline industry was oligopolistic and therefore would prevent the free entry of competitors. However, there was some consensus that the airline industry could perform in a competitive manner. This rationale resulted in what can be called the *theory of contestable markets*, which substitutes potential competition for the active participation of many sellers.[2]

For this theory to work, several conditions had to be met. First, barriers to entry could not exist. Such barriers could include physical barriers, informational barriers, and capital barriers.[3] Second, economies of scale could not be present. In the airline industry, this meant that operating many aircraft could not have a cost advantage over operating a single aircraft. Third, consumers had to be willing and able to switch quickly among carriers.[4] Finally, existing carriers had to be prevented from responding to new entrants' lower prices, assuming that the entrant possessed a lower cost structure than the incumbent.[5]

Although the theory of contestable markets proved to be correct in the early days of deregulation, incumbent airlines have been able to remove the potential threat of new entrants in today's operating environment, thus weakening the theory's application.[6] This conclusion points to the importance of understanding the market structures of the modes and how they will behave in a deregulated environment. It also leads to the conclusion that the passenger airline industry is indeed an oligopoly, and thus is subject to the potential abuses of this type of market.

Relevant Market Areas

A general statement classifying the market structure of the entire transportation industry cannot be made because it is necessary to view structures in particular market areas. In the railroad industry, for example, there exists a variety of different services, involving the transportation of thousands of different commodities between tens of thousands of different stations or geographic points, via a multiplicity of different routes and under various conditions of carriage.[7] The market structure in transportation must describe the situation at any one point, and even then the situation will differ between commodities. Therefore, to determine pricing in transportation, we must describe the situation between two points, for one commodity, in one shipment size, moving in one direction.[8]

For example, a particular railroad that provides service between Pittsburgh and Cincinnati might find that the movement of ordinary steel approximates what we have described as monopolistic competition. There is likely to be a large number of other carriers, especially common and contract motor carriers, that provide essentially the same service.

However, for the movement of a very large, sophisticated generator, the railroad might face an oligopolistic market on the move between Pittsburgh and Cincinnati because none of the motor carriers might be able to haul such a large piece of equipment and the railroad might be competing with only a few water carriers. It is possible to find some commodity where the railroad would be operating in a monopolistic position because of restrictions on operating authorities. Finally, there might even be a product for which the situation approaches pure competition. In fact, this might be true for certain steel products, given the availability of rail, motor, water, and private carrier. In summary, the relevant market situation for transportation consists of one commodity, moving between two points, in one shipment size, in one direction.

The market structure for a particular mode of transportation in one market could be described in more detail. This is especially true with respect to the railroad industry, the water carrier industry, and the pipeline industry. A typical situation in each of these industries could be described and made to fit one of the economic models previously mentioned. For example, it could be stated that between two particular cities the water carriers are faced with oligopolistic conditions. From this, the general pricing behavior of the industry could be discussed.[9] However, there is intermodal competition present in transportation, and it is necessary to take this fact into consideration to adequately describe market situations. Also, as has been stated, the situation varies by commodity.

The complexity of the situation does not eliminate the validity of the economic models described above. It only means that in order to make use of these models knowledge of the situation that exists in a particular market must be obtained. Although this might seem to be too much to expect at first, it can be accomplished. The elaborate classification system for rates (discussed later in this chapter) distorts the situation somewhat, but in our economy commodity rates are the most important in terms of total intercity ton-miles. Commodity rates are competitive on commodities between specific points. In setting prices, a carrier must have knowledge of the relevant market area. With this knowledge, it is possible to use one of the economic models described. Although there will be instances when carriers might find it expedient to generalize in adjusting prices, a much narrower focus is customary in the day-to-day negotiation and analysis of these prices.

The deregulation that has occurred in transportation between 1978 and 1996 has made these conclusions even more appropriate. Although it is true that there has been a general increase in competition, the competition has been uneven among market areas, commodities, and shipment sizes. The new competitive environment has made carriers and shippers more sensitive to the importance of the relevant market area concept. More prices are being negotiated by shippers and carriers and are taking into account the particular demand and supply situations for the movements affected.

The important point about this analysis is that, although transportation competition has indeed become more intense in the last three or four decades, the intensity is uneven. Therefore, all four types of markets can be found in transportation industries.

This makes pricing very challenging. In addition, the derived nature of transportation demand further complicates the pricing situation.

Cost-of-Service Pricing[10]

There are two alternative concepts for **cost-of-service pricing**: basing prices on marginal cost or basing prices on average cost. To give adequate treatment to each alternative, some simplifying assumptions will be made and exhibited using Figure 4-1. The assumptions are that (1) the firm's product or service (such as transportation) is homogeneous, (2) only one group of customers is involved, (3) this group of customers is responsible for all costs, and (4) the firm possesses some degree of monopoly power, as indicated by a downward sloping demand curve as seen in Figure 4-1.

If the firm desires to maximize its profits (see Figure 4-1), it will produce quantity Q_m and charge price P_m. By doing so, the firm would be making excess profits in the economic sense (that is, earning a rate of return on its invested assets in excess of that needed to attract and retain financial capital from investors). This result is good for the firm's investors (shareholders). However, it is not good from the standpoint of optimal allocation of resources for the economy at large, because the price is above **average cost** and the firm is not producing and selling as much as it would (Q_a) if its selling price was set equal to the average cost (P_a). This is a basic result of the firm's exercise of monopoly power.

This result might induce government regulation of the firm's pricing. If regulation is imposed, the regulatory agency has two alternatives for attempting to improve economic efficiency in the economy at large and to increase the economic well-being of existing and prospective buyers of the firm's output. By ordering the firm to set its price at P_z, the firm's output and sales would increase from Q_m to Q_z, the firm's **marginal cost** would equal its average cost of production, and the firm would neither earn excess profit nor incur a loss on any of the additional (marginal) units of output that it sells. Conceptually, this is identical to the outcome that would result under pure

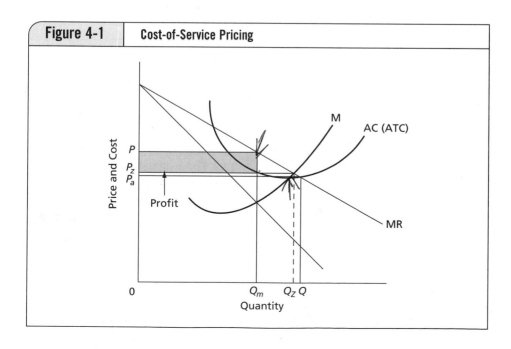

| Figure 4-1 | Cost-of-Service Pricing |

competition, where the forces of the market would cause a firm to sell its output at the going market price and where (assuming the firm is in a state of perfect equilibrium) the market price would be equal to both the firm's marginal cost and average cost.

It should be noted here that some advocates of regulation have argued that ordering a firm to set price equal to average cost is more socially desirable, because the firm's customers would be obtaining more output (Q_a) at an even lower price (P_a). However, critics of this approach point out that the units of output between Q_z and Q_a are being sold at a price (P_a) that is less than the marginal cost of producing them and hence that buyers of these units are receiving a subsidy from investors in the firm.

In Adam Smith's terminology, the value in use is not as great as the cost of producing the additional output. Therefore, there are alternate uses in which the resources used to produce this additional output are valued more highly by consumers. When stated in this manner, the argument is based upon logic usually advanced under a label of "welfare economics."[11] Under the marginal-cost solution presented in Figure 4-1, there would be excess profits because price is above the average cost. However, this need not be a problem because the excess profits can be used to pay taxes.

One of the arguments frequently raised against a strict marginal-cost approach to pricing is that, under decreasing cost conditions, if the firm equates marginal cost with demand, then it will necessitate the firm's operating at a loss (see Figure 4-2). However, the advocates of a strict marginal-cost approach would still present the argument that individuals are willing to pay the marginal cost of the additional output between Q_m and Q_r and therefore it should be produced. There is one obvious solution and that is to allow the government to make up the deficit through a subsidy.[12] These subsidies could be offset by the taxes collected in the previous example. These are also additional ways to offset governmental subsidies.

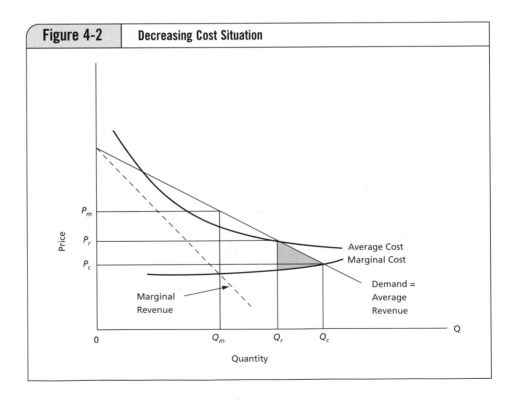

Figure 4-2   Decreasing Cost Situation

Thus far in this discussion, no attempt has been made to substantiate one approach or the other. The arguments advanced by advocates of each approach have been presented. Before any critique can be presented of these alternate approaches, the assumptions that were made at the outset should be examined.

The assumption that only one group of customers is served is not the typical situation, except in very special cases among transportation companies. Likewise, costs are not usually separable according to the classes of customers receiving the same type of service, but rather, common costs are quite typical, particularly with respect to railroads. Already mentioned is that output is not homogeneous in many instances; rather, what exists are heterogeneous or multiple services. Transportation firms are not peculiar in this respect because so many firms have common costs.

The presence of **common costs** raises some problems for cost-of-service pricing, particularly the average-cost approach. If rates are based upon average or fully allocated costs, it becomes necessary to apportion these costs by some arbitrary means. Average cost pricing with fixed or common costs or both makes these costs price-determining when they should be price-determined. In other words, fixed costs per unit depend on the volume of traffic, and the volume of traffic depends on the rate charged. To some extent then, cost is a function of the prices; the prices are not a function of the cost.[13] In fact, it could be argued that not only do costs determine prices, but also that prices determine cost; in other words, the situation is analogous to the chicken and the egg argument.

The presence of common costs does not raise the same theoretical problem for marginal-cost pricing because no arbitrary allocation of these costs is technically necessary. However, problems might be encountered because marginal cost can only be determined with large blocks of output such as a trainload or even a truckload. The output unit to be priced can be smaller with LTL shipments. There are some additional problems of a more practical nature, however, with respect to strict marginal-cost pricing. For example, in transportation, marginal costs could fluctuate widely, depending on the volume of traffic offered. The requirement of published rates would necessitate the averaging of these marginal costs to stabilize them, which would make them unequal with theoretical marginal costs.

Some theoretical and practical problems with cost-of-service pricing have been raised. An obvious question is whether cost-of-service pricing has any relevance for establishing prices. Prices charged by transportation companies are actually one of the criteria that guide intelligent shippers in selecting the mode of transportation or carrier that is most appropriate for their shipment. When the modal choice or carrier decision is made properly, the shipper will balance the carrier's price against the carrier's service characteristics such as transit time, reliability, and loss and damage record.

For the transportation decision to be properly made, the price charged should reflect the cost of providing the service to ensure carrier and economic system efficiency. The price(s) of carriers should be related to cost, but not to some arbitrary allocation of cost.

Railroads and pipelines require large, indivisible capital inputs because of their rights-of-way, terminals, and so on. The associated high fixed costs that are common costs to most of the traffic, if averaged over the units of traffic, will have to be allocated on an arbitrary basis, which will in turn lead to unwise and uneconomical pricing decisions. Adherence to an average cost or fully allocated cost approach does not make any sense in such situations.

Cost-oriented prices should be related to what we have defined as marginal cost or variable cost. Such costs, measured as precisely as possible, should serve as the conceptual floor for individual prices. Some traffic will move if prices are above marginal or variable cost, whereas other traffic will move at prices close to marginal cost, particularly under competitive circumstances. In other words, differential pricing seems to make sense in most instances, but the rationale needs further explanation.

In the presentation of cost-of-service pricing, mention was made of **decreasing cost industries**. Some transportation firms fall into this category. If prices are based on strict marginal cost, the firm experiences a loss. A subsidy could be paid, but this is not likely to be done. Therefore, the firm has to recover its fixed costs. To accomplish this on the basis of an average-cost approach is not acceptable. However, it can be accomplished by using marginal cost as a floor for prices and using the value of service, or demand, to establish how far above this minimum the rate or price should be set.

Value-of-service pricing is sometimes defined as **charging what the traffic will bear**. In actuality, this phrase can assume two meanings. First, it can be used to mean that prices are set so that on each unit the maximum revenue is obtained regardless of the particular costs involved. That is, no service should be charged a lower price when it could bear a higher price. The second meaning, which can be more conveniently expressed in a negative form and which is germane to this discussion, is that no service should be charged a price that it will not bear when, at a lower price, the service could be purchased. This lower price will always cover the marginal cost incurred by the company in providing the service.

The differences in the elasticities of demand for the different services will determine the actual level of the prices. The presence of indivisibilities in the cost structure necessitates the dissimilar pricing. Therefore, the greater the amount of the indivisibilities in the cost structure, the greater the need for dissimilar pricing and the consequent practice of segregating services according to demand elasticity.

One final point should be discussed, and that is the desirability of dissimilar pricing. Dissimilar pricing allows common and fixed costs to be spread out over large volumes of traffic. In other words, dissimilar pricing might render economical benefits because prices might be lower than they otherwise would be. It is not unusual to hear statements in the railroad industry that the prices on captive traffic subsidize competitive traffic; coal, for example, will not move unless the rates are relatively low. It could be argued that, as long as the coal rates cover more than the marginal cost of the movement, they allow the railroad to charge lower rates on other traffic.

As previously mentioned, the variable or marginal cost of providing the service should serve as the floor for carriers when setting prices. This relies entirely on how marginal or variable cost is defined, as we will see in this discussion. With this mentality, a carrier will be able to recover related costs of providing a service, at least in the short run. This relationship can be seen in Figure 4-3. In this example, a carrier's variable cost for a particular move is $90, its average cost (also called *fully allocated cost*) is $100, and its potential price is $110 (which could result in a $10 profit). This example assumes that (1) the carrier knows its costs and (2) it is able to charge a price that will result in a profit. This second assumption can be called *value-of-service pricing*, which will be discussed in the next section.

It can be said that dissimilar pricing is the logical approach for pricing in regulated industries. Cost indivisibilities necessitate the practice of discriminatory pricing, but this was approached within what might be called a cost framework. Marginal cost sets the minimum basis for prices, whereas fixed or common costs are, in effect, allocated on the basis of demand elasticity.

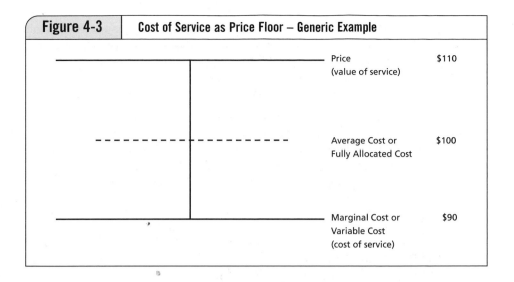

| Figure 4-3 | Cost of Service as Price Floor – Generic Example |

Price (value of service) $110

Average Cost or Fully Allocated Cost $100

Marginal Cost or Variable Cost (cost of service) $90

Global Perspectives

Air Cargo Remains Soft

A report issued by the Geneva-based International Air Transport Association (IATA) may have caused considerable alarm overseas, but many U.S. shippers were telling *LM* that it could have been worse. "Had our members not pre-planned for certain cost factors after the steep hike in fuel charges earlier in the year, our carriers might have been hit harder by this development," said David Castelveter, a spokesman for the Air Transport Association (ATA). "In a relative sense, our carriers are looking a little better because they took their lumps earlier when cutting back on expenses and services was imperative," he added. But that does little to diminish the overall impact of IATA's forecast for 2009, Castelveter admitted, noting that it showed an industry loss of $2.5 billion. All regions except the U.S. are expected to report larger losses in 2009 than in 2008.

Source: *Logistics Management,* January 2009, p. 4. Reprinted by permission.

Value-of-Service Pricing

Value-of-service pricing is a frequently mentioned and often criticized approach to pricing that has generally been associated with the railroad industry. Part of the problem associated with value-of-service pricing is that a number of different definitions of it are offered by various sources. Therefore, a workable definition of the term will be developed.

One rather common definition of value-of-service pricing in transportation is pricing according to the value of the product; for example, high-valued products are assessed high prices for their movement, and low-valued commodities are assessed low prices. Evidence can be found to substantiate this definition by examining the class-rate structure of railroads.

Several points are in order here. First, even if a cost-based approach is taken to setting prices, high-valued commodities would usually be charged higher prices because they are typically more expensive to transport. There is generally more risk involved in moving high-valued commodities and more expensive equipment is necessary. Second, the value of the commodity is a legitimate indicator of elasticity of demand; for example, high-valued commodities can usually bear higher prices because transportation cost is such a small percentage of the final selling price.

This concept can be seen in Figure 4-4. The demand curves of two different types of commodities for transportation services are shown. The high-value item has a steeply sloping demand curve implying price inelasticity. On the other hand, the low-value item has a gradual slope, implying price elasticity. To see how these elasticities relate to how a transportation firm can set prices based on product value, consider a price increase from price P_1 to price P_2. When the price of the transportation service increases for the high-value product, a small quantity-demanded decrease is observed from quantity Q_1 to quantity Q_2. For the same price increase, the low-value product cannot absorb the increased price. This inability to support the added price of the service is seen as a drop in the quantity demanded from Q_1 to Q_2. Clearly the decrease in quantity demanded for the low-value product is of a larger magnitude than the decrease for the higher-value product for the same price increase.

In a situation where a carrier has a complete monopoly, to consider value-of-service pricing only in terms of the commodity's value would not lead to serious traffic losses. It would be analogous to the idea behind progressive income taxes; that is, setting prices upon the ability or willingness to pay.[14] But where alternatives are present at a lower price, shippers are not willing to pay higher prices based upon the value of the product alone. This is one of the reasons why the motor carriers were able to make serious inroads in rail traffic during their early development. They undercut the prices on high-valued commodities when the railroads were the most susceptible to competition. In essence, the value of the commodity gives some indication of demand or the ability to bear a charge, but competition also will affect the demand for the service, that is, the height and slope of the demand curve.

Value-of-service pricing also has been defined as **third-degree price discrimination** or a situation in which a seller sets two or more different market prices for two or

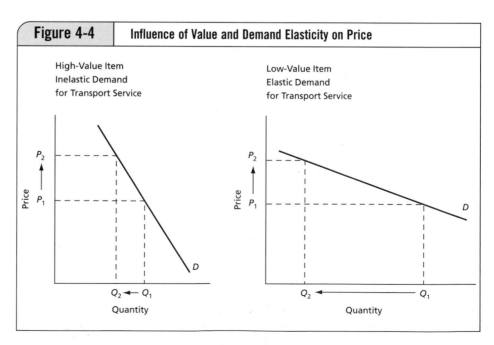

Figure 4-4 | **Influence of Value and Demand Elasticity on Price**

High-Value Item
Inelastic Demand
for Transport Service

Low-Value Item
Elastic Demand
for Transport Service

ame commodity or service.[15] Three ... practice third-degree price discrimi- ... ayers into groups or submarkets ac- ... this separation enables the seller to ... e second condition is that the seller ... n the submarkets. That is, the buyer must not buy in the lower-priced market and sell in the higher-priced markets. Third, the seller must possess some degree of monopoly power.

Another name given to value-of-service pricing is **differential** pricing. Differential pricing can be done based on several methods of segregating the buyers into distinct groups. It can be done by commodity (such as coal versus computers), by time (seasonal discounts or premium rates), by place (as Figure 4-5 demonstrates), or by individual person. It should be noted, however, that discrimination based on an individual person is illegal per se on traffic that remains economically regulated by the STB.[16]

These conditions for third-degree price discrimination can be fulfilled in the transportation industry, as well as in other regulated industries. For example, in transportation shippers are separated according to commodities transported and between points of movement. The previous discussion of the relevant market area in transportation implied that there were different or separable customer-related markets—for example, one commodity between each pair of shipping points, each with a separate elasticity.

Another relevant point is the nature of "essentially the same commodity or service."[17] Actually, many transportation companies sell multiple or heterogeneous services that are technically similar. For example, rail movements of television sets or glassware are very different in terms of time, equipment, terminal facilities, and so on.

Value-of-service or differential pricing makes sense from the perspective of the railroads, considering their high level of fixed costs and need to attract traffic. Remember that railroads will experience declining average costs with increases in volume. If shipments are priced properly, this could mean increased revenues from higher volumes with more profit.

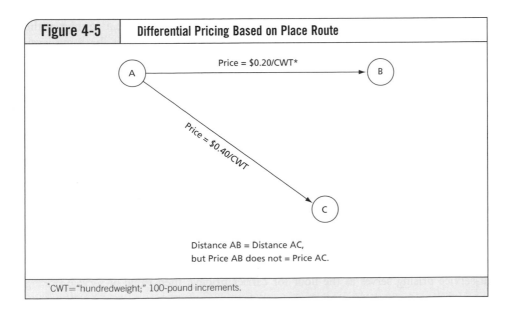

Figure 4-5	Differential Pricing Based on Place Route

Price = $0.20/CWT*

A → B

Price = $0.40/CWT

A → C

Distance AB = Distance AC,
but Price AB does not = Price AC.

*CWT="hundredweight;" 100-pound increments.

cost, which will now be included in the average cost figure. Marginal cost now becomes the added cost of loading the shipment and the reduced fuel efficiency, which will be assumed to be $20. Figure 4-7 shows these relationships. On the headhaul, the price of $110 covers both the average cost of $100 and the marginal cost of $90. On the backhaul, the $90 is allocated as a fixed cost over the units of output to result in an average cost of $50. Now the $80 price charged covers both the average cost and marginal cost and results in a profit, just as the price produced a profit in the headhaul example. In this example, value of service provided the price ceiling and cost of service provided the price floor, as shown in Figure 4-3. The point of showing how different price floors can be justified is that prices will be set depending on how costs are defined. In Figure 4-6, backhaul variable costs were defined from an accounting perspective, that is, those costs directly related to the return move. In Figure 4-7, backhaul variable costs were defined

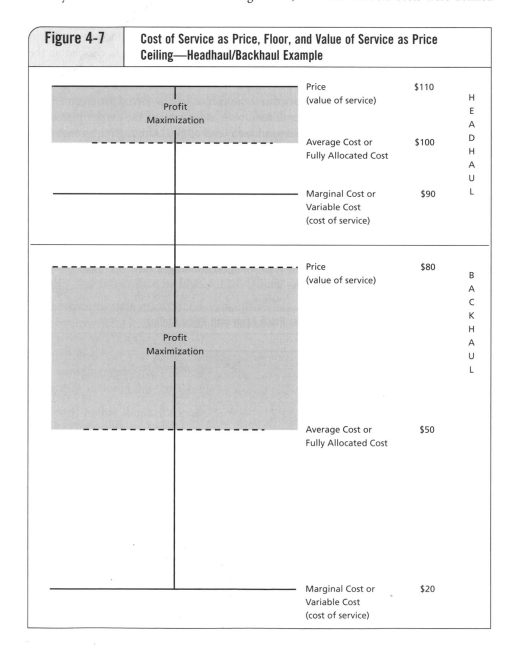

Figure 4-7 **Cost of Service as Price, Floor, and Value of Service as Price Ceiling—Headhaul/Backhaul Example**

Profit Maximization

Price (value of service) $110   HEADHAUL

Average Cost or Fully Allocated Cost $100

Marginal Cost or Variable Cost (cost of service) $90

Price (value of service) $80   BACKHAUL

Profit Maximization

Average Cost or Fully Allocated Cost $50

Marginal Cost or Variable Cost (cost of service) $20

from an economic perspective, that is, those costs that would be avoided if the carrier, in fact, returned empty. These two definitions result in two distinct perspectives on the profitability of the move for the carrier and would probably affect pricing and operations decisions of the carrier. Thus, when using costs as a base for price, care must be taken to identify the proper role and definition of those costs in the pricing decision.

Rate Making in Practice

A complete understanding of carrier cost economics and behavior is a necessary prerequisite to effective management of carrier pricing. This section presents an overview of the general forms of pricing that are employed by carriers of all types. The form of each rate is discussed and analyzed, along with the primary inducements for the carrier and its users.

The overall carrier pricing function revolves around costing, rates, and tariffs. Carriers employ costing personnel who are responsible for determining the overall cost and productivity of the carrier operations as well as the specific routes, customer services, and equipment needs. The work of cost analysts should serve as a pricing input to rate personnel who are responsible for establishing specific rates and general rate levels for the carrier. Tariffs are the actual publications in which most rates are printed or are found on carrier websites. Some firms print their own tariffs, which are often referred to as *individual tariffs*, or they use a rate bureau that is common to many carriers to establish and publish rates. These tariffs are referred to as *bureau tariffs*.

General Rates

These are the class, exception, and commodity rate structures in the United States. The **class rate** system provides a rate for any commodity between any two points. It is constructed from uniform distance and product systems. **Exception rates** are designed so that carriers in particular regions can depart from the product scale system for any one of many possible reasons, which will be discussed later. **Commodity rates**, on the other hand, are employed for specific origin–destination shipping patterns of specific commodities. Each one of these three systems has a particular purpose.

It would be simple if all transportation services were sold on the basis of ton-miles; that is, we would have to pay x dollars to move one ton one mile. But, in fact, transportation services are not sold in ton-miles; they are sold for moving a specific commodity in a specific shipment size between two specific points—for example, moving 10,000 pounds of glass from Toledo to New York City. This fact gives some insight into the enormous magnitude of the transportation pricing problem. There are thousands of important shipping and receiving points in the United States. Theoretically, the number of different possible routes would be all the permutations of these points. The result is in the trillions of trillions of possible rates. In addition, it is necessary to consider the thousands and thousands of different commodities and products that might be shipped over any of these routes. There are also the different modes to consider and different companies within each mode. It also might be necessary to consider the specific supply–demand situation for each commodity over each route.

Class Rates Because it is obviously impossible to quote trillions and trillions of rates, the transportation industry has taken three major steps toward simplification. Figure 4-8 summarizes this class rate simplification.

The first step consolidated the thousands of shipping points into groups by dividing the nation into geographic squares. The most important shipping point for all other shipping points (based on tonnage) in each square serves as the **rate base point** for all other shipping points in the square. These grouped points are found in a groupings tariff. This reduces the potential number of distance variations for rate-making purposes. The distance from each base point to each other base point was determined by the railroads and placed on file with the Interstate Commerce Commission (ICC, now the STB) and published in the National Rate Basis Tariff. The distance between any two base points is referred to as the **rate basis number**. The first simplifying step reduced the number of possible origins and destinations for pricing purposes. (See Tables 4-1 and 4-2 for examples of grouping and rate basis number tariffs.)

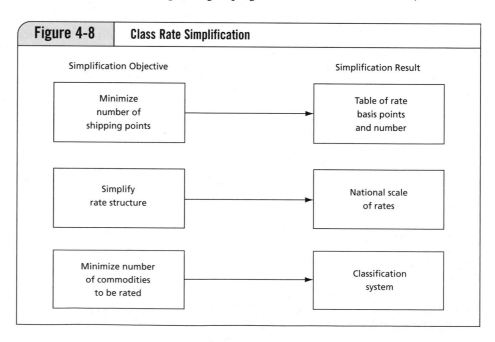

Figure 4-8 | **Class Rate Simplification**

Table 4-1	Groupings Tariff Example[a]	
STATE	**POINT**	**APPLY RATES FROM OR TO**
Michigan	Climax	Battle Creek
	Coleman	Clare
	Comstock	Kalamazoo
	Columbiaville	Flint
	Crossvillage	Cheyboygan
Ohio	Clay Center	Toledo
	Clifford	Chillicothe
	Clement	Dayton
	Cleves	Cincinnati
	Climax	Marion

[a]Alphabetical listing of points by states from and to which rates apply.

Source: Tariff ICC CMB 575-C.

| Table 4-2 | Rate Basis Numbers Tariff Example |

And Points Taking the Following Basing Points	Between Points Taking the Following Basing Points			
	Chilicothe OH	Cincinnati OH	Columbus OH	Dayton OH
	Rate Basis Numbers			
Cheboygan, MI	550	570	490	510
Clare, MI	400	420	360	380
Flint, MI	275	300	227	214

Source: Tariff ICC CMB 575-C.

The second step deals with the thousands and thousands of different items that might be shipped between any two base points. The railroads have established a national scale of rates that has been placed on file with the ICC (now the STB) and gives a rate in dollars per hundredweight (cwt), which is dollars per cwt for each rate basis number. (The motor carriers established a similar rate structure.) The actual rate to move a commodity considered the commodity's transportation characteristic by means of the classification, the third simplification step.

The third step simply groups together products with similar transportation characteristics so that one rating can be applied to the whole group. Now one rate is quoted for the group into which a number of different commodities have been placed, thereby reducing the number of rates quoted by the carriers. Items that are placed into class 125 will be charged 125 percent of the first-class rate found in the uniform scales of rates. This percentage number is called a *class rating*, and it is the group into which the commodity is placed for rate-making purposes. Table 4-3 is a classification example from the National Motor Freight Classification.

Table 4-3	National Motor Freight Classification			

ITEM	ARTICLES	CLASSES		
		LTL	TL	MW
156300	PLASTIC MATERIALS, OTHER THAN EXPANDED, GROUP: subject to item 156100 156300 Sheet or Plate, NOI. Self-supporting (rigid), see Note, item 156302, other than in rolls or coils, in boxes, crates or Packages 248, 384, 930, 1029, 2187, 2207 or 2310			
Sub 1	Exceeding 9 feet, 6 inches in two dimensions or 20 feet in one dimension	85	45	30
Sub 2	Not exceeding 9 feet, 6 inches in more than one dimension nor 20 feet in one dimension	60	35	30
156500	PLASTIC OR RUBBER ARTICLES, OTHER THAN EXPANDED, GROUP: Articles consist of Plastic or Rubber Articles, other than foam, cellular, expanded or sponge articles, see Item 110, Sec. 15 and Note, item 156502, as described in items subject to this grouping.			
156600	Articles, NOI, in barrels, boxes or crates, see Note, item 156602, also in Packages 870, 1078, 1170, 1241, 1273, 1409, 1456, 2195, 2212, 2213 or 2230:			
Sub 1	LTL, having a density of, subject to Item 170:			
Sub 2	Less than one pound per cubic foot, see Note, item 156608	400		
Sub 3	One pound per cubic foot, but less than two pounds, see Note, item 156608	300		
Sub 4	Two pounds per cubic foot, but less than four pounds, see Note, item 156608	250		
Sub 5	Four pounds per cubic foot, but less than five pounds, see Note, item 156608	150		
Sub 6	Six pounds per cubic foot, but less than 12 pounds, see Note, item 156608	100		
Sub 7	12 pounds per cubic foot, but less than 15 pounds, see Note, item 156608	85		
Sub 8	15 pounds or greater per cubic foot	70		
Sub 9	TL		100	10
			70	16
			60	21
			45	30
155000	Personal effects, other than household effects or furnishings, of commissioned or enlisted personnel of the U.S. Army, Air Force, Navy, or Marine Corps, or deceased veterans, moving on government bills of lading, see Note, item 155024, in bags, traveling bags, boxes, or in army trunk lockers or navy cruise boxes or foot lockers securely locked or sealed:			
Sub 1	Each article in value in accordance with the following, see Note, item 155022:			
Sub 2	Released value not exceeding 10 cents per pounds	100	70	16
Sub 3	Released to value exceeding 10 cents per pounds, but not exceeding 20 cents per pounds	125	77½	16
Sub 4	Released to value exceeding 20 cents per pounds, but not exceeding 50 cents per pound	150	85	16
Sub 5	Released to value exceeding 50 cents per pounds, but not exceeding $2.00 per pound	200	110	16
Sub 6	Released to value exceeding $2.00 per pound, but not exceeding $5.00 per pound	300	150	16

Source: National Motor Freight Classification 100-H.

Classification Factors The factors that are used to determine the rating of a specific commodity are the product characteristics that impact the carrier's costs. In particular, the ICC has ruled and the STB has maintained that four factors are to be considered: product density, storability, handling, and liability. Although no specific formulas are used to assign a commodity to a particular class, the four factors are considered in conjunction by a carrier classification committee. An individual carrier can establish a commodity classification that differs from the national classification; this individual carrier classification is termed an exception and takes precedence over the national classification.

Product density directly impacts the use of the carrier's vehicle and the cost per hundredweight. The higher the product density, the greater the amount of weight that can be hauled and the lower the cost per hundredweight. Conversely, the lower the product density, the lower the amount of weight that can be hauled and the higher the cost per hundredweight hauled.

As shown in Table 4-4, only 6,000 pounds of a product that has a density of 2 pounds per cubic foot can be loaded into the trailer, which means the cost per hundredweight shipped is $6.67. However, 48,000 pounds of a product with a density of 16 pounds per cubic foot can be hauled at a cost of $0.83 per hundredweight. Therefore, the higher the product density, the lower the carrier's cost per weight unit and the lower the classification rating assigned to the product.

Stowability and handling reflect the cost the carrier will incur in securing and handling the product in the vehicle. Product characteristics such as excessive weight, length, and height result in higher stowage costs for the carrier and a corresponding higher classification rating. Likewise, products that require manual handling or special handling equipment increase the carrier's costs and are given a higher rating.

The final classification factor, **liability**, considers the value of the product. When a product is damaged in transit, the common carrier is liable for the value of the product. Because higher-valued products pose a greater liability risk (potential cost), higher-valued products are classified higher than lower-valued products. In addition, products that are more susceptible to damage or are likely to damage other freight increase the potential liability cost and are placed into a higher classification rating.

Table 4-4	Product Density and Carrier Cost Per Hundredweight (cwt) Hauled		
	PRODUCT DENSITY		
	16 lb/ft^3	10 lb/ft^3	2 lb/ft^3
Shipment Weight (lb)[1]	48,000	30,000	6,000
Carrier Cost[2]	$400.00	$400.00	$400.00
Cost/cwt[3]	$0.83	$1.33	$6.67

[1]Shipment weight = product density × 3,000 ft^3 assumed capacity of 48-ft trailer.

[2]Carrier cost assumed for a given distance to be the same for each shipment weight.

[3]Carrier cost/shipment weight/100.

In Table 4-3, the stowability and handling factors are evidenced in the classification of Item 156300. Plastic sheets or plates that exceed 9 feet, 6 in (Sub 1) have a higher rating than the same product that does not exceed 9 feet, 6 in (Sub 2). The density factor is embodied in the classification item 156600, Subs 1 through 8; the higher the density, the lower the rating. Finally, product liability is a primary factor in the classification of Item 155000, personal effects of military personnel; the higher the declared value of the shipment, the higher the rating.

Determining a Class Rate The procedure for determining a class rate for moving a specific commodity between two points is outlined in Figure 4-9. The first step is to determine the rate base points for the specific origin and destination from the groupings tariff. Next, from the rate basis number tariff, determine the rate basis number for the relevant rate basis points. The class rating for the particular commodity being shipped is found in the classification. Finally, the rate is found in the class rate tariff for the appropriate rate basis number and class rating. The shipping charge for moving a product between a specific origin and destination is determined by multiplying the class rate, which is in cents per hundredweight, by the total shipment weight in hundredweight.

As an example, the total shipping charges for moving 11,000 pounds of plastic sheets, exceeding 9 feet, 6 in, from Crossvillage, Michigan, to Clifford, Ohio will be determined. From the groupings tariff (Table 4-1), it can be seen that the rate basis point for Crossvillage is Cheboygan, Michigan, and that for Clifford it is Chillicothe, Ohio. Next, the rate basis numbers tariff (Table 4-2) indicates that the rate basis number for rate basis points Cheboygan and Chillicothe is 550. From the classification (Table 4-3), it can be seen that the class rating for plastic sheets (Item 156300, Sub 1) is 85. Consulting the class tariff (Table 4-5) for a rate basis number of 550 and a class rating of 85, the resulting class rate is 846 cents per hundredweight for the weight group M10M (minimum of 10,000 pounds).

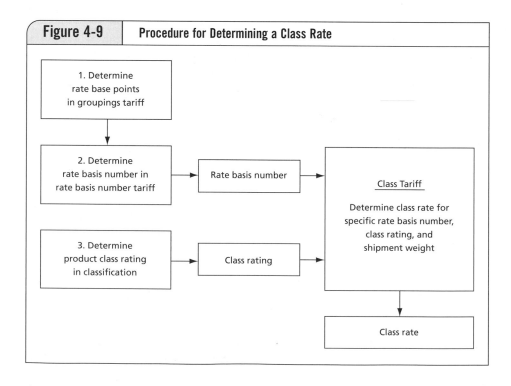

Figure 4-9	Procedure for Determining a Class Rate

1. Determine rate base points in groupings tariff

2. Determine rate basis number in rate basis number tariff → Rate basis number →

3. Determine product class rating in classification → Class rating →

Class Tariff

Determine class rate for specific rate basis number, class rating, and shipment weight →

Class rate

Table 4-5	Sample Class Rate Tariff				
			CLASSES (cents/100 lb)		
RATE BASIS NUMBER	**MINIMUM CHARGE**	**WEIGHT GROUP**	**200**	**100**	**85**
201 to 250		L5C	3,850	1,860	1,650
	4,500	M5C	3,105	1,500	1,325
		M1M	2,231	1,078	957
		M2M	1,825	882	781
		M5M	1,370	662	582
		M10M	1,264	611	540
		M20M	813	393	319
		M30M	650	314	255
		M40M	586	283	229
501 to 550		L5C	4,556	2,201	1,957
		M5C	3,775	1,824	1,633
	4,500	M1M	2,900	1,401	1,264
		M2M	2,488	1,202	1,092
		M5M	2,035	983	888
		M10M	1,933	934	846
		M20M	1,459	705	640
		M30M	1,292	624	572
		M40M	1,223	591	547

The computation of total shipping charges is as follows:

Shipment weight in cwt = 11,000/100 cwt
Shipping charges at class rate = $8.46/cwt $\times$ 110 cwt = $93.06

The term *tariff* is commonly used to mean almost any publication put out by a carrier or publishing agency that concerns itself with the pricing of services performed by the carrier. All the information needed to determine the cost of a move is in one or more tariffs.

Exception Rates An exception rate is a modification (change in rating, minimum weight, density group, and so on) to the national classification instituted by an individual carrier. Exception ratings are published when the transportation characteristics of an item in a particular area differ from those of the same article in other areas. For example, large-volume movements or intensive competition in one area might require the publication of a lower exception rating; in this case the exception rating applies,

Table 4-6	Example of Commodity Rate				
ITEM	COMMODITY	FROM	TO	RATE (cents per 100 lb.)	MINIMUM WEIGHT (lb)
2315	Rubber (reclaimed, dispersed, liquid, or paste)	Akron, OH		726	2,000
		Barberton, OH	Warren, MI	518	5,000
		Ravenna, OH		496	10,000
		Cleveland, OH			

rather than the classification rating. The same procedures described above apply to determining the exception rate, except now the exception rating (class) is used instead of the classification rating. There does not have to be an exception rate for every class rate.

Commodity Rates A commodity rate can be constructed on a variety of bases, but the most common is a specific rate published on a specific commodity or group of related commodities between specific points and generally via specific routes in specific directions. Commodity rates are complete in themselves and are not part of the classification system. If the commodity being shipped is not specifically stated, or if the origin–destination is not specifically spelled out in the commodity rate, then the commodity rate for the particular movement is not applicable.

When the commodity rate is published, it takes precedence over the class rate or exception rate on the same article between the specific points. A sample is shown in Table 4-6. The commodity rate in the table applies only to reclaimed, dispersed, liquid, or paste rubber. In addition, the commodity is direction-specific and applies from Akron, Barberton, Ravenna, and Cleveland, Ohio, to Warren, Michigan. This commodity rate is not applicable from Warren to Akron, for example.

This type of rate is offered for those commodities that are moved regularly in large quantities. Such a pricing system, however, completely undermines the attempts to simplify transportation pricing through the class-rate structure. It has caused transportation pricing to revert to the publication of a multiplicity of rates and adds to the complexity of the pricing system.

Rate Systems Under Deregulation

General rate structures were the basis of tariffs published by rate bureaus. These rate-making bodies consisted of carriers that collectively met, established rates, published them in tariff form, and sold them on a subscription basis. Deregulation changes in both rail and motor modes have prohibited rate bureaus from discussing or voting on rates that involve only a single carrier. Similarly, joint rate making is limited to only those carriers involved in a movement and not all carriers in the bureau.

The diminished role of the rate bureau in carrier rate making has resulted in a plethora of individual carrier tariffs. In addition, the greater reliance upon the marketplace to control carrier rates has enabled the shippers to greatly increase negotiations, resulting in rate reductions, discounts, and contract rates. Although deregulation has somewhat diminished the use and application of the class, exception, and commodity tariff systems, various features of these tariff systems are widely used today for the pricing of small LTL freight.

On the Line

Home Delivery Carriers Offer Many Pricing Options

During the many years I've been writing this column, I never discussed pricing options offered by for-hire carriers that specialize in making deliveries to private residences, apartments, dormitories and similar types of premises.

We're not talking here about the likes of UPS Ground, FedEx Ground, or the U.S. Postal Service, but for-hire home delivery carriers that primarily specialize in delivering larger size products such as new furniture, kitchen cabinets, appliances, etc. You'll find these carriers in every major city in the U.S.

A handful serving the furniture industry cover the entire country such as Home Direct USA, based in Hillside, Ill., and Mainstreet Delivery, headquartered in Green Bay, Wis. These are non-asset-based companies using small, independent home delivery carriers scattered throughout the U.S. and in some instances, Puerto Rico. Other carriers, such as Purnell Furniture Services, headquartered in Manassas, Va, and Cory Home Delivery out of Secaucus, N.J. are regional in territorial coverage and handle much of the East Coast.

Many of these companies got their start by going into retailers and taking over the warehousing and home-delivery operations that the retailers had long been performing with their own drivers and delivery vehicles. The one unique thing about these carriers is the wide variety of pricing options that they can offer their customers, be they retail stores, catalog companies, or companies selling over the internet. Below are some of those pricing options.

Varying according to different size products: An excellent example is furniture delivery carriers that make a separate charge for a sofa, a lower one for chairs, and yet a different charge for set-up tables.

As a percent of invoice price: Some of their customers want a set percent of their invoice to cover the cost of delivery, making it easier to quote a delivered price.

By the cube of the product: A notable example is the delivery of kitchen cabinets. Actually, there are two different pricing methods offered—one for delivery to the customer's garage and the other for unpacking it and bringing it into the kitchen.

Per package, with the charge varying by weight: Some of these home delivery carriers are delivering packages in competition with UPS Ground, FedEx Ground, and the USPS, many times at a very competitive price.

Varying according to the value of the product: For example, home delivery carriers serving the furniture industry have customers selling high-priced furniture, other customers dealing in medium-priced products, and still others offering low-end lines. These carriers charge a smaller fixed percent to customers with high-end lines, an even higher fixed percent on medium-priced lines, and yet an even higher fixed percent on customers in the low-end priced furniture business.

The vast majority of for-hire home delivery carriers price their service with a fixed price delivery to points within a set delivery zone, such as a radius of 50 miles. If they make deliveries to points beyond that zone, a higher charge applies.

Extra charges are assessed for performing "deluxing" prior to delivery—touching up scratched surfaces, polishing, etc. Assembly of a product once it is in the home, such as a bedroom set, is another type of additional charge.

Source: Ray Bohman, *Logistics Management,* January 2009, p. 23. Reprinted by permission.

The product classification feature of the former class rate system will no doubt survive for some time to come. This system of describing and classifying products simplifies the entire product description processes for all carriers. Carriers that are not even a part of the classification process often refer to these groupings to simplify their rate-making processes.

The class rate system also serves as a benchmark against which specific carrier rates and contract rates are created. Discount plans for specific shippers often are published as a percentage from the published class or exceptions-based rate.

Commodity rates published by individual carriers are similar in form to those published by the former rate bureaus. Most individual carriers publish commodity rates in a form similar to the one shown in Table 4-6.

Many innovative carriers have simplified their own class and commodity rate structures further. One way of accomplishing this is by providing shippers with small tariffs for moves from one or a few shipper points to any points within three-digit zip codes throughout the country. Thus, instead of describing the thousands of points in the United States, as in the rate base-point system, a maximum of 1,000 groupings is used. For a five-state region, one carrier has 85 three-digit groupings.

Many large motor carriers have computerized and/or web-based zip code tariffs. The shipper enters into the computer the three-digit zip code for the origin, destination, and class rating of the commodity being shipped. The computer program searches for the appropriate rate and determines the freight charges with any applicable discounts. These computerized zip code tariffs are simply a variation of the class rate structure, relying on the classification rating and zip codes to delineate the product being shipped and the origin and destination (rate basis points) of the shipment.

Another variation on the commodity tariff system is the **mileage rate**. The mileage rate is quoted in cents per mile and not in cents per hundredweight. For example, the shipper pays $1.25 per mile times the number of miles the shipment moves, regardless of the shipment weight, which is limited by the physical or legal operating constraints.

In summary, the innovative rate structures being used in today's deregulated environment are variations of the class and commodity rate structures. The next section discusses the special rates used by carriers.

Special Rates

A myriad of special rate forms have evolved over the years either as a result of special cost factors or to induce certain shipment patterns. In their basic form, these special rates appear as class, exception, or commodity rates.

Character-of-Shipment Rates

One set of special rates relates to the size or character of the shipment. Carriers generally have certain fixed costs for each shipment. Many rate forms have been developed that take advantage of the fact that additional units or weight in each shipment do not incur additional amounts of these fixed costs.

LTL/TL Rates   Less-than-truckload (LTL) shipments require several handlings. Each one of these handlings requires dock personnel, materials-handling equipment, terminal investment, and additional communications and tracking effort. A truckload (TL) shipment, on the other hand, is generally loaded by the shipper and moved intact to the destination, where the consignee unloads it. No intermediate handlings are required, nor does it have to be loaded or unloaded by carrier personnel. The direct movement also avoids intermediate terminals. As a result of these factors, larger TL shipments have lower rates than LTL shipments.

Multiple-Car Rates Railroads offer volume discounts for moves of more than one carload that are shipped as a single string of cars from one point to another. The cost of moving several cars in a single shipment is proportionally less than the cost of each car moved singly. For example, the multiple-car movement of 10 cars can be handled by the same effort (empty car drop-off, pickup, intermediate and delivery efforts, and documentation) as a single-car shipment. The only basic difference is the additional weight moved in the larger string of cars. Because of this economy of movement, railroads offer such rates in coal, grain, fertilizer, chemical, and many other basic commodity moves.

Incentive Rates The term **incentive rates** generally applies to a rate designed to induce the shipper to load existing movements and equipment more fully. These special rates usually apply only to weight or units loaded over and above the normally shipped quantities. For example, suppose an appliance manufacturer typically ships in carload quantities that only fill a car to 80 percent of its actual capacity. That is, the carload rate minimum is 40,000 pounds and the car is typically loaded to 48,000 pounds, but 60,000 pounds of appliances can be physically loaded into it. The carrier would prefer to have this car more fully loaded. In an incentive rate situation, the carrier would offer a rate lower than the carload rate that would only apply to the weight above the 48,000-pound norm in this example. It is more economical for the carrier to handle more weight in existing moves than to handle additional moves. By inducing the shipper to load each car more fully, fewer cars and moves would be required over the course of a year, and the same actual volume would be shipped.

Unit-Train Rates Unit trains are integrated movements between an origin and destination. These trains usually avoid terminals and do not require intermediate switching or handling of individual cars. In many situations, the shipper or consignee provides the car investment. The railroad experiences economies through high car utilization and reduced costs of movement because the rates are low in comparison to individual moves. Again, it is more economical to handle larger single movements than many individual moves. Rail carriers many times use this type of rate for trailer on flatcar (TOFC) or container on flatcar (COFC) movements.

Per-Car and Per-Truckload Rates Per-car or per-truckload rates are single-charge rates for specific origin–destination moves regardless of shipment commodity or weight. These rates also apply to container movements where the carriers' costs of movement are dominated by moving the equipment and not specifically by the weight of the shipment.

Any-Quantity Rates Any-quantity (AQ) rates provide no discount or rate break for larger movements. That is, there exists an LTL rate but no TL rate for large shipments. The AQ rates apply to any weight in a shipment. They are usually found with large, bulky commodities such as boats, suitcases, and cages where no economies are realized by the carrier for larger shipments.

Density Rates Some rates are published according to density and shipment weight, rather than by commodity or weight alone. These rates are common in air container shipments. For example, a density rate is published as, say, $10 per hundredweight for shipments up to 10 pounds per cubic foot, $9 per hundredweight for 11 to 20 pounds per cubic foot, and $8 per hundredweight for 21 pounds per cubic foot and up. These are applied when the carrier assesses rates on the basis of weight but does not experience lower costs for lighter-weight containers. Here, in fact, the carrier would experience a loss of revenue (due to a low weight) when moving a given amount of cubic footage.

A motor-carrier variation on the density rate is the linear foot rule. The generalized linear foot rule applies on shipments that weigh more than 2,000 pounds and occupy more than one linear foot of space for every 350 pounds. If the shipment meets these criteria, the carrier reconstructs the weight of the shipment based on 350 pounds times the number of linear feet of space occupied and eliminates any discounts the shipper has negotiated. Air carriers use a similar approach to handling low-density articles. All rates except household goods are exempt.

Area, Location, or Route Rates

A number of rates relate to area, location, or route. These special rates deserve consideration and discussion.

Local Rates Local rates apply to any rate between two points served by the same carrier. These rates include full-cost factors for pickup, documentation, rating, billing, and delivery.

Joint Rates Joint rates are single rates published from a point on one carrier's route to another carrier's destination. They are usually lower in total charges than the combination of the local rates because of through-movement economy.

Proportional Rates Many carriers experience a competitive disadvantage when their line is part of a through line that competes with another, more direct line. If a combination of local rates were charged, the through-movement cost might still be higher than the charges over the direct route. In this situation, the carrier might publish a proportional rate (lower than the regular local rate) that applies only to through moves to certain destination points beyond its line.

Differential Rates The term *differential rates* generally applies to a rate published by a carrier that faces a service time disadvantage compared to a faster carrier or mode. For example, water carriers often publish differential rates that are below those of railroads. In this way, the lower rate somewhat overcomes the longer transit time disadvantage inherent to the water carriers. The term *differential* is also found in situations where an extra charge is assessed for high-cost services such as branch lines. With all the recent mergers, this type of rate making has fallen from widespread use.

Per-Mile Rates Some rail, motor, and air carriers provide rates that are based purely upon the mileage involved. This is a common practice in bulk chemical truck moves and air charter movements. Railroads also use these rates in special train movements (high, wide, and heavy). Similarly, special moves, such as the movement of circus trains and some postal moves, are based on these rates.

Terminal-to-Terminal Rates Terminal-to-terminal rates, often referred to as *ramp-to-ramp rates*, apply between terminal points on the carrier's lines. These rates require the shipper and consignee to perform the traditional pickup and delivery functions. Many air freight rates and some piggyback rates are found in this form.

Blanket or Group Rates These rates apply to or from whole regions, rather than points. For example, all shippers of lumber from an area in Oregon and Washington are generally treated as having the same origin. Destinations eastward are grouped into zones in which all receivers in an entire state pay the same rates regardless of the special origin point in the Pacific Northwest. Blanket systems are found in food shipments from California and Florida. These rates equalize shippers and consignees because plant location is not a factor in determining the rate charged.

Time/Service Rate Structures

The Staggers Rail Act of 1980 specifically sanctioned rail contract rates, many of which can be classified as time/service rate structures. These rates are generally dependent on the transit time performance of the railroad in a particular service. One such contract provides for a standard rate for a transit time service norm. The shipper pays a higher rate for faster service and a lower rate for slower service. Another contract calls for additional shipper payments to the carrier for the fast return of empty backhaul shipper-leased cars. These rate forms either place incentives or penalties in areas where they tend to create desired results, or they reduce undesirable performance.

Contract Rates Contract services are commonplace in motor carriage and rail moves, as well as in water and some air moves. These services are governed by contracts negotiated between the shipper and carrier, not by generally published tariffs. Some specific contract service features that are typically found are described here.

One basic contract service feature calls for a reduced rate in exchange for a guarantee of a certain minimum tonnage to be shipped over a specified period. Another contract service feature calls for a reduced rate in exchange for the shipper tendering a certain percentage of all tonnage over to the contracting carrier. In both these instances, a penalty clause requires the shipper to pay up to the regular rate if the minimum tonnage is not shipped.

Another type of rail contract service feature calls for the rate to be higher or lower depending on the specific type of car supplied for loading and shipment, called a **car-supply charge**. The higher rates apply on cars whose contents have not been braced or blocked by the shipper; the higher charge is used to compensate the carrier for a potentially higher level of damage to the contents and ultimately to the higher liability level of the carrier. These are also the same cars that represent higher capital investment or per diem expense for the railroads.

A few contract service features require the shipper to pay a monthly charge to the railroad that supplies certain special equipment for the shipper's exclusive use. This charge tends to increase the shipper's use of the cars; the shipper no longer views them as free capital goods that can be used for temporary storage or loosely routed and controlled. Here the shipper firm has the incentive to use these cars in a way that benefits the firm and the carrier.

Many different rate and service configurations are found in motor carriage. These contract rates call for such services as scheduled service, special equipment movements, storage service in addition to movement, services beyond the vehicle (such as retail store shelf stocking by the driver), small package pickup and movement, bulk commodity movement, or hauling a shipper-owned trailer.

A great degree of flexibility surrounds the contracts of both rail and motor carriage. Carriers and shippers are relatively free to specifically tailor contract services to particular movements, equipment, and time-related services. The key in any contract service is to identify the service and cost factors important to each party and to construct inducements and penalties for each.

Deferred Delivery The deferred delivery rate is common in air transportation. In general, the carrier charges a lower rate in return for the privilege of deferring the arrival time of the shipment. For example, air express companies offer a discount of 25 percent or more for second- or third-day delivery, as opposed to the standard next-day delivery. The deferred delivery rate gives the carrier operating flexibility to achieve greater vehicle utilization and lower costs.

Other Rate Structures

Several other rate forms serve particular cost or service purposes.

Corporate Volume Rates A rate form called the *corporate volume rate* came into existence in 1981. It is a discounted rate for each LTL shipment that is related to the total volume of LTL shipments that a firm ships via a specific carrier from all shipping points. Generally, the more volume a shipper tenders to a particular carrier, the greater the discount.

The corporate volume rate is not widely used today, but the principle of gaining lower rates for shipping larger volumes via a carrier is the basis of many negotiated rates. The corporate volume concept brings the full market power of the shipper (total dollars spent on moving all inbound and outbound company freight) to bear on negotiations. Also, the practice of placing blocks of freight up for bid, such as all the freight moving into and out of the southeastern United States, uses the corporate volume approach to gain special rates from the accepted bidder.

Discounts In the motor carrier industry, a discount is a common pricing practice for LTL shipments moving under class rates. The typical discount ranges from 25 to 50 percent, with some discounts as high as 60 to 65 percent, off the published class rate. The discounts might apply to specific classes of LTL traffic moving between given origins and destinations, or all LTL commodities moving between any origin and destination. For the smaller shipper that does not have the corporate volume to effectively negotiate lower rates, the discount is a viable alternative to achieving reduced rates.

Loading Allowances A loading (unloading) allowance is a reduced rate or discount granted to the shipper that loads LTL shipments into the carrier's vehicle. Motor carriers are required to load and unload LTL shipments and their LTL rate structures include this loading and unloading cost. The shipper/receiver that performs this function is incurring a cost that would have been incurred by the carrier. Thus, the carrier agrees to reimburse the shipper for this expense in the form of a lower rate.

Aggregate Tender Rates A reduced rate or discount is given to the shipper that tenders two or more class-rated shipments to the carrier at one time. Usually, the aggregate shipment weight must equal 5,000 pounds or some other minimum established by the carrier. By tendering two or more shipments to the carrier at one time, the shipper reduces the carrier's pickup costs by reducing the number of times the carrier goes to the shipper's facility to pick up freight. With the aggregate tender rate, the shipper reaps part of the cost-reduction benefit that the carrier realizes from the multiple shipment pickup.

FAK Rates FAK rates, also known as *all-commodity rates* or *freight-all-kinds rates*, are rates expressed in cents per hundredweight or total cost per shipment. The specific commodity being shipped is not important, which means the carrier is basing the rate on the cost of service, not the value of service. The FAK rate is most valuable to shippers that ship mixed commodity shipments to a single destination, such as a grocery distributor shipping a wide variety of canned goods, paper products, and so on, to a local warehouse.

Released Value Rates Released value rates are lower than the regular full-value rates that provide for up-to-total-value carrier compensation in the event of loss or damage. Instead, released rates only provide for carrier obligation up to certain limited dollar amounts per pound shipped. They traditionally are found in air freight, household goods, and a small number of motor- and rail-hauled commodities. The 1980 and 1995 regulatory changes allowed flexible use of this rate form in most types of service and commodities.

Empty-Haul Rates An empty-haul rate is a charge for moving empty rail or motor equipment that is owned or leased by, or assigned to, a particular shipper. The existence of this type of rate tends to induce the shipper to fully load all miles of the equipment movements.

Two-way or Three-way Rates The terms *two-way rates* and *three-way rates* apply to rates that are constructed and charged when backhaul or triangular moves can be made. The intent here is to tie a fronthaul move with what would have been another firm's backhaul move. In this way, neither firm incurs the penalty for empty backhauls. Some bulk chemical motor carriers offer these rates. They reduce total transportation charges for the shippers, and the carrier's equipment is more fully utilized than it would be otherwise.

Spot-Market Rates "Spot-market" rates can be used to facilitate the movement of the equipment or product. For example, if an excess supply of empty trailers begins to accumulate in a geographic region, spot-market rates can be quoted to allow the trailers to begin moving full back to their origin. These are similar to those types of prices used in the buying and selling of commodities on the "spot market." This is also common in air freight. Today, carriers and shippers can use internet-based auctions to fill empty vehicles or move freight with spot-market rates.

Menu Pricing Carriers are beginning to provide more and more value-added services for shippers, such as loading/unloading, packaging, merge-in-transit, and sorting, along with traditional transportation services. Menu pricing allows the shipper to pick and choose those services the carrier should perform, and the shipper is charged accordingly. This concept is the same as that used in a la carte menus in restaurants. This type of pricing also requires the carrier to understand and know its costs in providing these services.

The regulatory standards legislated in 1980 and 1995, as well as altered administrative STB policies, have created a realm of flexibility and creativity in rate forms. Carriers are relatively free to develop rate systems to benefit them and shippers in ways that were neither common in the past, nor even existent. Any pricing system, however, should induce the buyer to buy in ways beneficial to the seller, be simple to understand and apply, and maximize the financial resources of the seller.

Many carriers have published their rate forms and structure in computerized form or on websites. Computerization of the former rate structures in the 1960s and 1970s was frustrated by the multitude of product classifications, locations, and footnote items that applied to specific movements. Tariffs of today are often greatly simplified, and computers are capable of greater memories and computational processes.

Pricing in Transportation Management

For many years, carriers relied on tariffs as their price lists for their services. Under traditional economic regulation, little incentive was present for carriers to differentiate themselves through either service enhancements or pricing strategies. Today, however, both of these differentiating tactics are critical to carriers in all modes, regardless of market structure. Unfortunately, however, many carriers still rely on the tariff mentality when setting prices as a competitive weapon. This way of thinking normally uses cost as a base and pays little or no attention to price as a part of the marketing mix. Many carriers will admit that they know their costs but do not know how to price.

This section will present a basic discussion on pricing for transportation management. Its intent is to introduce some common pricing strategies and techniques that are commonly used in such industries as retailing. Further in-depth discussions on these topics can be found in any basic marketing textbook.[19]

Factors Affecting Pricing Decisions

Many carrier pricing decisions are based on some reaction to a stimulus from the business environment. In transportation, the environment comprises many constituencies, four of which include customers (market), government, other channel members, and competition.

The discussion presented on value-of-service pricing in this chapter focused on the role of the market to determine prices. Obviously, a profit-maximization–oriented carrier will not set a price in the long run that prohibits the movement of freight or passengers. The carrier's price will be set at the level that maximizes its return. This, however, is dependent on what the market perceives to be a reasonable price and/or what the market is forced to pay (in monopolistic situations). The concept of price elasticity also plays an important role in the market's impact on carrier prices. For example, business travelers might be willing to absorb increases in air fares in exchange for the convenience of short-notice reservations, whereas leisure travelers might not. Customers then have a formidable impact on carrier prices.

Transportation was economically regulated by the federal government for well over 100 years because of potentially monopolistic abuses. Part of this regulation dealt with carrier prices in the forms of how they are constructed and how they are quoted. Most of the economic transportation regulation falls under the responsibility of the STB. After the deregulatory efforts of the late 1970s through the 1990s, however, the Justice Department also entered the carrier pricing arena to monitor for antitrust violations. In some respects, these government agencies help mitigate the imperfections in the marketplace to control carrier pricing. As such, governmental controls affect how carriers price their services. (Government impact on carrier pricing is discussed at length in Chapter 3, "Transportation Regulation and Public Policy.")

In the case of carriers, other **channel members** can include other carriers in the same mode and in different modes. For example, interline movements between different carriers that involve revenue splits will certainly impact how each carrier prices its services. If one carrier decides to raise its price, the other carrier either has to reduce its price or risk losing business, given that the market has a high price elasticity. This can be especially true in airline movements using two different trunkline carriers or using trunkline/commuter combinations. Another case involves interline agreements between railroads for track usage. Because there is no single transcontinental railroad, it is quite likely that a shipment will have to use the tracks of more than one railroad. If costs increase, rail carriers might have to increase their prices to customers, reduce their operating margins, or risk losing tonnage on that move.

Finally, competitors will impact carrier-pricing strategies. History has shown that even in transportation oligopolies (such as airlines and LTL motor carriers), price leaders that offer discounts to customers will find that competitors will match those discounts, even at the risk of reducing industry profits. This could be a symptom of the continual pressure on carrier customers to reduce transportation costs in their firms. Across-the-board price increases are also usually matched by all the major competitors in a particular mode. However, occasions do occur when competitors do not follow price leader actions. An attempt by one airline to simplify its pricing structure by reducing the number of special fares was not matched by its competitors. Because of this, that airline was forced to abandon its original simplification strategy and return to normal airline pricing tactics.

Carriers then must respond to changes and directions from their operating environment. Sometimes these changes might not favor the carriers, such as when government regulations force carriers to make a change that reduces efficiency. However, these environmental forces do exert pressure on carrier-pricing strategies and price levels.

Major Pricing Decisions

Every firm involved in delivering either a product or service faces major pricing decisions. These decisions can range from the very simple to the extremely complex. However, pricing decisions can be grouped into three categories. First, a carrier faces a decision when setting prices on a new service. For example, Federal Express had no precedent when setting prices on its first overnight delivery service. Such a decision could be difficult because it is based on little knowledge concerning the elasticity of the market to prices and the actual cost of providing the service. Also, if the price is set high enough to generate substantial profits, competitors will be enticed to enter the market at perhaps a lower price. On the other hand, if the price is set too low, although significant traffic might be generated, the carrier will not be maximizing its profits.

Second, a carrier must make decisions to modify prices over time. Market changes, operating changes, and service changes will require prices to be changed.

An important aspect of this decision is how and when to announce the changes to the market. For example, a major price increase by a carrier after announcing record company profits might get negative reactions in the market. In a manufacturing or retailing environment, price increases are sometimes announced in advance so customers can increase purchases to help offset the higher price. However, in transportation, services cannot be inventoried, so prior notification of a price increase does not accomplish the same objective, yet prior notification does allow for customers to seek alternative sources of supply.

Finally, carriers will make decisions initiating and responding to price changes. The concept of a *price leader* within an industry is not new. If a carrier is the price leader, then that carrier initiates the change; if not, then the carrier responds to the change. In transportation, where many of the markets are oligopolistic, downward price changes can be dangerous because of their potential to decrease industry revenues. Upward price changes can make a carrier the sole high-price service provider if competition does not follow the change, so how this decision is made can have a substantial impact on market share and profits.

Although there might be other types of price decisions, these represent the major ones that carriers will make. These can be considered strategic decisions because of the importance they have on carrier market position within the industry. For example, People's Express once offered a low-price, no-frills airline service and did not expect other carriers to match the low fares. However, some of the major trunk lines actually offered fares below People's, even though it meant a loss. With a high debt and stiff competition, People's Express eventually went out of business. Pricing then is a major marketing decision for every carrier.

Establishing the Pricing Objective

Pricing objectives for a carrier should reflect overall company objectives and reflect, in many ways, how the carrier will compete in its markets. Pricing objectives might also change for a particular service offering as it progresses through its product life cycle. Carriers with multiple markets might also establish various pricing objectives for these markets. For example, passenger airlines have separate pricing objectives for first-class and coach markets as well as for business and leisure travelers. This section will present several different pricing objectives that can be utilized in the transportation industry.

Especially in the case of ailing passenger airlines, **survival-based pricing** is aimed at increasing cash flow through the use of low prices. With this price level, the carrier attempts to increase volume and also encourage the higher utilization of equipment. Because an empty airline seat cannot be inventoried and is lost at takeoff, the marginal cost of filling that seat is small. Survival pricing then tries to take advantage of the marginal cost concept. Closely related is a **unit volume pricing** objective. This attempts to utilize a carrier's existing capacity to the fullest, so the price is set to encourage the market to fill that capacity. Multiple pickup allowances in the LTL industry, space-available prices in the freight airline industry, and multiple-car prices in the railroad industry are examples of this type of pricing objective.

Another price objective is called **profit maximization**, which can occur in the short run or in the long run. Carriers using this type of pricing usually are concerned with measures such as return on investment. This type of objective also can utilize what is called a **skimming price**. A skimming price is a high price intended to attract a market that is more concerned with quality, uniqueness, or status and is insensitive to price.[20] For example, although a high-cost move, pricing for the maiden flight of the Concorde was certainly aimed at those who would be willing to pay a high price because of the limited number of seats. This strategy works if competition can be kept out of a market through high investment costs or firm loyalty.

Many times a skimming price strategy is followed by a **penetration price** strategy. This can lead to a sales-based pricing objective, which can be an effective strategy because (1) a high price can be charged until competition starts to enter; (2) a higher price can help offset initial outlays for advertising and development; (3) a high price portrays a high-quality service; (4) if price changes need to be made, it is more favorable to reduce a price than to raise it; and (5) after market saturation is achieved, a lower price can appeal to a mass market with the objective of increasing sales.[21] A sales-based pricing objective also follows the life cycle approach of using skimming during the introduction and growth stages and penetration during the maturation stage. The recent reintroduction of luxury passenger railroad service might be a good example of this type of strategy. In transportation, this strategy would more likely be successful with passenger movements because of the reliance it places on the price–value relationship.

A **market share pricing** objective can be used in an industry whose revenues are stagnant or declining. This objective tries to take market share from competitors through the use of lower prices. This strategy is used frequently in passenger airlines and the LTL motor carrier industries. In some cases, this strategy assumes that competitors' offerings are substitutes and that competitors are not in a position to match the lower prices; if the services were not substitutes, a lower price would not provide a competitive advantage. For example, an airline that lowers its fares for business travelers to gain more of this market but does not offer the same number of departures and arrivals as a competitor might not succeed at gaining any market share.

Finally, a **social responsibility pricing** objective forgoes sales and profits and puts the welfare of society and customers first.[22] For example, after the tragic incident in New York City on September 11, 2001, many carriers offered to carry such items as food, clothing, building supplies, and medical supplies into the devastated area at greatly reduced prices or for free.

Because carriers in the various transportation industries service multiple markets, it is quite possible for them to employ several pricing objectives at one time. A carrier must be careful when setting an overall company pricing strategy to assure that these multiple pricing objectives are complementary, not conflicting.

Estimating Demand

Probably one of the most difficult tasks associated with pricing is estimating demand. In a perfectly competitive market, unit demand will decrease as price increases. This is reflected in the traditional demand-and-supply curve offered in basic economic theory. However, transportation carriers do not function in perfectly competitive markets. Demand estimation can become very tedious and difficult. However, certain concepts and procedures can be used in this process. One of these is the concept of *price elasticity*. Price elasticity refers to the change in demand because of a change in price. In an established market for a carrier, this relationship should be well developed to the point where demand implications from a price change should be easy to estimate. The example of business versus leisure travelers in the airline industry can be used to explain this concept. Business travelers are relatively price inelastic because demand for business travel by air does not fluctuate widely with increases in price. However, leisure travelers are very price elastic and might tend to delay travel or seek travel by an alternative mode if there is an increase in air fares. In a new market, estimations of price elasticity can be made by comparing the new market with a similar existing market.

A direct attitude survey might also be used in determining demand under a new pricing structure. For example, asking customers and/or potential customers how much business they would provide at certain price levels might produce some feel of how sensitive demand is to price. Caution has to be used in this method in how this question is asked because customers will usually tend to favor the lowest price.

Finally, a market test is a possible way to determine potential demand when market testing is feasible. This might involve a carrier introducing a new service at a high price in one area and at a higher price in another area to see how sensitive demand is to price. Important in this method is choosing test market areas that resemble the entire market for which the service is applicable.

Although not a science, demand estimation is a critical part of pricing strategy. Demand estimation results in potential revenue estimation. (Some of the theory behind demand estimation was presented earlier in this chapter, under the topic "Value-of-Service Pricing.") With revenue estimated, costs should next be established.

Estimating Costs

A significant portion of this chapter is devoted to the concepts of costs and cost-of-service pricing, so a detailed explanation of either is not necessary here. However, a decision must be made as to which costs should be included in the total cost analysis. In the example given under value-of-service pricing, the fuel expense and driver wages generated on a backhaul can be considered a fixed cost and, as such, need not be included in the backhaul pricing decision.

Another cost relationship that must be examined is how costs behave at different levels of output or capacity. The existence or nonexistence of scale economies in transportation, for example, will affect how costs behave at different capacity levels. This information can be used to determine such factors as break-even points. Regardless of the methods used, the cost of providing a service must be calculated to determine the attractiveness of a market for a carrier.

Price Levels and Price Adjustments

With demand and cost estimates generated, it is possible to set the actual price. Many methods for doing this exist, including demand-based methods, cost-based methods, profit-based methods, and competition-based methods. Lengthy discussions of these can be found in any basic marketing-text chapter on pricing.[23] However, a discussion of price adjustments is warranted because of the federal government regulations on such concepts as rebates.

Discounts are a reduction from a published price that rewards a buyer for doing something that is beneficial for the supplier.[24] In transportation, LTL versus TL prices reflect carrier savings from larger shipments, a portion of which is passed on to the customer in the form of a lower price. This could be called a quantity discount. Airlines use a form of seasonal discounts to encourage vacation passengers to travel during carrier off-peak periods. Cash discounts, relatively new to the transportation industry, reward customers who pay their bills within a stated period of time. A common form of a cash discount is "2/10, net 30," which means that the customer can take a 2-percent discount if the bill is paid within 10 days, or else pay the full amount within 30 days. This helps speed the cash flow for carriers, which is important for their financial stability.

Geographic adjustments are common in the transportation industry. Although not directly used by carriers, geographic adjustments are used by shippers and receivers to compensate for transportation costs in the final price to the customer. One common type of geographic price is FOB origin or FOB destination pricing. In FOB origin pricing, the buyer is responsible for transportation costs; in destination pricing, the shipper is responsible (see Figure 4-10).

Uniform-delivered pricing, a form of FOB destination pricing, offers a final price to customers for a product that includes all transportation costs. Related to this is **zone pricing**, in which every customer within a certain zone pays exactly the same price for a product based on average transportation costs within the zone.

When using discounts and allowances in the transportation industry, an important rule to remember is that a discount or allowance passed on to a customer must be the result of a reduction in carrier costs because of an action by the customer. Also, the discount or allowance given to the customer may not exceed the cost savings to the

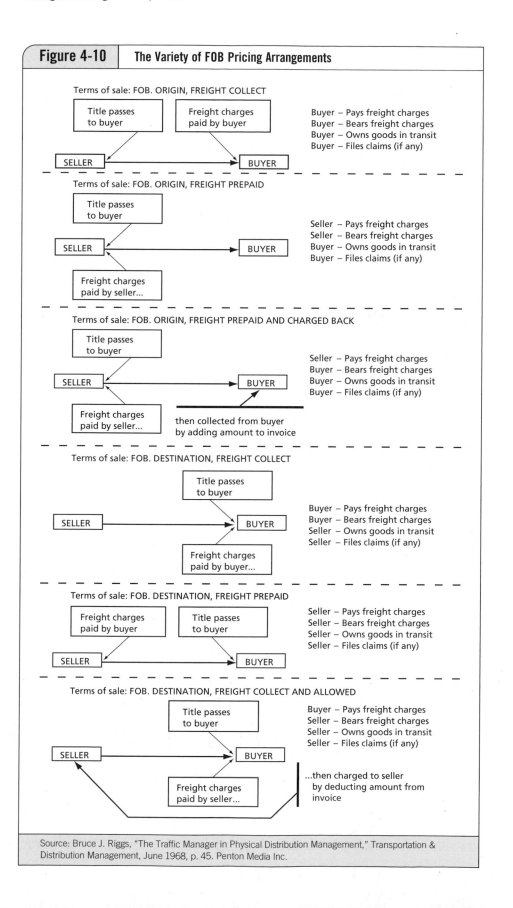

Figure 4-10 | The Variety of FOB Pricing Arrangements

Terms of sale: FOB. ORIGIN, FREIGHT COLLECT

Title passes to buyer
Freight charges paid by buyer
SELLER → BUYER

Buyer – Pays freight charges
Buyer – Bears freight charges
Buyer – Owns goods in transit
Buyer – Files claims (if any)

Terms of sale: FOB. ORIGIN, FREIGHT PREPAID

Title passes to buyer
SELLER → BUYER
Freight charges paid by seller...

Seller – Pays freight charges
Seller – Bears freight charges
Buyer – Owns goods in transit
Buyer – Files claims (if any)

Terms of sale: FOB. ORIGIN, FREIGHT PREPAID AND CHARGED BACK

Title passes to buyer
SELLER → BUYER
Freight charges paid by seller...
then collected from buyer by adding amount to invoice

Seller – Pays freight charges
Buyer – Bears freight charges
Buyer – Owns goods in transit
Buyer – Files claims (if any)

Terms of sale: FOB. DESTINATION, FREIGHT COLLECT

Title passes to buyer
SELLER → BUYER
Freight charges paid by buyer...

Buyer – Pays freight charges
Buyer – Bears freight charges
Seller – Owns goods in transit
Seller – Files claims (if any)

Terms of sale: FOB. DESTINATION, FREIGHT PREPAID

Freight charges paid by buyer
Title passes to buyer
SELLER → BUYER

Seller – Pays freight charges
Seller – Bears freight charges
Seller – Owns goods in transit
Seller – Files claims (if any)

Terms of sale: FOB. DESTINATION, FREIGHT COLLECT AND ALLOWED

Title passes to buyer
SELLER → BUYER
Freight charges paid by seller...
...then charged to seller by deducting amount from invoice

Buyer – Pays freight charges
Seller – Bears freight charges
Seller – Owns goods in transit
Seller – Files claims (if any)

Source: Bruce J. Riggs, "The Traffic Manager in Physical Distribution Management," Transportation & Distribution Management, June 1968, p. 45. Penton Media Inc.

carrier. Violating either of these rules of thumb exposes the carrier to the jurisdiction of the STB (rebates) and the Justice Department (antitrust and rebates).

Most Common Mistakes in Pricing

As previously mentioned, carriers have not had many years of experience in setting and managing prices on a strategic level. However, just like firms in any other industry, they are prone to certain mistakes. The first common mistake is to make pricing too reliant on costs. Although it is important to know the costs of providing a service, many other factors play a role in setting the appropriate price for a market. Competitive factors, customer preferences and values, and government regulations will affect the level at which the price will be most beneficial to the carrier.

The second common mistake is that prices are not revised frequently enough to capitalize on market changes. Under the previous regulatory environment, it was difficult for carriers to change prices because of the requirement of public notice and the burden of proof on the carrier. However, today's environment has allowed tremendous freedom and the flexibility for carriers to change prices. Unfortunately, for some carriers, the traditional mentality remains and can prevent a carrier from entering a market or, in some cases, creating a new market.

Setting the price independently of the marketing mix is a third common mistake. The **marketing mix**, also known as the "4 Ps," consists of product, price, promotion, and place. A carrier's product or output is transportation; its promotion is how it creates demand or advertises itself to customers; price is what it charges for its product or output; place is how it delivers its service to customers. All of these interact within a carrier's organization to provide access to and, it is hoped, success in current and potential markets. Managing one of these areas independently of the others will result in a suboptimization of the carrier's resources and its profits.

Finally, price is sometimes not varied enough for different service offerings and market segments. A "one price for all" mentality does not work in the transportation industry. As previously stated, carriers service multiple markets with differing service/price requirements. Airlines use a concept called *yield management pricing*, a form of value-of-service pricing, which relates price to the availability of capacity and the willingness of passengers to pay, or to address this situation.[25] Charging one price for all services is not going to maximize the profits for the carrier.

Pricing is a complex and challenging process that applies to all business entities. Pricing is also critical to a business's competitive advantage, position within its markets, and overall profitability. It must be managed within the context of the carrier's overall strategic plan, not independently of it.

SUMMARY

- The market structure for a carrier will be related to its cost structure; having a knowledge of this cost structure is necessary for the development of carrier prices.
- Cost-of-service pricing relies on the marginal cost of providing a service.
- Value-of-service pricing relies on the average cost of providing the service or on what the market will bear.
- Because of the high number of possible freight rates for commodities, tariffs were constructed to simplify them into class, exception, or commodity rates.
- Various types of special rates exist that allow carriers and shippers the flexibility to tailor rate structures to meet market needs.
- Pricing in transportation can be a strategic advantage if managed within the context of corporate strategy.
- Setting and managing prices in transportation are affected by actions of government, customers, competition, and other channel members.

STUDY QUESTIONS

1. Compare and contrast pure competition with monopoly from a pricing perspective. If you were a shipper, which would you prefer? Which would a carrier prefer?

2. Describe an oligopolistic market structure. What alternatives to price competition exist in such markets? Why would these alternatives be important to shippers?

3. What is value-of-service pricing? Is this approach to pricing valid today?

4. What is cost-of-service pricing? What is the relationship between value-of-service pricing and cost-of-service pricing?

5. What is a released value rate and how does its use affect a shipper's transportation costs?

6. What are the major forces that affect carrier pricing strategies?

7. How might pricing strategies differ among carriers in competitive markets, oligopolistic markets, and monopolistic markets?

8. What are the various factors used in classifying commodities for tariff purposes?

9. What are the differences among class, exception, and commodity rates?

10. Why were tariffs created? Are they still useful in today's transportation environment?

NOTES

1. For a more thorough discussion of contestable market theory, see W. J. Baumol, J. C. Panzar, and R. D. Willig, *Contestable Markets and the Theory of Industry Structure,* New York: Harcourt, Brace, Jovanovich, 1982.

2. Stanley E. Fawcett and Martin T. Farris, "Contestable Markets and Airline Adaptability Under Deregulation," *Transportation Journal,* Vol. 29, No. 1, 1989, pp. 12–24.

3. Ibid., p. 17.

4. Ibid., p. 14.

5. Ibid.

6. For a more detailed discussion of this conclusion, see Fawcett and Farris, op. cit.

7. Winthrop M. Daniels, *The Price of Transportation Service,* New York: Harper and Brothers, 1942, p. 1.

8. John R. Meyer, et al., *The Economics of Competition in the Transportation Industries,* Cambridge, MA: Harvard University Press, 1959, p. 205.

9. For an excellent analysis of industry pricing behavior, see Meyer, *The Economics of Competition,* pp. 203–211.

10. This section is based on the discussion in J. J. Coyle, "Cost-of-Service Pricing in Transportation," *Quarterly Review of Economics and Business,* Vol. 57, 1964, pp. 69–74.

11. Harold Hotelling, "The General Welfare in Relation to Problems of Taxation and of Railway and Utility Rates," *Econometrics,* Vol. 6, No. 3, 1938, p. 242.

12. R. W. Harbeson, "The Cost Concept and Economic Control," *Harvard Business Review,* Vol. 17, 1939, pp. 257–263.

13. Ibid.

14. George W. Wilson, "Freight Rates and Transportation Costs," *The Business Quarterly,* Summer 1960, pp. 161–162.

15. John J. Coyle, "A Reconsideration of Value of Service Pricing," *Land Economics,* Winter 1964, pp. 193–199.

16. George W. Wilson, *Theory of Transportation Pricing,* Bloomington, IN: Indiana University, 1985, p. 160.

17. For an extended discussion, see Coyle, "A Reconsideration of Value of Service Pricing," pp. 195–198.

18. This example is adapted from Wilson and Smerk, "Rate Theory," pp. 7–10.

19. See, for example, Eric N. Berkowitz, Roger A. Kerin, Steven W. Hartley, and William Rudelius, *Marketing,* 3rd ed., Homewood, IL: Richard D. Irwin, 1992.

20. Joel R. Evans and Barry Berman, *Marketing,* New York: Macmillan, 1982, p. 532.

21. Ibid.

22. Berkowitz, et. al., op. cit., p. 321.

23. Berkowitz, et. al., op. cit., pp. 339–352.

24. Ibid., p. 354.

25. For a discussion of yield management pricing, see Sheryl Kimes, "The Basics of Yield Management," *The Cornell H.R.A. Quarterly,* November 1989, pp. 14–19; Walter J. Relihan III, "The Yield Management Approach to Hotel Room Pricing," *The Cornell H.R.A. Quarterly,* May 1989, pp. 40–45; Peter P. Belobaba, "Application of a Probabilistic Decision Model to Airline Seat Inventory Control," *Operations Research,* Vol. 37, No. 2, 1989.

CASE 4-1

Hardee Transportation (A)

Jim O'Brien has realized for quite some time that some of Hardee's customers are more profitable than others. This is also quite true for certain freight lanes. However, Hardee has traditionally structured its prices around discounts off their published tariff rates. Most of the discounts have been based on freight volume only. Jim knows that his drivers and dock people do more for certain customers than move volume; they count freight during loading, sort and segregate freight on the dock, weigh shipments, and do some labeling.

Jim foresees some of the new service demands from his customers being very difficult to cost and price because they won't necessarily be based on freight volume. Some of these new demands will include merge-in-transit, event management, continuous shipment tracking RFID capability, and dedicated customer service personnel. Traditionally, Hardee has used average cost pricing for its major customers. Some of his pricing managers have urged Jim to consider marginal cost pricing. However, Jim has developed a keen interest in value-of-service pricing methods versus the traditional cost-of-service pricing.

The problem with both approaches for Hardee is that they have no form of activity-based costing or any other methodology that will allow them to really get a handle on where their costs are hidden. Jim knows what Hardee pays its drivers, knows the costs of equipment and fuel, and knows the overall costs of dispatch and dock operations. Hardee's average length of haul is 950 miles and its loaded mile metric is 67 percent.

CASE QUESTIONS

1. What would be the advantages/disadvantages of using cost-of-service versus value-of-service pricing for Hardee's customers? When discussing cost-of-service pricing, what type of cost (average versus marginal) would make more sense for Hardee?

2. How would you develop a methodology for Hardee to price its existing services? Its evolving services? Would you use the same or different strategies for each?

CASE 4-2

Hardee Transportation (B)

One of Jim O'Brien's customers has presented him with an opportunity for a significant amount of freight moving into a new market for Hardee. Hardee is a truckload carrier primarily moving freight in the East/West market in the United States. Although it has some movements in and out of Canada and Mexico, Hardee has focused on moving freight in eastward and westward directions. Hardee has dispatch centers located throughout the United States which have some dock capacity.

The new move would be between Pittsburgh and Miami. Hardee has avoided this market because of the lack of backhaul opportunities that exist outbound from Florida. However, this new move offers a significant increase in volume for Hardee. A complicating factor in this move is the request that Hardee perform sorting and segregation at its dispatch centers. Each shipment will consist of straight (one product) pallet loads of various types of consumer goods freight destined for a retailer's distribution center in Miami. Sorting and segregation at Hardee's locations would consist of breaking the pallets and sorting the freight by the retailer's store locations, then repalletizing into rainbow (mixed products) pallets for each store.

Hardee has never experienced this type of request before. Jim knows that he needs to put some type of costs to this move to make sure that the moves are profitable. Because of the large volume involved, not covering Hardee's costs in pricing could result in large losses for Hardee. The relevant information for costing this move is as follows:

Equipment Cost Data

Equipment Purchase Price

1. Line-haul tractors = $80,000
2. Line-haul trailers = $24,000

Depreciation

1. Tractors = 5-year straight line
2. Trailers = 8-year straight line

Interest

1. Tractors = 10 percent APR for 5 years
2. Trailers = 10 percent APR for 8 years

Fuel

1. $2.10 per gallon for diesel
2. Line-haul tractors = 6.5 miles per gallon

Labor

1. Line-haul drivers = $0.42 per mile
2. Pick-up and delivery (PUD) drivers = $30 (fully loaded) per hour
3. Dock workers = $25 (fully loaded) per hour

Miscellaneous

1. Insurance cost = $0.05 per mile

2. Maintenance cost = $0.15 per mile

3. Billing cost = $5.00 per freight bill

4. Tractors and trailers are available for use 20 hours per day (80 percent uptime), 365 days per year

5. Administrative/overhead cost = 8 percent of total cost of move

6. Dock facility cost = $15 per hour

7. Line-haul vehicle averages 45 mph between origin and destination.

Route and Time of Move

The shipment (40,000 pounds) originates at a customer location in Pittsburgh, located 20 miles from Hardee's dispatch center. A PUD driver is dispatched from the Hardee location at 8:30 a.m. on January 12, 2010, and arrives at destination at 9:00 a.m. the same day. The shipment is loaded from 9:00 a.m. to 12:00 p.m. The PUD driver departs the customer location at 12:00 p.m. and arrives back at the Hardee dispatch center at 12:30 p.m.

The sort process starts at 12:30 p.m. and ends at 8:30 p.m. on January 12. It requires unloading the trailer, sorting, and repalletizing the load. This operation requires two dock workers, each working the same trailer for 8 hours in the dispatch center.

The line-haul portion begins with the vehicle being dispatched from the Pittsburgh location at 8:30 p.m. on January 12 and traveling to Charlotte, North Carolina, a distance of 481 miles, and arriving at Charlotte at 7:12 a.m. on January 13. The driver rests from 7:12 a.m. until 3:12 p.m. The trip continues with the vehicle departing Charlotte at 3:12 p.m. on January 13 and traveling to Jacksonville, Florida, a distance of 399 miles, arriving at Jacksonville at 12:06 a.m. on January 14. The driver rests from 12:06 a.m. until 10:06 a.m. The line-haul portion concludes with the vehicle departing Jacksonville at 10:06 a.m. and traveling to the customer's location in Miami, a distance of 369 miles, and arriving at the distribution center at 6:18 p.m. on January 14.

The line-haul driver stays with the vehicle while it is being unloaded (2 hours unload time). The driver then deadheads at 8:18 p.m. from the customer's distribution center and arrives at a Hardee dispatch center located in Miami at 8:48 p.m., a distance of 15 miles from the distribution center.

CASE QUESTIONS

1. What are the pick-up, sort, line-haul, and delivery costs to Hardee for this move?

2. What is the total cost of this move? Cost per cwt? Cost per revenue mile?

3. If Hardee would put two drivers in the tractor for the line-haul move, there would be no rest required for drivers during the line-haul move. What would happen to total costs?

4. Assume that Hardee has no loaded backhaul to return the vehicle and driver to Pittsburgh. How would you account for the empty backhaul costs associated with this move? Would you include those in the headhaul move? How would this impact your pricing strategy?

APPENDIX 4A
Cost Concepts

Accounting Cost

The simplest concept or measure of cost is what has sometimes been labeled accounting cost, or even more simply as money cost. These are the so-called bookkeeping costs of a company and include all cash outlays of the firm. This particular concept of cost is not difficult to grasp. The most difficult problem with accounting costs is their allocation among the various products or services of a company.

If the owner of a motor carrier, for example, was interested in determining the cost associated with moving a particular truckload of traffic, all the cost of fuel, oil, and the driver's wages associated with the movement could be quickly determined. It might also be possible to determine how much wear and tear would occur on the vehicle during the trip. However, the portion of the president's salary, the terminal expenses, and the advertising expense should be included in the price. These costs should be included in part, but how much should be included is frequently a perplexing question. The computation becomes even more complex when a small shipment is combined with other small shipments in one truckload.

Some allocation would then be necessary for the fuel expense and the driver's wages.

Economic Cost

A second concept of cost is economic cost, which is different from accounting cost. The economic definition of cost is associated with the alternative cost doctrine or the opportunity cost doctrine. Costs of production, as defined by economists, are futuristic and are the values of the alternative products that could have been produced with the resources used in production.

Therefore, the costs of resources are their values in their best alternative uses. To secure the service or use of resources, such as labor or capital, a company must pay an amount at least equal to what the resource could obtain in its best alternative use. Implicit in this definition of cost is the principle that if a resource has no alternative use, then its cost in economic terms is zero.

The futuristic aspect of economic costs has special relevance in transportation because, once investment has been made, one should not be concerned with recovering what are sometimes referred to as **sunk costs**.[1] Resources in some industries are so durable that they can be regarded as virtually everlasting. Therefore, if no replacement is anticipated, and there is no alternative use, then the use of the resource is costless in an economic sense. This is of special importance in the railroad industry.

Railroads have long been regarded as having durable and therefore costless resources. That is, some of the resources of railroads, such as concrete ties, some signaling equipment, and even some rolling stock, are so durable and so highly specialized that they have no alternative production or use potential. So the use of such resources, apart from maintenance, is costless in an economic sense. Consequently, in a competitive pricing situation, such resources could be excluded from the calculation of fixed costs. Also, such specialized resources can be eliminated in comparing cost structures.[2]

Although the economic logic of the above argument on the use of durable, specialized resources is impeccable, it is frequently disregarded by pricing analysts and regulators. In a sense, the elimination of such costs from pricing calculations defies common sense. From the money or accounting cost perspective, these costs usually should be included.

The conclusion that must be drawn is that economic costs differ from money or accounting costs. Money costs are by their very nature a measure of past costs. This does not mean that money costs do not have any relevance in the economic sense. Past costs do perform a very important function because they provide a guide to future cost estimates. However, complete reliance should not be put upon historical costs for pricing in the transportation industry.

Social Cost

A third category of costs—social costs—might also be considered. Some businesses might not concern themselves with social costs unless required to do so by law. These costs take into consideration the cost to society of some particular operation and, in fact, might outweigh money cost. For example, what is the cost to society when a company releases its waste materials into a stream? Today many regulations and controls are administered by various regulatory agencies to protect society from such costs. These agencies make the business organizations responsible for social costs. (For example, strip-mine operators are customarily required to backfill and plant.) In spite of such controls, however, there are still instances when chemicals or other hazardous materials are discharged or leak out and society has to bear the cost of the cleanup operations as well as the health hazards.

This discussion is not trying to castigate business organizations or suggest that all investment decisions result in negative social costs because, in fact, there can be social benefits from business investments. However, to ensure that the discussion is complete, social costs must be considered.

Analysis of Cost Structures

There are two general approaches to an analysis of a particular cost structure. Under one approach, costs can be classified as those that are directly assignable to particular segments of the business (such as products or services) and those that are incurred for the business as a whole. These two types of cost are generally designated as separable and common costs, respectively. Usually, common costs are further classified as joint common costs or conjoint common costs. **Separable costs** refer to a situation in which products are necessarily produced in fixed proportions. The classic example is that of hides and beef. Stated simply, the production or generation of one product or service necessarily entails the production or generation of another product. In terms of transportation, joint costs occur when two or more services are *necessarily* produced together in fixed proportions. One of these services is said to be a by-product of the other. The most obvious illustration is that of the backhaul situation; the return capacity is the by-product of the loaded trip to the destination.[3]

It is a generally accepted fact that large transportation companies, especially railroads, have a significant element of common costs because they have roadbed, terminals, freight

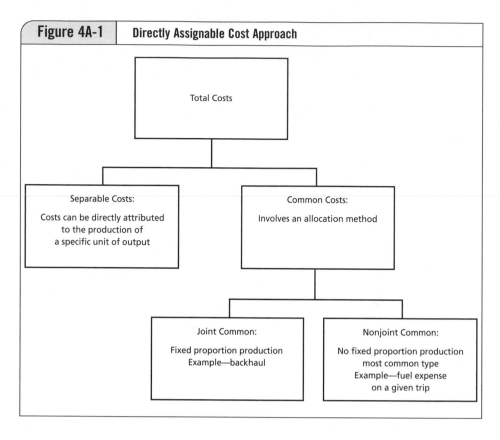

Figure 4A-1 | **Directly Assignable Cost Approach**

yards, and so on, the cost of which is common to all traffic. However, the only evidence of true jointness appears to be the backhaul.[4] Nonjoint common costs are those that do not require the production of fixed proportions of products or services. Nonjoint common costs are more customary in transportation. For example, on a typical train journey on which hundreds of items are carried, the expenses of the crew and fuel are common costs incurred for all the items hauled (see Figure 4A-1).

A technique for allocating costs directly to activity centers has been implemented in both the carrier and shipper communities. **Activity-based costing (ABC)** identifies costs specifically generated by performing a service or producing a product. ABC does not allocate direct and indirect costs based on volume alone; it determines which activities are responsible for these costs and burdens these activities with their respective portion of overhead costs.

One application for ABC today by both carriers and shippers is the calculation of customer profitability.[5]

Under the other basic approach to analyzing a particular cost structure, costs are divided into those that do not fluctuate with the volume of business in the short term and those that do. The time period here is assumed to be that in which the plant or physical capacity of the business remains unchanged, or the short run. The two types of costs described are usually referred to as *fixed* and *variable* costs, respectively.

In the first approach, the distinction between common and separable costs is made with the idea that costs can be traced to specific accounts or products of the business.

In the second approach, the distinction between fixed and variable is made to study variations in business as a whole over a period of time and the effect of these variations upon expenses. In other words, with fixed and variable costs the focus is on the fact that some costs increase and decrease with expansion and contraction of business volume, whereas other costs do not vary as business levels change.

Because of the two different approaches to studying costs, it is possible that a certain cost might be classified as common on one hand and variable on the other, or common under one approach and fixed under the other, and so on, for all the possible combinations. Therefore, the only costs directly traceable or separable are the variable costs, which are also separable. For example, fuel expense is generally regarded as a variable cost, but it would be a common cost with a vehicle loaded with LTL traffic.

The second approach of cost analysis—namely, fixed and variable costs—is important and should be discussed further. As indicated previously, **total fixed costs** are constant regardless of the enterprise's volume of business. These fixed costs can include maintenance expenses on equipment or right-of-way (track) caused by time and weather (not use), property taxes, certain management salaries, interest on bonds, and payments on long-term leases. **Fixed costs per unit** of output decline as more volume is allocated to a fixed cost asset.

A business has a commitment to its fixed costs even with a zero level of output. Fixed costs might, in certain instances, be delayed, or to use the more common term, deferred. The railroads frequently delay or defer costs. For example, maintenance of railroad rights-of-way should probably be done each spring or summer, particularly in the northern states. Freezing and thawing, along with spring rains, wash away gravel and stone (ballast) and may do other damage. Although this maintenance can be postponed, just as, for example, house painting might be postponed for a year or two, sooner or later it has to be done if the business wants to continue to operate. There is a fixed commitment or necessity that requires the corrective action and associated expense.[6] The important point is that total fixed expenses occur independently of the volume of business experienced by the organization.

Variable costs, on the other hand, are closely related to the volume of business. In other words, firms do not experience any variable costs unless they are operating. The fuel expense for trains or tractor–trailers is an excellent example of a variable cost. If a locomotive or vehicle does not make a run or trip, there is no fuel cost. Additional examples of variable costs include the wear and tear on tractor–trailers and the cost for tires and engine parts. Thus, variable cost per unit remains constant regardless of the level of output, while total variable costs are directly related to the level of output.

Another related point is that railroads and pipelines, like many public utility companies, are frequently labeled as decreasing cost industries. The relevance of this phenomenon to pricing was discussed earlier in this chapter, but it also deserves some additional explanation now. Railroads and pipelines have a high proportion of fixed costs in their cost structures. There is some debate about the percentage, but the estimates range from 20 to 50 percent. Contrast this with motor carriers whose average is 10 percent. As railroads produce more units, the proportion of fixed costs on each item will be lower. More importantly, this decline will occur over a long range of output because of the large-scale capacity of most railroads.

An example of the above situation is useful here. Assume that a particular railroad incurs $5 million of fixed costs on an annual basis. In addition, assume that the railroad is analyzing costs for pricing purposes between Bellefonte, Pennsylvania, and Chicago. In its examination of cost, the railroad determines that the variable cost on a carload is $250 between Bellefonte and Chicago.

Although it might be unrealistic, assume that the railroad only moves 10 cars per year. The cost would be as follows:

Fixed cost $5,000,000

Variable cost $2,500 (10 cars × $250)

Total cost $5,002,500

Average cost $500,250 per car

If it moves 1,000 cars, the cost would be:

Fixed cost $5,000,000

Variable cost $250,000 (1,000 cars × $250)

Total cost $5,250,000

Average cost $5,250 per car

If it moves 100,000 cars, the cost would be:

Fixed cost $5,000,000

Variable cost $25,000,000 (100,000 × $250)

Total cost $30,000,000

Average cost $300 per car

The relationship is easy to see. If the number of cars increased in our example, the average cost would continue to decline. Theoretically, average cost would have to level out and eventually increase due to decreasing returns, but the important point is that the high proportion of fixed costs and the large capacity cause the average cost to decline over a great range of output (see Figure 4A-2). There would be a point, however, at which additional cars would require another investment in fixed cost, thus shifting the average cost curve.

The significance of the declining cost phenomenon to a railroad is that volume is a very important determinant of cost and efficiency. Furthermore, pricing the service to

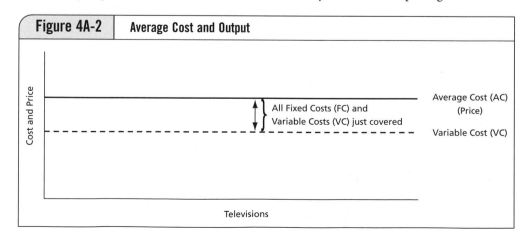

Figure 4A-2 | **Average Cost and Output**

attract traffic is a critical factor in determining profitability, particularly where there is competition from alternate modes of transportation.

Another cost concept that is of major importance in this analysis is marginal cost, because of its key role in understanding pricing decisions. Marginal cost can be defined as the change in total cost resulting from a one-unit change in output, or as additions to aggregate cost for given additions to output. This latter definition probably makes more sense in transportation because of the difficulties of defining the output unit. Marginal cost also can be defined as the change in total variable cost resulting from a one-unit change in output, because a change in output changes total variable cost and total cost by exactly the same amounts. Marginal cost is sometimes referred to as *incremental cost*, especially in the transportation industry.

There is one other type of cost that should be mentioned because of its importance in price decision—**out-of-pocket costs**. Out-of-pocket costs are usually defined as those costs that are directly assignable to a particular unit of traffic and that would not have been incurred if the service or movement had not been performed. Within the framework of this definition, out-of-pocket costs could also be either separable costs or variable costs. Although the above definition states that out-of-pocket costs are specifically assignable to a certain movement, which implies separable costs, they can definitely be considered as variable costs because they would not have occurred if a particular shipment had not been moved. The definition also encompasses marginal cost because marginal cost can be associated with a unit increase in cost.

The vagueness of the out-of-pocket costs definition has left the door open to the types of cost included as a part of the total cost calculation. The difficulty lies in the fact that from a narrow viewpoint, out-of-pocket costs could be classified as only those expenses incurred because a particular unit was moved. For example, the loading and unloading expense attributable to moving a particular shipment, plus the extra fuel and wear and tear on equipment (relatively low for railroads) could be classified as out-of-pocket costs. On the other hand, a broad approach might be used in defining out-of-pocket costs in regard to a particular shipment, thereby including a share of all of the common variable expenses attributable to a particular movement between two points.

The confusion surrounding the concept of out-of-pocket costs would seem to justify elimination of its use. However, the continued use of the term would be acceptable if its definition was made synonymous with the definition of one of the particular economic costs that its definition implies—marginal costs—because this term is important in price and output decisions and evaluations of pricing economics. Typically, out-of-pocket costs are most important to the firm's accounting system because they are payments that must be made almost immediately as an operating expense. The out-of-pocket cost concept is useful in that it is used as a way to estimate the amount of liquid funds that a transportation firm must keep on hand for daily operations.[7]

Figure 4A-3 gives a good breakdown of the methods of cost analysis. It illustrates the close relationship between the three cost concepts of variable, marginal, and out-of-pocket costs.

Although attention is devoted to cost structure in the separate chapters dealing with each of the modes of transportation, some consideration will be given in this section to an analysis of modal cost structures. Such discussion is useful and necessary background to the analysis of the approaches to pricing.

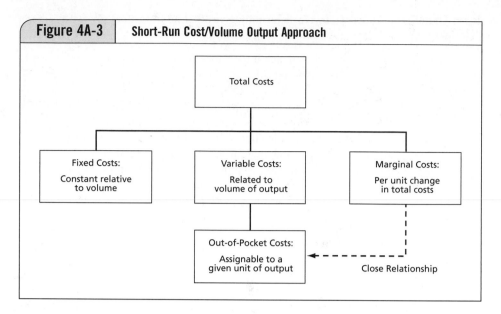

Figure 4A-3   Short-Run Cost/Volume Output Approach

Rail Cost Structure

One of the characteristics of railroads, as previously noted, is the level of fixed costs present in their cost structures. It is a commonly accepted fact that a relatively large proportion of railway costs are fixed in the short run. At one time it was believed that more than half of rail costs were fixed, and some individuals estimated that these costs ran as high as 70 percent of total cost. The exact proportion of fixed expenses is subject to some debate; however, it is generally accepted that fixed expenses constitute a significant portion of railroad total costs, ranging from 20 to 50 percent. The high proportion of fixed costs can be explained by railroad investment (in such things as track, terminals, and freight yards), which is much larger than the investment of motor carriers, for example. For this reason, railroads are generally regarded as having increasing returns, or decreasing costs per unit of output.[8]

As has been indicated, a significant amount of railroad costs also include common expenses because replacement costs of a stretch of track are shared by all traffic moving over it. This is also true with respect to other items of cost, including officers' salaries. Some of these common costs are also fixed costs, while others are variable costs (refer to Chapter 6, "Railroads").

Motor Carrier Cost Structure

The motor carrier industry is exemplified by a high proportion of variable costs. It has been estimated that variable costs in the motor carrier industry are 90 percent or more of total costs.[9] This high degree of variability is explained to a large extent by the fact that motor carriers do not have to provide their own right-of-way because roads are publicly provided. It is true that motor carriers do pay fuel taxes and other taxes to defray the cost of providing the highways, but these expenses are variable because they depend on the use made of the highway.

The economic concept of the "long run" is a shorter period in the motor carrier industry than in the railroad industry. The operating unit, the motor carrier vehicle, has a shorter life span than the rail operating unit. It is smaller and therefore more adaptable to fluctuating business conditions. The capital investment required is smaller too, and fleets can be expanded and contracted more easily.

The motor carrier situation varies greatly with respect to common costs. Companies that specialize in LTL traffic will have a significant proportion of common cost, whereas contract carriers with only two or three customers who move only TL traffic will have a high proportion of separable costs. Other companies that carry a mixture of TL and LTL traffic will be in the middle of the two extremes (refer to Chapter 5, "Motor Carriers").

Other Carriers' Cost Structures

Information on water carrier cost structure is less prevalent because many companies are privately owned or exempt from economic regulation. The cost structure is probably very similar to that of motor carriers because their right-of-way is also publicly provided. There are some differences, however, because the investment per unit of output is greater, and a large volume of traffic is necessary to realize mass movement potentialities.[10] (See Chapter 8, "Water Carriers and Pipelines").

The pipeline companies have a cost structure similar to that of railroads. The fact that they have to provide their own right-of-way and the fact that their terminal facilities are very specialized mean that they have a large element of fixed and usually sunk costs. They also usually have significant common costs because they move a variety of oil products through the pipeline (see Chapter 8, "Water Carriers and Pipelines").

The airline companies have a cost structure similar to that of water carriers and motor carriers because of the public provision of their right-of-way. Also, terminal facilities are publicly provided to a large extent, and the airlines pay landing fees based upon use. Airlines tend to have a significant element of common cost because of small freight shipments and the individual nature of passenger movements; for example, airlines very seldom sell a planeload to one customer (see Chapter 7, "Airlines").

The differences in the cost structures of the modes of transportation and their differing service characteristics make pricing of their services very important. If motor-carrier service is better than rail service, motor-carrier prices can exceed rail prices. The cost structure of the motor carrier might dictate that their prices can exceed rail prices. The cost structure of the motor carrier might dictate that their prices have to be higher than the rail prices. The critical question is what the relationship between demand and cost (supply) is in such cases.

NOTES

1. William J. Baumol, et al., "The Role of Cost in the Minimum Pricing of Railroad Services," *Journal of Business,* Vol. 35, October 1962, pp. 5–6. This article succinctly presents the essence of sunk versus prospective costs.

2. A. M. Milne, *The Economics of Inland Transport,* London: Pitman and Sons, 1955, p. 146.

3. Robert C. Lieb, *Transportation, the Domestic System,* 2nd ed., Reston, VA: Reston Publishing, p. 138.

4. This problem was argued in the economic journals at an early date by two notable economists. See F. W. Taussig, "Railway Rates and Joint Cost Once More," *Quarterly Journal of Economics,* Vol. 27, May 1913, p. 378; F. W. Taussig and A. C. Pigou, "Railway Rates and Joint Costs," *Quarterly Journal of Economics,* Vol. 27, August 1913, pp. 535 and 687; A. C. Pigou, *The Economics of Welfare,* 4th ed., London: Macmillan, 1950, Chapters 17 and 18. An excellent discussion of this debate is contained in D. P. Locklin, "A Review of the Literature on Railway Rate Theory," *Quarterly Journal of Economics,* Vol. 47, 1933, p. 174.

5. For a more thorough discussion of this topic, see Terrance L. Pohlen and Bernard J. LaLonde, "Implementing Activity-Based Costing (ABC) in Logistics," *Journal of Business Logistics,* Vol. 15, No. 2, 1994, pp. 1–23.

6. For an excellent discussion, see George W. Wilson and George W. Smerk, "Rate Theory," in *Physical Distribution Management,* Bloomington, IN: Indiana University, 1963, pp. 2–4.

7. Wayne K. Talley, *Introduction to Transportation,* 1st ed., Cincinnati, OH: Southwestern, 1983, p. 27.

8. George W. Wilson, *Essays on Some Unsettled Questions in the Economics of Transportation* (Bloomington, IN: Foundation for Economic and Business Studies, 1962), pp. 32–33.

9. Interstate Commerce Commission, Bureau of Accounts and Cost Finding, *Explanation of Rail Cost Finding Principles and Procedures,* Washington, DC: Government Printing Office, 1948, p. 88.

10. John R. Meyer, et al., *The Economics of Competition in the Transportation Industries,* Cambridge, MA: Harvard University Press, pp. 112–113.

APPENDIX 4B

LTL and TL Costing Models

As mentioned in this chapter, understanding costs for costing purposes is critical to a carrier's ability to price in order to maximize profits. Costing and pricing can be extremely complex exercises, depending on the amount and complexity of inputs. However, examining LTL and TL operations, it might be evident that defining their activities for costing purposes can be relatively simple. The purpose of this appendix is to offer basic and simplistic costing models for LTL and TL that can be used to get a feel for the costs associated with a particular move. Obviously, these are not complex models and would need to be adjusted for actual costing purposes.

Operational Activities

The examination of LTL and TL operations might result in the conclusion that they are significantly different in how they operate. Actually, they are very similar. The major difference between the two is in the dock rehandling that is associated with the LTL operations, not the TL. However, to move a shipment, both operations provide a pickup service, a line-haul service, and a delivery service. These three activities, along with dock rehandling for LTL, can be used to begin to break out the appropriate costs associated with a move.

Cost/Service Elements

Within each operational activity, those cost/service elements that will actually be responsible for shipment costs need to be identified. These cost/service elements can be defined as time, distance, and support. The time it takes a carrier to pick up, cross-dock, line-haul, and deliver a shipment will impact its fixed costs, such as depreciation and interest, because these costs are allocated and determined by units of time. The distance a carrier has to move a shipment during these operational activities will affect its variable costs, such as fuel and wages. Support costs, such as equipment insurance and maintenance, are considered semi-fixed and semi-variable because they will exist if no activity takes place but will increase as activity increases. Finally, shipment billing can be considered a fixed cost because normally the cost to generate a freight bill is not related to shipment size or distance.

Having identified four operational activities (pickup, cross-dock, line-haul, and delivery) and three cost/service elements (time, distance, and support), it is possible to develop a costing methodology that will allow the approximation of costs that a carrier could incur for moving a shipment.

TL Costing

This section will present a simplified TL costing model that can be used to approximate the costs of moving a shipment between two points. This model can be used for calculating headhaul costs but does not include an adjustment for a possible empty return trip. However, as will be seen, headhaul costs could be adjusted to compensate for variable costs of an empty backhaul.

The following scenario is used.

Shipment and Equipment Characteristics The shipment consists of 400 cartons at 90 pounds each with each carton measuring 3 cubic feet. Carriers' trailers have a weight capacity of 40,000 pounds and 2,880 cubic feet. The shipment weighs 36,000 pounds (90 percent of weight capacity) and occupies 1,200 cubic feet (almost 50 percent of trailer cubic capacity).

Equipment Cost Data

Equipment Purchase Price

1. Line-haul tractors = $80,000
2. Trailers = $24,000

Depreciation

1. Tractors = 5-year straight line
2. Trailers = 8-year straight line

Interest

1. Tractors = 10 percent APR for 5 years
2. Trailers = 10 percent APR for 8 years

Fuel

1. $2.10 per gallon for diesel
2. Line-haul tractors = 6.5 miles per gallon

Labor Cost

1. Line-haul drivers = $0.42 per mile
2. PUD operation drivers = $22.00 per hour

Miscellaneous

1. Insurance cost = $0.03 per mile
2. Maintenance cost = $0.15 per mile
3. Billing cost = $1.95 per freight bill
4. Tractors and trailers are available for use 365 days, 24 hours per day
5. Administrative/overhead cost = 10 percent of total cost of move

Route and Time of Move   The shipment originates on June 1, 2010, from Pennsylvania State University (located 35 miles from the carrier's dispatch/maintenance facility). A line-haul tractor and trailer are dispatched from the terminal at 7:30 a.m. (all times are Eastern Standard Time) and arrive at the shipper's dock at 8:30 a.m. The shipment is loaded from 8:30 a.m. to 12:00 p.m. Driver and tractor remain at Penn State during loading to visit the famous Nittany Lion statue. Driver and vehicle return to the carrier's terminal at 1:00 p.m. to pick up paperwork.

Total time for pickup = 5.5 hours

Total distance for pickup = 70 miles

The vehicle and the driver depart from the terminal at 1:00 p.m. on the same day for Dallas, Texas. The driver operates from 1:00 p.m. to 11:00 p.m. and travels 450 miles. The driver rests from 11:00 p.m. to 7:00 a.m. (on June 2) in Knoxville, Tennessee, and then operates another 8 hours (7:00 a.m. to 3:00 p.m.) and 375 miles. The driver rests again from 3:00 p.m. to 11:00 p.m. in Memphis, Tennessee. The driver concludes the trip by traveling 450 miles from 11:00 p.m. to 9:00 a.m. (June 3) to the consignee in Dallas, George Bush's summer home.

Total time for line-haul = 44 hours or 1.83 days

Total distance for line-haul = 1,275 miles

The trailer is unloaded from 9:00 a.m. to 12:00 p.m. with the driver and tractor remaining at the home to tour the museum dedicated to George Bush's college baseball days. The driver and vehicle then go to the carrier's Dallas terminal, located 45 miles from Bush's home, arriving at 1:00 p.m. to wait for further dispatch instructions.

Total time for delivery = 4 hours

Total distance for delivery = 45 miles

Cost Analysis Using the equipment cost data and the distance traveled and time elapsed for the shipment, an approximate cost for this move can be calculated. This analysis can be seen in Table 4B-1. In a real costing situation, certain changes might need to be made to the cost data included in this example. Tractor fuel economy, for example, might need to be increased or maintenance cost per mile might need to be decreased. The cost analyst would need to determine the appropriate levels for each cost element, depending on the type of equipment and nature of the move.

Pickup As can be seen in Table 4B-1, the pickup operation generated seven types of costs. *Depreciation expense* per hour is calculated by:

equipment cost/years depreciation/365/24.

This formula gives the hourly cost for depreciation for both the tractor and the trailer. *Interest expense (includes both principal plus interest)* per hour can be calculated using any interest payment calculator. The appropriate formulas can be found in tables in any introductory finance text.

Fuel cost per gallon and tractor fuel economy determine *fuel cost per mile*. This formula is:

fuel cost per gallon/miles per gallon

Labor, maintenance, insurance, and billing costs are given and are relatively easy to calculate. *Total pickup costs for this move are $185.46.*

Line-haul Notice that the line-haul costs categories for this move are the same as for the pickup operation, except for the billing expense. This is simply because only one freight bill needs to be generated for this move. This will also be seen by the absence of a billing cost in the delivery section.

Also, during the pickup operation, the driver was paid by the hour because waiting time was involved. In the line-haul section, the driver was paid by the mile. Obviously, pay scales for drivers will be determined by company or union policies. *Costs in the line-haul section are calculated in the same manner as they were in the pickup section.* Obviously, however, the time and distance generated by the line-haul activity are used. *Total line-haul costs for this move are $1,393.00.*

Table 4B-1	TL Costing Example			
I. Pickup				
1. Depreciation:	tractor	5.5 hr @ $1.83/hr =		$10.07
	trailer	5.5 hr @ $0.34/hr =		$1.87
2. Interest:	tractor	5.5 hr @ $2.33/hr =		$12.82
	trailer	5.5 hr @ $0.50/hr =		$2.75
3. Fuel		70 miles @ $0.32/mile =		$22.40
4. Labor		5.5 hr @ $22/hour =		$121.00
5. Maintenance		70 miles @ $0.15/mile =		$10.50
6. Insurance		70 miles @ $0.03/mile =		$2.10
7. Billing				$1.95
		TOTAL PICKUP COST		$185.46
II. Line-haul				
1. Depreciation:	tractor	44 hr @ $1.83/hr =		$80.52
	trailer	44 hr @ $0.34/hr =		$14.96
2. Interest:	tractor	44 hr @ $2.33/hr =		$102.52
	trailer	44 hr @ $0.50/hr =		$22.00
3. Fuel		1,275 miles @ $0.32/mile =		$408.00
4. Labor		1,275 miles @ $0.42/mile =		$535.50
5. Maintenance		1,275 miles @ $0.15/mile =		$191.25
6. Insurance		1,275 miles @ $0.03/mile =		$38.25
		TOTAL LINE-HAUL COST		$1393.00
III. Delivery				
1. Depreciation:	tractor	4 hr @ $1.83/hr =		$7.32
	trailer	4 hr @ $0..34/hr =		$1.36
2. Interest:	tractor	4 hr @ $2.33/hr =		$9.32
	trailer	4 hr @ $0.50/hr =		$2.00
3. Fuel		45 miles @ $0.32/mile =		$14.40
4. Labor		4 hr @ $22/hr =		$88.00
5. Maintenance		45 miles @ $0.15/mile =		$6.75
6. Insurance		45 miles @ $.03/mile =		$1.35
		TOTAL DELIVERY COST		$130.50

(continued)

Table 4B-1	Continued		
IV. Total cost			
1. Pickup, line-haul, delivery			$1708.96
2. Administrative/overhead (10%)			$170.90
		TOTAL TL COST	$1879.86
V. Revenue needs			
1. Per cwt ($1879.86/360) = $5.22			
2. Per revenue mile ($1879.86/1310 miles) = $1.44			

Delivery The delivery activity generates the same type of costs as did the pickup activity, except for billing. Again, the time and distance associated with delivery need to be used in calculating costs. *Costs for delivery are calculated in the same manner as they were in the pickup section. Total costs for delivery for this move are $130.50.*

Total Cost Adding the costs associated with pickup, line-haul, and delivery generates the total cost for this move of $1,708.96. Remember, however, that a 10-percent additional cost is added to make a contribution to the carrier's administration and overhead, so the *total cost for this move is $1,879.86.*

Revenue Needs Carriers quote prices in many forms. Two of the more common methods are price per hundredweight (cwt) and price per revenue, or loaded, mile. In this example, although profit has not yet been added, to recover the fully allocated or average cost for this move, the carrier would quote a *price per cwt of $5.22 ($1879.86/ 360.00 cwt)* or a *price per revenue mile of $1.44 ($1879.86/1310 miles).*

Once again, this model is a simplified version of those used by carriers. Certain adjustments and additions would need to be made to this model to make it more reflective of an actual move. However, it does give the analyst some idea of the approximate costs associated with a shipment.

LTL Costing

This section will present a simplified version of an LTL costing model. LTL costing is more difficult than TL costing because it requires arbitrary allocations of common and fixed costs to individual shipments. Although this does not make costing an LTL shipment impossible, it does require that the individual using the costs understand that averages and allocations were used. Thus, the resulting costs might not be as accurate as would be desired. However, this model will produce ballpark estimates for the cost of moving an individual shipment. *All* of the formulas for calculating depreciation costs, interest costs, and fuel costs are the same as those used in the TL costing example.

Shipment and Equipment Characteristics The shipment to be costed consists of 15 cartons, each weighing 40 pounds and measuring 16 cubic feet. The carrier's trailers have a weight capacity of 40,000 pounds and 2,880 cubic feet. This shipment then occupies 1.5 percent of the trailer's weight capacity and 8.3 percent of its cubic capacity. Because the cubic feet requirement is greater, it will be used to allocate costs in the line-haul move.

Equipment Cost Data

Equipment Purchase Price

1. PUD tractor = $55,000
2. LH tractor = $80,000
3. PUD trailer = $18,000
4. LH trailer = $24,000

Depreciation

1. Tractors = 5-year straight line
2. Trailers = 8-year straight line

Interest

1. Tractors = 10 percent APR for 5 years
2. Trailers = 10 percent APR for 8 years

Fuel

1. $2.10 per gallon for diesel
2. PUD tractors = 7.5 miles per gallon
3. LH tractors = 6.5 miles per gallon

Labor Cost

1. PUD drivers = $22.00 per hour
2. Dock handlers = $20.00 per hour
3. LH drivers = $22.00 per hour

Miscellaneous

1. Terminal variable cost per shipment at both origin and destination = $1.00
2. Terminal fixed cost per shipment at both origin and destination = $1.50
3. PUD equipment maintenance cost = $0.15 per mile
4. LH equipment maintenance cost = $0.15 per mile
5. PUD equipment insurance cost = $0.03 per mile
6. LH equipment insurance cost = $0.03 per mile
7. Billing cost = $1.95 per bill
8. Equipment is available 365 days, 24 hours per day
9. Administrative/overhead cost = 10 percent of total cost of move

Route and Time of Movement The shipment is picked up by the carrier's driver in a PUD city tractor/trailer unit on June 1, 2010, as one of 23 stops made by the driver that day from 7:30 a.m. to 6:30 p.m. The stops covered a total of 60 miles within the Altoona, Pennsylvania, satellite terminal service area. The shipment was one of four handled by the carrier at this particular shipper's location. Once the pickup vehicle returns to the Altoona terminal, it takes 15 minutes to move the shipment from the city unit across the dock to the line-haul trailer.

Total time for pickup = 11 hours
Total distance for pickup = 60 miles
Total dock time = 15 minutes

The line-haul tractor/trailer departs from the Altoona terminal at 11:00 p.m. on June 1 and arrives at the Cleveland break-bulk terminal, which is approximately 200 miles from the Altoona satellite, at 4:00 a.m. on June 2. The shipment moves from the line-haul trailer across the dock to a PUD city tractor/trailer unit in 15 minutes.

Total time of line-haul = 5 hours

Total distance for line-haul = 200 miles

Total dock time = 15 minutes

The shipment is delivered to the Cleveland consignee by the PUD driver in a PUD city tractor/trailer unit on June 2 as one of 16 stops made by the driver over the period from 7:30 a.m. to 6:00 p.m. The stops covered a total of 45 miles in the Cleveland area. This shipment is one of three delivered to this particular consignee by the driver.

Total time for delivery = 10.5 hours

Total distance for delivery = 45 miles

Cost Analysis With the equipment cost data and route and time of movement, an individual LTL shipment can be costed. This analysis can be seen in Table 4B-2. Once again, *the calculations for depreciation, interest, and fuel costs are the same as they were in the TL example.*

Pickup In this example, a PUD tractor and trailer were used in the pickup operation. This is specialized equipment that really has no alternative uses in the line-haul operation. As such, when this equipment is done with the PUD operation during the day, it will normally sit idle at the satellite terminal. This explains why a full day's depreciation and interest are charged to both the PUD tractor and PUD trailer, even though they were only utilized for 11 hours during this particular day. Some arguments might exist that this places an excessive cost burden on these shipments through fixed-cost allocation. This might be true. However, the cost analyst must make the decision as to where fixed costs will be recovered. If not through this allocation, then fixed costs must be covered by some other method so debt can be serviced and plans for equipment replacement can be implemented.

The fuel, labor, maintenance, and insurance cost calculations are relatively straightforward. *Total route costs for this move are $353.18.* Remember, however, that this cost is for all shipments picked up and delivered by the driver during the day. This calculation is for the cost of only one shipment. To do this, first divide the total route cost by the number of stops made by the driver. *This results in a route cost per stop of $15.36.* Second, divide the per stop cost by the number of shipments at the shipper's location that had the individual shipment. *This results in a route cost per shipment of $3.84.* Both the stop cost and the shipment cost are averages that assume that each stop is basically the same and each shipment is the same. Adjustments could be made to these figures to more accurately reflect the time and distance actually used for the individual shipment. Remember, however, the per-shipment-route costs used in this example are averages.

Shipment costs are those assigned to each individual shipment that are not generated by the PUD operation. Billing, terminal variable cost, and terminal fixed cost are not dependent on shipment size but are allocated to each shipment. The shipment took 15 minutes for its cross-dock operation resulting in the dock charge of $5.00.

Table 4B-2	LTL Costing Example			
I. Pickup				
A. Route Costs				
1. Depreciation:	PUD tractor	1 day @ $30.14/day =	$30.14	
	PUD trailer	1 day @ $6.16/day =	$6.16	
2. Interest:	PUD tractor	1 day @ $38.40/day =	$38.40	
	PUD trailer	1 day @ $8.88/day =	$8.88	
3. Fuel		60 miles @ $0.28/mile =	$16.80	
4. Labor		11 hr @ $22/hr =	$242.00	
5. Maintenance		60 miles @ $0.15/mile =	$9.00	
6. Insurance		60 miles @ $0.03/mile =	$1.80	
	SUBTOTAL		$353.18	
	# Stops		23	
	COST PER STOP		$15.36	
	# Shipments at stop		4	
	ROUTE COST PER SHIPMENT			$3.84
B. Shipment Costs				
1. Billing			$1.95	
2. Terminal variable cost			$1.00	
3. Terminal fixed cost			$1.50	
4. Dock		0.25 hr @ $20/hr =	$5.00	
	INDIVIDUAL SHIPMENT COST		$9.45	
C. Total Pickup Cost Per Shipment				$13.29
II. Line-haul				
1. Depreciation:	LH tractor	5 hr @ $1.83/hr =	$9.15	
	LH trailer	5 hr @ $0.34/hr =	$1.70	
2. Interest:	LH tractor	5 hr @ $2.33/h. =	$11.65	
	LH trailer	5 hr @ $0.50/hr =	$2.50	
3. Fuel		200 miles @ $0.32/mile =	$64.00	
4. Labor		5 hr @ $22/hr =	$110.00	

(continued)

Table 4B-2	Continued		
5. Maintenance		200 miles @ $0.15/mile =	$30.00
6. Insurance		200 miles @ $0.03/mile =	$6.00
	TOTAL LINE-HAUL FULL TRAILER		$235.00
	% capacity occupied by shipment		8.3%
	SHIPMENT LINE-HAUL COST		$19.51
III. Delivery			
A. Route Costs			
1. Depreciation:	PUD tractor	1 day @ $30.14/day =	$30.14
	PUD trailer	1 day @ $6.16/day =	$6.16
2. Interest:	PUD tractor	1 day @ $38.40/day =	$38.40
	PUD trailer	1 day @ $8.88/day =	$8.88
3. Fuel		45 miles @ $0.28/mile =	$12.60
4. Labor		10.5 hr @ $22/hr =	$231.00
5. Maintenance		45 miles @ $0.15/mile =	$6.75
6. Insurance		45 miles @ $0.03/mile =	$1.35
	SUBTOTAL		$335.28
	# Stops		16
	COST PER STOP	$20.96	
	# Shipments at stop		3
	ROUTE COST PER SHIPMENT		$6.99
B. Shipment Costs			
1. Terminal variable cost			$1.00
2. Terminal fixed cost			$1.50
3. Dock		0.25 hr @ $20/hr =	$5.00
	INDIVIDUAL SHIPMENT COST		$7.50
C. Total Delivery Cost Per Shipment			$14.49
IV. Total Cost Per Shipment			
1. Pickup, dock, line-haul, delivery			$47.29
2. Administrative/overhead (10 percent)			$4.73
	TOTAL COST PER SHIPMENT		$52.02
V. Revenue Needs			
1. Per cwt ($52.02/6)			$8.67

Total shipment cost for this move is $9.45. Combining the route cost per shipment and the shipment cost results in a total pickup cost per shipment of $13.29.

Line-haul Depreciation and interest for the line-haul equipment is charged only for the actual time the shipment is on this equipment. This is the same as in the TL example. Unlike the PUD equipment, this assumes that the line-haul equipment has alternative uses and is 100 percent utilized. Again, actual utilization rates can be used to adjust the allocation of depreciation and interest charges.

As previously mentioned, the shipment occupied 8.3 percent of the cubic capacity of the line-haul trailer. This is the basis used for allocating line-haul costs in a *line-haul cost per shipment of $19.51*. This allocation method assumes that all shipments in the line-haul trailer have approximately the same pounds per cubic foot requirement and that the trailer would probably be cubed out. The analyst might want to make adjustments for this based on the known average weight and cube per shipment in the carrier's system.

Delivery The calculations for delivery cost are the same as those used for pickup costs. For route shipment cost, 16 stops and 3 stops per shipment are used to determine the *average route cost per shipment of $6.99*. Shipment costs are also the same, except that billing cost is not included, resulting in a *shipment cost of $7.50 and a total delivery cost per shipment of $14.49.*

Total Shipment Cost Combining the pickup cost of $13.29, the line-haul cost of $19.51, and the delivery cost of $14.49 results in a total cost per shipment of $47.29. Remember, like the TL example, a 10 percent cost is added to cover administrative and other overhead expenses, resulting in a *total cost for the shipment of $52.02.*

Revenue Needs Although prices are quoted in many different forms in the LTL industry, one popular form is in price per cwt. Taking the total shipment charge of $52.02 and dividing it by 6 cwt results in a *price per cwt of $8.67*. Remember this price does not yet include an allowance for profit for the carrier.

Conclusion

Determining the cost for a particular shipment can be a very complex and time-consuming task.

Detailed data requirements and knowledge of a carrier's operations are necessary inputs to developing accurate costs. However, a simplified approach can be taken to shipment costing that does not need these complex requirements and results in approximate shipment costs. Thus, the advantage of these costing models is their simplicity and ease of calculation. Their disadvantage is that they use general data, allocations, and averages to determine shipment costs. The analyst must trade off these characteristics to determine the level of complexity needed for costing and whether these models will provide a sufficient level of cost detail.

Suggested Readings

Chapter 1 Transportation: Critical Link in the Supply Chain

Burnson, Patrick, "The State of Logistics: Under the Weather," *Logistics Management* (July 2008): 29–32.

Fitzgerald, Tina, Tim Brown, and Elizabeth Stewart, "Subway's Journey to Green," *Logistics Management* (April 2009): 22–27.

Moser, George, and Peter Ward, "Which TMS Is Right for You?" *Logistics Management* (July 2008): 59S–64S.

Quinn, John Paul, "Mid-year Rate Outlook: Uncertainty Persists," *Logistics Management* (July 2008): 44–48.

Tanowitz, Marc, and David Rutchik, "Squeezing Opportunity Out of Higher Fuel Costs," *Supply Chain Management Review,* Vol. 12 (2008): 34.

Chapter 2 Transportation: Critical Link in the Economy

Berman, Jeff, "Obama's Focus on Infrastructure May Spur Economic Recovery," *Logistics Management* (January 2009): 15–16.

O'Reilly, Joseph, "Night Moves," *Inbound Logistics* (May 2009): 28–30.

"Pocket Guide to Transportation 2009," *Bureau of Transportation Statistics* (January 2009).

Salzman, Randy, "What's Down the Road for Surface Transportation?" *World Trade* (May 2009): 32.

Schulz, John D., "Donahue Declares Infrastructure Investments a Must," *Logistics Management* (February 2009): 15–16.

Chapter 3 Transportation Regulation and Public Policy

"Building Highways, Again," *Traffic World* (December 15, 2008): 13–14.

Burnson, Patrick, "Time's Up!" *Logistics Management* (February 2009): 37–38.

Farris, M. Theodore, II, and Terrance L Pohlen, "Deregulation Delayed Is Deregulation Denied: Appealing the Wright Amendment," *Transportation Journal,* Vol. 45, No. 4 (Fall 2006): 67–71.

Skalberg, Randall K., "The U.S. Harbor Maintenance Tax: A Bad Idea Whose Time Has Passed?" *Transportation Journal,* Vol. 46, No. 3 (Summer 2007): 59–70.

"Truckers Urge: 'Eisenhower-like Commitment' in Highway Bill Funding," *Logistics Management* (May 2009): 20–21.

Chapter 4 Costing and Pricing for Transportation

Baatz, Elizabeth, "Pricing Across the Transportation Modes: Price Trends," *Logistics Management* (September 2008): 13.

Bohman, Ray, "The Importance of Freight Classification in Today's Pricing Market," *Logistics Management* (February 2009): 19–20.

Bohman, Ray, "Home Delivery Carrier Offer Many Pricing Options," *Logistics Management* (January 2009): 23.

"FedEx Hits Reverse," *Traffic World* (January 5, 2009): 29.

Quinn, John Paul, "Window of Opportunity: 2009 Logistics Rate Outlook," *Logistics Management* (January 2009): 29–32.

Sailor, Tim, "Part and Parcel," *Traffic World* (December 15, 2008): 19–22.

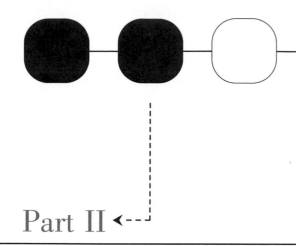

Part II

The first four chapters of this text provided a background of the environment faced by the transportation industry. Chapters 1 and 2 discussed the role of transportation in the economy and in the firm, respectively. Chapter 3 discussed the nature of transportation and public policy and how they affect the transportation industry. Chapter 4 provided a basic discussion of the economics of costs and pricing for transportation providers.

Part II of this text focuses on each of the five modes of transportation. Each modal chapter contains an industry overview, operating and service characteristics, cost structure, and current challenges and issues.

Chapter 5 focuses on the motor carrier industry and differentiates between both truckload (TL) and less-than-truckload (LTL) carrier operations. The impact of volatile diesel fuel prices on industry profits is highlighted in the Transportation Profile. A detailed discussion of LTL network structures and network decisions is also offered in this chapter. Finally, the new Federal Highway Trust Fund Tax rates on motor carriers are discussed.

Chapter 6 examines the railroad industry and its current operations. Special attention is given to recent attempts by the federal government to reregulate the railroad industry. A detailed discussion of new service innovations, including TOFC and COFC, is given focusing on the growth of intermodal carloadings in the railroad industry. Because volatile fuel prices have substantial impacts on all transportation modes, a comparison is made in this chapter between railroad fuel efficiency and the other modes of transportation.

The airline industry is the topic of **Chapter 7**. As with the other modal chapters, a discussion of the impact of volatile fuel prices on the airline industry is offered. Along with this cost impact, labor costs in the airline industry are also discussed. This chapter offers a comprehensive view of aircraft operating characteristics as well as a listing of the top airports in the United States. Because safety is critical in passenger air travel, a comparison of passenger fatalities between airlines and other passenger modes is offered.

Finally, **Chapter 8** presents a discussion of bulk carriers (water and pipeline). The historical development and significance of these modes are presented along with a discussion of the current status of each mode. The cost structures of each mode are presented along with their impacts on carrier operations and competitive advantage. Finally, the basics of intramodal and intermodal competition for each mode are examined.

Chapter 5

MOTOR CARRIERS

Learning Objectives

After reading this chapter, you should be able to do the following:

- Understand the development of motor carriers and their contributions to the U.S. economy
- Be familiar with the different types of firms in the motor carrier industry
- Appreciate the market forces shaping the motor carrier industry
- Gain knowledge of the service characteristics of motor carriers
- Identify the different types of vehicles and terminals used in the motor carrier industry
- Understand the impact of fuel and labor on the motor carrier cost structure
- Be aware of current issues facing the motor carrier industry

Transportation Profile

Fuel Eats Away Profits and Capacity

The truckload (TL) sector's hopes for a recovery in 2009 can be summarized in two words—fuel and capacity.

Fuel costs in some cases have exceeded labor as the highest expense for some big TL carriers and have surged to record-breaking levels, while fuel surcharges have helped blunt the record rise in diesel costs.

Shippers are paying as much as 50 percent in surcharges on a typical TL freight bill. But some TL carrier executives admit privately there is no sufficient business model to cope with $135-a-barrel crude oil or $4.50-a-gallon diesel.

But some shippers are pushing back on fuel surcharges; and that is causing much angst among TL executives who worry how high fuel surcharges can rise before shippers revolt—or bolt.

All this has caused many large TL carriers to reduce their over-the-road capacity in favor of shorter regional freight routes and intermodal for longer hauls. Among the carriers doing this are J.B. Hunt, Werner Enterprises, and Knight Transportation. All told, TL capacity dropped 3.6 percent the first two months of this year, according to a survey by the American Trucking Associations (ATA), the largest drop in capacity since it began its survey in 1997.

There are exceptions: Schneider National, the nation's second largets TL carrier, has increased over-the-road capacity by 7 percent in the past 15 months. Celadon, a major north-south TL carrier which gets about half of its $501 million annual revenue from traffic in and out of Mexico, says it raised capacity by a similar amount in the past 15 months.

The overcapacity that has plagued the TL sector since the record level of Class 8 trucks sales in 2006 (280,000 units sold, compared to 145,000 last year) is just about over, analysts say. Thom Albrecht, trucking analyst for Stephens, Inc., is anticipating that supply and demand will be close to equilibrium by the end of this year's third quarter.

He says it's too early to tell whether truckload rates will recover in a "V-shaped" manner or at a more gradually paced "U-shaped" curve. Still, Albrecht says the stage is being set for 2009 to represent a "meaningful recovery" for the TL sector.

Such a recovery may come at the expense of some smaller, less financially stable carriers. Already nearly 1,000 mostly small TL carriers have ceased operations this year. Albrecht is predicting "at least a couple thousand more casualties" this year as the pain of $4.50 per gallon diesel fuel prices (or higher) takes their toll.

So, the word for TL shippers in 2008 is this: Enjoy the break in rates that you've experienced over the past two years because when the recovery hits, capacity may not be sufficient. That will surely mean sharply higher rates.

Source: John Schultz, *Logistics Management,* July 2008, p. 36. Reprinted by permission.

Introduction

The motor carrier industry played an important role in the development of the U.S. economy during the 20th century, and it continues this role in the 21st century. The growth of this industry is noteworthy considering it did not get started until World War I, when converted automobiles were utilized for pickup and delivery in local areas. The railroad industry, which traditionally had difficulty with small shipments that had

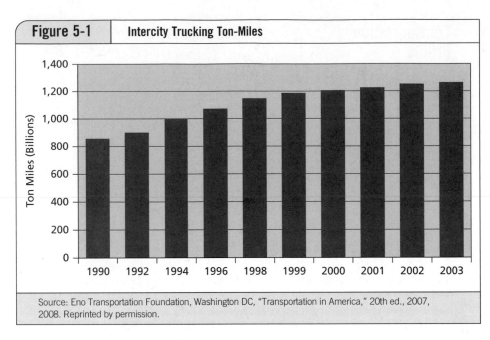

Figure 5-1 | **Intercity Trucking Ton-Miles**

Source: Eno Transportation Foundation, Washington DC, "Transportation in America," 20th ed., 2007, 2008. Reprinted by permission.

to be moved short distances, encouraged the early motor carrier entrepreneurs. It was not until after World War II that the railroad industry began to seriously attempt to compete with the motor carrier industry, and by that time it was too late.

The United States has spent more than $128.9 billion to construct its **interstate highway system** and in the process has become increasingly dependent on this system for the movement of freight. The major portion of this network evolved as the result of a bill signed into law in 1956 by President Dwight D. Eisenhower to establish the National System of Interstate and Defense Highways, which was to be funded 90 percent by the federal government through fuel taxes.

As the interstate system of highways developed from the 1950s to 1980, motor carriers steadily replaced railroads as the mode of choice for transporting finished and unfinished manufactured products. In 1950 the railroad industry moved 1.4 billion tons of freight on an intercity basis, whereas motor carriers moved 800 million tons. In 1980 railroads moved 1.6 billion tons, compared to more than 200 billion tons by motor carriers. By 2006 motor carriers were handling 10.7 billion tons (see Figures 5-1 and 5-2).

Industry Overview

Significance

In 2006 the United States paid over $645.6 billion for highway transportation, approximately 83.8 percent of the total 2006 Nation's Freight Bill.[1] Motor carriers transported 1,264 billion revenue freight ton-miles in 2003, or 31 percent of the ton-miles transported by all modes.[2] During 2005, approximately 8.7 million people were employed in the motor carrier industry, with an average annual compensation of $51,683.[3] These figures clearly demonstrate the significant role that motor carriers play in our society and the dependence of U.S. companies on motor carrier service. Finally, motor carriers logged 432.9 billion miles used for business purposes in 2006 (excluding the government and farm sectors).[4]

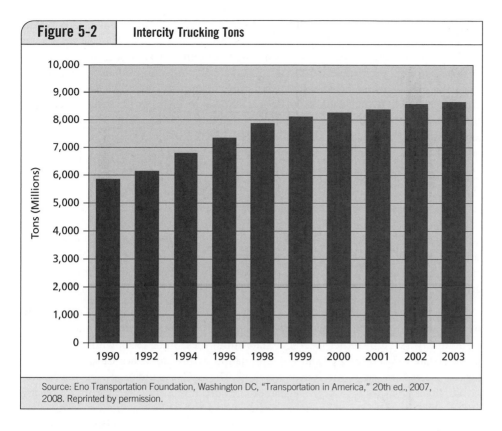

Figure 5-2 | Intercity Trucking Tons

Source: Eno Transportation Foundation, Washington DC, "Transportation in America," 20th ed., 2007, 2008. Reprinted by permission.

Types of Carriers

The first major division of motor carriers is between for-hire and private carriers. The **for-hire** carrier provides services to the public and charges a fee for the service. The private carrier provides a service to the industry or company that owns or leases the vehicles, and thus does not charge a fee, but obviously the service provider incurs cost. Private carriers might transport commodities for-hire, but when operating in such a capacity, the private carrier is really an exempt for-hire carrier.

For-hire carriers can be either local or intercity operators, or both. The local carriers pick up and deliver freight within the commercial zone of a city. The intercity carriers operate between specifically defined commercial zones to include the corporate limits of a municipality plus adjacent areas beyond the corporate limits determined by the municipal population. Local carriers frequently work in conjunction with intercity carriers to pick up or deliver freight in the commercial zone.

The for-hire carriers may be common and/or contract operators. The common carriers are required to serve the general public upon demand, at reasonable rates, and without discrimination. The contract carriers serve specific shippers with whom the carriers have a continuing contract; thus, the contract carrier is not available for general public use. Contract carriers also typically adapt their equipment and service to meet shipper needs. Shippers must choose to use a commercial carrier or to operate their own private fleet. The decision is based on what is best for their business. Trade-offs exist for both options, but the decision will ultimately be determined by the needs of the shipper.

Another important distinction is between the truckload (**TL**) and less-than-truckload (**LTL**) carriers. The truckload carriers provide service to shippers who tender sufficient volume to meet the minimum weights required for a truckload shipment and truckload rate or who will pay the difference. Less-than-truckload carriers provide service to shippers who tender shipments lower than the minimum truckload quantities, such as 50 to 10,000 pounds. Consequently, the LTL carrier must consolidate the numerous smaller shipments into truckload quantities for the line-haul (intercity) movement and disaggregate the full truckloads at the destination city for delivery in smaller quantities. In contrast, the TL carrier picks up a truckload and delivers the same truckload at the destination.

A hybrid type of carrier that has developed can best be characterized as a "heavy LTL" motor carrier. Shipment sizes carried by this type of carrier are in the upper end of what can be considered LTL shipments (that is, 12,000 to 25,000 pounds). This carrier utilizes consolidation terminals (like LTL carriers) to fully load trailers but does not utilize break-bulk facilities for deliveries. Rather, it delivers from the trailer, much like a "pool" carrier, charging line-haul rates plus a charge for each stop-off (like TL carriers). This type of carrier specializes in shipment sizes less than the TL carriers haul and more than LTL carriers haul. It has some fixed costs (because of the consolidation terminals) but not as much as in the LTL industry.

Finally, interstate common carriers might be classified by the type of commodity they are authorized to haul. Historically, motor carriers were required to have operating authority issued by either federal or state authorities. Since 1996, with the repeal of the Interstate Commerce Act and the elimination of the Interstate Commerce Commission, such authority is no longer required. The ICC Termination Act of 1995 removed virtually all motor carrier regulation and preempted the states from exercising any economic control over the motor carrier industry. Carriers are now only required to register with the Federal Motor Carrier Safety Administration and provide proof of insurance. They can then transport any commodity they wish, with only household goods and related items being subject to any economic oversight.

Number of Carriers

The motor carrier industry consists of a large number of small carriers, particularly in the TL (truckload) segment of the industry. As illustrated in Figure 5-3, as of 2008 a total of 616,187 interstate motor carriers were on file with the Office of Motor Carriers. Of these carriers, 87 percent operate with six or fewer vehicles.[5] This figure supports the small firm composition of the for-hire carrier industry. Keep in mind that many businesses do use their own private fleet.

A further explanation of the large number of small carriers is the limited capital needed to enter the TL industry. A motor carrier can be formed with as little as $5,000 to $10,000 equity, and the balance can be financed with the vehicle serving as collateral for the loan. However, LTL carriers have terminals that increase the capital requirements and thus add a constraint to entry.

There is a significant difference between TL and LTL carriers, both in terms of number and start-up costs. The great growth that occurred in the 1980s, when regulated carriers more than doubled, happened primarily in small TL carriers because of the low start-up costs indicated earlier.

The LTL segment of the motor carrier industry requires a network of terminals to consolidate and distribute freight, called a "hub-and-spoke" system. The large LTL carriers moved to expand their geographic coverage after 1980, and many of them eliminated their TL service. Because of this relatively high level of fixed costs, the LTL

Figure 5-3	U.S. Distribution of Motor Carriers

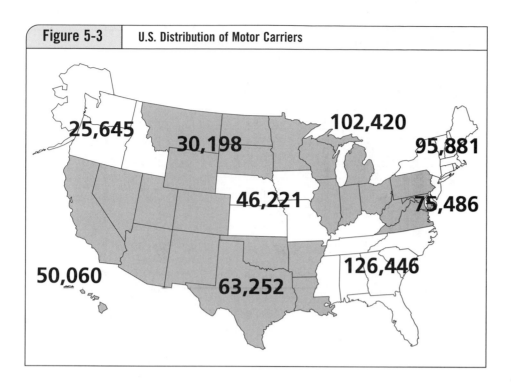

industry has continued to consolidate. In August 2003, Yellow Corporation announced that it would buy Roadway Corporation for $1.1 billion. After it was approved by the appropriate government agencies, this consolidation created a company that controls approximately 29 percent of the national LTL carrier market.[6]

Perhaps a brief description of an LTL operation would be helpful here. Shippers that have small shipping requirements use LTL carriers (for example, the cubic capacity of a 53-foot trailer is not needed for the shipment). Also, the LTL shipper typically has shipments headed for more than one destination. The LTL carrier collects the shipments at the shipper's dock with a **pickup and delivery (PUD)** vehicle. This vehicle, as its name implies, does the collection and delivery of all shipments. After a PUD vehicle has finished collecting and delivering shipments, it returns to a consolidation or break-bulk facility. Once at the consolidation facility, the packages collected are sorted by their final destination. The next part of the trip is called the **line-haul** segment. For this portion of the trip, the shipments are loaded into 28-foot, 48-foot, or 53-foot trailers. If 28-foot trailers are used, they are hooked together in combinations of twos and threes, depending on the state's trailer configuration permitted over the route of travel. The 28-foot trailer is used in this situation because it is easier to unload two 28-foot trailers at separate bays than to unload one 48-foot or 53-foot trailer at one bay. Another reason for using the 28-foot trailer is because LTL carriers find that it is easier to utilize the capacity of a 28-foot trailer. After the line-haul portion of the trip, the trailers are unloaded at another break-bulk facility and are then sorted and reloaded into a PUD vehicle to be delivered to the receiver.

The TL segment of the industry has been experiencing some limited concentration. Carriers such as J. B. Hunt and Schneider National have become increasingly larger. The ability of the larger TL carriers to compete effectively with small TL companies with their value-added services might change the structure of the TL segment.

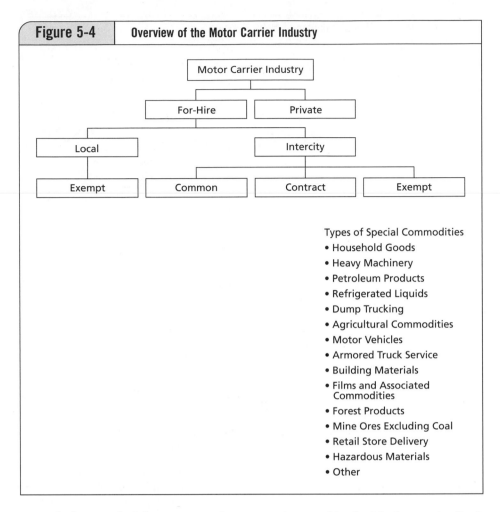

Figure 5-4 | Overview of the Motor Carrier Industry

Types of Special Commodities
- Household Goods
- Heavy Machinery
- Petroleum Products
- Refrigerated Liquids
- Dump Trucking
- Agricultural Commodities
- Motor Vehicles
- Armored Truck Service
- Building Materials
- Films and Associated Commodities
- Forest Products
- Mine Ores Excluding Coal
- Retail Store Delivery
- Hazardous Materials
- Other

With the repeal of the Interstate Commerce Act, combined with changes in distribution patterns, a climate was created in which new TL carriers could easily enter the business (see Figure 5-4). The "trucking recession" of 1994 and 1995, during which capacity greatly exceeded demand, removed many of the weaker firms either through bankruptcy or merger. However, low start-up costs in this sector still enabled new entrants to attempt success in this area.

Market Structure

When discussing the motor carrier industry, consideration must be given to the commodities hauled. Motor carrier vehicles, both for-hire and private, primarily transport manufactured, high-value products. These vehicles carry more than a majority of the various manufactured commodity categories. The commodity list includes food products and manufactured products, consumer goods, and industrial goods. In addition, these vehicles transport almost all of the sheep, lambs, cattle, calves, and hogs moving to stockyards.[7]

Motor carriers transport less of commodities such as grain, primary nonferrous metal products, motor vehicles and equipment, and paper and allied products. Because such commodities generally must move long distances and in large volumes, shipping them by rail and water is usually less expensive.

From a market structure perspective, the TL market can be considered as monopolistic competition. With the low entrance to market requirements (that is, capital), individuals can easily obtain equipment and begin operation within a specific geographic region. The LTL market, on the other hand, is oligopolistic in nature. This is the result of the significant investment needed by these carriers in break-bulk and other facilities. As such, barriers to entry exist in the LTL industry.

Competition

Motor carriers compete vigorously with one another for freight. With the large number of for-hire motor carriers, rivalry between firms can be intense. However, the most severe competition for for-hire carriers often comes from the private carrier.

As indicated earlier, the TL motor carrier industry offers few capital constraints to entry. With a relatively small investment, an individual can start a motor carrier business and compete with an existing carrier. Thus, freedom of entry, discounting, and lack of regulatory constraints appear to dominate the industry and suggest that competition between firms can control the industry. Such a conclusion has been the basis for greater reliance on the marketplace and less reliance on regulation. Even though the LTL segment is more concentrated, there is still intense competition between the top carriers. Other competitors include United Parcel Service, FedEx, and FedEx Ground.

Certain segments of motor carriers have higher capital requirements than others, as indicated, and therefore have some degree of capital constraint for entry. The major segment that has extensive capital requirements for entry is the LTL carrier. The LTL carrier must invest in terminals and freight-handling equipment that are simply not needed by the TL carrier. Special equipment carriers—carriers of liquefied gases or frozen products—usually have larger investments in equipment and terminals than those involved with general freight. The large TL carriers like J. B. Hunt and Schneider National also have significant capital investment.

On the whole, the motor carrier industry, especially for contract carriers, has been market oriented. Meeting customer requirements has been a common trait of motor carriers. The small size of the majority of for-hire carriers allows them to give individualized attention to customers. As carriers have grown in size, this close carrier–customer

---

Global Perspectives   *Border Brawl*

The Mexican government has placed tariffs on 90 American agricultural and manufactured exports as payback for the U.S. Congress' decision to officially nix the cross-border trucking pilot program between the U.S. and Mexico. The program was eliminated as part of the recently passed $410 billion Omnibus Appropriations Act, H.R. 1105, which was signed by President Barack Obama. Launched in September 2007, the program permitted up to 100 carefully-screened Mexican trucking companies into the U.S. for international deliveries and to operate beyond the 20-to-25 mile commercial zones along the U.S. Southwest border. But since its inception, the program was plagued by obstacles and set-backs, including a September 2008 Senate vote to terminate the program and a July 2007 amendment that intended to remove funding.

Source: *Logistics Management,* April 2009, p. 2. Reprinted by permission.

relationship has been strained. However, the responsiveness to customer demands for service still dominates all motor carrier organizations, and shippers expect carriers to respond to their needs.

Operating and Service Characteristics

General Service Characteristics

The growth and widespread use of motor carrier transportation can be traced to the inherent service characteristics of this mode. In particular, the motor carrier possesses a distinct advantage over other modes in the area of accessibility. The motor carrier can provide service to virtually any location as operating authority of the for-hire carrier no longer places restrictions on the areas served and commodities transported. Motor carrier access is not constrained by waterways, rail tracks, or airport locations. The U.S. system of highways is so pervasive that virtually every shipping and receiving location is accessible via highways. Therefore, motor carriers have potential access to almost every origin and destination.

The accessibility advantage of motor carriers is evident in the pickup or delivery of freight in an urban area. It is very rare to find urban areas not served by a pickup–delivery network. In fact, motor carriers provide the bridge between the pickup and delivery point and the facilities of other modes; that is, the motor carrier is referred to as the universal coordinator.

Another service advantage of the motor carrier is speed. For shipments going under 800 miles, the motor carrier vehicle can usually deliver the goods in less time than other modes. Although the airplane travels at a higher speed, the problem of getting freight to and from the airport via motor carrier adds to the air carrier's total transit time. In fact, the limited, fixed schedules of the air carriers might make motor carriers the faster method even for longer distances. For example, a delivery to a destination 800 miles away might take 17.8 hours by motor carrier (800 miles at 45 mph). Although the flying time between airports is 1.5 hours, 3 hours might be needed for pickup and 3 hours for delivery, plus time for moving the freight from one vehicle to another. If the airline has scheduled only one flight per day, the shipment could wait up to 24 hours before being dispatched. The motor carrier, however, proceeds directly from the shipper's door to the consignee's door. This service advantage became evident in the wake of September 11, 2001, when U.S. air traffic was shut down. The U.S. Post Office issued a statement alerting customers of delays for any package or letter traveling more than 800 miles because any Post Office shipment moving over 800 miles travels by air and under 800 miles travels by motor carrier.

When compared to the railcar and barge, the smaller **carrying capacity** of the motor carrier vehicle enables the shipper to use the TL rate, or volume discount, with a lower volume. Many TL minimum weights are established at 20,000 to 30,000 pounds. Rail carload minimum weights are often set at 40,000 to 60,000 pounds, and barge minimums are set in terms of hundreds of tons. The smaller shipping size of the motor carrier provides the buyer and seller with the benefits of lower inventory levels, lower inventory-carrying costs, and more frequent services.

Another positive service characteristic is the smoothness of transport. Given the suspension system and the pneumatic tires used on their vehicles, the motor carrier ride is smoother than rail and water transport and less likely to result in damage to the cargo (although there can still be some cargo damage with motor carrier transportation). This relatively damage-free service reduces the packaging requirements and thus packaging costs.

Lastly, the for-hire segment of the motor carrier industry is customer or market oriented. The small size of most carriers has enabled or even forced the carriers to respond to customer equipment and service needs.

Equipment

Many of the motor carrier service advantages emanate from the technical features of the transportation vehicle. The high degree of flexibility, the relatively smooth ride, and the small carrying capacity of the vehicle are the unique characteristics that result in greater accessibility, capability, frequency of delivery and pickup, cargo safety, and lower transit time.

The motor carrier vehicle can also be loaded quickly. A railroad operation needs to collect a number of freight cars to be pulled by one power unit; the motor carrier has just one or two. The ability to operate one cargo unit eliminates the time needed to collect several cargo units.

The other dimension of motor carrier equipment flexibility is the lack of highway constraint. Unlike the railroad and water carriers, the motor carrier is not constrained to providing service over a fixed railway or waterway. The motor carrier can travel over the highway, paved or unpaved, servicing virtually every conceivable consignee in the United States.[8] There are, however, gross vehicle weight and axle weight restrictions on vehicles while traveling the highway system.

In most cases, equipment represents the largest operating asset that a carrier maintains. With all of the different types and locations of equipment, positioning becomes critical to successful operations. Seasonal influences such as holidays or harvest times must also be considered, as they can drastically alter demand.

TL and LTL carriers need to make two types of equipment decisions: type of tractor (power) and type of trailer. In a TL operation, equipment positioning at terminals is not as important as in an LTL operation. However, power must be specified to be able to handle the size and length of the load, along with the terrain over which it travels. Many different specifications for tractors can be used, including single axle and twin axle, with different engine and drive train combinations. Decisions regarding trailers include length (28 feet, 45 feet, 48 feet, 53 feet, and so on) and trailer type (dry van, refrigerated, ragtop, container, flatbed, and so forth). These decisions will be made in light of market demands and the type of carrier operation.

LTL carriers must make the same types of equipment decisions as TL carriers along with deciding where to deploy this equipment. Similar to an airline equipment decision, LTL carriers need to position certain types of equipment at certain terminals. For example, city delivery vehicles and tractor–trailer combinations (either 28-foot or 40-foot trailers) will be positioned at PUD terminals, whereas line-haul trailers (usually 45, 48, or 53 feet) and line-haul tractors (single or twin axle) will be assigned to breakbulks. Compounding the LTL decision is the inclusion of 28-foot trailers (also called *pups, twins,* or *double bottoms*) in the equipment decision. Having the right mix of power and trailers at a particular terminal location determines the ability to efficiently serve customers.

Types of Vehicles

Motor carrier vehicles are either line-haul or city vehicles. Line-haul vehicles are used to haul freight long distances between cities. City straight trucks are used within a city to provide pickup and delivery service. On occasion, line-haul vehicles also will operate within a city, but the line-haul vehicle is normally not very efficient when operated this way.

Line-Haul Vehicles The line-haul vehicle is usually a tractor–trailer combination of three or more axles (see Figure 5-5). The cargo-carrying capacity of these vehicles depends on the size (length) and the state maximum weight limits. A tractor–trailer combination with five axles (tandem-axle tractor and trailer) is permitted in most states to haul a maximum of 80,000 pounds gross weight (110,000 pounds in Michigan). For a vehicle to run with more than five axles, a permit is required. If the empty vehicle weighs 30,000 pounds, the maximum net payload is 50,000 pounds or 25 tons.

The net carrying capacity of line-haul vehicles is also affected by the density of the freight. A 53 × 8 × 8-foot trailer has 3,392 cubic feet of space. If the commodity has a density of 10 pounds per cubic foot, then the maximum payload for the vehicle is

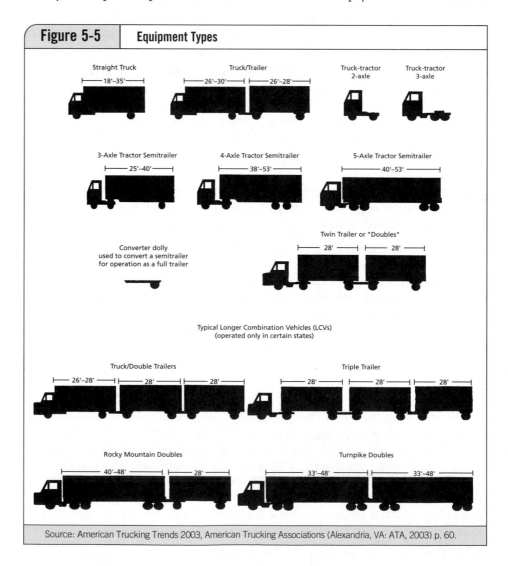

| Figure 5-5 | Equipment Types |

Source: American Trucking Trends 2003, American Trucking Associations (Alexandria, VA: ATA, 2003) p. 60.

33,920 (3,392 ft^3 × 10 lb/ft^3). Shippers of low-density freight (below 16 lb/ft^3) advocate increased payload capacity of motor carrier vehicles.

City Straight Trucks City vehicles, or "straight trucks," are normally smaller than line-haul vehicles and are single units (see Figure 5-5). The city truck has the cargo and power unit combined in one vehicle. The typical city truck is approximately 20 to 25 feet long with a cargo unit 15 to 20 feet long. However, there is growing use of small trailers (28 feet) to pick up and deliver freight in the city. These trailers can also be used for line-haul, which increases efficiency. Shipments can be "loaded to ride," meaning they will not require handling at the origin terminal.

Special Vehicles In addition to the line-haul and city vehicle classifications, the following special vehicles are designed to meet special shipper needs:

- Dry van: Standard trailer or straight truck with all sides enclosed
- Open top: Trailer top is open to permit loading of odd-sized freight through the top
- Flatbed: Trailer has no top or sides; used extensively to haul steel
- Tank trailer: Used to haul liquids such as petroleum products
- Refrigerated vehicles: Cargo unit has controlled temperature
- High cube: Cargo unit has drop-frame design or is higher than normal to increase cubic capacity
- Special: Vehicle has a unique design to haul a special commodity, such as liquefied gas or automobiles

The Department of Transportation's Federal Motor Carrier Safety Administration has established many rules and regulations governing the specifications of motor carrier vehicles. These regulations cover such areas as the number of lights on the vehicle, the type of brakes used, tire specifications, and other operating parts.[9] The overall allowable length, weight, and height of the vehicle are prescribed in the various states.[10]

Terminals

Some motor carrier operations, namely TL operations, might not require terminals for the movement of freight. The carrier uses the shipper's plant for loading and the consignee's plant for unloading. Typically, TL terminals normally provide dispatching, fuel, and maintenance services. Some carriers, such as Schneider National, are expanding the services offered by their terminal facilities to include restaurant and hotel offerings to give their drivers alternatives to truck stops. These terminals are designed primarily to accommodate drivers and equipment, but not freight.

Heavy LTL carriers use terminals for loading, or consolidation, only. However, as indicated earlier, LTL freight operations do require terminals. Some of the large LTL carriers, such as Yellow/Roadway, have more than 500 terminals. A driver will leave a terminal to make deliveries throughout the country but will always return to his or her domicile. A driver's domicile is the terminal that the driver originally left. The terminals used by motor carriers can be classified as pickup or delivery, break-bulk, and relay. A discussion of functions performed at each type of terminal follows.

Pickup and Delivery Terminals (PUD) The terminal is a key facility in the operation of an LTL hub-and-spoke system. This section will present an expanded discussion of the types and roles of the terminals in this system.

The most common type of terminal found in the LTL system is the PUD terminal. These are also called *satellite* or **end-of-the-line (EOL)** terminals. The PUD terminal serves a local area and provides direct contact with both shippers and receivers. The basic transportation service provided at this terminal is the pickup and/or delivery of freight on peddle runs. A **peddle run** is a route that is driven daily out of the PUD terminal for the purpose of collecting freight for outbound moves or delivering freight from inbound moves. A PUD terminal will have several peddle runs in its customer operating area. Figure 5-6 gives an example of how a peddle run is designed. The PUD terminal is located in Altoona, Pennsylvania. Attached to it are four peddle runs, one each to Tyrone, State College, Lewistown, and Huntington. Every Monday through Friday morning, a driver will depart the Altoona terminal and deliver freight to customers located on that driver's assigned peddle. During and after the deliveries, freight will be picked up from customers and returned with the driver to the Altoona terminal at the end of the day. When all the drivers return at the end of their shifts, the Altoona terminal will have freight to be consolidated and moved outbound from customers in Tyrone, State College, Lewistown, and Huntington to customers in other areas of the country.

Note that there are two elements of a peddle run, one called **stem time** and the other called **peddle time**. Stem time is the time that elapses from when the driver leaves the terminal until the driver makes the first pickup or delivery; it is also the time that elapses from when the driver makes the last pickup or delivery until returning to the terminal. This is nonrevenue-producing time because no shipments are handled. A carrier would want to locate PUD terminals in such a way that this nonrevenue-producing travel time is minimized. (This aspect of LTL service will be discussed later in this chapter.) The other type of time is peddle time. This is the time during which the driver is actively involved in the pickup and delivery of freight. This is revenue-producing time because it occurs when shipments are handled. Obviously, carriers would want to maximize the amount of time a driver spent performing these activities.

| Figure 5-6 | Terminal Peddle Run |

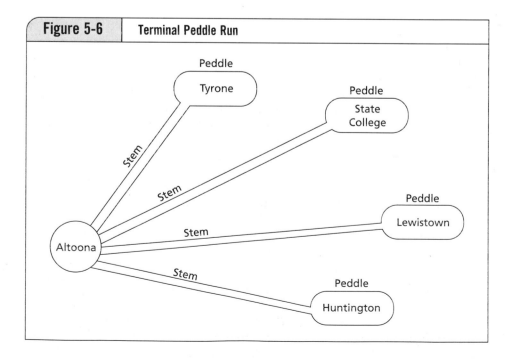

The basic terminal services performed at these facilities are consolidation and dispersion. For example, freight moving inbound to Altoona from other terminals (passing through a break-bulk) will be broken into individual deliveries by peddle run to be handled by the driver during that particular shift. Freight that is brought back by the peddle drivers for movement outbound from Altoona will be consolidated into line-haul trailers for subsequent movement to the appropriate break-bulk. This is a basic cross-dock type of operation with a direction of freight flow across the dock that changes depending on whether the move is inbound or outbound.

The dispatch operation provided at the PUD terminal is critical to the operating efficiency of the peddle runs. Freight can be picked up on peddle runs in one of two ways. First, a customer on a peddle run might have a standing order for a pickup every day at 10 a.m. The PUD driver is aware of this, so the customer has no need to notify the carrier in advance for the pickup. Second, a customer might call or e-mail the local PUD terminal to order service for a pickup. This is where the local dispatcher becomes involved. The dispatcher records the nature of the shipment and required time of pickup and assigns that shipment to the driver on the appropriate peddle run. The PUD driver will periodically call in to or receive a satellite message from the dispatcher to determine the order and frequencies of new pickup requests. Obviously, the dispatcher needs to be familiar with the geography of the peddle runs and the capacity of the PUD drivers and trailers to efficiently route freight with the appropriate vehicle.

Other services that are provided at the PUD terminal might include tracing, rating and billing, sales, and claims. However, some carriers are beginning to centralize these functions at break-bulks or other locations by taking advantage of telecommunications technology. For example, some LTL carriers use the Internet for tracing purposes. When the customer accesses the carrier's website, the shipper keys in the pro number or waybill number (also called a tracking number) and the system provides the current status of the shipment.

Break-Bulk Terminals Another type of terminal found in an LTL hub-and-spoke system is called a **break-bulk**. This facility performs both consolidation and dispersion (or break-bulk) services. Customers will rarely have contact with the operations at the break-bulk facility. The main purpose of this terminal is to provide an intermediate point where freight with common destinations from the PUD terminals is combined in a single trailer for movement to the delivering PUD terminal. This can be seen in Figure 5-7. Break-bulks will have many PUD terminals assigned to them as primary loading points. For example, assume that a shipper in Toledo, Ohio, wanted to send an LTL shipment to a customer in Pottstown, Pennsylvania. The Toledo PUD terminal is attached to the Cleveland, Ohio break-bulk, and the Philadelphia PUD terminal, which

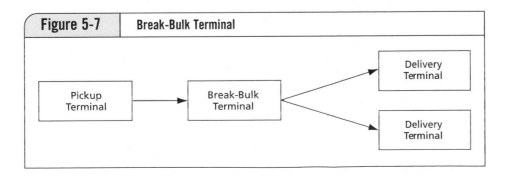

| Figure 5-7 | Break-Bulk Terminal |

handles the Pottstown peddle, is attached to the Lancaster, Pennsylvania, break-bulk. At the completion of the peddle run, the Toledo driver brings the shipment back to the Toledo PUD terminal. There it is sorted and combined with other shipments going to the Lancaster break-bulk service area. (This could include all PUD terminals covering significant portions of Pennsylvania, New York, New Jersey, and parts of Maryland.) These shipments are consolidated into one trailer that will be dispatched to the Lancaster break-bulk.

Once the trailer arrives in Lancaster, it will be unloaded, and all of the freight destined to Philadelphia and its peddle runs will be loaded into an outbound trailer. This trailer will be dispatched from the break-bulk and will arrive at the Philadelphia terminal to be unloaded in the early morning so the freight can be segregated into peddle delivery vehicles for an early morning delivery schedule. So, just as with the airline hub-and-spoke system, the LTL system utilizes the full capacity of its vehicles in the line-haul operation.

Break-bulk facilities also serve as driver domiciles. City drivers located at a PUD terminal will always remain in their local area during their shift and will be able to return home when it is over. Line-haul drivers, however, might or might not be able to return home after a trip, depending on the length of haul they are assigned. For example, a *turn* means that a line-haul driver is assigned a load to be taken from the break-bulk (domicile) to a PUD terminal that is no more than 5.5 hours away. Because of DOT-mandated driving limits, that line-haul driver can make the trip, drop the trailer, and pick up another shipment destined back to the break-bulk within the hours-of-service driving limit. However, a movement that requires more than 5.5 hours driving time in one direction will require a layover; that is, when the driver reaches the destination, a 10-hour rest period is required before that driver will be able to take a return load back to the break-bulk and return to the domicile. Therefore, at the maximum, a driver facing an 11-hour run with an 10-hour layover and an 11-hour return trip will return to the domicile within 32 hours of the original departure. Sometimes, however, a return load is not immediately available, which will delay the driver's return.

Relay Terminals **Relay terminals** are different from the PUD and break-bulk terminals in that freight is never touched. The relay terminal is necessitated by the maximum hours-of-service regulation that is imposed on drivers. Under DOT enforcement, drivers were permitted to drive a maximum of 11 hours after 10 consecutive hours off duty. At the relay terminal, one driver substitutes for another who has accumulated the maximum hours of service. (The term **slip seat** also has been used to describe the relay terminal operation.)

As indicated in Figure 5-8, the location of the relay terminal is a maximum driving time of 11 hours from an origin. If the relay terminal is located 5.5 hours from an origin, the driver can drive to the relay terminal and return within the maximum 11 hours. (This is also called a turn.)

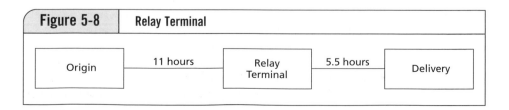

Figure 5-8   **Relay Terminal**

Using the example given in Figure 5-8, assume that the driving time is 15 hours between origin and destination. Without the relay terminal, the transit time is 26 hours. After 11 hours of driving, the driver goes off duty for 10 consecutive hours. Upon resuming duty, the driver drives 5 hours to the destination. The total elapsed time is 26 hours (11 + 10 + 5). The driver drives 11 hours to the relay terminal, and another driver takes over and drives the vehicle to the destination. In this instance, the relay terminal reduces the transit time by 10 hours, the mandated driver off-duty time. Under the new driver hours-of-service rules, relays still play an important role in LTL motor carrier operations. However, some carriers might have to rethink their relay structure because of the new, extended driver hours.

An alternative to the relay terminal is the use of a sleeper team—two drivers. While one driver accumulates the off-duty time in the sleeper berth of the tractor, the other driver is driving. The sleeper team has been most successful for long trips with many destinations.

Terminal Management Decisions

Many types of operating decisions need to be made when utilizing terminals in a carrier's network. Along with making these decisions, carrier management must also consider their strategic implications. This section will address a few of these types of decisions.

Number of Terminals In many modes, this is a relatively simple decision. For example, passenger airline terminals will be located close to major population centers. This decision, however, usually does not belong to the carrier but to some local government agency. Railroads must also make this decision but are limited by geography and track locations for terminal sites. Railroads will not normally have many terminals in their networks. The mode with probably the most difficult decision in this area is LTL motor carriage, primarily because of the vast numbers of terminals in these systems and the relatively small investment needed to develop a terminal site.

The obvious question for an LTL motor carrier is, "How many terminals should we have?" The obvious answer is, "It depends." First, the degree of market penetration and customer service desired by the carrier will help determine the number of terminals to establish. In theory, the more terminals closer to the customer, the better the service. This also has proven to be true in practice. Realistically, at some point additional terminals will result in no incremental increase in service and might even detract from service.

Second, the dilemma of small terminal versus long peddle must be addressed. Figure 5-9 represents this situation. In Example 1, assume that a carrier's market is the state of Pennsylvania, with one terminal located in Harrisburg with peddle runs to Erie, Scranton, Pittsburgh, and Philadelphia. This network utilizes only one terminal but has extremely long and expensive stem times for its peddle runs. The terminal must also be large to accommodate the volume of freight that will come from these four peddles. Example 2 shows a network that utilizes two terminals, each having two peddle runs with significantly shorter stem times. Each terminal in this scenario is smaller than the one terminal in Example 1. Thus, Example 2 has doubled the number of terminals but decreased stem times for customer PUD. The small-terminal-versus-long-peddle decision would be made based on the service implications of establishing terminals closer to customers versus the cost of adding another terminal.

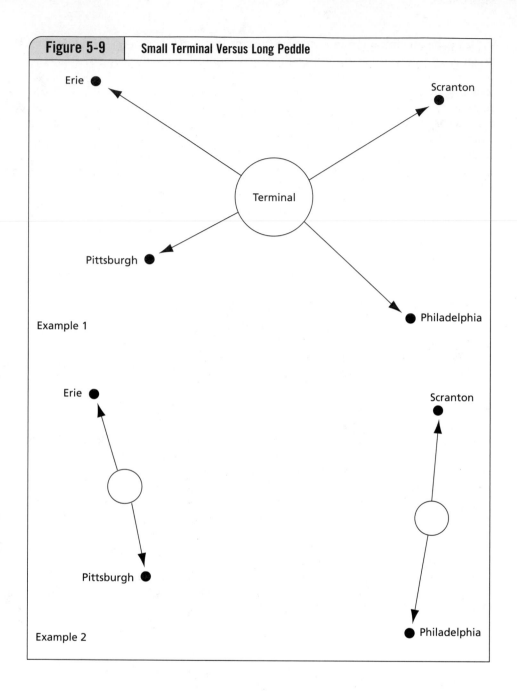

| Figure 5-9 | Small Terminal Versus Long Peddle |

Example 1

Example 2

Many times when shippers are making distribution system decisions, they assume that manufacturing facilities are fixed and that warehouse decisions must be made based on this fixed network. This assumption is also part of the terminal decision process for LTL motor carriers, except their "manufacturing facilities" are break-bulk terminals. Whether or not another terminal can be added to a break-bulk's operating region might simply be a question of available capacity at that break-bulk. Normally, each PUD terminal is assigned at least one door at a break-bulk. To add another PUD terminal means eliminating an existing terminal, physically adding another door to the break-bulk, or improving the productivity at the break-bulk to turn trailers in doors more than once per shift.

Locations of Terminals Closely related to the decision of how many terminals to establish is the decision of where to establish them. As previously mentioned, for airlines and railroads, this decision can be relatively simple because of geographic, government, and demand variables. LTL carriers, however, must consider some other variables. First, the DOT limits the amount of time a driver can continuously operate a vehicle before a rest period is required. Currently, this limit is 11 hours, so optimally PUD terminals should be located no more than 11 hours away from a break-bulk. This would allow a driver to complete the run in one trip. Second, PUD terminals should be located to minimize the distance that freight would need to be backhauled to the break-bulk. The assumption here is that freight flows from east to west and north to south in the United States. When a shipment is picked up, the idea is to send that freight in one of these directions as soon as possible. For example, given that a carrier has two break-bulks, one in Lancaster, Pennsylvania, and the other in Columbus, Ohio, where would a PUD terminal based in Pittsburgh send its freight? Based on the assumption made earlier about freight flows, Pittsburgh would send its freight to Columbus; that is, a shipment picked up by a Pittsburgh peddle driver would begin its east–west journey more productively by being sent to Columbus because if it were sent to Lancaster, it would conceptually duplicate this distance when it began its journey from Lancaster to the west (actually passing right by Columbus). Finally, market penetration and potential will help determine terminal location. As mentioned in the decision process for determining the number of terminals, getting closer to the customer can many times improve the level of service given to that customer.

Recent trends in the LTL sector have seen significant reductions in the number of terminals as these carriers strive to provide overnight and second-day delivery to more and more customers. To do this, many interterminal runs have been realigned with the resultant elimination of intermediate handling. This has resulted in increased load factors and reduced transit times. Less handling has also improved the claims experience for the LTL carriers. The long-haul LTL carriers will still favor the hub-and-spoke operation, whereas the regional carriers will still look toward fewer terminals with more direct runs.

Cost Structure

Fixed Versus Variable Cost Components

The cost structure of the motor carrier industry consists of high levels of variable costs and relatively low fixed costs. Approximately 70 to 90 percent of the costs are variable, and 10 to 30 percent are fixed. The public investment in the highway system is a major factor contributing to this low fixed-cost structure because the highway is the motor carrier's "right of way." In addition, the motor carrier is able to increase or decrease the number of vehicles used in short periods of time and in small increments of capacity. Lastly, the carriers as a group (with the exception of the LTL carrier) do not require expensive terminals. The small investment in terminals also contributes to low fixed costs. The bulk of the motor carrier's cost then is associated with daily operating costs—the variable costs of fuel, wages, maintenance, and highway user fees (such as fuel tax and vehicle registration).

The discussion of motor carrier cost will begin with the vehicle operating costs of long-distance fleets transporting products in tractor–trailers. These data can be compared only to similar operations; that is, comparisons cannot be made to local motor

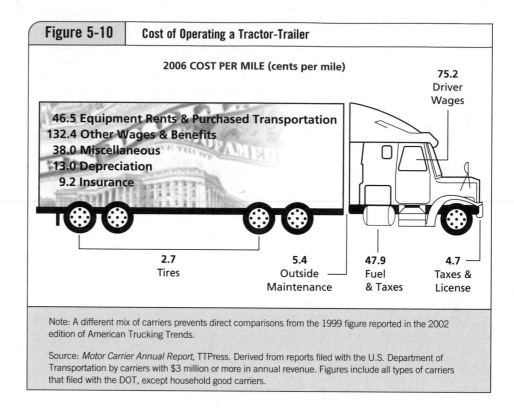

Figure 5-10 | Cost of Operating a Tractor-Trailer

2006 COST PER MILE (cents per mile)

75.2
Driver
Wages

46.5 Equipment Rents & Purchased Transportation
132.4 Other Wages & Benefits
38.0 Miscellaneous
13.0 Depreciation
9.2 Insurance

2.7
Tires

5.4
Outside
Maintenance

47.9
Fuel
& Taxes

4.7
Taxes &
License

Note: A different mix of carriers prevents direct comparisons from the 1999 figure reported in the 2002 edition of American Trucking Trends.

Source: *Motor Carrier Annual Report*, TTPress. Derived from reports filed with the U.S. Department of Transportation by carriers with $3 million or more in annual revenue. Figures include all types of carriers that filed with the DOT, except household good carriers.

carrier operations (PUD). Figure 5-10 indicates that in 2006 the total cost to operate a tractor–trailer was 375.0 cents per mile. As indicated, approximately 80 percent of the cost to operate an intercity tractor–trailer is variable. The remaining 20 percent is associated with the fixed costs: vehicle interest; depreciation and interest on terminals, garages, and offices; management; and overhead (such as utilities). For carriers handling LTL freight, the fixed cost is higher; that is, additional terminals, management, and overhead expenses are required to handle small-sized shipments.

The two categories with the largest share of the variable costs are labor and fuel. A discussion of each of these two variable costs will follow.

Labor The cost of drivers accounts for 20 percent of the total costs per vehicle mile, as shown in Figure 5-10. Labor costs (wages plus fringe benefits) usually absorb about 55 percent of a carrier's revenue dollar. That is, 55 cents out of every dollar in revenue goes to labor. The average annual wage in 2005 was $51,683.[11]

The over-the-road (intercity) driver is typically paid on a mileage basis, such as 42.0 cents per mile; local drivers are paid by the hour. Over-the-road drivers are normally paid an hourly rate for operating delays resulting from loading/unloading, accidents, weather, and the like.

The DOT enforces maximum hours of service regulation. As of January 3, 2004, the DOT's **driving time regulations** permit drivers to drive a maximum of 11 hours after being off duty for 10 consecutive hours. A driver is permitted to be on duty a maximum of 14 hours after 10 consecutive hours off duty. In addition, no driver can drive after accumulating 60 hours on-duty in 7 consecutive days, or 70 hours in 8 consecutive days.

On the Line

HOS Regulations Here to Stay

The good news for shippers entering 2009 is that there is no news. There's going to be no change in the current hours of service (HOS) regulations governing approximately three million long-haul truck drivers. The Federal Motor Carrier Safety Administration (FMCSA), in a move welcomed by both shippers and carriers, has decided to maintain the current HOS regulations. This just may end up an eight-year legal and procedural battle to revise the HOS regulations, which went largely unchanged from 1935 until FMCSA first offered its first revision back in 2000.

In one of the final truck-related regulations issued by the Bush administration, FMCSA said it was adopting as final its interim final rule of Dec. 17, 2007. That allows drivers to drive 11 hours within a 15-hour work day with a 34-hour restart provision.

Both provisions had been challenged in court by Public Citizen, Advocates for Highway Safety, unions, and other groups on procedural grounds.

The final rule was scheduled to be published in the Federal Register and became effective Jan. 19, the final day of the Bush administration.

"There have been procedural rules that have been identified by the court. We are properly addressing the concerns of the court," FMCSA Administrator John Hill said in a conference call. "I feel confident that moving forward is the best public policy at this time."

Both shippers and carriers have adapted to the new rules that went into effect in 2003, despite court challenges. The biggest change was a push by carriers to urge shippers to become more efficient at their loading docks since driver waiting time was no longer counted as off-duty time, but rather part of the drivers' work day.

Any changes to these rules would be highly disruptive to shippers and carriers. Some shippers have made changes to their practices to adapt. Carriers, on the other hand, have fine-tuned their networks to adapt to the required 11- and 15-hour requirements. Any further changes, they say, would be costly and inefficient.

Drivers are limited to 60 hours driving in seven days, or 70 in eight days, while allowing those clocks to be reset by taking 34 straight off-duty hours. Previously, the rule had allowed for 10 hours of driving in a 15-hour period, but allowed drivers to log on and off duty whenever they wanted.

FMCSA's Hill said he decided to propose keeping the current rules rather than create confusion within the trucking industry and the enforcement community by issuing further revisions. He called uncertainty "the enemy of enforcement and compliance."

There are still signs, however, that the incoming Obama administration might be sympathetic to the Teamsters union, Public Citizen, and other safety advocates who might try one more time to challenge these rules in court.

There are strong objections by some in Congress regarding HOS. Rep. James Oberstar, D-Minn., chairman of the House Transportation and Infrastructure Committee, said he was "disappointed that FMCSA is going down a path of trying to continue new standards for daily and weekly maximum driving time, when these standards have twice been rejected by the courts."

Source: *Logistics Management,* January 2009, pp. 16–17. Reprinted by permission.

The most pressing labor issue facing motor carriers, particularly TL carriers, is the shortage of qualified drivers. Part of the problem is that the federal government, as part of an overall safety program, imposed stringent driver licensing requirements. Since April 1992, all operators of vehicles over 26,000 pounds gross vehicle weight must hold a commercial driver's license (CDL). Although CDLs are issued by the driver's home state, the requirements are mandated by the federal DOT. Along with the new licensing requirements, the DOT also imposed stringent rules dealing with drug and alcohol abuse. Poor driving records and inability to pass the CDL test eliminated many marginal drivers.

The hardships imposed by the very nature of long-haul motor carrier operations have also impacted the availability of drivers. Drivers are frequently away from home for long periods and often have to assist with the loading and unloading of trailers. This lifestyle is not as attractive as other career choices, so the available pool from which drivers might be drawn has declined. The motor carrier industry has undertaken several initiatives to counteract the problem of driver retention and recruitment. They have raised the per-mile and per-hour pay rates, scheduled drivers home more frequently, and worked with shippers and consignees to make freight more "driver-friendly" (that is, easier to load/unload, tarp, brace, and so on).

Fuel Since 1974 the higher price of fuel has resulted in a rise in the relative proportion of fuel cost to total cost. For example, in 1976 fuel cost was 11.6 cents per mile or 19.8 percent of the total cost per mile, but in 1985 fuel cost was 24.6 cents per mile or 21.1 percent of total cost. In 2006 fuel cost was higher at 47.9 cents per mile or about 12.8 percent of total costs (see Figure 5-10). Carriers have experienced a 426 percent increase in diesel fuel prices from 1976 to 2007—approximately 53 cents per gallon in 1976 to about $2.79 per gallon in 2007. Ever since 1974 fuel prices have changed more frequently over a larger range due to fluctuations in supply.

Included in the price of the diesel fuel is a highway user tax imposed by both the federal and state governments. The fuel tax plus other taxes for highway use are payments made by the carrier to the government for the construction, maintenance, and control of the highways. In 2006 the motor carrier industry paid $37.4 billion in federal and state highway user taxes.[12] The federal fuel tax is 24.4 cents per gallon of diesel fuel plus a state average of 24.5 cents per gallon.[13]

Economies of Scale

There do not appear to be major economies of scale for large-scale motor carrier operations. Economies of scale are realized through more extensive use of large-sized plants or indivisible inputs. However, the extensive use of indivisible inputs is not characteristic of all motor carrier operations. In addition, the large number of small firms, especially in the TL segment, suggests that small-sized operations are competitive. The concentration of the LTL business is indicative of economies of operation in this segment.

In the short run, certain economies exist in the greater use of indivisible inputs such as terminals, management specialists, and information systems. The average cost of such inputs will decrease as output (greater use) increases. Such economies of use justify the rather large-sized firms that operate transcontinentally, especially in the LTL segment. Carriers that operate over wide geographic areas require more terminals, more elaborate information systems, and more management specialists than those carriers that operate over narrow geographic areas.

For TL operations, very limited investment is required for terminals, but information systems are becoming increasingly important to efficient operations. Computers in tractors, direct satellite communication to drivers, and bar coding with optical scanners are a few examples of the sophisticated information systems and technology that now exist in the motor carrier industry. Many of the TL carrier inputs (vehicle, labor, fuel) can be increased one vehicle at a time in response to the small increases in demand.

Operational cost trade-offs exist between large and small carriers. A large-scale operation affords savings in purchase economies of equipment and in such inputs as fuel, parts, and interest in loans. (The small carrier might enjoy some of these purchase economies from larger retailers of motor carrier vehicle suppliers, such as truck stops.) On the other hand, large LTL motor carriers might be unionized and thus pay higher labor rates, but the motor carrier industry is less unionized today than it was in 1980.

Overall, long-term economies of scale appear not to be significant in TL motor carrier transportation and are present to some degree in the LTL segment. This degree of scale economies has implications for competition and the market's capability to control such competition.

Operating Ratio A measure of operating efficiency used by motor carriers is the **operating ratio**. The operating ratio measures the percent of operating expenses to operating revenue.

$$Operating\ Ratio = (Operating\ expenses/Operating\ revenue) \times 100$$

Operating expenses are those expenses directly associated with the transportation of freight, excluding nontransportation expenses and interest costs. Operating revenues are the total revenues generated from freight transportation services; nontransportation services are excluded. Motor carriers might use the operating ratio to support a rate increase request. The closer the operating ratio is to 100, the more indicative of the possible need to raise rates to increase total revenues. In today's market, however, a rate increase might not be a feasible solution. Carriers are more likely to seek supply chain solutions with shippers and receivers to reduce operating expenses, thus increasing operating margin.

An operating ratio of 94 indicates that 94 cents of every operating revenue dollar is consumed by operating expenses, leaving 6 cents of every operating dollar to cover interest costs and a return to the owners. LTL motor carrier operating ratios usually range between 93 and 96, whereas the TL segment could see ratios in the low to mid 80s. The operating ratio is also a benchmark or barometer of financial viability. Obviously, if the operating ratio is equal to or greater than 100, there is no revenue available to cover fixed or overhead costs or to return a profit to owners or stockholders. Increasing revenues and/or reducing costs are viable approaches to resolving the problem of a high operating ratio.

Since the founding of the United States, the federal government has felt that it has the responsibility to provide highways to meet the national defense and commerce needs of the country. At first, the federal government was the sole financier of highways, but over the years, state and local governments have assumed a greater role. Today, the state and local governments assume the responsibility for maintaining the highways, while the federal government provides up to 90 percent of the construction cost of new highways with the designated network. The Federal Highway Administration (FHWA), part of the DOT, oversees the National Highway System (NHS). The NHS was defined in 1995 and consists of the 46,876-mile interstate highway system and 113,124 miles of existing state and federal noninterstate highways. Although the NHS includes slightly over 4 percent of the total road mileage, this network sees the transportation of more than 75 percent of intercity freight traffic.

The Intermodal Surface Transportation Efficiency Act (ISTEA) has been replaced by the Transporation Equity Act for the Twenty-first Century (TEA21), which has continued the role of FHWA in this area. Additional funds were added under TEA21, which remained in place until 2004. More than $73 billion was expected to be spent on roads and related projects during this period.

Funding Highway users—motor carrier vehicle and automobile operators—pay for the construction, maintenance, and policing of highways through highway user taxes. The total amount of taxes paid depends on the use of the highway. The motor carrier incurs a cost for the use of the highway that is related to its amount of use. This situation contributes to the high variable cost structure of the motor carrier.

Federal and state governments assess highway user taxes. The federal highway user taxes are paid into the Federal Highway Trust Fund. From the Federal Highway Trust Fund, the federal government pays 90 percent of the construction costs for the interstate system and 50 percent of the construction costs for all other federal-aid roads. Table 5-1 indicates items taxed and the rate assessed by the Federal Highway Trust Fund.

The state also assesses highway user taxes to defray the cost of construction, maintenance, and policing of highways. The state taxes include fuel taxes, vehicle registration fees, ton-mile taxes, and special-use permits.

Table 5-1	Federal Highway Trust Fund Tax Rates
COMMODITY	**TAX**
Gasoline	18.4 cents/gallon
Diesel fuel	24.4 cents/gallon
Special Fuels:	
General rate	18.4 cents/gallon
Liquefied petroleum gas	18.3 cents/gallon
Liquefied natural gas	24.3 cents/gallon
M85 (from natural gas)	9.25 cents/gallon
Compressed natural gas	18.3 cents/126.67 cubic feet
Tires	0 to 3500 pounds no tax
	Over 3500 pounds 9.45 cents for each 10 pounds in excess of 3500.
New truck and trailer sales	12% of manufacturer's sales price on trucks weighing more than 33,000 lb. and trailers exceeding 26,000 lb.
Highway vehicle use tax	For trucks weighing 55,000 lb. or more, $100 + $22 for each additional 1,000 lb. up to a maximum of $550

Source: Federal Highway Administration, Highway Trust Fund Primer.

Implied in the highway user tax concept is the philosophy that the highway predominantly confers benefits on specific groups and individuals. Although the general public benefits from increased mobility and the availability of a wide variety of goods and services, the motor vehicle user is presumed to be the major benefactor and therefore is expected to pay a larger share of the costs. An analogy that illustrates this concept is the property owner who pays property taxes that include an assessment for streets (access to the property). Much debate exists as to whether motor carrier vehicles pay a fair share of the total cost of highways. In 2006 motor carriers paid $37.4 billion in federal and state highway user taxes.[14] The central issue is whether motor carriers should pay for the added construction and maintenance costs caused by their heavier weight.

Because each state must pay for the maintenance, policing, and construction of the highways within its boundaries, each state attempts to ensure receipt of taxes for using its highways. For a motor carrier operation over many states, this means buying vehicle registrations in many states and maintaining records of miles driven in a particular state so that the state will receive a fuel tax or ton-mile tax. Such record-keeping adds a cost to the carrier's operation.

Current Issues

Safety

Some members of the motor carrier industry have come to realize that improved safety can mean improved profitability. After the regulatory reform that took place in the early 1980s, motor carriers found themselves with more direct control of their economic and operating policies. Deficiencies in safety can translate into decreased profitability because of expensive claims for lost or damaged goods, increased insurance premiums, accidents, fines, and so on. These consequences are not unique to the motor carrier industry; in fact, they apply to the entire transportation industry.

The FMCSA has developed rules under which its inspectors determine whether a carrier is fit from a safety rule compliance perspective. The system includes three categories: Satisfactory, Conditional, and Unsatisfactory. The FMCSA has the right to force a carrier to stop operating after a specific period has passed if the carrier has received an Unsatisfactory rating and improvement is not made. The period varies depending on the type of traffic the carrier is transporting. If the carrier is hauling nonhazardous materials, they must cease operations 60 days after his or her safety rating is found to be Unsatisfactory. If the company hauls hazardous materials, the period is reduced to 40 days. This only applies if the carrier does not correct the problems discovered in the FMCSA safety audit. There is also an appeal process that allows the carrier to correct any concerns as might be necessary.

The carrier might be allowed to continue to operate if there is a good faith effort on its part to correct the defects. Government regulations require that the FMCSA review a carrier who is found in violation within 45 days of that company's request. If the carrier transports hazardous materials, the time period for review upon request drops to 30 days.

Many shippers seek safety fitness information as part of their selection process, so there is considerable pressure on carriers to operate safely. Many transportation contracts contain clauses that permit the shipper to cancel the contract if the carrier's safety rating is Unsatisfactory.

A major related concern is that of alcohol and drug abuse. It has been estimated that American industry pays $50 to $100 billion for the effects and results of substance abuse in the workplace every year, either for the cost of accidents or losses in productivity. In response to this problem, the motor carrier industry has begun to move toward drug screening for its employees. Drug and alcohol testing are required in the following circumstances:

- As a requirement for employment
- As a part of a regular physical exam required of current employees
- For cause, required after any accident
- On a random selection basis

Drug and alcohol rules require motor carriers to have an anti-drug program, as well as drug testing that includes random and postaccident testing. All fleets, regardless of size, are required to have a complete program, including random and postaccident testing in place. These rules apply to the owner/operator as well. Many states have drug-testing programs of their own as well with which the carrier must comply.

When proper care is taken to implement a substance abuse program, most drivers support the program because it makes their job safer. Proper care in implementing a substance abuse program involves relating substance abuse to health problems, while leaving moral judgments to the individual. Such care also includes setting consistent policies that are enforceable and apply to every employee, making policies for violations known, and providing counseling and rehabilitation services for those employees who have substance abuse problems. Support for employees with problems is critical for any substance abuse program to be successful.

Other areas of safety concerns are drivers' hours-of-service and fatigue issues. Before January 3, 2004, the hours-of-service rules dated from before World War II and did not reflect modern realities. Under a complex formula of allowed driving and required rest periods, a driver can be on duty for no more than 60 hours in 7 days or 70 hours in 8 days. As previously discussed, these rules have been altered to address today's changing environment.

Another safety issue receiving attention deals with vehicle size and weight. As shown earlier, there are a number of different sizes of vehicles, and each has its own weight-carrying regulations. Recent studies have analyzed increasing total gross vehicle weight to 94,000 pounds with the addition of a third axle to the trailer. The studies have also addressed increased use of triples. All these issues include safety concerns and will require federal legislation before any changes can be made. In addition to safety, there are significant economic issues for the motor carrier industry because these larger vehicles will improve productivity and lower cost.

Technology

The use of satellite technology has a major impact on the motor carrier industry. Using global positioning technology (GPS), satellites are being used to track vehicles throughout their movement from origin to destination. The use of satellites allows the carriers to pinpoint the location of the vehicle and relay this information to the customer. The interaction between the driver, using an on-board computer, and a home-base computer allows route or arrival adjustment for poor weather or road conditions, and these adjustments can be communicated to the customers.

One area where satellite communication has had a very positive effect is in the movement of hazardous materials. For example, phosphorous pentasulfide (P_2S_5), a very dangerous chemical if not handled properly, is shipped by Bee Line Trucking for

---

Transportation Technology   *Scrutiny Rules the Day*

It certainly shouldn't surprise anyone that logistics and supply chain operations are being asked to cut back on their Warehouse Management Systems (WMS), Transportation Management Systems (TMS), Global Trade Management Systems (GTM), Yard Management Systems (YMS), and other SCM spending. In fact, the current economy has prompted 41 percent of respondents (to *Logistics Management's* 7th Annual Software Survey) to more carefully analyze their SCM investments, while 34 percent plan to freeze software investment in 2009. Sixteen percent say they'll move forward with investments in software this year, while 15 percent expect to upgrade existing programs in lieu of buying new packages.

"When things started going south for the economy in the fourth quarter, the big question was: What is IT spending going to look like moving forward?" says ARC's (Adrian) Gonzalez. "With only 16 percent of companies ready to make software investments and over twice that (34 percent) planning to freeze budgets, software vendors are probably concerned." Of the SCM vendors he communicates with, Gonzalez says that most are seeing more "delays" than "cancellations" of orders.

"A lot of shippers are waiting to see what happens in the second quarter of this year," adds Gonzalez. "Customers still expect to move forward, but it is a question of when, with projects being pushed out a bit."

Of the 41 percent of shippers who say they're planning to purchase SCM software sometime in the next 12 months, the bulk (31 percent) will invest in WMS, with 29 percent interested in TMS. Other SCM packages of interest include ERP (18 percent), GTM (13 percent), and YMS (10 percent).

With 32 percent of respondents currently using on-demand supply chain solutions, Gonzalez says he's surprised that more shippers aren't considering this alternative to purchase-and-install systems, particularly for TMS. Among those companies that plan SCM purchases over the next 12 months, just 36 percent are looking at on-demand options. "I really would have expected more companies to be looking at on-demand," says Gonzalez, "which is resonating strongly out in the market right now, particularly for those companies that have tightened their budgets."

Adapted From: Bridget McCrea, *Logistics Management*, April 2009, p. 39. Reprinted by permission.

---

the Monsanto Company, a corporation in the food, medicine, and health industries. The two companies have teamed up to provide safe transportation for this dangerous chemical. The satellites used in the transport allow communication between the driver and a terminal in San Diego, which forwards the information on location and status to both Bee Line and Monsanto. This tracking allows for quick reaction to any accidents or spills, and the computers can give the name of the authority in the area to call in case any emergency action needs to be taken. Satellite communication will continue to play a role in improved safety and customer service for motor carriers into the future.

LTL Rates

Since the early 1980s the LTL segment of the motor carrier industry has used discounts from published tariffs as a means of pricing segments to attract traffic of large shippers. The Interstate Commerce Commission (ICC) was eliminated under the ICC Termination Act of 1995 (ICCTA1995) and with it, most of the last vestiges of motor carrier rate regulation. Although certain portions of rate oversight were transferred to the then newly created Surface Transportation Board, for all practical purposes LTL rates are subject to the free-market environment. In addition, the common carrier obligation to serve was preserved, but absent was an enforcement mechanism, which the marketplace will control as well. As it currently stands, the shipper has more choices for LTL today than existed during the height of regulation.

A limited amount of antitrust immunity was also preserved, but only for classifications, mileage guides rules, and general rate adjustments. Individual carrier rates are subject to antitrust action but cannot be challenged on the basis that the rate is unreasonably high. This is a direct reversal of the situation that existed under the old ICC.

There is no longer any requirement to file tariffs, and contracts can be used instead. Although carriers are still required to maintain rates, rules, and classifications, they only need be furnished to the shipper upon request. In a departure from previous regulation, rates need not be in writing to be enforceable. Shippers, however, must exercise due caution because federal oversight and enforcement is greatly diminished.

This law also reduced the time for recovery of disputed freight charges from 3 years to 18 months. If either the carrier or the shipper feels that the charges are incorrect, they must file suit no longer than 18 months from the date of the shipment. The lack of tariffs might make this more difficult unless the shippers have obtained the carrier's prices and rules in writing before tendering the shipment to the carrier.

Financial Stability

Another major concern in the motor carrier industry is financial stability. The operating ratios of many motor carriers have been in excess of 95 percent, and some companies have operating ratios of over 100. The high operating ratios are a clear indicator of the financial plight of many motor carriers and an indication of the low competitive rates.

Immediately after the initial lessening of economic regulation in 1980, a large number of motor carriers failed as the competitive environment became severe. Of the top 100 motor carriers in 1980, fewer than 10 were still in business in 1990. Only one new LTL was formed in this period that survived to the 1990s. The failures after 1990 were fewer but usually involved larger firms that could not continue to compete. In some cases, the unionized carriers were victims of labor unrest or shipper concerns about stability. In other cases, mergers and buyouts reduced the number of Class I carriers. Recent consolidations have also occurred in the TL sector as the larger carriers have taken over smaller firms to achieve market share. In 2007 a total of 1,985 motor carrier firms failed, mostly those having at least five trucks.

Overcapacity has periodically been a severe problem for the motor carrier industry most recently during the recession of 2008 and 2009. Given that there is a finite amount of freight to be transported at any one time and there is little, if anything, that carriers can do to influence this, market share changes generally occur at the expense of one carrier over another. These periods of overcapacity also lead to severe pricing pressure, which can cause weaker carriers to exit the market. Shippers often exploit these factors and the spot market can drive prices below costs as carriers seek to move empty equipment.

Shippers have become increasingly cognizant of the failure rate among motor carriers, and many have introduced a financial evaluation of carriers into their overall decision framework for selecting carriers. When a carrier goes out of business, the interruption of service could have serious consequences.

SUMMARY

• Table 5-2 offers a summary of motor carrier industry characteristics.

Table 5-2	Summary of Motor Carrier Industry Characteristics
• General Service Characteristics	• Low Investments/Equipment
• Investments/Capital Outlays	• 90% Variable Costs, 10% Fixed
• Cost Structure	• Pure Competition
• Ease of Entry	• Compete on Price/Service
• Market Structure	• High-Valued Products
• How They Compete	• Large Number of Small Carriers (With Few Exceptions)
• Types of Commodities	• Long Distance/Metropolitan Destinations
• Number of Carriers	
• Markets in Which They Compete	
• Accessibility, Speed, Reliability, Frequency, and Lower Loss and Damage Rates	

• Motor carriers have developed rapidly during the 20th century and now represent one of the most important modes of transportation for freight movement in the 21st century. U.S. business and most individuals depend in whole or in part upon motor carriers for the movement of goods.

• The public provision (federal, state, and local government units) of highways has played a major role in the development of the motor carrier industry because of the ubiquitous level of accessibility provided by the comprehensive U.S. highway system.

• The private carrier is a very important part of the motor carrier industry and a viable option to large and small companies requiring special services, such as grocery or food deliveries. The need of U.S. industry for dependable and controlled service has also contributed to the development.

• For-hire motor carriers can be classified in a number of useful ways, including local versus intercity, common versus contract, regulated versus exempt, general versus specialized, and TL versus LTL.

• One of the manifestations of deregulation has been the tremendous growth in the TL segment of the motor carrier business, especially among the small truckload carriers, which has significantly escalated the degree of intramodal competition.

• The LTL segment of the motor carrier industry has experienced increased concentration; that is, the larger carriers have generated a larger share of the total tonnage, as they have aggressively expanded and marketed their services.

• The motor carrier industry plays a major role in the movement of manufactured and food products (that is, higher-valued, time-sensitive traffic) because of its generally higher quality of service compared to other modes of transportation.

• The general service characteristics of motor carriers, including accessibility, speed, reliability, frequency, and lower loss and damage rates, have given motor carriers an advantage over other modes.

• Motor carriers offer a variety of equipment for use by shippers that reflect the distance of service and customer requirements.

- The cost structure of motor carriers is dominated by variable costs largely due to the carriers' ability to utilize a publicly provided right-of-way (highways) where payment is based upon user charges such as fuel taxes and licenses.
- Labor costs are an important element of the motor carrier industry, which tends to be much more labor intensive than other modes. Increased equipment size and more nonunion drivers have lessened the impact of wage costs during the 2000s.
- In contrast to railroads, motor carriers are regarded as having limited economies of scale; that is, small-scale operations are viable and competitive. The major exception would be the LTL carriers with their required investment in terminals. There is increasing evidence that there are some economies of scale among large LTL carriers.
- Public funding of highways and the level of user charges paid by motor carriers continue to be arguable issues because it is frequently maintained that motor carriers do not pay their fair share.
- A number of current issues face motor carriers, including safety, substance abuse, technology, undercharge claims, and state regulation.

STUDY QUESTIONS

1. The motor carrier industry is probably the most visible segment of the transportation system in the United States, but in many ways the motor carrier is also the most significant element of the freight transport industry. What factors account for the motor carrier's visibility and significance?

2. The railroad industry played a significant role in the development and growth of many cities and geographic regions during the 19th century. What role, if any, have motor carriers played during the 21st century in terms of economic development?

3. Private carriage is more important in the motor carrier segment of our transportation industry than any of the other four major modal segments. What factors have contributed to private carriage becoming so prevalent in the motor carrier area?

4. The so-called local carrier is also almost unique to the motor carrier industry. Why?

5. Compare and contrast the TL segment of the motor carrier industry with the LTL segment in terms of infrastructure, cost structure, market structure, and operating characteristics.

6. What is the nature of intramodal and intermodal competition in the motor carrier industry? How have the motor carriers fared in terms of intermodal competition since 1980?

7. Describe the general service characteristics of motor carriers and explain how these service characteristics have contributed to the growth of the motor carrier industry.

8. The cost structure of the motor carrier industry is affected by its infrastructure (such as highways and terminals). Discuss the cost structure of motor carriers and how it is affected by the infrastructure. Should there be changes made in public policy with respect to the motor carriers' use of public highways?

9. Describe how fuel and labor have impacted motor carrier cost structures and how they have altered motor carrier operations.

10. What are the major issues facing motor carriers in the 21st century? How should these issues be addressed?

NOTES

1. American Trucking Associations, Inc., *American Trucking Trends, 2008–2009,* Washington, DC: American Trucking Associations, 2008.

2. *Transportation in America,* 20th ed., Washington, DC: Eno Transportation Foundation, 2007.

3. Ibid.

4. American Trucking Associations, op. cit.

5. Ibid.

6. "Yellow and Roadway Get it Together," *Logistics Management,* August 2003, p. 19.

7. American Trucking Associations, Inc., *American Trucking Trends, 1977–1978,* Washington, DC: American Trucking Associations, p. 27.

8. There are no notable exceptions to this ability to serve. Shippers located on an island are served by water or air transportation. Other unique examples exist where the motor carrier is physically unable to provide the transportation.

9. For a complete listing of federal equipment specifications, see the U.S. Department of Transportation, Federal Highway Administration, Bureau of Motor-Carrier Safety, *Federal Motor Carrier Safety Regulations,* Washington, DC: U.S. Government Printing Office, 2008.

10. Through police powers contained in the U.S. Constitution, each state has the right to establish regulations to protect the health and welfare of its citizens. Vehicle length and height laws are within these police powers, as are vehicle speed and weight laws.

11. *Transportation in America*, op. cit.

12. American Trucking Associations, 2008-2009, op. cit.

13. Ibid.

14. Ibid.

CASE 5-1

Hardee Transportation

Jim O'Brien of Hardee Transportation has his hands full with the requests from his largest customer. However, a new and possibly greater issue has presented itself to Jim: the new hours-of-service rules. Hardee's freight lanes and customer pickup and delivery (PUD) operations are set to reflect the previous 10 hours of maximum drive time for his drivers. The dispatch centers and bobtail patterns to service customer trailer pools are also set up on the previous rules.

Jim's customers don't necessarily agree with his concerns. They argue that drivers will actually have more continuous drive time under the new regulations. They also argue that the reduced on-duty hours for drivers will reduce driver fatigue and result in fewer accidents, lowering Hardee's operating costs. Jim doesn't agree. Even though driving hours are increased, total driving time might actually be reduced. If PUD times are increased at certain customer locations, driving time is reduced to comply with the 14-hour on-duty time.

This is a great concern for Jim because some of his largest customers have the longest PUD times. Plus, some of these customers also require that the driver bobtails to their shipping locations. Jim has approached his sales team with the request that they require their customers to reduce loading and unloading times. If they can't, Hardee has no choice but to either increase detention charges or seriously consider dropping those customers. Obviously, these two options were not well-received by the sales organization. Sales perceived these actions to be against Hardee's service strategy and were fearful that some customers may rebel.

CASE QUESTIONS

1. Using the information in this chapter, how would you tell Jim to proceed?

CASE 5-2
Squire Transportation

Squire Transportation (Squire) is a large national truckload (TL) carrier in the United States covering routes going both east-west and north-south. Squire's average length of haul is 1,200 miles with approximately 10 percent empty miles. Squire runs predominantly single driver tractors hauling 53-foot trailers. For years, Squire has relied on relatively inexpensive diesel fuel and nonunion drivers to keep its operating costs low. The location of its major customers requires either bobtailing tractors (repositioning without pulling trailers) or dead-heading equipment (running tractor-trailers empty) to pick up loads for delivery. These practices worked well when diesel prices were at the $1-per-gallon level.

However, the recent volatility of diesel prices has put a strain on Squire's operating costs. Drivers must refuel at truck stops where diesel prices are averaging $3 to $4 per gallon. Repositioning equipment is becoming cost prohibitive, but customers demand on-time pickups for on-time deliveries. Although these increasing diesel prices can be passed on to Squire's customers in the form of fuel surcharges, many customers are beginning to revolt against these rising surcharges. Squire's management can either accept these higher operating costs, thus reducing their profits, or begin to examine the implementation of regional TL operations.

CASE QUESTIONS

1. If you were advising Squire's management team on their impending decision, what would you tell them?

2. Is there an alternative to reduce the impacts of high diesel prices other than to develop regional operations?

3. If not, how would you advise Squire to develop a regional operation?

Chapter 6

RAILROADS

Learning Objectives

After reading this chapter, you should be able to do the following:

- Appreciate the contributions of the railroad industry to the development of the U.S. economy
- Gain an understanding of the size and types of firms in the railroad industry
- Discuss the relevance of intermodal and intramodal competition in the railroad industry
- Know the major types of commodities hauled by the railroads
- Recognize the different types of equipment used in the railroad industry
- Discuss the nature of costs in the railroad industry and how they impact pricing decisions
- Understand the importance of intermodal carloadings on the growth of the railroad industry
- Be aware of the current issues facing the railroad industry today

Transportation Profile

Senate to Consider Stiffer Rail Competition Rules

Freight railroads are facing their stiffest legislative challenges in three decades, as a bill that would make the first changes to the industry's competitive environment since 1980 is slated for a Senate vote in a matter of weeks.

The measure (S. 146), sponsored by Sen. Herb Kohl (D-Wis.), would expose railroads to antitrust laws, trim the power of the Surface Transportation Board—which currently sets rail competition policy—and permit lawsuits in state courts on rail competition policies.

Kohl's spokeswoman, Lynn Becker, told Transport Topics on May 6 that the Senate will consider the measure when its session resumes on June 1. "There hasn't been a vote on this issue since the Staggers Rail Act of 1980," Marty Durbin, vice president of federal affairs for the American Chemistry Council, told TT on May 7. "We consider it quite historic to actually make significant changes in freight rail policy. The current policy puts us in a position where the railroads are able to have monopoly-like power."

The Staggers act freed the railroads from major rate and service restrictions, allowing the industry to regain profitability that reached record level over the past five years.

Railroads continue to staunchly oppose Kohl's measure, which has been awaiting floor action since it was passed 14-0 by the Judiciary Committee in March. The bill "would cause dual oversight of railroad activities, resulting in overlapping and conflicting regulation," said Tom White, a spokesman for the Association of American Railroads. "Elements of rail labor have also come out strongly against the legislation because it would threaten the ability of the nation's railroads to expand their networks and could threaten the jobs of railroad workers."

Among the unions that side with AAR is the Transportation Communications International Union, which represents the industry's clerical workers.

"Customers were promised two things in the Staggers Act: access to competition and protection from monopolistic practices," said Robert Szabo, executive director of Consumers United for Rail Equity, known as CURE, whose members include the American Chemistry Council, as well as coal and grain shippers. "They have not gotten either."

Szabo's group has been attempting for more than two decades to change the competitive landscape, claiming that prices for shipping those bulk products typically are 50 percent higher when customers don't have a choice of railroads.

Becker said Kohl is "cautiously optimistic" that the Senate will pass S. 146. A companion House bill has not moved yet.

Tim Lynch, senior vice president of American Trucking Associations, said ATA has not taken a position on Kohl's bill, although he said that trucking has been subject to antitrust rules for decades and that "the water is not that cold."

Meanwhile, Senate Commerce Committee Chairman Jay Rockefeller (D-W.Va.) and committee member Frank Lautenberg (D-N.J.) have signaled their intention to pursue legislative changes as well. Neither has introduced a bill in this congressional session, but they have asked the STB to postpone hearings on rail competition this month while they develop legislation.

Durbin, who described Kohl's bill as "one step," said it was up to Rockefeller's committee to "get to the heart of the matter" by taking steps such as introducing rail competition where it doesn't exist today and changing STB procedures to decide rate cases faster and more fairly.

AAR's White said the group wouldn't comment on any proposed legislation by Rockefeller. "Our view is that railroads and shippers would both be best served by legislation that recognizes the need for a balanced and fair regulatory system and recognizes the enormous investments railroads must continue to make in order to expand rail capacity," White said.

CURE's Szabo said a particular sticking point was fourth-quarter rail profits that rose, despite an 8 percent decline in traffic. "Increasing revenue from declining volumes of freight?" Szabo observed. "The answer is obvious: the railroads are exploiting their monopoly power ... during the worst economic recession since the 1930s."

White responded: "For most of last year, rail traffic remained at fairly high levels—within a couple of percentage points of 2007. As those declines have continued, it should be noted that almost all of the Class I railroads reported double-digit drops in earnings during the first quarter."

Source: Rip Watson, *Transport Topics,* May 11, 2009, pp. 1, 27. Copyright © 2009 by T.T. Publishing. Reprinted by permission.

Introduction

The offering of scheduled common carrier freight and passenger service to the public began in the United States in 1830, with the start of operations on 13 miles of road between Baltimore and Ellicott's Mills, Maryland. At the start of the U.S. Civil War in 1860, 30,626 miles of road were in service. By then, rail transportation had proven overwhelmingly superior in both price and service quality to animal-powered road transportation, and superior in service quality to water transportation on lakes, rivers, and canals, and on the ocean between different ports within the United States.

During the first 30 years of its existence, the railroad industry evolved from a population of unconnected carriers focused on short-haul traffic to the completion of longer-distance lines located largely between the Atlantic seaboard on the east, the Mississippi River on the west, the St. Lawrence River and Great Lakes on the north, and the Potomac and Ohio Rivers on the south. The Civil War slowed but did not stop rail construction during the 1860s. Most notable was the completion in 1869 of the first rail link between the Midwest and the Pacific Coast. Total road mileage reached 52,922 in 1870. That year marked the beginning of the greatest boom in growth of railroad mileage. By 1900, total mileage stood at 196,346, accessing all parts of the country and providing shippers and travelers with a national network of carriers that connected with one another. Movement of traffic between connecting railroads was facilitated by the industry's almost universal adoption of standard track guage (track guage is the distance between the inside edge of the running rails of a rail track) of 4 feet 8 1/2 in (1435 mm.) and adherence to rolling stock design standards that permitted freight and passenger cars owned by one railroad to be run on the lines of another.

By 1900, the economic superiority of rail transportation had supplanted water transportation, on canals in particular but also on rivers, for many products and for almost all passenger traffic. Transportation of freight and passengers in horse-drawn vehicles continued, but only as short-distance feeders of traffic to and from rail terminals and from ocean, lake, and river ports. Rail transportation's cost and service quality advantages made possible the settlement and economic development, both agricultural and industrial, of landlocked areas in all parts of the United States. Many cities and towns were either founded or experienced significant growth because they stood at key points in the rail network.

The post-1870 boom in railroad network expansion was financed largely by private capital. In some locations, particularly in the East and Midwest, this led to overbuilding of the network. Some promoters of rail projects did not have profit from operation of a completed railroad as their objective. Instead, they sought profit from construction of a railroad and/or from its sale after completion to an already-existing parallel railroad that wanted to prevent erosion of its revenue base by rate competition from the new entrant. Much of this overbuilt capacity remained in operation until the 1970s and 1980s, when it was rationalized in the wake of financial failure of its owners.

Rail transportation remained the dominant, largely unchallenged, mode of intercity freight and passenger movement through the first two decades of the 20th century. However, erosion of its dominance began during the 1920s with the beginning of large-scale government-funded construction of hard-surface roads and superior service and/or cost characteristics of motor carriers and automobiles. Additional competition came from a revival of inland water transportation, which was aided by government-financed navigation improvements on rivers and by privately financed construction of oil pipelines. Air transportation emerged as a serious contender for rail passenger and mail traffic during the 1930s. Overall, the railroad industry suffered significant decline in relative importance after 1920. However, its role in freight transportation remains important in the 21st century.

The railroad industry has stabilized in relative importance during the first part of the 21st century. This trend has been well documented and can be attributed in part to the following factors: alternate transport modes with superior services and/or cost characteristics (primarily motor carriers and pipelines); a resurgence in water transportation; and the changing needs of the U.S. economy. In 2006 railroads transported only 43 percent of the total intercity ton-miles transported by all modes.[1] It is important to note that, on an actual basis, rail ton-miles have continued to increase and railroads are still the largest carrier in terms of intercity ton-miles, but not in terms of tonnage or revenues.

Starting in 1984, the railroad industry adopted a new depreciation accounting system, and **return on investment (ROI)** shot up to 5.7 percent. In 2007 ROI again showed an increase to 9.87 percent.[2] Consequently, some rail stocks have become more attractive investments.

The railroads are still vital to our transportation system and play an important role in our economy. For example, in 2003 rail revenues accounted for approximately 12.7 percent of the nation's freight expenditures.[3] Railroads in 2007 employed 186,112 people.[4] Investment is another indication of importance. In 2007, rail investment in new plant and equipment was over $117 billion. In 2007, for example, rail locomotive and freight car acquisition increased sharply over 2006, increasing more than 50 percent.[5] These indicators have been hailed as further evidence of the success of the Staggers Rail Act of 1980.

As mentioned earlier, in 2006 the railroads shipped about 43 percent of all ton-miles moved by all transport modes in the United States. This percentage of total ton-miles has been declining since its peak of 75 percent in 1929. However, actual ton-miles have, for the most part, been steadily increasing. In 1980 a total of 932 billion ton-miles of domestic intercity freight was moved. The figure dropped to 810 billion ton-miles in 1982 due mostly to the recession of 1982 to 1983. In 2006 the ton-miles moved were 1,853 billion, representing 43 percent of transportation's total 4,309 billion.[6]

These figures highlight the fact that, even though railroads continue to move record amounts of goods, they are capturing less of the total transportation market because other modes have been growing even faster. However, there are indications that railroads may experience a resurgence on a relative basis because of more aggressive marketing and growth in intermodal traffic. Between 2000 and 2007, intermodal traffic increased from a little over 9 million loadings to just over 12 million, an increase of 31 percent.[7] Intermodal shipments have become more attractive as fuel prices escalate and highway congestion increases.

Industry Overview

Number of Carriers

The U.S. freight railroad industry consisted of 565 different railroads in 2007. Of them, 7 were designated by the Surface Transportation Board (STB) as Class I companies (see Table 6-1), meaning that they each generated revenue of $359.6 million or more annually. The balance of 558 non-Class I rail carriers are identified by the Association of American Railroads (AAR) as either "regional" or "local" lines. Regional status applies to linehaul railroads operating at least 350 route miles and/or earning annual revenue of at least $40 million but less than the Class I revenue threshold. Local status applies to linehaul railroads below the regional criteria (commonly referred to as short lines) plus railroads that provide only switching and terminal service. Some regional, short line, and switching and terminal railroads are stand-alone companies. Others are subsidiaries of holding companies such as Genesee & Wyoming, Inc., and RailAmerica, Inc. RailAmerica is one of the largest. In 2009, its 42 subsidiary railroads operated in 26 states and 3 Canadian provinces over track totaling more than 8,000 miles.

Road mileage declined during the same 50-year period (see Table 6-2). Road mileage expanded rapidly during the initial construction period of 1830 to 1910 and reached a peak of 254,251 miles in 1916.[8] By 1929 road mileage was down to 229,530, and in 2007 it had been reduced to about 94,440 road miles.[9] This reduction is traceable largely to the abandonment of duplicate trackage that was built during the boom periods of the industry's developmental years that was no longer needed because of technology advances, market shifts, the rail merger movement, and intermodal competition.

Competition

The competitive position of the railroad industry has changed dramatically after the first two decades of the 20th century. Today, the industry is faced with intense intermodal

Table 6-1	Railroads in 2007			
RAILROAD	NUMBER	MILES	EMPLOYEES	REVENUE ($BIL)
Class I	7	94,313	167,216	$52.9
Regional	33	16,930	7,805	1.8
Local	523	28,891	11,791	2.1
Total	563	140,134	186,812	$56.8

Source: Association of American Railroads, *Railroad Facts,* Washington, DC, 2008, p. 3.

Table 6-2	U.S. Railroad Miles and Trackage (Class I)	
YEAR	**MILES OF ROAD***	**MILES OF TRACK****
1995	108,264	180,419
1996	105,779	176,978
1997	102,128	172,564
1998	100,570	171,098
1999	99,430	168,979
2000	99,250	168,535
2001	97,817	167,275
2002	100,125	170,048
2003	99,126	169,069
2004	97,662	167,312
2005	95,830	164,291
2006	94,942	162,056
2007	94,440	161,114

*This represents the aggregate length of roadway of all line-haul railroads exclusive of yard tracks, sidings, and parallel lines.

**This includes the total miles of railroad track owned by U.S. railroads.

Source: Association of American Railroads, *Railroad Facts,* Washington, DC, 2008, p. 45.

competition, particularly from the motor carrier industry, and selective intramodal competition. Consolidations within the industry have created a situation in which only seven Class I railroads generate 93 percent of railroad revenue.

The industry's economic structure has developed into a fine example of differentiated oligopoly. In other words, there are a small number of very large railroads, and they serve somewhat different market areas. Their major source of competition is intermodal in nature.

Intramodal Today, only a few railroads serve a particular geographic region. This situation gives rise to an oligopolistic market structure because there are a small number of interdependent large sellers. Barriers to entry exist because of the large capital outlays and fixed costs required, and, consequently, pricing of commodity movements not easily diverted to motor carriers and water carriers can be controlled by the existing railroad firms. For this reason, economic regulations enacted by Congress and administered by the ICC before 1980 brought the geographic coverage and the rate-making procedures of the railroads under federal scrutiny and control.

With the merger trend discussed earlier, the intramodal competition has been reduced. Many cities now have only one railroad serving them. Even major rail centers such as Chicago or Kansas City have seen the number of carriers serving those areas significantly reduced. Shippers are concerned that there will not be enough effective intramodal competition to preserve railroad-to-railroad competition.

Intermodal As noted earlier, the relative market share of railroad intercity ton-miles has been steadily declining because of increased intermodal competition. Inroads into the lucrative commodity markets have been facilitated by governmental expenditures on infrastructure that have benefited competing modes. For example, the government has provided an extensive local and national highway system, especially the interstate network, for motor carrier use.

Customers look for consistent on-time performance. Railroads need to provide this level of service to stay competitive. Railroad companies usually cannot deliver freight early because the customer then has to find a place to store it.

In addition, through improvements and maintenance of the inland waterway system by the U.S. Army Corps of Engineers, the government has also provided the right-of-way for water carriers. Because of the governmental programs and the response of the railroad industry to change, railways now account for 15.2 percent of total tonnage and 39.4 percent of total ton-miles shipped (see Table 6-3).

Overall, the railroads have been rate-competitive. Government expenditure programs aimed at promoting other modes, together with intermodal competition, forced the railways into making a determined effort to forestall industry decline by becoming more competitive. The Staggers Rail Act, which removed significant economic regulation, has allowed railroads to be much more price-competitive through contract rates and more tailored response to customers' service requirements.

Mergers Historically, many mergers have taken place in the railroad industry, and the size of the remaining carriers has correspondingly increased. Early rail mergers grew out of efforts to expand capacity to benefit from large-volume traffic efficiencies

Table 6-3	Railroad Intercity Ton-Miles and Tonnage			
YEAR	*TON-MILES	PERCENT OF TOTAL	**TONNAGE	PERCENT OF TOTAL
1950	597	56.1	1421	46.7
1960	579	44.1	1301	36.1
1970	771	39.8	1572	31.1
1980	932	37.5	1589	28.7
1990	1,091	34.9	1738	16.4
1995	1,375	37.4	1911	15.5
2000	1,534	38.5	2139	15.3
2001	1,558	39.0	2121	15.2
2003	1,610	39.4	2161	15.2

*Billions.
**Millions.
Source: Eno Transportation Foundation, Washington, DC, *Transportation in America*, 20th Ed. 2007.

and economies. Later, **side-by-side** combinations were made to strengthen the financial positions of many of the railroads and eliminate duplication. More recently though, **end-to-end mergers** were created to provide more effective intermodal and intramodal competition.[10] Customer service and reliability can be improved by these mergers because the many types of operating costs, such as car switching, clerical costs, and record-keeping, can be reduced. However, such improvements, in some instances, have been slow to develop.

Previously we noted that the number of railroads (see Table 6-1) and the number of miles of track (see Table 6-2) have declined. One of the major reasons for this decline in both the number of companies and the miles of track has been the significant number of mergers or unifications that have occurred in the railroad industry during the past 30 years. A total of 28 mergers have taken place during the past 30 years, and 50 unifications overall. The latter included not only mergers but also consolidations and outright purchases for control. The decade of the 1970s was very active, but the tempo of rail consolidations in the 1980s was hyperactive.

In 1920 there were 186 Class 1 railroads; by 2008 the number had declined to 7. One reason for this drop was the way in which railroads are classified by revenue; as it was adjusted for inflation, fewer roads qualified. The primary reason, however, was the accelerating trend of mergers. After the Staggers Act was passed in 1980, there was a significant increase in mergers and acquisitions so that as of 1999 there were only four major rail lines: Norfolk Southern, CSX Transportation, Union Pacific, and the Burlington Northern Santa Fe.

Global Perspectives

The Mexican Connection

The route from China to the United States might be taking a different route if the Mexican government and the Kansas City Southern Railway (KCS) have their way. Both entities are involved in developing the port of Lazaro Cerdenas along the southern coast of Mexico to become the new entry to the United States for containers arriving from China. The KCS has established a partnership with the Texas Mexican Railway Company and the Panama Canal Railway Company to form what is called the NAFTA Railway. Containers arriving at Lazaro Cerdenas would be loaded onto KCS flatcars and moved to Kansas City in the United States, where KCS has agreements with the Canadian National Railroad, BNSF, and the Norfolk-Southern Railroad to move these containers throughout the United States. This route would provide international container shipments an alternative to the highly utilized Port of Long Beach.

The Mexican government is also proposing a $4 billion construction project to develop the Port of Punta Colonet, about 150 miles south of Tijuana. The project would include port developers as well as railroads to construct the port and new rail lines to link Punta Colonet with the United States. The Union Pacific railroad, which owns a stake in the Mexican railroad Ferromex, could be a leading contender for the rail link between the new port and the United States.

These new developments also have their critics. Environmentalists fear the port construction will damage the areas' plants and wildlife. U.S. labor unions have expressed concern about the loss of American jobs that might result from shifting container arrivals from U.S. to Mexican ports. The port development process in Mexico has slowed from lawsuits and other legal battles, leading other critics to doubt that the projects will be undertaken any time soon.

Abandonments Recall that in 1916, at its peak, the railroad industry owned 254,037 miles of road. Today, more than half of that is gone, enough to circle the Earth three times. The early overexpansion left extensive amounts of excess trackage in many areas, and the railroads had to abandon significant portions of rail trackage to remain competitive. Parallel and overlapping routes, therefore, have been eliminated wherever possible.

Many factors led to the abandonment of track around the country. In the late 1950s, the government began the construction of the Interstate Highway System. This allowed motor carrier service to decrease transit time, which caused shippers to use these carriers. To effectively compete with motor carriers for time-sensitive traffic, railroads had to focus on efficient routes. In the 1970s and 1980s, bankruptcies forced the abandonment of portions of railroad systems such as the Rock Island, Penn Central, and Milwaukee Road. In 1980, partial deregulation gave rail companies greater freedom to buy, sell, or abandon unprofitable track. Once the railroad companies abandoned the tracks, they sold the rails and ties to scrap dealers.

The land used for rights-of-way, abandoned by the railroads, could also be used unless the original deed required the return when the property was no longer being utilized for railroad purposes.

In some cases, all or part of the right-of-way was turned into hiking trails with some bridges left in place. The program, Rail to Trails Conservancy, has been highly successful in adding over 10,000 miles of trails to the country's recreational facilities. In other cases, the land and sometimes even the track was left in place as part of a program known as "rail-banking." The theory behind this is should the line be needed in the future, it would be much easier to restore it. In one case, a major railroad company reopened a major line after it was closed for over 10 years.

Even though the railroad industry reduced its road mileage by more than half, the lines remaining still carried a major share of the existing freight. The abandonments included both rural branches and mainlines made duplicate by mergers of parallel carriers. The ICC, and later the STB, still regulate abandonments, but changes in the law made it much easier for railroad companies to shed unprofitable lines. Not all the lines were scrapped, as discussed above, and regional and short-line operators took over some of this property.

New developments, such as unit trains carrying one commodity like coal or grain from one shipper to one consignee, helped the railroads operate more profitably. As more and more traffic was concentrated on fewer and fewer routes, overhead costs were spread over more businesses. Each time a railroad interchanged a car to another line, there was the chance for delay. As mergers reduced the number of railroads, fewer interchanges were needed.

Operating and Service Characteristics

General Service Characteristics

Commodities Hauled In the 19th century, when the railroads were the primary source of transportation, they moved almost every available type of product or raw material. Today, the railroad system has evolved into a system that primarily transports large quantities of heavyweight, low-value commodities (or bulk products).[11] However, intermodal

Table 6-4	Carloads Originated by Commodity			
	CARLOADS (THOUSANDS)		CHANGE	
COMMODITY GROUP	2007	2006	CARS	PERCENT
Miscellaneous Mixed Shipments*	8,465	8,536	–71	–0.8
Coal	7,480	7,574	–94	–1.2
Chemicals and Allied Products	2,069	1,969	99	5.1
Farm Products	1,681	1,590	91	5.7
Motor Vehicles and Equipment	1,639	1,714	–75	–4.4
Food and Kindred Products	1,493	1,487	7	0.4
Nonmetallic Minerals	1,398	1,470	–73	–4.9

*The miscellaneous mixed shipments category (STCC 46) is mostly intermodal traffic.
Source: Association of American Railroads, Washington, DC, 2008, p. 25.

containers and trailers, carrying high-value finished products, make up a significant portion of many railroads' movements. Motor carriers concentrate on the handling of small-volume, high-value finished goods, whereas water and pipelines carry the larger volumes of the lowest-value types of bulk commodities. The railroads therefore find themselves engaged in intense competition with these other modes for the opportunity to ship many product categories. Although railroads still handle a wide variety of commodities, more than 83 percent of total rail carloadings in 2007 involved the movement of bulk materials. Table 6-4 lists the products with almost 31.5 million carloadings carried by the railroads in 2007. Of the seven commodities shown in the table, only two, motor vehicles and equipment and miscellaneous and mixed shipments (intermodal), are not bulk commodities.

Coal Railroads are the primary haulers of coal, accounting for 43.8 percent of the total tonnage transported in 2007.[12] Table 6-4 indicates that 7.48 million carloadings moved in 2007, up by more than 94,000 from 2006 levels. Coal is an alternative energy source that will probably continue to be an important commodity shipped by the railroads, and this tonnage may increase if there are political challenges in the Middle East that limit the supply of petroleum and related products.

Farm Products When considered together, farm and food products constitute the third largest commodity group hauled by railroads. Total movement by rail amounted to about 3.2 million carloads in 2007.[13] The growth in domestic markets and the increase of exports to foreign customers have been steady for many years. For example, the exportation of grain and its related products accounted for more than 50 percent of the total grain market. Because of this growth, distribution patterns might change, but the transportation of farm products will continue to be an important rail commodity movement.

Chemicals Chemicals and allied products, a great number of which are classified as hazardous by the U.S. Department of Transportation (DOT), are transported in specially designed tank cars. A total of 177 million tons of this highly rated traffic traveled by rail in 2007.[14] Railroads can safely transport chemicals in comparison with highway movements, and this safety has been steadily increasing for years. This type of long-haul bulk material is ideally suited for rail movement. Interestingly, motor carriers move more chemicals, and they compete vigorously for this traffic.

Transportation Equipment   Transportation equipment carloadings, which are linked to the relative health of the domestic automobile industry, have increased to more than 5 percent of total carloadings, but decreased by over 75,000 carloads from 2006 to 2007.

Although the commodities shipped by the railroad industry have changed over the years, with the emphasis placed on the movement of low-value, high-volume bulk materials, the railroads are still a possible mode of transport for many different types of goods, including both high-value merchandise and raw materials alike.

Traffic Shifts   As indicated previously, the demand for freight transportation is a derived demand; that is, transportation demand is based upon the demand for products to be moved. Consequently, economic conditions have an impact upon the demand for transportation service. This is especially true for railroads because they primarily move basic raw materials and supplies (such as coal, chemicals, and so on).

There was almost universal agreement that the U.S. economy was recovering during the last three quarters of 2003. In spite of the economic upturn, standard rail carload shipments during this period did not reflect the economic good news of 2003. However, intermodal movements by rail increased by 6.9 percent during this period. This trend toward intermodal moves could prove to be very beneficial to the railroad industry and allow them to be more competitive with the motor carriers.

Constraints

Railroads are constrained by fixed rights-of-way and therefore provide differing degrees of service completeness. For example, if both the shipper and receiver possess rail sidings, then door-to-door service can be provided. However, if no sidings are available, the movement of goods must be completed by some other mode.

The railroad system, although composed of individual companies, provides a truly nationwide network of service. Each railroad serves a specific geographic region, and freight and equipment are exchanged at interchange points. For example, a shipment between Philadelphia, Pennsylvania, and Portland, Oregon, might be handled by two or three railroads, depending on the route chosen. The through service is unique, but multiple handlings can create rate-division problems and delays in delivery.

Although on-time delivery performance and the frequency of service had deteriorated in the past, improvements have been made in recent years. The current position of the industry has been restored to competitive levels on selected movements (particularly over long distances). Railroads dominate the market for hauling 30,000 pounds or more over distances exceeding 300 miles. The industry hopes to expand its service to certain short-haul markets and selected lanes for manufactured products. Reliability and transit time, along with equipment availability, have improved to make railroads competitive in these markets.

Strengths

The large carrying capacity of rail freight cars and the economies of scale in freight train operations enable the railroads to handle large-volume movements of low-value commodities over long distances. Motor carriers, on the other hand, are constrained by volume and weight to the smaller truckload (TL) and less-than-truckload (LTL)

Table 6-5	Types and Number of Freight Cars in Service in 2007			
TYPE	TOTAL	CLASS 1 RAILROAD	OTHER RAILROADS	CAR COMPA- NIES AND SHIPPERS
Boxcars	121,570	68,776	39,638	13,156
Plain Box	16,329	1,257	5,085	9,987
Equipped Box	105,241	67,519	34,553	3,169
Covered Hoppers	411,503	110,360	20,513	280,630
Flatcars	172,243	95,733	23,622	52,888
Refrigerator Cars	22,092	16,361	2,457	3,274
Gondolas	217,775	98,129	21,941	97,705
Hoppers	166,421	68,799	11,241	86,382
Tank Cars	269,076	1,033	21	266,022
Others	5,029	981	1,031	3,017
Total	1,385,709	460,172	120,463	805,074

Source: Association of American Railroads, *Railroad Facts,* Washington, DC, 2008, p. 52.

markets. Furthermore, although pipelines compete directly with the railroads, they are restricted largely to the movements of liquid and gas (and then only in one direction).

This kind of carload capacity, along with a variety of car types, permits the railroads to handle almost any type of commodity. For the most part, the industry is not constrained to weight and volume restrictions, and customer service is available throughout the United States. In addition, railroads are able to use a variety of car types to provide a flexible service because the rolling stock consists of boxcars, tankers, gondolas, hoppers, covered hoppers, flatcars, and other special types of cars (see Table 6-5).

Another important service is that the **liability** for loss and damage is usually assumed by the railroads. Railroads, however, have had a comparatively high percentage of goods damaged in transit. In 2007 the total pay-out of freight claims for U.S. and Canadian railroads decreased to $96 million from $105 million in 2006.[15] Such damage occurs because rail freight often goes through a rough trip due to vibrations and shocks from steel wheels riding on steel rails. In addition, the incidence of loss is usually higher than on other modes because of the high degree of multiple handlings. Excessive loss and damage claims have tended to erode shipper confidence in the railroad's ability to provide adequate service.

To regain traffic lost to other modes and gain new traffic share, the railroads have placed an increasing amount of attention on equipment and technology. For example, to decrease damage to freight, improved suspension systems and end-of-car cushioning devices have been applied to freight cars assigned to the movement of shock-sensitive products.

Also, the Association of American Railroads has developed a quality certification program (M-1003) to ensure freight car quality and technical specifications. Finally, equipping cars with instrumentation packages to measure forces that might cause damage reduces the damage potential. One area that has received much attention has been the intermodal area, namely, trailer-on-flatcar (**TOFC**) and container-on-flatcar (**COFC**) service. Of special importance in the COFC market is the use of double-stacks, which significantly improve railroad productivity. The railroads realized the necessity of improving the TOFC and COFC services to compete effectively with motor carriers. The developments include terminal facilities for loading and unloading, as well as changes in the railcars, trailers, and containers. However, the changes have not stopped here. The railroads have invested a significant amount of money recently in improving right-of-way and structures to enhance service by preventing delays.

Microprocessors have found use in the railroad industry, particularly in communications and signaling. Computer chips are also being used in vital safety-related circuits. Fiber optics are used to improve communications, which will in turn improve service and revenues. The railroad industry hopes that these service-related improvements will increase its traffic.

Equipment

The **carload** is the basic unit of measurement of freight handling used by the railroads. A carload can vary in size and capacity depending on the type of car being used. Historically, the number of carloadings has declined since the turn of the century; there was a total of almost 37 million carloads in 1929. In 2007, the total railroad carloads equaled 31.5 million.[16] This decline has occurred primarily because of the introduction of larger cars and the increase in productivity per car type. Absolute tonnage has increased (see Table 6-3).

The increases in average carrying capacity of railroad freight cars over the past 50 years have been dramatic. In 2007 the average carrying capacity per car stood at almost 99.5 tons, compared to 46.3 tons in 1929.[17] Most of today's new cars have more than twice the capacity of the typical boxcar used 50 years ago. However, the carrying capacity of a new or rebuilt car could easily exceed 100 tons, and the trend of increasing average capacity will continue in the near future. A car with a 100-ton capacity probably represents the most efficient size with the present support facilities. Today's standard car gross vehicle weight is 263,000 pounds, with efforts being made to increase this to 286,000. However, bridge and track structures must be able to handle these weights.

The railroads own and maintain their own rolling stock. The characteristics of these cars have changed considerably to suit customer requirements; for example, the conventional boxcar had been de-emphasized but has seen resurgence in the past few years. Today's car fleet is highly specialized and is designed to meet the needs of the individual shipper. Following is a list of eight generalized car types:

- Boxcar (plain): Standardized roofed freight car with sliding doors on the side used for general commodities
- Boxcar (equipped): Specially modified boxcar used for specialized merchandise, such as automobile parts
- Hopper car: A freight car with the floor sloping to one or more hinged doors used for discharging bulk materials

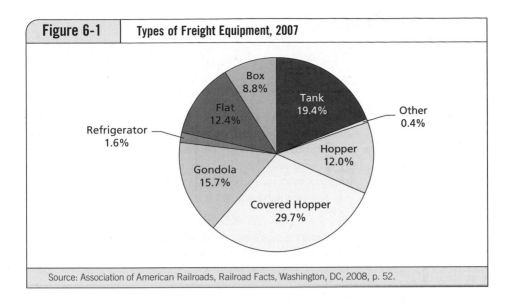

Figure 6-1 | **Types of Freight Equipment, 2007**

Source: Association of American Railroads, Railroad Facts, Washington, DC, 2008, p. 52.

- Covered hopper: A hopper car with a roof designed to transport bulk commodities that need protection from the elements
- Flatcar: A freight car with no top or sides used primarily for TOFC service machinery and building materials
- Refrigerator car: A freight car to which refrigeration equipment has been added for controlled temperature
- Gondola: A freight car with no top, a flat bottom, and fixed sides used primarily for hauling bulk commodities
- Tank car: Specialized car used for the transport of liquids and gases

The total number and percentage of freight cars in service in 2007 are shown in Table 6-5 and Figure 6-1. The boxcar has been surpassed in use by the covered hopper car, which is followed closely in number by the tank car. In addition, the largest increase in total new cars was in covered hopper cars. The composition of the railroad fleet has shifted from the accommodation of manufactured commodities to the movement of bulk goods. In 2007 more than 85 percent of the total fleet was designed for the transport of bulk and raw materials.

Class I railroads own almost 42 percent of the rolling stock in use, private companies hold title to the remainder (see Table 6-5).[18] Car companies and shippers are becoming increasingly more important in the ownership of railroad cars. In 1991 they owned almost all of the specially designed tank cars in use, and in the past several years they have purchased a substantial number of covered hopper cars, more than 30,000.

To remain competitive with the other modes of transportation, the railroads have increased their capacity. The average freight train load also has increased; in 2007 more than 3,274 tons per load were carried as compared to barely 800 tons per load in 1929.[19] This increase in capacity is necessary if more bulk commodities are to be shipped longer distances in the future.

Service Innovations

The railroad cost structure makes it necessary to attract large and regular volumes of traffic to take advantage of scale economies and to operate efficiently. In recent years, rail management has developed or re-emphasized a number of service innovations to increase traffic volume.

The concept of piggyback service was designed by railroad management to increase service levels to intermodal customers. Piggyback traffic, which includes both TOFC and COFC services, accounted for 15.2 percent of total loadings in 1986, occupying a little less than 3 million cars and ranking second behind coal in total rail carloadings. In 2007 more than 12 million trailers and containers were loaded.[20] As can be seen in Table 6-6, intermodal carloadings increased until 2000, when there was a modest decline of 2.7 percent. When discussing piggyback service, consideration must be given to the individual concepts of TOFC and COFC movements.

TOFC service transports highway trailers on railroad flatcars. It combines the line-haul efficiencies of the railroads with the flexibility of local motor carrier pickup and delivery service. On-time deliveries, regularly scheduled departures, and fuel efficiency

Table 6-6	Intermodal Carloadings
YEAR	**TRAILER AND CONTAINERS**
1980	3,059,402
1985	4,590,952
1990	6,206,782
1992	6,627,891
1993	7,156,628
1994	8,128,228
1995	7,936,172
1996	8,143,258
1997	8,698,308
1998	8,772,663
1999	8,907,626
2000	9,176,890
2001	8,935,444
2002	9,312,360
2003	9,955,605
2004	10,993,662
2005	11,693,512
2006	12,282,221
2007	12,026,660

Source: Association of American Railroads, *Railroad Facts,* Washington, DC, 2008, p. 26.

are the major reasons for the present growth and future potential of TOFC service. For example, a 100-car train (which places two trailers on each flatcar) is more economical to run than 200 trucks over the road. Fuel is saved and railroad economies of scale are realized. Traffic congestion, road damage, and maintenance and repair costs are all reduced because of the reduction of number of trucks out on the highways.

Table 6-6 shows that the intermodal movement of trailers and containers grew rapidly during the 1980s and 1990s. This growth was stimulated by the advent of double-stack containers used in international trade. Also, the railroads have placed new emphasis on their intermodal business after a number of years of doubting its profitability. In recent years, the railroads have largely segregated their intermodal traffic from regular freight, with most of the intermodal trains operating on a priority schedule.

One result of the new schedules has been more reliable service for shippers, which has led to increased growth in loadings. The railroads have also simplified their billing procedures and made their computers accessible to customers for service innovations.

The growing use of TOFC by motor carrier companies has also contributed to the recent growth. United Parcel Service (UPS) has been a supporter of rail intermodal service for some time and is the largest single customer of some railroads. The LTL carriers began using intermodal service during the 1980s to handle their surges of traffic, and as rail service has become more reliable, they are using the rail service on a continuing basis. New labor agreements allow union motor carriers to substitute rail for over-the-road up to a certain percent of the total traffic. The biggest change came when two of the largest truckload carriers, Schneider National and J. B. Hunt, purchased equipment to use rail intermodal service on an extensive basis. This commitment by these two large carriers has had a significant influence on the growth of rail intermodal service. Figure 6-2 shows the flows of traffic in the United States.

Figure 6-2	Intermodal Traffic Flows

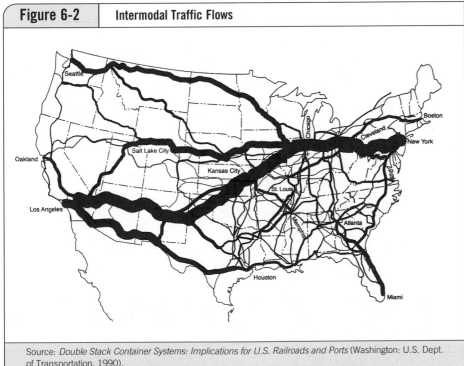

Source: *Double Stack Container Systems: Implications for U.S. Railroads and Ports* (Washington: U.S. Dept. of Transportation, 1990).

Note: Line thickness corresponds to intermodal volume.

COFC is the form of transportation for shipping containers and is equivalent to domestic TOFC for trailer movements. A container does not have wheels and must therefore be placed on a flatbed trailer for ramp-to-door delivery. The amount of handling is reduced because the container can be loaded and sealed at the origin and shipped directly to the consignee. Economies are realized because putting finished goods in containers means not only lower packaging and warehousing costs but also faster transit times because time and effort are saved in the loading, unloading, and delivery of goods. In addition, the TOFC piggyback plans can apply to COFC shipments with the substitution of the container for the trailer in the movement. Furthermore, land-bridge traffic, which substitutes railroads for ocean vessels for part of the journey, has become more widely used in international commerce because it facilitates the handling of export–import commodities.[21] The double stacking of the containers on traffic to and from West Coast ports has improved the productivity of the rail COFC service dramatically.

On the Line

Economic Downturn Impacts Railroads

The current economic situation in the United States is having a negative effect on railroad freight movements. The Association of American Railroads reported that from August 2008 to August 2009 carloads decreased by 16.4 percent and intermodal loadings decreased by 16.7 percent. The biggest decline in carloads was for metallic ores and metals (down 50 percent), while the smallest decline was in coal (down 9.1 percent). For the same period, trailer intermodal loadings declined 35.2 percent while container intermodal loadings declined by 12.1 percent.

However, the decline in carloads in August 2009 was the lowest since February 2009, and intermodal loadings were up 11,500 units from July 2009. This might show some indication that the decline in freight movements by the U.S. railroads has slowed and that the "bottoming out" of the economy has arrived.

The decline in rail freight has had a negative impact on the profitability of both the railroads and intermodal marketing firms. The HUB Group, a large intermodal marketing firm, reported that the economic downturn was cutting their fourth-quarter earnings. The Kansas City Southern Railroad also expected weaker-than-normal profits. Part of this is attributed to the weakening of the Mexican peso against the U.S. dollar; about 50 percent of the KCS tracks are in Mexico.

Even with declining freight movements, intermodal rail prices increased 2.8 percent in July 2009, and overall rail freight prices were up 0.1 percent during the same period. As the economy continues to rebound, with rail capacity tight, there seems to be an opportunity for the U.S. rail industry to seek further price increases across both carloads and intermodal loadings.

The **unit train**, which evolved from the rent-a-train concept for the movement of goods, specializes in the transport of only one commodity, usually coal or grain, from origin to destination. Many times the shipper owns cars, and the train is, in effect, rented to the shipper for a particular period of time. For example, a typical utility coal unit train move would involve the transportation of 10,000 tons of coal in 100 hopper or gondola cars, each with a 100-ton capacity. The movement would be directly from the mine to an electric power-generating station with no stops in transit, and loading and unloading would be accomplished while the train was moving. Because of the single commodity nature of the concept and the need to maintain regularly scheduled movements, empty backhauls occur. However, this drawback is offset by the high revenue-producing capabilities of the unit train resulting from the improved overall car utilization.

Rail management has responded by increasing the use of computers and communications to help improve discipline and maintain control over rail operations. Elaborate information and communication systems have been developed so that a railroad's progress, status, and reliability can be monitored on an online basis. Car ordering and billing is simplified, while cars are traced and located, and orders are expedited at a faster rate. Computers are not a panacea, but they do help bring about increased efficiencies without any loss in service quality.

Cost Structure

Fixed Costs

The railroad industry's cost structure in the short run (a period when both plant and capacity remain constant) consists of a large proportion of indirect fixed costs rather than variable costs.[22] This situation exists because the railroads, along with the pipelines, are the only modes that own and maintain their own network and terminals.

In addition, railroads, like other modes, operate their own rolling stock. In the past, it has been estimated by some managers that up to two-thirds of the industry's cost did not vary with volume.[23] Today it is believed that this figure is closer to 30 percent. The investment in long-lived assets has had a major impact on the cost characteristics of the industry. Cost structures were presented in Chapter 4.

The major cost element borne by the railroad industry, and not found in the cost structure of other modes (excluding pipelines), is the operation, maintenance, and ownership of rights-of-way. **Rights-of-way** describe what a carrier's equipment uses to provide movement. For example, the railroads operate trains on tracks they own and maintain, while the motor carriers use highways. Initially, a large capital investment is required and annual maintenance costs become a substantial drain on earnings. Capital expenditures in 2007 alone amounted to $9.1 billion.[24]

Another major component of the railroad industry's high fixed costs is the extensive investment in private terminal facilities. These terminal facilities include freight yards, where trains are sorted and assembled, and terminal areas and sidings, where shippers and connecting railroads are serviced. Because of the ownership of fixed assets, the railroads as a group are not as responsive as other modes to the volume of traffic carried. Motor and water carriers, as well as the airline industry, are able to shift resources more quickly in response to changes in customer demand because of their use of "free" rights-of-way. Motor carriers, for instance, pay for their costs through user charges, tolls, and various taxes (such as fuel taxes). These charges are related and vary directly with the volume handled, thereby creating a variable rather than a fixed cost for the user. Circumstances place the railroads at a disadvantage.

The investment for equipment in rail transport, principally for locomotives and various types of rolling stock, has been enormous. In 2007 more than $8.6 billion was spent on equipment.[25] The Class I railroads operated 24,143 locomotives and some

580,635 freight cars in 2007.[26] Other railroads, car companies, and shippers owned or leased about 500,000 cars. The costs associated with equipment are both fixed and variable depending on which costs are used and what time period is being considered.

It is apparent that the railroads have a high proportion of expenses that are fixed and constant in the short run. However, they also have costs that vary substantially with volume.

Semivariable Costs

Semivariable costs, which include maintenance of rights-of-way, structures, and equipment, have accounted for more than 40 percent of railroad outlays in recent years and have amounted to more than $10 billion per year. These figures, however, are deceptive because some railroads that were in poor financial health in the 1960s and 1970s had allowed their physical plants and equipment to deteriorate at alarming rates. The Federal Railroad Administration estimated that the industry has deferred more than $4 billion in maintenance expenses in some years.[27] Railway management in financially weak railroads found it necessary to forego maintenance to pay expenses, such as increased fuel and labor. Recently, maintenance schedules have been implemented on a regular basis so that service would not further deteriorate, and additional business would not be lost.

Variable Costs

Variable costs are one of the immediate concerns of railroad management, accounting for a large proportion of every revenue dollar spent by the railways. Labor cost is the largest single element of variable costs for railroads. Fuel and power costs are the next largest group of variable costs. Together these two categories account for a major portion of variable costs.

Labor In 2007 the cost of labor was $14.4 billion or $0.264 cents of every revenue dollar.[28] The average hourly gross earning for all employees was $27.37, with an average annual earning of $69,367. Train and engine employees received an annual earning of $73,202, whereas maintenance workers received about $59,486. Together, these groups accounted for 78 percent of all the wages paid by the railroads.[29]

Railroad labor is represented by many different unions as opposed to the motor carrier industry, the vast majority of whose unionized employees are members of one union, the Teamsters. There are three major classifications of labor unions: operating, nonoperating craft, and nonoperating industrial. Each represents a different category of employee. The large number of unions has created difficulties for railroad management because each union guards its rights. Recently, some unions have merged and have shown much more flexibility in allowing innovation.

Railroad management believes that some of the work rules for the operating unions are either out of date or inefficient. The railroad industry has been reducing the size of the standard train crew wherever possible. Many positions, such as that of fireman, a carryover from the steam engine era, are no longer needed. Changes in how crews are paid have allowed railroads to gain operating efficiencies. Furthermore, "seniority districts," or the establishment of artificial boundaries beyond which an employee is not authorized to work, is a barrier to operating efficiency. Progress has been made with these issues, but they have not been completely resolved.

The railroad industry has been addressing work rules and staffing requirements in a very aggressive manner in the past several years. Several railroads have negotiated new crew agreements that have reduced the number of personnel required for trains. Conrail started a program in 1981 to buy off unnecessary brakemen and firemen; this program eliminated more than 1,900 positions, yielding a savings of $85 million.[30]

Starting in 1982, rail management took steps to remove cabooses from freight trains. It has been estimated that the elimination of cabooses saved as much as $400 million per year. The rail unions agreed that railroads could drop cabooses by local agreement, if possible, and by arbitration, if necessary.[31] Two-person crews are now the standard, with both riding on the locomotive.

Railroad managers feel that continuing changes in modifying or eliminating work rules for rail employees must be implemented in the near future if the industry is to survive in its present form. Mutual trust and cooperation should replace impediments between labor and management that restrict productivity gains, labor-savings methods, and technological advances. Progress in other industries has indicated the productivity gains that are possible.

Fuel Fuel costs make up the second largest percentage of the revenue dollar. Fortunately, railroads have very efficient propulsion units, and productivity and fuel efficiency have increased dramatically since 1929. In the past 50 years, the railroads have more than doubled the revenue of ton-miles while reducing the locomotive units to less than one-half the 1929 level. Thus, the industry has been able to partially offset the increase in fuel costs by making locomotives more efficient. In 2007, $8.9 billion was spent on fuel, showing an increase of $5.6 billion from the 1980s level of $3.3 billion. This is a result of using more fuel-efficient engines and other train devices, such as wind-resistance designs.[32] The railroad's efficiency in the use of fuel is an important factor in making intermodal movements more attractive for motor carriers.

Economies of Scale

As previously indicated, railroads have a high level of fixed costs as contrasted with variable costs. Fixed costs, such as property taxes, are incurred regardless of traffic volume. Variable costs, on the other hand, vary or change with the volume of traffic moved; that is, they rise with increases and fall with decreases in traffic levels.

The development of any railroad requires a very large capital investment because of the cost incurred in buying land, laying tracks, building bridges, providing terminals, and providing right-of-way facilities. In addition, equipment investment is significant. Maintenance of right-of-way structures also results in fixed costs because it is usually the weather rather than use that necessitates such expenditures. The same is also true to some extent of equipment maintenance because the equipment spends so much time in freight yards and on sidings.

All costs are generally regarded as being variable in the long run because, as traffic increases, capacity is reached and new investment is needed in plants and equipment. However, because railroads are so large and facilities are durable, the short run can be a long period of time.

The focus here is primarily on the short run. Consequently, special note should be made of the impact of the high level of fixed costs in the railroad industry. When fixed costs are present, a business will operate under conditions of increasing returns until capacity is reached. In other words, an increase in output (traffic) will not be accompanied by a proportionate increase in total costs because only the variable costs will increase. This will mean a decline in the per-unit costs because the fixed costs will be spread out over an increased number of units with subsequent unit-cost declines.

Consider several examples that illustrate the impact of fixed costs and economies of scale. Suppose that C. B. N. Railroad carries 200 million tons of freight at an average charge of $0.035 per ton. It has fixed costs of $3.5 million and variable costs of $2.5 million:

Fixed Costs	$3.5 million
Variable Costs	+ $2.5 million
Total Costs	$6.0 million
Revenue	$7.0 million
Profit	$1.0 million
Cost Per Ton	$0.03

Assume a 20-percent increase in traffic at the same average charge of $.035 per ton and no need to increase plant size:

Fixed Costs	$3.5 million
Variable Costs	$3.0 million
Total Costs	$6.5 million
Revenue	$8.4 million
Profit	$1.9 million
Cost Per Ton	$0.0271

It is obvious from the above example that, if average revenue stays the same, the economies of scale not only lower costs per unit but also increase profit.

Financial Plight

As noted previously, the railroad industry once enjoyed a virtual monopoly on the efficient and dependable transportation of passengers and freight. Railroads played a very important role in achieving various national objectives during the 19th century. Because of this, the government promoted the growth of the industry until a distinct change in public attitudes toward railroads became apparent.

The establishment in 1887 of the Interstate Commerce Commission (ICC), which was created to regulate maximum rates and to prevent discrimination to protect the rail shipper, marked the beginning of this change. In later years, the ICC's objective was to promote competition between modes of transportation while ensuring the financial health of the regulated carriers. However, this objective was never completely accomplished.[33] Competition tended to be restrained under the regulatory environment prior to 1975.

Over the decades, competition from other modes of transportation increased dramatically. By the 1950s, more people selected buses and planes for transportation, rather than using rail transportation. The rail industry's share of the intercity freight market also declined to less than 50 percent during this time. Although competition from other modes became progressively more intense, the railroads were subject to strict regulations that frequently treated them as if they were still the dominant form of freight transportation.[34] Government funds were used to provide rail competitors with their rights-of-way without fully charging them the cost of constructing or maintaining them as with the rail industry. Between 1946 and 1975, the federal government spent more than $81 billion on highways, $24 billion on airports and supervision of airways, $10 billion on inland waterways, and only $1.3 billion on railroads.[35]

The financial position of the railroads grew increasingly worse after World War II. During the 1970s, the railroad industry's return on investment remained near 2 percent and never exceeded 3 percent. The railroads were plagued by decreasing market shares, poor future prospects, and high debt ratios. At least 20 percent of the industry was bankrupt by 1970. These poor conditions were evident in delayed or poor maintenance, increasing claims for damages, and accidents that cost the industry many of its much-needed customers. The railroads' share of intercity freight revenues had fallen from 72 percent in 1929 to less than 18 percent in the mid-1970s.[36]

It became obvious that the railroad industry could not continue to survive under these conditions and that the main obstacle that needed to be cleared from the railroads' path to survival was probably excessive regulation that restricted their ability to compete. Poor earnings made it difficult for the railroads to earn or borrow sufficient funds to make improvements in track and rail facilities.[37]

Legislation Reform

The Rail Passenger Act of 1970 created the government-sponsored National Railroad Passenger Corporation (**Amtrak**), which relieved the railroads of their requirement to provide passenger operations that were not profitable but considered necessary for fulfillment of public benefit needs.[38]

The **Regional Rail Reorganization Act of 1973 (3R Act)** attempted to maintain rail freight service in the Northeast by creating the Consolidated Rail Corporation (Conrail), which was formed from six bankrupt northeastern railroads. The act also created the United States Railroad Association (USRA) as the government agency responsible for planning and financing the restructuring. By 1980, the federal government had granted Conrail more than $3.3 billion in federal subsidies to cover its operating expenses.[39]

Conrail proved to be very successful and was "spun off" by the sale of its stock to the investing public in 1987. Conrail's management was able to rationalize the excess track while preserving and improving service. In 1996, CSX and Conrail announced their intention to merge. This raised opposition from the Norfolk Southern (NS). This triggered a bidding war for Conrail stock between CSX and NS. Ultimately, the bidding war was settled by agreement between CSX and NS to split Conrail.

The **Railroad Revitalization and Regulatory Reform Act of 1976 (4R Act)** had two primary purposes. The first was to provide authorization for federal funding for the startup of Conrail. The second was to provide greater commercial freedom to all railroads in the United States by reducing some aspects of economic regulation that had constrained railroads to compete for freight traffic as effectively as they otherwise could have.[40]

The **Staggers Rail Act of 1980** made major reductions in the comprehensive framework of economic regulation of the railroad industry that had evolved over the years since 1887. Among the more significant changes was legalization of contract rate-making. This enabled rail carriers to attract business with the use of confidential contracts tailored to conditions that were specific to shippers' needs. This gave railroads freedom identical to what had prevailed for many years in the motor carrier and water

Table 6-7	Summary: Railroad Industry Characteristics
• General service characteristics	• In competition with motor carriers; shippers of bulk products
• Investments/capital outlays	• High investments/equipment, track
• Cost structure	• High fixed costs, low variable costs
• Ease of entry	• Low
• Market structure	• Oligopoly/monopoly
• Ways in which they compete	• Price (intramodal) and service (intermodal)
• Types of commodities	• Low-value, high-volume bulk commodities
• Number of carriers	• Small number of large carriers
• Markets in which they compete	• High-value chemicals, long-haul but large commodities

industries.[41] The freedoms provided by the Staggers Act aided in driving improvement of the railroad industry's financial performance and condition during the decades that have followed its enactment.

The **ICC Termination Act of 1995** eliminated the ICC and transferred economic rail regulation to the Surface Transportation Board (STB), which is part of the DOT. Some critics contend that the STB has been too lenient in administering the remaining modest controls over railroad rates and services it is empowered to administer. Shippers of some types of commodities contend that railroad competition for the movement of their products is insufficient to prevent them from obtaining rates and service levels that would be attainable if railroad market power were constrained by more regulation by the STB.

Improved Service to Customers

As shown in Table 6-6, intermodal traffic has expanded by 484 percent during the period of 1980 to 2007, while productivity measures also have shown an increase.[42] An important indicator of improved performance is the railroads' continued good safety record. Train accidents declined by over 70 percent from 1980 to 2007. Consequently, injuries and fatalities also have fallen.

Many signs indicate that deregulation has brought improvement to the railroads (improved financial status) and to their customers. The industry has changed dramatically in many ways, including providing more tailored service and equipment and negotiating contract rates for volume movements. The railroads have worked hard to improve their operating performance times and reliability. Table 6-7 provides a comprehensive summary of railroad characteristics for review.

Current Issues

Alcohol and Drug Abuse

Alcohol and drug abuse has affected almost every workplace in the United States. Many industries, including the rail industry, are taking a close look at the problem and at possible methods of dealing with it.

The problem of substance abuse can be brought on by the very nature of railroad work. Long hours, low supervision, and nights away from home can lead to loneliness and boredom, which can then lead to substance abuse. Because of this situation, the railroads have been dealing with the problem of substance abuse for a century. Rule G, which was established in 1897, prohibits the use of narcotics and alcohol on company property. Rail employees violating this rule could be subject to dismissal; however, the severity of this punishment led to the silence of many rail workers who did not want to jeopardize the jobs of their coworkers.

To deal with this problem, the railroad industry has attempted to identify and help employees with substance abuse problems. The industry has established **employee assistance programs (EAPs)** that enable these troubled employees to be rehabilitated.

Employees can voluntarily refer themselves to EAPs before a supervisor detects the problem and disciplinary actions become necessary. However, a Rule G violation—substance abuse while on the job—usually necessitates removal of the employee from the workplace to ensure his or her safety and the safety of coworkers. Employees who are removed can still use EAPs for rehabilitation and can apply for reinstatement after they have overcome their problem.

Railroad EAPs have proven to be very effective. A recent Federal Railroad Administration report found that the rate of successful rehabilitation has risen by 70 percent. The success of these programs depends largely on support from rail workers as well as all levels of management.[43]

Energy

The energy shortages of the 1970s made the United States increasingly aware of the need to conserve natural resources. The U.S. government, for example, decided to reduce the quantity of fuels and petroleum products that are imported into the country. Americans want to preserve and, wherever possible, clean up the environment. The railroads today are in a favorable position, especially when compared to motor carriers, because they are efficient energy consumers. For instance, a train locomotive uses less fuel than a tractor–trailer in pulling the same amount of weight. Revenue ton-miles per gallon of fuel consumed by the railroads increased by almost 86 percent from 1980 to 2007.[44] Table 6-8 shows the relative energy consumption for the various modes of transportation.

Table 6-8	Relative Fuel Efficiency of Transportation Modes			
	TRILLION BTU*		**PERCENT OF TOTAL BASED ON BTU'S**	
MODE	2005	2006	2005	2006
Trucks	5088.2	5187.8	18.5%	18.7%
Air	2476.6	2496.2	9.0%	9.0%
Water	1121.8	1205.8	4.1%	4.4%
Pipe	841.6	842.1	3.1%	3.0%
Rail	656.8	669.6	2.4%	2.4%

*BTU = British thermal units.

Source: *Transportation Energy Data Book,* Oak Ridge National Laboratories, Department of Energy, Washington, DC, 2008, Table 2.6.

A study by the U.S. DOT concluded that railroads are more energy-efficient than motor carriers, even when measured in terms of consumption per ton-mile.[45] In addition to being more energy-efficient, railroads cause less damage to the environment than do trucks. In 1980, railroad emissions (0.9 grams per net ton-mile) were 75 percent less than truck emissions.[46] Railroads, in comparison to trucks—a major competitor—are able to move large amounts of freight with less energy and less harm to the environment.

The railroads economically shipped 905.6 million tons of energy-yielding products in 2007; 94 percent of these loadings were coal movements.[47] Because coal, which can be converted into electricity, is an abundant substitute for oil, electric utility companies can convert their present processes to coal whenever economically possible. Because the railroads already transport approximately three-quarters of all the coal moved, they would be able to increase service to the utilities and capture more of the market by using high-volume unit coal trains.

Hence, the railroads can be an important factor in the development of the nation's energy policy.

Technology

To become more efficient and consequently more competitive, the railroad industry is becoming a high-tech industry. Computers are playing a large role in every mode of transportation, and the railroads are no exception. A line of "smart" locomotives is being equipped with onboard computers that can identify mechanical problems, and the legendary red caboose was phased out by a small device weighing 30 pounds that attaches to the last car of the train. This electric device transmits important information to engineers and dispatchers alike, including information about the braking system. Other applications of computer technology are as follows:

- Advanced Train Control Systems (ATCS): A joint venture between the United States and Canada that will use computers to efficiently track the flow of trains through the entire rail system
- Rail yard control: Computer control of freight yards that is used to sort and classify as many as 2,500 railcars a day
- Communications and signaling: Provides quick and efficient communications between dispatchers, yard workers, field workers, and train crews
- Customer service: By calling a toll-free number, customers can receive information on the status of their shipments, correct billing errors, and plan new service schedules
- Radio Frequency Identification (RFID) tags to track equipment and shipments and improve visibility.

The role of high technology and computers will continue to expand and increase the ability of the railroads to provide progressively higher levels of customer service.[48]

Transportation Technology

PTC: Look Beyond the Safety Aspects

If you think Positive Train Control (PTC) is simply a train collision avoidance system, then you are behind the times. Installing PTC on the majority of the freight, passenger, commuter, and some short line locomotives is going to unlock a stream of data the railroads have only previously imagined.

If you are a railroad C-Level executive you are now able to see the clear signal to the railroad of the future. Taking advantage of this opportunity should be the subject of discussion from the board room to the people in operations centers, service design offices, field and terminal managers running operations, train crews, and those maintaining the railroads' assets. The other railroad groups who can leverage this data are strategic planners, marketing and sales, yield managers, customer service representatives, and sourcing managers, all of whom will have real-time data sources to improve service to the customer, manage revenue, and control costs.

The main objective of PTC is to create a safer operating environment for everyone. The by-product of the PTC, GPS, radios, and high-speed/high-volume data transmission equipment being installed on locomotives, track, signal, and communications infrastructure will create a mountain of data. When you turn the mountain of data into actionable information you will be running the railroad of the future. Taking advantage of real-time data with highly analytical speed computing overlaying new business processes to deliver "do it now," "do it this way," and "do it safely" packets of action information, with the supporting information, will help the railroads achieve their customer service goals and internal revenue and cost targets.

Source: Adapted from Jim Wilson, *Railway Age,* May 2009, pp. 22–23.

Future Role of Smaller Railroads

As noted, the deregulation of the railroad industry in 1980 led to a number of important changes. The consolidation among so-called Class I railroads has been noted in this chapter. The obvious outcome was a reduction in the number of carriers in this category, but interestingly, it led to an increase in the number of regional and small rail carriers. These small and regional rail carriers typically took over part of the infrastructure abandoned by the large railroads who spun off parts of their system that had low traffic levels and/or were deemed not to be needed for market success.

The small and regional carriers often have to operate at a cost disadvantage compared to the large rail system carriers who have the advantage economies of scale. However, the smaller rail companies have some advantages given that they are more flexible and adaptable in meeting the needs of their customers (shippers). They are usually not unionized, which also helps to make them more flexible. Another possible advantage is local ownership of the rail companies and the related willingness to accept lower returns and/or pay closer attention to customer needs to promote regional economic development.

It should also be noted that some local and state governments have provided financial assistance, primarily for infrastructure improvements, for the formation of short lines that have come into being in recent years. This community support is usually based upon a need to continue the rail service for the economic benefit of existing and potential new businesses. Although motor carrier transportation has often filled the need of smaller communities for transportation service, rail service may be viewed by some communities as a necessary ingredient for the economic viability of the area. Consequently, many communities have had the advantage of continuing rail service that would not have been possible otherwise.

The large Class I railroads have been frequent targets for criticism about the service they provide to their customers. The smaller lines are usually viewed in a more favorable light because of their responsiveness at the local level. However, the small and regional rail carriers are usually more vulnerable if a large shipper decides to close its operations. The future role of some of those carriers is somewhat uncertain because of these factors.

Customer Service

As suggested in this chapter, the large Class I railroads are perceived by some shippers as not being customer focused. This criticism has grown in intercity transport during the 1990s as mergers continued to occur. The new, larger companies appeared insensitive to shipper needs and concerns about equipment and service. Some of the service and equipment issues are attributable to the challenges inherent in combining relatively large organizations with unique systems and procedures, and problems always occur in spite of serious up-front planning.

The extent to which those equipment and service problems have persisted during the last several years is indicative of the legitimacy of shipper complaints. There are differences among the "majors" or Class I railroads in terms of their customer service focus, but unfortunately some shippers are inclined to lump them altogether as being unsatisfactory. Consequently, this is a major issue for railroads, and improvements need to be made to increase rail market shares of freight traffic.

Drayage for Intermodal Service

As indicated previously in this chapter, one of the constraints on rail service is the fixed nature of the rail routes and the high cost of adding rail segments to provide direct service. Consequently, the beginning and/or the end of a rail movement may depend upon motor carrier service. This is, obviously, especially true for intermodal service using trailers or containers. The pickup and delivery of trailers and containers in conjunction with a line-haul rail movement is usually referred to as *local drayage*.

When the railroads are carrying the trailers or containers of a motor carrier as a substitute for the motor carrier providing the line-haul service, local drayage is not an issue because the motor carrier will provide these links. However, when the railroad is the land carrier, it will have to arrange for local drayage for pickup and delivery. Motor carriers that are willing and able to provide this service for the railroads are becoming scarce and charging relatively high rates for the service. In some instances, the pickup and delivery time adds significantly to the total transit time. This is another area that needs attention to improve rail service.

SUMMARY

- The railroads played a significant role in the economic and social development of the United States for about 100 years (1850–1950) and continue to be the leading mode of transportation in terms of intercity ton-miles, but they no longer dominate the freight market.

- The railroad segment of the transportation industry is led by a decreasing number of large Class I carriers, but the number of small Class III carriers has been increasing in number since the deregulation of railroads in 1980.

- Intermodal competition for railroads has increased dramatically since World War II, but the level of intramodal competition has decreased as the number of Class I railroads has decreased. The increased intermodal competition has led to more rate competition.

- Mergers have been occurring among railroads for many years, but the pace has accelerated during the past 30 years, leading to rapid decrease in the number of Class I railroads.

- In recent years, the railroads have become more specialized in terms of the traffic they carry, with the emphasis being on low-value, high-density bulk products; however, there is some evidence of a resurgence of selected manufactured products such as transportation equipment.

- In recent years, railroads have been emphasizing new technologies and specialized equipment to improve their service performance and satisfy customers.

- Intermodal service (TOFC/COFC) has received renewed interest since 1980, and there has been a dramatic growth in the movement of such traffic by railroads.

- Long-distance truckload carriers and other motor-carrier companies such as UPS have also begun to use rail intermodal service.

- The railroads have a high proportion of fixed costs because they provide their own right-of-way and terminal facilities. Because the large railroads are multistate operators, the amount of fixed expenditures is significant.

- The cost of labor is the single most important component of variable costs for railroads, but the railroad industry has been striving to reduce labor costs on a relative basis by eliminating work rules that were a carryover from another era.

- The high level of fixed costs helps give rise to economies of scale in the railroad industry, which can have a dramatic impact upon profits when the volume of traffic increases.

- The financial plight of the railroads has improved since deregulation in 1980 as railroads have been able to respond more quickly and aggressively to market pressures from other modes, particularly motor carriers.

- A number of important issues are facing railroads at present, including substance abuse, energy, technology, small railroads, and local drayage.

STUDY QUESTIONS

1. Railroads no longer dominate the freight transportation market but they still lead the market in terms of freight ton-miles. What factors contribute to their leadership in this area? Why is their share of the total expenditures for freight movement so small if they lead in freight ton-miles?

2. Since the passage of the Staggers Rail Act of 1980, there has been an increase in the number of small railroads (Class III). Why has this number increased while the number of Class I railroads has decreased?

3. Explain the difference between intramodal and intermodal competition in the railroad industry. Which form of competition is most beneficial to shippers? Why?

4. One of the significant factors in rail development has been the number of mergers that have occurred, but there have been different types of mergers that have occurred over time. Discuss the major types of mergers and explain why they occurred. Will mergers continue to occur in the rail industry? Why or why not?

5. What factors have contributed to the decline in the volume of higher-value freight by the railroads? What changes, if any, could the railroads make to attract back more higher-value freight from motor carriers?

6. Railroads have abandoned a significant number of miles of track (over 260,000 miles) since 1916. Why has this trend developed? Will it continue into the future? Why or why not?

7. The railroad industry has developed a number of new types of equipment to replace the standard boxcar. What is the rationale supporting the diversification of equipment?

8. The railroad industry's cost structure is different than that of the motor carrier industry. What factors contribute to this difference? What impact do these differences have for the railroads in terms of pricing, competitiveness, and investment?

9. Discuss the major current issues facing the railroad industry. Select one of these major issues and present appropriate recommendations for resolving the issue.

10. What factors have contributed to the success of intermodal rail service? What barriers exist to future expansion?

NOTES

1. Association of American Railroads, *Railroad Facts,* 20th edition, Washington, DC, 2008, p. 32.

2. Ibid., p. 18.

3. *Transportation in America,* 20th edition, Washington, DC, Eno Transportation Foundation, 2007, p. 32.

4. Association of American Railroads, op. cit., p. 3.

5. Ibid., pp. 44.

6. Ibid., p. 32.

7. Ibid., p. 26.

8. U.S. Department of Commerce, Bureau of the Census, *Historical Statistics of the United States: Colonial Times to 1975,* Washington, DC: U.S. Government Printing Office, 1960, p. 429.

9. Association of American Railroads, op. cit., p. 45.

10. The National Commission of Productivity, *Improving Railroad Productivity,* p. 161.

11. The commodity groups included here are metals and metal products; food and kindred products; stone, clay, and glass products; and grainmill products.

12. Association of American Railroads, op. cit., p. 29.

13. Ibid., p. 25.

14. Ibid., p. 25.

15. Ibid., p. 62.

16. Ibid., p. 24.

17. Ibid., p. 52.

18. Ibid., p. 51.

19. Ibid., p. 37.

20. Ibid., p. 39.

21. Association of American Railroads, press release, Washington, DC, 1979, p. 342.

22. Fixed costs remain the same over a period of time or a range of output (such as labor costs). Semi-variable costs contain some fixed variable elements (such as setup costs on a production line).

23. R. J. Sampson and M. I. Farris, *Domestic Transportation: Practice, Theory, and Policy,* 4th edition, Boston: Houghton Mifflin, 1979, p. 59.

24. Association of American Railroads, op. cit., p. 44.

25. Ibid., p. 15.

26. Ibid., pp. 49, 51.

27. U.S. Department of Transportation, *A Prospectus for Change in the Freight Railroad Industry,* Washington, DC: U.S. Government Printing Office, 1978, p. 65.

28. Association of American Railroads, op. cit., p. 11.

29. Ibid., p. 57.

30. Frank Wilner, *Railroads and the Marketplace,* Washington, DC: Association of American Railroads, 1988, p. 7.

31. Ibid., p. 2.

32. Association of American Railroads, op. cit., p. 61.

33. Ibid, p. 11.

34. Ibid., p. 9.

35. Frank Wilner, *Railroads and the Marketplace,* Washington, DC: Association of American Railroads, 1988, p. 7.

36. Ibid., p. 9.

37. Ibid., pp. 8–12.

38. Ibid., p. 2.

39. Consolidated Rail Corporation, *Summary of Business Plan,* Philadelphia: Consolidated Rail Corporation, 1979, p. 5.

40. Wilner, op cit., p. 15.

41. Ibid.

42. Association of American Railroads, op. cit., p. 26.

43. Association of American Railroads, *What Are the Railroads Doing About Drug Abuse?,* Washington, DC: 1986, pp. 1–4.

44. Association of American Railroads, op. cit., p. 40.

45. Wilner, op cit., p. 15.

46. Ibid.

47. Association of American Railroads, op. cit., p. 29.

48. Association of American Railroads, *High Technology Rides the Rails,* Washington, DC, 1988, pp. 1–3.

CASE 6-1

CBN Railway Company

CEO John Spychalski is concerned about a problem that has existed at CBN railroad for almost 20 years now. The continuous problem has been that the locomotives used by the company are not very reliable. Even with prior decisions to resolve the problem, there still has not been a change in the reliability of these locomotives. Between 2006 and 2007, 155 new locomotives were purchased and one of CBN's repair shops was renovated. The renovated shop has been very inefficient. Spychalski estimated that the shop would complete 300 overhauls on a yearly basis, but instead it has only managed to complete an average of 160 overhauls per year.

The company has also been doing a poor job servicing customers (that is, providing equipment). CBN has averaged only 87 to 88 percent equipment availability, compared to other railroads with availability figures greater than 90 percent. Increased business in the rail industry has been a reason for trying to reduce the time used for repairing the locomotives. CBN's mean time between failure rate is low—45 days—compared to other railroads whose mean time between failure rates is higher than 75 days. This factor, Spychalski feels, has contributed to CBN's poor service record.

CBN is considering a new approach to the equipment problem: Spychalski is examining the possibility of leasing 135 locomotives from several sources. The leases would run between 90 days to 5 years. In addition, the equipment sources would maintain the repairs on 469 locomotives currently in CBN's fleet, but CBN's employees would do the actual labor on the locomotives. The lease arrangements, known as "power-by-the-mile" arrangements, call for the manufacturers doing the repair work to charge only for maintenance on the actual number of miles that a particular unit operates. The company expects the agreements to last an average of 15 years. John Thomchick, the executive vice president, estimates that CBN would save about $5 million annually because the company will not have to pay for certain parts and materials. Problems with the locomotives exist throughout CBN's whole system, and delays to customers have been known to last up to five days. Spychalski and Thomchick feel that the leasing arrangement will solve CBN's problems.

CASE QUESTIONS

1. What are potential advantages and disadvantages of entering into these "power-by-the-mile" arrangements?

2. What should be done if the problem with the locomotives continues even with the agreements?

3. Do you think that the decision to lease the locomotives was the best decision for CBN? Explain your answer.

CASE 6-2
Railroad Reregulation

Freight railroads were first economically regulated in the United States with the passage of the Act to Regulate Commerce of 1887. This legislation was in response to desires by several states to prevent the railroads from employing monopolistic practices. Railroads are considered natural monopolies because of their large fixed costs and natural barriers to entry into the industry. Monopolistic practices usually take the form of excessive prices and poor service to captive shippers. The 1887 Act was designed to prevent these practices and created the Interstate Commerce Commission to monitor railroad pricing and service activities.

In 1980, the Staggers Act was passed in an attempt to give more pricing freedom and market exit/entry freedom to the railroads. Part of the rationale of this Act was to allow railroads to operate in a more market-oriented environment and to take advantage of value-of-service pricing to increase industry profitability. In 1995, the ICC Termination Act was passed to provide even more freedom in pricing, exit/entry, and service to railroads. This Act also abolished the ICC and created the Surface Transportation Board (STB) to monitor railroad competitive practices.

Between 1996 and 2009, the railroads have enjoyed a resurgence in profitability. Their ability to freely price and to be exempt from antitrust laws allowed railroads to manage capacity more efficiently and expand their markets and products. During this time, railroads dramatically increased their volumes of TOFC and COFC business, becoming a significant business partner to the motor carrier industry in the United States.

Recently, however, there has been a push by Congress and a group known as Consumers United for Rail Equity (CURE) to pass legislation to once again economically reregulate the railroad industry and reduce the powers of the STB over rail competitive practices. The major argument for this legislation is that the railroads are once again employing monopolistic practices for shippers of bulk commodities such as grain, coal, and chemicals. The assertion is that railroads are charging excessively high prices to shippers of commodities of low value, thus making these commodities less price competitive in the market. This is coupled with the assertion that many of these bulk shippers are "captive" and don't have access to multiple railroads to ship their products.

The railroad industry disputes these claims and asserts that it is using its pricing as a competitive strength in a free-market economy and that reregulation would reduce industry profits, thereby forcing an industry consolidation which would further inhibit capacity and eventually result in higher prices.

CASE QUESTIONS

1. If you were asked to prepare an argument representing the interests of the railroad industry against reregulation, what would your main points be?
2. If you were a representative of CURE, what would your arguments be to reregulate the industry?
3. If you were a representative of the motor carrier industry, would you be for or against railroad reregulation? What would your arguments be?
4. What would be your position if you represented a group of shippers whose freight moved primarily by TOFC or COFC?

Chapter 7

AIRLINES

Learning Objectives

After reading this chapter, you should be able to do the following:

- Appreciate the importance of air transportation in the U.S. economy
- Gain knowledge of the types and number of carriers in the U.S. airline industy
- Understand the level of competition in the U.S. airline industry
- Become aware of the operating and service characteristics of airline transportation
- Be familiar with the different types of equipment used by airlines
- Appreciate the impacts of fuel and labor costs on airlines cost structures
- Understand the concepts of economies of scale and density in the airline industry
- Be aware of current issues facing airlines today

Transportation Profile

Carriers Alter Course

Boeing's *World Air Cargo Forecast 2006/2007* projected the air cargo industry to grow roughly 6 percent per year through 2025. Its new forecast won't be released until November, but Boeing's executives remain optimistic: "We continue to see growth despite the difficulties facing the industry," says Tom Crabtree, Boeing Commercial Airplanes regional director of business strategy.

According to Crabtree, that optimism is due to the fact that carriers are currently upgrading their fleets with passenger planes that aircraft manufacturers are converting with more fuel-efficient engines, and with factory-built freighters that accommodate increasingly higher payloads.

What's driving these changes? In a word: Fuel. The high cost of fuel is affecting the financial health of nearly every air carrier in the global market. To put a little perspective on just how much: According to James May, CEO of the Air Transport Association of America, U.S. airlines are projected to spend nearly $60 billion on fuel in 2008, $18 billion more than in 2007. The increase in fuel is the equivalent of employing 244,000 airline workers or purchasing 261 narrow-body jets.

Northwest, which plans to merge with Delta Air Lines, recently posted a quarterly net loss of $4.1 billion, partly due to higher fuel charges. United Airlines reported a $537 million loss and is cutting more than 1,100 jobs and numerous flights.

In an attempt to help cut costs, American Airlines (AA) implemented a Fuel Smart program that encourages employees to provide ideas that conserve fuel and energy. According to the carrier, the program saved AA approximately 96 million gallons in 2007. "In 2008, we expect to increase our rate of fuel savings by another 15 million gallons," says David Brooks, AA's Cargo Division president.

What's ahead? Observers expect tighter FAA inspections and carbon emissions standards. There may also be further industry consolidation, but this may create opportunities for carriers as well. "We may be able to add additional capacity in certain markets, which would be a good thing for shippers," stated Wally Devereaux, Southwest Airlines cargo sales and marketing director.

Source: Adapted from Karen E. Thuermer, "Carriers Alter Course," *Logistics Management*, July 2008, p. 42. Reprinted by permission.

Introduction

From the first flight, which lasted less than 1 minute, to space shuttles orbiting the earth, air transportation has come a long way in a short period of time. Wilbur and Orville Wright made their first flight in 1903 at Kitty Hawk and sold their invention to the federal government. In 1908 the development of air transportation began with the **U.S. Post Office** examining the feasibility of providing air mail service. Although airplanes were used in World War I, the use of airplanes for mail transport can be considered the beginning of the modern airline industry. Passenger transportation services developed as a by-product of the mail business and began to flourish in selected markets. Since that time, airplanes have become faster, bigger, and relatively more fuel-efficient. Although the level and degree of technological improvement have slowed in the airline industry, there is still opportunity for further innovation.

Airline travel is a common form of transportation for long-distance passenger and freight travel and the only reasonable alternative when time is of the essence. The tremendous speed of the airplane, coupled with more competitive pricing, has led to the growth of air transportation, particularly in the movement of passengers.

Industry Overview and Significance

In 2007 for-hire air carriers had total operating revenues of $173.1 billion, of which $107.0 billion (61.8 percent) came from passenger service.[1] In 2003 air carriers transported 15.2 billion revenue ton-miles, or approximately 0.4 percent of total intercity ton-miles.[2] Employment in the air carrier industry totaled 560,997 people in 2007, with an average annual compensation of over $74,786 for persons employed by scheduled carriers.[3]

The airline industry is very dependent on **passenger revenues** to maintain its financial viability. However, to characterize airlines simply as movers of people presents too simplistic a view of their role in our transportation system. The airlines are a unique and important group of carriers that meet some particular needs in our society. Although their share of the freight movement on a ton-mile basis is small, the type of traffic that they carry (high-value, perishable, or emergency) makes them an important part of our total transportation system. Emphasis upon total logistics cost in a quick-response lead-time environment will continue to contribute to their growth in freight movements.

Types of Carriers

Private Carriers

Air carriers can be segmented into for-hire carriers and private carriers. A **private air carrier** is a firm that transports company personnel or freight in planes to support its primary business. The preponderance of private air transportation is used to transport company personnel, although emergency freight is sometimes carried on private airplanes as well. Rarely, however, is a private air carrier established to routinely carry freight. The private air carrier is subject to the federal safety regulations administered by the Federal Aviation Administration (FAA) of the U.S. Department of Transportation.

For-Hire Carriers

The for-hire carriers are no longer regulated on an economic basis by the federal government and cannot be easily categorized into specific types because carriers provide many types of services. For our purposes, the for-hire carriers will be discussed according to type of service offered (all-cargo, air taxi, commuter, charter, and international) and annual revenue (majors, nationals, and regionals).

A classification frequently used by U.S. air carriers is one based on annual operating revenues. The categories used to classify air carriers in terms of revenue are as follows:

Majors — annual revenues of more than $1 billion

Nationals — annual revenues of $100 million to $1 billion

Regionals — annual revenues of less than $100 million

U.S. **major carriers** have $1 billion or more in annual revenues and provide service between major population areas within the United States such as New York, Chicago, and Los Angeles. The routes served by these carriers are usually high-density corridors, and the carriers use high-capacity planes. The U.S. majors also serve medium-sized population centers such as Harrisburg, Pennsylvania. Examples of major U.S. carriers are American, United, Delta, US Airways, and Southwest.

U.S. **national carriers** have revenues of $100 million to $1 billion and operate between less-populated areas and major population centers. These carriers operate scheduled service over relatively short routes with smaller planes. They "feed" passengers from outlying areas into airports served by the U.S. majors. Today, many of the U.S. national carriers operate over relatively large regional areas and are stiff competition for the U.S. majors on many routes. Examples of U.S. nationals include Midwest, Sun Country, and PSA Airlines.

Regional carriers have annual revenues of less than $100 million and have operations similar to the nationals. The carriers operate within a particular region of the country, such as New England or the Midwest, and connect less-populated areas with larger population centers. Included in the regional category are carriers such as Air Midwest, Big Sky, and Piedmont.

The **all-cargo carrier**, as the name implies, primarily transports cargo. The transportation of air cargo was deregulated in 1977, permitting the all-cargo carriers to freely set rates, enter and exit markets, and use any size aircraft dictated by the market. Examples of all-cargo carriers include FedEx and UPS Airlines.

Commuter air carriers are technically regional carriers. The commuter publishes timetables on specific routes that connect less-populated routes with major cities. As certified carriers abandon routes, usually low-density routes, the commuter enters into a working relationship with the certified carrier to continue service to the community. The commuter then connects small communities that have reduced or no air service with larger communities that have better scheduled service. The commuter's schedule is closely aligned with connecting flight schedules at a larger airport. Many commuter firms use turboprop aircraft to feed the major hubs of the major airlines. Today, however, some commuters are adding regional jets that not only continue to feed these hubs but also offer direct service to larger metropolitan areas. Many commuter operators are franchised by the majors, such as US Airways Express.

The **charter carriers**, also known as air taxis, use small- to medium-size aircraft to transport people or freight. The supplemental carrier has no time schedule or designated route. The carrier charters the entire plane to transport a group of people or cargo between specified origins and destinations. Many travel tour groups use charter carriers. However, a big customer for charters is the Department of Defense; it uses charter carriers to transport personnel and supplies. For example, Operation Iraqi Freedom (OIF) relied upon charters for some of their moves of personnel and supplies. The rates charged and schedules followed are negotiated in the contract.

Many U.S. carriers are also international carriers and operate between the continental United States and foreign countries, and between the United States and its territories (such as Puerto Rico). Because service to other countries has an effect on U.S. international trade and relations, the president of the United States is involved in awarding the international routes. Examples of international carriers include United and American. Many foreign carriers, such as British Air and Air France, provide services between the United States and their country.

Market Structure

Number of Carriers

A look at carrier revenues shows a concentration of earnings by a small group of majors, nationals, and regionals. (Table 7-1 provides numbers for these three categories.) Table 7-1 shows that a majority of air movements are made by 151 carriers. The largest increase in number of carriers has occurred among the regionals. In fact, 82 percent of total industry revenue was generated by the top 10 carriers (see Table 7-2).

Private air transportation has been estimated to include approximately 60,000 company-owned planes, with over 500 U.S. corporations operating private air fleets. In addition, thousands of planes are used for personal, recreational, and instructional purposes.

Deregulation in 1978 was expected to result in a larger number of airlines competing for passengers and freight traffic. The number of major airlines did increase initially, but as Table 7-1 indicates, the number of airlines has remained steady over the last several years, with 2007 seeing an increase. Available seat miles for 2007 increased by 3.1 percent from 2006 as some carriers are increasing the size of their aircraft.[4] The number of flights increased from 11.3 million in 2006 to 11.4 million in 2007. However, the number of late departures increased to 128,259 in 2007 from 100,690 in 2006.[5]

Competition

Intermodal

Due to their unique service, air carriers face **limited competition** from other modes for both passengers and freight. Air carriers have an advantage in providing time-sensitive, long-distance movement of people or freight. Airlines compete to some extent with motor carriers for the movement of higher-valued manufactured goods; they face competition from automobiles for the movement of passengers and, to a limited extent, from trains and buses. For short distances (under 800 miles), the access time and terminal time offsets the speed of the airline for the line-haul.

Table 7-1	Number of Carriers						
CARRIERS	2001	2002	2003	2004	2005	2006	2007
Majors	15	14	15	19	20	20	21
Nationals	39	35	32	35	33	32	34
Regionals	46	92	103	86	86	89	96
Total	**100**	**141**	**150**	**140**	**139**	**141**	**151**

Source: Air Transport Association, *2008 Economic Report.*

Table 7-2	Top 10 Airlines by Various Rankings—2007

#	PASSENGERS (THOUSANDS)		#	REVENUE PASSENGER MILES (MILLIONS)	
1	Southwest	101,910	1	American	138,417
2	American	98,165	2	United	117,376
3	Delta	72,924	3	Delta	103,279
4	United	68,362	4	Continental	81,380
5	US Airways	57,829	5	Northwest	72,907
6	Northwest	53,687	6	Southwest	72,320
7	Continental	48,974	7	US Airways	61,222
8	AirTran	23,741	8	jetBlue	25,722
9	jetBlue	21,304	9	Alaska	18,446
10	Alaska	17,544	10	AirTran	17,233

Bolded airlines = ATA members.

#	FREIGHT TON-MILES (MILLIONS)		#	TOTAL OPERATING REVENUES ($MILLIONS)	
1	FedEx	10,965	1	FedEx	23,250
2	UPS Airlines	6,802	2	American	22,833
3	Polar	4,958	3	United	20,049
4	American	2,129	4	Delta	19,239
5	Northwest	2,067	5	Continental	14,105
6	United	2,012	6	Northwest	12,735
7	Delta	1,128	7	US Airways	12,055
8	Continental	972	8	Southwest	9,861
9	Evergreen Intl.	752	9	UPS Airlines	4,910
10	ABX	645	10	Alaska	3,076

Source: Air Transport Association, *2008 Economic Report.*

Intramodal

Competition in rates and service among the air carriers is very intense, even though the number of carriers is small. As noted, passenger air carrier regulation was significantly reduced in 1978, and new carriers entered selected routes (markets), thereby increasing the amount of competition (see Chapter 4 for a discussion of the Theory of Contestable Markets). Also, existing carriers expanded their market coverage, which significantly increased intramodal competition in certain markets. Table 7-2 indicates that the top 10 air carriers accounted for about 82 percent of the total operating revenue. Carriers may also have **excess capacity** (too many flights and seat miles on a route) and attempt to attract passengers by selectively lowering fares to fill the empty seats. In 2007 airline prices fell 3.0 percent (not adjusted for inflation). During this same period, inflation (measured by the Consumer Price Index) rose 2.8 percent.[6]

New entrants to the airline market initially cause overcapacity to exist on many routes. To counter this and add passengers to their aircraft, carriers reduce prices and fare wars begin. This causes financially weaker carriers to exit the market. This is especially true of carriers with high operating costs (many times due to high-cost union labor contracts), high cost of debt, or high levels of fixed costs. (Many of these maintain high fixed investments in hub-and-spoke terminal operations.) The remaining carriers begin to enjoy economies of density (discussed later in this chapter), and the cost per passenger mile will decrease and margins will increase, even in the existence of relatively low fares. So, even with the discounted prices in today's airline market, many carriers have been able to remain profitable.

Service Competition

Competition in airline service takes many forms, but the primary service competition is the **frequency and timing** of flights on a route. Carriers attempt to provide flights at the time of day when passengers want to fly. Flight departures are most frequent in the early morning (7:00 a.m. to 10:00 a.m.) and late afternoon (4:00 p.m. to 6:00 p.m.).

In addition to the frequency and timing of flights, air carriers attempt to differentiate their service through the **advertising** of passenger amenities. Carriers promote such things as on-time arrival and friendly employees to convince travelers that they have the desired quality of service. jetBlue Airways was the first airline in the world that offered live satellite television free of charge on every seat in its fleet.[7] Frequent flyer programs and special services for high-mileage customers are popular examples of other services to attract loyal customers.

A postderegulation development in service competition was **no-frills service**. The no-frills air carrier (for example, Southwest Airlines) charges fares that are lower than that of a full-service air carrier. However, passengers receive limited snacks and drinks (coffee, tea, or soft drinks). Southwest offers passengers an opportunity to purchase a boxed meal at the gate before they enter the aircraft. Another hallmark of such carriers is that they only provide one class of service. Also, the passengers provide their own magazines or other reading materials. Overall, there are fewer airline employees involved in no-frills services operations, which contributes to lower costs. The no-frills carriers have had a significant impact on fares where their service is available.

Cargo Competition

For cargo service, competition has become intense. As a result of the complete deregulation of air cargo in 1977, air carriers have published competitive rates, but these rates are still higher than those available via surface carriers. Freight schedules have been published that emphasize low transit times between given points. To overcome accessibility problems, some carriers provide door-to-door service through contracts with motor carriers. Major airline freight companies (such as FedEx and UPS Airlines) have their own fleets of surface delivery vehicles to perform the ground portion of this door-to-door service.

Although the number of major and national carriers is small (approximately 56), the competition among carriers is great. An interesting development has been the number of surface carriers that have added air cargo service, such as UPS. Competition for nonpassenger business will become even greater as more carriers attempt to eliminate excess capacity resulting from currently reduced passenger travel patterns. Another interesting dimension has been the growth in volume of express carrier traffic, which is an important reason for the attraction of surface carriers into this segment of the business.

Operating and Service Characteristics

General

As indicated above, the major revenue source for air carriers is passenger transportation. In 2007 approximately 61.8 percent of total operating revenues were derived from passenger transportation. This revenue was generated from about 769.2 million passenger enplanements in 2007.[8] Air transportation dominates the for-hire, long-distance passenger transportation market.

In 2007 approximately 14.2 percent of the total operating **revenues** were generated from **freight** transportation.[9] The majority of freight using air service is high-value and/or emergency shipments. The high cost of air transportation is usually prohibitive for shipping low-value routine commodities unless there is an emergency.

For **emergency shipments**, the cost of air transportation is often inconsequential compared to the cost of delaying the goods. For example, an urgently needed part for an assembly line might have a $20 value, but if the air-freighted part arrives on time to prevent the assembly line from stopping, the opportunity value of the part might become hundreds of thousands of dollars. Thus, the $20 part might have an emergency value of $200,000, and the air freight cost is a small portion of this emergency value.

Examples of **commodities** that move via air carriers include mail, clothing, communication products and parts, photography equipment, mushrooms, fresh flowers, industrial machines, high-priced livestock, racehorses, expensive automobiles, and jewelry. Normally, basic raw materials such as coal, lumber, iron ore, or steel are not moved by air carriage. The high value of the products that are shipped by air provides a cost-savings trade-off, usually but not always from inventory, that offsets the higher cost of air service. The old adage "Time is money" is quite appropriate here.

Speed of Service

Undoubtedly, the major service advantage of air transportation is speed. The terminal-to-terminal time for a given trip is lower via air transportation than via any of the other modes. Commercial jets are capable of routinely flying at speeds of 500 to 600 miles per hour, thus making a New York to California trip, approximately 3,000 miles, a mere six-hour journey.

This advantage of high terminal-to-terminal speed has been dampened somewhat by reduced frequency of flights and congestion at airports. As a result of deregulation, the air traffic controllers' strike of 1981, and lower carrier demand, the number of flights offered to and from low-density communities has been reduced to increase the utilization of a given plane. As previously noted, commuter airlines have been substituted on some routes where major and national lines find the traffic volume to be too low to justify using large planes. The use of commuters requires transfer and rehandling of freight or passengers because the commuter service does not cover long distances.

Air carriers have been concentrating their service on the **high-density routes** like New York to Chicago, for example. In addition, most carriers have adopted the hub-and-spoke terminal approach, in which most flights go through a hub terminal; Atlanta (Delta) and Chicago (United) are examples. These two factors have aggravated the air traffic congestion and ground congestion at major airports and have increased total transit time while decreasing its reliability. Also, some carriers have been unable to expand because of limited "slots" at major airports. At hub airports, these slots are controlled by the dominant carrier, making it difficult for new carriers to offer service at that hub.

The shippers who use air carriers to transport freight are primarily interested in the speed and reliability of the service and the resultant benefits, such as reduced inventory levels and inventory carrying costs. Acceptable or improved service levels can be achieved by using air carriers to deliver orders in short time periods. Stock-outs can be controlled, reduced, or eliminated by responding to shortages via air carriers.

Length of Haul and Capacity

For passenger travel, air carriers dominate the long-distance moves. In 2007 the average length of haul for passenger travel was 1,078 miles for air carriers. The capacity of an airplane is dependent on its type. A wide-body, four-engine jet has a **seating capacity** of about 370 people and an all-cargo carrying capacity of 16.6 tons. Table 7-3 provides capacity and operating statistics for some of the more commonly used aircraft in both domestic and international markets.

Normally, small shipments that are time-sensitive are moved by air carriers. Rates have been established for weights as low as 10 pounds, and rate discounts are available for shipments weighing a few hundred pounds. Adding freight to the baggage compartment on passenger flights necessitates rather small-size shipments and thus supports rate-making practices for these shipments.

In addition to small shipment sizes, the packaging required for freight shipped by air transportation is usually less than other modes. It is not uncommon in air transportation to find a palletized shipment that is shrink-wrapped instead of banded. The relatively smooth ride through the air and the automated ground-handling systems contribute to lower damage and thus reduce packaging needs.

Accessibility and Dependability

Except in adverse conditions such as fog or snow, air carriers are capable of providing **reliable** service. The carriers might not always be on time to the exact minute, but the variations in transit time are small. Sophisticated navigational instrumentation permits operation during most weather conditions. On-time departures and arrivals are within 15 minutes of scheduled times. Departure time is defined as the time the aircraft door

| Table 7-3 | Aircraft Operating Characteristics—2007 | | | | | | |

MODEL	SEATS	CARGO PAYLOAD (TONS)	SPEED AIRBORNE (MPH)	FLIGHT LENGTH (MILES)	FUEL (GALLONS PER HOUR)	OPERATING COST $ PER HOUR	OPERATING COST $0.01 PER SEAT MILE
B747-200/300*	370	16.60	520	3,148	3,625	9,153	5.11
B747-400	367	8.06	534	3,960	3,411	8,443	4.6
B747-100*	–	46.34	503	2,022	1,762	3,852	–
B747-F*	–	72.58	506	2,512	3,593	7,138	–
L-1011	325	0.00	494	2,023	1,981	8,042	5067
DC-10*	286	24.87	497	1,637	2,405	7,374	5.11
B767-400	265	6.26	495	1,682	1,711	3,124	2.71
B-777	263	9.43	525	3,515	2,165	5,105	3.98
A330	261	11.12	509	3,559	1,407	3,076	2.51
MD-11*	261	45.07	515	2,485	2,473	7,695	4.75
A300-600*	235	19.12	460	947	1,638	6,518	5.93
B757-300	235	0.30	472	1,309	985	2,345	2.44
B767-300ER*	207	7.89	497	2,122	1,579	4,217	4.38
B757-200*	181	1.41	464	1,175	1,045	3,312	4.47
B767-300ER	175	3.72	487	1,987	1,404	3,873	5.08
A321	169	0.44	454	1,094	673	1,347	2.05
B737-800/900	151	0.37	454	1,035	770	2,248	3.88
MD-90	150	0.25	446	886	825	2,716	4.93
B727-200*	148	6.46	430	644	1,289	4,075	6.61
B727-100*	–	11.12	417	468	989	13,667	–
A320	146	0.31	454	1,065	767	2,359	4.14
B737-400	141	0.25	409	646	703	2,595	5.48
MD-80	134	0.19	432	791	953	2,718	5.72
B737-700LR	132	0.28	441	879	740	1,692	3.28
B737-300/700	132	0.22	403	542	723	2,388	5.49
A319	122	0.27	442	904	666	1,913	4.22
A310-200*	–	25.05	455	847	1,561	8,066	–
DC-8*	–	22.22	437	686	1,712	8,065	–

(continued)

Table 7-3	Continued						
						OPERATING COST	
MODEL	SEATS	CARGO PAYLOAD (TONS)	SPEED AIRBORNE (MPH)	FLIGHT LENGTH (MILES)	FUEL (GALLONS PER HOUR)	$ PER HOUR	$0.01 PER SEAT MILE
B737-100/200	119	0.11	396	465	824	2,377	6.08
B717-200	112	0.22	339	175	573	3,355	12.89
B737-500	110	0.19	407	576	756	2,347	6.49
DC-9	101	0.15	387	496	826	2,071	6.86
F-100	87	0.05	398	587	662	2,303	8.46
B737-200C	55	2.75	387	313	924	3,421	19.89
ERJ-145	50	0.00	360	343	280	1,142	8.63
CRJ-145	49	0.01	397	486	369	1,433	9.45
ERJ-135	37	0.00	357	382	267	969	9.83
SD 340B	33	0.00	230	202	84	644	11.6

*Data Includes cargo operations.

Source: Air Transport Association, *2003 Annual Report.*

is closed and, in the case of passenger aircraft, the vehicle is pushed away from the gate. Arrival time is defined as the time when the aircraft wheels touch down on the runway.

Poor **accessibility** is one disadvantage of air carriers. Passengers and freight must be transported to an airport for air service to be rendered. This accessibility problem is reduced when smaller planes and helicopters are used to transport freight to and from airports, and most passengers use automobiles. Limited accessibility adds time and cost to the air service provided. Even with the accessibility problem, air transportation remains a fast method of movement and the only logical mode when distance is great and time is restricted. The cost of this fast freight service is high, about three times greater than motor carrier and 10 times greater than rail. Nevertheless, the high speed and cost make air carriage a premium mode of transportation.

Equipment

Types of Vehicles

As previously mentioned, there are several different sizes of airplanes in use, from small commuter planes to huge, wide-body, four-engine planes used by the nationals. These various-sized planes all have different costs associated with using them; these costs will be addressed later in the section titled "Cost Structure." Table 7-3 compares some of the major aircraft types in terms of seats, cargo payload, speed, fuel consumption, and operating cost per hour. Airlines have many options to select from when purchasing equipment.

On the Line

FedEx Set to Reduce Aircraft Assets

Making good on its pledge to reduce expenses by about $1.0 billion for Fiscal 2010, FedEx took a step in that direction with the decision to permanently remove various aircraft used by its FedEx Express subsidiary by May 31. The aircraft being removed includes ten Airbus A310-200 aircraft and four Boeing MD10-10 aircraft owned by the company. "This decision reflects management's ongoing efforts to optimize the company's express network in light of continued excess aircraft capacity due to weak economic conditions and the expected delivery of newer, more fuel-efficient aircraft in fiscal year 2010," stated FedEx in an 8-K filing.

Source: Adapted from "FedEx set to reduce aircraft assets," *Logistics Management,* May 2009, p. 1. Reprinted by permission.

Terminals

The air carriers' **terminals** (airports) are financed by a government entity. The carriers pay for the use of the airport through landing fees, rent and lease payments for space, taxes on fuel, and aircraft registration taxes. In addition, users pay a tax on airline tickets and air freight charges. Terminal charges are becoming increasingly more commonplace for passenger traffic. Table 7-4 summarizes the various types of taxes paid by carriers, shippers, and passengers in the airline industry.

Table 7-4	Federally Approved Taxes and Fees: 1972–2009		
	1972	1992	2003
FEE	**AIRPORT AND AIRWAY TRUST FUND (FAA)**		
Passenger Ticket Tax[1a]	8.0%	10.0%	7.5%
Flight Segment Tax[1a]	–	–	$3.60
Frequent Flyer Tax[2]	–	–	7.5%
International Departure Tax[3]	$3.00	$6.00	$16.10
International Arrival Tax[3]	–	–	$16.10
Cargo Waybill Tax[1b] (domestic)	5.0%	6.25%	6.25%
Commercial Jet Fuel Tax	–	–	$0.043
Non-commercial Jet Fuel Tax	$0.07	$0.175	$0.218
Non-commercial AvGas Tax	$0.07	$0.15	$0.193
	ENVIRONMENTAL PROTECTION AGENCY (EPA)		
LUST Fuel Tax[4] (domestic)	–	$0.001	$0.001
	LOCAL AIRPORT PROJECTS		
Passenger Facility Charge	–	up to $3	up to $4.50

(continued)

Table 7-4	Continued			
		1972	1992	2003
FEE		**DEPARTMENT OF HOMELAND SECURITY (DHS)**		
September 11th Fee[5]		–	–	$2.50
Aviation Security				
Infrastructure Fee[6]		–	–	varies
APHIS Passenger Fee[7]		–	$2.00	$5.00
APHIS Aircraft Fee[7]		–	$76.75	$70.50
Customs User Fee[8]		–	$5.00	$5.50
Immigration User Fee[9]		–	$5.00	$7.00

[1a] Applies only to domestic transport or to journeys to Canada or Mexico within 225 miles of the U.S. border.
[1b] Applies only to flights within the 50 states.
[2] Applies to the sale, to third parties, of the right to award frequent flyer miles.
[3] Does not apply to those transiting the United States between two foreign airports; $8.00 on flights between the mainland United States and Alaska/Hawaii.
[4] Congress created the Leaking Underground Storage Tank (LUST) trust fund in 1986.
[5] Funds TSA at up to $5.00 per one-way trip and $10.00 per round trip since 2/1/02; suspended 6/1/03–9/30/03.
[6] Funds TSA since 2/18/02; suspended 6/1/03–9/30/03.
[7] Funds agricultural quarantine and inspection services conducted by CBP.
[8] Funds inspections by U.S. Customs and Border Protection; passengers arriving from Canada, Mexico, U.S. territories and possessions, and adjacent islands are exempt.
[9] The majority of collections fund inspections by U.S. Customs and Border Protection and a smaller portion of the collections fund certain activities performed by U.S. Immigration and Customs Enforcement that are related to air and sea passenger inspections.

Source: Air Transport Association, 2009.

The growth and development of air transportation is dependent upon adequate airport facilities. Therefore, to ensure the viability of air transportation, the federal government has the responsibility of financially assisting the states in the construction of airport facilities. The various state and local governments assume the responsibility for operating and maintaining the airports.

At the airport, the carriers perform passenger, cargo, and aircraft servicing. Passengers are ticketed, loaded, and unloaded, and their luggage is collected and dispersed. Cargo is routed to specific planes for shipment to the destination airport or to delivery vehicles. Aircraft servicing includes refueling; loading of passengers, cargo, luggage, and supplies (food); and maintenance. Major aircraft maintenance is done at specific airports.

As carrier operations become more complex, certain airports in the carriers' scope of operation become **hubs**. Flights from outlying, less-populated areas are fed into the hub airport, where connecting flights are available to other areas of the region or country.

For example, Chicago, Denver, and Washington-Dulles are major hub airports for United Airlines. Flights from cities such as Toledo and Kansas City go to Chicago, where connecting flights are available to New York, Los Angeles, and Dallas. Delta Airlines uses the Atlanta and Cincinnati airports in the same way. By using the hub airport approach, the carriers are able to assign aircraft to feed passengers into the hub over low-density routes and to assign larger planes to the higher-density routes between the hub and an airport serving a major metropolitan area. In essence, the hub airport is similar to the motor carrier's break-bulk terminal.

Airport terminals also provide services to passengers, such as restaurants, banking centers, souvenir and gift shops, and snack bars. The Denver airport also includes some major general purpose attractions similar to a shopping mall. The success of the Pittsburgh airport has resulted in other airports expanding restaurants to include many popular chains (McDonald's, TGI Friday's, Pizza Hut, and so forth) and popular shops for clothing, accessories, books, and other items.

Cost Structure

Fixed Versus Variable Cost Components

Like the motor carriers, the air carriers' cost structure consists of high variable and low fixed costs. Approximately 80 percent of total operating costs are variable and 20 percent are fixed. The relatively low fixed-cost structure is attributable to government (state and local) investment and operations of airports and airways. The carriers pay for the use of these facilities through landing fees, which are variable in nature.

As indicated in Table 7-5, 37.9 percent of airline operating costs in 2007 were incurred for flying operations and amounted to $62.14 billion; maintenance costs equaled 10.2 percent of total operating costs. Both of these expenses are variable costs. The next major category of expense is aircraft and traffic servicing, which totaled $22.3 billion in 2007 and about 13.6 percent of total operating costs. In 2007 depreciation accounted for about 4.3 percent of total operating expenses.

Table 7-5	U.S. Scheduled Airlines Operating Costs				
	($BILLIONS)				
EXPENSE	2003	2004	2005	2006	2007
Flying Operations	37.0	45.70	54.9	59.8	62.15
Maintenance	13.4	14.55	15.45	15.90	16.68
Passenger Service	9.21	9.52	9.27	8.76	8.91
Aircraft and Traffic Servicing	19.59	20.54	21.25	21.31	22.31
Promotion and Sales	8.24	8.60	8.63	8.42	8.54
General and Administrative	8.34	8.80	9.06	9.78	10.58
Depreciation and Amortization	6.69	6.91	6.78	6.93	7.10
Transport Related	15.59	21.35	25.18	26.50	27.64
Total Operating Costs	118.10	135.95	150.47	157.40	163.89

Source: Air Transport Association, *2008 Economic Report.*

Table 7-5 provides a comparison of operating costs for 2003, 2004, 2005, 2006 and 2007. The cost of flying operations increased from 2003 to 2007, as did total operating expenses. From 2003 to 2007, every cost item increased except for passenger service and promotion and sales.

The increased price competition in the airline industry has caused airlines to try to operate more efficiently by cutting costs where possible. There has been much effort put forth to decrease labor costs because the airline industry tends to be labor-intensive compared to other modes, such as railroads and pipelines. The airlines have negotiated significant labor cost reductions with many of the unions represented in the industry.

Fuel

Escalating **fuel costs** have caused problems in the past for the airlines. The average price per gallon of fuel for domestic operations was about 89 cents in 1983 compared to 57 cents in 1979 and 30 cents in 1978. It dropped to under 60 cents in 1986 but rose again in 1990 to above the 1983 level. It decreased again by 1998 to about 55 cents per gallon. By December 2007 the price per gallon of aviations fuel was $2.10 per gallon.[10]

The impact that such fuel increases have had can be shown by analyzing fuel consumption for certain aircraft that are commonly used today. The Air Transportation Association's annual report shows that the number of gallons of fuel consumed per hour for the following planes is as follows (see Table 7-3):

367-seat 747	3,411 gallons/hour
286-seat DC-10	2,405 gallons/hour
148-seat 727	1,289 gallons/hour
101-seat DC-9	826 gallons/hour

Using a cost of $0.77 per gallon, the fuel cost per hour is $7,163.10 for a 747, $5,050.50 for a DC-10, $2,706.90 for a 727, and $1,734.60 for DC-9. Consequently, rapidly escalating fuel costs in recent years have caused airlines to suffer financially in an already depressed pricing market.

When fuel costs rise, carriers scrutinize planes in the fleet as well as routes served. More **fuel-efficient** planes have been developed and added to carrier fleets. In the short run, carriers are substituting smaller planes on low-density (low demand) routes and eliminating service completely on other routes. Commuter lines have provided substitute service on the routes abandoned by major and national carriers. The average cost per gallon of fuel increased from $1.97 to $2.10 from 2006 to 2007 and fuel consumption increased by 187 million gallons (1.03 percent increase) from 2006 to 2007, resulting in additional fuel expense of 2.94 billion.[11]

Labor

In 2007, average salaries and wages increased by 2.7 percent but were offset by a reduction in average benefits and pensions of 11.9 percent. In 2007 carriers employed 560,997 people at an average annual compensation of $74,786.[12] Average compensation includes wages and fringe benefits.

Airlines employ people with a variety of different skills. To operate the planes, the carrier must employ pilots, copilots, and flight engineers. The plane crew also includes the flight attendants who serve the passengers. Communications personnel are

Table 7-6	Average U.S. Airline Pilot Hourly Wages—2008	
	5-YEAR FIRST OFFICER	**10-YEAR CAPTAIN**
Delta	$94.00	$152.00
Northwest	$82.00	$137.00
Continental	$95.00	$167.00
United	$82.00	$133.00
US Airways	$75.00	$122.00
Southwest	$119.00	$194.00
American	$97.00	$163.00
Amerijet	$50.00	$85.00
Source: Airline Pilot Central, 2009.		

required to tie together the different geographic locations. Mechanics and ground crews for aircraft and traffic service provide the necessary maintenance and servicing of the planes. The final component of airline employment consists of the office personnel and management. Overall employment has decreased as airlines have moved aggressively to reduce costs to improve their competitiveness and lower prices in selected markets.

Strict safety regulations are administered by the FAA. Acceptable flight operations, as well as hours of service, are specified for pilots. Both mechanics and pilots are subject to examinations on safety regulations and prescribed operations. FAA regulations also dictate appropriate procedures for flight attendants to follow during takeoff and landing.

The wages paid to a pilot usually vary according to the pilot's equipment rating. A pilot who is technically capable (has passed a flight examination for a given type of aircraft) of flying a jumbo jet will receive a higher compensation than one who flies a single-engine, six-passenger plane. Table 7-6 shows the average pilot compensation for the major airlines in the United States for narrowbody aircraft. Southwest averages the highest pilot wages, whereas Amerijet has the lowest. Pilot wages have decreased by 2.4 percent from 2006 to 2007.[13]

Equipment

As mentioned earlier, the cost of operating airplanes varies. Larger planes are more costly to operate per hour than smaller planes, but the cost per seat-mile is lower for larger planes. That is, the larger plane has the capacity to carry more passengers; thus, the higher cost is spread out over a large number of output units.

Table 7-3 shows the hourly operating costs for four aircraft used by major carriers in 2002. The cost per block hour was $8,443 for the 367-seat 747 and $2,071 for the 101-seat DC-9. However, the cost per seat-mile was $0.0046 for the 747 and $0.00686 for the DC-9. This reduced operating cost per seat-mile for the larger planes indicates that economies of scale exist in aircraft.

Economies of Scale/Economies of Density

Large-scale air carrier operations do have some **economies of scale**, which result from more extensive use of large-size planes or indivisible units. Of the small number of major and national carriers, approximately 17 transport over 78 percent of the passengers, indicating that large-scale operations exist.

The information contained in Table 7-3 suggests the existence of economies of scale with large-size planes. Market conditions (sufficient demand) must exist to permit the efficient utilization of larger planes (that is, if the planes are flown near capacity, the seat-mile costs will obviously decrease). Contributing to the existence of economies of scale for aircraft is the inability to inventory an unused seat. For example, a 367-seat 747 is about to close its doors with 10 seats empty. If the plane takes off with the empty seats, the seats are "lost" for that flight because the airline cannot inventory the excess capacity for another flight that might be overbooked. On the other hand, the marginal cost of filling those 10 empty seats right before the doors on the aircraft are closed are negligible. This is the same concept of economies of scale as found in the railroad industry. The marginal cost of adding one more rail car to a train right before departure is negligible.

Another factor indicating large-scale operations for air carriers is the integrated **communication network** required for activities such as operating controls and passenger reservations. Small local or regional carriers find the investment required for such a communication system rather staggering, but without the communication system, the emerging carrier cannot effectively operate (provide connecting service with other carriers and ticketing to passengers). Such carriers have purchased passenger reservation systems from large carriers to be competitive.

The air carrier industry overall has a cost structure that closely resembles that of motor carriers. Long-run economies of scale, as compared to short-run economies of plane size and utilization, are not significant in the air carrier industry. Industries characterized by high variable-cost ratios (airlines and motor carriers) can relatively easily add equipment to a given market. As such, the ability to decrease fully allocated cost per mile by adding aircraft does not exist. On the other hand, when high fixed-cost industries (pipe and rail) add fixed capacity, they can decrease fully allocated cost per mile by adding volume to the fixed capacity. In high fixed-cost industries, however, capacity is not easily added in small increments.

Economies of density exist when a carrier has significant volume between an origin–destination pair to fully utilize capacity on forward-haul movements as well as utilize significant capacity on back-haul movements. This concept can exist across all modes of transportation. Southwest Airlines uses this concept aggressively when deciding which markets to enter, choosing those city pairs that offer high volumes of potential passengers to fill outbound aircraft. Table 7-7 shows the top 25 passenger markets in the United States. Of these, 11 have New York City as the originating point. jetBlue, based out of JFK Airport in New York, currently serves Fort Lauderdale, Orlando, San Juan, Tampa, and West Palm Beach. Economies of density, then, are important for all airlines to achieve to fully utilize capacity in a given market. History has shown that this has been a successful strategy for new entrants to the airline passenger market.

Over the years the federal government has provided direct operating **subsidies** (that is, public service revenues) to air carriers. The subsidies have been provided to ensure

Table 7-7	Top 25 Domestic Airline Markets—2007[1]		
	PASSENGERS (DAILY AVERAGE)		
1	New York	Chicago	4,839
2	New York	Fort Lauderdale	4,777
3	New York	Orlando	4,423
4	New York	Los Angeles	3,776
5	New York	Atlanta	3,518
6	New York	San Francisco	2,908
7	Honolulu	Kahului	2,660
8	New York	Las Vegas	2,418
9	New York	West Palm Beach	2,363
10	New York	Miami	2,305
11	New York	Boston	2,275
12	New York	Tampa	2,249
13	Chicago	Las Vegas	2,192
14	Dallas/Ft Worth	Houston	2,147
15	Washington DC	New York	2,083
16	Washington DC	Chicago	2,071
17	Dallas/Ft Worth	New York	2,001
18	Chicago	Los Angeles	1,988
19	Chicago	Orlando	1,968
20	Chicago	Phoenix	1,874
21	Orlando	Philadelphia	1,852
22	Honolulu	Lihue	1,847
23	San Juan	New York	1,811
24	Los Angeles	San Francisco	1,790
25	Los Angeles	Las Vegas	1,174

[1]Includes all commercial airports in a metropolitan area.

Source: Air Transport Association, *2008 Economic Report.*

air carrier service over particular routes where operating expenses exceed operating incomes. The subsidies enable regional carriers to provide service to less-populated areas that otherwise would probably not have air service.

Rates

Pricing

Airline pricing for passenger service is characterized by the **discounts** from full fare. Seats on the same plane can have substantially different prices depending on restrictions attached to the purchase, such as having to stay over a weekend or having to purchase the ticket in advance. Businesspeople generally pay more for their airline travel due to the more rigid schedules they are on and the fact that they usually depart and return during the high-demand times. jetBlue, Southwest, and AirTran have aggressively discounted prices in major passenger markets. However, inflation-adjusted airfares declined by 1.4 percent in 2007 and declined by 51.9 percent between 1978 and 2007.[14] The price of seats on different flights and the price of the same seat on a particular flight can vary due to competition with other airlines, the time and day of departure and return, the level of service (first class versus coach or no-frills service), and advance ticket purchase. Discount pricing has continued throughout the 2000s as airlines have attempted to increase their "payload." Industry load factors in 2007 are 79.9 percent, up from 79.2 percent in 2006.[15] This is a result of aggressive pricing as well as more systematic allocation of capacity to markets.

Cargo pricing is dependent mainly on weight and/or cubic dimensions. Some shipments that have a very low density can be assessed an over-dimensional charge, usually based on 8 pounds per cubic foot. This over-dimensional charge is used to gain more appropriate revenue from shipments that take up a lot of space but do not weigh much. An exaggerated example of a shipment to which this rule would apply is a shipment of inflated beach balls. Other factors affecting the price paid to ship freight via air transportation include completeness of service and special services, such as providing armed guards.

Operating Efficiency

An important measure of operating efficiency used by air carriers is the **operating ratio**. The operating ratio measures the portion of operating income that goes to operating expenses:

$$\text{Operating Ratio} = (\text{Operating Expense}/\text{Operating Income}) \times 100$$

Only income and expenses generated from passenger and freight transportation are considered. Like the motor carrier industry, the air carrier industry's operating ratio was in the low to mid-90s between 1994 and 2000, ranging from 96.9 in 1994 to 94.7 in 2000. The operating ratio for the industry in 2007 was 94.7.[16] The overall profit margin is small, and a loss is incurred when the operating ratio exceeds 100.

Another widely used measure of operating efficiency is the load factor (previously discussed). The load factor measures the percentage of a plane's capacity that is utilized.

$$\text{Load Factor} = (\text{Number of Passengers}/\text{Total Number of Seats}) \times 100$$

Airlines have raised plane load factors to the 70 to 80 percent range. The particular route and type of plane (capacity) directly affect the load factor, as does price, service level, and competition.

Again, referring to Table 7-3, the relationship among load factor, cost, plane size, and profitability can be seen. Assume that a route requires one hour to traverse and has a load factor of 65 percent; the average operating cost per passenger for a 747 is $35.39 ($8,443 per hour/(367 [capacity] = 0.65 [load factor])). If the demand drops to 80 passengers on the route, the load factor for the 747 would be 21.8 percent (80/367), and the hourly operating cost per passenger would be $105.54 ($8,443/80). At this level of demand, the carrier would substitute a smaller capacity plane, such as a 727 or DC-9. With 80 passengers, the load factor for the DC-9 would be 79.2 percent (80/101) and the average operating cost would be $25.89 ($2,071/80). The small aircraft would be more economical to operate over this lower-density route, and the carrier would substitute this more efficient plane (DC-9) on this hypothetical route.

Equipment substitution, however, might not be possible, and substitution might result in excess capacity. The jumbo planes have large carrying capacities that might not be utilized in low-demand routes. Thus, large-capacity planes are used on high-demand routes such as New York–Chicago and New York–Los Angeles, and smaller capacity planes are used on low-demand routes such as Toledo–Chicago and Pittsburgh–Memphis.

Current Issues

Safety

The issue of **airline safety** is of great importance to the airline industry. Any incident involving airplanes receives a great deal of publicity from the media because of the large number of people affected at one time. (Accidents involving motor vehicles affect only a few people in each incident but affect a greater number of people than do airline accidents in the long run.)

Several factors affect airline safety. First, airport security has come under close scrutiny over the past several years. On September 11, 2001, four aircraft were hijacked and two were flown into the Twin Towers in New York City, killing and injuring thousands of people. As a result, airport security has reached an all-time high, causing more delays at airport terminals. The U.S. government created the Office of Homeland Security to be the agency that monitors and manages the security of the U.S. borders.

Air travel is more popular than ever, as indicated previously, but there is still great concern about safety. The 1990s had some significant air disasters among major carriers, including TWA, American, USAirways, SwissAir, and the ValuJet crash in the Florida Everglades. In addition, the frequent reportings of near collisions, minor accidents, and airplane recalls have heightened public awareness of the air safety problem. However, air travel is still the safest way to travel. Table 7-8 shows the trend of aircraft accidents from 1997 through 2007. The spike in 2001 was caused by the incident in New York City on September 11. Table 7-9 shows that even though there is a significant loss of life in an airline tragedy, air travel is still the safest mode for passenger travel, with automobiles being the most dangerous.

Finally, as with other transportation modes, the issue of substance abuse concerning pilots and ground crews has become important. Strict drug-testing policies and alcohol consumption guidelines are in effect for pilots and other aircraft personnel. In spite of these concerns, airline travel is still a very safe form of transportation; however, these issues are currently being addressed by the airlines to ensure that airline transportation remains safe.

Security

The aftermath of the tragic air fatalities of 9/11 gave rise to the establishment of the Department of Homeland Security as well as the Transportation Security Administration (TSA). Both of these agencies are responsible for the safety of passengers while in airports and in flight. New screening procedures have been established at airports for

Table 7-8	U.S. Air Carriers Operating Under 14 CFR 121—Scheduled Service				
YEAR	DEPARTURES (MILLIONS)	TOTAL ACCIDENTS	FATAL ACCIDENTS	FATAL ACCIDENT RATES[1]	FATALITIES
1997	8.1	43	3	0.030	3
1998	8.3	41	1	0.009	1
1999	8.6	40	2	0.018	12
2000	9.0	49	2	0.018	89
2001	8.9	41	6	0.019	531
2002	9.3	34	0	0.000	0
2003	10.8	51	2	0.020	22
2004	11.4	23	1	0.009	13
2005	11.6	33	3	0.027	22
2006	11.3	26	2	0.019	50
2007	11.4	24	0	0.000	0

[1]Fatal accidents per 100,000 departures; excludes incidents resulting from illegal acts.

Source: National Transportation Safety Board. Air Transport Association, *2008 Economic Report.*

Table 7-9	U.S. Passenger Fatalities Per 100 Million Passenger Miles			
YEAR	AUTOS[1]	BUSES[2]	RAILROADS[3]	AIRLINES[4]
1997	0.93	0.01	0.05	0.01
1998	0.86	0.05	0.03	0.00
1999	0.84	0.07	0.10	0.005
2000	0.81	0.01	0.03	0.02
2001	0.78	0.02	0.02	0.06
2002	0.78	0.06	0.05	0.00
2003	0.74	0.05	0.02	0.005
2004	0.71	0.05	0.02	0.002
2005	0.68	0.07	0.10	0.004
2006	0.67	0.02	0.10	0.01
10-Yr. Avg.	0.78	0.04	0.04	0.01

[1]Passenger cars/taxis; drivers considered passengers; data from the National Safety Council Fatality Analysis Reporting System.
[2]Does not include school buses; data from the National Safety Council Fatality Analysis Reporting System.
[3]Data from the Federal Railroad Administration.
[4]Large and commuter scheduled airlines, excluding cargo; from the National Transportation Safety Board.

Source: Air Transport Association, 2009.

Transportation Technology

Freight Forwarders Cite Serious Issues Regarding Air Cargo Security Screening

Despite significant progress being made in screening cargo on passenger planes, there are still major challenges ahead on the path to safeguarding air cargo in this country according to the Airforwarders Association (AfA).

Testifying last month before the House Homeland Security Subcommittee on Transportation Security and Infrastructure Protection, Brandon Fried, executive director of the AfA, acknowledged the progress made in reaching the 50 percent air cargo screening milestone (as mandated by H.R. 1 Implementing Recommendations of the 9/11 Commission Act), but warned that there are three primary challenges still facing the TSA in achieving the 100 percent screening goal by the August 2010 deadline.

"The ease of attaining the first portion of the screening mandate should be both a sign of encouragement and caution," said Fried. "It proves that our industry and its airline partners can collectively rise to any challenge. However, serious issues have yet to be resolved, including the lack of approved pallet screening technology, ongoing financial barriers to participation, and the future of air cargo security policy in general."

Noted experts, including the Government Accountability Office (GAO), have stated that abandoning a risk-based security program in favor of screening may actually make the nation less safe.

"The Transportation Security Administration has limited resources, both financially and in terms of personnel, and it is an unwise use of those finite dollars and employees to treat each piece of cargo as if it had the same threat level," said Fried.

In an interview with *LM*, GAO spokesman Stephen M. Lord said TSA does not expect to meet the mandated 100 percent screening deadline as it applies to inbound air cargo.

"In part that is due to existing inbound screening exemptions and challenges it faces in harmonizing security standards with other nations," he said. "We are really focusing on compliance in 2010."

Meanwhile, TSA has taken several key steps to meet the mandate, including establishing a new requirement for 100 percent screening of cargo transported on narrow-body aircraft; revising or eliminating most screening exemptions for domestic cargo; creating the Certified Cargo Screening Program (CCSP) to allow screening to take place at various points in the air cargo supply chain; and establishing a screening technology pilot.

Source: Patrick Burnson, *Logistics Management*, April 2009, p. 17.

passengers and new guidelines developed for carry-on luggage. Another area of security conern is for freight loaded onto passenger-carrying aircraft. This freight, most times arranged for movement by air freight forwarders, has not been subject to a high level of security screening in the past. However, new legislation passed in the United States is calling for 100 percent screening of all freight loaded onto passenger-carrying aircraft. The intent of this legislation is to prevent unnecessarily dangerous freight from threatening the lives of passengers in an aircraft. Aircraft security is, and will continue to be, an important issue in defending the United States from terrorist acts.

Technology

Because the airline industry must offer quick and efficient service to attract business, it constantly needs more sophisticated equipment. With other modes such as railroads and water carriers, travel times are measured in days; however, air carriers measure travel time in hours.

For this reason, the airline industry has developed automated information-processing programs like the Air Cargo Fast Flow Program, which was designed by the Port Authority of New York/New Jersey. The Fast Flow Program is a paperless system that speeds the processing of air freight cargo through customs processing, which was found to take 106 out of 126 hours of processing time for international shipments. The system allows the air freight community to tie into customs-clearing systems and thus reduce paperwork and time requirements dramatically. The system also will provide better tracking of shipments and better communication between connecting carriers. These improvements will allow customers to receive their inbound shipments faster than ever before.

The FAA and the federal government are proposing an entire overhaul to the current air traffic control system that would rely on the use of GPS navigational aids. This would increase the capacity for aircraft in operating space as well as reduce travel times between origin/destination pairs. However, this change would also require new technology on current and new aircraft. The plan will cost billions of dollars and take years to develop but will offer airlines an opportunity to reduce operating costs and increase service.

SUMMARY

- The airline industry began its development in the early part of the 20th century, and its growth was influenced to a great extent initially by government interest and policy.
- The airline industry is dominated by revenue from passenger service, but air freight revenue is growing in importance.
- Both private and for-hire carriers operate as part of the airline industry, but private carrier service is predominantly passenger movement.
- For-hire carriers can be classified based on service offered (all-cargo, air taxi, charter, and so on) or annual operating revenue (majors, nationals, or regionals).
- All-cargo carriers and commuter operators have grown in importance in recent years and play a more important role in the total airline industry.
- A relatively large number of airline companies exist, but a small number (10) account for more than 82 percent of the total revenue.
- Deregulation of airlines was rationalized to some extent with the argument that an increase in the number of carriers would increase competition. Initially, there was an increase followed by a decrease; today the number is higher.
- Airlines are unique in that they face limited intermodal competition, but intramodal competition is very keen in terms of pricing and service and has been exacerbated by unused capacity.
- Airline service competition is usually in terms of frequency and timing of flights, but special passenger services and programs are important.
- The express portion of air freight has grown dramatically. A growing number of commodities use air freight service, and increased growth is expected.
- Speed is the major advantage of airlines for both passengers and freight, but the airlines' speed of service has been offset recently by congestion and fewer flights.
- The higher cost of airline service can be a trade-off against lower inventory and warehousing costs, as well as other logistics-related savings.
- Airline carriers are essentially long-haul service providers for passengers and freight because the cost of takeoffs and landings makes short hauls relatively uneconomical.
- Airlines usually provide service for small shipments where value is high and/or the product may be perishable.
- Airlines offer a generally reliable and consistent service, but their accessibility is limited.
- Airlines use different types of equipment that limits their carrying capacity, but their overall equipment variety is also limited.
- Airlines use publicly provided airways and terminals, but pay user charges on both, which helps make their cost structure highly variable.
- Major and national airlines use a hub approach to their service, which contributes to operating efficiency but often adds travel time.
- Fuel and labor costs are important expense categories for airlines and have received much managerial attention. The low fuel cost of the late 1990s helped the airlines improve their profitability; today, however, rising fuel prices are having a negative impact on industry profits.
- Economies of scale and economies of density exist in the airline industry, making larger-scale carriers usually more efficient, based on equipment, markets, and communications.
- In the era of deregulation, discount pricing has become very popular, and it has made the rate schedules of airlines for passenger services complex.

- Airline safety is an important issue, but overall airlines have a very good record.
- Traditionally, airlines have capitalized on new equipment technology to improve their operating efficiency and to expand capacity. In recent years, technology improvements have come in a variety of other areas.

STUDY QUESTIONS

1. What are the types of carriers as defined by revenue class? Who are some of the members of each class? Do you think the members of each class would compete against or work together with members of the other classes? What about members of their own class? Use examples obtained from advertising or websites.

2. Discuss the ways in which air carriers compete with each other. How have regulatory changes affected this competition?

3. What is the major advantage of air carriers? How does this advantage impact the inventory levels of those firms using air transportation? Explain how this advantage relates to the choice of modes when choosing between air carriage and other modes of freight and passengers transport.

4. Discuss the length of haul and carrying capacity of the air carriers. Explain how they both favor and hinder air carriers from a competitive standpoint.

5. What is the role of government in air transportation? Include both economic and safety regulations in your answer.

6. How does fuel cost and efficiency affect both air carrier costs and pricing?

7. What is the current situation of labor within the air industry? Are unions a major factor? How does skill level vary within the industry? Do you think this situation is similar to other modes? If so, which one(s)? Explain why.

8. Do air carriers have economies of scale at any level? Economies of density? Discuss and support your answer with examples.

9. How do air carriers price their services? Is the weight or density of the shipment a factor? Explain this factor as part of your answer. How does air carrier pricing relate to the value of the goods being transported?

10. What are the current issues facing the air industry? Discuss how each impacts the industry, its customers and employees.

11. What is the cost structure of the air industry? How does it compare with other modes? How does this affect pricing, particularly for passengers? Be sure your answer includes examples from either advertising or the Internet.

NOTES

1. Air Transport Association, *2008 Economic Report,* Washington, DC: 2008, p. 6.

2. Eno Foundation, *Transportation in America,* Washington, DC, 20th edition, 2007, p. 40.

3. Air Transport Association, op. cit., p.14.

4. Ibid., p. 6.

5. Bureau of Transportation Statistics, *Airline On-Time Data,* Washington, D.C., 2009, Table 1.

6. Air Transport Association, op. cit., p. 11.

7. Hoover's Online, June 7, 2004, http://www.jetblue.com/learnmore/factsheet.html.

8. Air Transport Association, op. cit., p. 6.

9. Ibid., p. 6.

10. Ibid., p. 12.

11. Bureau of Transportation Statistics, Washington, DC, 2009.

12. Air Transport Association, op. cit., pp. 12–13.

13. Ibid., p. 14.

14. Ibid., p. 11.

15. Ibid., p. 6.

16. Ibid., p. 7.

CASE 7-1

Airspace Airlines

Airspace Airlines is a regional passenger airline operating in the southeastern United States. It operates as an independent airline between certain origin/destination pairs but also operates as a contract carrier for Delta out of the Atlanta airport. Airspace currently has a fleet of aging turboprop aircraft with an average capacity of 35 passengers. The average trip length for Airspace is 250 miles. Airspace employs only Airline Pilot Association union pilots.

Jim Gray is the vice president of operations for Airspace and is faced with the challenge of minimizing the impacts of fuel and labor costs on Airspace operating profits. The operating cost per seat mile for his fleet of aircraft is approximately $0.12. Maintenance costs are 15 percent of operating costs and are higher than the industry average. Pilot wages average $45 per hour. Airspace averages 50 departures per day out of the Atlanta airport.

Delta has approached Airspace about increasing the number of departures it offers out of Atlanta. Delta is also asking for a lower fare structure to help boost its profits. Jim knows that his current fleet will not be able to meet an increased demand and is pessimistic that he can lower operating costs without significantly reducing fuel costs and increasing pilot productivity. However, he is certain that the future financial viability of Airspace relies on a continued relationship with Delta.

CASE QUESTIONS

1. What suggestions would you give Jim to help Airspace lower its operating costs?

2. How would you help Airspace implement those plans?

3. What constraints can you identify that would prevent Airspace from implementing your suggestions?

4. How would you suggest Jim respond to Delta's requests for more flights at a lower cost?

CASE 7-2
US Airways

The U.S. airline industry has faced growing intramodal competition, as well-increased fuel and labor costs over the past several years. Carriers such as Airtran, jetBlue, and Southwest have collectively changed the financial operating results for many of the traditional airlines. Companies such as American, Delta, United, and US Airways have seen these rising costs and increased competition as a threat to their survival. Both United and US Airways had declared reorganization under bankruptcy and have emerged successfully. Delta and Northwest have decided that a merger would be the most successful plan for both airlines.

However, none have struggled as has US Airways. Their relatively short-haul, Northeast-dominated routes have made US Airways extremely susceptible to low-cost competition. This case is based on facts found in the popular press and is intended to present the current state of US Airways and its competitors. It will present a synopsis of the operating strategies and characteristics of US Airways and three of its competitors: AirTran, jetBlue, and Southwest. A summary of 2007 operating characteristics for these four airlines can be found in Table 7-10.

AirTran

Based in Atlanta, AirTran Airways makes nearly 700 departures daily to 55 cities (mostly Eastern and Midwestern destinations). Its top competitors are Delta, Southwest, and US Airways. AirTran's strategy is to focus on both business and leisure travelers using low fares. Its labor costs are among the lowest in the industry. It is the world's largest operator of Boeing 717s and will take more deliveries of the Boeing 737-700 on 2007. AirTran, unlike Southwest, operates a hub-and-spoke network out of its Atlanta hub. Revenues have increased from $1.89 billion in 2006 to $2.31 billion in 2007, with net income increasing from $14.7 million to $52 million during the same period. AirTran is facing significant competition in Atlanta from Delta and from US Airways in Orlando.

jetBlue

Based in John F. Kennedy International Airport in New York City, jetBlue was one of the fastest-growing airlines in the United States. Revenues grew from $2.36 billion in 2006 to $2.84 billion in 2007, with net income increasing from a loss of $1.0 million to a gain of $18.0 million during the same period. It currently operates 104 Airbus 320 aircraft to 53 cities. jetBlue's strategy is to offer low fares in one class of service on its aircraft. It is one of the only airlines to offer 36 channels of live satellite television free at every seat. jetBlue was the first U.S. airline to introduce "paperless cockpit" flight technology and the only U.S. airline to be 100 percent ticketless. Its routes are point-to-point and rely mostly on nonstop, long-distance flights. Right now, its main competitors are American, Southwest, and United. However, its Florida market is in direct competition with US Airways.

Southwest

Located in Dallas, Texas, Southwest has enjoyed 38 profitable years. Southwest was the first of the new low-cost, no-frills airlines. Passengers sit wherever they want and free meals are not served onboard. Meals may be bought at the gate and brought onboard. Southwest locates its operations in major cities but not at major airports. For example,

Table 7-10	2007 Annual Operating Characteristics			
	AIRTRAN	**JETBLUE**	**SOUTHWEST**	**US AIRWAYS**
1. Aircraft	137	134	520	356
2. Employees	8,002	9,695	33,436	32,602
3. Departures	262,000	196,000	1,162,000	525,000
4. Revenue Passengers (000)	23,741	21,304	101,910	57,829
5. Revenue Passenger miles (millions)	17,233	25,722	72,320	61,222
6. Available Seat Miles (millions)	22,680	32,148	99,636	75,790
7. Operating Revenue ($millions)	2,309	2,843	9,861	12,055
8. Operating Profit ($millions)	137	166	790	524
9. Net Profit ($millions)	52	18	645	350
10. Aircraft				
• A320	0	104	0	75
• A319	0	0	0	319
• A321	0	0	0	28
• A330	0	0	0	9
• B737	50	0	520	87
• B757	0	0	0	43
• B767	0	0	0	10
• B717-200	87	0	0	0
• E190	0	30	0	11
11. Hubs	Atlanta	JFK/NYC	Chicago Los Angeles Dallas	Philadelphia, Charlotte
12. Rank 2007				
• Passengers	8	10	1	5
• Revenue Passenger Miles	10	8	6	7
• Revenue	12	11	8	7

Source: Air Transport Association, *2008 Economic Report*, pp. 22–23.

in Chicago Southwest has avoided the congestion and high cost of using O'Hare and has opted for using Midway Airport. Southwest's growth was well planned. It entered specific market pairs where economies of density were present. Its low-cost structure (nonunion labor) allowed it to attract both business and leisure travelers from existing carriers by offering much lower fares. It only utilizes Boeing 737s in its fleet. Its major rivals are American (at Dallas), Delta, and jetBlue. A new entrant called Song, a low-cost subsidiary of Delta, will begin to provide some significant competition to Southwest in its major markets. However, Southwest made a significant strategic move into the main markets serviced by US Airways. Its first move was into Baltimore (a Piedmont hub operated by US Airways), making US Airways downplay its significance in its hub-and-spoke network servicing the Southeast. Recently Southwest made a major move into Philadelphia, the major hub in the US Airways network.

US Airways

US Airways, originally known as Allegheny Airlines, is one of the original major hub-and-spoke airlines in the U.S. Based in Arlington, Virginia, US Airways has major hubs in Pittsburgh, Philadelphia, and Charlotte, North Carolina. Rising labor and fuel costs, coupled with its relatively short-haul network in the Northeast, forced US Airways into bankruptcy reorganization (it successfully emerged from the restructuring in 2003). US Airways currently has the highest operating cost per mile of any major U.S. airline. The unions have made many wage and operating concessions to help bring US Airways out of bankruptcy. However, continued pressure from nonunion, low-cost airlines has presented major challenges for US Airways to grow back to profitability.

US Airways predominantly utilizes feeder, or commuter, airlines (that is, US Airways Express) to bring passengers from small metropolitan areas to its major hubs where it consolidates passengers into larger aircraft traveling to more distant locations. Its major hub was in Pittsburgh. However, rising costs at the Pittsburgh International Airport have forced the airline to cut flights significantly from this hub and focus its efforts on the Philadelphia International Airport. Basing its major operations in the Northeast also brings with it delays and cancellations because of weather.

US Airways has begun to introduce regional jets into some of its medium markets, hoping to reduce its operating cost per mile and to compete with the low-cost airlines. Traditionally, the main competitors for US Airways were United, American, and Delta (all union, hub-and-spoke carriers). However, its new competitors are AirTran, jetBlue, and Southwest.

CASE QUESTIONS

1. If you were the CEO of US Airways, what would you do to confront the competition from its low-cost competitors?

2. Can US Airways survive by remaining the same carrier it is today?

3. If you were AirTran, jetBlue, or Southwest, how would you continue to take market share away from US Airways?

4. Do American, Delta, and United still pose competitive threats to US Airways?

Chapter 8

WATER CARRIERS AND PIPELINES

Learning Objectives

After reading this chapter, you should be able to do the following:

- Understand the importance of domestic waterways in the development of the economy of the United States and particularly of cities located contiguous to the waterways

- Appreciate the role and significance of the water carrier industry at the present time in the U.S. economy and how it complements and competes with the other basic modes of transportation

- Discuss the various types of water carriers and their roles in the overall water carrier system

- Understand the competitive environment for water carriers on an intramodal as well as an intermodal basis

- Discuss the service and operating characteristics of water carriers as well as their cost structure and equipment challenges

- Understand the current issues faced by the water carrier industry in the 21st century

- Appreciate the development and current position of the pipeline industry in the economy

- Discuss the types of pipeline companies and their role in the transportation system

- Understand the nature of the operating and service characteristics of pipeline carriers and what makes them unique in the transportation system

- Discuss the cost structure and rates of pipelines

Transportation Profile

Mon Valley Coal and Aggregates Company: A Sequel

Andy Kersnick and his son, Mike Kersnick, were having a heated discussion about the future of their family business, the Mon Valley Coal and Aggregates Company of Monessen, Pennsylvania, which was located in the so-called Mon Valley along the Monongahela River in the southwestern part of the state. Andy, who was currently the CEO (after having succeeded his retired father-in-law, Joe Hulich), and Mike, who was COO currently, were involved in a strategic planning session trying to map out a future course of action for their company. Both Andy and Mike recognized the need to transform their organization, but they had different visions about the future strategic direction of the Mon Valley Coal and Aggregates Company.

The company was founded in the early 1900s when Monessen was a bustling steel town along the Monongahela River south of Pittsburgh. The town benefited from good rail service and access to the Ohio River via the Monongahela. The company got its start distributing coal from the rich reserves in Pennsylvania and West Virginia to the numerous steel plants along the river. Other raw materials were added over time as opportunities developed, especially the road system which needed aggregates for construction and related purposes.

The company was at a crossroads again because most of the steel mills located in towns along the river had closed and so had their suppliers. Business volume and profits had significantly declined, and drastic action was needed if the Kersnicks wanted to continue operating the business.

A key to the success of Mon Valley Coal and Aggregates Company was an efficient and effective transportation strategy. Historically, the company accepted large shipments of materials by barge or by rail hopper car. Its location on the river made either approach a viable alternative. Deliveries to customers were usually made by truck. In fact, Mon Valley had its own fleet of trucks for deliveries but was considering other options, namely, for-hire carriers.

The closing of the Monessen Steel Mill had changed the economics of the company because it could no longer justify the large-volume deliveries required by rail and barge. About ten years ago, Mon Valley had made a strategic change from coal as their primary product to aggregates for road construction and to home-heating oil. Andy felt at that time that they could extend their market boundary for coal using barge transportation for delivery to customers in the Midwest via the Ohio River, and/or rail shipments to the Port of Toledo and then barge on the Great Lakes to appropriate locations. Both strategies had been moderately successful, which had provided some financial stability for Mon Valley.

Andy also eliminated having all shipments stop in Monessen for eventual delivery to customers, which had contributed to the cost of doing business. Eliminating the stop-off allowed them to price their product more competitively for the Midwest market area. He also felt that the increase in oil prices over the last ten years had increased the opportunity for coal sales to public utility companies and other businesses, especially coal retailers who sold for home use. He was also counting on a revival of interest in barge service and government investment in port facilities in the Monessen area. Mike was of the opinion that they should change to all-truck transportation to minimize their inventory levels. Andy wanted to put more emphasis on aggregates because he anticipated increased expenditures for road construction in Southwestern Pennsylvania to stimulate economic development.

Introduction

Water carriers and pipelines are frequently overlooked by the general public. Most people are aware of trucks, planes, and trains, but they have limited appreciation of the role and contribution of water and pipeline carriers to businesses and our economy. These two modes of transportation are a very important part of our transportation system and overall infrastructure, particularly for certain types of products. In this chapter, we will explore the role and importance of water carriers and pipelines to a modern transportation system to gain an understanding and appreciation of their significance.

Brief History of Water Transportation

The inland or domestic waterways (rivers, lakes, and oceans) have provided an important link for freight and people movement for centuries. Waterways are a natural highway, and even some motive power (currents and wind) can be provided by nature. Water transportation has, of course, been improved by modern technology and federal investment to enhance motive power, vessel carrying capacity, and even the waterways by building dams and canals and dredging to increase the potential of water transportation for economic development. Today, there are 26,000 navigable kilometers of waterways in the Unites States.[1]

Water transportation played an important role in the early development of the United States, providing the settlers with a link to markets in England and Europe. In addition, many of our major cities developed along the coasts and still thrive in those locations. As the internal sections of the country developed, water transportation along the rivers and the Great Lakes linked the settlements in the wilderness with the coastal cities and also gave rise to interior cities such as Pittsburgh, Cincinnati, and Memphis. The natural highway, or waterway, was the only viable form of economical transportation available until the railroads were developed and was a prime determinant of population centers, as well as industrial and commercial concentration at port cities along the rivers and Great Lakes. Early private and public sector construction projects in transportation included the Erie, C&O, and other canals to provide inexpensive water transportation.

This chapter focuses on the basic economic and operating characteristics of domestic water and pipeline transportation. An overview is given first, followed by a consideration of types of carriers, market structure, operating and service characteristics, equipment cost structure, and current issues.

Water Transport Industry Overview

Significance of Water Transport

Water transportation remains a viable mode of transportation for the movement of products and especially of basic raw materials. Domestic water carriers compete with railroads for the movement of bulk commodities (such as grains, coal, ores, and chemicals) and with pipelines for the movement of bulk petroleum, petroleum products, and chemicals. The significance of water transportation will be examined from the perspectives of ton miles, market share, and freight expenditures.

In 2004, over \$330 billion was spent in total on freight transportation classified as consumer freight expenditures bill, which was an increase of 2.7 percent over 2003.[2] Water carriers accounted for about 12 percent of the total freight expenditures. Truck transportation expenditures dominated the market with 56 percent of the total spent on freight movements. The water carrier share, excluding international data, had a slight decline from 2.6 to 2.5 percent of freight expenditures from 2000 to 2004.[3]

The distribution of domestic intercity freight as measured in ton-miles has changed dramatically since the advent of transportation deregulation. Motor carriers have been the biggest beneficiary, as noted previously, but water carriers have not fared as well. Barge (river) traffic stayed steady from 2006 to 2007, and Great Lakes traffic declined by 6 percent in the same period.[4] From 2000 to 2005, waterborne transportation had a total decline of 9 percent in ton-miles. In contrast to 1990, when water transportation accounted for over 23 percent of ton-miles, there has been a decline to just under 13 percent of ton-miles for 2005.[5] To give a broader sense of the trend over the last decade, from 1996 to 2006 water transportation ton-miles declined 29 percent.[6]

In terms of ton-miles, waterborne transportation accounted for 13 percent of all transported freight in 2005.[7] Coastwise and internal water transportation accounted for 45 percent and 46 percent, respectively, of all waterborne traffic. Coastwise domestic shipping has historically not been included in the data for domestic water transportation's share of intercity ton-miles because of the long distances involved (for instance, from the Atlantic Coast to the Pacific Coast through the Panama Canal). Such movements generate high ton-mile figures for a relatively small tonnage figure. For example, if coastwise shipping had been included in 1980, the water carrier share would have been 33.3 percent instead of 16.4 percent. However, the 2001 figures still would have declined to 15.6 percent (as opposed to 13.2 percent noted above).[8]

As of 2007, domestic waterborne freight topped 1 billion short tons, with inland transportation accounting for 61 percent of the tonnage.[9] Water carriers collectively (coastwise, lakes, internal, intraport, and intraterritory) had an overall decrease in tonnage of 4.7 percent in 2007 compared to 2000 because tonnage shipped declined from 1,069 million to 1,021 million tons.[10]

Water transportation is the second most efficient form of transportation, in terms of energy costs per dollar of gross output, or the market value of goods and services produced. The most efficient form is rail, with 6 percent of its energy inputs as a percentage of output, while water transportation has 9 percent and air travel has 21 percent.[11] However, water transportation energy costs have risen more rapidly than for other modes.

Strong competitive pressures pushed average freight rate levels down for some modes during the 1990s. However, prices for producers or manufacturers have increased 16 percent during the last decade, but average freight rates for barge shipments have decreased by 8 percent. Rail rates also declined during this period, reflecting the competitiveness of the marketplace, especially intermodal competition.

It is obvious that the water carriers' importance in the U.S. transportation system declined over the past decade. However, many manufacturers and suppliers would experience serious problems in maintaining their competitive position without the availability of low-cost water transportation. The decline in water transportation is attributable in part to the transformation of the U.S. economy from basic manufacturing to service industries and technology. The focus on logistics and supply chain management has also impacted water transportation because companies have switched

Transportation Technology   *Shipment Visibility for the Alaskan Trade*

Most carriers have struggled with the challenge of providing shipment visibility for themselves and for their customers. Federal Express has been a leader in this area and has established a level of visibility which allows their customers and their customer's customer to track and trace shipments on a real-time basis on their own computers. This type of visibility provides a level of customer service which has many benefits in terms of efficiency and effectiveness. It is also very helpful to Federal Express in being able to respond to unexpected interruptions and delays. For the most part, Federal Express, UPS, and the Postal Services have been able to implement and execute their shipment visibility using bar codes and various types of scanners. Their fast service, small shipments, and controlled environment allows this type of technology to be effective as well as efficient.

Other modes of transportation have difficulty with bar coding technology, which is passive in nature; that is, the bar code has to be "read" by a scanner. Radio Frequency Identification tags (RFID), which can emit a signal, are more appropriate for some of the other modes of transportation, as they can tag a container, trailer, or car to track the progress of the shipment. However, the RFID tags have some challenges. One of the early challenges was the cost of each RFID tag and appropriate attachment to the container or trailer to prevent damage and protect against severe weather conditions and rough handling. Over the course of the last decade, the cost of RFID tags has been significantly reduced and the quality increased.

One of the major intermodal shipping lines on routes linking the lower 48 states with Alaska and several other major locations announced the ocean industry's first fully-functional intermodal RFID program to Alaska, which will provide their customers with real-time shipment visibility during all phases of transit. It will be matched with their web-based event management system. This integrated system will provide real-time shipment information throughout the container's transit from the origin loading facility through to final destination. The program will also include the installation of RFID readers at distribution centers, terminals and key Alaska highway routes. A leading grocery retailer in the Alaska market is participating in the pilot testing program to monitor shipments from its Pacific Northwest distribution centers to stores across Alaska. The unparalleled visibility of shipment containers will provide many opportunities for improved supply chain efficiency and visibility.

Source: Adapted from Internet Press Release, Horizon Lines, May 21, 2009.

to carriers offering better service (for instance, using motor carriers to offset other costs such as carrying cost for inventory, warehousing cost, packaging cost, and so forth).

Types of Carriers

Like motor carriers, the first major classification of the domestic water carrier industry is between for-hire and private carriers. A **private carrier** cannot be hired and only transports freight for the company that owns or leases the vessel. Private water carriers are permitted to transport, for a fee, exempt commodities; when they are hauling such exempt goods, they are technically exempt for-hire carriers. Bona fide private water carriers (transporting company-owned freight and exempt commodities) are excluded from federal economic regulation, as are water carrier shipments of three or fewer commodities within the same barge unit.

The **for-hire water carriers** consist of regulated and exempt carriers that charge a fee for their services. Exempt carriers, as indicated above, are excluded from the federal economic regulations administered by the **Surface Transportation Board** (STB). When authority was transferred to the STB under the **ICC Termination Act of 1995**, the STB's authority was expanded over domestic water traffic. In addition to inland river traffic, the STB has jurisdiction over port-to-port traffic when both ports are in the United States as well as transportation between the United States and its territories. Water carriers are exempt from economic regulation when transporting bulk commodities, both dry and liquid. Because the majority of freight transported by domestic water carriers consists of bulk commodities, exempt carriers dominate the for-hire segment of the industry.

Regulated water carriers are classified as either common or contract carriers. Economic regulation, similar to that controlling motor carriers (for instance, operating certificates, rates, and so forth), is administered by the STB. Although the majority of water traffic is exempt from regulation, a small number of regulated common and contract carriers do exist.

The domestic water carrier industry is most commonly classified by the waterway used. Carriers that operate over the inland navigable waterways are classified as **internal water carriers**. Internal water carriers use barges and towboats and operate over the principal U.S. rivers—the Mississippi, Ohio, Tennessee, Columbia, and Hudson—plus smaller arteries. Internal water carriers dominate the north–south traffic through the central portion of the United States via the Mississippi, Missouri, and Ohio rivers. The volume of freight moved on the major inland waterways is listed in Table 8-1 for six years from 1980 to 2006.

The Great Lakes carriers operate along the northeastern portion of the United States and provide service between ports on the five Great Lakes that border the states of New York, Pennsylvania, Ohio, Michigan, Indiana, Illinois, Wisconsin, and Minnesota. The lake ships normally remain on the lakes, but access to Atlantic and Gulf ports is possible via the Saint Lawrence Seaway. This Great Lakes-to-Atlantic traffic is classified as a coastal operation.

Table 8-1	Freight Carried on Major U.S. Waterways: 1980–2006					
IN MILLIONS OF TONS (4.0 REPRESENTS 4,000,000)						
	1980	1990	2000	2003	2005	2006
Atlantic Intracoastal Waterway	4	4.2	3.1	1.9	2.7	2.6
Great Lakes	183.5	167.1	187.5	156.5	169.4	173
Gulf Intracoastal Waterway	94.5	115.4	113.8	117.8	116.1	122.6
Mississippi River System	584.2	659.1	715.5	676.8	678	702.1
Mississippi River mainstem	441.5	475.3	515.6	478	454.6	497.7
Ohio River System	179.3	260	274.4	261.3	280.1	270.7
Columbia River	49.2	51.4	55.2	47.2	51.5	52.3
Snake River	5.1	4.8	6.7	5.3	5.3	5.2
Source: U.S. Army Corps of Engineers, Waterborne Commerce of the United States, annual.						

Coastal carriers operate along the coasts serving ports on the Atlantic or Pacific oceans or the Gulf of Mexico. Intercoastal carriers transport freight between East Coast and West Coast ports via the Panama Canal. Coastal and intercoastal carriers use oceangoing vessels, but some operators use oceangoing barges (18,000-ton capacity). Currently, large quantities of petroleum, crude and refined, are moved between points on the Atlantic and Gulf of Mexico. Likewise, oil from Alaska moves via coastal carriers to refineries along the Pacific coast.

Number and Categories of Carriers

The domestic for-hire water carrier industry consists of a limited number of relatively small firms. The latest numbers available from the Bureau of Transportation Statistics are for 2006, when it was reported that there were 682 vessel operators in service, and that number had decreased from 1,114 in 2000.[12]

Including support activities such as port and harbor operations and navigation services, total employment for water transportation is 154,500.[13] Vessels on the Mississippi and Gulf intracoastal water account for 27.6 percent of U.S. vessels, and Great Lakes vessels represent 4.7 percent; the remainder of the vessels navigate the coastal areas, including the Atlantic, Pacific, and Gulf of Mexico.[14] Based upon operating revenues for hauling domestic freight, the inland waterways (rivers and canals) were the most important, followed by the coastal waterways and then the Great Lakes carriers. Operating revenues on the inland waterways have remained relatively constant over the last decade, whereas revenue on the Great Lakes has increased about 23 percent because of an increase in higher-valued freight movements. Freight revenue on the coastal waterways declined about 40 percent during the 1990s as explained below. Water carriers have experienced increased competitive pressure, but the intensity has varied from segment to segment, with carriers operating along the coastal waterways experiencing the greatest impact of the competition, especially from railroads and pipeline carriers.[15]

Competition

Water carriers vigorously compete for traffic with other modes and, to a limited degree, with other water carriers. The relatively small number of water carriers results in a limited degree of competition. Because the number of carriers on a given waterway is limited, there is little incentive for the water carriers to compete with one another by lowering rates because they realize that the rate decrease will most likely be matched.

The major water carrier competition is with two other modes, namely rail and pipelines. Water carriers compete with railroads for the movement of dry bulk commodities such as grain, coal, and ores. For example, the movement of grains from the Midwest to New Orleans (for export traffic) is possible by rail as well as by water carrier. The water carriers can use the Mississippi and Missouri River systems to connect the plains states with New Orleans. Both modes move sizable amounts of grain along this traffic corridor.

Rail and water carriers compete heavily to move coal out of the coal-producing states of Pennsylvania, West Virginia, and Kentucky. The water carriers are capable of transporting coal via the Ohio and Mississippi rivers to Southern domestic consuming points (utilities), as well as to export markets.

On the Great Lakes, water carriers compete with railroads for the movement of coal, ores, and grain. Iron ore and grain originating in Minnesota, Michigan, and Wisconsin are moved across the Great Lakes to other Great Lakes ports, or out of the Great Lakes region via the Saint Lawrence Seaway to Atlantic and Gulf ports or to export markets.

The Port of Toledo has become an interchange point between rail and water carriers for the transport of coal. Railroads haul coal out of the coal-producing states to Toledo, where the coal is loaded onto lake ships for movement to northern Great Lakes ports. In essence, the railroads have helped to overcome the water carrier accessibility problem by moving coal from the mines to Toledo, which suggests that the modes are partners rather than competitors. Because the cost of the water–rail combination is lower than the all-rail route, shippers continue to request the combined water–rail service.

Water carriers and pipelines are vigorous competitors for the movement of bulk liquids. Bulk liquids (petroleum, petroleum products, and chemicals) account for about one-third of the total tonnage transported by domestic water carriers. Bulk liquids are important commodities to both modes, and vigorous competition exists for moving bulk liquids along the Gulf, Atlantic, and Pacific coasts, as well as the Mississippi River system.

To a very limited degree, water carriers compete with trucks. However, trucks are usually used to overcome the accessibility constraints of water carriers because trucks tie inland areas to the waterways for pickup and/or delivery. Shipment quantities argue against an all-motor carrier movement for long hauls because one barge can transport the equivalent of 58 tractor-trailers.

Operating and Service Characteristics

Commodities Hauled and Related Characteristics Figure 8-1 indicates the relative importance of the major commodities moved on the Inland waterway system in terms of their annual volume. In 2007, water carriers hauled 164.8 million short tons of petroleum, which represents 26.5 percent of the total short tons hauled that year.[16] Water carriers were second to pipelines but only transported about one-third of the ton-miles hauled by pipelines. The water carrier share of the refined petroleum movements experienced a surge in 2003 and 2004, but has generally been lower than pipeline's share of petroleum transport.[17] Chemicals accounted for about 8.2 percent of the

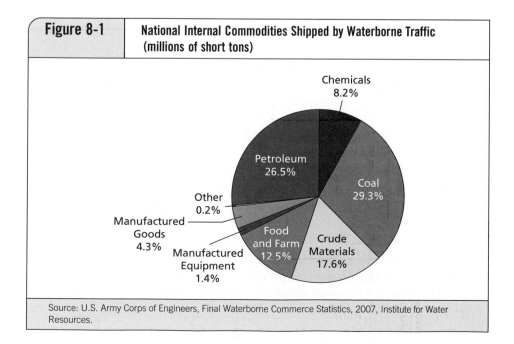

Figure 8-1	National Internal Commodities Shipped by Waterborne Traffic (millions of short tons)

Source: U.S. Army Corps of Engineers, Final Waterborne Commerce Statistics, 2007, Institute for Water Resources.

water carrier total. Coal and coke represent about 29 percent of the total freight moved by water carriers. Crude materials transported by water carriers are typically raw materials such as forest products, pulp, sand, and metal ores, accounting for 17.6 percent. Agricultural products account for about 15 percent of the total.[18] It is obvious that water carriers are important for low-value, bulk movements of liquid and dry materials. The low rates of water carriers are attractive to the shippers of such commodities.

Water carriers are considered to be medium-to-long-haul carriers. Their carrying capacity is relatively large, which makes short hauls with frequent stops uneconomical. However, the length of haul varies by segment from about 400 miles for inland water carriers to over 1,500 miles for coastal carriers. As noted, the carrying capacity is large. Barges are capable of carrying 1,500 to 3,000 tons, and lake carrier vessels can carry about 20,000 tons. A 1,500-ton load represents the typical carrying capacity of 15 railcars or about 50 trucks. The long hauls and the large carrying capacity combined with fuel efficiency allow water carriers to offer low-cost service—about 72 cents per ton-mile on average.[19]

The low cost of the water carrier comes with some service disadvantages that need to be considered by shippers. Water carriers are relatively slow, with average speeds on inland rivers, for example, of 5.5 to 9 miles per hour. The limited accessibility of the water carrier usually necessitates pickup or delivery by another mode of transportation to bridge the accessibility gap. The transfer between modes will obviously add to the total cost.

Service can also be disrupted by weather. Rivers and lakes freeze during the winter months in the Northern states, which can interrupt service for several months. Drought conditions can lower water levels and restrict traffic flow. Conversely, heavy rains can cause flooding, which is also disruptive to service. The waterways are a natural highway, but Mother Nature can also constrain the flow of traffic.

Overall, water carriers are an attractive alternative for low-value traffic, where transportation rates are a significant part of the total delivered cost and price of the good. However, the poor service characteristics may add costs for the user, which have to be traded off against the low rate to calculate the true total cost.

Equipment

Types of Vehicles Because most domestic water carriers transport bulk materials, they use ships with very large **hold** openings to facilitate easy loading and unloading. Watertight walls dividing the holds allow a ship to carry more than one commodity at a time. However, most carriers will carry a limited variety of products at one time. The importance of the major types of equipment utilized on the Inland waterways is indicated in Figure 8-2 in terms of their percentage of the total fleet.

The largest ship in the domestic water carriage industry is the tanker. A **tanker** can carry anywhere from 18,000 to 500,000 tons of liquid, generally petroleum or petroleum products. Due to oil spill problems, the use of double-hulled tankers has become preferable to the use of the more conventional single-hulled tankers. However, the building of these ships has diminished greatly since 1991.

Another type of vessel is the **barge**, a powerless vessel towed by a tugboat. Barges are most commonly used by internal waterway carriers. Additional barges can be added to a tow at very little additional cost. Consequently, barge transportation offers a capacity flexibility comparable to railroads, at lower rates.

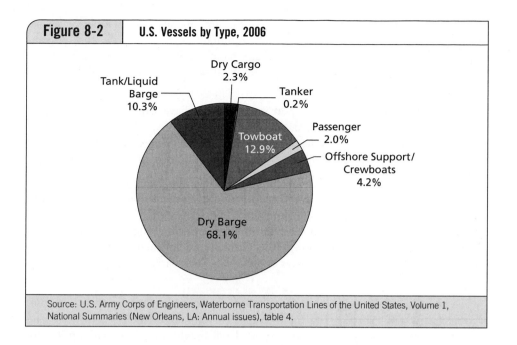

Figure 8-2 | **U.S. Vessels by Type, 2006**

Dry Cargo 2.3%
Tank/Liquid Barge 10.3%
Tanker 0.2%
Towboat 12.9%
Passenger 2.0%
Offshore Support/ Crewboats 4.2%
Dry Barge 68.1%

Source: U.S. Army Corps of Engineers, Waterborne Transportation Lines of the United States, Volume 1, National Summaries (New Orleans, LA: Annual issues), table 4.

Fuel As seen in Figure 8-3, the majority of fuel used by water transportation is residual fuel oil, also known as heavy fuel oil. This is the remainder, or residue, of fuel after crude oil is distilled. Diesel, also typically extracted from crude oil, makes up about a quarter of fuel consumption in water transportation.

Terminals Water carrier terminals are often provided by the public. Most ports are operated by local government agencies, and many ports have publicly operated storage facilities. It has been recognized for a long time that water transportation is a catalyst to economic activity in the community, and it is this belief that has spurred public investment in the operation of ports.

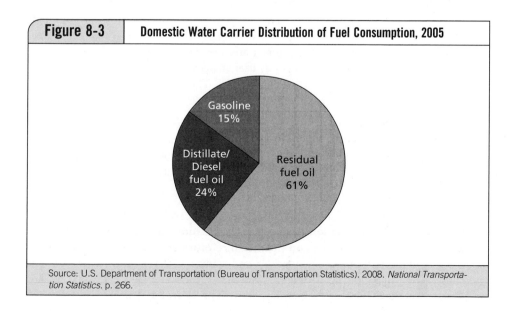

Figure 8-3 | **Domestic Water Carrier Distribution of Fuel Consumption, 2005**

Gasoline 15%
Distillate/ Diesel fuel oil 24%
Residual fuel oil 61%

Source: U.S. Department of Transportation (Bureau of Transportation Statistics). 2008. *National Transportation Statistics*. p. 266.

Some volume users of transportation invest in and operate port facilities or **shipper terminals**. Individual firms that handle such commodities as grain, coal, and oil commonly build docks, terminals, and commodity-handling facilities to meet their unique needs. The water carriers have the opportunity to use these private facilities owned by shippers.

Over the past few decades, major port improvements have centered on the mechanization of materials-handling systems, especially for internal waterway ports. Efficient handling of larger volumes of bulk commodities has been a prerequisite for ports that desire to remain economically competitive with other ports along the waterway and for water carriers that seek to be competitive with other modes.

The port facilitates ship loading and unloading, which means that the port must be equipped with cranes, forklifts, and other handling equipment. Certain commodities like oil, grain, and coal require more technically advanced loading equipment, such as pneumatic loaders and railcar dumping equipment. Such materials-handling equipment reduces unproductive port delays and enables water carriers and ports to remain economically viable.

The port also facilitates the transfer of freight from one mode to another. The port is usually served by railroads and motor carriers. Terminals at the port will have railroad sidings to handle inbound and outbound rail freight as well as parking lots for motor carrier equipment. Ports play a key role in promoting the efficiency of intermodal transportation.

Because barges and ships carry larger loads than rail or motor carrier vehicles, storage facilities are necessary at the port. The storage areas receive cargo from many trucks and railcars. This freight is held until sufficient volume is obtained to be handled effectively by barge or ship. Conversely, when a loaded vessel arrives at port, the freight is unloaded, stored, and then dispatched in hundreds of railcars or trucks at some later date.

Cost Structure

Fixed Versus Variable Cost Components The basic cost structure of water carriers consists of relatively high variable costs and low fixed costs. Like motor carriers and air carriers, water carriers do not provide their own highways (rights-of-way). The waterways are provided by nature (except canals) and are maintained, improved, and controlled by the government. The carriers pay **user charges**—lock fees, dock fees, and fuel taxes—for the use of government-provided facilities. These user charges are directly related to the volume of business and therefore are considered variable costs.

The **operating costs** for water carriers are approximately 85 percent variable and 15 percent fixed. Fixed costs include depreciation and amortization and general expenses. The major variable expenses are line-operating costs, operating rents, and maintenance. Line-operating costs are those expenses associated with renting operating equipment and facilities.

Infrastructure As indicated above, the domestic water carriers' low fixed costs can be attributed in part to **public aid** in the area of infrastructure. For water carriers, the major public aid is the construction and maintenance of waterways. The construction of canals with public fund opens new markets and sources of revenue for water carriers. The construction of locks and dams on rivers makes the waterways navigable for domestic water carriers. The dredging of the Mississippi River, for example, is performed by the **Army Corps of Engineers** to maintain channel depth and width. Port facilities are maintained by federal and local monies.

An example of a major public aid for domestic water carriers is the **Tennessee Tombigbee** (Tenn-Tom) **project**. Opened in 1985, the project connects the Tennessee River and the Warrior River via the Tombigbee River. Another example of public aid was when, in 1986, the federal government built two 1,200-foot locks and a new dam at Lock and Dam Number 26 on the Mississippi River system.

Critics of waterway projects like Tenn-Tom often refer to them as "**pork barrel projects**," suggesting that they are funded by government funds for the benefit of only a small number of the legislators' constituents. Critics question their value to society and maintain that these projects probably would not have been constructed if the actual users or local taxpayers had to assume the full burden of the costs. The U.S. Army Corps of Engineers has been responsible for conducting benefit/cost analysis to determine if such projects deserve to be funded by federal dollars, but critics question whether the Corps' analysis are realistic and whether the projects' expected benefits will ever be realized.

Labor Water transportation is not labor-intensive. In 1997, 2.72 million ton-miles of freight were transported for each water carrier employee. This compares to 4.74 million ton-miles for each rail employee, 0.4 million ton-miles for each motor carrier employee, and 39.3 million ton-miles for each pipeline employee.[20]

Labor is required at the terminal to load and unload general commodities. The freight is moved from the dock onto the ship and into the appropriate hold for the voyage (and vice versa for unloading). In addition, labor is required to handle the loading of freight from connecting modes, such as truck and rail, and to store the freight waiting to be loaded onto the ship or connection carriers.

Domestic water carriers usually do not require much labor at the terminal, because the carriers primarily transport bulk commodities that can be loaded mechanically. Great Lakes carrier companies have developed ships that are equipped with automatic unloading devices that reduce the amount of labor required to unload the ships.

Current Issues

Drug and Alcohol Abuse The grounding of the Exxon tanker *Valdez* off the shores of Alaska in March 1989 exemplifies the need for strong measure against drug and alcohol abuse in the water transportation industry. The captain of the *Valdez* was found to be intoxicated at the time the ship ran aground and spilled 10 million gallons of oil off Alaska's shores. The full impact of this disaster will not be known for many years to come; however, it is known that the environmental damage resulted in the deaths of hundreds of animals, including some endangered species, and the loss of income and jobs for many of Alaska's citizens (such as fishermen, for example).

In recognition of the problem of substance abuse, the U.S. Coast Guard now tests American seamen for drug abuse before they are issued a seamen's license and before they can be employed. Seamen are also tested randomly during their employment.

Port Development Because of today's environmental concerns, ports are having trouble keeping pace with the accelerated developments in global trade. Ports are now having to balance competitive economic concerns with the concerns of the public, which, rightly or wrongly, often view ports as a main source of air, water, and noise pollution.

An example of the struggle would be the problems the Port of Oakland, California, faced in trying to get permission to dredge its harbors to a lower depth in order to berth new, larger vessels. Without the dredging, Oakland's competitiveness would decrease. But proposals for dumping the spoil from the dredging were denied at every turn. Soon another problem developed. The city's mayor decided to siphon port revenues into the city's coffers to alleviate budget problems. After local and international businesspeople united in support of the port's autonomy, the mayor backed down. Months later, thanks to the concerted efforts of two U.S. representatives and California's governor, the port got approval to dredge and dump the spoil in a cost-effective spot in the bay. Although that issue was resolved, now California is considering a bill that would allow the state to take revenue from the ports to replenish the state's depleted treasury.

Global Perspectives

Ports: An Essential Link

Ports are the critical link between the United States and foreign countries for global commerce and between waterborne transport and the surface modes of transport within the United States, which provide the connection to businesses and consumers. Port development and growth through capacity additions, efficiency, and technological improvements are essential to the economy. The forecasted growth in global trade is expected to bring even more pressure on U.S. ports, particularly on the West Coast. Maritime policy and transportation policy at large must align to ensure that U.S. ports are prepared to handle the increase in volume in an efficient and environmentally responsible manner and are able to compete with the ports of neighboring countries.

The U.S. port infrastructure makes the important connection between the maritime trading system, represented by the world fleet, and the U.S. economy and U.S. consumers and producers. There are more than 300 ports in the United States, and they vary greatly in ownership, size, and the types of cargo and vessels handled. Ports may be operated by a state, a county, a municipality, a private corporation, or a combination. Many ports are complex entities, involving facilities for transportation by several modes of transportation: water, rail, or motor carrier.

The ports are the nodes on the maritime network through which commerce flows, and they have developed with little federal coordination, intervention, or support. Having been initially driven by the location of population nodes, ports have developed in the most urbanized parts of the U.S. coastline. Although this pattern of development takes advantage of proximity to workforces and markets, the increasingly expensive, finite spaces where the large vessels of today can berth for loading and unloading have led to a set of very large facilities that create additional congestion on adjacent infrastructure. The existence or lack of railway and road infrastructure has often either facilitated or stymied port development.

Although the federal government has the effective role of being a spokesperson for the national interest in port development, neither the Maritime Administration nor any other federal entity has the statutory authority for this role. No federal entity determines the national optimal direction in overall port development. Nor does any federal entity study efficient freight routing through the broader multimodal transportation system.

Source: Adapted from "An Evaluation of Maritime Policy in Meeting the Commercial and Security Needs of the United States," prepared by HIS Global/Insight, Inc., U.S. Department of Transportation, Maritime Administration, January 2009, p. 25.

Another current issue facing North American ports is the growth of multicarrier alliances, leading to the expansion of the already gargantuan ships. An increase from 6,000 20-foot equivalent units (TEUs) to 8,000 TEUs has many ports worried for the future. The larger the ships are, the deeper they go, meaning that many of the smaller ports will need to begin the dredging process as soon as possible to be able to compete in the future. The dredging process would allow ports to make their waterways deeper and wider in order to accommodate these new, larger ships and allow them to stay competitive. However, as indicated above, the approval process for the dredging is problematic.

Brief History of Pipelines

Pipelines have played an important role in the transportation industry in the post-World War II era. Originally, pipelines were used to feed other modes of transportation, such as railroads or water carriers. The Pennsylvania Railroad initiated the development of pipelines in the oil fields of Pennsylvania in the 19th century and then sold out to the Standard Oil Company, establishing the precedent of pipelines being owned by the oil companies. Early in the 20th century, the oil companies operated the pipelines as integrated subsidiaries and often used them to control the oil industry by not providing needed transportation service to new producers. Consequently, after World War II, in a decision rendered by the U.S. Supreme Court known as the **Champlin Oil Case**, pipelines were required to operate as common carriers if there was a demand by shippers of oil for their services. This decision was coupled with the growth in demand for gasoline after World War II and the need to move oil and oil products from the oil fields in Texas and Oklahoma to the markets in the Northeastern states.

Pipeline Industry Overview

The pipeline industry is unique in a number of important aspects, including the type of commodity hauled, ownership, and visibility. The industry is relatively unknown to the general public, which has little appreciation of the role and importance of pipelines. Pipelines are limited in the markets they serve and very limited in the commodities they can haul. Furthermore, pipelines are the only mode with no **backhaul**; that is, they are unidirectional with products that only move in one direction through the line.

Significance of Pipelines

As seen in Table 8-2, pipelines accounted for 20 percent of the total ton-miles shipped in the United States in 2005.[21] This figure is comparable to the share of water carriers, and pipelines' relative position, on a strict tonnage basis, is comparable to that of all water carriers. Few people in the United States would guess that pipelines compare to motor carriers and rail companies in terms of traffic relevance. Pipelines are virtually unknown to the general public but represent a key component in our transportation system. Oil and oil products represent two-thirds of the ton-miles transported by pipeline, and natural gas makes up the other third.[22]

As shown in Table 8-3, the pipeline network grew steadily until the early 1980s, allowing pipelines to move an increased amount of tonnage. However, Table 8-3 does not adequately reflect the increase in total capacity because it does not show the diameter of pipelines. As we will discuss later, pipeline diameters have increased in recent

Table 8-2	Pipeline Share of U.S. Ton-miles of Freight	
YEAR	TON-MILES SHIPPED (BILLIONS)	TOTAL TRANSPORTATION INTERCITY TON-MILES (%)
1980	905	26.9
1985	821	24.8
1990	864	23.9
1995	932	22.7
2000	927	21.4
2005	942	20.6

Source: Bureau of Transportation Statistics. 2008. *National Transportation Statistics*. Washington, DC.

years, and the larger diameters have increased capacity significantly because of the increased volume that can move through the pipeline. The larger diameter has also allowed the total oil network shown in Table 8-3 to decrease since the early 1980s to about 160,000 miles in 2005. As of 2006, natural gas pipelines (includes transmission and distribution lines) represented about nine times the mileage of oil pipelines.[23]

The tonnage comparison shown in Table 8-2 is a sharp contrast to the revenue picture indicated in Table 8-4. Here the low rates of the pipeline, which are discussed later in this chapter, are reflected in the very low percentage of the total intercity revenue paid to all pipeline carriers. The pipelines account for approximately 4 percent of the total transportation revenues, compared to motor carriers, for example, which account for more than 75 percent of the total revenue.

Table 8-3	Pipeline Network (Thousands of Miles)	
YEAR	OIL PIPELINE	NATURAL GAS PIPELINE
1960	191	631
1970	219	913
1980	218	1052
1985	214	1119
1990	209	1189
1995	182	1277
2000	177	1369
2005	160	1478

Source: U.S. Department of Transportation (Bureau of Transportation Statistics). 2008. *National Transportation Statistics*. Washington, DC, p. 23.

Table 8-4	Revenue Position of Pipelines
YEAR	**OIL PIPELINE (MILLIONS USD)**
1960	895
1970	1,376
1980	7,548
1985	8,910
1990	8,506
1995	9,077
2000	8,958
2001	9,066
Source: Eno Transportation Foundation. 2002. *Transportation In America,* 19th ed., Washington, DC.	

Types of Carriers

As noted earlier, due to the decision rendered by the U.S. Supreme Court in the Champlin Oil Case, many pipelines operate as common carriers. Hence, although some private carriers exist today, the for-hire carriers dominate the industry. Common carriers account for approximately 90 percent of all pipeline carriers.

Ownership

With some exceptions, oil companies have been the owners of the oil pipelines. Beginning with Standard Oil Company buying out the Pennsylvania Railroad and developing pipelines more extensively in order to control the industry and enhance its market dominance, oil companies have been the principal owners of pipelines. The federal government entered the pipeline business briefly during World War II when it developed two pipelines to bring crude oil and oil products from the oil fields of the Southwest to the Northeast to ensure an uninterrupted flow of oil. These two pipelines, known as the Big Inch and the Little Inch, were sold to private companies after the war.

Some pipelines are joint ventures among two or more pipeline companies because of the high capital investment necessary for large-diameter pipelines. Individual, vertically integrated oil companies control the largest share of the pipeline revenues, followed by jointly owned pipeline companies. Railroads, independent oil companies, and other industrial companies control the remaining percentage.

Number of Carriers

Like the railroad industry, the pipeline industry has a small number of very large carriers that dominate the industry. In 2006 there were approximately 2,297 total pipeline operators.[24] The oligopolistic nature of the industry is demonstrated by the fact that 20 major integrated oil companies control about two-thirds of the crude oil pipeline mileage.[25]

There are a number of reasons for the limited number of pipeline companies. First, startup costs (capital costs) are high. Second, like railroads and public utilities, the economies of scale are such that duplication or parallel competing lines would be uneconomic. Large-size operations are more economical because capacity rises more than proportionately with increases in the diameter of the pipeline and investment per mile decreases, as do operating cost per barrel. For example, a 12-in pipeline operating at capacity can transport three times as much oil as an 8-in pipeline.

The procedural requirements for entry and the associated legal costs also contribute to the limited number of companies. An additional factor is the industry itself, which has been dominated by the large oil companies that joined together in the post-World War II era to develop pipelines from major fields and entry ports.

Oil Carriers   The pipeline industry experienced rapid growth after World War II, but the rate of growth (percentage increase) has since decreased dramatically. Freight ton-miles increased to 942 billion in 2005, compared to 932 billion in 1995. There were corresponding changes in other data, including the number of employees, which also decreased. Overall, however, oil pipelines play a major role in our transportation network because, as previously mentioned, they transport about 13 percent of the total freight ton-miles in the United States.[26]

Natural Gas Carriers   Another part of the pipeline industry is involved with the transportation of natural gas, which, like oil, is an important source of energy. The movement data for natural gas are recorded in cubic feet, rather than ton-miles. The industry is comparable in size to the oil pipeline industry in terms of the number of companies and, as in the oil pipeline industry, there has been a growth in the number of companies since 1975. It should be noted that there has been a reclassification of some companies since 1975, so the growth numbers are not exactly comparable. Natural gas pipelines represents about 7 percent of domestic ton-miles of freight.[27] Finally, operating revenues have increased by about 41 percent between 2000 and 2005.[28]

Operating and Service Characteristics

Commodities Hauled   Pipelines are specialized carriers in that they transport a very limited variety of products. The four main commodities hauled by pipeline are oil and oil products, natural gas, coal, and chemicals.

Oil and Oil Products   The majority of pipeline movements are crude oil and oil products. In 2007, pipelines moved about 66 percent of the total ton-miles of crude oil and petroleum products. Pipelines in total (including natural gas) experienced a 5.6 percent increase in freight ton-miles shipped from 1990 to 2006.[29]

The total volume of petroleum transported domestically in the United States declined slightly during the 1990s. However, the split by modes between pipeline and water carrier has changed for several reasons. A pipeline was built across Panama during the 1980s, virtually eliminating long movements of Alaskan crude oil tankers around South America. The Alaskan crude oil is now transshipped via the pipeline to Atlanta tankers for Gulf and Atlantic Coast deliveries to refineries. Also, another large crude oil pipeline has been built, providing service from the West Coast to Midwest refineries and reducing the need for tanker movements even further.

The length of haul in the oil pipeline industry is medium in length compared to other modes. Crude oil movements average about 800 miles per shipment, and product lines average about 400 miles per movement. The average shipment size for these movements is very large. (This will be discussed later in the section titled "Equipment.")

Natural Gas Natural gas pipelines are an important part of our total pipeline network. They account for the second largest number of intercity miles of pipeline. (This figure does not include all their transmission and distribution pipeline mileage, only intercity miles.) The natural gas pipeline companies produce about 10 percent of the gas they transport. Independent gas companies produce the remaining 90 percent and transport it via the pipelines. Similar to oil pipelines, the natural gas pipelines operate as public carriers.

Coal Coal pipelines are frequently called **slurry lines** because the coal is moved in a pulverized form in water (one-to-one ratio by weight). Once the coal has reached its destination, the water is removed and the coal is ready for use. Coal pipelines are primarily used for transporting coal to utility companies for generating electricity. The large slurry pipeline that operates between Arizona and Nevada covers 273 miles and moves 5 million tons of coal per year. Coal pipelines use enormous quantities of water, which causes concern in several Western states where their installation has been proposed, because there is a scarcity of water and the water is not reusable (as there is no backhaul).

Chemicals Chemical lines are another type of product line, although only a limited number of different types of chemicals are carried by pipelines. The three major chemicals are anhydrous ammonia, which is used in fertilizer; propylene, which is used for manufacturing detergents; and ethylene, which is used for making antifreeze.

Relative Advantages

A major advantage offered by the pipeline industry is low rates. Pipeline transportation can be extremely efficient with large-diameter pipelines operating near capacity. Average revenues for pipeline companies are below one-half of a cent per ton-mile, which is indicative of their low-cost service.

Two additional user cost advantages complement the low rates. First, pipelines have a very good **loss and damage record** (L and D). This record is attributed in part to the types of products transported, but it is also related to the nature of the pipeline service, which provides underground and completely encased movement.

The second important cost advantage is that pipelines can provide a warehousing function because their service is slow. In other words, if the product is not needed immediately, the slow pipeline service can be regarded as a form of free warehousing storage. (Products move through pipelines at an average of 3 to 5 miles per hour.)

Another positive service advantage of pipelines is their dependability. They are virtually unaffected by weather conditions, and they very rarely have mechanical failures. Although the service time is slow, scheduled deliveries can be forecasted very accurately, diminishing the need for safety stock. The risk of terrorism is reduced when the pipelines are buried in the ground.

Relative Disadvantages

Although the pipelines' slow speed can be considered an advantage due to its use as a free form of warehousing, in some instances the pipelines' slow speed can be considered a disadvantage. For example, if a company's demand is uncertain or erratic, it will have to hold higher levels of inventory to compensate for possible shortages because the pipeline will not be able to deliver an extra amount of the product in a short period of time.

Pipelines are also at a disadvantage when it comes to completeness of service because they offer a fixed route of service that cannot be easily extended to complete door-to-door service. That is, they have limited geographic flexibility or accessibility. However, because the source of the pipelines and the location of the refineries are known and are fixed for a long period of time, the fixed-route service factor may not be a critical problem. Frequently, pipelines depend on railroads and motor carriers to complete delivery, which adds to user costs.

The use of pipelines is limited to a rather select number of products: crude oil, oil products, natural gas, coal, and a limited number of chemicals. There is interest in using pipelines for other products because of their cost advantage, but the technology for such use has not yet been fully developed. Capsule and pneumatic pipelines can carry and extend the low-cost, high-volume, reliable service to other bulk products. Frequency of service (the number of times a mode can pick up and deliver during a particular period) is a characteristic of interest to some users. On one hand, the large tenders (shipment size requirements) and slow speed of pipelines reduces the frequency. On the other hand, service is offered 24 hours a day, seven days a week.

Pipelines are generally regarded as somewhat inflexible because they serve limited geographic areas and limited points within that area. Also, they carry limited types of commodities and only offer one-way service. Finally, the operations technology precludes small shipment sizes.

In summary, pipelines offer a good set of services for particular types of products, but they have some serious limitations for many other products.

Competition

Intramodal **Intramodal competition** in the pipeline industry is limited by a number of factors. First, there are a small number of companies—slightly more than 100. The industry, as noted previously, is oligopolistic in market structure, which generally leads to limited price competition. Second, the economies of scale and high fixed costs have led to joint ownership of large-diameter pipelines because the construction of smaller parallel lines is not very efficient. Finally, the high capital costs preclude duplication of facilities to a large extent.

Intermodal The serious threats to the pipeline industry are in terms of traffic diversion to other modes of transportation. Technically, pipelines compete with railroads, water carriers, and motor carriers for traffic. However, even with these forms of transportation, the level of competition is limited. The most serious competition is water tanker operations, because their rates are competitive with pipelines. However, the limited coverage of water carrier service also limits its effective competitiveness. Trucks have increased the number of products they carry that can also be carried by pipelines. However, truck service complements rather than competes with the pipeline because trucks often perform a distribution function (delivery) for pipelines.

Once a pipeline has been constructed between two points, it is difficult for other modes to compete. Pipeline costs are extremely low, dependability is quite high, and there is limited risk of damage to the product being transported. The major exception is coal slurry pipelines because the need to move the pulverized coal in water can make the costs comparable to rail movements. Water carriers come closest to matching pipe-line costs and rates as indicated.

Equipment

The U.S. Department of Transportation estimates that the total pipeline investment is in excess of $21 billion, based on historical costs. Also, the department estimates it would cost about $70 billion to replace the system at today's costs.[30] This great invest-ment in the equipment is necessary to finance the complex operation of getting oil from the well to the market.

From 1980 to 2006, oil pipeline infrastructure (in standard miles) dropped 22.5 per-cent, while the natural gas infrastructure rose 45.9 percent.[31]

Pipelines can be grouped into other categories in addition to for-hire or private car-riers. For instance, they are frequently classified as gathering lines or trunk lines, parti-cularly in reference to the movement of oil. The trunk lines are further classified or subdivided into two types: crude and product lines. The gathering lines are used to bring the oil from the fields to storage areas before the oil is processed into refined pro-ducts or transmitted as crude oil over the trunk lines to distant refineries. Trunk lines are used for long-distance movement of crude oil or other products, such as jet fuel, kerosene, chemicals, or coal.

Early in the history of the oil industry, the refineries were located primarily in the eastern part of the United States, and thus the long-distance movement of oil was basi-cally the movement of crude oil. The state of technology in the industry also made it much easier to control leakage with crude oil than with refined oil products such as gasoline or kerosene. After World War II, however, refineries were developed at other locations, especially in the Southwest, when better technology (limited seams and weld-ing techniques) made the long-distance movement of oil products easy to accomplish.

When comparing gathering lines and trunk lines, there are several important differ-ences to note. First, **gathering lines** are smaller in diameter, usually not exceeding 8 in, whereas trunk lines are usually 30 to 50 in in diameter. Gathering lines are frequently laid on the surface of the ground to ensure ease of relocation when a well or field runs dry. Trunk lines, on the other hand, are usually seen as permanent and are laid underground.

The term **trunk line** is often used in conjunction with oil movements and can refer to crude oil trunk lines or oil product lines. Oil trunk lines move oil to tank farms or refineries in distant locations, whereas oil product lines move the gasoline, jet fuel, and home heating oil from refineries to market areas. Technically, however, any long-distance movement via a large-diameter, permanent pipeline implies a trunk-line movement. Therefore, when coal, natural gas, or chemicals move via pipelines, such movement is usually classified as trunk-line movement.

Commodity Movement

Gathering lines bring oil from the fields to a gathering station, where the oil is stored in sufficient quantity to ship by trunk line to a refinery. After the oil is refined, the various products are stored at a tank farm before they are shipped via product line to another tank farm with a market-oriented location. A motor carrier most frequently makes the last segment of the trip, from the market-oriented tank farm to the distributor or ulti-mate customer.

Trunk lines, as indicated previously, are usually more than 30 in in diameter and are the major component of the pipeline system. Stations that provide the power to push the commodities through the pipeline are interspersed along the trunk line. For oil movements, pumps are located at the stations, which vary in distance from 20 to 100 miles, depending on the viscosity of the oil and the terrain. Figures 8-4 and 8-5 illustrate the major interstate and intrastate pipelines in the United States.

The pumping stations for large-diameter pipelines can provide 3,000 to 6,000 horsepower. Compressors are used for the movement of natural gas, and pumps are used for the liquid items that move through the pipelines.

Computers at the pumping stations continually monitor the flow and pressure of the oil system. Any change indicating a leak is easily detected. Routine visual checks and searches by airplane are sometimes used to locate leaks. Great care is rendered, not only because of the potential losses but also because of the lawsuits that could ensue as a result of damage to property and the environment.

In the oil segment of the pipeline industry, sophisticated operating and monitoring techniques are used because of the different petroleum products moving through the product lines and the different grades of crude oil moving through the crude oil lines. There are 15 grades of crude oil and a range of products including jet fuel, kerosene, and aviation fuel. When two or more grades of crude oil or two or more products move through a system at one time, the "batches" may need to be separated by a rubber ball called a batching pig. However, this is not always necessary because the different specific grades of the products helps to keep them separated. Any mixing (slop) that does occur is only minor amounts of high-grade products mixed into lower-grade items. Usually, products are scheduled 1 month in advance with kerosene moving first,

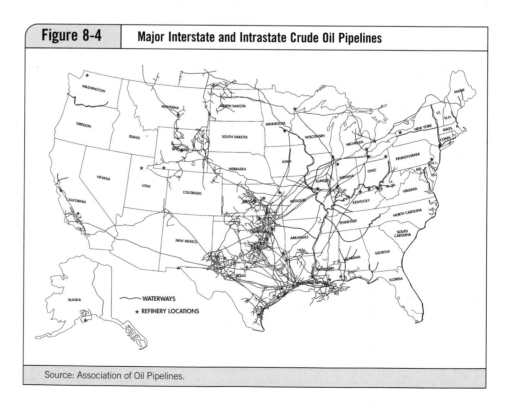

| Figure 8-4 | Major Interstate and Intrastate Crude Oil Pipelines |

Source: Association of Oil Pipelines.

Figure 8-5	Major Interstate and Intrastate Product Pipelines

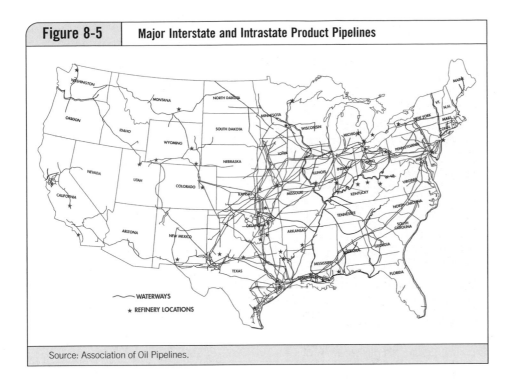

WATERWAYS
★ REFINERY LOCATIONS

Source: Association of Oil Pipelines.

then high-grade gasoline, then medium-grade gasoline, then various other products, with home heating oil last. Before the cycle starts again, the pipeline is usually scoured to prevent mixing problems.

Cost Structure

Fixed- Versus Variable-Cost Components Like the railroad industry, the pipeline industry has a high proportion of fixed costs with low capital turnover. The pipeline owners have to provide their own right-of-way by purchasing or leasing land and constructing the pipeline and pumping stations along the right-of-way. The property taxes, amortizations of depreciation, return to investors, and preventative maintenance all contribute to the high ratio of fixed to variable expenses.

In addition to the right-of-way costs, the terminal facilities of pipelines contribute to the high level of fixed costs. The same types of expenses associated with the right-of-way, such as depreciation and property taxes, are incurred by the pipeline terminals.

As stated previously, the pipeline industry has significant economies of scale. The high fixed costs and the economies of scale help to explain the joint ownership and investment in large-diameter pipelines. Pipelines do not operate vehicles like other modes of transportation because the carrying capacity is the pipe itself, which is best regarded as part of the right-of-way. This unique element of the pipeline operation helps to explain the low variable costs because vehicles are frequently a major source of variable expense. Table 8-5 shows the operating characteristics, revenues, and net income of oil pipeline companies.

Labor costs are very low in the pipeline industry because of the high level of automation. One example is the Trans-Alaska Pipeline System, built at a cost of $9.2 billion

Table 8-5	Petroleum Pipeline Companies—Characteristics 1980–2006						
	173 represents 173,000						
	Covers pipeline companies operating in interstate commerce and subject to the jurisdiction of the Federal Energy Regulatory Commission						
Item	Unit	1980	1990	2000	2003	2005	2006
Miles of Pipeline - Total	1,000	173	168	152	140	131	140
Gathering Lines	1,000	36	32	18	14	14	12
Trunk Lines	1,000	136	136	134	126	118	129
Total Deliveries	Mil. Bbl.	10,600	11,378	14,450	13,236	12,732	12,768
Crude Oil	Mil. Bbl.	6,405	6,563	6,923	6,941	6,675	6,668
Products	Mil. Bbl.	4,195	4,816	7,527	6,295	6,057	6,101
Total Trunk Line Traffic	Bil. Bbl.-miles	3,405	3,500	3,508	3,591	3,485	3,536
Crude Oil	Bil. Bbl.-miles	1,948	1,891	1,602	1,609	1,571	1,578
Products	Bil. Bbl.-miles	1,458	1,609	1,906	1,982	1,914	1,958
Carrier Property Value	Mil. dol.	19,752	25,828	29,648	32,018	29,526	32,686
Operating Revenues	Mil. dol.	6,356	7,149	7,483	7,704	7,917	8,517
Net Income	Mil. dol.	1,912	2,340	2,705	3,470	3,076	3,743

Source: PennWell Publishing Co., Houston Texas, Oil & Gas Journal, annual (copyright)

and operated by 450 employees. The pipelines employ about 8,000 people compared to about 10 million in the motor carrier industry for comparable ton-miles on an intercity basis. Another variable cost is the cost of fuel for the power system.

Rates Pricing in the pipeline industry is unique compared to its major modal competitors. First of all, pipelines do not use the freight classification system that underlies the class rates of railroads and motor carriers. The limited number and specialization of commodities make such a practice unnecessary. A crude oil pipeline or natural gas pipeline has little need for an elaborate classification system.

Even though pipelines have high fixed costs, the differential pricing practices common in the railroad industry are virtually nonexistent among pipelines. The nature of operation (one-way movement, limited geographic coverage of points, limited products, and so forth) provides little opportunity to provide differential pricing practices. Pipelines quote rates on a per-barrel basis (one barrel equals 42 gallons). Quotes for rates are typically point-to-point or zone-to-zone. Also, minimum shipment sizes, usually called tenders, are required; these range from 500 barrels to 10,000 barrels.

Pipeline rates are very low, which is reflected in the fact that they carry about 20 percent of the total intercity ton-miles and receive only about 4 percent of the total revenues.

On the Line

The Politics of Global Pipelines

Similar to other modes of transportation, pipelines can provide the links for bringing nations together because they can establish political and economic alliances based upon convenience and/or necessity. In today's world, they can be viewed as one of the trade routes of the 21st century. Pipelines can be a vital delivery system for water, oil, oil products, and natural gas. They help sustain the economic and, perhaps, social wellbeing of some countries.

For countries that produce oil but do not have ports, pipelines carry material resources for hundreds, or even thousands, of miles. Pipelines, therefore, allow foreign revenue to flow into the producing country to support the local citizenry, and they can provide social capital to support economic improvements.

Pipelines can enable wealth, development, power, economic stability, global leverage, and so forth, but they also can lead to political tensions. It has been estimated by several sources that there are over a million miles of oil and natural gas pipelines crisscrossing the globe among independent nations. They are arteries of modern commerce in some parts of the world.

Pipelines crossing national boundaries create a need for interdependence and collaboration, which can give rise to national issues as well as international issues. Pipelines can be a major influence on political strategy and foreign policy. The United States, for example, consumes more oil than it produces and for political and security reasons purchases oil from a variety of sources. Some of those sources are landlocked, which necessitates pipeline transportation, usually to a port in another country where the oil can be transshipped to a tanker ship for movement to a designated refinery.

When new oil sources are discovered in a landlocked country, it usually necessitates the development of a pipeline to unlock the newly discovered resource. Russia is a good example of such a situation. Russia is one of the largest exporters of oil. The former Soviet Republics around the Caspian Sea also figure into this equation. Consequently, the United States is supporting development of pipelines designed to transport crude oil from the Caspian Port Baku, Azerbaijan, through Tbilisi, Georgia, to the port of Ceyhan in Turkey. This is only one example and there are others.

Pipelines have been described as an almost invisible part of the U.S. transportation infrastructure, but they are much more visible in global situations as described above. They connect nations and provide the basis for economic and political alliances, which, in turn, may promote stability in the geographic areas of the pipeline. Economic interdependence can help to stabilize alliances, as long as there are not any outside influences that disrupt or impede the flow of oil through the pipelines. In this age of terrorism and political unrest in the Middle East and South America, there is a continuing threat of disruption and permanent interruption.

Source: Adapted from Steve Goldstein. "Pipeline Diplomacy." *The Philadelphia Inquirer,* October 26, 2003, pp. C1 and C3.

SUMMARY

- Water carriers played a key role in the development of many cities and regions both globally and domestically.

- The water carrier system is still a viable part of the total transportation system and competes with the railroad system and pipelines for the movement of bulk, low-value commodities.

- The domestic water carrier system can be classified in terms of inland carriers (rivers, canals, and Great Lakes) and coastal/intercoastal carriers. Both types are important components of the water carrier system.

- Intramodal competition among water carriers is not as important as intermodal competition with railroads and pipelines. All three of these modes compete for long-distance movements of bulk commodities.

- Water carriers offer low-cost services, but their transit time is slow and can be interrupted by weather conditions. Accessibility and potential product damage are also service disadvantages.

- Water carriers have relatively low fixed costs because they use a right-of-way provided by the government for which they pay user charges, like motor carriers and airlines.

- Water carriers are not labor-intensive for their movement operations but may require more labor in terminal areas for certain types of freight.

- The development of pipelines began in the 19th century in Pennsylvania by the Pennsylvania Railroad, but subsequently the ownership and development were taken over by the oil companies, who operated them as integrated subsidiaries.

- Ownership of pipelines by oil companies has continued to the present, but some oil pipelines are now owned by non-oil companies. Also, joint ownership by several companies has become common because of the large investment of capital necessary for construction.

- The pipeline industry is a large component of our transportation industry (more than 20 percent of intercity ton-miles), but it is largely invisible to many people.

- Because of market-control tactics used by some oil companies, an important U.S. Supreme Court ruling after World War II required pipelines to operate as common carriers even if owned by an oil company.

- Pipelines are very specialized in terms of the commodities that they carry. Most of the traffic is oil and oil products, but they also carry natural gas, chemicals, and coal.

- Only a small number of pipeline companies operate in the U.S. (about 100), and they have limited intramodal competition.

- Pipelines are low-cost carriers when operated near capacity, but they have high levels of fixed cost because of the heavy investment necessary in infrastructure. They need volume to lower unit costs.

- Pipeline service is relatively slow and has limited accessibility, but it is very reliable in terms of delivery with little or no loss and damage.

- Intercity pipeline service is provided by large-diameter (30–50 in) pipelines called trunk lines. Small-diameter pipelines, called gathering lines, are used to bring the oil from the producing area to the terminals for storage before processing and/or transporting.

- Pipelines are a highly automated, efficient form of transportation. Oil moves in one direction in large volumes at a steady, slow speed.

- Although there is always concern about safety and the environment, pipelines have been a relatively safe mode of transportation.

STUDY QUESTIONS

1. The integrated ownership of pipelines was initially used by some oil companies to gain control of oil-producing area. How did they use their market power to gain market control? What other reasons can be offered for integrated ownership? Are these reasons valid in today's business environment?

2. The pipeline industry has approximately 100 companies, as compared to the motor carrier industry with more than 50,000. How do you account for this difference, given the fact that they both carry approximately the same volume of intercity ton-miles?

3. The typical pipeline company has high fixed costs. What economic factors account for this situation? What special problems does this present?

4. Pipelines account for more than 20 percent of the intercity ton-miles but less than 5 percent of the revenue paid by shippers to transportation companies. What factors account for this contrast? Is this situation likely to change? Why or why not?

5. The economic and market position of the pipelines has been described as mature and stable with little likelihood of significant growth in the near future. Do you agree? Why or why not?

6. Water carriers played a dominant role in the transportation system of the United States in the 18th and 19th centuries. Why has their relative position declined during the 20th century? Are they still an important component of the total transportation system? Why or why not?

7. What would be the impact of higher fuel charges on the water carrier industry? Provide a rationale for raising their user charges.

8. Technology often offers the potential of improving efficiency and effectiveness of transportation companies, but water carrier do not appear to have applied much new technology to improve their service. What impediments slow technological progress in the water carrier industry?

9. Intermodal competition is more intense than intramodal competition for water carriers. Why?

10. Why are pipelines unknown to many individuals? Do you think the pipelines should advertise to change this?

NOTES

1. U.S. Department of Transportation, Bureau of Transportation Statistics. 2008. *National Transportation Statistics.* Washington, DC: p. 346.

2. Eno Transportation Foundation and Upper Great Plains Transportation Institute. 2007. *Transportation in America.* Washington, DC.

3. U.S. Department of Transportation, Bureau of Transportation Statistics, 2008. *National Transportation Statistics.* pp. 88–89.

4. U.S. Army Corps of Engineers. *Waterborne Commerce of the United States.* Washington, DC: pp. 30–64.

5. U.S. Department of Transportation, Bureau of Transportation Statistics. 2008. *National Transportation Statistics.* Washington, DC: pp. 88–89.

6.   Ibid.

7.   Ibid.

8.   Ibid.

9.   U.S. Army Corps of Engineers, Institute for Water Resources. 2007. *Final Waterborne Commerce Statistics.* Washington, DC: p. 1.

10. Ibid.

11. U.S. Dept of Transportation, Maritime Administration. 2006. "U.S. Water Transportation Statistical Snapshot." Washington, DC.

12. U.S. Army Corps of Engineers. Annual issues. *Waterborne Transportation Lines of the United States,* Volume 1, National Summaries. New Orleans, LA: table 13.

13. U.S. Census Bureau. U.S. Table 1031. *Transportation and Warehousing—Establishments, Employees, and Payroll by Kind of Business (NAICS Basis): 2000 and 2005.* Washington, DC.

14. U.S. Army Corps of Engineers. 2007. *Summary of the United States Vessel Inventory.* Washington, DC: p. 4.

15. Eno Foundation. 2007. *Transportation in America,* 19th ed. Washington, DC: Author.

16. Ibid.

17. Ibid.

18. U.S. Army Corps of Engineers, Institute for Water Resources. 2007. *Final Waterborne Commerce Statistics.* Washington, DC: p. 4.

19. U.S. Department of Transportation, Bureau of Transportation Statistics. 2008. *National Transportation Statistics.* Washington, DC: pp. 87–228.

20. Ibid.

21. Ibid.

22. Ibid.

23. Ibid.

24. Ibid.

25. Ibid.

26. Ibid.

27. Ibid.

28. Ibid.

29. Ibid.

30. U.S. Department of Transportation, Bureau of Transportation Statistics. 2002. *National Transportation Statistics.* Washington, DC: pp. 193–195.

31. Federal Highway Administration. 2008. *Freight Facts and Figures.* Table 3-1: Miles of Infrastructure by Transportation Mode. Washington, DC.

CASE 8-1
Great Lakes Carriers

During the summer of 2008, Ben Heuer, president and chief operating officer of Great Lakes Carriers (GLC), and E. Kate Weber, vice president of business development, visited with the port directors of every major port on the Great Lakes. Their objective was to seek additional business for GLC's bulk cargo division with a related objective of exploring potential demand for a container ship operation on the Great Lakes.

GLC was founded in 1940 by Ben's grandfather with one ship hauling coal and iron ore from the mines along the Great Lakes to the steel mills in Indiana, Ohio, and surrounding areas. Today the company has a fleet of 12 bulk ore vessels that haul iron ore from Duluth to various Ohio ports as well as grain from the upper Great Lakes area to Chicago, Buffalo, and Erie. The demand for the movement of both commodities has decreased during the past decade—iron ore movements decreased because of increased foreign steel production, and railroads have increased their share of the grain movement with new larger hopper cars.

Kate suggested to Ben that there was a limited amount of container ship service on the Great Lakes and that this might be an opportunity for GLC to diversity. Container traffic between the United States and the EU can move via railroad to the port of Montreal, where it is transloaded to an oceangoing container ship. Substantial NAFTA container traffic (USA–Canada) moves via either railroad or truck to major cities adjacent to the Great Lakes. Lastly, the area surrounding the Great Lakes is a major manufacturing region with large volumes of traffic moving among the major port cities. New RFID technology could provide GLC with a competitive advantage for higher-value container traffic where visibility could help improve supply chain efficiency and effectiveness. Kate also believed that they could charge higher rates with RFID tags and explore the possibility of diversifying even further into logistics-related services.

Ben and Kate discussed the type of vessel that would be needed to move containers and concluded that current GLC vessels could not be retrofitted for container operations. Furthermore, the new ship would have a maximum carrying capacity of about 1,000 containers because of the size limitations imposed by the locks on the Saint Lawrence Seaway. The typical oceangoing container ship has a minimum carrying capacity of 2,500 containers.

The proposed operation would consist of weekly sailing schedules beginning in Duluth and stopping at Chicago, Detroit, Toledo, Cleveland, Buffalo, and Montreal. Containers would be picked up and delivered at each port along the route. The transit time from Duluth to Montreal wass estimated to be five to seven days, compared to four to fivedays by rail and two days by truck. For intermediate origin-destination pairs, such as Chicago to Cleveland, the transit time was estimated to be three days, which compared favorably with railroad service; however, the truck transit time was one day. The rate for the container service was estimated to be 40 percent of the current truck rate and 75 percent of the current rail rate, but the RFID program may allow higher rates because it would be a premium service and differentiate GLC from the rail and motor carriers.

The meetings with the port directors confirmed that the volume of grain and iron ore being handled by Great Lakes carriers was on the decline and the predictions for the next five years were for a continued decline. The lack of container ship service on the Great Lakes was also confirmed and the port directors, in general, were enthusiastic about the possibility of GLC initiating such service. They were also interested in the advantages of the RFID technology even though it would require some additional investment for them.

As the 2009 Great Lakes shipping season came to a close, Ben and Kate began the planning and analysis of container ship business with a goal of having a decision made by the start of the next shipping season.

CASE QUESTIONS

1. What marketing data would you want to have available to make the decision?

2. What cost data would you need to make a rational decision?

3. What are some of the logistics supply chain issues that GLC should consider?

4. What is your recommendation regarding the RFID Technology? Why?

5. Based on what you know, what recommendation would you make to the GLC Board of Directors regarding a container ship operation?

CASE 8-2
CNG Pipeline Company

At the weekly brainstorming session, John Spychalski, president of CNG Pipeline Company (CNG), suggested that they build a new pipeline from Elizabeth, New Jersey, to the Midwest to move refined petroleum products, gasoline, and diesel fuel. Following some discussion, he asked the strategic planning group to consider the idea before the next brown-bag session.

Skip Grenoble, vice president for strategic planning, thought that John was not considering the cost and impact of this idea. How could CNG obtain land to build the pipeline, let alone obtain the necessary capital to finance the project? Then there was the question of the existing refineries located in Ohio, Indiana, and Illinois. Skip knew refined petroleum products were being transported from the Gulf of Mexico refineries via barge and pipeline to the Midwest market areas currently.

Skip turned over the project to Evelyn Thomchick, chief strategy analyst, to develop a preliminary analysis of the viability of building a new pipeline. In the span of six days Evelyn found the following strategic issues for the project:

- At least four Midwest refineries were being planned for closure within the next five years because of environmental and cost considerations.
- A number of major refineries were considering building new refineries offshore, closer to the sources of foreign oil. Both cost and environmental considerations suggested this consideration.
- The New Jersey–Midwest corridor was one of the most-developed land regions in the United States with the highest land values.
- The demand for refined petroleum products was expected to increase, but the keen interest in alternative sources of energy, more fuel-efficient cars, and sustainability issues were matters of some concern.
- The project would require approximately 10 years to complete, including the time to obtain land via the eminent domain process.
- The capital requirements for the project were estimated at $800 billion.

CASE QUESTIONS

1. Do you feel the project has any merit for further investigation? Why or why not?

2. What additional information is needed beyond that provided by Evelyn Thomchick to make a better decision?

3. What is your political assessment of building a pipeline that will traverse five states?

Suggested Readings

Chapter 5   Motor Carriers

Bernstein, Mark, "Wireless Takes to the Road," *World Trade,* (April 2008): 26.

Burnson, Patrick, "Parcel Express Roundtable: Slugfest," *Logistics Management* (January 2009): 33–36.

Cantor, David E., Thomas M. Corsi, and Curtis M. Grimm, "Safety Technology Adoption Patterns in the U.S. Motor Carrier Industry," *Transportation Journal,* Vol. 45, No. 3 (Summer 2006): 20–45.

"Critical Issues in the Trucking Industry," *The American Transportation Research Institute* (October 2008).

Donath, Max, "Homeland Security and the Trucking Industry," *The American Transportation Research Institute* (July 2005).

Schulz, John D., "Only the Strong Will Survive," *Logistics Management* (April 2009): 46S–54S.

Schulz, John, "Cutting LTL Costs: Going to the Bench," *Logistics Management,* (February 2009): 35.

Zuckerman, Amy, "Transportation Management Systems Give Shippers Power to Make Smarter Trucking Choices," *World Trade,* (January 2008): 34.

Chapter 6   Railroads

Berman, Jeff, "Senate Committee Endorses Railroad Antitrust Legislation," *Logistics Management* (April 2009): 15–16.

Berman, Jeff, "2008 Annual Report—Railroads: Volume Is Down, But Business Is Up," *Logistics Management,* (July 2008): 38.

Berman, Jeff, "Study Says Railroad Fuel Surcharges Exceeded $6.5 Billion," *Logistics Management,* (October 2007): 19.

Boyd, John D., "Carloads in Reverse," *Traffic World* (January 5, 2009): 26.

McCue, Dan, "The Changing Landscape of U.S. Railroads," *World Trade,* (January 2009): 30.

Sheys, Kevin, "Rail Safety Is No Paper Chase," *Traffic World* (January 5, 2009): 7.

Chapter 7   Airlines

Abeyratne, Ruwantissa, "Competition in Air Transport—The Need for a Shift in Focus," *Transportation Law Journal,* Vol. 33, Iss. 2 (2005–2006): 29.

Cheng, Yung-Hsiang, and Chian-Yu Yeh, "Core Competencies and Sustainable Competitive Advantage in Air Cargo Forwarding: Evidence from Taiwan," *Transportation Journal,* Vol. 46, No. 3 (Summer 2007): 5–21.

Sowinski, Lara, "Air Cargo Flies a New Heading," *World Trade,* (August 2008): 34.

Theurmer, Karen E., "Air Cargo: Flying Low," *Logistics Management,* (May 2009): 31.

Theurmer, Karen E., "2007 State of Logistics Report/Air Cargo: Nowhere to Go But Up," *Logistics Management,* (July 2007): 42.

Wong, Jehn-Yih, and Pi-Heng Chung, "Retaining Passenger Loyalty through Data Mining: A Case Study of Taiwanese Airlines," *Transportation Journal,* Vol. 47, No. 1 (Winter 2008): 17–29.

Chapter 8   Water Carriers and Pipelines

"Discussion of Effects of Long-Term Gas Commodity & Transportation Contracts on the Development of Natural Gas Infrastructure," *Interstate Natural Gas Association of America* (2005).

Farris, M. Theodore, "Are You Prepared for a Devastating Port Strike in 2008?" *Transportation Journal,* Vol. 47, No. 1 (Winter 2008): 43.

Higginson, James K., and Tudorita Dumitrascu, "Great Lakes Short Sea Shipping and the Domestic Cargo-Carrying Fleet," *Transportation Journal,* Vol. 46, No. 1 (Winter 2007): 38.

Ives, Buddy, "Pipeline Activity May Slow But Won't be at Crawling," *Pipeline and Gas Journal,* Vol. 236 (March 2009): 64.

Jewell, Michael T., "The Evolving Pipeline Regulations: Historical Perspectives and a New Model for Pipeline Safety in the Arctic National Wildlife Refuge," *Transportation Law Journal,* Vol. 34 (2007): 173–189.

Shister, Neil, "Ocean Transport Adjusts to New Realities," *World Trade,* Vol. 21 (June 2008): 48.

Warner, Bruce E., and Mark S. Shaffer, "Carbon Capture and Sequestration (CSS): A Pipedream or a Real Business Opportunity for Gas Pipeline Developers?" *Pipeline and Gas Journal,* Vol. 236 (May 2009): 5.

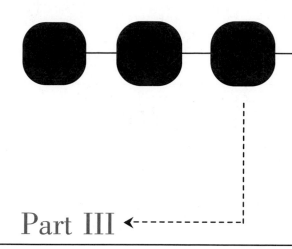

Part III

The first eight chapters of the textbook provide a solid foundation of transportation knowledge. The topics have focused on key issues regarding the role of transportation and the modal options available to freight shippers. We now turn to the strategic activities and challenges involved in the movement of goods through the supply chain. The six chapters in Part III focus on a variety of critical transportation management issues.

Chapter 9 examines the topic of transportation risk management. Companies must proactively work to understand and mitigate the potential freight flow disruptions that exist across the supply chain. Following a general overview of key concepts and the risk management process, the chapter focuses on transportation risk reduction strategies, methods, and outcomes. Special attention is given to the increasingly important topic of supply chain security.

The next two chapters address the ever-expanding role of global transportation in the supply chain. **Chapter 10** focuses on the extensive set of planning activities related to the timely and efficient movement of freight between countries. Effective choice of trade terms, accurate documentation, and logical mode, carrier, and route selection will facilitate global freight flows.

The execution activities related to these flows are the focus of **Chapter 11**. International freight must be properly packed, transported, and cleared through Customs. This chapter discusses the key options for moving freight globally. Also highlighted are the key service providers who streamline the freight flows and minimize border crossing complications.

Chapter 12 explains the roles and industry composition of third party logistics (3PL) providers. Given the financial and service impact of transportation on supply chain success, many companies are turning to external freight movement experts. This chapter discusses the structure of the 3PL industry, customer characteristics, and relationship options. Specific issues related to establishing and managing 3PL relationships are addressed, along with a discussion of current and future 3PL industry issues.

While 3PLs and for-hire carriers are vital supply chain participants, private fleets remain a major force in freight transportation. **Chapter 13** discusses the importance of private transportation and fleet management to companies large and small. Key highlights include discussions of the rational for using a private fleet, the types of private transportation, and current practices in fleet management.

Transportation is a dynamic field that must constantly adapt to the world it serves. As supply chain requirements expand, economic conditions change, and technological innovations emerge, transportation professionals must respond accordingly. **Chapter 14** tackles the major issues of environmental sustainability, fuel price volatility and availability, and infrastructure inadequacy, as well as other challenges. Emerging transportation strategies are also discussed in this forward-looking wrap up.

Chapter 9

TRANSPORTATION RISK MANAGEMENT

Learning Objectives

After reading this chapter, you should be able to do the following:

- Understand the nature of transportation risk and disruptions
- Explain the concept of risk management
- Describe the general process for managing transportation risk
- Identify the primary categories and types of transportation risk
- Understand the key factors in risk assessment
- Discuss the four techniques for managing transportation risks
- Appreciate the challenge of balancing transportation security and global trade efficiency
- Recognize key transportation security regulations and initiatives

Introduction

As strange as it may seem, pirates really do exist in the 21st century. It's a growing problem and not merely an action movie genre. As the Transportation Profile highlights, companies are at risk of their freight being stolen or hijacked for ransom as it flows through dangerous trade lanes. In 2008 alone, more than 100 vessels were attacked off the coast of Somalia. Other hot spots include the waters near Indonesia, Malaysia, India, the Philippines, Brazil, and Ecuador.

Piracy is just one of the threats that organizations face when moving goods. Major incidents—hurricanes, pandemics, labor unrest, and terrorism—create societal problems and significant business challenges. From a transportation standpoint, they are disruptive events that result in supply chain disorder and discontinuity. The outcomes can vary dramatically from minor inconveniences and delivery delays to tremendous problems that threaten a company's image and financial outlook.

Companies cannot idly stand by and hope for the best when they move freight. They must actively work to limit exposure to legitimate hazards. This chapter focuses on the management of transportation risk and service disruptions. We will discuss the general concepts of disruption, risk, and business continuity, as well as the risk management process. Specific issues related to transportation risk management strategies will be addressed, followed by a discussion of expected outcomes. Throughout the chapter, you will gain an understanding of the true challenges involved in the movement of goods as well as the methods available to mitigate transportation risk.

Risk Concepts

Risk is an everyday part of life. Whenever we get behind the wheel of our cars, the potential exists for us to be involved in an accident, to be delayed due to congestion, or to get lost. Although the likelihood of anything bad happening may be remote, each of these risks poses an unpleasant consequence for us—costs, missed appointments, stress, and so on.

The same issues arise when companies put freight in a container, railcar, or trailer. The freight can potentially be stolen, damaged, lost, or delayed while in motion or at rest in a port, trucking terminal, rail yard, or other intermediate facility. That is, freight is at risk of many disruptions from the time it leaves the origin location until it reaches its final destination.

So what exactly are disruptions and risks? A review of dictionary entries and magazine article descriptions would create a dizzying variety of definitions. For the purpose of this chapter, we will use the following characterizations as the foundation of our discussion:

>   **Disruption**—an event that results in a displacement or discontinuity; the act of causing disorder.[1]

>   **Transportation Disruption**—an unplanned or unanticipated event that interrupts the normal flow of goods and materials through the supply chain. These disruptions expose companies within the supply chain to operational and financial risks.[2]

>   **Risk**—a hazard or a source of danger that has a possibility of incurring loss or misfortune.[3]

>   **Transportation Risk**—a future freight movement event with a probability of occurrence and the potential for impacting supply chain performance.

Problems arise when the threat of transportation disruptions and hazards become reality and the supply chain is negatively affected. Unfortunately, these disruptions are common and costly. A 2008 Aberdeen Group study revealed that 99 percent of the companies surveyed had suffered a supply chain disruption in the past year, with 58 percent suffering financial losses as a result.[4]

At minimum, these disruptions are nuisances, creating extra work and delays. Recovery efforts hurt productivity, involve expensive expediting efforts, and require premium freight services. At worst, disruptions inflict long-term damage to a company's image, profitability, and stock price.

Until recently, the true impact of these supply chain disruptions was unknown. Research by Professors Kevin Hendricks and Vinod Singhal has helped to quantify the impact of supply chain glitches on company performance. Their findings indicate that these disruptions result in:

- Significant stock prices declines of nearly nine percent
- Lower operating performance levels over the ensuing few years
- Inventory increases and asset turnover decreases [5]

These eye-opening findings, along with a number of high profile events like the 9/11 terrorist attacks, have prompted supply chain managers to pay more attention to risk. These managers are actively engaged in efforts to reduce the probability of disruptions through a process called risk management:

> **Risk Management**—the variety of activities undertaken by an organization to control and minimize threats to the continuing efficiency, profitability, and success of its operations[6]

How does risk management work? Going back to the driving example, it is possible for you to plan a car trip so that the likelihood of getting delayed or lost is minimized. By studying traffic patterns, mapping out a route, and printing step-by-step directions (or using a GPS navigation system), you can develop a plan to greatly reduce the risk of a trip disruption. This proactive planning initiative will reduce your potential for getting caught in rush hour traffic, being forced into construction detours, or becoming lost. Of course, your risk management plan isn't totally foolproof because unpredictable events such as accidents may still occur.

Another key component of managing risk is to prepare for the inevitable freight-related problems. Developing planned responses to deal with high probability risks— like hazardous winter weather in Minnesota—is far more effective than waiting until problems occur to develop solutions. This process of proactive planning for fast recovery from disruptions is called business continuity planning:

> **Business Continuity Planning**—the processes and procedures an organization puts in place to ensure that essential functions can continue during and after a disruption or disaster.[7]

Business continuity planning efforts focus on developing and testing the resources, actions, procedures, and information needed to deal with a crisis situation. In transportation management this involves having readiness plans to reestablish full functionality of delivery processes as swiftly and smoothly as possible. Poor advanced planning will produce ineffective, slow disruption recovery and a protracted interruption of freight flows.

As you might expect, risk management and business continuity planning are not simple tasks. They demand significant time and expertise, involve financial investment, and require frequent revision. Hence, risk management activities must be driven by the top management of companies across a supply chain if transportation disruptions risks are to be minimized. They must view risk management as critical tool for protecting profitability and implement detailed, cyclical processes to control risk. A four-step risk management methodology is discussed in the next section.

Transportation Risk Management Process

Risk management is an integral part of effective transportation management. It is an iterative process that enables continual improvement in rational decision making. Risk management is the process of identifying risk, its causes and effects, and its ownership with a goal of increasing overall understanding in order to manage, reduce, transfer, or eliminate threats to supply chain success.

The objectives of the **risk management process** include the following:

- Define the key objectives and scope of the risk management process.
- Identify risk issues through structured brainstorming, data gathering exercises, and interviews.
- Allocate responsibilities for each identified risk, to provide further details of background, consequence, and management information.
- Assess each risk against an agreed consistent scale for likelihood and potential impact on operations.
- Compare risk significance to identify the top risks requiring urgent management attention.
- Develop detailed management action plans and responses for each risk.
- Provide a framework to implement actions and monitor their effectiveness.
- Provide a baseline for the process, allowing risks to be reevaluated and further threats to be identified.[8]

These objectives are addressed through implementation of the four-step risk management process outlined in Figure 9-1. Step 1 involves identification of the potential threats and disruptions to which the organization is susceptible. Step 2 focuses on evaluation and prioritization of the risks. The more vulnerable the organization's transportation process is to a potential risk, the more attention it should receive. Step 3 requires the organization to develop proactive risk management and mitigation strategies. Structural and procedural changes may be required to execute the strategy. Step 4 promotes continuity, vigilance, and process improvement. Ongoing testing of strategies, evaluation of their success, and scanning for new risks are needed to achieve maximum protection. Each step is described in detail below.

Step 1—Risk Identification

Accurate and detailed **risk identification** is vital for effective risk management. Thus, the first step in developing an effective transportation risk management program is to identify potential disruptions that can occur to freight that is moving through the supply chain. This involves a concerted effort to discover, define, describe, document,

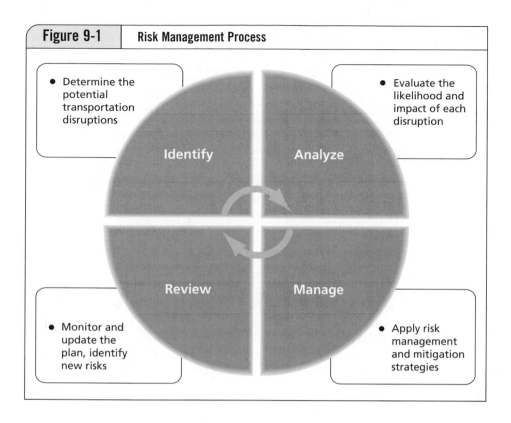

Figure 9-1 | **Risk Management Process**

- Determine the potential transportation disruptions

Identify

- Evaluate the likelihood and impact of each disruption

Analyze

Review

Manage

- Monitor and update the plan, identify new risks

- Apply risk management and mitigation strategies

and communicate risks before they become problems and adversely affect freight flows.

The goal of risk identification is to capture as many transportation disruption risks as possible. During this process, all possible transportation risks that can occur along the global and domestic segments of the supply chain should be recorded. Both inbound and outbound transportation processes should be studied as well.

There are various techniques that can be used for risk identification. Useful techniques include:

- **Brainstorming** is common risk identification technique used to develop a high-level list of risks. Meetings are held with knowledgeable participants who identify threats, concerns, and possible issues in an unstructured setting. The goal is to create a dialogue that triggers new thoughts, produces a large number of ideas, and refines them into a stronger, more complete list of risks than any one individual could develop.

- Interviews and surveys can be used to capture transportation risk information from individuals. Their knowledge and lessons learned from experience with disruptions are collected quickly and efficiently.

- Historical data and documented knowledge provide a collection of information about specific transportation activities, service providers, and trade lanes. Detailed data regarding actual disruptions (frequency, service impact, and recover costs) can be gleaned from these sources to create a strong, fact-filled risk identification list.

Regardless of the technique used, it is essential to include managers, supervisors, and hourly personnel in the initiative to ensure that no risks go undetected.

This process will produce a long list of potential disruptions. Rather than trying to assess each one independently, it is beneficial to organize the disruptions by similar characteristics. The process of categorizing the disruptions into broad risk categories will streamline the risk management process and limit duplication of efforts.

Such efforts are valuable in transportation management, given the wide array of problems that can occur as freight is transferred from one supply chain partner to another. Although the exact categorization may vary by company type, primary mode used, and region of the world, there are six common risk categories related to freight transportation: product loss, product damage, product contamination, delivery delay, supply chain interruption, and security breach.

Product Loss We have all seen news reports of cargo being stolen, but you may not realize the magnitude of this problem. The International Cargo Security Council reports that cargo theft in the United States exceeds $60 billion per year, or $205 per citizen. However, the economic loss to a firm goes far beyond the value of lost goods. Indirect costs of cargo theft include sales lost to stolen goods, added expenses to expedite the shipment of replacement goods, disrupted customer service, and damaged brand value. Other indirect costs include claims processing and the potential impact on insurance rates and coverage. Many security experts estimate the indirect costs are three to five times greater than the direct cost of the loss.[9]

Product loss is not limited to criminals stealing entire shipments. Product loss includes any type of action or negligence that leads to product not reaching the intended buyer. This includes:

- **Product Pilferage**—the theft of part of the contents of a shipping package by freight handlers, equipment operators, and managers can be a problem. It is a particular challenge with iPods, smart phones, pharmaceutical products, and other high-value goods that can be easily concealed and later sold for cash.

- **Shipment Jettison**—in the movement of freight via water, it may be necessary to cast all or part of a ship's cargo overboard to save the ship, crew, and other cargo from perils such as catastrophic weather, running aground, or fire. The master of the ship has the absolute right to jettison cargo when he reasonably believes it to be necessary, and the owners of the ship incur no liability. If the ship is carrying goods of more than one shipper, the rule of **general average** provides for apportioning the loss among all the shippers because all have benefited by the master's action.

- **Piracy and Hijacking**—as discussed in the Transportation Profile, these product loss risks are on the rise. Not only do these crimes create financial losses for companies but they often put ship crews and truck drivers at risk of being kidnapped, injured, or killed. There is also a strategic security concern issue because the money generated from these crimes may be used to fund, train, and assist terrorists.

Product Damage Though it would appear to be a relatively mundane risk, product damage is a potential peril that arises every time a shipment is handled. Employee inattention, negligence, and poor training all contribute to this very costly problem. Damaged product loses much, if not all, of its value. Repaired products can't be sold as new at full price. Otherwise, damaged product may need to be salvaged to recoup some value, or discarded, incurring a total loss. The cost of freight claims processing and product replacement add to the financial impact of damage incidents.

Product damage can result from a wide array of actions or inactions on the part of freight handlers and equipment operators. Specific damage risks include:

- Equipment Accidents—though the number of accidents involving U.S. commercial vehicles is declining, there were 368,000 reportable accidents involving large trucks in 2006. The cost of such accidents is very high, averaging $91,112 per incident for cargo damage, vehicle damage, injuries and medical costs, loss of revenue, increased insurance rates, and other direct costs.[10] Accidents involving other modes also contribute to **freight damage**.

- Poor Freight Handling—a failure to use caution when moving product in/out of equipment can increase the risk of damage. Fragile goods require protection from impact, tilting, shaking, and rough handling. These hazards must be avoided to safeguard product integrity.

- Improper Equipment Loading—the long distance movement of freight may involve a rough ride, especially for rail and ocean transportation. Freight damage risks are high if the load is not properly secured and stacked. If too much space is left between freight, product may shift and fall. If product is improperly stacked (heavy product loaded on top of lightweight product), product may be crushed.

Product Contamination A particular risk to food, pharmaceutical goods, and other consumables is the possibility that product becomes contaminated while en route from origin to destination. Customers may reject a delivery of goods if there is evidence of possible contamination. They do not want to assume the risk of product loss or the responsibility for disposal.

Product contamination risk increases along with trip distance and time in transit. The longer the goods are out of your control, the more opportunity exists for natural or man-made contamination issues to arise. Primary **freight contamination** risks include:

- Climate Control Failure—environmentally sensitive goods such as fruit, vegetables, electronics, biomedical samples, and chemicals often require transportation within a strict temperature or humidity range. Failure to provide a stable climate inside the container during transit will result in product degradation, spoilage, or contamination.

- Product Tampering—the deliberate contamination of goods after they have been manufactured is a risk that is remote but potentially devastating. Multiple individuals handle freight as it moves from the production facility to retail store shelves, making it difficult to fully safeguard product integrity. Given the threat of lawsuits and brand damage, the mere hint of tampering can lead to a swift reaction by the affected companies. Clearing product from store shelves, restocking the supply chain, and rebuilding consumer confidence is a major financial challenge.

- Exposure to Contaminants—the risk of freight coming in contact with potentially undesirable substance (physical, chemical or biological) occurs when different types of freight are commingled. Contamination issues also arise if transportation equipment is used to move different commodities on consecutive trips (for instance, filling a railroad tank car with food grade oil after it was used to transport an industrial solvent).

Delivery Delay There are few things more frustrating than not receiving a scheduled delivery of a time-sensitive shipment like concert tickets. If they arrive a day late, the tickets are rendered worthless and you missed a great event. Companies who rely upon **just-in-time delivery** of inventory to keep their production lines running experience the same frustration, only to a much higher level of financial pain. If a critical shipment is delayed a few hours, production lines will stop and the lost productivity cost may be hundreds of thousands of dollars. These companies are at huge risk if delivery commitments are not kept.

There are numerous **delivery delay** risks. Some transportation perils result from other supply chain strategies such as sourcing goods from low-cost manufacturers in the Far East. This strategy significantly increases supply chain complexity and distance, boosting the possibility of late deliveries. Other risks are out of the company's control, though it is important to recognize their potential impact. Common delivery schedule disruptors include:

- **Congestion**—overburdened roadways, railways, and port facilities impede product flows and create bottlenecks in the supply chain. As equipment sits idly in traffic and average speeds drop, slower-than-anticipated transit times are achieved and delivery windows are missed. The nuisance of U.S. roadway congestion costs the country $78 billion a year in wasted fuel, lost productivity, and delivery delays.[11]

- Poor Weather—as environmental conditions deteriorate, it becomes more challenging to maintain an accurate delivery schedule. Companies located in or delivering to customers in areas of extreme climate conditions—frequent cold, snow and ice conditions, hurricane zones, and so on—must factor these uncontrollable issues into freight movement planning and delivery commitments.

- Equipment Malfunction—mechanical breakdowns of delivery vehicles can cause product to get stranded en route. Likewise, problems with freight handling equipment at ports (such as container cranes) and other freight transfer facilities can slow the flow of products moving in or out of the terminal. Both types of malfunctions will delay shipments beyond their scheduled delivery times.

Supply Chain Interruption Many transportation risks are created by poor execution of day-to-day operations. Ineffective decision making, employee errors, and basic glitches cause temporary disruptions of freight flows. Such risks pale in comparison to the devastating effects of supply chain interruptions that bring transportation operations to a grinding halt. The cost of such disruptions is high and recovery time is prolonged.

Although they don't occur frequently, these problems often fall outside the control of the company. Recent examples of transportation-altering **supply chain interruptions** include:

- Carrier bankruptcy—in times of economic slowdown or high energy prices, financially unstable transportation companies are unable to survive. Their demise causes capacity challenges for customers who previously depended upon the carrier for service. These customers are quickly forced to seek out new service providers whose rates are likely to be much higher. The trucking industry has been particularly hard hit of late with nearly 2,000 companies going out of business in 2007 and 2,690 ceasing operations in the first three quarters of 2008.[12]

- Labor disruptions—many transportation companies and facilities rely upon unionized labor for freight handling and movement. When work-related disputes occur or labor contracts expire, a labor strike risk is created. Some strikes can be predicted in advance, though others are sudden "wild cat" strikes that occur with little warning and create havoc. For example, a 2002 contract dispute between the International Longshoremen and Warehouse Union (ILWU) and the Pacific Maritime Authority (PMA) led to a ten-day

closure of U.S. Pacific Coast ports. Severe supply chain interrupt~~~
curred at a cost of $15.6 billion to the U.S. economy.[13]

- **Capacity shortages**—during peak economic growth, transportation capacit~~~
  stretched to the point that carriers are often unable to provide enough equipment and operators to service all demand. Transportation companies are
  able to increase rates or apply peak season surcharges to freight. At the same
  time, there is a risk of service quality failures due to facility congestion,
  equipment shortages, and operator inexperience.

Security Breach The increase in terrorist attacks, organized crime activity, and
illegal immigration fosters tremendous effort to secure international borders. Transportation companies are now heavily involved in the development of policies and
procedures to better control freight and limit supply chain exposure to problems.
A failure to properly protect in-transit freight leaves the transportation company, its
customers, and the general public vulnerable to acts that threaten security. Repeated
failures lead to government calls for time-consuming freight inspections and costly
countermeasures.

There is no shortage of security challenges facing organizations, especially with
shrewd criminals scheming to exploit system flaws and security vulnerabilities. Common points of exposure are:

- Lax security processes—supply chain security and **resiliency** are not optional;
  they must be built into global transportation operations. Companies must
  think about their potential security vulnerabilities and develop appropriate
  defenses. A failure to establish strong security practices will make the company a prime target for intentional transportation disruptions.
- Unprotected transfer facilities—many transportation companies fail to do the
  simple things like lock doors, fence in facilities, and require security badges
  to limit access to freight and transportation equipment. Ease of facility entry
  and access will only promote product theft, deliberate contamination, or catastrophic disruptions (such as hiding a bomb in a freight container).
- Shipment control failures—freight **visibility** and access control are the keys to
  protecting in-transit goods from harm. When freight is "off the radar
  screen," security risks and disruption opportunities increase. Improperly
  controlled freight containers can provide hiding spots for stowaways attempting to illegally enter a country. Often, the stowaways contaminate the
  container's contents and cause legal headaches for authorities.

Although we have identified six categories of risk and discussed 18 specific risks, the
list is not by any means comprehensive. The perils of transportation are many and
varied. Hazardous materials dangers, the corrosive nature of saltwater, border crossing
issues, military conflicts, and a host of other issues constantly threaten to disrupt transportation operations. Managers must remain vigilant to possible threats and constantly
analyze transportation risk.

Step 2—Risk Assessment

Evaluating transportation risks is a challenging proposition because they do not affect
organizations equally. Risks and their potential impact are influenced by supply chain
strategy, modes used, and operational capabilities. For example, if a company focuses
on just-in-time delivery of materials for their assembly plant, delivery delays pose a
high risk of shutting down the production line. In contrast, delivery delays are not as
big of an issue to the company that keeps a month's worth of raw materials on hand.

e which risks are of direct pertinence and significance to

...essment is to evaluate the risks identified during Step 1
...er to determine how serious each risk is to the organization.
...ion, two parameters are typically evaluated:

...e likelihood of the risk occurring
...consequences if the risk does occur

...sessed in terms of the transportation risk's effect on time, cost,

...nt of risk should also be studied. **Risk proximity** attempts to addresses
...en will the risk occur?" Certain disruptive events, such as hurricanes
...ve specific time windows during which they are likely to impact the
...by thinking now about these seasonal risks, the organization may be able
...ategies to effectively manage the risks. A natural tendency is to take a re-
...ach to risk after the problem occurs. This "fire-fighting" mode is neither
...t nor service quality-oriented.[14]

Risk assessment can be qualitative or quantitative in nature. **Qualitative risk analysis**
provides a baseline evaluation of risks in a rapid and cost-effective manner. These
judgmental approaches seek to classify each risk in terms of low, medium, or high
probability and impact (see Figure 9-2). Experts from the organization should participate in the process of assigning each risk to the matrix. For example, theft by piracy

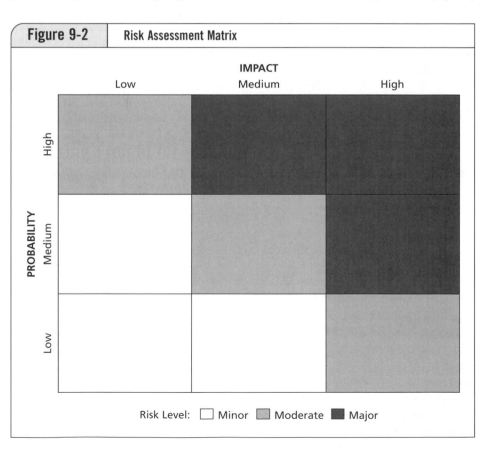

Figure 9-2 — **Risk Assessment Matrix**

may be a high-impact, medium-probability risk for freight moving through the Gulf of Aden. In contrast, piracy would be a low-impact, low-probability risk for domestic freight moving from Atlanta to Dallas.

An issue landing in a "Major Risk" category is deemed to be unacceptable. The organization must spend time, money, and effort on a proactive strategy to reduce the likelihood of occurrence and limit consequences in the event of that particular disruption. The organization should also address issues in the "Moderate Risk" and "Minor Risk" categories through contingency planning. However, the level of management attention is tempered by the reduced risk potential.

Quantitative risk analysis often builds upon the foundation created by qualitative analysis. Those risks falling into the "Major" risk level category may warrant detailed assessment of available data to evaluate their relative danger levels. Quantitative analysis incorporates numerical estimates of frequency or probability and consequence. In practice, a sophisticated analysis of risk requires extensive data which can be expensive to acquire or is often unavailable. Fortunately, few decisions require sophisticated quantification of both frequency and consequences.

Risk assessment is a time consuming task. To be of value, this activity needs to generate useful information for the organization. One option is to create a risk assessment report that highlights risk management priorities and "red flag" issues:

1. Relative ranking or prioritization of risks—the overall risk ranking is determined by either the calculated risk level or expert ratings of risks.

2. List of risks requiring immediate response—the most urgent risks commonly need responses in the short term. By sorting according to urgency (that is, the relative ranking list), it is easy to identify the most severe risk events which need immediate action.

3. List of risks for additional analysis and response—risks which need additional analysis and management strategy development are identified. This usually consists of the major risks not needing immediate response and some moderate risks.

4. Watch list of low priority risks—risks which are not urgent and require action in the distant future are commonly detailed on a monitoring list. This typically includes the remaining "Moderate Risks" and all "Minor Risks."

5. List of risks grouped by categories—placing risks in categories (such as theft risks, damage risks, and so on) reveal areas of risk concentration and highlights common causes of risk.

6. Risk trends—as risk analysis is repeated over time, problematic trends may emerge (for instance, a minor impact issue is occurring more frequently or generating higher costs than expected) which warrant further analysis.

Risk assessment is an invaluable activity for identifying critical transportation challenges and primary disruption concerns. This effort ensures that organizations will focus scarce resources on relevant risk management and mitigation strategies.[15]

Step 3—Risk Management Strategies

Using the output from the risk assessment, the next step is to create a coherent strategy for managing and mitigating transportation risks in a cost-effective manner. The mitigation strategy identifies specific efforts, actions, and procedural changes that must be taken by management to reduce high priority risks. The goal is to lower the probability of risk occurrence and/or minimize the negative impact if the risk occurs. A risk can never be totally eliminated, but its frequency and effect on the organization can be reduced if properly addressed.

Mitigation strategies must not be haphazardly applied to disruption risks. First, the strategies must be in sync with the overall supply chain strategy and corporate strategy. Second, mitigation strategies and actions must focus on high priority issues. Third, the mitigation action must be reasonable in terms of cost and time to implement versus the likelihood of success. Otherwise, money and effort will be wasted on low priority risks or ineffective risk remedies. Finally, a standardized process should be used to implement disruption mitigation actions as discussed in the On the Line feature.

Each **risk mitigation** strategy should produce an action plan that identifies:

- roles and responsibilities for developing, implementing and monitoring the strategy
- resources required to carry out the planned actions
- timelines
- conditions present in order for risk level to be acceptable

A well-developed plan plays an important role in decreasing the risk of transportation disruptions as well as their effect on the supply chain and company performance. These plans typically focus on one of four techniques to manage and mitigate risk: avoidance, reduction, transfer, or retention.[16]

Risk Avoidance   The simplest way to eliminate a risk is to not perform an activity that carries risk. While this strategy provides absolute protection from a transportation disruption, it also means losing out on the potential gains that come from accepting some risk. For example, a company could avoid transportation risks by refusing to accept a customer's order. No freight needs to be shipped, meaning that the risk of in-transit freight loss or damage is eliminated. However, the company also misses the revenue and profit opportunities related to accepting the order.

One alternative to this very conservative pure avoidance strategy would be to take steps to remove the risk. When possible, the ideal solution is to keep the risk from happening. Tools like root cause analysis can be used to pinpoint the reasons why a disruption occurs. Processes can be revised to eliminate the disruption's causes and greatly minimize the risk. For example, if an investigation revealed that all thefts occurred when a specific trucking company was used, the simple solution would be to never use that carrier again. Hence, that particular theft risk would be removed.

Another avoidance strategy would be to sidestep the specific exposure. In the case of freight loss or damage risk, the seller could choose to work only on an **F.O.B. Origin** basis. That is, the seller simply requires the buyer to take ownership of the goods at the seller's location and assume all responsibility for transporting the goods. The seller evades the liabilities that come with owning in-transit freight without sacrificing the sale. Of course, some customers may prefer to purchase goods on a delivered basis (**F.O.B. Destination**) and seek out more accommodating sellers.

On the Line

Disruptions—When Good Supply Chains Go Bad

Between the publicity given to high profile supply chain failures and the financial impact research on glitches, the awareness of supply chain disruptions is at an all time high. As interest levels grow, so does the number of disruption assessment tools to evaluate and mitigate risk. While these tools are each slightly different, they converge on four common actions.

The foundation of any risk mitigation process is to *acknowledge the disruptions* that can occur in the supply chain. Organizations must map their supply chains and identify their particular bottlenecks and risks. For example, fresh produce importers must understand that the longer a supply chain is stretched geographically, the more fragile and brittle it becomes. Lengthened transit times, increased congestion, and greater security issues are three disruption scenarios that must be evaluated. Similarly, the risks related to sole sourcing, lean initiatives, and centralized distribution must be assessed in terms of disruption vulnerability and potential cost.

Next, companies should *mitigate potential disruptions* with the potential to impact supply chain performance and costs. Steps must be taken to create a more resilient supply chain—one that reduces the likelihood of disruptions and absorbs them with minimal impact. Resiliency can be achieved in the fresh produce chain through enhanced security, process redundancies, and flexibility. Redundancy means having the same capabilities at multiple locations or sources in case of disruptions at the primary operation. Flexibility strategies such as supplier diversity and leveraging multiple modes of transportation allow the organization to ward off emerging problems.

The third component of disruption risk mitigation is to *establish quick response capabilities* for the most likely supply chain glitches. Organizations must take the time to develop contingency plans that focus on failure modes (for example, your primary transportation provider has no capacity) rather than specific reasons for the failure (a bankruptcy, labor strike, or weather issue). This will limit the number of scenarios that have to be considered by the organization, making the contingency planning effort more effective. The goal is to decouple causes from the failure modes and be able to react when bad things happen.

It is not enough to merely think up scenarios and develop contingency protocols. Once the plans are created, there is value in running periodic simulations of supply chain disruptions and practicing the implementation of appropriate responses. These stress tests help the organization assess the strengths and weaknesses of their contingency plans. It is also helpful to have funds set aside in a risk-management budget that is separate from the normal operating budget. This pool of money can be used to quickly implement robust contingency plans which ultimately limit the cost of the disruption.

Finally, organizations must *monitor their performance* in regards to actual disruptions. They should assess what happened in the supply chain, how well they responded, and how the disruption could be prevented in the future. These audits also help the organization evaluate and refine their contingency plans. Such efforts promote continuous improvement of supply chain performance.

It is critical to coordinate the four disruption mitigation components in a comprehensive program. While the effort is neither simple nor free, effective investment of time and money can reduce the frequency and severity of supply chain disruptions. Ultimately, this will help an organization steer clear of severe, long-range costs.

Source: Brian J. Gibson, "When Good Supply Chains Go Bad," *Blueprints: The Produce Professionals' Quarterly Journal*, Vol. 5, No. 2, 2006. Reprinted by permission of Blue Book Services/Produce Reporter Co.

Risk Reduction Given that many risks cannot be totally eliminated or avoided, it is important for companies to proactively mitigate or limit risk. This involves adopting risk management strategies that reduce the likelihood of a disruption and/or limit the severity of financial loss. For example, a company could attempt to reduce the risk of theft or hijacking by hiring armed guards to travel with high value freight. This strategy could be effective at reducing risk to a more acceptable level, but it may be expensive and/or raise other risks.

There are numerous types of strategies to pursue the goal of risk reduction. Some companies will use a **hedging strategy** to offset or balance out the risks presented by a single option. This diversification avoids the inflated risk of having "all your eggs in one basket." In transportation, companies can disperse their freight among multiple carriers to reduce the financial risk of a sole sourced carrier bankruptcy or service interruption.

A **postponement strategy** seeks to limit risk by delaying a commitment of resources. Trucking companies could reduce the risk of productivity losses by delaying the dispatch of drivers until after a customer has loaded a trailer and submitted proper documentation. This will reduce driver wait time and maximize the use of available service hours for transporting freight.

A **buffering strategy** provides additional resources to reduce risks related to capacity shortages or performance problems. An air freight carrier may have extra jets available to reduce the impact of equipment failures. They may also have a few pilots on call each day to be prepared for volume spikes. Both buffering actions will reduce the likelihood of freight delays.

Given the vast array of transportation risks, it is impossible to discuss in detail the reduction strategies that have been developed. Table 9-1 highlights a variety of risk reduction strategies that align well with the six risk categories and 18 specific risks discussed earlier.

Risk reduction requires that companies be proactive in establishing plans to deal with the high-probability/high-impact risks that emerge from the identification and analysis processes. The strategies discussed briefly below will help companies reduce a variety of common transportation risks that affect all modes.

- Develop and maintain relationships with quality carriers—effective transportation service providers are reliable, reasonably priced, and have an excellent reputation for protecting freight. Transportation buyers must make a concerted effort to balance service dependability, cost efficiency, and safety when selecting modes and carriers. Hiring high quality carriers, actively monitoring their performance, and focusing on continuous improvement of transportation processes will reduce the risk of delays and damage.
- Use protective product packaging—freight may be handled by forklifts, conveyors, cranes, and multiple transportation vehicles on the way to its final destination. To minimize the risk of concealed product damage or contamination, protective materials like cardboard, bubble wrap, foam packing peanuts and forms, plastic bags, and other materials should be used inside shipping cartons. Insufficient packaging increases the risk of product damage and limits carrier liability in freight claim situations.
- Properly secure freight inside containers—assuming that the ride will be rough encourages companies to safeguard their in-transit inventory. Loads should be secured and protected as needed by using blocking and cleats nailed to the floor, braces, straps, load bars, separators, or air bags and other void fill materials. In addition, load preparation through the use of stretch wrap, shrink wrap, banding, and edge protectors will stabilize and protect freight.

Table 9-1	Transportation Risk Reduction Strategies		
RISK CATEGORY	**SPECIFIC RISKS**	**REDUCTION STRATEGIES**	**ANTICIPATED OUTCOMES**
Product Loss	Theft and pilferage Piracy and hijacking Cargo jettison	Use generic packaging & descriptions Avoid lawless hot spots Strategic routing	Mitigate risk of financial loss, reduce customer delivery delays, and avoid replacement shipment expenses.
Product Damage	Operator accident Poor freight handling methods Improper equipment loading	Use protective packaging Establish training programs Monitor carrier performance	Enhance freight safety, reduce freight claims administration, and profit margin protection.
Product Contamination	Temperature control failure Product tampering Exposure to hazardous materials	Leverage pervasive automation Secure freight / lock containers Isolate dangerous freight	Safeguard brand equity, decrease potential for product liability lawsuits, and trim product recalls and inventory replacement costs.
Delivery Delay	Congestion Poor weather Equipment malfunction	Use event management software Employ dynamic re-routing tools Perform preventative maintenance	Proactive response to problems resulting in less wait time, greater delivery reliability, and improved customer satisfaction.
Supply Chain Interruption	Capacity shortage Carrier bankruptcy Labor disruptions and strikes	Contract with quality carriers Monitor carrier finances Establish alternate carriers & ports	Avoid major disruptions of product flows that can impact supply chain productivity, and product availability.
Security Breach	Shipment control breakdown Unprotected transfer facilities Lax security processes	Employ cargo tracking technology Screen & evaluate vulnerabilities Participate in C-TPAT and FAST	Greater protection against terrorist activity, fewer government inspections, and streamlined border clearance.

- Require the use of reliable equipment—allowing carriers to use defective or poorly maintained equipment to move your freight produces transportation risk. Poor vehicle maintenance raises the potential for delivery delays due to equipment breakdowns and inspection failures. Outdated or malfunctioning equipment increases the likelihood of product damage due to accidents, poor ride quality, leaks, and other problems. To avoid these problems work only with carriers that perform preventative maintenance, regularly upgrade or replace old equipment, and have a strong track record of equipment safety compliance.

- Leverage technology to maintain shipment control—monitoring in-transit freight not only provides peace of mind, it helps managers avoid potential problems and respond rapidly to disruptions. The Transportation Technology box highlights the importance of these capabilities to transportation companies like Cool Carriers that handle temperature- and humidity-sensitive freight. Visibility tools provide a seamless flow of timely information across the supply chain. Accurate knowledge of in-transit freight allows managers to be proactive in routing and scheduling to meet delivery windows. Exception management tools detect performance problems and alert the affected organization. Corrective action can be taken to resolve the situation before the supply chain is adversely impacted.

Risk Transfer The risk analysis activity may identify potential problems that an organization deems too problematic to manage or mitigate on its own. In these situations, the organization may seek outside assistance in controlling those risks. This risk transfer strategy provides a means to place liability on a third party should the risk occur. Of course, the third party doesn't freely accept the risk. They are paid by the customer to assume or share the risk.

Insurance is a common method of risk transfer. Individuals can purchase medical, life, property, and liability insurance. Transportation companies and their customers can also do the same to reduce their risks. For example, the financial risks stemming from commercial vehicle accidents and related lawsuits are very high. Rather than setting aside a large pool of money to self-insure against these possible problems, most transportation companies purchase coverage from insurance companies. They are using the strategy of risk transfer as the means to place financial liability on a third party (the insurance company) should the risk (a vehicle accident) occur.

Freight owners often purchase insurance as a means to transfer their risk of in-transit freight loss, damage, and delay. Most carriers assume very limited liability for these types of problems. For example, the U.S. Postal Service and parcel carriers limit their risk to $100 per shipment. If they should lose or damage your package containing a $500 digital camera, they will pay no more than $100. Hence, you either take a $400 gamble on their ability to deliver your package intact or you can transfer the risk to an insurer for a fee. The same options are available to companies shipping freight worth thousands of dollars. They can essentially self insure (accepting the limited carrier liability amount) or purchase insurance through the transportation company, a cargo insurance broker, or an insurance underwriter.

It is also possible to transfer risk to **third party logistics** service providers (3PLs). These experts—discussed in more detail in Chapter 12—are external suppliers that perform all or part of an organization's logistics services. Companies contract with 3PLs because these service providers have the knowledge, capacity, technologies, and capability to mitigate some risk factors. 3PLs provide a diverse array of transportation services, administrative support, and strategic planning. Some 3PLs cover the full spectrum of global freight management issues while other companies assist with specific risks like asset protection, cargo loss control, or hazardous materials movement.

Regardless of the 3PLs' role and the risk transfer provisions in 3PL contracts and insurance policies, organizations are not absolved of their responsibilities. They must remain vigilant of potential risks and continually strive to reduce their exposures. After all, they own the freight and must protect it along with their customer relationships.

Transportation Technology	*Trailer Tracking and Temperature Sensors Reduce Cost and Risk*

When you think of Florida, sunshine, the beach, and warm temperatures come to mind. And Cool Carriers, one of the state's larger trucking companies that focus on moving refrigerated freight, knows that correct temperatures inside the trailer can be the difference between profit and loss.

Based in Pompano Beach, Fla., Cool Carriers specializes in hauling perishable freight throughout the United States. Cool Carriers has received numerous awards for excellence in customer service and on-time delivery, yet Cool Carriers still had to rely on labor intensive manual polling of over 30 reefers to determine location.

"I have to know where my trucks are, but it was taking us nearly two hours every time we polled our fleet," said Tommy McWhorter, head of operations. "And just as important, I need to know that the temperature in our trailers is within customer specifications. The process was labor and time intensive but the information was essential to running our business."

Cool Carriers chose TransCore's Sense & Track™ trailer tracking system with temperature sensing modules added to each trailer. "Installing the systems across our fleet was painless," added McWhorter, "and it worked perfectly from the first time we used it. In as little as 30 seconds, we not only know the location, but the temperature status of every truck in our fleet. That saves us time and money while adding value to our customer service proposition."

ABOUT THE SYSTEM

TransCore's Global Wave® Sense & Track mobile terminal is a compact all-satellite communications device. Using a two-way protocol, it sends reports, receives commands, and can be polled throughout North America. It utilizes a third generation GlobalWave satellite modem that allows for fast GPS fixes with an accuracy of 35 feet or better and capable of providing location information in less than a minute, among the fastest response times in the industry.

The Sense & Track mobile terminal, when combined with sensors, becomes an integral part of the trailer, able to show loaded/empty status and provide data from other monitored systems such as load temperature and tire inflation. By adding cargo and door sensors, immediate alert notification can be sent when trailer doors are opened or closed along with empty/full load status information enhancing security for both the load and trailer, including reduction of theft.

Source: Adapted from "TransCore Trailer Tracking and Temperature Sensors Save Cool Carriers of Florida Two Hours Per Day," *EON News Brief,* March 26, 2008. Reprinted by permission.

Risk Retention Risk is inevitable, but not all risk is created equal. Organizations must evaluate risk and make a judgment and determine what, if anything, they will do about it. Those issues falling in the minor risk categories of Exhibit 9-2, particularly the low probability, low impact issues, warrant little attention. These risks have limited potential to negatively affect the supply chain. They present an acceptable level and the organization will retain the risks.

In other situations, the cost of mitigating a risk may outweigh the benefits realized. For example, the potential savings from a low deductible insurance policy may not be enough to offset the additional policy cost. A transportation company may have a $2,500 or $5,000 deductible on their collision insurance. They will retain all financial risks related to small accidents and deductible portion of larger incidents.

Finally, some risks are so large or catastrophic that they either cannot be reasonably mitigated or insured against. War and some natural perils are examples.

Regardless of the reason for retaining a risk, it cannot be ignored. It is vital that all accepted risks have a viable fallback plan. Retained risks must be monitored to ensure that any escalation is captured and appropriate strategies are then implemented.

Collectively, these four types of risk management strategies help organizations adhere to the Boy Scout motto: "Be Prepared." When organizations conscientiously evaluate risks, determine the best course of action (avoid, reduce, transfer, or retain), and establish business continuity plans for major and moderate risks, the negative consequences and duration of incidents will be reduced. Furthermore, the organization will likely improve performance on all transportation fronts—cost, safety, product protection, and delivery reliability.

Step 4—Risk Review and Monitoring

Risk management planning is not a static, one-time process. Organizations cannot analyze risks, develop plans, and simply assume that the plans can be perfectly implemented as needed. Instead, a testing and review process must be instituted to ensure that existing risk mitigation efforts and disruption recovery processes work as intended. Thus, risk management requires ongoing effort by the organization. As Figure 9-1 suggests, it is a circular or continuous process.

Conducting tests of risk management action plans is the only way to know that they will actually work when a true disruption occurs. These testing initiatives should demonstrate and measure the effectiveness of risk mitigation activities. The central concern at this stage is to validate the process and its ability to reduce or eliminate unacceptable risks.

A thorough testing program simulates disruptions and defines benchmarks for recovery processes. Separate test plans should be developed by the organization for each disruption scenario. It is important to accurately simulate each disruption's impact on inventory, physical plant, people, and external parties.

There are two stages to testing. First, well-communicated, controlled tests are conducted to walk the organization and their supply chain partners through the process. This identifies gaps in the risk management plan and gets everyone comfortable with reacting to each risk scenario. Then, surprise tests are carried out to see how the plan and people hold up under pressure. Without surprise tests, the organization doesn't know how well it will react when a real event occurs.[17]

Organizations must also periodically review and update risk management plans. Risks are not static, making it imperative for organizations to regularly reassess the likelihood and expected impact of risks. This will help the organization evaluate whether their previously selected plans are still applicable and effective. Also, the organization must be cognizant of emerging challenges that change risk profiles and introduce new risks. As economic conditions change, competitive threats arise, new regulations are enacted, and customer expectations grow, the organization must respond to these new and diverse risks.

Realize that risk management and mitigation plans are not perfect. Testing, experience, and actual disruptions will necessitate action plan changes and improvements to better deal with the risks being faced. The goal of the risk review stage is to establish a repeatable, measurable, verifiable validation process that can be run from time to time to continually verify the organization's ability to manage risk.

In summary, the risk management process described in this section outlines the steps that organizations must take to identify, monitor, and control transportation risk. The purpose of the process is to effectively address, prevent, and reduce risks that prevent the organization from meeting its goals. It must always be remembered that the key to risk management is active engagement. The process will fail if organizational commitment and contribution are lacking and risks are not efficiently identified, assessed, and pursued to their conclusion.

Supply Chain Security

The terrorist attacks on September 11, 2001 brought global commerce between the United States and the rest of the world to a halt. International and domestic air transportation was brought to a halt within hours and flights were suspended for days. Ocean vessels loaded with containers and other freight were prevented from loading or unloading in major U.S. ports, forcing many ships to anchor off the coast and wait for days to be unloaded. Fresh produce rotted and materials needed to keep assembly lines running did not arrive on time. It was a frightening period of time and the attacks showed just how vulnerable global supply chains were to intentional disruptions.

Before the events of September 11, 2001, ships would frequently arrive in U.S. ports and clear U.S. Customs in a matter of hours. Since that fateful day, enhanced security measures have made the arrival and clearance process more complex. Increased **cargo inspection**, much more paperwork, and longer time to enter the country are now a reality. Some shipments are given very close scrutiny because of their country of origin.

This tightening of U.S. borders has occurred during an era of unprecedented global trade growth. Given the importance of global trade to the U.S. economy, a delicate balance must be struck between security and the efficient flow of global commerce. If security is too tight it could impede the flow of goods, causing delays and decreased efficiency. If trade efficiency is overemphasized, security can be compromised.

Compounding the challenge of this dangerous environment is the variety of risks inherent in global trade. Some of the risks are purely physical in nature. Longer distances, greater product handling, multiple border crossings, and more intermediaries each make the supply chain more susceptible to loss, damage, and delay problems. Other challenges are manmade, motivated by political, ideological, or criminal intent. At minimum, they present theft risks; at worst they generate a number of deliberate threats including nuclear, chemical, biological, radiological, and high explosive weapons, weapon components, narcotics, currency, stowaways, and prohibited or restricted commodities. These issues add an urgent dimension to transportation risk that requires a joint effort between government and industry to limit the number and magnitude of security breaches.

Regarding this need for cooperation, the **Department of Homeland Security** states in its *Strategy to Enhance International Supply Chain Security*: "The international cargo supply chain security is a global issue that cannot be successfully achieved unilaterally. From a United States perspective the most effective supply chain security measures are those that involve assessing risks and identifying threats presented by cargo shipments before they reach the United States. For international containerized cargo, this assessment and identification is most effective if it is conducted before a container is loaded onto a vessel destined for the United States. Yet this is only half of the necessary calculus. The global supply chain is bidirectional, requiring domestic efforts to ensure the integrity of both inbound and outbound cargo. Such an effective cargo security strategy requires a multi-layered, unified approach that must be international in scope."[18]

Fortunately, a variety of proactive efforts are under way and there have been significant improvements in the security of the global supply chain since September 11, 2001. Numerous legislative acts and government programs have been developed. Transportation risk-related improvements include passage of the Maritime Transportation Security Act of 2002, creation of the **Container Security Initiative**, and development of **Advance Manifest Rules**. Additional improvements have been achieved via cooperative agreements with the United States' trade partners, both governmental and in the private sector, such as the **Customs-Trade Partnership Against Terrorism** and the **Free and Secure Trade** Program.

Maritime Transportation Security Act of 2002

The Maritime Transportation Security Act of 2002 (MTSA) is intended to protect U.S. ports and waterways from a terrorist attack. This law is the U.S. equivalent of the International Ship and Port Facility Security Code (ISPS), and was fully implemented on July 1, 2004. It requires vessels and port facilities to conduct vulnerability assessments and develop security plans. An important result of MTSA is to create a consistent security program for all the nation's ports to better identify and deter threats.

According to the MTSA, all tankers and other vessels considered at high risk of a security incident (such as barges, large passenger ships, and cargo and towing vessels) entering U.S. waters must have certified security plans that address how they would respond to emergency incidents, identify the person authorized to implement security actions, and describe provisions for establishing and maintaining physical security, cargo security, and personnel security. These plans must be updated at least every five years and be reapproved whenever a change is made to a tanker that could affect the vessel's security.

The tankers and other high-risk vessels must be equipped with automatic identification systems that will allow vessel tracking and monitoring while traveling on U.S. navigable waters. The U.S. Coast Guard can assign sea marshals to accompany tankers as they transit in and out of U.S. ports to ensure harbor safety and security.

The MTSA also specifies that all U.S. port facilities deemed at risk for a "transportation security incident," such as LNG marine terminals, fossil fuel processing and storage facilities, and cruise ship terminal facilities, must prepare and implement security plans for deterring such incidents to the "maximum extent practicable."[19]

Container Security Initiative

The **U.S. Customs and Border Protection** (CBP) created the Container Security Initiative (CSI) to address the threat to border security and global trade posed by the potential for terrorist use of a maritime container to deliver a weapon. The CSI program seeks to identify and inspect all containers that pose a potential risk for terrorism at foreign ports before they are placed on vessels destined for the United States. CBP has stationed multidisciplinary teams of U.S officers from both CBP and Immigration and Customs Enforcement (ICE) to work together with our host foreign government counterparts. Their mission is to target and prescreen containers and to develop additional investigative leads related to the terrorist threat to cargo destined to the United States.

The three core elements of CSI are:

- Identify high-risk containers. CBP uses automated targeting tools to identify containers that pose a potential risk for terrorism, based on advance information and strategic intelligence.
- Prescreen and evaluate containers before they are shipped. Containers are screened as early in the supply chain as possible, generally at the port of departure.
- Use nonintrusive inspection technology to prescreen high-risk containers to ensure that screening can be done rapidly without slowing down the movement of trade. This technology includes large-scale X-ray and gamma ray machines and radiation detection devices.

A reciprocal program, CSI offers participating countries the opportunity to send their customs officers to major U.S. ports to target oceangoing containerized cargo to be exported to their countries. Likewise, CBP shares information on a bilateral basis with its CSI partners. CSI is now operational at ports in North America, Europe, Asia, Africa, the Middle East, and Latin and Central America. CBP's 58 operational CSI ports now make approximately 86 percent of all maritime containerized cargo imported into the United States subject to prescreening prior to importation.[20]

Advanced Manifest Regulations

CBP published a series of advanced manifest rules which require carriers to submit a cargo declaration to CBP before cargo reaches the United States. These rules vary by mode and origin point. The purpose of the rule is to enable CBP to analyze container content information before a container is loaded and thereby decide on its load/do not load status in advance. In case of noncompliance with the rule, the most important consequence is denial of loading or unloading and a consequent disruption of cargo flows and supply chains. Furthermore, CBP may impose fines or other penalties on the carriers and others responsible for the submission of cargo declarations.

Targeted at ocean container freight, the 24-Hour Advance Vessel Manifest Rule applies to all vessels which will call at a U.S. port and all cargo destined for the U.S. or carried via U.S. ports to a non-U.S. destination. The rule applies whether the load port is a CSI port or not. To fulfill responsibilities when submitting cargo declarations to the CBP, the following information is required:

1. A precise description of the cargo or the six-digit Harmonized Tariff Schedule (HTS) number under which the cargo is classified and weight of the cargo, OR for a sealed container, the shipper's declared description and weight of the cargo. Generic descriptions such as 'FAK' (freight of all kinds), 'STC' (said to contain), 'general cargo,' 'toys,' 'chemicals' and similar are not acceptable.

2. Quantity of cargo expressed by the lowest external packaging unit (containers and pallets are not acceptable units).

3. Shipper's complete name and address or Automated Commercial Environment (ACE) identification number from all bills of lading.

4. Complete name and address of the consignee, owner or owner's representative or ACE identification number, from all bills of lading.

5. Internationally recognized hazardous material code where applicable.

6. Container numbers and seal numbers for all seals affixed to containers.

Additional rules, required by the Trade Act of 2002, mandated submission of advanced electronic data on all shipments entering and leaving the country. The rules address how CBP intends to collect advance cargo information electronically to identify high-risk shipments that could threaten the safety and security of the United States. These regulations permit better risk management against the terrorist threat, before cargo shipments reach the U.S. border ports of entry. Table 9-2 outlines the timeline of advanced manifest information for each mode.[21]

Customs-Trade Partnership Against Terrorism

The Customs-Trade Partnership Against Terrorism program (C-TPAT) is a voluntary government-business initiative to build cooperative relationships that strengthen and improve overall international supply chain and U.S. border security. C-TPAT recognizes

Table 9-2	U.S. Advanced Manifest Regulations	
MODE	**INBOUND FREIGHT**	**OUTBOUND FREIGHT**
Air & Air Couriers	4 hours prior to arrival in U.S. or "wheels up" from certain nearby areas	2 hours prior to scheduled departure from the U.S.
Ocean	24 hours prior to lading at foreign port	24 hours prior to departure from U.S. port where cargo is laden
Rail	2 hours prior to arrival at a U.S. port of entry	2 hours prior to the arrival of the train at the border
Truck	FAST: 30 minutes prior to arrival in U.S. Non-FAST: 1 hour prior to arrival in the U.S.	1 hour prior to the arrival of the truck at the border

Source: United States Customs and Border Protection

that CBP can provide the highest level of cargo security only through close cooperation with the ultimate owners of the global supply chain such as importers, carriers, consolidators, licensed customs brokers, and manufacturers. Through this initiative, CBP encourages businesses to ensure the integrity of their security practices and verify the security guidelines of their business partners within the supply chain.

C-TPAT offers trade-related businesses an opportunity to play an active role in the war against terrorism. By participating in this worldwide supply chain security initiative, companies will ensure a more secure and expeditious supply chain for their employees, suppliers, and customers. Beyond these essential security benefits, CBP offers benefits to certain certified C-TPAT member categories, including:

- A reduced number of CBP inspections (reduced border delay times)
- Priority processing for CBP inspections (front-of-the-line processing for inspections when possible)
- Assignment of a C-TPAT Supply Chain Security Specialist (SCSS) who will work with the company to validate and enhance security throughout the company's international supply chain.
- Potential eligibility for CBP Importer Self-Assessment program (ISA) with an emphasis on self-policing.[22]

C-TPAT is not just a big-company program. Medium and small companies can also participate directly in C-TPAT or employ its guidelines in their security practices. Thus far, it is a very popular program as indicated in the Global Perspectives feature.

Global Perspectives

C-TPAT Membership Nears 7,000 Mark

The Customs-Trade Partnership Against Terrorism (C-TPAT) continues to gain ground. U.S. Customs and Border Protection, which oversees the program, recently announced that membership has grown to just under 7,000 companies since the program began in 2003. C-TPAT is a voluntary government-industry partnership in which companies agree to submit extensive documentation on their supply chain security practices in exchange for preferential treatment of their import cargo at ports of entry.

CBP conducted 3,011 validations in 2007, a 27-percent increase from 2006. Last year marked the first time the agency re-verified supply chains it had previously evaluated; about 20 percent of last year's efforts were re-validations. In addition, CBP certified 2,601 new C-TPAT members and granted Tier III status to 17 companies. Tier III is the highest level of C-TPAT participation. It is granted to companies that exceed the minimum standards and have adopted best practices, such as using certain types of container-security devices.

CBP takes the validation process seriously. Based on its findings during validation exercises, the agency temporarily suspended or removed 112 companies from the program for security breaches or failure to meet C-TPAT's minimum criteria. Of those, 47 were conditionally or fully reinstated after they took corrective action.

Free and Secure Trade

The Free and Secure Trade (FAST) program is a direct outgrowth of the Smart Border Accords entered into between the United States and Canada and the United States and Mexico in the wake of the terrorist attacks of September 11, 2001.

FAST is designed to enhance the security and safety of North America while also bolstering the economic prosperity of the U.S., Canada, and Mexico by aligning, to the maximum extent possible, their commercial processing programs. The FAST program uses common risk-management principles, supply chain security, industry partnerships, and advanced technology to improve the efficiency of screening and clearing commercial traffic at ports of entry along the U.S./Canada and U.S./Mexico borders.

The FAST program provides expedited processing for participants that qualify under the stringent terms of the program. Participants qualify by enhancing the security of their manufacturing plants, warehouses, and shipping systems under the auspices of C-TPAT. FAST processing on the U.S./Mexico border also requires the foreign manufacturer to use high security seals properly placed in the approved manner when crossing the border.[23]

We have discussed a few of the security challenges and initial programs aimed at protecting the U.S. and its citizens. However, security is an ongoing concern. Savvy criminals, terrorists, and others who seek to do harm to the United States are always seeking new opportunities to exploit security weaknesses. Hence, security regulations and programs are constantly being scrutinized and improved. Newer initiatives such as the Safe Port Act of 2006, the detailed Advanced Manifest System 10 + 2 Rules, and the Transportation Workers Identification Credentials program are a few examples. Expect to see demands for more frequent container inspections, new freight protection technologies, and greater government-industry collaboration to emerge in this ongoing battle.

It is important to realize that there is also a business benefit to mitigating security risks. A 2006 study by Stanford University, the National Association of Manufacturers and IBM found that companies who improved supply chain security:

- Improved their asset visibility in the supply chain by 50 percent,
- Reduced their Customs inspections by 48 percent,
- Reduced inventory theft by 38 percent, and
- Improved on-time shipping to customers by 30 percent.[24]

Clearly, supply chain security is more than a necessary evil. Companies should look at it as an opportunity to improve transportation service and enhance the bottom line.

SUMMARY

- Transportation risks are potentially disruptive events that produce supply chain disorder. Uncontrolled risk can produce negative outcomes ranging from minor delivery delays to major product losses that affect financial performance.

- Organizations can reduce threats to the continuing efficiency and effectiveness of their transportation operations through a process of risk management.

- Despite best efforts to reduce risks, most cannot be totally eliminated and disruptions may occur. Business continuity planning focuses on dealing with and recovering quickly from these disruption episodes.

- Risk management is the process of identifying risk, its causes and effects, and its ownership with a goal of increasing overall understanding in order to manage, reduce, transfer, or eliminate threats to supply chain success.

- The perils of transportation are many and varied. Managers must remain vigilant to all types of risk and work to discover, define, document, and communicate risks before they adversely affect freight flows.

- It is not enough to identify risks. Managers must work to understand how serious each risk is to the organization. They must assess both the likelihood of a disruption risk occurring and the consequences of a disruption incident.

- Transportation managers must be proactive in developing specific action plans and procedural changes to address supply chain risks. Response options include risk avoidance, reduction, transfer, or retention.

- Risk is a never-ending challenge. Organizations must establish a repetitive, measurable, verifiable risk monitoring process to remain focused on existing and emerging transportation disruptions.

- Given their respective levels of importance to the U.S. economy and citizens, a delicate balance must be struck between transportation security and the efficient flow of global commerce.

- Security is not the responsibility or domain of a single group. Government and industry must collaborate on legislation, programs, and agreements to secure global supply chains. MTSA, AMR, C-TPAT, FAST, and other programs are solid examples of these cooperative initiatives.

STUDY QUESTIONS

1. Describe the concepts of disruptions and risks as they apply to transportation. Why are they important from financial and service standpoints?

2. Risk management consists of a series of steps that should be followed to reduce the consequences of disruptions. Briefly discuss these steps.

3. Six different categories of transportation risk were discussed in the chapter. Identify these categories, describe them, and give transportation examples for each risk categories.

4. Risk analysis is a critical component of risk management. When conducting this activity, what are the two components of risk that must be analyzed? Why are they important?

5. What are the key outputs of a risk assessment process? What should be done with these outputs?

6. What does it mean when a company tries to mitigate their transportation risk? How can they accomplish this?

7. What is the role of insurance in transportation risk management?

8. Why is risk management considered to be a continuous loop process?

9. Describe the challenges that governments and organizations face when addressing transportation security risks?

10. What steps is the U.S. government taking to reduce transportation security risks related to global trade?

11. What roles can business and industry play in the creation of globally secure transportation networks?

NOTES

1. "Wordnet Search, 3.0" Retrieved January 10, 2009 from: http://wordnetweb.princeton.edu/perl/webwn?s=disruption

2. Adapted from Handfield, Rob, "Avoid Supply Chain Risk," *sascom Magazine,* 2nd Quarter, 2007. Retrieved January 10, 2009 from: http://www.sas.com/news/newsletter/business/2007_06_26.pdf

3. "Wordnet Search, 3.0" Retrieved January 10, 2009 from: http://wordnetweb.princeton.edu/perl/webwn?s=risk

4. Viktoriya Sadlovska, Melissa Spinks, and Robert Shecterle, *Supply Chain Risk Management: Building a Resilient Global Supply Chain,* Boston, MA: The Aberdeen Group, 2008.

5. Kevin Hendricks and Vinod Singhal, "Association Between Supply Chain Glitches and Operating Performance," *Management Science,* Vol. 51, No. 5, 2005.

6. "Risk Management Definition and Additional Resources from BNET." Retrieved January 10, 2009 from: http://dictionary.bnet.com/definition/Risk+Management.html

7. "Business Continuity Planning (Continuity Planning and BCP) Definition." Retrieved January 10, 2009 from: http://www.bitpipe.com/tlist/Business-Continuity-Planning.html

8. Karl Davey, "Basic Risk Management Process," *Acquisition Community Connection,* (June 2003). Retrieved January 11, 2009 from: https://acc.dau.mil/CommunityBrowser.aspx?id=17752&lang=en-US

9. Michael Wolfe, "In This Case Bad News is Good News," *Journal of Commerce,* July 26, 2004, p. 38.

10. "Commercial Motor Vehicle Facts." Retrieved January 11, 2009 from: http://www.fmcsa.dot.gov/facts-research/facts-figures/analysis-statistics/cmvfacts.htm

11. David Schrank and Tim Lomax, *The 2007 Urban Mobility Report,* College Station, TX: Texas Transportation Institute, 2007.

12. Rosalyn Wilson, *19th Annual State of Logistics Report,* Oak Brook, IL: Council of Supply Chain Management, 2008.

13. M. Theodore Farris II, "Are You Prepared for a Devastating Strike in 2008?" *Transportation Journal,* January 2008.

14. "JISC InfoNet – Qualitative Risk Analysis." Retrieved January 15, 2009 from: http://www.jiscinfonet.ac.uk/InfoKits/risk-management/qual-analysis

15. "Anticlue: Qualitative Risk Analysis." Retrieved January 15, 2009 from: http://www.anticlue.net/archives/000817.htm

16. Mark S. Dorfman, *Introduction to Risk Management and Insurance 9th Edition,* Englewood Cliffs, NJ: Prentice Hall, 2007.

17. Jim LeTart, "Six Steps to Secure Global Supply Chains," *Supply and Demand Chain Executive,* July 28, 2008. Retrieved January 15, 2009 from: http://www.sdcexec.com/online/article.jsp?siteSection=6&id=10581&pageNum=1

18. United States Department of Homeland Security, *Strategy to Enhance International Supply Chain Security,* (July 2007). Retrieved January 18, 2009 from: http://www.dhs.gov/xlibrary/assets/plcy-internationalsupplychainsecuritystrategy.pdf

19. United States Department of Energy, "The Maritime Transportation Security Act of 2002." Retrieved January 18, 2009 from: http://www.eia.doe.gov/oil_gas/natural_gas/analysis_publications/ngmajorleg/mtransport.html

20. United States Customs and Border Protection, "CSI in Brief." Retrieved, January 18, 2009 from: http://www.cbp.gov/xp/cgov/trade/cargo_security/csi/csi_in_brief.xml

21. United States Customs and Border Protection, "Rules for Improving Cargo Security." Retrieved, January 18, 2009 from: http://cbp.customs.gov/xp/CustomsToday/2004/March/Other/rules_cargosecurity.xml

22. United States Customs and Border Protection, "C-TPAT Overview." Retrieved, January 18, 2009 from: http://cbp.gov/xp/cgov/trade/cargo_security/ctpat/what_ctpat/ctpat_overview.xml:http://cbp.gov/xp/cgov/trade/cargo_security/ctpat/what_ctpat/ctpat_overview.xml

23. United States Department of Homeland Security, "Free and Secure Trade (FAST) Implementation on the US/Mexico Border." Retrieved January 18, 2009 from: http://www.dhs.gov/xnews/releases/press_release_0309.shtm

24. Barchi Peleg-Gillai, Gauri Bhat, and Lesley Sept, *Innovators in Supply Chain Security: Better Security Drives Business Value,* Washington DC: The Manufacturing Institute, 2006.

CASE 9-1

Young Again Pharmaceuticals

Cliff Crandall, senior director of transportation for Young Again Pharmaceuticals (YAP), is gearing up for his company's most critical product rollout in more than a decade. YAP has developed a breakthrough liquid suspension that reverses the ageing process for anyone over 35 years of age. Available only by prescription, the new product has been dubbed "Twenty-something in a Bottle" by the media. Demand is expected to be very high despite the outlandish price tag of $395 for a month's supply.

The product is being manufactured in YAP's San Juan, Puerto Rico laboratory and will be distributed to major retail pharmacies in the United States and Canada. Crandall is responsible for selecting the mode and contracting with carriers to deliver the product. He is concerned about the safe and timely delivery of the initial product shipments in May to the retailers' distribution centers. The product is high value, somewhat fragile, and of interest to thieves. Some product, stolen from the laboratory, has already appeared on auction websites.

In an effort to make effective transportation decisions and minimize YAP's risks, Crandall decided to hold a brainstorming session with his logistics team before signing any carrier contracts. The discussion of key risks produced the following list of concerns:

- "If shipments are late or incomplete, retailers will penalize us with vendor chargebacks. You know they will hit us with small fines for delivery mistakes."
- "I'm worried about shipment delays or freight loss from hurricanes in the Atlantic Ocean."
- "You've got to consider temperature sensitivity issues. If the product freezes, we won't be able to sell it."
- "I've been reading about all the piracy problems experienced by ocean carriers. You know, a 20-foot container of our product has a retail value of nearly $275,000."
- "I'm more concerned about theft of individual cases at ports and while the product is on the road."
- "We're looking at border delays and Customs fines if we don't properly document and mark our freight."
- "Our brand image will take major damage if the product gets into unauthorized distribution channels due to theft or misdirected deliveries."
- "The company sustainability push has led to reduced packaging and biodegradable packing materials. If the cartons get wet or bounced around, we're going to end up with a lot of damaged, unsellable product."
- "Those major East Coast ports can get very congested during peak shipping season. That will cause delays."

By the time the meeting was over, Crandall realized that he needed to spend some time looking into these issues. While he was pretty sure that some problems were remote, Crandall thought that it would be wise to evaluate each one. His new concern became how to conduct an effective risk assessment.

CASE QUESTIONS

1. Assess the risks identified in the brainstorming session. Create and populate a table similar to Figure 9-2.

2. Based on your answer to Question 1, what are the three primary risks that you believe YAP must address? Why?

3. What do you recommend that YAP do to mitigate each of the three risks identified in Question 2?

4. What should YAP focus on after attempting to mitigate these transportation risks?

CASE 9-2

Tiger Golf

Ricky Magness, vice president of procurement for Tiger Golf Unlimited (TGU), is looking to bring his company out of a slump. Sales have been flat and TGU is a mere six months away from the most important industry event of the year, the PGA Merchandise Show. During the trade show, TGU will introduce a new line of golf clubs that almost magically correct the most common maladies of golfers—slices, worm burners, and duck hooks. The company is very excited about the product line and has staked its future on this rollout. Demand is expected to be very high and profits will soar—if Magness can find a low cost manufacturer to build the product and fill the U.S. supply chain immediately following the PGA Merchandise Show.

Magness has been traveling the globe in search of a high quality, low cost supplier for the clubs. He is also wary of product espionage that could lead to copycat clubs filling the market too quickly. After conducting a thorough analysis of twelve different manufacturers, Magness has narrowed his consideration to three potential suppliers:

- Supplier 1 is located in Kuala Lumpur, Malaysia. The company has experience making golf products, boasts excess factory capacity, and produces a tremendous knock-off of the Callaway Big Bertha line of golf clubs. Product prices are reasonable but ocean freight rates and insurance costs are high due to required transit through the Malacca Straits. The product is made available at the Port of Kelang and is 670 MYR (Malaysian Ringgit) per set.

- Supplier 2 is located in Wulumuqi, China. The company is a former state-owned maker of Red Army military supplies. The far inland location creates a very low labor cost but increases the length of supply lines and the distribution channel. The factory-based cost of the product is $149 U.S. per set.

- Supplier 3 is located in Edinburgh, Scotland. The company is a world-class manufacturer of golf clubs and is used by nearly every major club manufacturer in the United States and Europe. They are somewhat constrained by factory capacity and road congestion to the port, but promise to meet all deadlines. The cost of the product, delivered to the Port of Charleston, South Carolina is £165 (British Pound) per set.

Before making a final supplier selection, Magness thought that it would be wise to confer with Moe Hanna, TGU's vice president of logistics, and Larry Himmer, the director of transportation. The three executives met at company headquarters to compare the options. Hanna was impressed by the thoroughness of the supplier evaluation process and production cost analysis. In contrast to his boss, the transportation director launched into a tirade. He gave a very impassioned speech about off-shore manufacturing risks and possible transportation disruptions. Himmer also kept talking in acronyms about new security regulations and more paperwork requirements.

By the time the meeting was over, Magness was worried. Had he missed something in his analysis or was Himmer ranting aimlessly about a nonissue? Magness decided that the analysis of the three potential suppliers should take on another dimension—supply chain risk and what could be done about it.

CASE QUESTIONS

1. What issues should Magness evaluate in his assessment of transportation risks?

2. Analyze each supplier option that Magness is considering. What specific risks does each supplier option present?

3. Which supplier would you recommend that Magness choose to best balance company goals with supply chain risk?

4. What types of security issues and requirements will confront TGU if they off-shore manufacturing?

Chapter 10

GLOBAL TRANSPORTATION PLANNING

Learning Objectives

After reading this chapter, you should be able to do the following:

- Discuss the relationship between international trade and global transportation
- Identify the three critical flows in global supply chains
- Recognize the importance of proper global transportation planning
- Understand the role of Incoterms in determining transportation responsibilities, risks, and costs
- Describe the payment term options available to exporters and importers
- Appreciate the value of timely, accurate global freight documentation
- Analyze the key issues in effective international transportation mode and carrier selection
- Evaluate the critical factors in route design for international shipments

Transportation Profile	Global Trade Hits 60 Year Low

After decades of growing world imports and exports, a severe global trade slump hit in late 2008. The problem, according to *Business Week,* is that globalization and risky actions by banks, investors, and consumers created soaring global debt. Michael Mandel notes, "The huge trade surpluses in such countries as China, Japan, and Germany created a flood of liquidity that pushed up asset prices and encouraged borrowing around the world. In turn, the high debt levels boosted consumption and investment and fueled demand for imports. Moreover, cheap credit made it easy for importers and exporters to finance their globe-spanning transactions."

When the recession set in and the financial bubble burst, "creative" financial institutions, leveraged businesses, and overextended consumers found themselves in severe trouble. The days of easy credit ended quickly as banks endured a liquidity crisis and severely curtailed lending. Heavy job losses occurred as companies went into survival mode, and the real estate market stagnated as prices plummeted and foreclosures skyrocketed in the United States and other countries. The impact on global trade was swift and devastating. The volume of world trade in 2009 was expected to decline by 11.9 percent, according to the International Monetary Fund (IMF). Such a decline has not been experienced since the Great Depression 60 years ago.

As 2010 nears, two questions loom. First, which countries will be hardest hit by the trade decline? Second, when will a turnaround occur? Unfortunately, there is no consensus answer to either question.

Early on, China was viewed as very vulnerable because of its heavy export activity and the rapid decline of U.S. imports. However, the decline experienced by China was far less severe than those of Taiwan and Japan. And emerging market economies like China and Brazil have begun to rebound. The United States, for all its challenges and predictions of its demise, experienced an uptick of exports in the summer of 2009.

Although the volume of trade remains well below precrisis levels, imports and exports appear to have touched bottom, according to a *Wall Street Journal* article. The IMF predicts a modest global trade increase of 2.5 percent in 2010.

If this occurs, an upward turn in trade could spur production and encourage hiring in exporting economies that are still plagued by high unemployment. However, others warn that the global economic turnaround is tentative and will not be evenly distributed among countries or industries. Also, concerns of rising protectionism and low employment growth could portend weak global demand.

There are many more predictions being put forth and the correct answers will not be known until the recovery is well under way. Volatility and uncertainty are the only guarantees at the moment.

Source: Adapted from Michael Mandel, "China Hangs Tough as Trade Crates," *Business Week,* Jan. 26, 2009, p. 28. Reprinted by special permission, copyright © 2009 by The McGraw-Hill Companies, Inc; and Sudeep Reddy, John W. Miller, and Alex Frangos, "Trade Upturn Hints at a Recovery," *Wall Street Journal,* October 10, 2009.

Introduction

The global economy is going through a highly volatile period as highlighted in the Transportation Profile. Diesel and bunker fuel prices have been largely unpredictable, thanks to the wild swings in crude oil prices (peaking at nearly $150 per barrel before

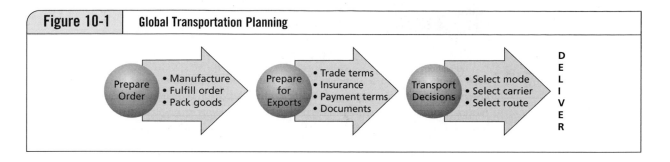

Figure 10-1 | **Global Transportation Planning**

plummeting to less than $40 per barrel in 2008). Demand for industrial and consumer products has contracted after years of unprecedented growth, due to rising prices and a global recession, and companies have struggled to secure needed financing because of the global credit crunch.

What do all these issues have in common? They create extreme challenges in the market for global transportation services. Just a few short years ago during the global trade boom, ports were testing the limits of their capacity, ocean carriers were placing orders for new ships, and freight customers were scrambling to find available containers and berths to move product to free-spending consumers. However, in a very short span of time, global trade has contracted and the transportation industry has scrambled to weather the lean times. Transportation rates have dropped and capacity is ample— good news for freight customers but not for the transportation service providers.

Despite the current economic conditions and cries for reducing import/export activity by protectionists, global trade remains a huge activity. Well over $14 trillion dollars in global merchandise export activity is anticipated for 2009, according to the World Trade Organization.[1] This level of activity, while well below the $15.8 trillion merchandise export peak in 2008, drives an ongoing need for effective global transportation services. Global transportation companies and their customers must effectively plan and manage in the current cost control focused economy. They must also position their organizations for future growth opportunities in anticipation of a more healthy global economy.

Navigating the choppy waters of a global recession is no easy task for transportation managers. However, they should not lose sight of the fundamental issues and practices that generate effective, efficient freight flows. This chapter focuses on the need for proper planning before freight leaves the exporter's shipping dock. We will discuss the global transportation industry in terms of its size, options, and critical flows. Specific planning issues related to trade terms and payment terms will be covered, followed by an overview of key transportation documents. Chapter 10 will wrap up with coverage of mode, carrier, and route selection. Throughout the chapter, you will gain a greater appreciation of the importance of the global transportation planning activities outlined in Figure 10-1.

Overview of Global Transportation

The United States is a large trading partner in the world. The United States trades with nearly all nations of the world, producing nearly $1.3 trillion in goods exports and more than $2.1 trillion in goods imports in 2008.[2] This level of foreign trade creates a tremendous level of transportation activity between the United States and its trading partners around the world. These key partners are identified in Table 10-1.

Table 10-1	U.S. Trading Partners – 2008		
COUNTRY	**GOODS EXPORTS ($ IN BILLIONS)**	**COUNTRY**	**GOODS IMPORTS ($ IN BILLIONS)**
Canada	261.4	China	337.8
Mexico	151.5	Canada	335.6
China	71.5	Mexico	215.9
Japan	66.6	Japan	139.2
Germany	54.7	Germany	97.6
United Kingdom	53.8	United Kingdom	58.6
Netherlands	40.2	Saudi Arabia	54.8
South Korea	34.8	Venezuela	51.4
Brazil	32.9	Korea	48.1
France	29.2	France	44.0
Top Ten Total	796.6	Top Ten Total	1,383.0
Grand Total	**1,291.3**	**Grand Total**	**2,112.5**

Source: U.S. Census Bureau, *FT900: U.S. International Trade in Goods and Services*, February 11, 2009.

The ten countries identified in Table 10-1 account for 62 percent of U.S. goods exports and 65 percent of U.S. goods imports. The geographic dispersion of these primary trading partners creates a need for sizable global transportation flows. Globally, more than $750 billion was spent on transportation services in 2007 to facilitate merchandise flows. Transportation accounts for 22.8 percent of world exports of commercial services, not including spending on passenger transportation.[3] On a weight basis, more than 8 billion tons of product moved in the international seaborne trade in 2007.[4]

Global transportation service is provided by all modes of transportation, including pipelines. Traffic between the United States, Canada, and Mexico is largely handled by truck and rail companies. However, non-North American freight moves via air and water transportation, with 80 and 90 percent of the global trade in goods moving via water transportation. Hence, the issues discussed in Chapter 10 and Chapter 11 will revolve around the movement of goods via these two modes.

Global Trade Agreements Stimulate Transportation Activity

The growth of global trade has been fueled by the establishment of **free trade agreements** (FTAs) around the world. This type of agreement is a pact between two or more countries or areas in which all participants agree to lift most or all tariffs, quotas, special fees and taxes, and other barriers to trade between the entities. The purpose of FTAs is to allow faster and more business between the countries or areas, which should benefit all participants. The FTA driven growth in trade between countries has led to a greater need for international freight transportation.

The United States participates in both **bi-lateral trade agreements** and **regional trade agreements**. According to the Office of the U.S. Trade Representative, the United States pursues comprehensive free trade agreements to expand opportunities for American workers, farmers, ranchers, and service providers. Currently, the United States has FTAs in effect with 14 countries: Israel, Canada, Mexico, Jordan, Chile, Singapore, Australia, Morocco, the Dominican Republic, El Salvador, Guatemala, Honduras, Nicaragua, and Bahrain.[5]

Regional trade initiatives are also a key part of U.S. trade strategy. They include the Free Trade Area of the Americas, aimed at uniting the Western Hemisphere in a free trade zone; the Enterprise for ASEAN Initiative, designed to promote trade in Asian countries; the Middle East Free Trade Initiative; and the North American Free Trade Agreement (NAFTA), which links the United States, Mexico and Canada in a free trade area of 427 million people.[6]

NAFTA was signed by leaders of Canada, the United States, and Mexico on December 17, 1992 and was ratified by Congress in early 1994. NAFTA establishes free trade between these three countries and provides the way the Agreement is to be interpreted. The treaty states that the objectives of the three countries are based on the principles of an unimpeded flow of goods, most-favored-nation (MFN) status, and a commitment to enhance the cross-border movement of goods and services. MFN status provides the lowest duties or customs fees, if any, and simplifies the paperwork required to move goods between the partner countries. NAFTA supersedes the 1988 Canada–U.S. Free Trade Agreement.

An example of the trading arrangement between the United States and Mexico that is made possible by NAFTA is a unique international operation known as a **maquiladora**. A maquiladora is a U.S. manufacturing or assembly operation located along the U.S.–Mexico border, or other locations specified by the Mexican government. U.S. raw materials and component parts are sent to the maquiladora, where the semifinished or finished product is manufactured or assembled. All or part of the maquiladora's output is subsequently returned to the United States without any Mexican import duties being paid. The U.S. companies with maquiladora operations are taking advantage of the lower labor rates in Mexico.

Although NAFTA and other trade agreements have been largely successful, work remains to be completed. One of the primary ongoing NAFTA challenges is cross-border transportation between the United States and Mexico.

Canadian motor carriers now have the same rights in the United States as U.S. truckers have in Canada. Historically a foreign carrier was not allowed to pick up and deliver shipments within the United States. Canadian carriers are now allowed to transport domestic U.S. traffic when such transportation is incidental to a return trip to Canada. For example, a Canadian trucker could deliver a load in Chicago, pick up a shipment for Detroit, and upon arrival in Detroit pick up a shipment destined to Canada.

The same accessibility is not currently available between the United States and Mexico. Under NAFTA, the United States and Mexico agreed to phase out restrictions on cross-border cargo services that allowed carriers to travel only short distances beyond their national borders. Initially, Mexican truckers would be able to travel throughout Texas, New Mexico, Arizona, and California in 1995. American truckers would have similar rights in Mexican border states. By 2000, all restrictions on cross-border trucking were to have been lifted. U.S. trucks would be able to conduct cross-border transportation to and from any point in Mexico; Mexican trucks would be able to carry cargo across the border to and from any point in the United States.[7]

Just prior to the 1995 implementation, the United States announced it would not lift restrictions on Mexican trucks, citing concerns with truck safety and illegal drug smuggling. The issue became contentious, with both countries limiting access to foreign trucks. In 2001, a NAFTA dispute settlement panel found the U.S. trucking restrictions to be in breach of its NAFTA obligations. After much back and forth dialogue, Mexico agreed in 2007 to cooperate in a joint demonstration program as a step towards full NAFTA implementation. The program allowed up to 100 trucking firms from Mexico to transport international cargo beyond the commercial zones along the U.S.–Mexico border and up to 100 U.S. trucking firms to transport international cargo into Mexico.

The Trucking Pilot Program began on September 6, 2007, and was originally designed to run for one year. By an exchange of letters between the United States and Mexican Transportation Secretaries on August 4, 2008, the Trucking Pilot Program was extended up to an additional two years to ensure that it could produce sufficient data to evaluate its safety impact. However, the recently passed omnibus spending bill ended funding for the program. President Obama signed the bill into law on March 11, 2009.

The failure to extend the program has led to retaliation by Mexico. Officials announced increased tariffs on 89 U.S. import products on March 18, 2009. In response, President Obama has tasked the Department of Transportation (DOT) and others to propose legislation to meet the NAFTA agreement that mandates allowing Mexican-licensed trucks to travel beyond commercial zones along the U.S.–Mexico border.[8] How soon action is taken and the NAFTA transportation provisions are implemented remains to be seen.

Logistics Channel Issues in Global Transportation

Global transportation involves more than the physical flow of goods via the modes mentioned above. As in any supply chain, the global flow of goods is supported by effective information flows between the **exporter** and **importer**. The flow of payments is also critical to timely completion of the transaction. Wood et al. (2002) used the concept of logistics channels or networks to describe the planning and execution of these key flows. These include the transaction channel, the communication channel, and the distribution channel.[9] Each is discussed briefly below.

Transaction Channel Activities   When purchasing goods, paying for them, and preparing for their movement, the buyer (importer) must take steps to protect its financial interests and reduce risk. The importer must effectively negotiate details with the seller (exporter) that go beyond the basics of product quality, price, and quantity. In global transactions, it is also important to clarify the location and point in time at which legal title for the goods transfers from the exporter to the importer.

Why is this so important? **Transfer of ownership** is linked to responsibility for the goods in transit. This responsibility include making key decisions regarding mode and carrier selection, **insurance** coverage, and **routing**. The transfer of ownership also determines who is responsible for payment of transportation services, insurance, and import duties. Finally, ownership determines responsibility for compliance with government regulations, management of the goods while in transit, and financial **liability** in the event of freight damage, loss, or delay. **Terms of trade**, discussed later in this chapter, help to clarify the point of transfer and the responsibilities of each party to the transaction.

Another key transaction channel activity is payment for the goods. In a global transaction, both the exporter and importer are at greater risk than in a domestic transaction. The exporter is concerned about the risk of nonpayment by the importer. Payment in advance of shipment would be the ideal choice for the exporter. However, the importer may have some apprehensions about shipment delivery and product quality. Hence, the preferred option would be payment after delivery. There are other options to moderate the risks faced by each party. These **terms of payment** options will be discussed shortly.

Communication Channel One of the major challenges in global transportation is maintaining visibility and control of freight as it move across borders and is handed off between carriers and intermediaries. Timely information sharing and the use of technology can vastly improve shipment visibility. Proper freight documentation ensures compliance with government regulations and facilitates the uninterrupted flow of goods through potential bottlenecks at border crossings and ports.

Paperwork may seem like a simple issue in this era of information technology but there are still communication channel challenges. A much larger number of documents are involved in a global transaction than in a purely domestic one. Different documents are required by the country of export, the country of import, transportation companies, banks, and the importer. Many of the documents are not yet in electronic format and copies must be distributed to each party involved in the transaction. SITPRO, a United Kingdom-based organization involved in simplifying trade processes, highlighted these paperwork challenges in a recent study. SITPRO found that each import shipment of perishable food generates over 150 documents (not all transportation related) as it moves through the cold chain from farm to store shelf.[10] Documentation and other communication channel issues are discussed later in this chapter.

Distribution Channel Managing an extended transportation network increases the potential for disruptions, with distance and complexity being the main culprits. Also, freight travels through multiple facilities and is touched by numerous intermediaries. Also, transportation infrastructure, regulations, and service options vary from country to country. As a result, global freight is at greater risk of erratic and extended transit times, freight stoppages, visibility problems, and loss of control than domestic freight.

Rather than raising their hands in surrender, global transportation managers must actively manage the distribution channel. They must recognize and act upon the need for effective transportation planning in terms of mode, carrier, and route selection. Properly matching freight to the most appropriate mode will facilitate safe and cost-efficient distribution of goods. Vigilant carrier selection processes will lead managers to reputable transportation service providers with significant experience in key markets, extensive capabilities, and a strong customer orientation. Optimal route selection from among the wide variety of options will provide for greater freight protection and more consistent service. These three distribution channel issues are covered in more detail at the end of the chapter. Other important distribution channel issues include freight protection (proper packing and loading of goods) and process control (measuring and monitoring transportation performance).

While global transportation managers must address the extended distances, longer transit times, and multiple carriers involved in the distribution channel, careful consideration of all three channels is essential to success. Managers must focus on the ownership transfer, freight control, and payment issues in the transaction channel. Also, managers must understand documentation requirements and the need to interact with multiple governments, sometimes unfamiliar sellers, and a variety of transportation service providers in the communication channel. Finally, managers must work toward coordinating decision across the three channels and making conscientious tradeoffs between them as needed.

Global Transportation Challenges

Moving freight across oceans and country borders is no simple task. Compared to domestic freight movement, global transportation of goods over long distances creates a variety of significant challenges: longer and more variable transit time, risk of in-transit product damage or loss, higher delivery and **accessorial service** expenses, and greater in-transit inventory carrying costs. These challenges must be accurately weighed against the obvious labor cost benefits of sourcing goods globally or moving production offshore.

Transportation managers must also be cognizant of broader issues that impact the availability and cost of global transportation services. Proper long-range planning of the transportation function requires that managers take the time to monitor business trends, government intervention, and consumer demand. Failure to respond to changes in these macrolevel issues will produce unnecessary risk, capacity challenges, and a competitive disadvantage.

While there are no shortages of external issues, the following challenges are worthy of further attention by global transportation managers:

Trade Level Fluctuation Significant increases in global trade activity can create major transportation challenges. From 2002 to 2007, the global transportation system came under significant pressure as global trade hit record levels. Ocean carrier capacity was at a premium, containers were hard to find, and rates rose. Major ports also suffered from severe **congestion** problems as they struggled to keep up with the heavy volume of traffic moving through their facilities. Similar problems will arise with the next trade boom. Transportation managers must prepare for these demand-driven capacity and congestion issues through strong alliances with major transportation service providers, contracts that secure long term capacity, and creative use of alternate ports and routes.

Declines in global trade activity can also wreak havoc on the transportation industry. While port congestion issues dissipate and containers become readily available, carrier capacity is not guaranteed. Many ocean and air carriers reduce frequency of service and retire older equipment during economic downturns to reduce costs and protect their pricing structure. Transportation managers must monitor transportation industry activity and work with their service providers to avoid getting caught in the capacity squeeze.

Carrier Consolidation Retailing, banking, and automobile manufacturing aren't the only industries that have been hard hit by the global recession. Air carriers are struggling to remain competitive in this very challenging environment with a 4 percent drop in cargo traffic during 2008.[11] In response, air carriers have become more selective about the routes they serve and frequency of service. Industry consolidation has also continued with the Delta/Northwest merger and the Lufthansa takeover of BMI in 2008. This carrier shrinkage diminishes cargo capacity and direct service availability, particularly to smaller markets. Transportation managers must monitor the industry dynamics and steer business toward financially stable air carriers with suitable routes.

In the ocean transportation industry, carrier capacity and route cuts have not had the intended effect of maintaining freight rates. Under the weight of mounting debt, fuel costs, and diminished traffic, financially strapped carriers are either going out of business (for instance, Senator Lines ceased operations on February 28, 2009), developing strategic alliances, or merging operations. Even the largest carriers are involved, with Neptune Orient Line bidding for Hapag-Lloyd (the world's fifth largest container line) in 2008. Concerns of oligopolistic competition, less choice, and eventual rate increases are being voiced by exporters and importers alike.[12] Transportation managers can negotiate lower rates during the lean times for the carriers but will have less choice and face higher prices as freight volume increases.

Security Risks As Chapter 9 highlighted, global transportation managers face a heightened level of risk unlike their domestic counterparts. Protection against terrorism has become a necessity in the post-9/11 world. Paperwork containing more detailed information must be shared in a timely fashion with government agencies, inspection of freight will continue to increase, and efforts to secure supply chains will become more extensive. All of these requirements will generate greater transportation cost and higher potential for freight delays.

Theft remains a major challenge in global transportation. Ship hijackings are on the rise and pirates are more brazen with the prospects of huge ransom payoffs. More than $150 million in ransom was paid in 2008 by ocean carriers.[13] Likewise, product theft from ports and other facilities continues to impact global transportation. Global cargo theft is a $50 billion per year problem and is growing.[14] Transportation managers must leverage security technology; choose transportation routes, ports, and service providers wisely; and disguise their freight to minimize exposure of their freight to terrorism, hijacking, tampering, and theft.

Shifts in Regional Sourcing Over time, production activity migrates from one region of the world to another. In the late 20th century, electronics manufacturers moved production from the United States to Mexican maquiladora plants to leverage low cost labor. Similarly, textile and clothing manufacturing moved offshore to Central America. As China, India, and other countries began to open their economies to the world, sourcing shifted from the Americas to Asia. In these sourcing shifts, transportation managers are challenged to secure adequate capacity of high quality service. Also, it is imperative that transportation and logistics cost increases related to longer supply chains do not offset the manufacturing labor savings.

The recent crude oil price spike led to higher transportation rates and **fuel surcharges**. This cost burden, combined with rising labor costs in China and problems with extended supply chains, has led companies to reassess their Asian outsourcing strategy.[15] The migration may reverse, as companies reconsider "near-sourcing" production in Mexico and other Latin American countries. As the Global Perspectives feature indicates, shorter routes to market mean lower costs and lower risks, making near-sourcing much more appealing than a few years ago. Again, transportation managers will need to develop strong relationships and cost competitive contracts with service providers to support the modified flow of goods.

The four issues discussed above have a direct impact on the flow and cost of global freight. However, there are numerous other challenges around the world that transportation managers must heed. Government **regulation** and intervention, volatile fuel prices, sustainability and global warming issues, and the financial industry meltdown each present potentially negative implications for the transportation industry and its customers. Transportation managers must remain vigilant of these external issues and their potential for disrupting the global supply chain.

Global Perspectives

Transportation Issues Encourage Near-Sourcing

In the immortal warning of the *Jaws* movie poster, "Just when you thought it was safe to go back into the water," so it is with near-sourcing.

"Last spring and summer," recalls Charlie McGee, Vice President of International Development for Averitt, "near-sourcing was hot as firecrackers." The competitive advantages that had been driving U.S. supply chains in a mad dash to China over the previous decade had seemingly all turned sour. Now, though, he's seen that wave of enthusiasm begin to ebb.

The pressures to bring sourcing closer to home came to a focus when hefty ocean fuel surcharges (remember $150 a barrel oil?) were wiping out much of the savings from cheap labor. "Lots of people started to rethink their overall supply chains," observed McGee. "Near-sourcing got pretty strong legs." This was especially true with products which are less labor intensive, like tooling and metals. The Americas started looking good again.

"We have seen a migration of both manufacturing and assembly of finished goods from Asian origins back to the Americas ... most aggressively over the past couple of years," agrees Bryan Lusby of C.H. Robinson. "It doesn't appear that any one sector is driving the move," he observes. "We are seeing supply chain re-engineering from high tech to apparel. But in general, it appears that the high cost, high duty goods are on the forefront of the activity."

There was a certain déjà vu quality to this migration, Mexico had seen an influx of U.S.-bound production before, in the 1990s—which then subsequently departed for China.

"Obviously the groundwork for much of this movement to Mexico was laid with the inception of NAFTA," says Lusby. "But many companies chose to source their manufacturing and procurement from Asia. The reasons were pretty straightforward in terms of total landed cost, as well as confidence in the supply chain dynamics ... as well as the quality of goods being produced."

WHAT CHANGED?

"The cost benefits of labor began to be outweighed by the ever increasing transportation rates for ocean and airfreight," continues Lusby. "This was driven in part by better capacity planning on the carrier sides, keeping rates on an upward trend, especially when combined with the ever increasing fuel surcharges. Additionally, the numerous examples of finished goods quality issues—from lead paint in toys to tainted food products—posed real threats to U.S. suppliers and American consumers."

Risk mitigation is another big factor that has prompted reappraisal of offshore supply chains, particularly the vulnerability associated with a distant China link. Cheap production may have been the irresistible lure in the beginning, but over time it has become clear that there is vulnerability associated with a globally stretched supply chain.

As Forrester Research recently noted, "Leading companies look beyond low cost labor and favorable tax breaks and complete detailed site selection assessments that include factors like the probability of disruption scenarios, geopolitical stability, transportation infrastructure, currency fluctuations, and IP protection laws.

The arguments for near-sourcing—lower transport costs, enhanced supply chain flexibility and responsiveness, better visibility, less logistics bottlenecks—seemed compelling, as Charlie McGee noted, until the economic downturn. The financial breakpoints, which were all pointing toward near-sourcing, suddenly eased off as the price of fuel precipitously declined. Compounding this was the excess supply in ocean transport, driving down costs. "Near-sourcing is happening more slowly, more gradually," he observes. "That's the pace that will likely be maintained." But the long-term trend is for the 're-Americanization' of a significant share of production. Little by little, people are realizing that there is no cost difference in buying and sourcing in Asia than in Mexico. And with Mexico, you get faster cycle time and reduced transportation costs. But the shift doesn't happen in one fell swoop."

Source: Adapted from Neil Shister, "Near-sourcing: The Way Forward," *World Trade,* April 2, 2009. Reprinted with permission from World Trade Magazine.

Export Preparation Activities

Long before global freight is loaded and transported to its destination, key decisions must be made and requirements completed. Four primary export preparation activities are choosing the terms of trade, securing freight insurance, agreeing upon the terms of payment, and completing the required freight documentation. These preshipment steps help to clarify responsibilities of the exporter and importer, protect each party's financial interests, improve freight control and visibility, and facilitate problem-free transport.

Terms of Trade

When a company purchases goods from an international supplier, the buyer typically focuses on product price, quality, and quantity of goods. However, transportation issues must also be considered and a number of relevant activities must take place:

- Clearing the goods for export
- Organizing the transport of goods from origin to destination, often involving multiple moves and modes
- Clearing customs in the country of import
- Arranging payment for transportation, insurance, and duties

The terms of trade specified in the contract determine which of these responsibilities are handled by the exporter (the international supplier) and which are managed by the importer (the company making the purchase). Terms of trade are extremely important because they show precisely where the exporter's responsibilities end and where the importer's responsibilities begin. They govern decision making authority for movement of the product, establish when the ownership and title of the goods pass from the exporter to the importer, and clarify which organization incurs delivery-related costs. In short, the terms of trade facilitate international trade by streamlining the process for determining responsibilities and risks related to the international transport of goods.

A very challenging situation would arise for exporters and importers if each country established their own terms of trade. Inconsistencies, changes, and interpretation issues would hamper trade. Fortunately, a harmonized set of selling terms has been established by the **International Chamber of Commerce** (ICC) to reduce some of the confusion and complexity involving international shipments. Widely known as **Incoterms**, these *In*ternational *C*ommercial *Terms* make international trade easier and facilitate the flow of goods between different countries. As described by the ICC, "Incoterms are international rules that are accepted by governments, legal authorities, and practitioners worldwide for the interpretation of the most commonly used terms in international trade. They either reduce or remove altogether uncertainties arising from differing interpretations of such terms in different countries."[16]

Since 1936, Incoterms have provided standard trade definitions for international sales contracts. They have been revised and refined six times since the original set was put into effect. The most recent set of trade rules, known as Incoterms 2000, refine the 1990 rules by providing additional information on the use of intermodal transportation and clarifying the loading and unloading requirements of both buyer and seller. Incoterms address matters relating to the rights and obligations of the parties to the contract of sale with respect to the delivery of goods sold. In practical terms, it isn't possible to effectively develop a contract price for goods until the exporter and importer agree upon the Incoterm to be used in the transaction.

There are 13 specific Incoterms available to exporters and importers. All apply to ocean transport, while only seven of them are appropriate for air, rail, truck, and intermodal transportation. Figure 10-2 indicates the proper usage of each Incoterm by mode. Also, Incoterms are typically expressed as three letter acronyms with a named location and the Incoterms version used to avoid any confusion. For example, a properly completed Incoterm description on a document would read: "DEQ, Long Beach, California, USA, Incoterms 2000" to indicate that the exporter is responsible for the goods until they are unloaded at the Port of Long Beach.

The terms are broken down into four primary groups. The E term is used when the importer takes full responsibility from point of departure; F terms are used when the main carriage is not paid by the exporter; C terms are used when the main carrier is paid by the exporter; and D terms are employed when the exporter takes full responsibility to the point of arrival. Each group is discussed in more detail below.

E Terms The E terms consist of one Incoterm, **Ex Works (EXW)**. This is a departure contract that gives the importer total responsibility for the shipment. The exporter's responsibility is to make the shipment available at its facility. The importer agrees to take possession of the shipment at the point of origin and to bear all of the cost and risk of transporting the goods to the destination. Table 10-2 identifies additional responsibilities of the E term.

F Terms The three F terms obligate the exporter to incur the cost of delivering the shipment cleared for export to the carrier designated by the importer. The importer

Figure 10-2 Incoterms Applicability by Mode

Table 10-2	Importer/Exporter Responsibility											
EVENT	EXW	FCA	FAS	FOB	CFR	CIF	CPT	CIP	DAF	DES	DEQ	EXW	DDP
Exporting packing, making, labeling	E	E	E	E	E	E	E	E	E	E	E	E	E
Export clearance	I	E	E	E	E	E	E	E	E	E	E	E	E
Transport from origin to port	I	E	E	E	E	E	E	E	E	E	E	E	E
Load main carrier	I	I	I	E	E	E	E	E	E	E	E	E	E
Select main transport	I	I	I	I	E	E	E	E	E	E	E	E	E
Unload main carrier	I	I	I	I	I	I	I	I	I	I	E	E	E
Cargo insurance	I	I	I	I	I	E	I	E	E	E	E	E	E
Import clearnace, pay duty & taxes	I	I	I	I	I	I	I	I	I	I	E	I	E
Transport from port to destination	I	I	I	I	I	I	I	I	I	I	I	E	E
	I = Importer			**E** = Exporter									

selects and incurs the cost of main transportation, insurance, and customs clearance. **Free Carrier (FCA)** can be used with any mode of transportation. Risk of damage is transferred to the importer when the exporter delivers the goods to the carrier named by the importer.

Free Alongside Ship (FAS) is used for water transportation shipments only. The risk of damage is transferred to the importer when the goods are delivered alongside the ship. The importer must pay the cost of "lifting" the cargo or container on board the vessel.

Free On Board (FOB) is used for only water transportation shipments. The risk of damage is transferred to the importer when the shipment crosses the ship's rail (when the goods are actually loaded on the vessel). The exporter pays for loading. See Table 10-2 for additional responsibilities on the F Terms.

C Terms The four C terms are shipment contracts that obligate the exporter to obtain and pay for the main carriage and/or cargo insurance. **Cost and Freight (CFR)** and **Carriage Paid To (CPT)** are similar in that both obligate the exporter to select and pay for the main carriage (ocean or air to the foreign country). CFR is only used for shipments by water transportation, whereas CPT is used for any mode. In both terms, the exporter incurs all costs to the port of destination. Risk of damage passes to the importer when the goods pass the ship's rail, CFR, or when delivered to the main carrier, CPT.

Cost, Insurance, Freight (CIF) and **Carriage and Insurance Paid To (CIP)** require the exporter to pay for both main carriage and cargo insurance. The risk of damage is the same as that for CFR and CPT. See Table 10-2 for additional responsibilities of the C Terms.

D Terms The D terms obligate the exporter to incur all costs related to delivery of the shipment to the foreign destination. There are five D terms; two apply to water transportation only and three to any mode used. All five D terms require the exporter to incur all costs and the risk of damage up to the destination port.

Delivered At Frontier (DAF) means the exporter is responsible for transportation and incurs the risk of damage to the named point at the place of delivery at the frontier of the destination country. For example, DAF, Laredo, Texas, indicates the exporter is responsible for making the goods available at Laredo, Texas. The importer is responsible for customs duties and clearance into Mexico. DAF can be used with all modes.

Delivered Ex Ship (DES) and **Delivered Ex Quay (or wharf) (DEQ)** are used with shipments by water transportation. Both terms require the exporter to pay for the main carriage. Under DES, risk of damage is transferred when the goods are made available to the importer on board the ship uncleared for import at the port of destination. The importer is responsible for customs clearance. With DEQ, risk of damage is transferred to the importer when the goods cleared for import are unloaded onto the quay (wharf) at the named port of destination.

Delivered Duty Unpaid (DDU) and **Delivered Duty Paid (DDP)** are available for all modes. DDU requires the exporter to incur all cost, except import duties, to the named place in the country of importation. Risk of damage passes to the importer when the goods are made available, duties unpaid, at the named place. (DDU is similar to DES.) DDP imposes the same obligations on the exporter as DDU, plus the additional responsibility of clearing the goods for import and paying the customs duties. (DDP is similar to DEQ.) See Table 10-2 for additional responsibilities of the D Terms.

Proper choice of Incoterms will go a long way toward the effective balancing of responsibilities for international transportation between the exporter and the importer. Key determinants of Incoterm selection include the relative expertise of each firm as well as their willingness to perform the required tasks. Other relevant factors include the type of product being sold, the mode of transportation being used, and the level of trust between the firms.[17]

Finally, it is important to realize that Incoterms do not cover every aspect of an international delivery. Incoterms do not constitute a contract between the exporter and importer. Figure 10-3 summarizes what responsibilities and obligations that Incoterms do and do not address.

Figure 10-3	Role of Incoterms

Incoterms are used to define the relationship between Exporter and Importer regarding:	Incoterms will not:
• Mode of delivery	• Define contractual rights
• Arrangement of customs clearances and licenses	• Specify transport details regarding delivery of goods
• Passage of title	• Define liabilities and/or obligations between the parties
• Transfer of risk and insurance responsibilities (i.e., who has to insure goods during transport)	• Dictate how the title of the goods will pass (although Incoterms dictate when they transfer)
• What the delivery terms are	
• How transport costs are shared between the parties	• Dictate obligations with regards to the goods prior to and after delivery
• When a delivery is completed	• Protect a party from his/her own risk of loss

Source: Transportgistics, *Deciphering Incoterms.* Available from http://www.transportgistics.com/decipheringincoterms.htm.

Cargo Insurance

One of the issues addressed by Incoterms is responsibility for insuring the freight. The organization assuming this role faces one of the most complex issues in global transportation. Cargo insurance is challenging because of the unique terminology, centuries-old traditions, and confusing set of regulations that limit carrier liability.

Regardless of the challenges, cargo insurance is critical. Importers and exporters are exposed to countless perils and financial risks when their freight moves through the global supply chain. They must determine their insurable interests and how to most effectively manage risk. Each of these insurance related issues are introduced below.[18]

Financial Risks Trying to recover financial losses from international carriers for freight damage or loss is difficult and time consuming. Thanks to regulations like the Carriage of Goods by Sea Act (COGSA), an ocean carrier's liability is limited to $500 U.S. per customary shipping unit. However, COGSA regulations eliminate this liability in 17 defensible situations. The regulation states that neither the carrier nor the ship shall be responsible for loss or damage arising or resulting from fire, perils of the sea, acts of God, acts of war, labor stoppage, insufficient packaging, and nine other circumstances.[19]

Similarly, an air carrier's liability is minimal in comparison to the true value of the cargo as air cargo tends to consist of expensive products. Also, liability is limited in cases of inherent defect, cargo quality or vice, defective packaging, acts of war or armed conflict, or an act of public authority carried out in connection with the entry, exit, or transit of the cargo. Carrier liability, as determined by the Warsaw Convention of 1929, was limited to $9.07 per pound. Subsequent changes to the regulations, most recently the Montreal Protocol No. 4, changed the liability level to 17 Special Drawing Rights (SDR) per kilogram. This is approximately $25.45 per kilogram based on current rates of $1.497 = 1 SDR.[20] Still, this amount will not adequately compensate an importer or exporter for the actual value of lost or damaged high value goods.

In both modes, the burden of proof is on the importer or exporter to prove that the carrier was at fault. With all the liability limitations provided in the regulations, substantiating carrier responsibility can be very difficult. If they cannot prove fault, importers and exporters have little legal recourse against international carriers.

Transportation Perils International cargo is subject to a wider array of loss and damage risks than domestic freight. This is due to the extended origin-to-destination distance, number of transfers between carriers, and varying climatic conditions. In particular, ocean freight faces considerable obstacles to loss- and damage-free delivery:

- Cargo movement—ocean freight is subject to a harsh ride with the ship moving in six different directions (heave, pitch, roll, surge, sway, and yaw) during a voyage
- Water damage—water from storms and waves can infiltrate cargo
- Overboard losses—cargo containers can be lost overboard during storms
- **Jettison**—cargo may be purposely dumped overboard to save the ship or prevent further cargo losses
- Fire—most dangerous cargo (chemicals, ammunition, and so forth) moves via ocean transport, creating fire and explosion risk
- Sinking—catastrophic storms and waves can overwhelm ships and cause them to sink along with the cargo
- Stranding—mechanical breakdowns, storms, groundings, and other problems can lead to damaged or delayed freight

- **General average**—loss or damage to another customer's freight is shared by all parties involved in the voyage
- Theft—cargo theft, particularly during dwell time at ports and overland transport, adds up to billions of dollars yearly
- Hijacking—pirate attacks on ocean ships is prevalent, with freight being delayed for ransom or stolen
- Other risks—freight contamination, vessel collision, government delays, and port strikes can cause freight loss[21]

International freight moving via air or rail face perils, though they are minimal compared to ocean freight. Air cargo is a very safe mode with limited risk of loss due to crashes or accidents. Movement risk exists as cargo can shift during takeoff or landing and turbulence can occur during transit. Cold temperatures can also be a problem for sensitive freight. Also, theft is an ongoing challenge, particularly when freight sits idle at air forwarder and freight terminal facilities.

Managing Risks   The financial threats and transportation perils for international cargo should not be ignored. Exporters and importers must actively manage these risks. They have three options at their disposal: **risk retention**, **risk transfer**, or take a mixed approach.

Retaining the risk is essentially a strategy of self-insurance. A company may determine that it is more economical to forego cargo insurance for the anticipated risks. The company is taking a calculated gamble that the potential loss or damage would be less expensive than the cost of insurance. The risk retention strategy can make sense for very large exporters and importers that can absorb occasional losses, ship low value goods or goods that are not susceptible to damage, or have extensive experience and extreme confidence in their carriers. Unfortunately, some companies retain risk through ignorance because they do not understand the scope of risks involved in international transportation or the limits of carrier liability.

Risk transfer means that a company shifts its potential problems to an insurance company through the purchase of a cargo insurance policy. There are a wide variety of policies available to the customer to cover both freight loss and General Average liability in ocean shipping.[22] Insurance can be obtained through carriers, freight forwarders, or directly from an insurance company. Insurance makes sense when a company's operations would be severely impacted by a loss; the goods are valuable, susceptible to damage, or a theft target; or the perceived risk is too high.

The mixed approach is a combination of self-insurance and risk transfer to an insurance company. Just as an individual may reduce their insurance policy costs through a higher deductible in the event of a loss, exporters and importers can use deductibles to reduce insurance costs. The company must take the time to identify and analyze its risks, determine if they are significant enough to transfer, and negotiate a customized contract with an insurance provider for the amount above the maximum financial exposure that it is willing to risk.

Insurable Interests   A company has an **insurable interest** in cargo when loss or damage to it would cause the company to suffer a financial loss or certain other kinds of losses. The owner of goods in transit has a financial stake in the safe arrival of the goods. This may be the importer or exporter, depending on the Incoterm used.[23] However, even if the importer doesn't own the goods during main transit (under DES, for instance), it still has an interest in making sure the goods arrive safely to the destination. Should the exporter not provide adequate insurance coverage of the goods, the importer can obtain supplemental coverage to protect itself against loss.[24]

Why is this important? An insurance contract is legally binding only if the purchaser has an insurable interest and the interest is insurable. Without it, the carrier is not obligated to pay loss and damage claims.

Terms of Payment

The financial transaction creates another area of risk for the exporter and the importer. Exporters are concerned about nonpayment for goods that are sold internationally. Often, they don't have personal experience with the importer, there may be limited information available on the creditworthiness of the importer, and there is limited legal recourse if the importer fails to pay for the goods. Also, the cost of litigation or mediation in the country of import is high. Hence, exporters are rightfully cautious about extending credit to global customers. Importers may also have concerns regarding payment timing and methods. When dealing with an unfamiliar supplier, an importer will not want to pay for goods without a guarantee that product quality, quantity, price, and delivery are consistent with the terms laid out in the contract.

Balancing the risks of the two parties can be challenging. Exporters would reduce their risk of nonpayment by demanding cash in advance. However, doing so creates a risk of losing business to a more aggressive competitor. Importers would reduce their risk of product problems by purchasing goods on **open account**. However, demanding this option may cause potentially excellent suppliers to walk away from the business. Fortunately, there are middle ground alternatives to facilitate trade without placing all financial risk on one party.

A **letter of credit** (LC) is a financial instrument that ensures that the exporter gets paid and the importer receives the goods as expected. The importer's bank issues the LC to the exporter. The customer's bank charges a fee to the importer to issue a LC. The LC essentially guarantees that the bank will pay the seller's invoice (using the customer's money or line of credit) provided that the goods are delivered in accordance with the terms stipulated in the LC. These terms should reflect the contractual agreement between the seller and buyer. LCs are often complex documents that require careful drafting to protect the interests of buyer and seller. Table 10-3 highlights key issues related to this payment term.

Drafts, sometimes called bills of exchange, are similar to an importer's check. Like checks used in domestic commerce, drafts carry the risk that they will be dishonored. However, in international commerce, title does not transfer to the importer until the draft is paid, or at least engages a legal undertaking that the draft will be paid when due.

A **sight draft** is used when the exporter wishes to retain title to the shipment until it reaches its destination and payment is made. Before the shipment can be released to the importer, the original ocean bill of lading (the document that evidences title) must be properly endorsed by the importer and surrendered to the carrier.

A **time draft** is used when the exporter extends credit to the buyer. The draft states that payment is due by a specific time after the buyer accepts the time draft and receives the goods (for example, 30 days after acceptance). By signing and writing "accepted" on the draft, the buyer is formally obligated to pay within the stated time.[25]

Table 10-3	International Terms of Payment			
METHOD	USUAL TIME OF PAYMENT	GOODS AVAILABLE TO BUYER	RISK TO SELLER	RISK TO BUYER
Cash in Advance	Before shipment	After payment	None	All – relies on seller to ship goods exactly as quoted and ordered
Letter of Credit	After shipment is made, documents presented to the bank.	After payment	Gives the seller assurance of payments. Depends on the terms of the letter of credit.	Assures shipment is made but relies on exporter to ship goods as described in documents. Terms may be negotiated to alleviate buyer's degree of risk.
Sight Draft	On presentation of draft to buyer.	After payment to buyer's bank.	If draft not honored, goods must be returned or resold. Storage, handling, and return freight expenses may be incurred.	Assures shipment but not content, unless inspection or check-in is allowed before payment.
Time Draft	On maturity of the draft	Before payment, after acceptance	Relies on buyer to honor draft upon presentation.	Assures shipment but not content. Time of maturity allows for adjustments, if agreed to by seller.
Open Account	As agreed, usually by invoice	Before payment	Relies completely on buyer to pay account as agreed	None

Source: Adapted from Foreign Trade On-Line, *International Terms of Payment*. Available from http://www.foreign-trade.com/reference/payment.cfm.

Freight Documentation[26]

Freight documents control the cargo on its journey from origin point in the country of export to its final destination in the country of import. Missing or incorrect paperwork can cause delays and additional costs. Recall, for example, the advanced manifest regulations discussed in Chapter 9. A failure to provide complete cargo information 24 hours prior to loading at an international seaport can lead to denial of loading, fines, and penalties. Paperwork errors can also lead to Customs clearance delays, additional inspection, and improper application of duty rates. Hence, proper and accurate documentation is critical to the timely and cost-efficient flow of international cargo.

Documentation requirements are governed by the customs regulations of the exporting and importing nations. Because these regulations differ, the number and types of documents required may vary widely, depending on the origin and destination of the shipment. Experts suggest that exporters and importers enlist the assistance of a freight forwarder to handle the formidable amount of documentation, as forwarders are specialists in this communication channel process.

In general, international cargo travels with four types of documents: invoices, export documents, import documents, and transportation documents. Each is briefly discussed below, with an emphasis on the transportation paperwork category.

Invoices A critical document in both international and domestic transaction is the invoice (or bill) for the goods. The exporter sends this document to the buyer requesting payment for the goods being sold. That sounds fairly straightforward, but the international invoice requirements are more complex and there are multiple types of invoices that may be involved in the transaction.

The most common billing document is the **commercial invoice**. This invoice accompanies the shipment unless the terms of payment dictate that the commercial invoice is sent directly to the importer or a bank involved in the transaction. Precision is the key for commercial invoices as they are often used by governments to determine the true value of goods when assessing customs duties. Governments that use the commercial invoice to control imports will often specify its form, content, number of copies, language to be used, and other characteristics.

As the sample commercial invoice in Figure 10-4 indicates, a commercial invoice must contain a precise description of the product, quantities, and value, as well as the country of origin. These factors are critical as they may impact the duty rates applied to the shipment. Other important information includes the Incoterms used in the transaction, delivery related charges paid by the exporter, and details regarding the companies engaged in the transaction (buyer, seller, shipping origin, and shipping destination). Payment terms and currency in which the payment is to be made should also be clearly stated.

Other types of invoices include the **pro-forma invoice** and **consular invoice**. The pro-forma invoice is a sales quote in an invoice format that may be required by the buyer to apply for an import license, contract for preshipment inspection, open a letter of credit, or arrange for transfer of hard currency. This document is used by the importer to better understand the total landed costs for a potential order and provides information for price quote comparisons. A consular invoice is a document prepared by the exporter and certified in the country of origin by a consul of the country of importation. It shows the transaction details and origin of the goods.

Export Documents Many countries require companies selling product abroad to keep track of the type of goods being exported. Much of this requirement is focused on maintaining accurate trade statistics but there are exceptions. In the case of strategic materials (such as military items, telecommunications equipment, computer technology, and so forth) and national treasures, the government wishes to maintain control of the outflow of goods. Sometimes, a government may prevent exporters from selling these materials to customers in certain countries. In other situations, government authorization is required to export these goods. An **export license** is the government document that authorizes the export of these specific goods in specific quantities to a particular destination.

The **Shipper's Export Declaration** (SED) is used to control exports and act as a source document for official U.S. export statistics. The SED must be prepared by the exporter for all shipments exceeding a nominal value ($500 for goods shipped via the U.S. Postal Service and $2,500 for goods moving via any other method of transportation). Also, SEDs must be prepared, regardless of value, for all shipments requiring an export license or destined for countries restricted by Export Administration regulations. The document is given to the transportation service provider for presentation to U.S. Customs and Border Protection at the port of export.[27]

A **Certificate of End Use** is a document intended to assure authorities in the exporting country that the product will be used for legitimate purposes (for example, enriched uranium will be used to operate a nuclear power plant rather than in nuclear weapons). End-use certificates are provided by the importing country's government. Other export documents may be required, depending on the country of export and the ultimate

Figure 10-4	Sample Commercial Invoice

COMMERCIAL INVOICE

DATE OF EXPORT	TERMS OF SALE	REFERENCE	CURRENCY
11/21/09	FAS - Qingdao, China	LL-01-23-1962	US DOLLAR

SHIPPER / EXPORTER	CONSIGNEE
Jinto Exports Intl. 2390 Xinhua East Hohhot, Niemongol, 00010 86-471-6607777	Moberg Enterprises 5549 Bobcat Ave. Athens, Ohio, US 45700 (740) 559-1000

COUNTRY OF ULTIMATE DESTINATION	IMPORTER *(IF DIFFERENT THAN CONSIGNEE)*
UNITED STATES	

COUNTRY OF MANUFACTURE
China

OCEAN BILL OF LADING NUMBER
95G630587-X1

FULL DESCRIPTION OF GOODS	WEIGHT (LBS.)	QUANTITY	UNIT VALUE	TOTAL VALUE
TC0085 TOOL CART	10230.00	220	58.00	12760.00
CJ01 ROLLING RACK	17500.00	500	35.00	17500.00
			0.00	0.00
SUB-TOTAL	27730.00	720		30260.00

TOTAL NO. OF PACKAGES	Shipped via Maersk AVON From Quingdao, China to New York, USA Container No: CIU32587440		
720		FREIGHT COSTS	3593.00
		INSURANCE COSTS	490.00
		ADDITIONAL COSTS	0.00
	TOTAL INVOICE VALUE		**$ 34,343.00**

I hearby certify that this invoice shows the actual price of goods described, that no other invoice has been issued, and that all particulars are true and correct.

SIGNATURE OF SHIPPER / EXPORTER

Sen Yiaboi

PRINT NAME HERE

destination of the cargo. They facilitate government collection of export taxes and control of export quotas.

Import Documents Numerous commercial documents are required by the governments of importing countries. The documents are intended to protect its citizens from inferior quality products, properly classify products for collection of duties, and limit the importation of products that the government finds inappropriate. Some import documents are quite onerous to obtain or complete. These documents create artificial trade barriers to protect certain industries from foreign competition.

The **Certificate of Origin** is a widely required import document. It is a statement that the goods were shipped from the country in which the exporter is located. The exporter's Chamber of Commerce attests to the shipment's origin but not the location of production. That information is provided by a **Certificate of Manufacture**. This document must be signed by the Chamber of Commerce in the exporting manufacturer's country. Both are used by importing countries to determine which tariff to apply to the goods.

A **Certificate of Inspection** attests to the authenticity and accuracy of the goods. An independent company inspects the goods and confirms that they conform to the description contained in the commercial invoice. This document is used in situations where the payment terms involve a letter of credit or documentary collection. Other types of import documents include **phyto-sanitary certificates** which ensure that plants being imported meet regulations regarding pests, plant diseases, chemical treatments, and weeds; a **certificate of analysis** which attests to the composition and purity level of products as stated in the commercial invoice; and a **certificate of certification** provided by an independent inspector that confirms goods conform to the manufacturing standards of the importing country.

Transportation Documents The disruption-free flow of goods also depends upon the availability of key transportation documents. Typically, freight carriers will not accept cargo unaccompanied by thorough and accurate paperwork. Otherwise, it will be difficult to create an accurate **manifest**. This internal carrier document lists the exact makeup of the cargo, its ownership, port of origin and port of destination, handling instructions, and other key information. Given the importance of an accurate manifest for security regulation compliance, carriers will just as soon leave cargo behind rather than risk Customs penalties and fines.

The primary transportation document is the **bill of lading**. This document acts as a contract of carriage between the transportation company and the cargo owner—either the exporter or importer, depending on the Incoterm used. As the contract, this document specifies the price and instructions for moving the freight. The bill of lading also serves as a receipt for the goods. When the transportation company signs the document, it is acknowledging that it has received the cargo in good condition in the right quantity. For international shipments, an **ocean bill of lading** is used for water transport and an **air waybill** is used for air carrier shipments. Figure 10-5 provides a sample ocean bill of lading.

Various bill of lading types exist. A **through bill of lading** is a contract that covers the specific terms agreed to by a customer and carrier. This document covers the domestic and international transportation of export merchandise. It differs from an **intermodal bill of lading** only in the liability of freight forwarders and carriers for freight problems. Finally, bills of lading may be negotiable or non-negotiable. If the bill of lading is non-negotiable, the transportation carrier is required to provide delivery only to the consignee named in the document. If the bill of lading is negotiable, the person with ownership of the bill of lading has the right of ownership of the goods and the right to reroute the shipment.

Additional documents facilitate the transport of international cargo. A **packing list** is a detailed inventory of the contents of a shipment. It is considerably more detailed and informative than a standard domestic packing list. The packing list itemizes the material in each individual package and indicates the type of package, such as a box, crate, drum, or carton. It also shows the individual net, legal, tare, and gross weights and measurements for each package (in both United States and metric systems).[28]

Figure 10-5	Sample Bill of Lading

MAPLE LEAF INTERNATIONAL CONTAINER LINES

OCEAN BILL OF LADING

SHIPPER/EXPORTER	BOOKING NO.	
	EXPORT REFERENCES	
CONSIGNEE/IMPORTER	FORWARDING AGENT FMC NO.	
	POINT AND COUNTRY OF ORIGIN OF GOODS	
NOTIFY PARTY	ALSO NOTIFY - ROUTING AND INSTRUCTIONS	

INITIAL CARRIAGE BY	PLACE OF INITIAL RECEIPT	
EXPORTING CARRIER	PORT OF LOADING	LOADING PIER TERMINAL
AIR/SEA PORT OF DISCHARGE	PLACE OF DELIVERY BY ON CARRIER	TYPE OF MOVE

PARTICULARS FURNISHED BY SHIPPER

MARKS AND NUMBERS	NO. OF PACKAGES	DESCRIPTION OF PACKAGES AND GOODS	GROSS WEIGHT	MEASUREMENTS

SHIPPERS DECLARED VALUE $_____ SUBJECT TO EXTRA FREIGHT   FREIGHT PAYABLE AT BY

CHARGES AS PER TARIFF AND CARRIERS LIMITS REFER TO CLAUSE 16 HEREOF

FREIGHT CHARGES	PREPAID	COLLECT	Received the goods, or packages said to contain goods herein mentioned, in apparent good order and condition unless otherwise indicated, to be transported and delivered as herein provided.
			The carriage is subject to the provisions of the U.S. Carriage of Goods by Sea Act of 1936. All the terms and conditions of the Carrier's regular form Bill of Lading, as filed with the Federal Maritime Commission available to any shipper or consignee upon request, are incorporated with due force and effect as if they were written at length herein, and all such terms and conditions so incorporated by reference are agreed by the Shipper to be binding and to govern the relations, whatever they may be between those included in the words "Shipper" and "Carrier" as defined in Carrier's regular form Bill of Lading. IN WITNESS WHEREOF the Carrier has signed and the Shipper has received THREE (3) original bills of lading, ONE of which being accompanied, the others to stand void.
			BY: _____
			As agent for Maple Leaf International
TOTAL CHARGES			**BL. No.**

A **shipper's letter of instructions** is a document that spells out the requirements for handling in-transit goods. It is an important document when the cargo is susceptible to damage or requires special attention (such as live animals and plants, temperature sensitive goods, and so forth). Special documentation may also be required for dangerous or hazardous goods.

Despite the widespread availability of Internet resources, **electronic data interchange**, and other information technology tools, the transportation industry is still largely paper-based. The **International Air Transport Association** (IATA) estimates that the average airfreight shipment generates up to 30 different paper documents. These paper-based processes are not cost effective, nor do they serve the pressing needs for security and speed that are the key characteristics of air cargo.[29] Similar challenges exist in the ocean transport industry.

The IATA has begun an initiative called *e-freight* to replace the most widely used paper documents (packing lists, invoices, certificate of origin, and others) with electronic messages. The goal is to reduce costs while improving transit times, accuracy, and the competitiveness of air freight. The IATA plans to replace 20 air freight documents with electronic messages by 2010 via the e-freight system. Average annual net benefits of up to $4.9 billion across the air cargo supply chain are envisioned.[30]

Government agencies are also developing technology based systems to remedy the paper chase. Substantial improvements have been made to computerize various documents and processes, but these automation improvements have not been made in all countries. Canada has a computerized system called the Pre-Arrival Review Process for Canadian imports. In the United States, Customs and Border Protection (CBP) has developed the Automated Brokers Interface System and the Automated Export System to facilitate trade. Automation of import border processing is the goal of Automated Commercial Environment (ACE), the CBP commercial trade processing system. ACE is intended to enhance border security while expediting legitimate trade.[31] The Transportation Technology feature reveals that the multiyear development effort is moving forward but problems have slowed the progress of ACE.

Transportation Technology

Creating the Automated Commercial Environment: A Multiyear Journey

Visit the U.S. Customs and Border Protection (CBP) website, and you will learn that the Automated Commercial Environment (ACE) is the United States' commercial trade processing system, designed to automate border processing, to enhance border security, and to foster our nation's economic security through lawful international trade and travel. ACE is intended to replace the current import processing system, called the Automated Commercial System (ACS). ACE is part of a multiyear CBP modernization effort that is being deployed in phases. As it is envisioned, ACE will provides a solid technology foundation for all border security initiatives within CBP, and will:

- Allow trade participants access to and management of their trade information via reports
- Expedite legitimate trade by providing CBP with tools to efficiently process imports/exports and move goods quickly across the border
- Improve communication, collaboration, and compliance efforts between CBP and the trade community
- Facilitate efficient collection, processing, and analysis of commercial import and export data
- Provide an information-sharing platform for trade data throughout government agencies

Initial work on the design and development of ACE began in August 2001. In late 2003, the ACE Secure Data Portal was introduced. The ACE Secure Data Portal is an interactive online tool that provides a single user-friendly gateway to access CBP information via the Internet. Almost any entity doing business with CBP can now establish an ACE portal account, thereby taking advantage of a consolidated approach for tracking activity in a single comprehensive, account-based view.

Since its initial rollout and enhancements, ACE has been deployed nationally to all land border ports. More than 15,500 ACE portal accounts have been established and more than $36 billion in duties and fees have been collected in ACE. Today, there are over 100 downloadable and customized reports available in the ACE Portal. The Reports feature can be used as a management business tool to analyze and track operational, financial, and compliance data. Other current functions include Periodic Monthly Statement processing, which allows users to consolidate periodic daily statements and pay on a monthly basis; the ACE Truck Manifest System, which supports electronic data interchange for the transmission of required electronic cargo information to create a secure and streamlined environment for processing and releasing cargo at the land borders; and Entry Summary, Accounts, and Revenue capabilities that provide enhanced account management functions, a single source for master data, and an integrated, account-based financial and entry summary processing system.

Still, the $3 billion project faces some challenges, according to a recent *Journal of Commerce* article. In 2008, new modules for electronic vessel and rail electronic manifests failed testing. This problem threw other new ACE features off schedule. Upon correction of the problems, CBP plans to introduce modules that will process the most common types of import entries. This will allow CBP to shut down ACS and shift needed funding to ACE and needed system upgrades.

Initially scheduled for completion by 2012, ACE remains a work in progress. Future phases will include account enhancements and reference data, as well as new business process functionality relating to post release and finance processes. Also scheduled for the future are Cargo Control and Release functions for all modes of transportation. This critical functionality will eventually allow CBP to provide technical updates to refresh, remodel, and remake the entire automated cargo control environment into a true multimodal manifest application. Cargo Control and Release will seamlessly support all modes of transportation and bring new functionality to the trade community and CBP field users.

Source: R. G. Edmonson, "Automated Commercial Environment," *Journal of Commerce,* January 12, 2009; and U.S. Customs and Border Protection, *ACE 101,* retrieved October 13, 2009 from www.cbp.gov/linkhandler/cgov/trade/automated/modernization/ace/ace101.ctt/ace101.pdf.

Transportation Planning

With the key export preparation activities addressed, the next phase of global transportation planning focuses on the selection of the modes, carriers, and routes by which goods will be delivered. While trade terms and documentation issues are fairly technical and their execution is methodical, global transportation managers have the opportunity to be strategic and innovative when choosing transportation providers and routes. These decisions must align with corporate strategies, control risk, and provide the required level of customer service. Also, the transportation costs generated by these planning decisions must not push the **total landed cost** for products beyond a competitive level in the marketplace.

Mode Selection

The fundamental decision in global transportation is mode selection—how will goods be transported from the origin to the destination? The exporter and/or the importer will be involved in this decision, depending upon the Incoterm used for the transaction. Each party will choose the mode for the portion of the delivery for which they are responsible.

There are five traditional modes of transportation—truck, rail, water, air, and pipeline—available to the global transportation manager. Each mode has inherent service and cost advantages. While these relative advantages were covered in previous chapters, a summary is provided in Table 10-4. In an international situation, **intermodal transportation** (a combination of two or more transportation methods that will be discussed in Chapter 11) can be particularly useful.

Choosing among the modal options requires the consideration of multiple issues, according to numerous research studies that have been conducted over the years. These studies commonly identify accessibility, capacity, transit time, reliability, and product safety as the key determinants in choosing a mode. Of course, cost is another critical consideration in modal selection. A brief discussion of each mode selection factor is provided below.

Table 10-4	Comparison of Modal Capabilities				
MODE	**STRENGTHS**	**LIMITATIONS**	**PRIMARY ROLE**	**PRIMARY PRODUCT CHARACTERISTICS**	**EXAMPLE PRODUCTS**
Truck	• Accessible • Fast & versatile • Customer service	• Limited capacity • High cost	Move smaller shipments in local, regional, and national markets	High value Finished goods Low volume	Food Clothing Electronics Furniture
Rail	• High capacity • Low cost	• Accessibility • Inconsistent service • Damage rates	Move large shipments of domestic freight long distances	Low value Raw materials High volume	Coal/coke Lumber/paper Grain Chemicals
Air	• Speed • Freight protection • Flexibility	• Accessibility • High cost • Low capacity	Move urgent shipments of domestic freight and smaller shipments of international freight	High value Finished goods Low volume Time sensitive	Computers Periodicals Pharmaceuticals B2C deliveries
Water	• High capacity • Low cost • International capabilities	• Slow • Accessibility	Move large domestic shipments via rivers, canals and large shipments of international freight	Low value Raw materials Bulk commodities Containerized finished goods	Crude oil Ores / minerals Farm products Clothing Electronics Toys
Pipeline	• In-transit storage • Efficiency • Low cost	• Slow • Limited network	Move large volumes of domestic freight long distances	Low value Liquid commodities Not time sensitive	Crude oil Petroleum Gasoline Natural gas

Accessibility Freight buyers must considers a mode's ability to reach origin and destination facilities and provide service over the specified route. The geographic limits of a mode's infrastructure or network and the operating scope authorized by governmental regulatory agencies also affect accessibility. For example, moving cargo from Valparaiso, Chile to Brisbane, Australia is limited to air or ocean transport. Intermodal transportation can be used to overcome accessibility problems.

Capacity The amount of product being moved can render a mode infeasible or impractical. Transportation managers must match the capacity of a mode to the size and nature of the product being moved. Some modes are well-suited to handling a large volume of goods in an economical fashion while others are better suited to smaller goods and shipments.

Transit Time Time is a key consideration in mode selection as transportation impacts inventory availability, stockout costs, and customer satisfaction. Transit time is the total elapsed time that it takes to move goods from the point of origin to its destination (that is, door to door). This includes the time required for pickup activities, terminal handling, linehaul movement, and customer delivery. Modal speed and ability to handle pickup and delivery responsibilities greatly affect transit time.

Reliability Many companies feel that transit time reliability is more important than speed in mode selection as it impacts their ability to plan supply chain activities. Reliability refers to the consistency of the transit time provided by a transportation mode. It is easier to forecast inventory needs, schedule production, and determine safety stock levels if it is known with some certainty when goods will arrive. Internationally, reliability is impacted by distance, port congestion issues, security requirements, and border crossings—especially when the two countries do not have a proactive trade agreement.

Safety Goods must arrive at the destination in the same conditions they were in when tendered for shipment at the origin. Proper precautions must be taken to choose a mode with the ability to protect freight from damage due to poor freight handling techniques, inferior ride quality, and accidents. Fragile products (including glass and computers, so on) must be shipped via modes with the best ride quality. Temperature sensitive goods (food, pharmaceuticals, some hazardous chemicals, and so on) must move on modes with consistent warming or cooling capabilities. Perishable goods (such as magazines, newspapers, and flowers) require modes with the fastest transit times.

Cost Transportation cost is an important consideration in the modal selection decision. Transportation costs include the rate for moving freight from origin to destination plus any accessorial and terminal fees for additional services provided.

Product value must be factored into the cost analysis. If a company spends too much on transportation relative to the value of a product, they will not be able to sell the product at a competitive price. Thus, water, rail, and pipeline are generally more suitable for low value commodities, while truck and air costs can be more readily absorbed by higher value finished goods.

Other factors impact mode selection. The nature of a product—size, durability, and value—may eliminate some modes from consideration as they cannot physically, legally, and/or safely handle the goods. Also, shipment characteristics—size, route, and required speed—are important considerations. Modal capacities must be matched to the total weight and dimensions of shipments, while modal capabilities must be matched to customer service requirements. Combined, these considerations tend to limit modal selection to two or three realistic options, one of which is intermodal transportation.

The general strategy regarding modal selection focuses on determining which mode or combination of modes best suits the requirements of the global transportation buyer. This long range decision requires an analysis of the best fit and balance between modal capabilities, product characteristics, supply chain requirements for speed and service, and transportation cost. Short of major price, infrastructure, service quality, or technological changes in the modes, the decision does not need to be revisited frequently.

Carrier Selection

After the modal decision has been made, the global transportation manager's attention turns to selecting individual service providers within the mode. Like the modal decision, carrier selection is based on a variety of shipment criteria and carrier capabilities: geographic coverage, transit time average and reliability, equipment availability and capacity, product protection, and freight rates.

A major difference between modal and carrier selection is the number of options available to the transportation manager. Numerous trucking options exist for short distance cross-border transportation. Multiple ocean and air carriers serve major trade routes for intercontinental cargo movement. However, the number of carrier options is shrinking in all primary modes. Difficult economic conditions have led to carrier mergers, bankruptcies, and service area consolidation.

Another difference is the frequency of the decision. Carrier selection requires more active and frequent engagement of the transportation buyer than does the more long-range modal selection decision. This engagement does not focus on choosing a new carrier for each freight move; it focuses more on the transportation buyer remaining vigilant and managing the performance of chosen carriers. It is critical to monitor each carrier's service level and freight rates on an ongoing basis. Should carrier performance deteriorate, it may be necessary to select new service providers.

The type of service provided within a mode impacts carrier selection. Most carriers have their roots in one of two types of service—direct service or indirect service. Direct service provides immediate point-to-point flows of goods. Chartering an entire ship for a voyage would be an example. Indirect service requires interim stops and/or transfer of freight between equipment. Using a portion of a regular-route containership is a common indirect option. Time and effort must be expended in evaluating service requirements and matching them to potential carrier capabilities, quality, and price.

Within a mode, most carriers have the capabilities to provide a similar level of service, but these service levels can and do vary greatly from one transportation company to another. Also, since the cost structures are essentially the same for carriers in a given mode, their rates tend to be aligned for a given movement. Given this similarity, transportation rates tend not to be the most important criterion in carrier selection. Service performance is the key determinant for this decision. Carrier selection research suggests that reliability of on-time delivery and on-time pickup, technical capabilities, carrier response to emergencies, information sharing, freight damage experience, carrier financial stability, and total transit time are among the most important criteria to transportation service buyers.[32]

Carrier selection strategy commonly focuses on concentrating the transportation buy with a limited number of carriers. Using a small group of carriers helps the organization leverage their purchasing dollars for lower overall rates, build relationships with service providers who gain a better understanding of freight flows and requirements over time, and allows the organization to effectively monitor performance of the carrier base. A core carrier strategy takes this concentration focus to a greater depth with the organization narrowing their carrier base to a select few service providers that have proven to be the best carriers in terms of service quality and cost efficiency. Even with these strong alliances, global transportation managers must remain vigilant, monitoring carrier performance, rates, and financial stability. Having a contingency plan with backup carriers will protect exporters and importers from prolonged capacity loss or disruptions.

Route Planning

Routing planning and delivery scheduling activities are not trivial—they involve big dollars, impact customers, and can cause major headaches if not properly managed. Conceptually, they are not difficult problems to understand but they are challenging to solve, particularly with the long distances and multiple route options involved in global transportation.

It would be easy to assume that route planning is the responsibility of the carrier chosen to move freight. In general, that is true, but global transportation managers must not take a total hands-off approach to this topic. They should be involved because effective routing impacts customer satisfaction, supply chain performance, and organizational success. Transit time and on-time performance depend heavily on proper scheduling and sequencing of stops. Effective routing also helps avoid unfriendly countries, poorly equipped ports, and congested border crossing points that may drastically delay cargo flows.

Efficiency is another major issue, given the sheer amount of money spent on transportation. Globally, over $1 trillion is spent on freight transportation services. Carriers and their customers must develop more efficient routes that maximize equipment capacity utilization. They also need to use routes that control expenses related to tolls, port costs, and other service surcharges. The On the Line feature reveals that ocean carriers are weighing multiple route options to limit these expenses.

Product safety is the third concern when developing routes, particularly for surface transportation. Major trouble spots for hijacking, product theft, and piracy such as the Gulf of Aden and the South China Sea should be factored into route planning. Land routes with poor quality roads and freight handling capabilities may also pose problems. Though more time consuming and potentially more expensive from a transportation standpoint, using an indirect or circuitous route may mitigate a much larger risk of product loss.

While these operational impacts are easy to understand, it is important to note that routing is not a standalone function that is planned independently of other global transportation processes. Routing decisions must be integrated into a larger transportation strategy that supports global supply chain excellence. Thus, the global transportation manager must coordinate mode selection, carrier selection, route planning and other transportation decisions. These decisions must also be properly aligned with global sourcing, inventory, and demand fulfillment strategies.

On the Line

Ocean Carriers Seek Creative Cost- Cutting Solutions

Given the combined challenges of slowing global trade, overcapacity, and depressed rates, ocean carriers are doing all they can to cut operating costs. Key strategies include the concept of "slow steaming," altering routes, and scrapping older, less efficient ships.

Slow steaming is viewed by ocean carriers as a way to reduce fuel expenses while having a positive impact on the environment. In 2007, Maersk Line initiated a comprehensive study on 110 vessels, which shows that despite the traditional policy of 40–60 percent as the minimum engine load, it is safe to go as low as 10 percent. This makes it possible for container ships to sail at half speed, thereby significantly reducing not only fuel costs but also CO_2 emissions.

Being able to select any given speed, down to 10 percent engine load, enables a more flexible voyage and schedule planning as well as reducing fuel expenses by 10 to 30 percent. For a post-Panamax container ship, it amounts to saving US $1 million, 3,500 tons of fuel, and cutting 10,000 tons of CO_2 emission per year, according to the Maersk website. The company has been recognized as the Sustainable Shipping Operator of the Year by Sustainable Shipping.

Altering routes to avoid expensive waterways, canals, and ports is possible because importers and exporters are not demanding fast services. The slower service allows companies to use ships as temporary in-transit warehouses, which frees up space in landside facilities. Ocean carriers benefit from not incurring the added operating costs.

For example, *Traffic World* reports that some container lines are routing their Asia-to-Europe vessels around the Cape of Good Hope at the southern tip of Africa. The voyage is longer, but the savings are significant.

Likewise, carriers are considering a route from Asia to the U.S. east coast around Cape Horn at the southern tip of South America. This avoids routing the ships through the Panama Canal and its expensive tolls. It is estimated that a ship loaded with 2,000 40-foot-long containers pays US $250,000 to transit the canal.

"Our calculations do indicate that it might very well be beneficial to go south of the Horn with some of our vessels," said Morten Englestoft, chief operating officer of Maersk Line in Copenhagen in the *Traffic World* article. "Given the significant cost of going through the (Panama) canal, we have to explore all the alternatives."

Such radical routing changes are possible only due to overcapacity in the ocean carrier industry, low fuel costs, and lack of discounts for Suez Canal and Panama Canal tolls, according to a *Logistics Management* article. Few carriers have actually taken action, but the threat of rerouting may be enough to pressure canal authorities to cut or freeze tolls.

Finally, carriers are planning to scrap smaller container ships as new, larger vessels are delivered. These megaships were ordered years ago when the industry was growing quickly. Though not currently needed, it is not feasible for carriers to now cancel the orders, as deposits of 30 to 40 percent were paid, according to *American Shipper*.

Ed Zaninelli, vice president of OOCL, believes that the new, larger ships will replace older, smaller ones. He says that it's cheaper to keep the larger ships running as they are more efficient—even if they are half empty on a voyage.

Source: Patrick Burnson, "Ocean Shipping: Cool, Calm Correction," *Logistics Management,* September 2009; Peter T. Leach, "Looking for Options," *Traffic World,* February 23, 2009; and "Who's Making Money?" *American Shipper,* July 2009.

SUMMARY

- Moving goods globally adds layers of complexity to transportation decision making. Extensive planning efforts must be made to prepare for these extended cargo movements.

- The global flow of goods must be supported by effective information flows between the exporter and importer, as well as the timely flow of payments to complete the transaction.

- Global transportation creates a variety of significant cargo challenges: longer and more variable transit time, risk of in-transit product damage or loss, higher delivery expenses, and greater in-transit inventory carrying costs.

- Four primary export preparation activities must be addressed before moving cargo: choosing the terms of trade, securing freight insurance, agreeing upon the terms of payment, and completing the required freight documentation.

- Proper choice from among the 13 Incoterms should be based on the relative expertise of the exporter and importer and will effectively balance responsibility for international transportation.

- Importers and exporters are exposed to unique financial risks and countless perils when their freight moves through the global supply chain. Hence, cargo insurance is a critical risk mitigation tool.

- Letters of credit and other payment tools can be used to balance the exporter's risk of nonpayment with the importer's risk of product problems and fraud.

- Four types of documentation are used to control global cargo: invoices, export documents, import documents, and transportation documents.

- Global mode selection involves the analysis of accessibility, capacity, transit time, reliability, safety, and cost. Often, only one or two of the five modes are realistic options given the product and shipment characteristics.

- Carrier selection is based on a variety of shipment criteria and carrier capabilities: geographic coverage, transit time average and reliability, equipment availability and capacity, product protection, and freight rates.

- Route planning for global shipments is important as it affects transportation cost, product availability, and cargo security.

STUDY QUESTIONS

1. Why is global transportation such an important issue?

2. Why is transportation planning an important aspect of global freight movement? What types of planning must be done?

3. Identify and describe the three channels involved in global transportation.

4. What types of transportation challenges must organizations take into account when considering global sourcing?

5. What is the role of trade terms in global transportation? Briefly describe the four groups of Incoterms.

6. What risks and perils are present in global transportation? Discuss how exporters and importers can manage these risks.

7. What payment options are available for international transactions? How does each option protect the interests of the exporter and the importer?

8. Why is documentation important to global transportation? Briefly describe the primary documents used to facilitate global cargo flows.

9. How do governments use the information contained in global freight documents?

10. What factors impact mode selection for global transportation?

11. How does global carrier selection differ from mode selection?

12. When developing transportation routes for global freight, what considerations should influence the decision maker?

NOTES

1. World Trade Organization, *World Trade 2008, Prospects for 2009,* March 23, 2009. Retrieved April 8, 2009 from: http://www.wto.org/english/news_e/pres09_e/pr554_e.htm

2. U.S. Census Bureau, *FT900: U.S. International Trade in Goods and Services,* February 11, 2009. Retrieved April 8, 2009 from: http://www.census.gov/foreign-trade/Press-Release/2008pr/12/

3. World Trade Organization, *International Trade Statistics 2008,* Retrieved April 10, 2009 from: http://www.wto.org/english/res_e/statis_e/its2008_e/its08_trade_category_e.htm#top

4. United Nations Conference on Trade and Development, *Review of Maritime Trade,* 2008.

5. Office of the United States Trade Representative, *Bilateral Trade Agreements.* Retrieved May 11, 2009 from: http://www.ustr.gov/Trade_Agreements/Bilateral/Section_Index.html

6. Office of the United States Trade Representative, *Regional Trade Agreements.* Retrieved May 11, 2009 from: http://www.ustr.gov/Trade_Agreements/Regional/Section_Index.html

7. United States Department of Transportation, *NAFTA Transportation Provisions.* Retrieved May 11, 2009 from: http://www.fmcsa.dot.gov/intl-programs/naftatrans.htm

8. "President Obama Blinks in NAFTA Truck Dispute," *Refrigerated Transporter.* Retrieved May 11, 2009 from: http://refrigeratedtrans.com/carriers-shippers/obama-nafta-dispute-0318

9. Donald. F. Wood, Anthony Barone, Paul Murphy, and Daniel Wardlow, *International Logistics* 2nd ed., (New York, NY: AMACOM, 2002).

10. Chris Gillis, "WCO Ponders Future," *American Shipper,* May 2008, 6–11.

11. International Air Transport Association, *Cargo Plummets 22.6 Percent in December,* January 29, 2009. Retrieved April 10, 2009 from: http://www.iata.org/pressroom/pr/2009-01-29-01.htm

12. Simon Heaney, "Top 20 Container Lines," *American Shipper,* September 2008.

13. Stephanie McCrumman and Ann Scott Tyson, "U.S. Negotiations with Somali Pirates Continue," *Washington Post,* April 9, 2009.

14. NaviTag Technologies, *Cargo Theft.* Retrieved April 10, 2009 from: http://www.navitag.com/product/industry.htm

15. Sean Murphy, "Will Sourcing Come Closer to Home?" *Supply Chain Management Review,* September 2008.

16. International Chamber of Commerce, "The 13 Incoterms – FAQs About the Basics." Retrieved April 13, 2009 from: http://www.iccwbo.org/incoterms/id3038/index.html

17. Pierre David, *International Logistics,* (Cincinnati, OH: Atomic Dog Publishing, 2004), 53.

18. For an extensive discussion of international insurance, see Pierre David, *International Logistics,* (Cincinnati, OH: Atomic Dog Publishing, 2004), Chapter 8.

19. CEVA, *The Basics of Cargo Insurance.* Retrieved April 13, 2009 from: http://loginet.eaglegl.com/web/insurance-basics.cfm

20. International Monetary Fund, *Currency Units per SDR for April 2009.* Retrieved April 13, 2009 from: http://www.imf.org/external/np/fin/data/rms_mth.aspx?SelectDate=2009-04-30&report Type=CVSDR

21. Pierre David, *International Logistics,* (Cincinnati, OH: Atomic Dog Publishing, 2004), 145–154.

22. Discussion of various insurance policy types can be found in Pierre David, *International Logistics,* (Cincinnati, OH: Atomic Dog Publishing, 2004), Chapter 8.

23. *Principles of Cargo (Marine) Insurance.* Retrieved April 13, 2009 from: http://resources.alibaba.com/topic/17982/Principles_of_Cargo_Marine_Insurance_.htm

24. Pierre David, *International Logistics,* (Cincinnati, OH: Atomic Dog Publishing, 2004), 155.

25. Unz & Co., *A Basic Guide to Exporting.* Retrieved April 14, 2009 from: http://www.unzco.com/basicguide/c12.html

26. Unless otherwise noted, information in this section is derived from Pierre David, *International Logistics,* (Cincinnati, OH: Atomic Dog Publishing, 2004), Chapter 7.

27. Unz & Co., *A Basic Guide to Exporting.* Retrieved April 14, 2009 from: http://www.unzco.com/basicguide/c10.html

28. Ibid.

29. International Air Transport Association, *IATA E-Freight: Vision and Mandate,* February 2009. Retrieved April 20, 2009 from: http://www.iata.org/NR/rdonlyres/9D0873C1-B76D-40A6-9895-25E04B2073B3/0/IATAefreightvisionandmandateFeb2008.pdf

30. International Air Transport Association, *IATA E-Freight: Generic Benefits Presentation,* April 2009. Retrieved April 20, 2009 from: http://www.iata.org/NR/rdonlyres/F53FBD30-F189-49CA-A58C-B3F5385AB558/0/IATAEFbenefitspresentationF.pdf

31. U.S. Customs and Border Protection, *ACE 101,* June 25, 2008. Retrieved April 20, 2009 from: http://www.cbp.gov/linkhandler/cgov/trade/automated/modernization/ace/ace101.ctt/ace101.pdf

32. Shane R. Premeaux, "Motor Carrier Selection Criteria: Perceptual Differences between Shippers and Motor Carriers," *Transportation Journal* (Winter 2002).

CASE 10-1

Music Explosion - Developing a "Sound" Global Transport Plan

Music Explosion (ME) produces those really annoying car speakers that rattle your windows. A typical set of ME speakers retails for $350 and weighs 10 pounds. However, they are a bit bulky at 6 cubic feet per set (1.5 × 1.5 × 1). The speakers are not overly susceptible to damage, though moisture can be a problem.

The company manufactures their "Blasters" speaker line in San Diego for U.S. distribution. The company's growth is waning and ME is preparing for expansion into the Pacific Rim, starting with Japan, Taiwan, and Australia, to turn things around. Nick Jagr, company president, has negotiated most of the issues to sell Blasters through automotive aftermarket retailers in those countries. You have been brought onboard to handle the transportation issues related to the company's initial effort in global fulfillment.

During your first day, Jagr holds a fast paced meeting that bounces across multiple topics. He occasionally mentions the global expansion project and makes some offhand comments that are relevant to your new position as director of global transportation. Since you want to make a positive day-one impression, you have taken as many notes as possible and written down numerous Jagr quotes. They read:

> "The local market for our product is sad, sad, sad. We need to join the global marketplace but don't want to play with fire. Let's take a measured approach."

> "Our negotiations are going well but these retailers want to nail down trade terms with those three letter acronyms before signing on the dotted line. I tried to tell them that you can't always get what you want, but they were pretty insistent on those trade terms."

> "We've got little experience with global freight. Still, we want to play some role in the transportation process or the retailers will ask for huge discounts. One buyer mentioned "Incoterms" and taking on responsibilities. We better get up to speed on that or they'll put us between a rock and a hard place."

> "I think that a middle-of-the-road transportation strategy is on target. We should manage the transportation process up to a point and then hand it over to our distributors and retailers. Somehow this relates to those Incoterms."

> "We have to tumble the dice and pick a mode of transport that balances service and cost. I like the idea of air freight."

> "I think that this international expansion is really going to work out well. Is it just my imagination, or are we still overlooking some transportation issues? One of the carriers vying for the business mentioned documentation as being critical."

After a few more rambling statements, Jagr got up and began to walk out of the meeting. Before leaving, he turned to you and said, "Welcome to the show. Get your initial thoughts for our global transportation strategy worked out and email it to me. Be quick, time is *not* on our side."

CASE QUESTIONS

1. Given the information in the case, which Incoterms group (E, F, C, or D) should ME pursue as the exporter? Why?

2. Based on your response to Question 1, what responsibilities and risks will ME assume?

3. Which mode of transportation should ME use to move Blasters to their new markets? What benefits does it bring?

4. Why should ME worry about something as mundane as paperwork? What documents must they prepare?

5. Identify and describe other global transportation issues that Jagr may be overlooking.

CASE 10-2
A Megapixel Opportunity

Alex Delvecchio is the senior electronics buyer for MegaShop, a discount chain with 1,800 stores in Canada, Mexico, and the United States. In preparation for the upcoming holiday season, Alex was reviewing the supplier options for digital camera model JX-25 sold under the MS Platinum private label. This particular model of camera is forecast to sell 40,000 units over the next 12 months.

He had received three proposals from suppliers in different countries. They were all reasonably priced, high quality cameras and worthy of further study, but Alex had some concerns about issues of delivery costs, risks, and foreign exchange rate exposure.

Option 1—continue to purchase cameras from Shinko Electric in Nagano, Japan. Product has been sourced from Shinko for the past 12 years. Sales have historically been on an open account, thereby simplifying the relationship. Quarterly shipments of 9,000 units are made in 40-foot containers under terms Incoterm CPT, Port of Long Beach. The price offered per unit for the upcoming holiday season is 19,500 JPY (Japanese Yen).

Option 2—purchase the cameras from Deep Impex, a Delhi, India–based manufacturer. Deep Impex has a solid reputation in the electronics industry and Alex nearly purchased cameras from them last year. Their offer is based on MegaShop taking a monthly delivery of 4,500 units in 20-foot containers under Incoterm FAS, Port of Mumbai. The price offered for the next year is 9,500 INR (Indian Rupees).

Option 3—purchase the cameras from Foto Technika, a distributor in Odessa, Ukraine. Foto Technika sources cameras from small contract manufacturers in Eastern Europe. Their offer is based on MegaShop taking a monthly delivery of 4,000 units in 20-foot containers under Incoterm EXW, Odessa (the Foto Technika distribution center). The price offered for the next year is $200 USD (U.S. Dollars).

As Alex considered his options, he consulted an online currency converter to evaluate the price offers. He found the following exchange rates:

1 USD = 98.77 JPY   1 USD = 50.36 INR   1 USD = 7.96 UAH (Ukraine Hryvnia)

CASE QUESTIONS

1. What is the current price per camera in USD for the Shinko Electric offer? What costs, responsibilities, and risks does MegaShop (the buyer) assume under CPT, Port of Long Beach?

2. What is the current price per camera in USD for the Deep Impex offer? What costs, responsibilities, and risks does MegaShop (the buyer) assume under FAS, Port of Mumbai?

3. What is the current price per camera in USD for the Foto Technika offer? What costs, responsibilities, and risks does MegaShop (the buyer) assume under EXW, Odessa Distribution Center?

4. What other transportation costs and issues must Alex consider to make an effective supplier selection?

5. Which of the three options would you recommend? Why?

Chapter 11

GLOBAL TRANSPORTATION EXECUTION

Learning Objectives

After reading this chapter, you should be able to do the following:

- Recognize the importance of intermodal service in global transportation execution
- Describe the intermodal options available to global transportation managers
- Discuss the importance of proper freight packing, documentation, and insurance
- Understand the government's role in safe and secure global transportation operations
- Discuss ocean transportation services, equipment options, and rate structures
- Describe international air transportation services, equipment options, and rate structures
- Understand the role of ancillary service providers in facilitating global freight flows
- Appreciate the critical roles that seaports and airports play in the global supply chain
- Articulate the customs clearance process for import goods
- Analyze current issues impacting the execution of global transportation

Transportation Profile

International Freight Challenges

The widespread availability of imported goods and books like *The World Is Flat* suggest that global access to goods is as simple as placing an order online. However, it isn't that simple, particularly when the transportation industry is experiencing turmoil. When times are good, capacity and infrastructure can't grow fast enough to handle the great volume of international trade. When times are tough, the available capacity quickly shrinks and transportation managers may have a difficult time finding available service quality and capacity.

The electronics and agriculture industries have recently run into the latter problem with air cargo capacity, according to *Traffic World*. A February 2009 article reports that "rising costs and declining demand pushed many passenger airlines to reduce flights late last year and in the first quarter, sharply curtailing the belly space available to shippers."

Between the lax import-export activity and modal shift from air to ocean service among cost-conscious companies, neither demand nor capacity is expected to grow any time soon. Trade via international air is expected to decline by one percent from 2008 through 2013, according to an August 2009 article in *American Shipper*.

Tougher security regulations also affect the flow of air freight. The Transportation Security Administration's (TSA) Certified Cargo Screening Program pressures forwarders and airlines to screen goods before loading. This goal can negatively impact service speed of airlines and air cargo companies. It also may affect product quality of perishable items like fruit and seafood, which are packed and sealed at specific temperatures for shipping. Opening the boxes for inspection compromises the temperature and puts the product at risk of contamination and spoilage.

The unpredictability of petroleum prices challenges all modes, but particularly air transportation. In 2008, every dollar increase per barrel drove an additional $464 million in fuel expenses for U.S. passenger and cargo airlines, according to the Air Transport Association. Historically, fuel expenses have ranged from 10 percent to 15 percent of U.S. passenger airline operating costs, but fuel averaged more than 35 percent in the third quarter of 2008. These costs are passed onto customers when possible through rate increases or fuel surcharges. Carriers unable to charge higher rates incur major financial losses and may not survive.

There is no single solution to help international carriers overcome these three challenges of capacity, regulation, and cost. Carriers must focus on the fundamentals—staying lean operationally, understanding and complying with regulations, getting ahead of trends such as volume shifts between trade lanes, maintaining customer service levels, and investing wisely in technology—to remain financially viable and competitive in a difficult economic environment.

Importers and exporters would be wise to develop relationships and contracts with such international carriers to minimize their own risks and challenges when moving freight globally.

Sources: Air Transport Association, "Energy/Fuel," Retrieved October 5, 2009 from http://www.airlines.org/economics/energy/; "Cherry Shipping Stemmed?" *Traffic World*, February 2, 2009; and, "International Air Freight 2008–2013: Turbulence Ahead," *American Shipper*, August 2009.

Introduction

If you watch the occasional transportation company advertisement on television, the focus is on simplicity and ease. "One call does it all" and "bringing the world closer" are common themes. Oh, if it were only so easy!

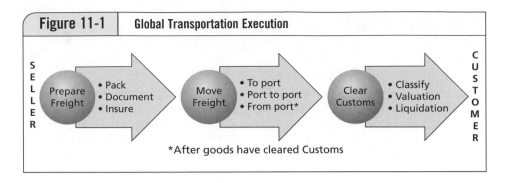

While the preparation of global shipments is a fairly straightforward activity, the real challenges begin when the freight starts to move. The global journey often involves multiple carriers from different modes, numerous border crossings, and long distances. The risk of disruptions, delays, damage, and other problems make for an eventful time whether you are importing electronics or exporting fresh produce, as revealed in the Transportation Profile feature. Whether the issue is securing enough capacity, dealing with governmental regulations, or some other unexpected problem, global transportation execution is anything but simple.

Overcoming these potential challenges to move products safely and quickly across borders requires great attention to detail and internal expertise. Flawless transportation execution also requires strong working relationships with capable transportation service providers. Following an overview of global freight flows, this chapter spotlights the key players in global transportation execution—transportation companies, third party logistics firms, port operators, and ancillary service providers. Chapter 11 wraps up with a discussion of Customs clearance. Throughout the chapter, you will gain a greater awareness of the many options available to global transportation managers (and challenges faced) as they seek to move freight with minimal complication and maximum efficiency. These key execution activities are outlined in Figure 11-1.

Overview of Global Freight Flows

The movement of goods internationally is a huge business, with spending in the world freight market estimated at $380 billion. In 2008, more than $964 billion worth of goods moved between the United States and its North American Free Trade Agreement partners, Canada and Mexico.[1] With all this freight flowing across borders, companies must proactively manage the process and make solid decisions regarding the type of service used, intermodal options, and freight preparation.

Global freight primarily moves via one of two service options—direct service or indirect service. Figure 11-2 provides a comparison of the two service types.

Direct service is commonly used in situations when international freight is moving relatively short distances between directly accessible origin and destination points. A single mode of transportation is used to move freight from the seller's location in one country to the customer's location in another country with no interim stop-offs or transfers to other modes or carriers. This on-demand type of service is effective for truckload moves across land borders, such as freight flowing from Canada to the United States or between countries on the European continent (for instance, Belgium and Italy). Relatively few

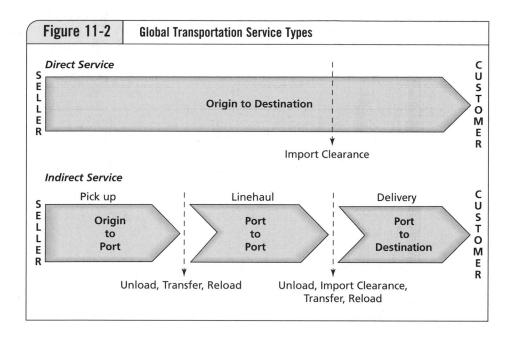

Figure 11-2 | Global Transportation Service Types

Direct Service

S E L L E R

Origin to Destination

Import Clearance

C U S T O M E R

Indirect Service

S E L L E R

Pick up — Origin to Port

Unload, Transfer, Reload

Linehaul — Port to Port

Unload, Import Clearance, Transfer, Reload

Delivery — Port to Destination

C U S T O M E R

companies have the ability to leverage this type of service via other modes as their facilities are often not accessible by train, pipeline, airplane, or ship.

Indirect service is used in situations where freight is moving long distances between continents or facilities that are not directly accessible by the mode of choice. In this type of service, freight flows are interrupted by interim stops and transfers of freight between carriers and modes. For example, freight moving from Dusseldorf, Germany to Santiago, Chile would involve three distinct moves—from the seller's location in Dusseldorf to the Port of Antwerp in Belgium via truck, from the Port of Antwerp to the Port of Valparaiso in Chile via ocean carrier, and onward to the customer in Santiago on a truck. Similar combinations are required for international air transportation as few companies are located directly adjacent to an airport. Typically, indirect service is accomplished by combining the services of different modes—that is, intermodal transportation.

Intermodal Transportation

Intermodal transportation involves the use of two or more modes of transportation in moving a shipment from origin to destination. It is often said that international transportation is intermodal transportation because so many goods moving from one country to another involve the use of multiple modes and carriers. Virtually everything moving across an ocean will involve truck or rail carriers for product pickup and delivery and an air or ocean carrier for the linehaul portion of the trip.

Shifting freight between modes may seem inefficient and time consuming, but the improved reach and combined service advantages created by intermodal transportation offsets these issues. The primary benefits of intermodalism include the following:

- *Intermodal transportation facilitates global trade.* The capacity and efficiency of ocean transportation allows large-volume shipments to be transported between continents at relatively low per unit costs. The speed of air transportation allows perishable goods to flow quickly between countries. The final domestic leg of the delivery can take place via truck. The ocean-truck combination makes product competitive across global markets by keeping the landed cost in check. The air-truck combination facilitates expedited distribution of "hot" commodities like fashion and rapid replenishment of products that are in high demand.

- *Greater accessibility is created by linking the individual modes.* The road infrastructure allows trucks to reach locations that are inaccessible to other modes, especially air transportation, water transportation, and pipelines. For example, air transportation can only move freight between airport facilities. Trucks provide the flow between the origin and departure airport as well as the arrival airport and the customer destination. Railroads can also facilitate the use of domestic river transportation and international ocean transportation. Getting low-sulfur coal from a Wyoming mine to a utility company in Japan would be best accomplished through a combination of rail and water transportation.

- *Overall cost efficiency can be achieved without sacrificing service quality or accessibility.* In other words, intermodal transportation allows supply chains to utilize the inherent capabilities of multiple modes to control cost and fulfill customer requirements. If a furniture manufacturer needed to move 20 loads of furniture from North Carolina to California for export, a combination of truck and rail transportation would improve upon truck-only service. The speed and accessibility of trucks would be used for the initial pickup and final delivery, while the cross-country transportation would be handled by the cost-efficient railroads.

Intermodal Transportation Options   It can be argued that flexibility is another valuable trait of intermodal transportation. Companies can use any combination of the five transportation modes that best suits their freight. In a global scenario, this can be valuable as transportation options may be very limited at origin points and/or destination points. That is, what works modally for one location may be unavailable for another location. Figure 11-3 highlights the most prevalent options for intermodal transportation.

Figure 11-3	Common Intermodal Combinations

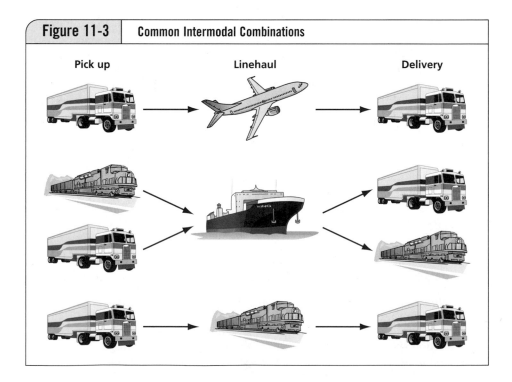

Pick up   Linehaul   Delivery

The accessibility of truck transportation makes it ideally suited for pickup and delivery of containerized international freight. Rail and barge transportation are an option for raw materials and other bulk commodities.

Large carriers (such as Canadian National, Neptune Orient Lines, and UPS) are establishing multimodal capabilities. This allows them to utilize the most efficient and economical combination of intermodal transportation for their international customers. In the majority of cases, the carrier makes the determination of what mode or modal combinations to use. After all, when customers drop overnight letters in the express delivery box, they are not concerned about the combination of modes used as long as the letters arrive on time!

Intermodal Freight Types Another valuable aspect of intermodalism is its ability to handle multiple types of freight. Whether the goods are commodities, component parts, or finished products, they can be transported by intermodal methods. The key is to have the right transportation equipment, freight handling capabilities, and transfer methods to effectively move goods between modes. The primary freight types are containerized freight and transload freight.

Containerized freight is loaded into or onto storage equipment (a container or pallet) at the origin and delivered to the destination in or on that same piece of equipment with no additional handling. For example, if a load of DVD players needed to be shipped from the factory to the market, the players would be loaded into a 40-ft container at the factory in Taiwan, transferred to the port via truck, and loaded on a containership bound for Los Angeles. Upon arrival, the container would be moved from the ship onto another truck and delivered to the retailer's distribution center.

The development of freight containers has made intermodal transportation of finished goods very economical. A standard dry box container looks much like a truck trailer without the chassis. It can be lifted, stacked, and moved from one piece of equipment to another. Dry boxes are widely used, though specialized containers are available for handling temperature-sensitive goods (refrigerated containers), commodities (tank and dry bulk cargo containers), and other unique cargoes.

A critical step in the growth of containerization and intermodalism was the development of container standards in the late 1960s. These standards defined sizes and fitting and reinforcement norms. Oceangoing containers are now built to common dimensional height and width specifications. This makes it possible to build transportation equipment to readily transport containers owned by any company and handling equipment to easily and safely transfer goods between modes.

There are five common standard lengths, 20 ft (6.1 m), 40 ft (12.2 m), 45 ft (13.7 m), 48 ft (14.6 m), and 53 ft (16.2 m). Container capacity is often expressed in **twenty-foot equivalent units (TEUs)**. An equivalent unit is a measure of containerized cargo capacity equal to one standard 20 ft (length) × 8 ft (width) container. For example, a 40-ft container is the equivalent of two TEUs. Figure 11-4 provides information regarding the capacity of widely available container sizes.

Although no universal statistics are kept on containerized intermodal transportation, there is strong evidence that containerization is growing in importance and volume. Today, approximately 90 percent of nonbulk cargo worldwide moves by containers stacked on transport ships.[2] The number of containers flowing from around the world through U.S. ports has increased nearly 30 percent between 2001 and 2005.

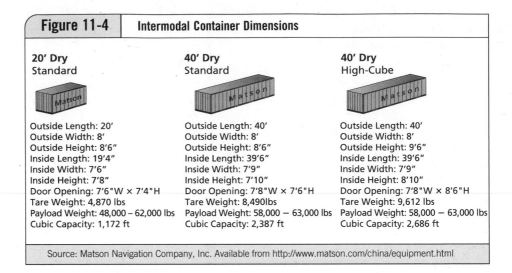

Figure 11-4 | **Intermodal Container Dimensions**

20' Dry
Standard

Outside Length: 20'
Outside Width: 8'
Outside Height: 8'6"
Inside Length: 19'4"
Inside Width: 7'6"
Inside Height: 7'8"
Door Opening: 7'6"W × 7'4"H
Tare Weight: 4,870 lbs
Payload Weight: 48,000 – 62,000 lbs
Cubic Capacity: 1,172 ft

40' Dry
Standard

Outside Length: 40'
Outside Width: 8'
Outside Height: 8'6"
Inside Length: 39'6"
Inside Width: 7'9"
Inside Height: 7'10"
Door Opening: 7'8"W × 7'6"H
Tare Weight: 8,490lbs
Payload Weight: 58,000 – 63,000 lbs
Cubic Capacity: 2,387 ft

40' Dry
High-Cube

Outside Length: 40'
Outside Width: 8'
Outside Height: 9'6"
Inside Length: 39'6"
Inside Width: 7'9"
Inside Height: 8'10"
Door Opening: 7'8"W × 8'6"H
Tare Weight: 9,612 lbs
Payload Weight: 58,000 – 63,000 lbs
Cubic Capacity: 2,686 ft

Source: Matson Navigation Company, Inc. Available from http://www.matson.com/china/equipment.html

Figure 11-5 highlights this growth. Experts predict that this trend will continue, with intermodal container volume reaching 80 million TEUs in 2015.

Other factors have contributed to the growth of containerized intermodal transportation. They include better information systems to track containers as they move through the supply chain and the development of intermodal terminals to facilitate efficient container transfers between modes. In addition, new generations of ocean vessels, railcars, and truck trailers are being built specifically to handle intermodal containers in greater quantity and with greater ease.

Transload freight includes goods that must be handled individually and transferred between transportation equipment multiple times. Transload freight primarily consists of bulk-oriented raw materials that must be scooped, pumped, lifted, or conveyed from one container to another when transferred between modes. Given the massive weight

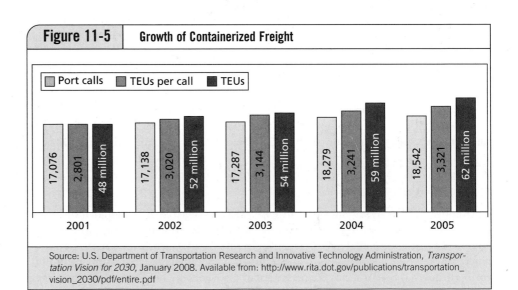

Figure 11-5 | **Growth of Containerized Freight**

Legend: ☐ Port calls ▨ TEUs per call ■ TEUs

2001: Port calls 17,076 | TEUs per call 2,801 | TEUs 48 million
2002: Port calls 17,138 | TEUs per call 3,020 | TEUs 52 million
2003: Port calls 17,287 | TEUs per call 3,144 | TEUs 54 million
2004: Port calls 18,279 | TEUs per call 3,241 | TEUs 59 million
2005: Port calls 18,542 | TEUs per call 3,321 | TEUs 62 million

Source: U.S. Department of Transportation Research and Innovative Technology Administration, *Transportation Vision for 2030*, January 2008. Available from: http://www.rita.dot.gov/publications/transportation_vision_2030/pdf/entire.pdf

and volume of these commodities requiring movement, water, rail, and pipeline are the primary modes employed. For example, orange juice concentrate may be picked up using a rail tank car, pumped into the hold of a cargo ship for the linehaul move, and then pumped into a tank truck for final delivery to the bottling facility.

Intermodal Routing The ability to use multiple modes of transportation also opens up alternative route options to all-water service. **Land bridge** transportation involves movement from one seaport to another using a combination of water and rail transport. This routing method is effective in part because the goods remain in the same container and a single bill of lading covers the entire intermodal journey. There are two primary land bridge routes used for global commerce: the Asia-America-Europe land bridge and the Asia-Europe land bridge.

The Asia-America-Europe land bridge uses a North American rail link to connect Asia and Europe. It is an alternative to moving freight across the Pacific Ocean, through the Panama Canal, and across the Atlantic Ocean. Instead, the freight moves via ocean carrier from an Asian port to a U.S. or Canadian port on the Pacific coast, then by train to an Atlantic coast port, and onward to Europe via ocean carrier. Despite the transfers between modes, the typical transit time is cut nearly in half versus all-water service. Also, ocean vessel size limitations are avoided when the ship does not have to use the Panama Canal. This allows ocean carriers to use much larger ships, which are more efficient, and to offer more frequent service.

The Asia-Europe land bridge involves moving freight via ocean from Japan and Southeast Asia to the Pacific harbors in Russia. From there, the freight moves across Russia via the Trans-Siberian Railway and onward to European destination countries by water, rail, and truck transportation. This routing avoids long-distance trips around the African continent or through the Suez Canal and the Mediterranean Sea.

A related routing option is the **mini-bridge**. This all-water alternative focuses on the combination of water and rail service with a port as the origin or destination point for the shipment. An example of an origin-focused mini-bridge is a shipment moving from Seattle to the Port of New York/New Jersey via rail and onward to Rotterdam via ocean carrier. A destination-focused mini-bridge is a shipment moving from Yokohama, Japan to the Port of Long Beach via ocean carrier with onward delivery to the Port of Savannah via rail. Such routes can save time, reduce costs, and avoid fees for using the Panama Canal.

A **micro-bridge** is similar to a mini-bridge with the main difference being the origin or destination point. This type of shipment originates or terminates at an inland port rather than an ocean port. For example, a shipment moving from Hong Kong to Atlanta would move via ocean to the Port of Oakland and onward to Atlanta via rail. This is much faster than moving the freight from Hong Kong through the Panama Canal to Charleston via ocean carrier and onward to Atlanta via truck or rail. Figure 11-6 provides examples of these three routing options.

Intermodal Challenges The most pressing issue in the intermodal transportation market is congestion. While the ocean carriers are adding capacity to meet the growing demand levels, transfer points can quickly get clogged with freight. During peak demand periods, U.S. seaport facilities along the Pacific coast have struggled to keep product flowing through their facilities in a timely fashion. Intermodal capacity problems in the rail industry have also surfaced. Equipment shortages, transfer facility congestion, and labor issues create delivery delays and supply chain disruptions.

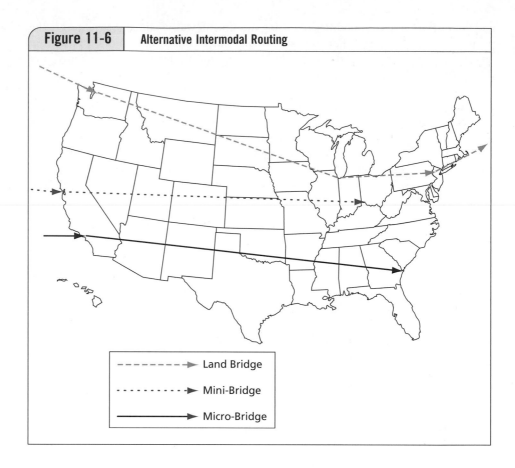

Figure 11-6 | Alternative Intermodal Routing

Land Bridge

Mini-Bridge

Micro-Bridge

Significant infrastructure investment, equipment purchases, and operator hiring will be needed to overcome existing challenges and prepare for the anticipated growth of intermodal transportation.

Preparing Freight for Movement

Recall from Chapter 10 the amount of planning that goes into moving freight across oceans and country borders. The risk of in-transit product damage and delays cannot be ignored by transportation managers in the execution phase of global transportation. During preparation for release of the freight to the transportation company, key precautions must be taken. These include preventing freight damage through protective packaging and proper packing, insuring the goods against key risks, and completing all necessary documentation.

Packing the Freight Exporters must pay attention to the stress that global transportation puts on packaged goods, particularly goods moving via ocean. Four potential in-transit problems should be kept in mind when choosing packaging materials: breakage, moisture, pilferage, and excess weight. While shipping containers provide some protection from these issues, it is critical to protect products as they are packed in shipping cartons and to protect the cartons when they are packed in the shipping container. To provide proper balance in the container, the weight must be evenly distributed.

There is a great deal of container handling and transfers during an indirect international move. Containers can get dropped or can collide with each other during the loading/unloading processes. Hence it is important to use protective packaging around each product. Also, it is important to secure the cartons within the container by packing the shipping cartons as tightly as possible. Gaps and empty spaces should be filled with dunnage, paper, or air bags to eliminate in-transit load shifting. This will avoid product being crushed, being banged around during transit, or spilling out of the container when the door is opened.

Moisture is a constant concern because condensation can accumulate inside the container. Another aspect of this problem is that cargo may also be unloaded in precipitation or the foreign port may not have covered storage facilities. It is important to use packages and packing filler made of moisture-resistant material. Plastic can be used inside cartons to protect freight and shrink wrap can be used around palletized or unitized product to create a moisture barrier.

Theft and pilferage are added risks. To avoid pilferage, avoid writing contents or brand names on packages. Other safeguards include using straps, seals, and shrink wrapping. The goal is to limit awareness of the contents of the cartons and eliminate the opportunity for undetected access to the shipment.

Finally, because transportation costs are determined by volume and weight, specially reinforced and lightweight packing materials have been developed for global transportation. Packing goods to minimize volume and weight while reinforcing them may save money, as well as ensuring that the goods are properly packed. It is recommended that a professional firm be hired to pack the products if the seller is not equipped to do so. This service is usually provided at a moderate cost.

Normally, air shipments require less heavy packing than ocean shipments, though they should still be adequately protected, especially if they are fragile and/or of interest to thieves. In many instances, standard domestic packing is acceptable, especially if the product is durable and there is no concern for display packaging. In other instances, high-test (at least 250 pounds per square inch) cardboard or tri-wall construction boxes are more than adequate.

While advertising and logos on cartons are not desirable, certain carton markings are important. The information provided on the outside of the cartons must comply with customs regulations of the country of destination, enable freight handlers and receivers to correctly identify shipments, facilitate proper handling of shipments, and adhere to environmental and safety regulations for hazardous materials. At minimum, each carton should prominently display the following information:

- Customer and destination information—business name, ship-to address
- Seller and origin information—business name, ship-from address, and country of origin
- Cargo information—weight in pounds and kilograms, size in inches and centimeters, cautionary and handling markings using international pictorial symbols, handling instructions, and package number (for example, "2 of 14")
- Hazardous materials markings should also be used as needed. These markings should follow the United Nations harmonized standards and internationally recognized symbols.

Insuring the Goods International cargo is subject to a wider array of loss and damage risks than domestic freight. This is due to the extended origin-to-destination distance, number of transfers between carriers, and varying climatic conditions. In particular, ocean freight faces considerable obstacles to loss- and damage-free delivery. Because of these obstacles, sellers and customers are exposed to significant financial risks when their freight moves through the global supply chain.

Before tendering freight to the transportation company, the exporter and importer must determine their insurable interests and understand how to most effectively manage risk. For most organizations, the appropriate response is to transfer the risk of financial loss through the purchase of freight insurance. A detailed discussion of freight insurance is provided in Chapter 10.

Completing the Paperwork Freight documents control international cargo on its journey from origin point in the country of export to its final destination in the country of import. Missing or incorrect paperwork can cause delays and additional costs. In general, international cargo travels with four types of documents: invoices, export documents, import documents, and transportation documents. These documents must be completed fully and accurately prior to tendering freight to the transportation company. A detailed discussion of freight documentation and paperwork is provided in Chapter 10.

Policy and Regulatory Issues Impacting Global Flows

Given the strategic nature of transportation, governments around the world take an active interest in freight movement. Key roles include regulation of the transportation industry, investment in transportation infrastructure, and promotion of international trade. Government agencies may also control the import and export of strategic materials.

While many governments have taken a market-focused approach toward carrier competition, this does not mean that they have adopted a hands-off approach to transportation regulation. Oversight is growing in areas where the transportation industry has the potential to impact the quality of life, the safety of citizens, and the growth of commerce. For example, the United Kingdom's Department for Transport's goal is transport that works for everyone. This means a transport system that balances the needs of the economy, the environment, and society. In support of this aim the Department has five strategic objectives, one of which is to support national economic competitiveness and growth by delivering reliable and efficient transport networks.[3]

In the United States, current policy and regulatory actions focus on transportation safety, environmental impact reduction, and security. Key policy priorities include the following:

- Protection of the traveling public is the primary driver of transportation safety regulation. Laws have been enacted to limit the size of freight equipment, combined freight and equipment weight, and travel speed. Current regulations also focus on driver qualifications, equipment safety, random drug testing of truck drivers, and control of hazardous material transport.

- Congestion, air pollution, greenhouse gas emissions, noise, and dependence on a volatile world oil market are examples of environment-related concerns. In response, the U.S. government has enacted legislation to address these and other environmental protection issues.

- Terrorism threats have led to security-focused legislation and programs that impact global transportation, such as the initiatives discussed in Chapter 9. These include the Maritime Transportation Security Act of 2002, the Container Security Initiative, and the Advanced Manifest Rules. A recent addition to the security effort has been passage of the Importer Security Filing, a regulation that supplements the Advanced Manifest Rules.

Global Perspectives

Understanding the 10+2 Import Requirements

The Customs and Border Protection (CBP) agency's Importer Security Filing (ISF) regulation has become commonly known as the 10+2 initiative because it requires importers and vessel-operating carriers to provide trade data (10 elements and 2 elements each, respectively) for nonbulk cargo shipments arriving into the United States via ocean. Melissa Irmen, vice president of products and strategy at Charlotte, N.C.-based trade solutions provider Integration Point, offers these tips for complying with the new regulations.

Remember that 10+2 pertains to goods transiting through the United States, not just imports. Carriers must file data for goods moving through the country for export and for freight remaining onboard the vessel.

Be aware of the "flexible enforcement" loophole. CBP will not assess liquidated damages for failure to meet the new requirements until Jan. 26, 2010. In the interim, the agency expects importers to make a good faith effort to comply.

Understand who is responsible for filing the data. The ISF importer bears responsibility for ensuring all 10 data elements are filed correctly, even if the information originates from another trading partner. The elements include: manufacturer name and address; seller name and address; container stuffing location; consolidator name and address; buyer name and address; ship-to name and address; importer of record number; consignee number; country of origin of the goods; and commodity harmonized tariff schedule number.

Engage your carriers. Carriers must file the container's status message and stow plan. You do not have to tie these elements to the importer data; CBP will make that correlation.

Don't wait until the last minute. Filings must be submitted 24 hours prior to the shipment's arrival in a U.S. port, or upon lading at a foreign port that is less than a 24-hour voyage to the closest U.S. port. To prevent delays, you can send ISFs in advance, even without the two most difficult to obtain data elements—container stuffing location and consolidator—as long as you provide these two remaining elements 24 hours prior to arrival.

Know what data can be amended. "Flexibility in interpretation" was introduced for data elements that cause the most concern for compliance, such as country of origin, ship-to party, and manufacturer. You can submit an initial response based on the best available data 24 hours prior to lading, but you must ensure that CBP receives the final data on time.

Learn how to file electronically, or engage a partner to do it for you. All ISF filings must be submitted via the Automated Manifest System (AMS) or the Automated Broker Interface (ABI). You may be a self-filer or you can choose to use an agent. If you don't have electronic submission capability, you'll need to engage a partner to handle it.

Transition now toward electronic filing. It's possible to meet the 10+2 requirements with manual data entry using commercially available documents. This allows you to test each channel in the supply chain while the electronic data integration is being built.

Know the penalties for compliance failure. The fine for failure to meet ISF requirements was reduced from the value of the shipment to $5,000 per shipment. However, the statement of what constitutes a violation—such as a misreported shipment or incorrectly stated line items on a filing—has not been issued yet.

Get help. Consult the CBP website (www.cbp.gov/xp/cgov/trade/cargo_security/carriers/security_filing/) for the most current information on the 10+2 regulations.

Source: Adapted from Deborah Catalano Ruriani, "10 Tips: Understanding 10+2 Requirements," *Inbound Logistics,* March 2009. Reprinted with permission.

It requires that ten additional pieces of information from the importer and two additional pieces of information from the carrier be provided to U.S. Customs and Border Protection (CBP) 24 hours before loading of the ship. The new regulation is commonly called the "10+2" rule. Additional information regarding "10+2" is provided in the Global Perspectives feature.

Effective management of freight flows requires that transportation managers take the time to understand and comply with government policies and regulations both at home and abroad. This includes both regulations that impact the flow of import goods as well as those that affect the flow of export goods. Failure to abide by these requirements at home and abroad will lead to delivery delays and potential penalties, including fines, freight confiscation, and/or denial of entry.

Global Transportation Providers

The global transportation market is served by carriers in all modes of transportation, including pipelines in North America and Eastern Europe. Intercontinental freight moves primarily via ocean and air freight. It is estimated that 98 percent of intercontinental containerized trade volume and 60 percent of trade value is moved via ocean carriers. The balance moves via air freight carriers.[4] However, intracontinental freight flows primarily via trucks. For example, 72 percent of European freight is handled by trucks on a ton-kilometer basis, as revealed by Figure 11-7. Because intracontinental freight flows are similar to domestic moves, this section primarily focuses on intercontinental ocean transportation and air transportation. Surface transportation and ancillary service providers are also briefly discussed.

Ocean Shipping

As mentioned previously, ocean shipping is an essential resource in global supply chains. The vast majority of containerized finished goods, as well as bulk materials

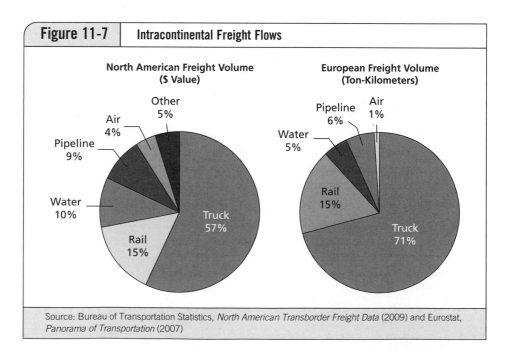

Figure 11-7 | **Intracontinental Freight Flows**

North American Freight Volume ($ Value)
- Other 5%
- Air 4%
- Pipeline 9%
- Water 10%
- Rail 15%
- Truck 57%

European Freight Volume (Ton-Kilometers)
- Air 1%
- Pipeline 6%
- Water 5%
- Rail 15%
- Truck 71%

Source: Bureau of Transportation Statistics, *North American Transborder Freight Data* (2009) and Eurostat, *Panorama of Transportation* (2007)

moving across oceans, travel via this mode. Ocean shipping is a very diverse industry with a variety of service options, equipment types, service providers, pricing alternatives, and key issues that must be addressed. No matter what the commodity, freight volume, and geographic requirements may be, there is an ocean carrier with the capability and capacity to move the cargo.

Service Options Ocean transportation service providers can be segmented into three different categories—liner services, charter services, and private services. Each type provides specific service features to global shippers as discussed below.

Liner service is provided by ships that travel on regularly scheduled voyages, following fixed routes with predetermined ports of call. Typically, a liner ship will serve a particular trade area, such as the trans-Pacific lanes between Asia and North America, trans-Atlantic lanes between Europe and North America, or Asia-Europe lanes. Some liner ships travel the globe on "round the world" schedules, eastbound or westbound, passing through the Panama Canal and the Suez Canal.

There are different types and sizes of liner ships, many of which are assigned to specific routes based on their size, **draft**, and cargo handling capabilities. Liner ships may carry containers, break-bulk shipments that require transload services, or a combination of freight types. Historically, the freight rates charged have been based on the shipping company's tariff or, if the company is a member of a liner conference, the tariff of that conference. Today, the service providers have more flexibility to negotiate contract rates with individual customers.

Charter service is provided by ships that are hired for a specific voyage or amount of time. It is similar to hiring a limousine service or taxi to give you tailored services (for instance, direct point-to-point service). The ship owner essentially leases the vessel to a **charterer** (the customer) who uses the ship to move its own cargo. Some charterers move cargo for other companies with the goal of making money on the difference between leasing costs and the price charged to other customers.

These charter or "tramp" ships operate in geographic regions defined by the individual customer according to the type of charter agreed to. Charter types include:

- A **voyage charter** is the hiring of a vessel and crew for a voyage between a load port and a discharge port. The charterer pays the vessel owner on a per-ton or lump-sum basis. The owner pays the port costs (excluding **stevedore services**), fuel costs, and crew costs.

- A **time charter** is the hiring of a vessel for a specific period of time. The owner still manages the vessel but the charterer selects the ports and directs the vessel where to go. The charterer pays for all fuel the vessel consumes, port charges, and a daily charter rate to the owner of the vessel.

- A **bareboat charter** is an arrangement for the hiring of a vessel whereby no administration or technical maintenance is included as part of the agreement. The charterer pays for all operating expenses, including fuel, crew, port expenses, and **hull insurance**.

- A **demise charter** shifts the control and possession of the vessel; the charterer takes full control of the vessel along with the legal and financial responsibility for it.

Freight rates may be on a per-ton basis over a certain route (such as iron ore moving between Brazil and China) or alternatively may be expressed in terms of a total sum—normally in U.S. dollars—per day for the agreed duration of the charter. Depending on the type of ship and the type of charter, normally a standard contract form called a **charter party** is used to record the exact rate, duration, and terms agreed between the ship owner and the charterer.

Private service is similar to operating a private truck fleet. Private ships are owned or leased on a long-term basis by the company moving the goods. Chiquita Brands International uses a private fleet of refrigerated ships to move bananas and other fruits from Central American plantations to the U.S. market. The return trip carries specialized shipping cartons and other supplies to the plantations. Oil and lumber products are also moved via private service. The economics of private shipping are similar to those of private motor trucks.

Equipment Types

According to the CIA Factbook, there were 36,241 registered commercial ships worldwide in 2008. Most ships fly a **flag of convenience**, with the owners registering their ships in countries that offer advantageous fees and regulations rather than in their home country. Popular countries for ship registration include Panama, Liberia, China, Malta, Singapore, and the Bahamas. These countries register ships of all types and sizes ranging from private yachts to oil **supertankers**.

Individual ships are designed differently and can be somewhat unique. This makes it difficult to classify ships according to specific types. Thus, we will talk about five general groups of ship types.

Containerships are built for the specific purpose of moving standardized 20-ft and 40-ft oceangoing containers. In general, these "box ships" hold containers under deck in specific slots created by vertical guides. After the hatch covers are put in place, the remaining containers are loaded above or on deck by stacking them on top of each other. These containers are secured via metal bars and twistlocks. Some newer ships have eliminated the hatch covers and decks and extended the vertical guides. This is done to increase the speed of loading and unloading at ports.

The number and size of containerships has flourished. **Panamax ships** capable of transiting the Panama Canal have grown, with the latest ships carrying up to approximately 5,000 TEUs. In 1996, Maersk created the first **post-Panamax ship**, a 6,400-TEU vessel that would not fit through the Panama Canal. Since then, the development of the post-Panamax fleet has been dramatic. Today 30 percent of the world's fleet, by capacity, is post-Panamax.[5] Recently, the Mediterranean Shipping Company's Daniela completed its maiden voyage from Asia to Europe with 13,800 TEUs onboard. Plans for a 22,000-TEU vessel are on the drawing board.[6] The top container lines in the world are presented in Table 11-1.

The combination of loading/unloading speed, intermodal transferability, and freight protection has make container shipping very popular. While a break-bulk ship might require many days to unload and load its cargo by small crane and manpower, a container ship can enter, unload, load, and clear a port in less than 12 hours using the huge portside container cranes. Such speed has brought about labor savings to both the shipper and the liner company, as well as increased ship (and capital) utilization. Because a ship is only earning revenue at sea, it is easy to see why containers have become a dominant form of packaged-goods international shipping.

Break-bulk ships are multipurpose vessels that are capable of transporting shipments of unusual sizes, unitized on pallets, in bags, or in crates. The ships tend to be smaller and have onboard cranes, giving them the flexibility to serve nearly any port. Many of these ships are engaged in specialized trades or specific trading lanes. The problem

Table 11-1	Top 10 Container Lines - 2008					
COMPANY	COUNTRY	TEUs	SHIPS OWNED	SHIPS CHARTERED	SHIPS ON ORDER
A.P. Moeller – Maersk	Denmark	2,036,600	242	321	94
Mediterranean Shipping Co.	Switzerland	1,313,600	—	—	52
CMA CGM Group	France	966,389	99	303	81
Evergreen Line	Taiwan	649,647	93	93	9
Hapag-Lloyd	Germany	505,812	62	77	14
COSCO Container Lines	China	459,586	82	59	65
APL	Singapore	443,267	38	92	31
China Shipping Container Lines	China	425,293	84	50	41
NYK Group	Japan	414,247	52	69	36
Hanjin Shipping Group	South Korea	379,281	26	66	38
Total of Top 10 Carriers		7,593,722	778*	1130*	461
Percent of World Fleet		**60.8%**			

*not including Mediterranean Shipping Co.

Source: Adapted from Simon Heaney, "Top 20 Container Lines," *American Shipper*, September 2008.

with break-bulk shipping is the labor-intensive loading, unloading, and load securing processes. Because each unitized piece of the shipment must be handled separately, port dwell times are longer, which is costly and time consuming. Hence, break-bulk shipping's share of international trade is decreasing.

Roll-on/roll-off (RORO) ships were created to move wheeled vehicles such as cars, trucks, farm equipment, and construction equipment that can be driven on and off the vessel. Since it would be costly and dangerous to use a crane to load this type of freight, the RORO ship has a ramp which drops down to the wharf, allowing vehicles to be quickly loaded or unloaded. The interior of the ship has many decks to store the cargo, similar to a parking garage. In some ships, the height of the decks can be adjusted to accommodate different sizes of rolling cargo.

Bulk carriers is a catch-all category for ships that are dedicated to the transport of a specific bulk commodity on a voyage basis. **Crude carriers** move petroleum products (crude oil, gasoline, diesel fuel, and so forth) in massive quantities. The size and draft of these ships severely limits the routes available, as they need deep water ports. **Dry-bulk carriers** have several holds in their hulls in which loose cargo like grains, coal, ore, and other commodities are loaded. These ships are generally small enough to move through the Panama Canal and serve smaller ports. **Gas carriers** move compressed gasses like liquefied natural gas and liquefied petroleum gas in specialized tanks. These unique ships are employed on long-term time charters and travel a stable schedule similar to liner ships.

Combination ships are multipurpose vessels that can handle different types of commodities and load types. A typical ship design has under-deck holds for bulk or break-bulk cargoes, a tweendeck to hold vehicles or break-bulk cargo, and a main deck which carries containers. These vessels are likely to have their own cranes and other equipment for loading and unloading cargo. The cargo flexibility, smaller size, and handling equipment help combination ships thrive in smaller markets and developing countries.

Rate Structure Ocean shipping rates are impacted by carrier cost structure, commodity, freight volume, origin and destination points, and ancillary services required. The type of service provided—liner or charter—has a major influence on rate structures. Our discussion of rates will be segmented by type of service.

The general cost structure of liner operations, as with most ship operations, is largely fixed and common in nature. Approximately 80 to 90 percent of total cost is fixed and 10 to 20 percent is variable. Liner companies tend to have large overhead costs for marketing, management, and business development.

A majority of the total costs of operating a ship is also fixed. Because cargo loading, unloading, and fuel are the only primary variable costs, the ship's operation cost is roughly the same regardless of the commodity or volume hauled. The problem of determining a cost per pound entails a difficult fixed-cost allocation process, which can be arbitrary at best. Ship operators will often determine unit costs in terms of cost per cubic foot of ship space used so as to better evaluate and price for the range of commodities handled.

Because the cost of owning and operating liner ships is relatively fixed, ship operators attempt to solicit and charge rates that will maximize the total revenue of the entire ship. This condition brings about the tendency to price according to the principles of value of service. That is, a floor of variable costs must be covered as a minimum; then the blend of high- and low-value-per-pound commodities, as well as the host of traffic elasticities, leads to pricing according to what the traffic will bear to maximize revenue.

Historically, the majority of liner rates were determined collectively by a group of carriers serving specific trade routes and ports. These shipping **conferences** are essentially legal cartels in which the carriers agree not to compete on price by publishing standardized rate **tariffs**. The conferences were allowed to exist with antitrust immunity by governments because of the high fixed-cost structure of the industry. Conferences exist for trans-Pacific, trans-Atlantic, and Asia-Europe trade routes, as well as all other major trade lanes of the world. Contract rates and independent rates were also available but with limited availability.

The 1999 implementation of the **Ocean Shipping Reform Act** (OSRA) altered the balance of ratemaking power in the liner industry. A primary goal of OSRA was to promote a more market-driven, efficient liner shipping industry. OSRA brought about many changes to the conference system, most notably the ability of large shippers to negotiate private, confidential contracts with liner companies. This enhanced ability to deal with individual carriers, the elimination of the "me-too" requirement for similarly situated customers, and the confidentiality of certain commercially sensitive service contract terms have fostered a shift to contract carriage. Carriers generally report that 80 percent or more of their liner cargo now moves under independently negotiated service contracts.[7]

As a result of OSRA and other reforms, many ocean conferences have lost significant membership, ceased operations, or shifted their focus. For example, the Trans-Pacific Stabilization Agreement (TSA) is now "a research and discussion forum of major ocean container shipping lines that carry cargo from Asia to ports and inland points in the U.S."[8] TSA member carriers are authorized under the applicable shipping laws of U.S. and Asian governments to meet and exchange market information, jointly conduct market research, develop voluntary, nonbinding guidelines for rates and charges, and establish common terms of service and standards. Like many other conferences, TSA no longer negotiates rates or files tariffs with the U.S. Federal Maritime Commission or with Asian governments.[9]

Charter shipowners also experience costs that are largely fixed in nature. Ownership costs present themselves in depreciation and interest costs. Fuel is not as greatly variable with the commodity weight load, as is ship speed or at-sea versus port time. The key is that the shipowner minimizes empty nonrevenue miles and days.

Charter rates are individually negotiated based on the type of charter (voyage or time) and services required. The market for ship chartering is a fluid supply-and-demand situation. At any given time, the charter rate situation can be one of feast or famine for shipowners. This market can fluctuate over both the short and long term. In the short run, the demand for a ship and charter rates at a single port area will depend on shipper movement needs and available ship supply within a time span as short as a month. Over longer periods, a market can be considered glutted or tight, depending on the number of ships or types of ships that are available in the world during the span of a year.

The charter rate negotiation process involves the two primary parties involved in chartering: the shipowner and the charterer (customer). **Shipbrokers** are usually employed to investigate the market and conduct the negotiations. In most cases, both parties will have their own brokers and negotiate through these representatives, who should do their best to preserve their respective principal's interests and intentions.

A successful negotiation will result in a charter party, a contract in which the shipowner agrees to place their ship, or part of it, at the disposal of the charterer for the carriage of goods from one port to another port on being paid freight, or to lease the ship for a specified period, the payment being known as hire money. The charter party states in written form the agreement between a shipowner and a charterer and factually records the agreement and the terms and conditions that have been negotiated.

Current Issues As transportation is a derived demand industry, global economic booms and busts directly impact the industry. When global trade is growing, as was the case up until 2007, the major issues revolve around capacity shortages, port congestion, and rate increases. However, global recessions create vastly different issues and problems. As trade volume dips, liner and charter carriers end up with an excessive amount of unused capacity. The result is precipitous rate drops despite many carriers removing ships from service to cut capacity. The survival of financially weak carriers is challenged and their only hope may be a merger or purchase.

While plummeting ocean rates are a real problem—anywhere from 20 to 60 percent declines in container transport prices in 2009[10]—the real conundrum is the growth of new capacity. Ocean carriers went on a ship ordering binge for 10,000-TEU-plus vessels in 2007. Because it takes years to build a new ship, the added capacity—35 ships in 2009, 49 in 2010 and 91 in 2011—comes at a time when it is not needed.[11] The additional TEU capacity will likely keep freight rates depressed in the near future, as highlighted by the On the Line article.

The ocean shipping industry faces other challenges moving forward. Fluctuating fuel prices and rising fees for port services and Panama Canal transits are ongoing

On the Line

The Worst of Times for Ocean Shipping Rates

The ocean shipping industry faces a real conundrum. The precipitous decline in global trade in 2008 and 2009 has dramatically impacted container shipping volume. Both transatlantic and transpacific container volumes are off 20–30 percent. At the same time, global fleet capacity is growing by more than 12 percent as ultralarge ships ordered earlier in the decade are being delivered by ship builders.

In response, the shipping industry has had to take dramatic capacity-reduction steps to offset the addition of these megaships, each capable of handling 13,000 or more containers. Carriers are aggressively scrapping older ships and idling other vessels. Reportedly, more than 500 ships are sitting empty along the coasts of Singapore and Malaysia.

Unfortunately, these efforts have had limited impact. Container rates are in a free fall, with some dropping below carrier operating costs or with carriers charging only minimal bunker (fuel) costs to move containers. Drewry Shipping Consultants report that the Honk Kong–Los Angeles container benchmark rate on July 6, 2009 dropped to $871 from $2,043 a year earlier.

The combination of declining volume and rate wars has led to severe industry financial problems. Maersk Line lost US $950 million through June 2009. The number could have been much worse, if not for aggressive cost cutting by the company. And the situation is worse at other carriers, with Mediterranean Shipping Company losing more than US $1 billion during the same time frame. The survival of many ocean carriers is at stake if losses like these continue to mount.

Overcapacity will continue to depress rates over the next few years. Rates will remain stagnant and ocean carrier viability will hang in the balance.

Therein lies a longer term problem. If carriers don't survive the current shakeout, then who will operate the laid-up capacity when the global economy improves? The potential for permanent capacity loss is high, and the shipping headaches of 2007—capacity shortages, port congestion, and container shortages—may resurface.

So what can importers and exporters do to protect themselves? They must take a longer-term perspective and avoid those tempting distressed rates that don't properly compensate ocean carriers. Here are some key suggestions from the articles referenced below:

- Pay close attention to transportation procurement risks—carrier bankruptcies, service termination, and cargo liens.

- Seek out financially stable ocean carriers with consistent service levels. Work closely to develop mutually beneficial contracts.

- Consider shorter-term contracts with lower volume commitments. Paying higher rates in exchange for space guarantees is not currently necessary.

Sources: Patrick Burnson, "Ocean Shipping: Cool, Calm Correction," *Logistics Management,* September 2009; Chris Gillis and Chris Dupin, "Decision Time," *American Shipper,* May 2009; adapted from John W. Miller, "The Mega Containers Invade," *The Wall Street Journal,* January 26, 2009. Copyright © 2009 by Dow Jones & Company, Inc. Reprinted by permission.

concerns, especially when economic conditions make it difficult to pass higher costs along to customers. Environmental legislation is on the rise to combat the "dirty" marine diesel fuel used to propel ships. Ship emissions are a major source of soot, sulfur dioxide, and smog-forming pollution. Also, freight protection headaches such as piracy threaten to drive operating and insurance costs higher.

International Air

Air cargo is a $50-billion business that transports 35 percent of the value of goods trad- ed internationally. While air cargo transportation remains a small and specialized mode in terms of tonnage, it is a critical part of the airline business and the supply chain. Air carriers transport small quantities of high-value, low-weight, semifinished and finished goods. Primary commodities moved globally as air cargo include compu- ters, precision instruments, electronics, pharmaceuticals, perishable foods, periodicals, and apparel. In this section, international air transportation characteristics are dis- cussed, including service options, equipment types, service providers, pricing alterna- tives, and key issues that must be addressed.

Service Options International air transportation is available in virtually every market of the world. Wherever passenger service is available, you can also find air cargo ser- vice. Two primary carrier types dominate this mode.

Air cargo carriers focus exclusively on the movement of freight, packages, letters, and envelopes. Like ocean carriers, customers have the option of using scheduled service or charter service. Many air carriers provide regularly scheduled service through a highly coordinated network of operations and equipment.

A niche group of air cargo carriers provide on-demand service for customers who need more immediate, direct transportation or the full capacity of the aircraft. Typically, air cargo charter services are used for emergency shipments (for instance, to prevent a production line shut down), for goods that will not fit in traditional aircraft, or for deliveries to locations where regularly scheduled service is not available. This service option provides an opportunity for customized services but at a very high cost.

One variation of air cargo carriers is a small group of **integrated carriers**. These com- panies have the capability to provide door-to-door service because they own ground delivery equipment as well as aircraft. They offer a consistent schedule of pickup and delivery windows and standard expedited service through their hub-and-spoke net- works. Because these carriers make air transportation of time-sensitive goods such a simple, well-controlled process, they have become key players in the global delivery of expedited movement of letters, small packages, and small shipments. They also are de- veloping capabilities and capacity to move larger volume shipments. Examples include FedEx, UPS, and DHL.

In contrast, **nonintegrated carriers** provide air transport service only from airport to air- port. They rely on air freight forwarders or the customer to provide delivery service to and from the airport. The advantage of these carriers is the speed and flexibility of un- scheduled direct service and the potential for same-day cargo movement. Key players in the nonintegrated international linehaul market include Cargolux and Polar Air Cargo.

Combination carriers move freight and passengers, often on the same trip, with cargo loaded in the belly of the aircraft. As demand has grown, some of the larger interna- tional carriers have created separate divisions or companies to focus on air cargo movement and provide scheduled service to meet the needs of global commerce. Of the top 10 carriers of air freight (scheduled freight ton-kilometers), seven are combination carriers led by Korean Air and Lufthansa. Table 11-2 provides a list of the top interna- tional air cargo carriers.

Equipment Types While there are many sizes of aircraft used for moving interna- tional cargo, the primary difference between equipment type focuses on the internal

Table 11-2	Top 10 Scheduled Air Cargo Carriers		
COMPANY	HOME COUNTRY	MILLIONS OF INTERNATIONAL FREIGHT TON-KILOMETERS FLOWN	
		2007	2006
Korean Air	South Korea	9,498	8,680
Lufthansa	Germany	8,336	8,077
Cathay Pacific	Hong Kong	8,225	6,914
Singapore Airlines	Singapore	7,945	7,991
FedEx Corporation	USA	6,470	6,136
China Airlines	China	6,301	6,099
Air France	France	6,123	5,864
Emirates	United Arab Emirates	5,497	5,027
Cargolux	Luxembourg	5,482	5,237
United Parcel Service	USA	5,077	

Source: International Air Transport Association, *World Air Transport Statistics – 53rd Edition*, 2008.

configuration of the plane. Some equipment is set up to carry strictly freight while others carry a combination of passengers and cargo. Each type is discussed below.

Air freighters are aircraft dedicated solely to the movement of freight. The main deck of the aircraft has no amenities and is set up to quickly move freight on and off the plane using a roller deck. A **roller deck** is a main deck equipped with rollers on the floor which allows palletized or containerized cargo to be pushed into position. In the air freight industry, these specially designed containers that fit properly inside the rounded fuselage are called **unit load devices** (ULDs). The pallets and ULDs are then secured to the aircraft floor using hooks and slings.

A wide variety of freighters are used around the world. They range from the Cessna Caravan that FedEx uses for small market pickup and delivery to the Anatov AN-124, a huge plane capable of handling oversized payloads. Due to the unique size of its cargo deck and loading door, the AN-124 can transport unique products (such as mining and power plant equipment) of up to 150 tons with dimensions as large as 13-ft high by 19-ft wide. The Boeing 747 Freighter (capacity of nearly 27,500 cubic feet and 124-ton payload) is widely used with more than 300 aircraft providing about half the world's dedicated-freighter capacity. Airbus hopes to take some of this market share with its A380-800F, the first commercial freighter with three full cargo decks and the capability to carry a 150-ton payload over distances of 5,600 nautical miles.

Cargo also travels on **passenger airplanes**. The passengers travel on the main deck or cabin of the plane while luggage and some cargo are loaded into the lower deck or belly of the aircraft. The cargo is commonly restricted to smaller individual shipments of cargo rather than full pallets or ULDs, due to the weight limitations of the aircraft, the capacity of the hold, and the exterior door size. Also, certain items considered hazardous or a fire threat (such as nonrechargeable lithium-ion batteries) are no longer allowed to be carried by passenger aircraft. The main benefit of using passenger airplanes for cargo is the frequency of service and ability to move critical shipments on the next flight out.

A third, hybrid type of equipment is the **combi airplane**. The term *combi* refers to the flexibility to move passengers and/or cargo on the main deck of the aircraft. A movable partition in the cabin separates the passengers from the cargo and allows flexibility to move more passengers or cargo based on demand. Combi aircraft typically feature an oversized cargo door, as well as tracks on the cabin floor to allow the seats to be added or removed quickly. Once thought of as a way to gain greater air transportation efficiencies, opportunities to use this type of aircraft are waning due to increased safety restrictions and security regulations.

Whatever the international shipment requirement may be, an aircraft with an appropriate combination of payload, range, and speed is likely available.

Rate Structure   The air carrier cost structure consists of high variable costs in proportion to fixed costs, somewhat akin to the motor carrier cost structure. Like motor and water carriers, air carriers do not invest heavily in facility infrastructure or byways. Governments around the world build airports and air cargo facilities terminals, as well as provide traffic control of the airways. Air carriers pay variable lease payments and landing fees for their use. Equipment costs, though quite high, are still a small part of the total cost.

Air cargo rates are based on the **value of service** or the **cost of service**. Value of service rates are demand based and consider the sensitivity of the cargo being shipped to freight rates. The less sensitive cargo is to rates, the higher the rate will be. On traffic lanes where demand is strong and plane capacity is limited, the air rates will be high, and vice versa for traffic lanes where supply exceeds demand. Also, products with high prices or emergency conditions surrounding the move will be charged high rates because the freight rate is a small portion of the landed selling price.

Cost of service factors also enter into air carrier pricing of cargo. Given the limited cargo-carrying capacity of a plane, space is at a premium. The utilization of this space is related to the **density** of the cargo, with low-density cargo requiring more space per weight unit than high-density cargo.

Air carriers calculate the **dimensional weight** (dim weight) of a shipment to evaluate the weight versus space issue. Freight carriers use the greater of the actual weight or dimensional weight to calculate shipping charges. Carriers calculate international air shipments as (Length × Width × Height)/(Dimensional Factor). The common dimensional factor for international freight is 166 for shipments measured in inches and 5,000 or 6,000 for shipments measured in centimeters.

For example, an international shipment weighing 1,500 pounds with 100 cartons measuring 16 in by 12 in by 18 in has a dim weight of 20.8 pounds per case (16 × 12 × 18/166) and a total dim weight of 2,082 pounds. Thus, the air carrier will charge the customer based the higher dim weight of 2,082 pounds instead of the actual weight of 1,500 pounds.

Dimensional weight favors shippers of dense objects and penalizes those who ship lightweight cartons. A carton of unpopped corn kernels will likely be charged by gross weight while a carton of popcorn will probably be charged by its dimensional weight. This is because the large box of popcorn takes up a lot of space but does not fill up a plane's capacity in terms of weight, making it an inefficient use of space.

The pricing of international air freight is governed by the International Air Transport Association (IATA) via The Air Cargo Tariff (TACT). TACT is generally considered to be a set of guidelines which contains comprehensive information regarding air cargo rules, regulations, rates, and charges. More than 100 airlines contribute information regarding 2.3 million rates and charges to TACT.[12] However, carriers are not required to use these rates and major carriers tend to develop their own rates based on the commodity and market competition.

TACT includes three types of international air carrier rates: general cargo, class, and specific commodity rates. The **general cargo rate** is a standard rate that applies to commodities for which there is no other applicable rate. The general cargo rate is available for any commodity, can vary with distance and direction, and/or is applicable between specific origin–destination pairs. Discounts are available for larger shipment sizes and may or may not include ground transportation to and from the airport.

The **class rate** is applicable to cargo grouped into classes. There is no classification system in international air transportation as is found in domestic surface transportation. The rate for a particular class expressed as a percentage of the general cargo rate is usually lower than the general cargo rate and can be door-to-door or airport-to-airport.

The specific **commodity rate** is applicable to a specific commodity between a specific origin–destination pair. The specific commodity rate is generally lower than the general cargo rate. A high minimum weight is usually required for each shipment. Because the air carrier utilizes the specific commodity rate to attract freight and to enable shippers to penetrate certain market areas, it may have a time limit. As with the other commodity-based rates, the specific commodity rate can be either door-to-door or airport-to-airport.

Container rates are also available for cargo shipped in a container. The rate is cost based, rather than value of service or commodity based. The rate applies to a minimum weight in the container. Some carriers offer a container rate discount per container shipped over any route of the individual carrier. The discount is deducted from the tariff rate applicable to the commodity being moved in noncontainerized form and a charge is assessed for returning the empty container.

Current Issues Traditionally, customers have been willing to pay a premium to transport high-value, time-sensitive goods that require superior protection while in transit. However, few of these products are proving to be highly recession proof. International air cargo volume was down dramatically in 2008 and the worst was yet to come. The IATA projects a 13 percent decline in 2009 and industry losses of $4.7 billion.[13]

In response, air carriers are "right-sizing" their networks by cutting route frequency, using fewer widebody aircraft, and eliminating service to unprofitable markets. Air carriers are also grounding aircraft in record numbers. Industry experts estimate that 2,300 jet airliners of the global fleet of 20,293 have been taken out of service, many of them parked in the California and Arizona deserts.[14] Also, passenger and cargo airlines have begun to revise their equipment orders. Carriers began to cancel or delay orders in 2008 and there are fears that up to one-third of the order backlogs for new planes could vanish in 2009 and 2010.[15]

The international air cargo industry also faces numerous cost obstacles to profitable growth. A primary challenge is the volatile cost of kerosene-type jet fuel. It is estimated that every additional penny paid for a gallon of jet fuel adds $195 million of cost to the

Transportation Technology

Global Trade Management Systems Facilitate Freight Flows

There was a time when U.S. companies could get by with manual global trade processes assisted only by a sharp mind, a pen, and a few forms. Using these three elements, companies were trading back and forth across the high seas in a way that complied with regulations, but provided very little in terms of visibility or accountability.

The terrorist attacks of September 11th changed all of that; and over time those events forced companies to rethink the way they handle their global trade activities. For most global shippers, however, new regulations and programs designed to take risk out of the supply chain have introduced a separate group of challenges that now need to be managed.

Combine the tightening global regulatory environment with the fact that more domestic shippers are involved with international trade, and it's easy to see why the need for Global Trade Management (GTM) systems continues to grow.

In fact, the GTM market grossed about $280 million in sales in 2007, according to Adrian Gonzalez, director of ARC Advisory Group's Logistics Executive Council. And to add to that future growth, the big ERP players like SAP and Oracle have either gotten into or are about to get into the game. Vendors like Management Dynamics, Kewill, Descartes, JPMorgan, and Infor also offer GTM systems that are continually being improved and tweaked to accommodate shippers' needs and demands.

Companies looking to pick among those offerings would be wise to examine the complexity of their own global trade operations before making a decision, adds Gonzalez. He advises that a firm that's handling a large volume of shipments going from China to the U.K., for example, should consider a best-of-breed solution; while a shipper that's handling imports from China, Mexico, or Canada to the U.S. might look at a smaller, niche vendor.

Much like in the TMS and WMS spaces, on-demand options are also becoming a popular choice for shippers looking for fast GTM startup times with low upfront investments. "We're seeing more on-demand used on the content side, since that changes regularly and is delivered via subscription," says Gonzalez, who calls GTM one of the faster-growing supply chain software categories.

Some of that growth will be driven by Oracle's move into the space, says Ian Hobkirk, former senior analyst of supply chain execution at the Aberdeen Group. Already armed with a world-class TMS, the vendor is "really putting a lot of horsepower into building a GTM solution," adds Hobkirk. "Shippers want to go to one source for their TMS and GTM, and right now there's no one out there offering that in an effective manner."

Also driving the market will be the continued impact of stricter rules governing global trade, says John Fontanella, vice president of research at AMR Research. "One of the main drivers is security regulations imposed in the U.S. and Europe, both of which are putting more responsibility on the shipper," says Fontanella, "which in turn requires capable, fully-developed GTM systems and the vendors to support and enhance them."

Vendors are answering the call and coming up with ways to replace manual processes with automated procedures that are easier for shippers to handle with less manpower. Here are two companies that are successfully using GTM systems in the course of business in lieu of the manual processes once used at their companies.

Source: Bridget McCrea, "Global Trade Management: Can You See Me Now?," *Logistics Management*, June 2008. Reprinted with permission.

industry. Some of these costs may be recouped through fuel surcharges but air carriers may find it difficult to pass along increased costs during economic downturns.

Another major cost issue is the expense of security mandate compliance. Homeland security fees, cargo screening costs, training, and related security expenses are estimated to have an annual impact of more than $4 billion on the industry, according to the Air Transport Association. Freight customers are moving toward new software systems to ease the financial burden of compliance. One valuable tool, Global Trade Management, is discussed in the Transportation Technology feature.

Clearly, the air cargo industry has experienced the perfect storm of rising costs, declining volume, and a global credit crisis. There are significant challenges and many questions regarding the ability of the international air freight market to rebound. The industry must control its costs and reevaluate its value proposition in light of changing customer freight patterns and competition from the ocean industry. Experts warn that the decades-long trend of air freight capturing a rising share of containerized trade flows will reverse as ocean carriers offer increasingly sophisticated and reliable time-definite service at a fraction of the cost of air transport.[16]

Surface Transport

Moving goods across adjacent land borders is the primary domain of trucks, rail, and pipeline service. Trucking is clearly the major player for intracontinental freight flows in North America and Europe. For example, 72 percent of European freight is handled by trucks on a ton-kilometer basis and the vast majority of U.S.-Canada freight movement is by truck. As issues related to U.S.-Mexico bilateral trucking service rules are resolved, this volume will also increase.

Despite the high volume of intracontinental truck traffic, the industry is hampered by a patchwork of domestic rules and regulations that impede international freight flows. There are few global standards for trucking or roadway infrastructure. Each country has its own regulations regarding equipment length, width, and carrying capacity. Safety regulations regarding driver hours of service, speed limits, and inspections are also inconsistent. Finally, many countries have mandated driving bans during certain times of the day and/or days of the week, making it difficult to plan delivery schedules. Motor carriers and their customers must understand the unique requirements of each country to ensure efficient and timely freight movement.

International rail service benefits from a standardized infrastructure and equipment. Still, North American and European rail traffic accounts for less than 20 percent of the total regional freight volume. Rail activity focuses on the movement of bulk raw materials and intermodal containers. Fuel price and tax issues, road congestion, and greenhouse gas emissions have created a push for more rail freight in Europe, though passenger trains have priority over all other traffic. Other challenges include inconsistent train operator regulations, limited investment in cargo transfer facilities, and infrequent service. Such issues will have to be overcome to make rail service a viable alternative for all but the least time-sensitive cargo.[17]

Ancillary Services

The complexity of international transportation makes it difficult for any importer or exporter to plan and execute global freight flows. In addition to transportation companies, customers can leverage the expertise of third party logistics (3PL) companies. These service providers facilitate the movement of goods via ocean and air by developing exceptional capabilities in one or more steps in the global freight flow process.

International Freight Forwarders The primary role of an international freight forwarder (IFF) is to help importers and exporters transport their goods. Many IFFs specialize in particular service areas, modes of transport, or markets. IFFs are often seen as the travel agents of international freight transportation. These service providers identify and book the best routes, modes of transport, and specific carriers for customers, based on their specific requirements.

IFFs can help an organization reduce its international air and ocean transportation costs. Because they arrange for the transport of many shipments, IFFs can consolidate freight going to a single destination. This allows the IFF to negotiate lower transportation rates than many individual customers could achieve on their own. In addition to cost savings, companies should consider using an IFF when the scale and complexity of freight transportation is high or when there is limited internal time, experience, and expertise to manage the process.

IFFs often offer a wide range of secondary trade-related services as well as their core transport ones. These include completion of freight documentation, Customs clearance services, insurance services, inventory management, and other value added logistics services. IFFs are also valuable sources of information regarding international trade. They can help organizations avoid the common errors and pitfalls of moving goods across borders.

Non Vessel-owning Common Carriers When an organization wishes to move small shipments in less than containterload (LCL) quantities, an effective service provider is a non vessel-owning common carrier (NVOCC). Unlike IFFs, who usually act as the organization's agent, NVOCCs are common carriers that provide service via containers rather than the entire ship.

NVOCCs book container berths on ships on a regular basis, allowing them to gain advantageous rates from the ocean carriers. They are able to resell the space to customers in smaller increments at favorable rates. The NVOCC combines the goods from multiple customers into a single load to fill a container. The container is then given to an ocean carrier for movement to the destination port. Upon arrival, the NVOCC receives the container and delivers the contents to each final destination.

Export Packers Given the challenges of properly packing, marking, and loading shipments, many companies seek the assistance of export packing companies. These service providers help customers who lack the equipment or expertise to protect in-transit products. Not only do they ensure that products arrive safely, export packers help save money by using economical packing materials, improving space utilization inside cartons and containers, and taking steps to prevent theft. Export packers also ensure that all packing regulations and marking requirements are met across the channel.

Port Operations and Customs Clearance

In a perfect scenario, exporters and importers would be directly accessible to their mode of choice with no need for freight transfer to other carriers or modes. Unfortunately, being located directly on the water, rail line, or runway is highly impractical for most organizations, as is the cost of owning all of the necessary freight handling equipment. Instead, they rely heavily on ports to provide the infrastructure, equipment, and labor needed to load, unload, and transfer freight between carriers. Without efficient port operations, it would be extremely difficult to achieve the tremendous volume of global trade of the last decade.

Intercontinental trade moves primarily through airports and seaports, while intracontinental trade moves directly from origin to destination through international gateways or indirectly through intermodal transfer terminals and **inland ports**. Seaports and airports are discussed in detail below.

Port facilities can be privately owned, though the vast majority of major international seaports and airports are government owned. The facilities are managed by a **port authority**, a governmental or quasigovernmental public agency charged with creating and supporting economic development in the port area. Most port authorities are financially self-supporting. These organizations own the land, develop the infrastructure, set user fees, and sometimes levy taxes. Some port authorities execute day-to-day port operations.

Seaports

Given that the vast majority of intercontinental cargo moves via ocean carriers, seaports play a critical role in global trade. A seaport is an area of land and water with related equipment to permit the reception of ships, their loading and unloading, and the receipt, storage, and delivery of their goods. There are thousands of seaports around the world, though the vast majority of international trade flows through a small group of major ports. For example, there are over 1,000 seaports in Europe handling a total of 3.5 billion tons of cargo per year, though only ten European ports handle more than 50 million tons annually. In the United States, there are more than 150 deep draft commercial seaports. Table 11-3 identifies the top global ports for various types of freight.

Infrastructure Before an exporter or importer determines which ports to use, they must consider infrastructure issues. These basic facilities, equipment, and services greatly impact the capabilities and capacity of a seaport. Some seaports have infrastructures that are tailored to containerized freight while others focus on bulk, break-bulk, or rolling freight. Hence, it is critical to match freight with the cargo handling capabilities of the port.

One important infrastructure issue is the depth of the water. Unobstructed deep water is needed in both the channel leading to the port and at the wharf to serve the growing population of post-Panamax ships. The turning radius of these large ships also requires the availability of a wide basin. Because most ports are not naturally deep, the waterway must be dredged regularly and occasionally deepened to handle large ships.

Wharfside freight handling capabilities are also critical. Seaports must offer an adequate number of ship berths to meet inbound and outbound demand. They also need the ability to quickly load and unload cargo. At a container port, gantry cranes wide enough to move containers on or off the largest ships are needed. This will avoid the time-consuming task of turning the ship around. At bulk ports, the port should have cranes, conveyors, elevators, and/or heavy lift equipment to facilitate timely freight transfer on and off ships. On-port freight handling equipment for moving cargo to and from the wharf is also needed.

Table 11-3	Major Seaports of the World							
THOUSANDS OF TONS					**TWENTY-FOOT EQUIVALENT UNITS**			
RANK	PORT	COUNTRY	MEASURE	TONS	RANK	PORT	COUNTRY	TEUS
1	Shanghai	China	metric	561,446	1	Singapore	Singapore	27,935,500
2	Singapore	Singapore	freight	483,616	2	Shanghai	China	26,152,400
3	Ningbo-Zhoushan	China	metric	471,630	3	Hong Kong	China	23,998,449
4	Rotterdam	Netherlands	metric	401,181	4	Shenzhen	China	21,103,800
5	Guangzhou	China	metric	341,363	5	Yingkou(Liaonian)	China	13,713,000
6	Tianjin	China	metric	309,465	6	Busan	South Korea	13,254,703
7	Qingdao	China	metric	265,020	7	Rotterdam	Netherlands	10,790,604
8	Qinhuangdao	China	metric	245,964	8	Dubai Ports	UAE	10,653,026
9	Hong Kong	China	metric	245,433	9	Kaohsiung	Taiwan	10,256,829
10	Busan	South Korea	revenue	243,564	10	Hamburg	Germany	9,917,180
11	Dalian	China	metric	222,859	11	Qingdao	China	9,430,600
12	Nagoya	Japan	freight	215,602	12	Ningbo	China	9,258,800
13	South Louisiana	US	metric	207,785	13	Guangzhou	China	9,200,000
14	Shenzhen	China	metric	199,190	14	Los Angeles	US	8,355,038
15	Kwangyang	South Korea	revenue	198,190	15	Antwerp	Belgium	8,175,951
16	Houston	US	metric	196,014	16	Long Beach	US	7,312,465
17	Antwerp	Belgium	metric	182,897	17	Port Kelang	Malaysia	7,118,714
18	Chiba	Japan	freight	169,202	18	Tianjin	China	7,102,100
19	Ulsan	South Korea	revenue	168,652	19	Tanjung Pelepas	Malaysia	5,500,000
20	Kaohsiung	Taiwan	metric	149,225	20	New York / New Jersey	US	5,299,105

Source: American Association of Port Authorities, *World Port Rankings – 2007*.

Finally, ports must have adequate marshaling yards, warehouse facilities and transit sheds for storage, and interchange capabilities to move freight between modes. Ports must also have strong information technology and security systems to maintain visibility, control, and safety of the freight.

Operations Although there are many organizations involved in the day-to-day operation of an international port—the port authority, ocean carriers and their agents, pilots, **stevedores**, **longshoremen**, **chandlers**, freight forwarders, **Customs brokers**, Customs agent, and landside carriers, to name the primary players—basic cargo flows are fairly straightforward.

On an export container move, a trucking company or railroad delivers the export freight to the port and checks in at the security gate. The container is then dropped at its assigned holding location. When the appropriate ship arrives, the container is retrieved and loaded on the ship.

At the point of import, the container is unloaded from the ship, after which it is moved to a storage area or loaded directly onto an outbound truck chassis or railcar. Prior to its release, the container will be scanned and possibly inspected by Customs for security purposes. The delivery carrier then moves the container from the port to the importer's facility.

Port authorities can assume the role of port landlord or operator. At a landlord port, the port authority builds the wharves, which it then rents or leases to a terminal operator such as a stevedoring company. The operator invests in cargo-handling equipment (forklifts, cranes, and so forth), hires longshoremen to handle cargo, and negotiates contracts with ocean carriers for ship loading or unloading services.

At an operational port, the port authority builds the wharves, owns the cranes and cargo-handling equipment, and hires the labor to move cargo on the port property. The port authority normally contracts with a stevedore company to hire and manage the longshoremen that move cargo between the ship and the wharf.

Current Issues To remain competitive, port authorities must remain vigilant of equipment innovations, regulatory changes, and congestion challenges. First, the size of containerships continues to increase because ocean carriers are motivated to achieve economies of scale. By 2012, it is predicted that 180 containerships of at least 10,000 TEUs will be sailing the world's oceans.[18] Waterways will need to be dredged, port authorities and terminal operators must invest in larger cranes, and sailing schedules will have to change to accommodate the longer unloading and processing times for these huge ships.

From a security standpoint, seaports must comply with existing and emerging governmental initiatives. In the United States, ports play a role in supporting the Container Security Initiative, the Security and Accountability for Every Port (SAFE) Act, and related programs. For example, under the SAFE Act, port operators must validate the credentials of all people working on the port and cooperate with CBP in the inspection of incoming containers for radiation problems.

Finally, seaports must prepare for future growth even during economic contractions. A lack of investment in facilities and technologies, coupled with anticipated international trade growth, may result in a return to port congestion problems. Also, shifts in global sourcing hotspots can alter freight flow patterns. For example, moving production from the Far East to the Americas to reduce transportation costs and delays would shift traffic to U.S. Gulf and eastern seaboard ports. Those ports must closely monitor sourcing trends and be ready to handle the increased volume.

Airports

International freight moves through thousands of cargo-friendly airports worldwide. An airport is broadly defined by the U.S. Federal Aviation Administration as any area of land or water used or intended for landing or takeoff of aircraft. It has adjacent areas used for airport buildings, facilities, and equipment, as well as rights of way to the buildings and facilities. **Cargo airports** are airports that, in addition to any other air transportation services that may be available, are served by aircraft providing air transportation of cargo only, with a total annual landed weight of more than 100 million pounds.[19]

Table 11-4	Major Cargo Airports of the World		
RANK	PORT	COUNTRY	METRIC TONS
1	Memphis International Airport	United States	3,695,561
2	Hong Kong International Airport	Hong Kong	3,656,724
3	Shanghai Pudong International Airport	China	2,598,795
4	Incheon International Airport	South Korea	2,423,717
5	Ted Stevens Anchorage International Airport	United States	2,361,088
6	Charles De Gaulle International Airport	France	2,280,049
7	Frankfurt Airport	Germany	2,111,116
8	Narita International Airport	Japan	2,099,349
9	Louisville International Airport	United States	1,973,965
10	Singapore Changi Airport	Singapore	1,883,894
11	Dubai International Airport	United Arab Emirates	1,824,992
12	Miami International Airport	United States	1,806,769
13	Los Angeles International Airport	United States	1,630,385
14	Amsterdam Airport Schiphol	Netherlands	1,602,584
15	Taiwan Taoyuan International Airport	China	1,493,120
16	London Heathrow Airport	United Kingdom	1,486,260
17	John F. Kennedy International Airport	United States	1,446,491
18	O'Hare International Airport	United States	1,324,820
19	Beijing Capital International Airport	China	1,303,258
20	Suvarnabhumi Airport	Thailand	1,173,131

Source: Airport Council International, *The 2008 World Airport Traffic Report.*

Most international airports are multipurpose airports that serve both passenger and cargo traffic. They handle the 32 percent of the intercontinental air freight moving in the belly of passenger planes and the majority of the 68 percent moving on air freighters.[20] Table 11-4 identifies the twenty largest cargo airports around the globe. However, some air freight companies are beginning to move away from the major international gateways to all-cargo airports. The purpose of these new facilities (including Alliance Airport in Fort Worth, Texas, Montreal-Mirabel International Airport in Canada, and Paris-Vatry Airport in France) is to provide alternative landing locations to congested international gateways and reduce operating costs.

Infrastructure Air cargo companies choose airport locations based on multiple factors. The first step is to create a short list of possible airports based on geography and then investigate any existing restrictions which may limit operations, such as capacity caps or noise limits that might block operations from that airport. Only when these hurdles have been cleared do freighter operators consider infrastructure issues such as runway length, terminal facilities, and freight forwarder presence, as well as landing fees, airport quality, and weather.[21] An ideal freight-friendly airport "offers around the clock operation, spacious ramps and aircraft parking, effortless transfer between the aircraft parking lot and warehouse, easy access to customers' logistics centers, and a strategic and geographical location easily accessible to its prime market."[22]

The runways of an airport determine the types of aircraft that can serve the facility. Longer runways are needed to support large aircraft and direct flights to and from far-away places. Runway and taxiway width has become another infrastructure issue due to the size and weight of the new Airbus A380. For example, runway and taxiway upgrades as well as taxiway, aircraft stand, and buildings relocations may be needed to provide sufficient wingtip clearance before the A380 enters service.

The number of runways is another major infrastructure issue as it determines the capacity of the airport. Multiple runways, as are found at most major international airports, support simultaneous takeoffs and landings. Single runway airports are severely capacity constrained and the slightest accident, malfunction, or weather issue immobilizes the entire operation.

Airports must also have the necessary equipment to efficiently handle cargo. Terminals are needed to facilitate fast intermodal transfers of freight, while warehouses are needed to protect and store cargo. Finally, hours of operation impact airport selection. Since air freighters tend to fly at night and use airports during off-hours to avoid congestion with passenger flights, it is imperative that noise regulations not limit airport availability to certain times of the day.

Operations Airport operations tend to be less complex but more time sensitive than seaport operations. First, there are not as many organizations involved in air freight movement and transfers. For example, airport authorities engage in general planning and operations but don't engage in freight handling activities. The primary freight responsibilities fall to the air cargo companies, cargo handling contractors, freight forwarders, trucking companies, and 3PL service providers. Of course, Customs bureaus will also have an active role in clearing freight at international gateways.

Export air cargo arrives at the international airport via truck or a domestic feeder flight from a smaller airport. In the United States, outbound cargo is subject to the Transportation Security Administration's (TSA) **Known Shipper Program**, under which the companies sending freight on U.S. flights must be identified by an air carrier or freight forwarder to TSA as legitimate shippers. Moving forward, all cargo traveling on narrow-body passenger aircraft will require 100 percent screening.

After screening and clearance, the cargo is loaded on the outbound international flight and flown to the destination airport. At the point of import, the cargo is unloaded from the aircraft, and moved to the terminal. Prior to its release from the airport, the cargo must be cleared by Customs or moved to a specialized warehouse. The freight forwarder or trucking company concludes the trip by moving the shipment from the airport to the importer's facility.

Current Issues Airports face many of the same challenges as seaports. They must flex capacity to deal with the current downturn in international air cargo volume while positioning the infrastructure and operations for future demand. Limited U.S. airport capacity has been added since the completion of Denver International Airport in 1995. Many airports around the world are at or near capacity with limited space to grow. Any prolonged weather problem or technical delay at a major international airport will have a domino effect on the operation of inbound and outbound flights that can last hours or days.

Airports are also impacted by new security regulations discussed previously in this chapter and in Chapter 9. This involves facility upgrades and new equipment to provide better airport access control and to help airlines comply with cargo screening requirements. Scanning of incoming air cargo began in 2008 to prevent terrorists from smuggling radioactive bombs into the United States, while scanning of all cargo on narrow-body passenger aircraft is mandated by the Department of Homeland Security as of October 1, 2009.

Ground safety improvements and preparations for the next generation of air traffic control systems will also be needed. The challenge will be finding the funding needed to support these initiatives.

Customs Clearance[23]

When import cargo reaches the destination country, it must be cleared through Customs. Each country's regulations and process may be unique, so it is important to fully understand the process. Depending on the product, country of origin, and other relevant issues, the Customs entry and clearance process can be complex and full of surprises. Many companies rely upon the expertise of Customs brokers to avoid the many pitfalls of Customs clearance. Figure 11-8 and the accompanying discussion provide a brief overview of the U.S. clearance process. A detailed discussion of the process can be found in the trade section of the CBP website (http://www.cbp.gov/xp/cgov/trade/).

In the United States, the importer of record (that is, the owner, purchaser, or licensed customs broker designated by the owner, purchaser, or consignee) will file entry documents for the goods with the port director at the goods' port of entry. Imported goods are not legally entered until after the shipment has arrived within the port of entry, delivery of the merchandise has been authorized by U.S. Customs, and estimated duties have been paid. It is the importer of record's responsibility to arrange for examination and release of the goods.

Entry Filing Entering merchandise is a two-part process consisting of (1) filing the documents necessary to determine whether merchandise may be released from CBP custody, and (2) filing the documents that contain information for duty assessment and statistical purposes. Many organizations, or their Customs brokers, file the key

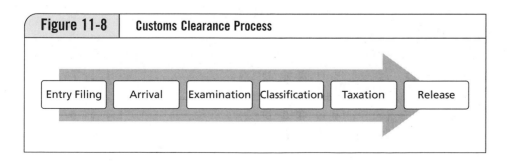

Figure 11-8	Customs Clearance Process

Entry Filing → Arrival → Examination → Classification → Taxation → Release documents prior to arrival to streamline the clearance process. Key filing documents include the entry manifest or application and special permit for immediate delivery, commercial invoice (if unavailable, a pro forma invoice can be used), packing lists, and other documents necessary to determine merchandise admissibility.

The entry must be accompanied by evidence that a bond has been posted with CBP to cover any potential duties, taxes, and charges that may accrue. Bonds may be secured through a resident U.S. surety company, but may be posted in the form of U.S. currency or certain government obligations. In the event that a customs broker is employed for the purpose of making entry, the broker may permit the use of his bond to provide the required coverage.

Arrival As the goods arrive at the seaport or airport, CBP is notified of arrival and unloading. Carriers participating in the **Automated Manifest System** can receive conditional release authorizations after leaving the foreign country and up to five days before U.S. arrival. If the application is approved, the shipment will be released expeditiously after it arrives. This process is useful for time-sensitive products, perishable goods (such as fruits and vegetables) and tariff quota merchandise.

Examination Following presentation of the entry documents and arrival of the shipment, it may be examined by CBP or the examination may be waived. Reasons for examining the goods and documents include determining: the value of the goods for Customs purposes and their dutiable status, whether the goods are properly labeled with their country of origin or other required markings, whether the shipment contains prohibited articles or illegal contraband, and whether the goods match the invoice. If no legal or regulatory violations have occurred, the clearance process continues. If problems are found, the shipment can be held pending correction, exported, or destroyed.

Classification All goods imported into the United States are subject to duty or duty-free entry in accordance with their classification under the applicable items in the U.S. Harmonized Tariff Schedule (HTS). The HTS comprises a hierarchical structure for describing all goods in trade for duty, quota, and statistical purposes. This structure is based upon the international Harmonized Commodity Description and Coding System, administered by the World Customs Organization in Brussels, Belgium. Access to the most current HTS is available from the U.S. International Trade Commission website (http://www.usitc.gov/tata/index.htm).

Taxation A **duty** is the tax that an importer must pay in order to bring goods into the country. When goods are dutiable, ad valorem, specific, or compound rates may be assessed. An ad valorem rate, the type of rate most often applied, is a percentage of the value of the merchandise. For example, a 5 percent ad valorem duty on a $50,000 shipment is $2,500.

Import duties vary from product to product and are dependent on the commodity being imported, its declared value, its country of origin, and other factors like antidumping legislation and quota controls. Import duty values can be as low as zero for trading partner countries like Canada and Mexico or as high as 100 percent (or more) of the product's declared value.

Release After the clearance requirements are completed and CBP has accepted the rate and amount of duty ascertained, the entry is considered to be liquidated. The goods can be released to the importer for onward domestic delivery of the goods.

In some situations, the importer may wish to postpone release of the goods. The goods are placed in a CBP **bonded warehouse** under a warehouse entry. The goods may remain in the bonded warehouse up to five years from the date of importation. At any time during that period, warehoused goods may be re-exported without paying duty, or they may be withdrawn for consumption upon paying duty at the duty rate in effect on the date of withdrawal. If the goods are destroyed under CBP supervision, no duty is payable.

While the goods are in the bonded warehouse, they may, under CBP supervision, be manipulated by cleaning, sorting, repacking, or otherwise changing their condition by processes that do not amount to manufacturing. After manipulation, and within the warehousing period, the goods may be exported without the payment of duty, or they may be withdrawn for consumption upon payment of duty at the rate applicable to the goods in their manipulated condition at the time of withdrawal. Perishable goods, explosive substances, or prohibited importations may not be placed in a bonded warehouse. Certain restricted articles, though not allowed release from custody, may be warehoused.

Another option for postponing release of goods is through the use of a **Foreign Trade Zone** (FTZ). FTZs are sites within the United States (in or near a U.S. Customs port of entry) where foreign and domestic goods are held until they are ready to be released into international commerce. Merchandise may enter a FTZ without a formal CBP entry or the payment of Customs duties or government excise taxes. If the final product is imported, duties are not paid until the goods are released into the U.S. market. Items that are processed in FTZs and then re-exported are charged no duties. While in the FTZ, goods may be assembled, repaired, stored, tested, sampled, repackaged or relabeled, cleaned, or combined with other products.

There is no time limit on goods stored inside a FTZ and certain foreign and domestic merchandise held in FTZs may be exempted from state and local inventory taxes. This allows firms to minimize their costs while their products are waiting to be shipped. In addition, quota restrictions are in some cases waived for items entering an FTZ. However, the restrictions would apply if the items were to enter the U.S. market.

Facilitating Role of Brokers   Customs brokers often have key responsibilities in the Customs clearance process. Customs brokers are the only persons who are authorized by the tariff laws of the United States to act as agents for importers in the transaction of their Customs business. They are experts at the entry process and can help importers avoid Customs clearance pitfalls that delay shipments and increase costs.

Customs brokers are private individuals or firms licensed by CBP to prepare and file the necessary Customs entries, arrange for the payment of duties found due, take steps to speed the release of the goods in CBP custody, and otherwise represent their principals in Customs matters. Other key duties include completion of documents, coordination of inland and ocean transportation, dockside inspection of cargo, and other duties as required by the importer. The fees charged for these services may vary according to the Customs broker and the extent of services performed.

SUMMARY

- Global transportation execution can be very challenging as it involves multiple carriers from different modes, numerous border crossings, and long distances. The risk of disruptions, delays, and damage also exists.

- When moving cargo internationally, direct exporter to importer moves are used for short-distance, cross-border movements by truck or rail. Indirect moves via ocean or air are used for intercontinental cargo movements.

- Intermodal transportation—the use of two or more modes of transportation in moving a shipment from origin to destination—is widely used to improve accessibility and cost efficiency of global transport.

- Intermodal freight is either containerized or requires transloading. The vast majority of finished goods move in containers due to their enhanced safety, handling speed, and service availability.

- Global transportation may subject freight to a variety of damage risks. It is critical to protect products as they are packed in shipping cartons and to protect the cartons when they are packed in the shipping container.

- Exporters and importers must be prepared to comply with a wide variety of government programs and regulations aimed at transportation safety, environmental impact reduction, and security.

- Ocean carriers have a huge role in global transport, moving 98 percent of intercontinental containerized trade volume and 60 percent of trade value.

- Ocean transport customers can choose between liner service and charter service, depending on their needs. A wide variety of ship types can carry an endless array of product types.

- Air cargo transportation is a small and specialized mode in terms of tonnage. However, it is a critical mode for time-sensitive, high-value freight and transports 35 percent of the value of goods traded internationally.

- International air cargo primarily moves on air freighters (68 percent) versus passenger planes and combi planes (32 percent). The rates are based on weight or space utilization (dim weight), whichever is higher.

- A variety of 3PL service providers—international freight forwarders, customs brokers, NVOCCs, and export packers—help exporters and importers move international freight quickly and efficiently.

- Seaports and airports are critical links in the global supply chain, providing the infrastructure, equipment, and labor needed to load, unload, and transfer freight between carriers.

- When cargo reaches the destination country, it must receive government approval to enter the country and travel to the final destination. Customs clearance involves entry, arrival, examination, classification, taxation, and release.

STUDY QUESTIONS

1. How does direct service differ from indirect service in global transportation? When is it advantageous to use each type?

2. What are the benefits and drawbacks of intermodal transportation for international freight?

3. What combination of intermodal services would be most beneficial for the following products?

    a. Lumber moving from British Columbia, Canada to Hickory, North Carolina

    b.   Seedless grapes moving from Valparaiso, Chile to Phoenix, Arizona

    c.   iPhones moving from Cupertino, California to Copenhagen, Denmark

4. If you need to move two TEUs of Adidas footwear from the factory in China to the European distribution center in Antwerp, Belgium, what route options should be considered? Which would you choose?

5. If you are moving international cargo to the United States, what security issues and regulations would impact your operations? How will you comply with these requirements?

6. What are the major trends and issues in ocean transportation? How does this impact global supply chain operations?

7. How has the Ocean Shipping Reform Act impacted the process for determining ocean transportation rates?

8. Given the high cost of international air freight service, why would companies choose this mode of transportation?

9. How are air cargo rates calculated? Calculate the cost of international air transportation for the following shipment: 200 cartons of fine jewelry weighing a total of 2,500 pounds. The carton dimensions are 18 in by 12 in by 12 in (L × W × H). The freight rate is $10.25 per pound.

10. What value do third party logistics companies bring to global transportation execution? Discuss the roles of

    a.   International freight forwarders

    b.   NVOCCs

    c.   Customs brokers

11. What roles do airports and seaports play in global transportation? How does cargo flow through these facilities?

12. Identify and briefly describe the six steps involved in the CBP Customs clearance process. What can individual companies do to streamline this process?

NOTES

1. Bureau of Transportation Statistics, *North American Transborder Freight Data.* Retrieved May 19, 2009 from: http://www.bts.gov/programs/international/transborder/TBDR_QA.html

2. C. E. Ebeling, "Evolution of a Box," *Invention and Technology,* Winter 2009.

3. Department for Transport, *DfT Aims and Objectives.* Retrieved May 19, 2009 from: http://www.dft.gov.uk/about/aimandobjectives

4. MergeGlobal Value Creation Initiative, "Insomnia," *American Shipper,* July 2008, 70.

5. GlobalSecurity.org, *Container Ship Types.* Retrieved May 20, 2009 from: http://www.globalsecurity.org/military/systems/ship/container-types.htm

6. Jonn W. Miller, "The Mega Containers Invade," *Wall Street Journal,* January 26, 2009.

7. Federal Maritime Commission, *The Impact of the Ocean Shipping Reform Act,* (2001). Retrieved May 19, 2009 from: http://www.fmc.gov/images/pages/OSRA_Study.pdf

8. Transpacific Stabilization Agreement, *About TSA.* Retrieved May 19, 2009 from: http://www.tsacarriers.org/about.html

9.   Ibid.

10. Eric Johnson, "Absolute Zero?" *American Shipper,* March 2009.

11. Mark Page, "Nowhere to Hide," *Journal of Commerce,* January 12, 2009.

12. International Air Transport Association, *The Air Cargo Tariffs.* Retrieved May 23, 2009 from: http://www.iata.org/ps/publications/tact.htm

13. Karen Theurmer, "Air Cargo: Flying Low," *Logistics Management,* May 2009.

14. Ibid.

15. Micheline Maynard, "High Fuel Costs Delay Airplane Orders," *New York Times,* August 1, 2008.

16. MergeGlobal Value Creation Initiative, "End of an Era?" *American Shipper,* August 2008.

17. Pierre David, *International Logistics,* (Cincinnati, OH: Atomic Dog Publishing, 2004).

18. Eckhardt-Herbert Arndt, "The New 12000 TEU Ship: A Challenge for Shipowners and Ports Alike," *ITJ Logistics Worldwide,* June 2008.

19. Federal Aviation Administration, *Airport Categories.* Retrieved May 25, 2009 from: http://www.faa.gov/airports_airtraffic/airports/planning_capacity/passenger_allcargo_stats/categories/

20. MergeGlobal Value Creation Initiative, "End of an Era?" *American Shipper,* August 2008.

21. John Gardiner, Ian Humphreys, and Stephen Ison, "Freight Operators Choice of Airports: A Three-Stage Process," *Transport Reviews,* Vol. 25, No. 1, 85–102, January 2005.

22. Schwartz, A. C. "Freighter-Friendly Offerings," *Air Transport World,* Vol. 39, No. 5, 2002.

23. This section is based on information contained in U.S. Customs and Border Protection, *Publication # 0000-0504: Importing into the United States: A Guide for Commercial Importers,* (2006). Retrieved May 25, 2009 from: http://www.cbp.gov/linkhandler/cgov/newsroom/publications/trade/iius.ctt/iius.pdf

CASE 11-1
Where There's Smoke ...

Smokehouse Seasonings Inc. (SSI) is a rapidly growing retailer of all things barbeque. They purchase unique grills, smokers, spices, sauces, and cooking utensils from around the globe. SSI's 12 stores are strategically located in six warm weather cities—Miami (4), Orlando (2), Atlanta (2), San Diego (2), Los Angeles, and Las Vegas. SSI also has a successful website.

Early on, SSI management focused on merchandising and building stores. Little thought was given to supply chain issues until a director of logistics was hired to improve SSI's global flows and processes. Rachel, the new director, started her role by holding a conference call with Bobby, SSI's transportation coordinator, and Mario, the company's senior buyer.

Rachel:	Thanks for dialing in on such short notice. I'll keep things brief. The "let's get it to the store, no matter what" attitude has got to go. My charge from the CEO is to reduce our international transportation spend without killing service quality.
Mario:	That all sounds good, but I don't understand why I'm on this call. You're talking about delivery issues and that's not my area. I don't see where the buying organization could cause your headaches.
Rachel:	I think that some of your decisions impact transportation and you could give us some insights.
Mario:	Well, I'll try.
Rachel:	Bobby, how are you making decisions regarding international routes and carriers?
Bobby:	Mario and people from his team give me information on the product vendor, location, shipment size, and how soon they want the product. I go to carriers that I'm familiar with and cut the best deals that I can manage.
Rachel:	What's your split between ocean and air?
Bobby:	I'd say it's about 50/50. We use air to expedite hot orders and anything less than a TEU worth of product. If I can fill up a container, I bring it through the Port of Los Angeles, strip the container, and send out smaller quantities via LTL service.
Mario:	No wonder why our margins are getting killed. You're always using that premium air service.
Bobby:	It's not my fault that your people wait until the last minute to finish a deal. If they would find suppliers in more strategically located cities, buy larger quantities, and give me more time, I could shift plenty of volume to ocean carriers.
Rachel:	Hold on, this is not the time to be pointing fingers. We need to focus on strategies and solutions.
Mario:	Maybe we're getting too big to try to manage this cargo flowing from around the world on our own. Every time I pick up a magazine, I'm reading about more regulation. Can't we look for some outside assistance?

Bobby: That's a possibility but I'm pretty darn good at what I do. With more stable cargo volume, we could try to initiate some ocean contracts and maybe even a charter or two. As for the air cargo, Mario has to get those suppliers to pack product in appropriate sized boxes. They use huge boxes that weigh next to nothing and are filled with packing peanuts.

Rachel: Now, we're getting somewhere. I want you to dig into these ideas and also come up with some new ideas for improving transportation. We'll talk about them in detail next Tuesday. I'll email you the dial-in information.

CASE QUESTIONS

1. Based on the conversation, what are the main causes of SSI's global transportation problems?

2. Given their product lines, is SSI using the right mix of global transportation services? Explain.

3. How can SSI leverage Mario's idea about external assistance with transportation?

4. What about the ideas that Bobby provided? Would routing, contracting, or chartering impact ocean service?

5. Is Bobby's complaint about product packing legitimate? What should be done?

CASE 11-2

As the Blade Turns

Revolving Wings (RW) is a Kalamazoo, Michigan manufacturer of equipment for the renewable energy sector. The company has a strong domestic market for their fiberglass composite wind turbine blades thanks to federal tax breaks offered to power companies. RW has some excess plant capacity thanks to a recent expansion and is investigating the opportunity to enter the export market. Demand for turbine blades is especially strong in India, where there is a strong commitment to renewable energy but a shortage of critical parts to meet the growing need for power generating capacity.

During its annual executive retreat, exporting is a major topic of discussion. After a presentation by the business development team and a similar evaluation by an industry analyst, RW's CEO sees the light. He quickly becomes a strong proponent of selling wind turbine blades to a power company near Bangalore, India. "Now all we have to do is figure out how to get the blades there quickly and without damage," says the CEO. "Darren, get your team on this one. I want some solid answers."

Darren Helm, RW's transportation director, knows this is a big opportunity for the company but it comes with tremendous challenges. Picking the right mode, finding ports that can handle the blades safely, and routing the freight are just a few of the issues that keep Helm awake the night after the CEO tagged him to lead the "export to India" project.

At his next staff meeting, Helm reminds his team: "These blades can be up to 148 ft long and weigh 12 tons. We have to first get them from the plant to the point of export. That's not easy, since we need to plan routes to avoid urban rush hours, sharp curves, narrow lanes, and weight-limited bridges."

"On top of those usual challenges, we have to find a high-quality international carrier to get the blades to India," Helm adds. "And don't forget the port challenges and final delivery to Bangalore."

Turning to you, Helm says: "Get me some answers fast! We need a plan of action for the CEO by Friday."

CASE QUESTIONS

1. What are the major problems and pitfalls that RW faces as it tries to go global with its product line?

2. What mode(s) of transportation would you recommend to Helm as most appropriate for moving the turbine blades domestically and internationally?

3. How would you route shipments of turbine blades from Kalamazoo to Bangalore? Why?

4. What role will ports play in the flow of turbine blades from the United States to India?

Chapter 12

THIRD PARTY LOGISTICS

Learning Objectives

After reading this chapter, you should be able to do the following:

- Understand the concept of third party logistics and its role in the movement of goods
- Identify the different types of third party logistics service providers
- Describe the four types of transportation activities that are outsourced
- Discuss the reasons why companies seek integrated third party logistics services
- Understand the size and scope of the third party logistics market
- Evaluate the reasons for outsourcing and the results achieved
- Summarize the process for outsourcing transportation and logistics activities
- Appreciate the current challenges and competitive issues in the third party logistics industry
- Compare the coordination roles of various service provider types
- Recognize the importance of information technology in managing outsourced activities

Transportation Profile

The Seven Abilities of Highly Effective 3PLs

The right logistics provider can bring you convenience, cost savings, and competitive advantage as you work to deliver the right product to the right place at the right time at the right price.

Execution is the key, central to responding to fluctuating pressures of production schedules, capacity, weather, or other influences on your strategic supply chain plans. A good third party logistics service provider (3PL) provides quality transportation management and process improvements that can lead to execution excellence.

Your 3PL should be able to deliver these seven services:

1. **Provide visibility.** Product in transit is, in essence, inventory. While it is not in your production or distribution facility, it is in your supply chain. Your 3PL should work with you to develop processes for gathering and reporting inventory status.

   Confirming transit time and required arrival dates should be central to each driver dispatch. As the status of each shipment is gathered via automated and manual procedures, you can verify that your rolling inventory will be delivered on time.

2. **Measure performance.** Your 3PL should measure performance and provide reporting so you can make informed decisions about your supply chain. The first step is to develop perspective across the organization's functional silos. Next comes managing transportation and total supply chain costs so you can maximize revenue opportunities.

3. **Create a low-cost network.** Low transportation rates alone do not equal low cost. The highest goal in transportation and logistics is to create the lowest-cost network possible that ensures product is where it needs to be, when it needs to be. A strategic, long-term approach to buying transportation can lead to better service and lower costs.

4. **Offer multimodal options.** Beyond capacity planning, multimodal strategies can help manage the risk of running out of inventory by alternating modes, varying transit times, and selecting carriers. Timely visibility to shipments, regardless of mode, provides valuable information you can use to help reduce costly out-of-stocks.

5. **Develop internal and industry rate benchmarks.** Achieving a true low-cost solution and identifying waste in your supply chain requires benchmarking rates by lane and identifying the low-rate carriers to create a low-cost network. When 3PLs develop both internal and external benchmarks, you can gauge how you are doing against both your historical results and the wider market.

6. **Conduct constraint-based bids.** Constraint-based biding tools use math to both optimize price and constrain carriers in different ways. Typical constraints can include maximum volume for a lane, minimum or maximum number of carriers servicing a facility, and penalties for not providing services such as EDI and drop trailers, or for a poor on-time percentage.

   Constraint-based bids, conducted by logistics professionals who understand and use the tools regularly, can help set a baseline for future improvements. The tools also provide cost savings and set the stage for managing long-term carrier relationships, as opposed to managing a large, disparate network.

7. **Establish reliable transit times.** On-time deliveries and effective carrier management are critical. 3PLs can help you determine key performance indicators of successful deliveries because such metrics vary from company to company. Then you can work with your 3PL to

develop operating procedures and data-gathering processes. The collaborative efforts of process mapping, data integrity, and timely reporting will positively influence successful deliveries.

When your product is where it is supposed to be, when it is supposed to be there, and at a planned total landed cost, maximum revenue is generated. That's the level of service you can expect a strategic 3PL to deliver.

Source: Adapted from Jim Butts, "The Seven Abilities of Highly Effective 3PLs," *Inbound Logistics*, September, 2006. Reprinted with permission.

Introduction

Outsourcing is a fact of life in the 21st century. The concept of managing all business activities in-house has given way to specialization or focusing on a company's core capabilities. Hence, many companies have outsourced their information technology (IT) processes to an external service provider that manages the systems, software, and equipment. This allows the company to focus on using the technology to operate the business rather than having to manage all the technical issues and challenges. This reliance on external experts is commonly used for accounting, payroll and tax preparation, advertising, human resources benefits administration, and numerous other activities. Many companies like Nike even outsource their production needs to contract manufacturers located around the world.

Transportation is another activity that is widely outsourced to external experts. Global companies like COSCO (China Ocean Shipping Company) Deutsche Post (owner of Exel and DHL), FedEx, Maersk, and UPS provide a wide variety of transportation and logistics services to individuals and companies around the world. These **third party logistics service providers** (3PLs) are experts in the management and flow of freight, allowing customers to focus their resources on other activities. Some of these larger organizations provide a one-stop shopping solution where customers can purchase all their transportation service needs, regardless of mode or geographic requirements.

Given the financial and service impact of transportation on a company's success, developing an effective transportation outsourcing strategy is critical. As the Transportation Profile suggests, you should not just hire the first 3PL that comes to the door. It is imperative to find a 3PL with a track record of providing quality transportation management and services that support execution excellence. How to accomplish this is the goal of Chapter 12. We will discuss the general structure of the 3PL industry, customer characteristics, and relationship options. Specific issues related to establishing and managing 3PL relationships will be addressed, followed by a discussion of current and future 3PL industry issues. Throughout the chapter, you will gain an understanding of the key benefits and challenges of outsourcing transportation requirements.

Industry Overview

If you were to Google for a definition of *third party logistics* or *3PL*, the responses would be numerous and varied. These explanations range from simple and arbitrary to extensive and detailed. Here are a few examples:

> **EyeforTransport:** supply of logistics related operations between traders by an independent organization.[1]

BusinessDictionary.com: arrangement in which a firm with long and varied supply chains outsources its logistical operations to one or more specialist firms, the third party logistics providers.[2]

Council of Supply Chain Management Professionals: outsourcing all or much of a company's logistics operations to a specialized company. The term "3PL" was first used in the early 1970s to identify **intermodal marketing companies** (IMCs) in transportation contracts. Up to that point, contracts for transportation had featured only two parties, the shipper and the carrier. When IMCs entered the picture—as **intermediaries** that accepted shipments from the shippers and tendered them to the rail carriers—they became the third party to the contract, the 3PL. Definitions have broadened to the point where these days, every company that offers some kind of logistics service for hire calls itself a 3PL. Preferably, these services are integrated, or "bundled," together by the provider. Services they provide are transportation, warehousing, cross-docking, inventory management, packaging, and freight forwarding. In 2008, legislation passed declaring that the legal definition of a 3PL is "A person who solely receives, holds, or otherwise transports a consumer product in the ordinary course of business but who does not take title to the product."[3]

Pulling the key points from these definitions, a 3PL firm may be defined as "an external supplier that performs all or part of a company's logistics functions."[4] This definition is purposely broad and is intended to encompass suppliers of services such as inventory management, warehousing, distribution, financial services, and transportation. This chapter will focus on the transportation aspects of the 3PL industry, though it is important to remember that transportation services provided by a 3PL must be well integrated with the customer's other logistical activities. The transportation focused 3PLs must also provide solutions to logistics challenges and supply chain problems.

Types of 3PL Providers

While many 3PLs promote themselves as **integrated service providers** with a comprehensive range of logistical capabilities, most have their origins and greatest level of expertise in a specific logistics activity. Hence, the easiest way to categorize these service providers is on the basis of their foundation service offerings. 3PLs are typically categorized as being transportation based, distribution based, forwarder based, financial based, or information based firms. Each of these is discussed briefly in the following paragraphs.

Transportation Based These 3PLs trace their origins to freight movement via truck, rail, air, or other modes of transportation. As customer requirements expanded, these transportation companies developed 3PL subsidiaries or major divisions to provide a broader set of capabilities to serve the marketplace. Not only do these organizations move freight, they may also manage transportation operations on behalf of customers, provide **dedicated contract carriage**, operate fulfillment centers, and develop logistics solutions, among other services.

Transportation-based 3PLs and their parent companies include APL Logistics; Neptune Orient Lines Limited, FedEx Global Supply Chain Services; FedEx Corporation, Schneider National; Schneider National Inc., and UPS Supply Chain Solutions; United Parcel Service of America Inc. among others. Some of the services provided by these 3PLs leverage the transportation assets of their parent companies, while other rely upon the assets of other companies. In all instances, these firms extend beyond the transportation activity to provide a more comprehensive set of logistics offerings.

Distribution Based These 3PLs suppliers originated from the public or contract warehousing business and have expanded into a broader range of logistics services. Based on their traditional orientation, these types of organizations are heavily involved in logistics activities such as inventory management, warehousing, and order fulfillment. Some have added transportation services to assist customers with the coordination, optimization, and execution of shipments via all modes. The combination of distribution and transportation capabilities creates a one-stop integrated logistics service offering so that customers have the option of working with a single 3PL.

Distribution based 3PLs range from single facility operators to global organizations with strategically located operations centers. Major players include Exel, DSC Logistics, Ozburn-Hessey Logistics, and UTi Integrated Logistics (formerly known as Standard Corporation). This category also includes a number of 3PL firms that have emerged from larger corporate logistics organizations. Prominent among these are Caterpillar Logistics Services; Caterpillar Inc., IBM Supply Chain Management Services; IBM Corporation, and Intral Corporation; The Gillette Company. These providers have significant experience in managing the logistics operations of the parent firm and, as a result, prove to be very capable providers of such services to external customers. While the idea that a 3PL firm may emerge from a corporate logistics organization is an interesting one, not all of these conversions have resulted in commercially successful 3PLs.

Forwarder Based This group of 3PLs includes **freight forwarders**, brokers, and agents that primary facilitate the flow of goods on behalf of customers. Though these companies do not own equipment, they arrange transportation services for LTL (less than truckload) shipments, air cargo, and ocean freight, as well as providing other transportation related services. Many are engaged in the support of international freight movement, booking cargo space with carriers, arranging freight movement to and from carrier facilities, preparing and processing documentation, and performing related activities.

While some of these organizations, such as C.H. Robinson Worldwide Inc., Hub Group Inc., and Kuehne + Nagel Inc. have extended their primary roles into a broader range of 3PL services, other forwarder based service providers have been absorbed by larger organizations seeking to enhance their service offerings. During the last ten years, Circle International Group Inc. merged with Eagle Global Logistics (which was later bought out by CEVA Logistics in 2008), UPS purchased Fritz Companies Inc., and FedEx acquired Tower Group International. Further merger and acquisition activity is expected in the future as freight forwarding companies seek to increase profitability through building economies of scale.

Financial Based This category of 3PL providers helps customers with monetary issues and financial flows in the supply chain. Their traditional roles include **freight rating**, freight payment, **freight bill auditing**, and accounting services. Some of the financial based 3PLs have added information systems tools to provide freight visibility (such as **tracking and tracing** capabilities) and assist customers with electronic payment, carrier compliance reporting, and freight claims management.

Primary players among this category include Cass Information Systems, Inc., Commercial Traffic Corporation, PowerTrack Network (U.S. Bank), and Transportation Solutions Inc. In addition, companies like GE Capital Solutions (General Electric) provide transportation equipment financing, leasing services, and asset tracking.

Information Based The Internet has provided an excellent platform for the growth of information based 3PLs. These companies have digitized many activities that were

Transportation Technology

Enhancing Freight Flows with TMS Capabilities

Sterling Commerce, a provider of supply chain management technology services and subsidiary of AT&T Inc., said this week it has added integrated parcel management capabilities to Sterling Transportation Management System (TMS), its flagship, Web-based TMS.

The company said this enhancement allows shippers to plan and execute transportation operations and processes across all modes, and, in turn, reduce costs, provide better shipment visibility, and track transportation spending while meeting shipping and delivery goals.

Incorporating parcel management capability into Sterling TMS helps customers figure out the best shipping alternatives with the lowest cost option, according to Richard Douglass, global industry executive, manufacturing and logistics at Sterling.

Decisions on mode and pricing are tabulated in the Sterling TMS with what the company describes as a "lowest cost mode selection" capability that builds upon existing tools within the application, which allows shippers to rate shipments across all modes and select the most cost-efficient mode that meets service and delivery expectations, based on volume, destination, and type of freight.

"This application is about trying to make things easier for the shipper to figure out the best way to ship and improve productivity and reduce the amount of time spent jumping around from system to system or looking at different rate tables," said Douglass. "It is about stream-lining and optimizing that whole process."

Another component of the integrated parcel management capabilities of Sterling TMS, according to the company, is its support for zone skipping, which allows a shipper to consolidate parcel shipments going to the same geographic region and then line-hauling them together closer to the destination before separating them into individual shipments.

A leading supply chain technology analyst recently wrote in a research report that parcel management applications in the future will represent a sizable segment of future transportation spending.

"Traditional TMS vendors have shied away from building software to support the function because it requires not only separate logic and content but also must be continually updated to stay in compliance with individual carrier rules," according to AMR Research analyst John Fontanella.

Source: Adapted from Jeff Berman, "Logistics Technology: Sterling Commerce Adds Parcel Management Capabilities to its TMS," *Logistics Management,* December 2008. Reprinted by permission.

---

previously performed manually or required the use of licensed software. Today, these information based 3PLs provide online freight brokerage services as well as cargo planning, routing, and scheduling. They also offer companies access to **transportation management systems**, warehouse management systems, and performance management tools via the Internet on a per use basis. This software as a service capability allows customers to avoid the high cost of licensed software implementation, instead paying for access on a variable cost basis.

Though many information based 3PLs have come and gone during the Internet era, a few strong players have emerged. Companies like Descartes Systems Group Inc., Sterling Commerce, and Transplace are among the leaders in creating robust information tools and online capabilities for the coordination, optimization, and control of transportation and logistics activities. Insights into the capabilities of Sterling's Internet based transportation management system can be found in the Transportation Technology feature.

The 3PL industry can be segmented in other ways as well. One common way to distinguish service providers is by the resources that they rely upon to fulfill customer requirements. 3PLs with tangible equipment and facilities are called **asset-based providers**. In contrast, 3PLs that leverage the resources of other companies are called **non-asset-based providers**. Each type is discussed below.

Asset Based Providers

When a 3PL owns many or all of the assets necessary to run its customers' transportation and logistics activities, it is known as an asset based provider. This category includes companies that own truck fleets, containers, aircraft, terminals and warehouses, material handling equipment, technology systems, and/or other resources. An asset based provider typically has its own labor force to perform the customers' work and management team to oversee the day-to-day operations. Having these internal resources allows the 3PL to leverage internal strengths and infrastructures to provide direct, immediate solutions.

This type of 3PL includes widely known companies such as Exel, FedEx, UPS, Menlo, and Saddle Creek. We are familiar with them because we see their vehicles on the road and pass by their facilities. FedEx, for example, has a network of company-owned facilities that are linked by FedEx vehicles and aircraft. Their various operating divisions— FedEx Home, FedEx Express, FedEx Freight, and so forth—are capable of moving shipments ranging from single packages to full truckloads, as well as managing customers' inventory and order fulfillment needs from FedEx-owned distribution centers.

Many customers choose to work with asset based providers because they have readily available **capacity**, permanent employees, and direct control of the customers' freight. They prefer to work with a single 3PL who will take total responsibility for the outsourced activity and assume accountability if problems occur. Customers can also maintain greater visibility of outsourced activities and inventory if they are handled by a technology savvy asset based provider who performs all activities internally rather than handing them off to other companies.

The primary concern with asset based providers is bias toward their internal resources. The argument is that these companies have made significant investments in physical assets and are tethered to those assets when developing solutions for customers. This internal focus may not always generate the most flexible solutions or produce the most cost-efficient transportation and logistics services for the customers.

Non-Asset Based Providers

When a 3PL contracts with other firms to provide transportation and logistics services rather than owning the required equipment and facilities, it is called a non-asset based provider. This type of provider acts as a service integrator and is not restricted to using any particular warehouse or transportation company in providing services to its customers. Non-asset based providers offer expertise in negotiating contracts with transportation companies and distribution centers in an effort to achieve the best combination of price and service for their customers.

From a transportation standpoint, companies like CEVA Logistics, C.H. Robinson, and Transplace are heavily involved in **freight management** and brokerage, helping customers with freight activities such as securing capacity at reasonable costs, scheduling pickups and deliveries, **routing and scheduling** shipments, and auditing freight bills.

Non-asset base providers may also focus on international freight flows via freight forwarding, **Customs brokerage**, and related activities. Finally, non-asset based providers may also provide strategic planning and technology services. Consulting firms like Accenture, Capgemini, and CSC Consulting and software firms fall into this category.

Customers view non-asset based providers as being more flexible than their asset based counterparts. Non-asset based 3PLs can be unbiased in their decision making as they are not limited to an internal infrastructure of assets. Because they are not restricted to using any particular transportation company or set of facilities to serve customers, they are free to objectively choose the best set of service providers and create innovative solutions for customers. This can lead to tailored services and lower overall costs for the customer.

There are also concerns with non-asset based providers. First, these companies do not have significant internal capacity to handle customers' requirements. This can be a problem during times of economic expansion when transportation equipment availability is squeezed. Also, there are more moving parts and relationships to manage when a non-asset based provider uses external service providers on behalf of their customers. It is imperative to have strong IT capabilities to maintain control and visibility of customers' freight that is dispersed among a variety of transportation and warehousing companies.

3PL Services and Integration

As the preceding discussion indicates, there are many types of 3PL service providers offering a vast array of capabilities. Name any type of transportation or logistics requirement that a customer may have and there is a 3PL able to support it. These customer requirements range from strategic supply chain design to daily operations. Within the transportation function, 3PLs provide four primary types of services: freight movement, freight management, intermediary services, and specialty services. Figure 12-1 highlights key capabilities within each service type.

Most of the service offerings related to freight movement and freight management are discussed in detail by other chapters. However, you may not be familiar with some of the intermediary and special services offered by 3PLs to their customers. Each service option is briefly described below.

Figure 12-1	**3PL Primary Transportation Offerings**

FREIGHT MOVEMENT	FREIGHT MANAGEMENT
• For hire carriage	• Carrier selection, routing, & scheduling
• Contract carriage	• Contract compliance
• Expedited service	• Performance analysis
• Time definite service	• Freight bill auditing and payment
• Intermodal service	• Transportation management systems
INTERMEDIARY SERVICES	**SPECIALTY SERVICES**
• Surface forwarding	• Dedicated contract carriage
• Air forwarding	• Drayage
• Freight brokerage	• Pool distribution
• Intermodal marketing	• Merge in transit
• Shippers associations	• Household good movement

Surface Freight Forwarding Surface freight forwarders pick up, assemble, and consolidate shipments and then hire carriers to transport and deliver the consolidated shipments to the final destination. They match demand with capacity and help customers obtain economic rates for the consolidated shipments. From the perspective of the customer, freight forwarders act as the carrier, and, therefore, are liable to shippers for loss and damage to freight that occurs during transit.

Air Freight Forwarding Air freight forwarders consolidate small shipments for long-haul movement and distribution. They primarily use the services of major passenger and freight airlines for long-haul service. The air freight forwarder serves the shipping public with pickup service, a single bill of lading and freight bill, one-firm tracing, and delivery service.

Freight Brokerage Brokers function as middlemen between the shipper and the carrier much the same as a real estate broker does in the sale of property. A broker is an independent contractor paid to arrange transportation. The broker normally represents the carrier and seeks freight on their behalf to avoid moving empty equipment. They may also represent shippers seeking capacity on the spot market.

Intermodal Marketing Companies IMCs are intermediaries between shippers and railroads and are also known as consolidators or agents. They are facilitators or arrangers of rail transportation service. They assume little or no legal liability; the legal shipping arrangement is between the shipper and the railroad, not the agent. Freight charge payment usually is made to the IMC who, in turn, pays the long-haul carrier.

Shippers Associations These nonprofit transportation membership cooperatives arrange for the domestic or international shipment of members' cargo with motor carriers, railroads, ocean carriers, air carriers, and others. The association aggregates cargo and ships the collective membership cargo at favorable volume rates.[5]

Dedicated Contract Carriage 3PLs offering this hybrid private/for-hire arrangement serve as a customer's private fleet with a customized turnkey solution. Dedicated contract carriage includes the management of drivers, vehicles, maintenance services, route design, delivery, and administrative support for a fixed price. Companies gain the advantages of a private fleet without the direct responsibility of capitalizing and operating it.

Drayage These companies provide local transportation of containerized cargo. Drayage companies specialize in short haul movement of intermodal containers from origin to ocean ports and rail yards and from these facilities to their ultimate destination. They are typically contracted by the rail or ocean carrier to provide these pickup and delivery services.

Pool Distribution As an alternative to direct LTL service, a 3PL may move a large quantity of product in bulk to a specific market or regional terminal. From there, the pooled freight is offloaded, sorted by customer, and then reloaded onto local delivery trucks for distribution to final destinations. Pool distribution can reduce transit times, maintain shipment integrity, reduce claim potential due to less handling, and generate cost discounts versus LTL rates.

Merge In-transit A merge-in-transit system unites shipments from multiple suppliers at a specified merge point located close to the end customer. It avoids the need for traditional warehousing, in which orders are assembled from inventory in stock for shipment. Merge-in-transit provides a number of customer benefits, including the delivery of a single, consolidated shipment, reduced order cycle time, and lower transportation costs with less inventory in the system.

Household Goods Movement This group of service providers is specifically organized to move the household goods of people and businesses. Household goods movers, often called van lines, are geared to serve the market with specialized vehicles, local agencies with warehouses for storage, and pickup and delivery equipment, as well as central dispatching operations.

While many 3PLs have expertise in some of these areas, leading 3PLs are pursuing two additional capabilities. First, they are developing integrated service offerings to accommodate customer desires for one stop shopping with a single service provider. Second, they are expanding service territories to meet the requirements of increasingly global customers.

These two customer driven moves go hand in hand. As customers embrace global sourcing and distribution, their supply chains become more complex and challenging. In turn, they need the assistance of highly capable 3PLs to develop integrated, cross-functional global supply chains. Transportation expertise is not enough to capture the attention of these increasingly sophisticated customers. 3PLs must also develop expertise in supply chain network design, process implementation and coordination, and day-to-day execution.[6] Doing all three requires strong IT tools, multimodal capabilities, and the ability to manage and streamline the flow of goods through the supply chain.

In response to the demand for integrated services, larger 3PLs (such as Deutsche Post, UPS, and FedEx) have embarked on an aggressive plan to expand and integrate their capabilities. Table 12-1 provides an example of this expansion, revealing how FedEx has acquired numerous companies since 1998. The company has leveraged the strength of its express delivery service to create a more diversified portfolio of transportation, e-commerce, and business services. FedEx Global Supply Chain (a division of FedEx Services) offers specialty 3PL services like critical inventory logistics, fulfillment services, transportation management, **cold chain** solutions, freight forwarding, brokerage, and **cross dock** services.

FedEx is not alone in the pursuit of integrated capabilities and global reach. Customers' increasing activity in global sourcing and distribution has driven 3PLs like Exel, CEVA Logistics, and Geodis Wilson to bolster their international resources through the creation of internal divisions, acquisition of smaller 3PLs, or the development of partner relationships with other 3PLs. They are building logistics expertise and well developed transportation networks to accommodate the growing volume of trade between key regions of the world.

Another option to address customers' global service requirements is to invest in strategically located transportation and distribution facilities. These assets can help an organization establish critical **hubs**, streamline flows, and support customer fulfillment needs. UPS has been very active in this regard, establishing a physical presence in Asia, Europe, and Latin America that allows the company to serve more than 200 countries and territories. The Global Perspective feature highlights their most recently opened international hub in Shanghai, China.

Table 12-1	FedEx Capability Expansion Timeline

YEAR	EVENT
1998	Acquires Caliber System Inc. comprised of small-package carrier RPS, LTL carrier Viking Freight, Caliber Logistics, Caliber Technology and Roberts Express.
1999	Acquires air freight forwarder Caribbean Transportation Services
2000	Company is renamed FedEx Corporation. Expanded service capabilities are divided into operating companies: FedEx Express, FedEx Ground, FedEx Global Logistics, FedEx Custom Critical and FedEx Services. FedEx Trade Networks is created with the acquisitions of Tower Group International and WorldTariff. FedEx Supply Chain Services became part of FedEx Services
2001	Acquires LTL carrier American Freightways
2002	FedEx Freight is created with rebranding of Viking Freight and American Freightways
2004	Acquires Kinko's
2006	Acquires LTL carrier Watkins Motor Lines
2007	Acquires international firms to enhance global capabilities: express company ANC (United Kingdom), Flying-Cargo Hungary Kft (Hungary), Prakash Air Freight Pvt. Ltd. (India), and DTW Group's fifty percent share of the FedEx-DTW International Priority express joint venture (China).

Source: FedEx Timeline, available at http://about.fedex.designcdt.com/our_company/company_information/fedex_history/fedex_timeline.

Global Perspectives

UPS Opens International Hub in Shanghai

UPS announced this week it has officially opened a new international hub in Shanghai, China. The company said this hub will provide shippers with improved access to China and expedite the movement of express packages and heavy freight on a global basis.

The hub is located at the Pudong International Airport in the Yangtze River Delta region. This hub will link all of China via Shanghai to UPS's international network, with direct access to the Americas, Europe, and Asia. It will also connect points served in China through a dedicated service by Chinese all-cargo airline Yangtze River Express. The Shanghai hub will also be connected to its intra-Asia air hub at the Clark Air Force in the Philippines, which is scheduled to be relocated to Shenzen in southern China in 2010.

UPS broke ground on the Shanghai hub in 2006, and it has been serving China since 1988, according to Mark Dickens, UPS International spokesman. But up until China became part of the WTO, UPS had to operate through Sinotrans, a Chinese service partner. And when it became wholly-owned in China in late 2005, Dickens said UPS quickly embarked on an expansion plan that included the Shanghai hub.

The Shanghai hub, according to UPS, has 117 conveyor belts, 47 docking bays, and a sorting capacity of 17,000 pieces per hour. Other features of the hub include:

- a collaboration with Shanghai Customs to deploy a Customs risk management system which minimizes unnecessary checks and expedites shipment clearance for delivery to recipients;
- an IT system at its dedicated Customs area comprised of automated import and export inspection geared to increase overall package flow efficiency;
- a "Shipper Build Area" at the General Cargo Handling Area that enables customers to perform onsite packaging before goods are loaded onto aircraft, as well as eliminating the practice of processing goods at a separate facility; and
- augmenting delivery time for shippers in eastern China by a full day, along with express and cargo shipment pickup times for China shipments being pushed back by one day and four hours, respectively, to provide shippers with improved flexibility to prepare shipments.

"With China being the world's factory in addition to having one of the world's fastest growing consumer classes, there was no question that UPS had to establish a major operational facility in China," explained Dickens. "The question, of course, was where. Shanghai has was selected for several reasons: the concentration of origin and destination volume associated with the Yangtze River Delta, Shanghai's connectivity to other points in China and beyond, the efficiency of the airport operations, room for expansion, and support from both the local and national governments."

And shippers, said Dickens, will see a lot of benefits as a result of the new Shanghai hub, including better connectivity to its global network. UPS will operate 80 flights a week in Shanghai to and from the United States, the Philippines, South Korea, Japan, and Europe, he said.

GLOBAL ECONOMIC IMPACT

At a time when the economy is shaky and credit markets frozen, Dickens said that UPS remains committed to finding new and better ways to serve its customers and grow its business. While he acknowledged UPS is seeing some reductions in volume in various global sectors, he said it is also seeing new growth, too.

During its third quarter earnings release in October, UPS said its daily export volume out of China grew by more than 10 percent over the same period in 2007. And one of its strongest trade lanes is Asia to Europe, where UPS's export volume was up more than 15 percent in the third quarter of 2008 as well.

Source: Adapted from Jeff Berman, "Global Logistics/Air Cargo: UPS Opens up New International Hub in Shanghai," *Logistics Management,* December 2008. Reprinted by permission.

3PL User Overview

In the previous section, you were introduced to different types of 3PLs and specific service providers, as well as brief references to 3PL customers. In this section, we dig into the customer aspects of 3PL. The key issues include who these customers are, why they outsource transportation and logistics activities to 3PLs, and what services they require. As you will learn, outsourcing has become a way of life for shippers, who rely heavily on 3PLs to help plan, execute, and control their supply chains.

Use of 3PL services has been growing for more than ten years. The aggressive growth and expansion of the global 3PL industry produced revenues of $487 billion in

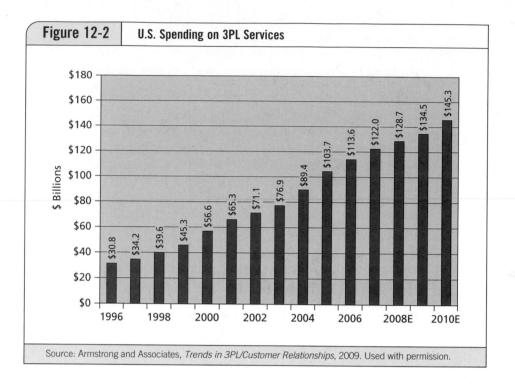

Figure 12-2 | **U.S. Spending on 3PL Services**

Source: Armstrong and Associates, *Trends in 3PL/Customer Relationships*, 2009. Used with permission.

2007. In the United States alone, 3PL gross revenues grew to $122 billion in 2007—an $8.4 billion increase over the previous year, according to consultants Armstrong & Associates Inc. in their annual study of service trends, 3PL market segment sizes, and growth rates.[7] Figure 12-2 highlights the growth in U.S. 3PL spending.

In the United States, 3PLs captured 16 percent of total logistics spending in 2008, up from 10 percent in 2002. Table 12-2 reveals that U.S. companies account for 25 percent of spending in the total global 3PL market. This spending, in both the domestic and international markets, is driven by large companies. The Armstrong study found that 77 percent of the Fortune 500 outsourced some or all of their logistics and supply chain functions to outside providers in 2008, up from 64 percent in 2005. The global Fortune 500—which includes U.S.-based multinationals—spent nearly $200 billion on 3PL services in 2008, up about $10 billion from 2007.[8]

Table 12-2 | **3PL Spending by Region (U.S. $ BILLION)**

	NORTH AMERICA	EUROPE	ASIA-PACIFIC	LATIN AMERICA	OTHER
3PL Spending	$143	$170	$113	$15	$46
Total Logistics Spending	$1,613	$1,696	$1,524	$247	$1,224

Source: Armstrong and Associates, *Trends in 3PL/Customer Relationships*, 2009. Used with permission.

Leading the use of 3PL services are the technology, automotive, and retailing industries. On average three services are provided by 3PLs for each customer relationship. Major 3PL users include General Motors, Procter & Gamble, Walmart, Ford, and PepsiCo. Each uses 30 or more 3PLs to help manage and operate their supply chains.[9] While 3PLs rely upon these Forture 500 clients for current revenues, future growth opportunities lie with small and midsize companies.

Reasons for Outsourcing

The most logical reason for using 3PL services is a lack of internal capabilities. Companies with little transportation and logistics expertise would be wise to outsource rather than attempting to build internal operations. Instead, they can leverage the knowledge, skills, networks, and resources of experienced 3PLs.

You may be surprised to find that Proctor & Gamble and Walmart, companies with premier supply chain capabilities, make extensive use 3PL services. They, like other companies, use 3PLs when it is appropriate to reduce costs, increase resource capacity, and fill gaps in expertise. For example, Walmart contracts with Exel to handle distribution of automotive tires to its U.S. stores. Walmart avoids the cost of building a dedicated tire warehouse, leverages Exel's inventory management capabilities, and reduces the need to expend energy on a product line that is not sold in all stores.

Numerous studies have identified why companies outsource or do not outsource their transportation and logistics requirements. Table 12-3 provides lists from two recent studies that highlight these factors. Note that there is some conflict between the results as a reason for outsourcing may also be listed as a reason for not outsourcing. Clearly, outsourcing transportation and logistics is not for every organization. Before choosing to use 3PL services, an organization should spend time developing clear transportation objectives and then analyze if and how 3PLs can provide key support.

Table 12-3	**Reasons For and Against 3PL Use**
REASONS FOR USING 3PL SERVICES	**REASONS AGAINST USING 3PL SERVICES**
Opportunity for cost reductions	Logistics is a core competency of company
Ability to focus on core competencies	Cost reductions would not be experienced
Opportunity to improve customer service	Control over outsourced function would diminish
Improve return on assets	Service level commitments would not be realized
Increase in inventory turns	Company has more expertise than 3PL providers
Productivity improvement opportunities	Logistics is too important to consider outsourcing
Imbibe more flexibility into logistics processes	Outsourcing is not a corporate philosophy
Access to emerging technology	Global capabilities of 3PL need improvement
Expansion to unfamiliar markets	Inability of 3PLs to form meaningful relationships
Ability to divert capital investments	Issues related to security of shipments

Source: B.S. Sahay and Ramneesh Mohan, "3PL practices: an Indian perspective, *International Journal of Physical Distribution & Logistics Management*, Vol. 36, No. 9, 2006; and, Georgia Tech and Capgemini LLC, *Eleventh Annual 3PL Study*, 2006.

Primary Activities Outsourced

While the use of 3PLs has grown dramatically, customer engagement patterns have not changed dramatically from year to year. Organizations predominantly use 3PL service providers for executing specific services rather than for fully managing their supply chains, according to Armstrong and Associates. Their 2009 study of nearly 4,000 shipper-3PL relationships revealed that 82 percent are "tactical" in nature, meaning 3PLs are used for specific tasks such as transportation or warehousing. Only 18 percent of the relationships are classified as "strategic," where a 3PL essentially takes over a customer's entire logistics and supply chain operation, says Armstrong. Many of the Fortune 500 customers are just too large for a single 3PL to manage independently.[10]

These **tactical services** often focus on transportation. The 2009 Georgia Tech-Capgemini annual study of 3PL customers (www.3plstudy.com), found that half of the most frequently outsourced activities are related to the movement and management of freight. Domestic and international transportation dominate 3PL usage in all four geographical regions as shown by Table 12-4. Customs clearance, freight forwarding, and **shipment consolidation** are also widely used services.[11]

Table 12-4	Activities Outsourced to 3PLs			
	NORTH AMERICA %	EUROPE %	ASIA-PACIFIC %	LATIN AMERICA %
Domestic transportation	78	92	91	70
International transportation	69	89	89	70
Warehousing	70	73	75	62
Customs clearance and brokerage	66	57	81	56
Forwarding	48	44	70	45
Shipment consolidation	46	43	55	38
Reverse logistics	31	42	41	34
Cross-docking	37	43	35	25
Transportation management	39	38	36	25
Product labeling, packaging, assembly, kitting	29	42	37	35
Freight bill auditing and payment	54	20	21	14
Supply chain consultancy provided by 3PLs	21	15	14	14
Order Entry, Processing, and Fulfillment	12	14	21	17

Table 12-4	continued			
	NORTH AMERICA %	EUROPE %	ASIA-PACIFIC %	LATIN AMERICA %
Fleet Management	9	15	14	15
LLP/4PL Services	11	13	14	12
Customer Service	11	10	12	22

Source: Georgia Tech and Capgemini LLC, *The State of Logistics Outsourcing: 13th Annual 3PL Study*, 2008, Fig. 6, p. 13. Copyright © 2008 C. John Langley, Jr., Ph.D., and Capgemini U.S. LLC. All rights reserved. Reprinted by permission.

The heavy use of tactical transportation activities does not mean that 3PLs should abandon their drive toward integrated global service capabilities. Over three-quarters of the participants in the Georgia Tech-Capgemini study look to their 3PLs for needed integration, rather than trying to accomplish it internally. 3PL customers, particularly those with mature and complex supply chains, prefer to work with **strategic services** providers that can integrate processes, people, and services. It is not surprising that these customers view IT as exceptionally critical to this integration capability.[12]

Results Achieved

3PL users are satisfied with their outsourcing results, according to the Georgia Tech-Capgemini study. The study participants, from across industries and around the globe, place a high value on their relationships with 3PL service providers. They credit 3PLs with helping them to attain goals related to service, cost, and customer satisfaction Figure 12-3

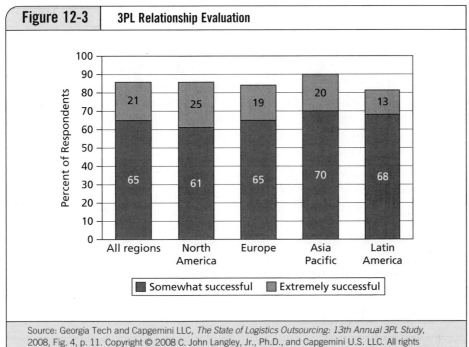

Figure 12-3	3PL Relationship Evaluation

Source: Georgia Tech and Capgemini LLC, *The State of Logistics Outsourcing: 13th Annual 3PL Study*, 2008, Fig. 4, p. 11. Copyright © 2008 C. John Langley, Jr., Ph.D., and Capgemini U.S. LLC. All rights reserved. Reprinted by permission.

highlights the success of these relationships, with 86 percent of all companies reporting that they are extremely or somewhat satisfied with their 3PL experiences.[13]

These positive evaluations are not surprising, given the quantitative results achieved on a year to year basis. The study participants consistently report logistics cost reductions in the range of 12 to 15 percent, fixed logistics asset reductions in excess of 20 percent, and **order cycle time** reductions of 20 to 30 percent. Also, 76 percent of the 2008 study respondents believe that 3PLs help customers accommodate significant variations in demand with fewer fixed assets. Finally, 67 percent of the respondents feel that 3PLs help them increase **service reliability**.[14]

Despite these achievements, 3PLs are not perfect. Only 12 percent of the study respondents reported having no problems with their 3PL providers. Customers have concerns regarding the following issues: unrealized service-level commitments, lack of **continuous improvements** and achievements in offerings, and cost reductions not realized. Also, insufficient IT capabilities and a lack of integration across regions and services must be addressed by 3PLs.[15]

Establishing and Managing 3PL Relationships[16]

The development of a 3PL relationship should not happen by chance. Unfortunately, a service purchaser may select a logistics service provider without much forethought or planning. Instead, the purchaser should carefully evaluate potential 3PL service providers and select the one whose capabilities, commitment level, and price match the buyer's requirements. This can be a time consuming process but it will greatly increase the likelihood of a mutually beneficial relationship.

Figure 12-4 outlines the steps involved in establishing and sustaining 3PL relationships. For purposes of illustration, let us assume that the model is being applied from the perspective of a manufacturing firm, as it considers the possibility of forming a relationship with a 3PL service provider.

Step 1: Perform Strategic Assessment This first stage involves the process by which the manufacturer becomes fully aware of its transportation and logistics needs and the overall strategies that will guide its operations. This audit provides a perspective on the firm's transportation and logistics activities, as well as developing a wide range of useful information that will be helpful as the opportunity to form relationships is contemplated. Some of the types of information that may become available as a result of the audit include:

- Overall business goals and objectives, including those from a corporate, divisional, and logistics perspective
- Needs assessment to include requirements of customers, suppliers, and key logistics providers
- Identification and analysis of strategic environmental factors and industry trends
- Profile of current logistics network and the firm's positioning in respective supply chains
- Benchmark, or target, values for logistics costs and key performance measurements
- Identification of gaps between current and desired measures of logistics performance (qualitative and quantitative)

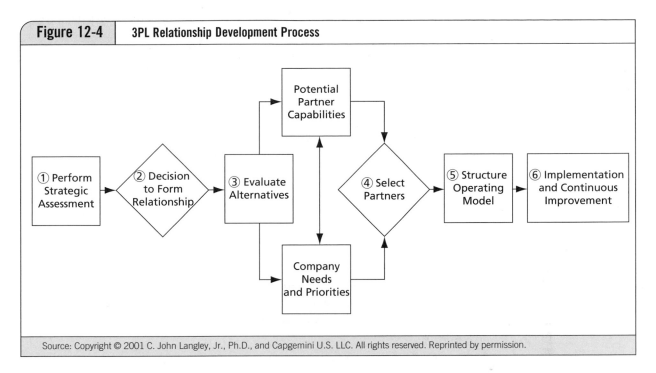

Figure 12-4 | **3PL Relationship Development Process**

Given the significance of most transportation and logistics relationship decisions, and the potential complexity of the overall process, any time taken at the outset to gain an understanding of one's needs is well spent.

Step 2: Decision to Form Relationship When contemplating a 3PL relationship, the first issue focuses on which of the service provider's capabilities are needed by the company. A suggested approach to making this decision is to make a careful assessment of the areas in which the company appears to have **core competency**. As Figure 12-5 indicates, for a firm to have core competency in any given area, it is necessary to have expertise, strategic fit, and ability to invest. The absence of any one or more of these may suggest that the use of 3PL services is appropriate.

Lambert, Emmelhainz, and Gardner have conducted significant research into the topic of how to determine whether a partnership is warranted and, if so, what kind of

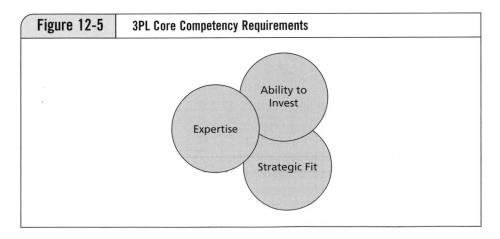

Figure 12-5 | **3PL Core Competency Requirements**

partnership should be considered.[17] Their partnership model incorporates the identification of "drivers" and "facilitators" of a relationship; it indicates that for a relationship to have a high likelihood of success, the right drivers and facilitators should be present.

Drivers are defined as "compelling reasons to partner." For a relationship to be successful, the theory of the model is that all parties "must believe that they will receive significant benefits in one or more areas and that these benefits would not be possible without a partnership." Drivers are strategic factors that may result in a competitive advantage and may help to determine the appropriate type of business relationship. Although there certainly are other factors that may be considered, the primary drivers include the following:

- Asset/Cost efficiency
- Customer service
- Marketing advantage
- Profit stability/Growth

Facilitators are defined as "supportive corporate environmental factors that enhance partnership growth and development." As such, they are the factors that, if present, can help to ensure the success of the relationship. Included among the main types of facilitators are the following:

- Corporate compatibility
- Management philosophy and techniques
- Mutuality of commitment to relationship formation
- Symmetry on key factors such as relative size, financial strength, and so on

In addition, a number of additional factors have been identified as keys to successful 3PL relationships. Included are factors such as: exclusivity, shared competitors, physical proximity, prior history of the potential partner, previous experience with the partner, and a shared high-value end user.

Step 3: Evaluate Alternatives Although the details are not included here, Lambert and his colleagues suggest a method for measuring and weighting the drivers and facilitators we have discussed.[18] Then they discuss a methodology by which the apparent levels of drivers and facilitators may suggest the most appropriate type of relationship to consider. If neither the drivers nor the facilitators seem to be present, then the recommendation would be for the relationship to be more transactional or "arm's length" in nature. Alternatively, when all parties to the relationship share common drivers, and when the facilitating factors seem to be present, then a more structured, formal relationship may be justified.

In addition to utilization of the partnership formation process, it is important to conduct a thorough assessment of the company's needs and priorities in comparison with the capabilities of each potential partner. This task should be supported with not only the availability of critical measurements and so on but also the results of personal interviews and discussions with the most likely potential partners.

Although transportation and logistics executives are significantly involved in the decision to form 3PL relationships, it is frequently advantageous to engage other corporate managers in the selection process. Representatives of marketing, finance, manufacturing, human resources, and information systems, for example, frequently have valuable perspectives to contribute to the discussion and analysis. Thus, it is important to assure a broad representation and involvement of people throughout the company in the partnership formation and partner selection decisions.

Step 4: Select Partners While this stage is of critical concern to the customer, the selection of a transportation or logistics partner should be made only following very close consideration of the credentials of the top candidate 3PLs. Also, it is highly advisable to interact with and get to know the final candidates on a professionally intimate basis.

As was indicated in the discussion of Step 3, it is likely that a number of executives will play key roles in the relationship formation process. It is important to achieve consensus on the final selection decision to create a significant degree of buy-in and agreement among those involved. Due to the strategic significance of the decision to form a transportation or logistics relationship, it is essential to ensure that everyone has a consistent understanding of the decision that has been made and of what to expect from the firm that has been selected.

Step 5: Structure Operating Model The structure of the 3PL relationship refers to the activities, processes, and priorities that will be used to build and sustain the relationship. As suggested by Lambert and his colleagues, components "make the relationship operational and help managers create the benefits of partnering."[19] A suggested list of components of the operating model includes:

- Planning
- Joint operating controls
- Communication
- Risk/Reward sharing
- Trust and commitment
- Contract style
- Scope of the relationship
- Financial investment[20]

Step 6: Implementation and Continuous Improvement Once the decision to form a 3PL relationship has been made and the structural elements of the relationship identified, it is important to recognize that the most challenging step in the relationship process has just begun. Depending on the complexity of the new relationship, the overall implementation process may be relatively short or it may be extended over a longer period of time. If the situation involves significant change to and restructuring of the company's transportation or logistics network, for example, full implementation may take longer to accomplish. In a situation where the degree of change is more modest, the time needed for successful implementation may be abbreviated.

Finally, the future success of the relationship will be a direct function of the ability of the involved organizations to achieve both continuous and breakthrough improvement. As indicated in Figure 12-6, there are a number of steps that should be considered in the continuous improvement process. In addition, efforts should be directed to creating the breakthrough, or "paradigm-shifting," type of improvement that is essential to enhance the functioning of the relationship and the market positioning of the organizations involved.

The ultimate goal of this six-step process is to develop productive relationships between companies and 3PL service providers that create outstanding customer service and cost-efficient operations. Like any relationship, both organizations must invest

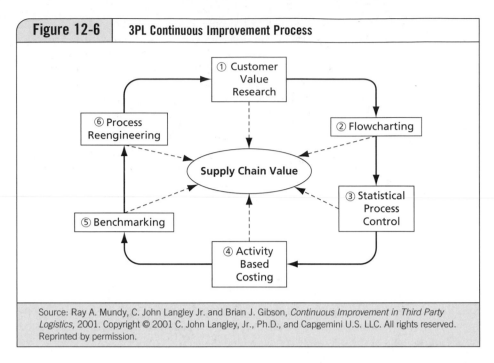

Figure 12-6 | **3PL Continuous Improvement Process**

time and energy into its development and sustainment. Both parties must share information, trust their counterparts, and be open to new ideas and methods. The most successful long-term 3PL relationships occur when the organizations collaborate on a regular basis, adopt a team approach to problem solving, and leverage each other's capabilities. The On the Line feature highlights the type of relationship that emerges when a company effectively chooses a 3PL provider and works closely with them to build competitive transportation capabilities. Such relationships may face challenges early on, but perseverance can lead to positive results for both parties.

On the Line   *3PL Relationship Eases Sunny Delight's Transition*

In August 2004, consumer products giant Procter & Gamble spun off the Sunny Delight beverage brand, selling it to Boston-based private equity firm J.W. Childs Associates. As part of the transition service agreement, Sunny Delight would have to wean itself completely off Procter & Gamble's systems, including its transportation system, within a year. "All at once, we were a business with $550 million in sales and no systems," says Jim Glendon, Sunny Delight's supply chain director.

As Sunny Delight began working out how it would manage transportation, it quickly rejected the idea of going it alone. Its core competency was making and marketing beverages, not transportation and logistics. "We could have hired a staff, developed our own expertise, negotiated with carriers, and put in our own TMS [transportation management system] et cetera, but we would never have had the scale, the knowledge of the industry, the expertise, the systems that a 3PL brings to the party," says Glendon.

The same factors that informed Sunny Delight's decision to outsource also influenced its selection process. "Our selection was based certainly on price but also on the systems capabilities, the scale, and the expertise of the provider," says Glendon. Lacking systems of its own,

Sunny Delight was especially keen to partner with someone who could provide instant access to sophisticated technology, he adds. "With everything else that we had to put in place—our WMS, our core accounting systems, all our plant systems, order shipping, billing, on down the line—if there was anything that made sense to outsource, that's what we wanted."

After evaluating five bids, Sunny Delight chose Transplace, a Frisco, Texas-based third-party logistics and technology company. Among other advantages, Transplace had done business with Procter & Gamble in the past and was familiar with the systems Sunny Delight had used when it was part of the P&G fold. That shared background promised to make the transition to a new transportation structure easier.

As Sunny Delight had hoped, the transition went smoothly. With assistance from the 3PL, the beverage company was able to get off Procter & Gamble's systems and onto its own by the mandated deadline.

Today, the two enjoy an almost seamless collaboration. "[Transplace] acts as if they are part of the business in terms of the sense of urgency and the sense of ownership that they feel toward the business. And that extends all the way from looking toward how can they improve results to their transportation coordinators answering the phone as Sunny Delight," says Glendon.

As an example of the partnership's depth, Glendon points to the quarterly review meetings with Sunny Delight's top carriers. "It's a joint meeting with Transplace and Sunny Delight," he reports. "So even though Transplace is paying the carriers every week, we want to make it clear to [the carriers] that this is a partnership, and they are speaking on our behalf."

But the story doesn't end there. Three years after the divestiture, Sunny Delight was ready to do some acquiring of its own. In October 2007, the company bought Fruit2O flavored water and Veryfine juice from Kraft.

Just as Transplace had helped ease Sunny Delight's separation from Procter & Gamble, it also helped its customer integrate the two new brands into its operations. Among other advantages, the 3PL's contacts and expertise proved helpful in arranging for the dry van service that would be needed to transport the Fruit2O and Veryfine products.

Working with dry van haulers was a first for Sunny Delight, which ships its own products via refrigerated trucks. "It was a whole different set of transportation needs," says Glendon. "We were looking at different carriers, and we needed to quickly get bids under way and carriers established." Speed was of the essence here because Sunny Delight had just 120 days after the deal was signed to integrate the two new brands into its system. But Glendon reports that, with Transplace's help, Sunny Delight was able to meet the project's deadline.

At the same time it was lining up carriers, Sunny Delight was also working to come up with an overall distribution plan—figuring out what products to store where, what transportation lanes to use, and how much volume to ship. Before the acquisition, the Kraft brands' products were being shipped from two Kraft plants and 12 mixing centers. After February 24, 2008, the beverages would be shipped from five Sunny Delight plants.

Once again, Transplace stepped in to help Sunny Delight work out the details. "They had an equal seat at the table in terms of understanding the scope, the requirement, and the timing," says Glendon. Not only did Transplace participate in all of the planning meetings and discussions, but it also dispatched a delegation to visit the Littleton, Mass., plant that Sunny Delight acquired as part of the deal. Before the handoff, Transplace managers went over all the details with the facility's management to make sure that they were familiar with the plant's standard operating procedures and had full information for carriers, including the location of the drop lot and guard house.

The support Transplace provided helped ensure that Sunny Delight was able to integrate the new brands into its operations "without a hitch," says Glendon. In fact, the project went so smoothly that when Sunny Delight recently made another acquisition, it set an even more ambitious timeline. In early October, it signed a licensing agreement with Kraft to produce and market the Crystal Light ready-to-drink bottled beverages (Kraft will continue to make and sell the powdered versions of Crystal Light). This time, Sunny Delight expects to fully integrate the new brand in 60 days. Glendon is confident that the company will easily make that goal.

Strategic Challenges for 3PL Users

Customers are generally satisfied with the quality of services provided by 3PLs but there are always opportunities to improve service and relationships. Table 12-5 highlights some of the key areas ripe for service enhancement. Although these issues appear to be the responsibility of the 3PL service providers, customers must take an active role in facilitating better performance. As customers consider their outsourcing options and seek to identify key opportunities to leverage the transportation capabilities of 3PL services providers, they must bear in mind a number of potential strategic issues: service requirements, coordination role, technology integration, goal cohesion, supply chain security, and future challenges. Each issue is discussed briefly below.

Service Requirements Before a customer sits down at the table with potential 3PL service providers, they must determine what types of services are required. During the strategic analysis of the 3PL relationship development process it is important for customers to decide if they are going to take a tactical or strategic approach toward outsourcing.

The tactical approach focuses on outsourcing individual requirements to 3PLs on an as-needed basis. Companies like Walmart and Proctor & Gamble will use 3PLs in a transactional fashion to fill in gaps in their capabilities or capacity. There is limited effort to fully integrate the 3PL into the customer's systems and **collaboration** is more tactical than strategic. Walmart's decision to use Greatwide Transportation for refrigerated product delivery instead of its own fleet is an example of a tactical 3PL service purchase.

In contrast, the strategic approach seeks to establish an integrated set of capabilities through extensive use of 3PL services. The ensuing relationship is one in which the organizations cooperate and willingly modify their business objectives and practices to help achieve long-term goals and objectives. The customer becomes more heavily reliant upon the 3PL to be a strategic service provider and a key influencer of the customer's logistics performance. An example of this approach is the decision by Goodyear Tire and Rubber to entrust Exel with its transportation load planning, **private fleet** operations, and order fulfillment.[21]

While there may be a temptation to think that the strategic approach is superior to or more advanced than the tactical approach, the important issue is that the choice of 3PL properly matches the customer's service needs. While there are highly effective

Table 12-5	Customer Challenges with 3PLs	
		Percent of Respondents
Service level commitment not realized		51%
Lack of continuous, ongoing improvements and achievements in offerings		42
Information technology capabilities not sufficient		39
Cost reductions not realized		36
Lack of project management skills		35
Ineffective management of key performance indicators		34
Unsatisfactory transition during implementation stage		30
Errors caused by excessive manual steps within business processes		28
Lack of global capabilities		27
Lack of consultative/knowledge-based skills		25
Lack of business process integration across regions and supply chain services		20
Inability to form meaningful and trusting relationships		17
Poor post-merger integration of acquired companies		13
No problems reported		12

Source: Georgia Tech and Capgemini LLC, *The State of Logistics Outsourcing: 13th Annual 3PL Study*, 2008, Fig. 5, p. 12. Copyright © 2008 C. John Langley, Jr., Ph.D., and Capgemini U.S. LLC. All rights reserved. Reprinted by permission.

relationships that leverage the strategic and integrative capabilities of 3PL providers, there are excellent tactical 3PL relationships that focus on a specific needs of the customers.

Coordination Role The growth and advancement of the 3PL industry has created a number of purchase options for customers. Today, they can choose from companies specializing in a limited number of services, integrated services, or strategic management services. The decision regarding which type of 3PL to use depends on the company's preference for coordination of key activities. Figure 12-7 highlights the hierarchy of 3PL service providers and their coordination roles.

Companies that choose not to use 3PL services conduct activities internally and assume the coordination role. As they begin to outsource, companies use **logistics service providers** for cost reduction of primary activities like transportation and warehousing but the coordination role remains in-house. As they begin to purchase value added services, customers should look for 3PLs with the integrated capabilities that we discussed earlier in the chapter. Because there are more activities and locations to manage, the coordination role is likely to be shared with a key 3PL. In a few cases, companies have aligned themselves with a service provider who has primary responsibility for

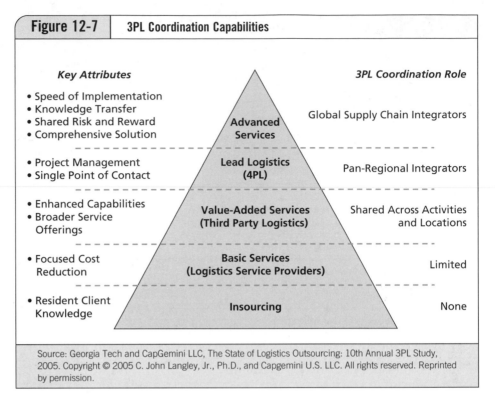

Figure 12-7 | **3PL Coordination Capabilities**

Key Attributes

- Speed of Implementation
- Knowledge Transfer
- Shared Risk and Reward
- Comprehensive Solution

- Project Management
- Single Point of Contact

- Enhanced Capabilities
- Broader Service Offerings

- Focused Cost Reduction

- Resident Client Knowledge

Advanced Services

Lead Logistics (4PL)

Value-Added Services (Third Party Logistics)

Basic Services (Logistics Service Providers)

Insourcing

3PL Coordination Role

Global Supply Chain Integrators

Pan-Regional Integrators

Shared Across Activities and Locations

Limited

None

coordination and control of transportation and logistics activities in a region of the world. These **lead logistics providers** or **fourth party logistics** companies (4PL) serve as the customer's supply chain integrator. In the future, advanced service providers are expected to emerge with the capabilities to coordinate transportation and logistics activities on a global basis.

In late 2008, Navistar International Corporation, a manufacturer of commercial and military trucks, chose Menlo Worldwide Logistics as its global lead logistics provider to support Navistar's movement into global markets. As the supply chain integrator, Menlo assumed responsibility for the management of Navistar's global transportation providers, regional warehouse management, lead time planning, and net landed cost modeling. Through the relationship, Navistar expects to build a world-class logistics capability that will make the company more profitable and better serve its customers.[22]

Technology Integration IT is a high priority issue for 3PL customers. Technology is viewed as a critical capability of 3PL service providers to improve communication, enhance shipment visibility and **event management**, and manage day-to-day warehouse and transportation operations, according to the Georgia Tech-Capgemini study. More than 92 percent of the study participants view IT capabilities as a necessary element of a 3PL service offering. However, only 35 percent report that they are satisfied with their 3PL service providers' IT capabilities, continuing a gap between expectations and performance that has lingered for more than seven years.[23]

Primary 3PL IT challenges include difficulty providing **shipment visibility** to customers and a lack of integration among internal 3PL systems. These two issues make it difficult for customers to achieve seamless information flows across their transportation and logistics networks. On the 3PL side, the lack of IT integration hampers their ability to coordinate internal activities, offer true integrated service capabilities, or effectively serve as a lead logistics provider. In the 3PL selection process, customers must scrutinize the current IT capabilities and future IT investment plans of potential service providers.

Goal Cohesion While 3PLs tout their customer focus and willingness to collaborate, they are in business to make money. This naturally leads to goals that are not always consistent with the desires of customers and creates the potential for conflict. To overcome this challenge, customers must work with their 3PLs to develop reasonable expectations and requirements that are achievable as well as provide the opportunity for service provider profitability.

A number of factors contribute to the creation of consistent goals and mutually beneficial outcomes according to the Georgia Tech-Capgemini study. The study cites strong personal relationships across the operational and executive levels of the organizations as greatly contributing to success. Also, strong contracts with detailed requirements and performance verification capabilities keep everyone focused on the same goals. Finally, attainable performance targets for cost and service must be established. Customers must then monitor **key performance indicators** to ensure that their 3PLs are driving toward their contractual goals and commitments.[24]

Supply Chain Security As Chapter 9 highlighted, there is no shortage of transportation related security concerns. As a company's supply chain becomes more global, the potential for security risk multiplies. The Georgia Tech-Capgemini study reveals that the chief security concern among 3PL users is theft, by a wide margin over natural disaster disruptions and product tampering risk. The ability of 3PLs to navigate the complex and changing pathway of government antiterrorism regulations is another factor that customers must consider when selecting a 3PL service provider.[25]

While 3PL users are largely satisfied with the level of security provider by 3PLs, steps can be taken to enhance security. The keys to avoiding theft and other security problems are fairly straightforward. Top measures 3PLs can use to maintain or enhance supply chain security are providing better physical security for material goods, developing security procedures in collaboration with customers, and providing proactive reports and alerts when shipments deviate from planned routes or schedules. 3PLs should also monitor freight at key transfer points, obtain C-TPAT and other certifications, and avoid high risk transportation routes (such as the Gulf of Aden, where more than 100 pirate attacks on ships occurred in 2008).

Future Issues and Challenges The 3PL industry has grown dramatically over the past ten years and is expected to expand in both dollar volume and capabilities. As customers extend their global activities, supply chain complexity will also grow. 3PLs, especially those developing far reaching physical networks, integrated logistics capabilities, and effective IT tools, will be well positioned to serve the transportation and logistics requirements of their customers. However, even the best 3PLs will be challenged by volatile fuel costs, economic instability, and shifting production and demand patterns.

To reach the required level of expertise, 3PLs will need to effectively position themselves for the future through internal growth, mergers, and strategic acquisition of competitors. As customers shift production from far away locations to nearby emerging markets where the cost of labor, shipping, and land is less expensive, 3PLs will need to establish a presence in these new regions. 3PLs will also need to enhance their breadth of capabilities and strategic services to serve customer desires for one stop shopping and lead logistics provider skills. Finally, 3PLs will need to be a driving force of transportation and logistics innovation to ensure that they can meet the cost-efficiency and service quality requirements of customers.

"These are certainly exciting, yet challenging, times for 3PL providers as we attempt to predict, analyze, and adapt to the various forces that will affect our customers' supply chains in years to come," notes Joe Gallick, senior vice president of sales for Penske Logistics.[26]

SUMMARY

- A third party logistics (3PL) service provider is defined as an "external supplier that performs all or part of a company's logistics functions." It is desirable that these suppliers provide multiple services and that these services are integrated in the way they are managed and delivered.

- The several types of 3PLs are transportation based, distribution based, forwarder based, financial based, and information based suppliers.

- Asset based providers serve customers with tangible equipment and facilities, while non-asset based providers leverage the resources of other companies.

- 3PLs provide a variety of transportation services, including: freight movement, freight management, intermediary services, and specialty services.

- Customer demands for integration of 3PL services have led to significant expansion and acquisition activities among major service providers.

- The 3PL industry is a growing and substantial force in logistics, with more than $487 billion spent globally on 3PL services in 2007.

- When outsourcing labor-intensive logistics operations, companies seek cost reduction, the ability to focus on core competencies, and service improvements.

- According to an annual study of 3PL users, customers are satisfied with their 3PL relationships and credit 3PLs with helping them attain goals related to reduction of operating costs, fixed asset investment, and order cycle time.

- There are six steps involved in the development and implementation of a successful 3PL relationship. The ultimate goal of the process is to develop outstanding customer service capabilities and cost efficient operations.

- Although the industry is poised for future growth, 3PLs must prepare for changing customer service requirements, develop coordination capabilities, invest in technology integration, establish cohesive goals, and help secure customers' supply chains.

STUDY QUESTIONS

1. Define the concepts of outsourcing and third party logistics. What role does transportation play in 3PL?

2. What are the basic types of 3PL firms? How do they facilitate the planning and execution of freight transportation?

3. Why would a company use an asset based 3PL service provider versus a non-asset based provider?

4. Why is service integration an important issue to the 3PL industry? What companies are developing these capabilities?

5. Discuss the reasons why some companies choose to use the services of 3PLs and why other companies do not use 3PL services.

6. What are some of the more frequently outsourced logistics activities? Less frequently outsourced?

7. To what extent are clients/customers satisfied with 3PL services? What can 3PLs do to improve customer satisfaction?

8. Describe the six steps involved in establishing and managing 3PL relationships. Which step(s) do you feel is (are) most critical?

9. If you were given the task of outsourcing your company's transportation operations, what types of capabilities would you seek in a 3PL service provider?

10. Discuss the challenges that 3PLs and their customers face as they seek to improve performance and reduce costs.

11. How would you distinguish between a logistics service provider, a value-added service provider, and a lead logistics provider? What role does each play in coordination of transportation and logistics activities?

12. Why is information technology an important issue to customers when outsourcing transportation and logistics activities?

NOTES

1. "EyeforTransport - Transportation Glossary." Retrieved February 20, 2009 from: http://events.eyefortransport.com/glossary/st.shtml#T

2. "Third party logistics (3PL) definition." Retrieved February 20, 2009 from: http://www.businessdictionary.com/definition/third-party-logistics-3PL.html

3. Council of Supply Chain Management Professionals, *Supply Chain Management Terms and Glossary,* (2008). Retrieved February 20, 2009 from: http://cscmp.org/Downloads/Public/Resources/glossary03.pdf

4. John J. Coyle, C. John Langley, Jr., Brian J. Gibson, Robert A. Novack, and Edward J. Bardi, *Supply Chain Management: A Logistics Perspective,* 8th ed., chap. 4, (Florence, KY: Cengage Learning, 2009).

5. "About AISA - The American Institute for Shippers' Associations." Retrieved March 15, 2009 from: http://www.shippers.org/shippers.html

6. Peter Bradley, "Third Party Logistics: A Successful Handoff?" *DC Velocity,* November 2005.

7. Armstrong and Associates, *Trends in 3PL/Customer Relationships,* 2009.

8. Ibid.

9. Ibid.

10. Mark B. Solomon, "3PLs Set Their Sights on Small, Mid-sized Players," *DC Velocity,* March 2009.

11. Georgia Tech and Capgemini LLC, *The State of Logistics Outsourcing: 13th Annual 3PL Study,* 2008.

12. Ibid.

13. Ibid.

14. Ibid.

15. Ibid.

16. Unless otherwise noted, information in this section is adapted from John J. Coyle, C. John Langley, Jr., Brian J. Gibson, Robert A. Novack, and Edward J. Bardi, *Supply Chain Management: A Logistics Perspective,* 8th ed., chap. 4, (Florence, KY: Cengage Learning, 2009).

17. Douglas M. Lambert, Margaret A. Emmelhainz, and John T. Gardner, "Developing and Implementing Supply Chain Partnerships," *The International Journal of Logistics Management,* Vol. 7, No. 2 (1996): 1–17.

18. Ibid.

19. Ibid.

20.   Ibid.

21.   Robert J. Bowman, "Goodyear's Logistics Outsourcing Program Faces a Moment of Truth," *Global Logistics and Supply Chain Strategies,* March 2006.

22.   "Navistar Selects Menlo Logistics as Global Lead Logistics Provider," *Business Wire,* October 10, 2008.

23.   Georgia Tech and Capgemini LLC, *The State of Logistics Outsourcing: 13th Annual 3PL Study,* 2008.

24.   Ibid.

25.   Ibid.

26.   Jeff Ashcroft, "Annual 3PL CEO Survey Reveals Impact of Economy on Global Supply Chains," *SupplyChainNetwork.com,* October 6, 2008. Retrieved April 2, 2009 from: http://www.supplychainnetwork.com/?p=402

CASE 12-1

Wardrobe Concepts Ltd.

Wardrobe Concepts Ltd. (WCL) is a rapidly growing semi-custom cabinet maker. Their premier product line is sold through a network of regional building products distributors. Recently, WCL has developed a strategy to sell a moderate line of cabinets called the Skyline Collection that will be sold through home store chains. At a recent industry trade show, interest in the new line was high and all indications point toward heavy demand for WCL products.

Shortly after the trade show, Joann Franzen, the vice president of marketing, met with her logistics counterpart, Shane Doane, to discuss the opportunity. Franzen wanted to discuss the demand forecast for the Skyline Collection. The meeting was also intended to address the strategy for product distribution.

Both agreed that the forecast was reasonable and relatively conservative, given the current economic conditions. However, the two disagreed on order fulfillment and distribution issues.

Franzen suggested that the WCL private fleet be used to move finished goods from WCL assembly plant in French Lick, Indiana to the retail outlets of Home Mart, a Midwest chains with 250 stores and WCL's first customer to consider signing a contract for the Skyline Collection. "As the inaugural reseller of the Skyline Collection, we need to give Home Mart exceptional service," said Franzen.

"I'm not so sure about that strategy," replied Doan. "Our fleet is relatively small and we use it to deliver high margin custom orders to no more than 30 different distributors. You're talking about a nearly tenfold increase in the number of delivery points." He also noted that the size of the initial Home Mart orders for display product and inventory would be large. Later, deliveries would be smaller replenishment orders and customer-specific buys.

Franzen replied: "I don't want some second rate for-hire trucking company damaging the product or delivering it late just because you're looking to save a few transportation dollars. You've got to maintain exceptional control over the movement of this product. Home Mart is just too important for us to cut corners."

"This isn't really the type of freight that for-hire carriers desire," stated Doan. "It is prone to damage, low weight, and takes up a great deal of the cubic capacity of a trailer. That means high transportation rates. We really need to come up with a middle ground solution to serve the customer effectively without busting our budget."

"I need to sell product and get contracts signed," responded Franzen. "You need to analyze this one on your own and come back to me with a viable order fulfillment and delivery solution. Give me a call tomorrow before my meeting with Home Mart. I want to get the contract finalized but need the transportation details specified before they will sign on the dotted line."

With his position firmly stated, Franzen got up and left the room without another word.

CASE QUESTIONS

1. What role can third party logistics play in the WCL-Home Mart supply chain? Is it a viable alternative to the WCL private fleet or for-hire transportation?

2. What type of 3PL service provider is best suited to serve the WCL-Home Mart supply chain? Why?

3. Does Doan need to investigate the use of an integrated 3PL or a lead logistics provider? Why or why not?

4. Given the situation and the marketing VP's concerns, identify and discuss the challenges of using 3PL services for the Home Mart deliveries.

CASE 12-2

Jetstream Aerospace

Jetstream Aerospace is a world leader in the design and manufacture of innovative aviation products and services for the regional, business, and amphibious aircraft markets. These product lines encompass such internationally known and respected names as Thrifty regional jets and Luxuria business aircrafts. Jetstream's global workforce of over 20,500 associates delivered 532 aircrafts in 2009, generating over $9 billion in sales and creating a remarkable $11.7 billion order backlog.

The company also provides aftermarket support for its aircraft. When an airplane breaks down or a critical part needs to be replaced, the clock begins ticking, eating valuable time and profits as the aircraft sits idle. Therefore, Jetstream's customers need fast response when an aftermarket service part is needed. Speed, in many cases, is more important than cost to the customers, who want their aircraft flying instead of sitting on the tarmac.

Unfotunately, Jetstream has struggled to provide the level of delivery service demanded by its customers. After a series of acquisitions, the company's service parts business was fragmented and disjointed, resulting in declining service quality and a threat to customer loyalty. Also, the customer base has become much more global, meaning that the company has to quickly deliver service parts to nearly every region of the world.

The topic of aftermarket service received great attention during the quarterly update meeting of senior management. Jetstream's CEO opened the discussion with, "Folks, I'm getting pretty tired of answering emails and calls from our major customers about planes being grounded because a $75 repair part wasn't in stock or couldn't be tracked during delivery. We need to figure out this problem and fix it fast. The goal is to regain our number one ranking in customer service by restoring market confidence in the Jetstream aftermarket support capabilities. Now get busy!"

The brainstorming session among the senior managers became very animated. They quickly outlined a set of goals: improved service quality, improved aftermarket parts velocity and responsiveness, and sustained sales growth and profitability through cost containment.

Next, a heated discussion ensued about how to accomplish the goals. A few managers advocated the idea of centralizing all customer service operations in Amsterdam at the company's distribution center near Schiphol International Airport. The rationale was greater inventory availability and better control of order fulfillment. Others wanted to set up a network of company-owned regional distribution facilities in Jetstream's major market areas. They felt that this arrangement would reduce distance to customers and improve order cycle times. A lone dissenter brought up the idea of hiring a 3PL to help manage the aftermarket business. Her justification was simple: "Jetstream is a great manufacturing company but is challenged in the service parts area. Why don't we bring in a company with logistics expertise to optimize our service parts business?"

The response was immediate and negative from the other managers. They felt that Jetstream was highly capable and didn't need outside help. "A few tweaks here and there are all we need," said the Director of Customer Relations.

His comment was gaining great support until the CEO cleared his throat and boldly stated: "Third party logistics? That sounds intriguing. Tell me more."

CASE QUESTIONS

1. Discuss the pros and cons of using third party logistics for Jetstream's aftermarket services. *see Fig 12-*

2. What potential risks exist with outsourcing the aftermarket services to a 3PL?

3. What transportation and logistics activities should be considered for outsourcing in this situation? Should Jetstream obtain these services on a tactical or strategic basis?

4. What type of 3PL service provider is best suited to meet Jetstream's aftermarket service goals? How should they go about finding a capable 3PL service provider?

Chapter 13

PRIVATE TRANSPORTATION AND FLEET MANAGEMENT

Learning Objectives

After reading this chapter, you should be able to do the following:

- Explain and define private transportation from a legal and practical perspective
- Appreciate the role and importance of private transportation among the various modal types—rail, air, water, pipeline, and trucking
- Discuss the advantages and disadvantages of private trucking
- Analyze the cost structure of private trucking and understand the various components of fixed and variable (operating) costs
- Understand how driver and equipment costs can be calculated for private carriage
- Discuss the role of leasing for private transportation and how it impacts the cost structure and operating costs of private trucking
- Appreciate the challenges associated with the daily operation of a private fleet
- Understand the issues associated with private fleet organization
- Discuss the importance of control for a private fleet to improve efficiency and effectiveness
- Understand the challenges and issues associated with regulations pertaining to private trucking

| Transportation Profile | The Silent Partner: Private Fleets |

Private carriage is an important part of the transportation system in the United States and in most other countries of the world. In fact, private transportation has a long history in the United States and was the primary component of the system until the development of the railroad and canal sectors in the 19th century. The large fixed cost and capital investment required for an effective rail system precluded individuals and the small companies that existed at that time from providing private service. Railroads were the first "big business" in the U.S. with absentee ownership. Subsequently, the other modes of transportation also developed larger companies that provided for-hire service to the general public.

While the motor carrier sector developed a large number of for-hire carriers, private carriage has always been a very important part of the motor carrier industry, as noted in Chapter 5. The development of public highways after World War I by the federal, state, and local governments provided an opportunity for small to large companies to purchase trucks. They provided private transportation on the publically provided infrastructure and paid user charges for that privilege. The list of private fleet operations reads like a Who's Who of Corporate America. Many of these companies found private motor carrier service to be an attractive and advantageous alternative to for-hire rail and water carriers.

The success of private trucking reflects the growth and development of the economy in the United States. Successful companies use technology and software to administer and manage their private fleets for service and profitability. America's private fleets include some of the largest names in U.S. business—Walmart stores, Verizon, Pepsi Bottling Group, and Safeway. Less– well-known companies, like Sysco Food Corp, provide essential day-to-day deliveries and services to many other industries. These private fleets often contract out to for-hire carriers for additional services and income.

Not only do private fleets haul products, they also help to provide essential services for many smaller service businesses—plumbers, contractors, electricians, and so forth. Combined, these small businesses operate sizeable private fleets. Private trucking provides a large slice of service and revenue to U.S. industry.

Source: Adapted from *America's Private Fleets*, National Private Truck Council.

Private Transportation

Private transportation may be construed as "do-it-yourself" rather than "buy it" transportation services. The firm engaged in private transportation is vertically integrated to perform the services provided by for-hire carriers. The private transportation decision is a classic "make" versus "buy" decision in which a company must determine if it is cheaper to make (engage in private transportation) or buy transportation (use a for-hire carrier).

In this chapter the private transportation issue is examined for all modes, but emphasis is given to private trucking, the most pervasive form of private transportation. Attention will be directed to the decision to enter into private trucking and the operation of a private truck fleet.

What Is Private Transportation?

Private transportation is *not* the opposite of public (government) transportation. Private transportation is a legal form of transportation defined in the Interstate Commerce Act as "any person who transports in interstate or foreign commerce property of which such person is the owner, lessee, or bailee when such transportation is for the purpose of sale, lease, rent or bailment, or in the furtherance of any commercial enterprise."

The above legal definition may be interpreted as follows: Private transportation is the movement of goods owned by a firm that also owns or leases and operates the transportation equipment for the furtherance of its primary business.

A private carrier does not provide service to the general public. Rather, the private carrier serves itself by hauling its own raw materials and finished products. The private carrier was permitted to haul goods for others (the public) in the past but only if such service was provided free of charge. Notable exceptions to this general prohibition against the private carrier charging a fee included the movement of exempt commodities and freight of firms that were 100 percent owned subsidiaries.

In the past, the Interstate Commerce Commission (ICC) strictly enforced the prohibition of private carriers hauling public goods for a fee. This enforcement was an extension of the control over entry for common and contract carriers, who must prove public convenience and necessity. However, the 1980 Motor Carrier Act greatly reduced controls over entry into the common and contract carrier fields, and grants of authority became easier to obtain even for an existing private motor carrier. After the abolition of the ICC in 1995, the responsibilities of regulating private transportation were transferred to the Surface Transportation Board.

Although private trucking is the most prevalent, private transportation is found in other modes as well. A brief analysis of private transportation in rail, air, pipeline, and water follows.

Private Rail Transportation

Private transportation in the railroad industry usually takes the form of privately owned railcars of other businesses that are moved by a common carrier railroad. Private rail transportation does not exist in the form of a business operating a rail service to transport goods or personnel on an intercity basis.

Many businesses do purchase or lease specialized rail equipment, such as hopper, temperature-controlled, and tank cars, to ensure an adequate supply of vehicles. It is common for agribusiness firms to own (or lease) a supply of hopper cars to haul grain from the farms to the grain elevators to end users during the harvest season. Railroads normally do not have a sufficient supply of hopper cars to meet the peak demands during the harvest season. Thus, many agribusiness firms have acquired a private fleet of rail equipment to ensure an adequate supply of railcars and continued operation of the company.

As stated above, no business owns a private railroad to transport its freight on an intercity basis since the cost of the infrastructure is prohibitive. The private railcars are moved intercity by a for-hire railroad. The railroad grants the shipper permission to have the private car moved over its lines, and the railroad provides an allowance from the normal rate to the shipper for use of the private railcar. This car allowance takes the form of either a mileage allowance or a reduction from the published rate for the specific commodity movement. The car allowance recognizes that the user is incurring a portion of the transportation expense (the capital cost of the vehicle) that is normally incurred by the railroad.

Private rail transportation usually includes the cost of a private siding or spur track that connects the railroad's track with the user's plant or warehouse. The rail transportation user desiring service to its door must provide and maintain the rail track on its property. In the absence of a private siding or spur track, the shipper must use a public side track and incur an additional transportation (accessibility) cost to move the freight between the public siding and the user's facility.

Some large manufacturing firms have built small railroads within the confines of their plants to shuttle railcars from building to building. Such private railroads may be construed as materials handling systems that move railcars loaded with goods such as raw materials. The switch engine performs the same function as the forklift; that is, the switch engine places the railcars in the proper location to permit loading and unloading. The switch engine of such private railroads does not operate outside the plant limits.

A number of large firms own for-hire railroads that primarily connect the owner's facilities with other for-hire railroads. These railroads are legally classified as for-hire common carriers, not private rail carriers. As an example, consider a large forest products company that owns and operates a short-line railroad in a rural community. The railroad is classified as a common carrier but provides service primarily to the area's major rail shipper, the forest products company.

Private rail transportation is not a common form of private carriage. Private rail transportation basically means that the user buys or leases railcars, provides rail tracks on its property and, in some limited cases, provides switching within the plant.

Private Air Transportation

Private air transportation, unlike the other modal forms of private carriage, is used extensively, if not exclusively, to transport people. The private airplane fleets are purchased and operated to typically serve the travel needs of executives. The company plane is normally used by upper management, with lower-level managers using commercial flights.

The private airplane fleet may also be used to transport freight in certain emergency situations. Documents that are needed to consummate an important sale or repair parts that will prevent an assembly line from closing are typical examples of emergency situations in which the corporate jet may be called upon for freight duty. The objective of the private air fleet is to serve the travel needs of management, not to make routine deliveries of freight.

The corporate jet can become somewhat of a status symbol. The private airplane projects an image of success—success both for the company and its managers. Within the organization, the manager who has access to the company plane may be viewed by contemporaries as having "made it."

The cost of flying via a company plane is expensive and, depending on the size and accommodation provided, can possibly be three, four, or more times greater than on commercial flights. Thus, the importance attached to managers using the private plane must be high enough to offset and justify the higher cost. Since the 9/11 incidents and the heightened security measures at public airports, many companies have increased their use of private or leased air service to save the time of their highly paid, valuable employees. The expense can be more easily justified under the current circumstances at large public airports.

Another good rationale or justification is to provide service to certain smaller and perhaps more remote communities where access is difficult and time consuming because of stops and/or plane changes. This is especially true for small communities that have lost some or all of their scheduled commercial flights because of a decrease in demand. The cost of the managers' time while waiting for commercial flights can and often does justify the expense of a private plane. As fuel costs have escalated, the cost trade-off has been more challenging, but the expense can be justified for the reasons explained above.

Private Water Transportation

The use of company-owned or leased ships and barges is quite common for the transportation of bulk, large-volume products. The private water carrier transportation of coal, ore, and oil is widely practiced. Most private domestic water transportation takes the form of barge operations. Firms lease or buy barges and towboats to push barges carrying their own bulk product over the inland waterways of the United States. Some firms operate ships that carry ore and coal over the Great Lakes and along the Atlantic, Gulf of Mexico, and Pacific coasts. The Great Lakes ships may also move through the St. Lawrence Seaway to and from the Atlantic ocean ports.

Private water transportation is most advantageous for the movement of bulk, low-value products that move in large volume between limited origins and destinations. As indicated above, coal, ores, and petroleum products are typical commodities moved by private water carrier fleets. These products are usually moved regularly and in large volumes from places such as mines, grain silos, and ports of entry to steel mills, electrical generating plants, refineries, processing mills, or storage facilities.

Relatively large investment (capital) is required to begin private water carrier operation. This investment includes the capital required for the vehicles (barges, towboats, and ships) and for the dock facilities. It should be noted that the dock facility expenses would be incurred if either private *or* for-hire water transportation were used. The shipper (receiver) is responsible for providing docking facilities to load and unload cargo at the shipper's plant just as the side track is used for rail operations to a shipper's plant. Public ports are available, but the private water carrier would be required to use some form of land transportation (truck or rail) to move the cargo between the public port and the shipper's plant and also usually pay a user fuel at the public dock or port.

The large capital investment requires regular, large-volume shipments to reduce unit costs. Usually, firms that operate private water fleets have plants adjacent to waterways. The mining, steel, petroleum, and agriculture industries are significant users of private water transportation.

Private Oil Pipeline Transportation

Private oil pipeline transportation exists in a constrained form similar to that found with some smaller railroads. Although the vast majority of oil pipelines are regulated and required to operate as for-hire transportation companies, it is common for the major oil companies to own for-hire oil pipelines. Essentially, the owners of the oil pipeline have invested in a transportation company that provides service to them as well as to other shippers of petroleum products. The regulation of oil company–owned oil pipelines is meant to ensure the independent, nonowner oil companies access to the pipeline transportation at reasonable rates as noted in Chapter 8.

The reason for the shipper-owned oil pipelines is basically economic. A huge investment is required to start a pipeline. The high fixed costs necessitate high traffic volume for the service to be economical. Like the railroads, duplicate or parallel oil pipelines create excess capacity and economic waste. Thus, shipper ownership, especially multiple shipper ownership, minimizes the high start-up cost barrier to entry and provides a guaranteed minimum amount of shipper-owner traffic to be moved through the oil pipeline. It should be noted again that there are some independent oil pipelines not owned by oil companies.

Private Trucking

Private trucking is the most frequently used and most pervasive form of transportation in the United States. Gary Petty, president and CEO of the **National Private Truck Council**, says that private fleets generate over $300 billion in revenue, accounting for nearly half of the truck transportation revenue in the United States.[1] Just over half of the tons of commodities shipped domestically are hauled by private carriers.[2] Private fleets contribute to 2.5 percent of the gross domestic product.

Previous to the dissolution of the ICC, the exact number of private fleets in operation was very difficult to determine because firms were not required to report private trucking operation. However, a new Department of Transportation (DOT) requirement that private trucking firms register with the DOT should provide more accurate data in the future. The U.S. Census Bureau estimates that there are 4 million private trucks on the road, as reported by the National Private Truck Council.

Whatever the number of private fleets, private trucking is an integral segment of the transportation system employed by the shipping public. At one time or another, almost every company will study or actually operate a private truck fleet, even if the fleet consists of only one truck. For this reason, an in-depth analysis of private trucking—from the reasons for private trucking to the operation of a fleet—is provided below.

Why Private Trucking? The primary reasons for a firm having a private truck fleet are improved service and lower costs. In either case, the private fleet operator is attempting to improve the marketability and profitability of its products. Through improved levels of service, the firm attempts to differentiate its product (lower transit time) and increase its sales and profits. Reduced costs permit the company to keep prices constant (a price reduction during inflationary times), to lower prices, or to increase profits directly. The advantages and disadvantages of private trucking are summarized in Table 13-1. This table provides a convenient reference for the discussion that follows about private truck transportation and can be a useful tool for the evaluation of the potential for private trucking in specific situations. Tables 13-2 and 13-3 provide insight into the specific types of costs for private trucking, and an example is provided to demonstrate how this information could be applied to determine whether private transportation was feasible.

Improved Service A private truck fleet permits a firm to have greater control and flexibility in its transportation system so it can respond to customer needs, both

Table 13-1   Advantages and Disadvantages of Private Trucking

ADVANTAGES	DISADVANTAGES
Improved Service Convenience, Flexible Operation, Greater Control, Lower Transit Times, Lower Inventory Levels, Reduced Damage, Driver/Salesperson, Last Resort (special needs) **Lower Cost** Reduced Transportation Costs (Eliminates Carrier Profit), Reduced Inventory Levels, Advertising, Bargaining Power With For-Hire Carriers, For-hire authority to backhaul, Lower Driver Turnover	**Higher Cost** Transportation Cost Higher Than For-Hire, Empty Backhaul, Lack of Managerial Talent, Added Overhead and Managerial Burden, Capital Requirements, Cargo Damage and Theft Responsibility, Liability for Accidents, Increased Paperwork, Breakdown on the Roads, Labor Union

Table 13-2   Private Truck Costs

FIXED COSTS	OPERATING COSTS
Depreciation (lease) Trucks, Trailers, Garage, Office	**Labor (drivers)** Wages, Fringe Benefits, FICA (Workers Compensation), Layover Allowances
Interest On Investment Vehicles, Garage, Office, Maintenance Equipment	**Vehicle Operating Costs** Fuel, Oil, Grease, Filters, Tires, Tubes, Maintenance (Labor and Parts), Road Service, Tolls
Management Costs Salaries, Fringe Benefits, Travel and Entertainment, FICA (Workers Compensation)	**Insurance** Liability, Collision and Comprehensive, Cargo
Office and Garage Costs Salaries, Utilities, Rent or Property Cost, Supplies, Communication	**License and Registration Fees** **Highway User Taxes** Fuel, Ton-Mile, Federal Use Tax

Table 13-3   Fixed Costs of Trucking*

COST ITEM	CENTS/MILE
Fixed Costs	
Depreciation on Vehicle	8.7
Interest on Vehicle	3.2
Depreciation and Interest on Other Items	1.6
Management and Overhead	13.6
Total Fixed	27.1

Source: U.S. Department of Agriculture.
*Based on Long Distance Haulers of Refrigerated Fruit.

external (for finished goods) and internal (for raw materials). This increased responsiveness is derived from the direct control that the private carrier has over the dispatching, routing, and delivery schedules of the fleet. Such control means the private carrier can lower transit times to the customer, lower inventory levels, and possibly lower stockouts.

Because the driver is really an employee of the seller, improved relations may result from private trucking. The driver now has a vested interest in satisfying customer needs and in being courteous. In addition, the private carrier driver would probably exercise greater care in handling freight and would reduce the frequency of freight damage.

Private fleets usually have higher driver retention due to better pay, benefits, and human resource policies. While national truckload carriers often have driver turnover over 100 percent, private fleets on average have 16 percent turnover.[3]

Some firms use the private truck as a moving store, calling on many customers along a route to take orders and to deliver merchandise. (The delivery milk truck, now virtually extinct, is a good example of the moving store.) For such merchandising operations, a for-hire carrier does not allow the firm to exercise the necessary control and direction, and private trucking is the only viable alternative.

The last-resort advantage of private trucking emanates from a lack of capable for-hire carrier service. Firms that ship products requiring special equipment (for example, cryogenics [liquid gas] require a pressurized tank trailer) have difficulty finding for-hire carriers with such special equipment and are virtually forced into private trucking to remain in business. In addition, firms that ship damaged products sometimes find it difficult to get for-hire carriers willing to provide service within a reasonable time frame or at a reasonable rate. This last resort is due to lack of in-house talent which means that the firm must hire outside managers for the specific purpose of managing the fleet. This usually increases management costs.

Capital availability has been a problem for some firms. The money tied up in truck, trailers, and maintenance facilities is money that is not available for use in the company's primary business. This capital problem can be eliminated by leasing the equipment.

As a private carrier, the firm bears the risk of loss and damage to its freight. To hedge against possible loss, the private carrier can buy cargo insurance or act as a self-insured carrier (merely absorb all losses). Customers receiving damaged goods will contact the seller (private carrier) for reimbursement, and failure (or delay) of payment is a direct indictment against the seller. When a for-hire carrier is used, the seller can "wash its hands" of the claim because the dispute is between the buyer and the carrier, assuming FOB origin terms of sale.

The risk of public liability resulting from a vehicle accident is incurred by private fleet. This risk can be mitigated by insurance, but the possibility of excessive court judgments is present.

The cost of paperwork and maintenance for long-distance, multistate operations is greater than for short-distance or local operations. The clerical costs associated with accounting for mileage driven in various states, gallons of fuel purchased in different states, and vehicle licenses or permits required by different states escalate as the scope of the private carriage operation becomes multistate.

Breakdowns away from the home terminal or garage requiring emergency road service are more expensive than normal maintenance service. The possibility of such emergency service increases as the operating scope increases. Breakdowns also reduce the service levels and have an impact on customer service and eventually sales and profits.

The final disadvantage of private trucking is the possible addition of another union, the Teamsters, into the company. It is quite common for private fleet drivers to be unionized by the Teamsters, and then the Teamsters attempt to represent the other employees who are not drivers. In some companies, the private fleet drivers are members of the union representing the nondriver employees.

Although there are disadvantages to private trucking, the fact that there are so many private truck fleets suggests that the advantages outweigh the disadvantages for many firms. The firm's analysis of costs and benefits of private trucking is critical at the evaluation stage as well as throughout the operation of the fleet.

Private Trucking Cost Analysis

Efficient and economical private truck operation requires a working knowledge of the actual cost of operating the fleet. The manager must know the facts affecting the individual cost elements of private trucking to make effective decisions that lower costs and improve service.

Fixed Costs Fixed costs are those that do not vary in the short run. For private trucking, these costs can be grouped into four areas: depreciation (lease payments), interest on investment, management, and office and garage. Fixed costs are approximately 27.1 cents per mile for fleets of long-distance haulers of refrigerated products.

The fixed cost per mile varies inversely with the number of miles operated per year. The greater the number of miles driven, the lower the fixed cost per mile; that is, the total fixed cost is spread over a larger number of miles. Therefore, most private truck fleet managers who refer to the scale economies associated with increased vehicle utilization are concerned with spreading fixed costs over a larger number of miles.

For example, if annual use equals 140,000 miles, total fixed cost for the operation described in Table 13-3 is $37,940 (140,000 miles × $0.271). If the vehicle is operated over 200,000 miles, approximately 43 percent greater utilization than the 140,000 miles per year, the fixed cost per mile would decrease to 19.9 cents per mile ($39,740 ÷ 200,000).

Interest on vehicles (investment) accounts for 3.2 cents per mile or approximately 12 percent of total fixed cost per mile, as indicated in Table 13-3. Because of the relatively low cost of borrowing money, vehicle interest cost has dropped from 25 percent in 1989 to 12 percent of total fixed costs in recent years.

Management and overhead (office and garage) costs are approximately 13.6 cents per mile or about 50 percent of total fixed costs. It is quite common to find management costs being understated in a private trucking operation. Management time, and therefore costs, is siphoned from the primary business of the firm to assist in managing the fleet. Rarely is this "free" management talent accounted for in the private fleet cost analysis.

Vehicle depreciation represented 32.1 percent of total fixed costs or 8.7 cents per mile. Vehicle costs have decreased in recent years but, in all likelihood, will rise in the future. The actual cost of a truck depends upon the size, carrying capacity, engine, and market conditions.

Operating Costs Operating costs are those costs that vary in the short run. Private trucking operating costs consist of fuel, driver wages, maintenance, insurance, license fees, tires, and user taxes. As indicated in Table 13-4, operating cost as reported by the American Transportation Research Institute (published 2008) was $1.73 per mile.

The total operating cost varies directly with the number of miles operated per year. The greater the number of miles operated, the greater the total operating costs. The operating cost per mile will remain approximately the same.

For example, total operating cost for 140,000 miles per year is $242,200 (140,000 miles × $1.73). If the mileage per year is increased to 200,000 miles, total operating cost will increase to about $346,000. In reality, license, insurance, and certain miscellaneous costs will remain constant per year and then decrease per mile; maintenance costs, however, will increase.

Fuel and oil costs represent 36 percent (63 cents per mile) of operating costs. After a spike in retail prices in late 2008, seen in Figure 13-1, diesel fuel prices have dropped off and have averaged about $2.20 per gallon over the first half of 2009. A diesel tractor averages about 4.5 to 5.5 miles per gallon, and a gasoline tractor averages a little

Table 13-4	Operational Costs of Trucking		
MOTOR CARRIER MARGINAL EXPENSE		**COSTS PER MILE**	**COSTS PER HOURS**
Vehicle-based			
Fuel-oil Costs		.634	$33.00
Truck/Trailer Lease or Purchase Payments		.206	$10.72
Repair and Maintenance		.092	$4.79
Fuel Taxes		.062	$3.23
Truck Insurance Premiums		.060	$3.12
Tires		.030	$1.56
Licensing and Overweight-Oversize Permits		.024	$1.25
Tolls		.019	$0.99
Driver-Based			
Driver Pay		.441	$16.59
Driver Benefits		.126	$6.56
Driver Bonus Payments		.036	$1.87
Total Marginal Costs		**$1.73**	**$83.68**
Source: American Transportation Research Institute, 2008.			

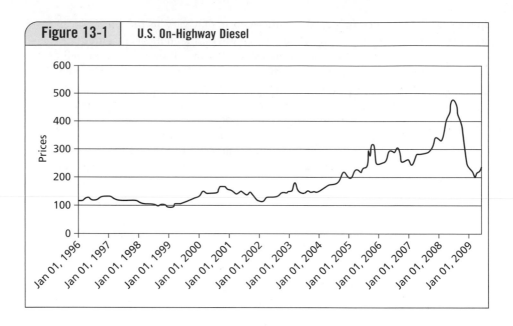

Figure 13-1 | U.S. On-Highway Diesel

less. For most transportation companies, fuel is the second highest operational expense, overshadowed only by labor costs; for some, fuel is becoming the foremost expenditure.[4]

From Table 13-4 we see that maintenance, repair, and tire costs were 12 cents per mile or 7 percent of total operating costs. Maintenance cost includes the cost of normal preventative maintenance such as oil lubrication and new tires and major and minor repairs.

The remaining operating costs—insurance, license, and miscellaneous—account for about 10 cents per mile. Insurance cost includes the cost of vehicle collision and comprehensive protection, public and personal liability, and cargo insurance. The company's rate of accidents determines the insurance premium assessed.

The cost of licensing and registering the vehicle is determined by the size of the vehicle and by the individual state and the number of other states in which the vehicle operates. The license fee for a given truck is not uniform among the states. Most states require a registration fee to use state highways. Thus, the greater the geographic scope of the private truck operation, the greater the license and registration cost.

Miscellaneous costs include such operating items as tolls, overload fines, and driver road expenses (lodging and meals). A private truck fleet manager must watch miscellaneous operating costs closely because miscellaneous costs can "hide" inefficient and uneconomical operations.

A fundamental requirement for an economical private truck fleet is knowing the costs. Once the costs are known and analyzed, effective decisions can be made. In the next section, attention is directed to the major operating decisions in private trucking.

On the Line   *Taking the Company Private*

Following the passage of the Motor Carrier Act of 1980, the for-hire sector of the motor carrier industry became increasingly competitive. As noted in Chapters 3 and 5, the Act essentially deregulated the motor carrier sector by eliminating many of the restrictions on rates. Routes and commodities allowed carriers and shippers an opportunity to negotiate rates and service levels but more importantly increased the number of carriers available to provide service in the best traffic lanes. This increased competition served to reduce many of the prevailing rates on those traffic lanes, sometimes by a substantial amount.

The level of competition, the lower rates, and the availability of service caused companies that had their own private fleets to reevaluate the costs and benefits of private trucking. Consequently, companies that historically had provided their own transportation service, such as Kimberly Clark, decided to outsource their transportation requirements. The quality of service provided by companies such as Schneider Trucking, plus the competitive rates, made this decision a logical choice in a number of situations for economic reasons. As indicated in this chapter and Chapter 5, there are other benefits to private trucking, such as control and advertising, which persuaded many companies to maintain their private fleets. But there is no question that there were numerous companies that outsourced all or part of their needed transportation services to for-hire carriers and logistics services companies during the 1980s and 1990s. Private fleets were viewed as a burden on the balance sheet, a cost center, and a noncore activity by a growing number of companies.

The 21st century has ushered in a renewed interest in private trucking. Increased rates, capacity shortages in some areas, and concerns about delivery service have caused companies to reconsider the private trucking option. This is particularly true of companies with predictable routings, the potential for backhauls, and demanding customers who expect "perfect orders." Some companies are also seeing advertising value with their names, logos, and so forth on the sides of their trucks. Of course, there could be a negative aspect in the case of an accident or some driver transgression. Changes in regulations give private carriers new opportunities to sell their unused capacity, which will be discussed in this chapter.

Private fleets still face the same issues as for-hire carriers, such as higher fuel charges, driver shortages, and road and infrastructure conditions. Private fleets usually have much lower driver turnover rates than for-hire carrier fleets with consequent customer service benefits. Another alternative for shippers is to purchase dedicated service from larger carriers. Dedicated service is analogous to buying guaranteed carrying capacity for the future, as discussed in Chapter 5. Many experts predict that we will see a resurgence in private trucking in the forthcoming years.

Source: Danielle Gallagher, Center for Supply Chain Research, The Pennsylvania State University, 2010.

Major Operating Decisions

Fleet operators try hard to improve fuel mileage because the savings potential is great. For example, assume the fleet depicted in Table 13-3 was able to increase vehicle mileage per gallon by 10 percent, from 5 miles per gallon to 5.5 miles per gallon. The total fuel cost savings for 140,000 miles per year would amount to $2,800 per truck or 9.1 percent. Such potential savings are usually sufficient justification for a $200 to $400 expenditure for an air deflector or for radial tires.

Driver cost (non-union) was 60.3 cents per mile or 35 percent of total operating cost, as given in Table 13-3. Over-the-road drivers are paid on the basis of the miles driven. City drivers are paid on an hourly basis. Table 13-5 provides an example of a union contract covering drivers in the Midwest.

As indicated in Table 13-5, over-the-road drivers were paid 42.0 cents per mile; this rate of pay was the same whether the tractor-trailer was loaded or empty. The rate was 43.0 cents per mile for driving a tractor pulling double trailers or twins. However, the over-the-road driver was paid $17.10 per hour for delays such as breakdowns. If we assume an over-the-road driver drives 125,000 miles per year (2,500 miles per week × 50 weeks), the fringe benefit *cost* equals 15.0 cents per mile ($18,803.70/125,000).

The city (pickup and delivery) driver was paid $17.36 per hour. To this hourly rate for city drivers (and over-the-road drivers) must be added the cost of fringe benefits, which amounted to $9.79 per hour. The 1993 total driver costs, then, were $27.15 per hour ($17.36 hourly rate plus $9.79 fringe benefits per hour) Fringe benefits represented 36.1 percent of the total city driver cost.

Table 13-5	Example of Driver Costs	
Driver Wages		
Over-the-Road		**City**
.42 cents/mile (5 axle combination) .43 cents/mile (double trailer) $17.10/hour (waiting)		$17.36/hour
Fringe Benefits		
Benefit	**Total Cost**	**Cost/Hour (1920 hrs/yr)***
Hospitalization ($112.70/week)	$5,860.40	$3.05
Pension ($88.00/week)	4,576.00	2.38
Holidays (10 days @ $138.88/day)	1,388.80	.72
Vacation (2.0 weeks @ $781.20/ week)**	1,562.40	.81
FICA (7.65%)	2,775.60	1.45
Federal Unemployment	64.00	.03
State Unemployment***	762.38	.40
Worker's Compensation***	1,814.12	.95
Total Fringe Costs	**$18,803.70**	**$9.79**

*Total hours possible = 52 weeks × 40 hours/week
Less: Vacation (80 hours), Holidays (80 hours) Hours worked/year
2,080 hours − 160 = 1,920

**Vacation is an average; Actual is based on years of service

***Varies by state (5% rate used)

Equipment The private trucking manager is concerned with two basic equipment questions: What type of equipment should be selected, and should this equipment be purchased or leased? Each of these questions is discussed below.

Choosing the type, size, make, model, type of engine, and so on of the vehicle used in private trucking seems to be an overwhelming challenge. However, the equipment used is determined by the firm's transportation requirements. The size of the shipment, product density, length of haul, terrain, city versus intercity operation, and special equipment needs are the equipment determinants to be examined. Table 13-6 provides a summary of the equipment selection factors and implications.

The size of the shipment and product density determine the carrying capacity desired in the vehicle. Shipments averaging 45,000 pounds will require five-axle tractor-trailer combinations. However, a low-density commodity such as fiberglass insulation requires a large carrying capacity, even though the weight of the shipment is low (10,000 pounds of fiberglass insulation can be carried in a trailer 40 feet long).

Long-distance operations, 300 miles or more one way and 75,000 or more miles per year, usually indicate the use of diesel-powered equipment. Diesel engines have a longer life and get better mileage than gasoline engines, but diesel engines have a higher initial cost. Some recent developments in diesel engine design have produced an economical, short-range, city diesel engine.

Table 13-6	Equipment Selection Factors and Implications
SELECTION FACTOR/CHARACTERISTICS	**EQUIPMENT IMPLICATION**
Shipment Size • Large Size Shipment (>35,000 lbs) • Small Size Shipment (<10,000 lbs)	Vehicles That Can Haul 80,000 lbs Vehicles That Can Haul 30,000 lbs
Product Density • Low Density (<15 lbs/feet cubed) • High Density (>15 lbs/feet cubed)	High Cube Capacity Vehicles (Trailers That Are 110 Inches High, 102 Inches Wide, and 57 Feet Long) Normal Cube Capacity
Length of Haul • <75,000 Miles Annually • >75,000 Miles Annually • Trips > 1,000 One-Way Miles	Gasoline Powered Diesel Powered Diesel Powered with Sleep Cells
City Operations	Gasoline Powered
Intercity Operations	Diesel Powered
Terrain • Mountainous • Level	Higher-Powered Engines Lower-Powered Engines
Special Needs • Controlled Temperature • Customer Required Unloading	Refrigerated Trailers Power Tailgate

For intercity operations, the tractor-trailer combination is commonly used along with a diesel engine if the distance justifies it. City operations use straight trucks that are gasoline powered. However, some city operations, furniture delivery for example, use small, single-axle trailers with gasoline-powered tractors. The reason for using trailers is to permit loading of one trailer while deliveries are being made with another; service to the customer is improved, and the firm reduces congestion and improves efficiency at the warehouse.

The terrain over which the vehicle travels affects the selection of certain equipment component parts such as the engine and drive train. For mountainous operations, the truck will require a high-powered engine and a low-geared drive train. For level, interstate highway operations, a lower-powered engine with a high-geared drive train is in order. Vehicles designed for mountainous operations usually are restricted to the mountainous regions because it makes sense to use different powered units in different regions.

Another transportation factor to be considered is the need for special equipment—refrigeration, power tailgates, high cube capacity, and so on. The nature of the product and customer requirements will dictate the type of special equipment to be considered.

A final consideration is the use of sleeper cabs for tractors. The sleeper cab adds several thousand dollars ($2,000–$4,000) to the initial price of the vehicle and is usually only considered when the trips are more than 1,000 miles one way. The sleeper permits the use of two drivers: One can accumulate the required off-duty time in the sleeper bed while the other driver continues to drive. The two-driver team produces lower transit time and better service. However, lower transit time also can be accomplished by substituting drivers at appropriate intervals.

The sleeper cab also can eliminate the cost of lodging for a one-driver operation. Instead of paying for a room, the driver accumulates the required eight hours off duty in the sleeping bed. However, there is a fuel cost to run the engine to produce heat or cooling for the driver in the sleeper. This fuel cost for a large diesel engine is 2 to 4 gallons of fuel per hour or $4.40 to $8.80 per hour (at $2.20 per gallon). The sleeper cost per eight-hour rest could be $35.20 to $70.40, which is comparable to current daily lodging costs. An increased focus on reducing idling time, reducing both fuel costs and emissions, is a trend that many firms are embracing. Using auxiliary power units (APUs) to provide secondary power to sleeper cabs can reduce fuel costs during non-driving hours.

Leasing   One of the disadvantages of private trucking, identified in Table 13-1, is the capital requirement for the equipment. Many firms are finding it difficult to buy money to use in the primary business; they cannot afford to buy a fleet of trucks as well. Leasing the equipment for a private truck operation reduces demands on company funds and enables existing capital to be used in the primary business of the company.

There are two basic types of lease arrangements available: the full-service lease and the finance lease. Both types are available with a lease-buy option that gives the lessee the option to buy the equipment, at book value, at the end of the lease.

The full-service lease includes the leased vehicle plus a variety of operating support services. The full service may require the lessor to provide fuel, license and registration, payment of highway user taxes, insurance, towing, road service, tire repair, washing, substitute vehicles for out-of-service equipment, and normal preventative maintenance. The more services requested by the lessee, the greater the lease fee. The full-service leasing fee consists of a weekly or monthly fixed fee per vehicle, plus a mileage fee.

In addition, the cost of fuel purchased from the lessor will be charged to the lessee. The full-service lease is a popular method of leasing trucks and tractors that require maintenance and other services.

The finance lease is only a means of financing equipment. Under the finance lease, the lessee pays a monthly fee that covers the purchase cost of the equipment and the lessor's finance charge. No services are provided by the lessor: All maintenance is the responsibility of the lessee. The finance lease is a common method of leasing trailers that require little maintenance.

As noted earlier, leasing increases working capital. Existing funds are not drained off into trucking equipment but remain available for use in the primary business. In addition, leasing sometimes does not have an impact on the borrowing limits negotiated with lending institutions.

Leasing permits a company to reduce or eliminate much of the risk associated with private trucking. A company can use full-service leasing to conduct a trial private trucking operation. The monthly fixed operating costs will be known throughout the lease period; this gives a great deal of certainty to the trial operation. If the trial private trucking is too expensive, the firm can quit operating at the end of the lease or even during the lease term if there is a cancellation clause. (However, there may be a cancellation penalty.) Most companies just starting a private trucking operation would be well advised to use full-service leasing,

Other advantages of leasing include purchase discounts for equipment, fuel, and parts that the lessee is able to realize through large-volume purchases. During the fuel shortages that occurred in 1973 and 1978, major full-service leasing companies offered a source of fuel, which kept many lessees' private fleets operating. The wide geographic scope of operation of major leasing companies offers full maintenance service throughout the country, which is especially important to private fleets that operate nationwide.

Leasing does have its disadvantages. First, leasing may cost more than owning. Further, for large fleets (30 or more vehicles), the private fleet operator already has a volume purchase advantage and expertise. Finally, some companies may have excess funds to employ, and a truck fleet may offer an acceptable return on investment.

The economic test of buying versus leasing is a comparison of the net present cost of buying versus leasing. The **net present cost** is a flow discounted cash approach that considers the cost and savings of both buying and leasing as well as the tax adjustments.

Fleet Operation and Control   The daily operation of a private fleet is a complex undertaking, and the discussion of daily operations is beyond the scope of this text. However, attention will be given to the operational areas of organization, regulation, driver utilization, the empty backhaul, and control mechanisms.

Organizing the Private Fleet   Once the fleet is in operation, intraorganizational conflicts may arise. These conflicts center on the incompatibility of departmental (user) demands and the private fleet goals.

The private fleet operating goals usually are to provide good service and to lower transportation cost. These goals, together, pose problems for the private fleet manager and open the door for intraorganizational conflict. For example, a division may request the fleet manager to provide fifth-day delivery to Houston from New York. To do so would increase transportation costs beyond what was incurred previously by private or for-hire trucks. Although the service is desirable to the customer, it is not cost efficient. The manager is unable to meet both goals.

To combat this conflict, the goal of the fleet is normally a cost-constrained service goal. That is, the goal is to provide good service at a given level of cost. Now the fleet manager can provide the best service that a given level of cost will permit.

Another organizational problem is the user's concept that private trucking is free transportation. Many shipments become emergencies that must be made, regardless of the cost, or a customer will be lost. A department may have the idea that the private fleet is already purchased (leased) so it should be used rather than sit idle. As pointed out earlier, operating cost represents a large portion of total costs, at $1.73 per mile; therefore, the truck is not free.

One organizational approach to eliminate the idea of free transportation is to establish the private fleet as a profit center. The income generated by the fleet is a paper or internal budget fee assessed to the using departments. The real costs are subtracted from the paper income to generate a paper profit. The manager's performance is evaluated on this paper profit. To guard against the idea that the private fleet must make a profit at any cost to the user, the departments must be given the option of using the private fleet or for-hire carriers (competition).

The profit center organizational structure was encouraged by deregulation provisions; basically, the provisions permitted private trucking to be operated as a for-hire carrier through intercorporate hauling and eased constraints to securing operating authority. A 2006 report from the National Private Truck Council indicated that approximately 53 percent of the private fleets surveyed had for-hire authority.

The use of a profit center concept is ideally suited for a fleet operation that is designed to operate as a for-hire carrier. By establishing the fleet as a profit center, the fleet is operated as a separate business entity with management responsible for profitability and asset utilization. The establishment of a separate corporate entity for the fleet that has secured operating authority permits the fleet to solicit business from other shippers, thereby increasing the fleet utilization, eliminating the empty backhaul, and possibly generating a profit for the parent firm.

The question of where to position the fleet in the organization (in which department) is another perplexing question. Usually a profit-center fleet is set up as a separate department reporting to the chief executive officer of the parent company. Placing the cost-center fleet under the control of the marketing, finance, production, or traffic departments tends to give the fleet the bias of the controlling department. For example, marketing tends to provide service at any cost, whereas traffic tends to minimize costs at the expense of service. The solution reached by a multifaceted manufacturing/retailing company was to place the private fleet under the control of the division that made the greatest use of the fleet. This division was charged with the cost of operating the fleet and was given credit (paper income via budget transfers) for service provided to other divisions.

Many private fleets are centralized. Centralized organization permits the fleet manager to provide service to many different departments and divisions, thus increasing the fleet utilization. A decentralized operation usually is found where separate divisions have different operating and vehicle requirements, which eliminates the possibility of joint divisional utilization of equipment and operating economies through centralized control.

Controlling the Private Fleet A key element to an effective and efficient private truck fleet is control over cost and performances. Table 13-7 is a list of cost and performance criteria for effective private truck fleet control.

Costs by function must be collected at the source. Fuel costs (and gallons) should be noted for each vehicle. This notation of functional costs at the cost source permits analysis of individual cost centers for the actual costs incurred. It is very difficult to analyze the fuel efficiency of individual vehicles in a fleet when fuel costs are aggregated for the entire fleet.

Further, the collection of functional costs by driver, vehicle, plant, and so on will permit analysis of problem areas within the fleet. The use of fleet averages only may conceal inefficient operations at particular markets or plants. However, functional costs by vehicle, plant, and driver can be compared to fleetwide averages, and a management-by-exception approach can be practiced. That is, if the specific costs (fuel cost/given driver) are within acceptable limits, nothing is done. Management action is taken when the specific costs are out of line with the desired level.

The performance criteria to be considered are miles operated (loaded and empty), human resource hours expended, vehicle operating hours, number of trips made, tonnage hauled, and the number of stops made. By collecting the above performance data, the fleet manager is able to measure the fleet's utilization and the drivers' productivity. Control measures such as overall cost per mile, per hour, and per trip can be computed and used in determining unacceptable performance areas in the fleet. Such information also is valuable to marketing and purchasing departments that determine the landed cost of goods sold or purchased.

Likewise, performance measures must be collected and identified at the source. Total fleet mileage and total fleet fuel consumption (gallons) will permit determination

Table 13-7	Private Cost and Performance Control Criteria	
COST	**PERFORMANCE**	
By function	Miles Operated	
Fuel (and gallons), Driver, Maintenance, Interest, Depreciation, Tires, Parts, Management, Overhead, License and Registration	By Vehicle, By Driver	
	Empty Miles	
	Total, By Location	
	Human Resource Hours	
	Total, Driving, Loading and Unloading, Breakdown	
Functional Cost	Vehicle Operating Hours	
By Vehicle, Driver, Plant, Market, Warehouse, Customer	By Vehicle	
	Number of Trips	
	By Vehicle/Time Period	
	Tonnage	
	By Vehicle	
	Number of Stops (Deliveries)	
	By Driver	

of overall fleet fuel efficiency. However, collection of fuel consumption and mileage per individual vehicle will provide the information necessary for purchasing fuel-efficient vehicles as replacements or additions to the fleet.

The performance criteria enable the fleet manager to analyze the productivity of drivers. The number of miles driven per day, the number of stops (deliveries) made per day, or the number of hours per run or trip are driver productivity measures that can be collected for each driver. From this productivity data, individual drivers who drive fewer miles per day, make fewer stops per day, or take a longer time to make a run than the standards (fleet average, for example) are singled out for further investigation and corrective action.

There are numerous examples of world-class service provided by private fleets that are owned or leased by companies because of the benefits that they provide. For example, Perdue Farms has a private fleet that includes 230 tractors, 235 drivers, and 750 trailers and travels 22 million miles a year. Their on-time delivery exceeds 99 percent, and they have been recognized as "Supplier of the Year" by several companies not only for the quality of their products but also for the quality of their trucking service that distributes to their customers. Perdue is not alone in this area; Walgreens has operated a private fleet since the company was founded over 100 years ago. Walgreens has tried for-hire carriers but feels that their private fleet offers them some real advantages in terms of not only service but also cost. Another good example is Pepsi, which operates the fourth-largest private fleet in the U.S.—5,937 trailers, 2,544 straight trucks, and 8,800 trailers. They have trucks on the road 24 hours a day, and they do not have to worry about capacity availability. It is estimated that private fleets represent over half of the U.S. trucking market and about 2.5 percent of the GDP of the United States.

Regulations   As stated earlier, bona fide private trucking is exempt from federal economic regulations. The private carrier need not secure authorization (certificate of public convenience and necessity) to transport the firm's products. Because private coverage is not for-hire service, no tariffs are published.

To be excluded from these economic regulations, the trucking operations must be truly private carriage. The trucking service must be incidental to and in the furtherance of the primary business of the firm—the primary business test. Thus, the transportation of the firm's raw materials and finished goods in private trucks is bona fide private trucking if the firm takes the normal business risks associated with such products. Normal business risk would include the existence of production facilities, sales outlets, product inventories, and a sales force for the products being transported.

A common problem many private fleets face is how to eliminate the empty backhaul. Miles traveled without a load add cost to the company, including the time consumed. In Figure 13-2, the cost of filling that backhaul can be calculated in comparison to leaving those miles empty.

Before the Motor Carrier Act of 1980, private fleets were prohibited from transporting subsidiary freight for a fee. Private fleets were then permitted to haul freight for subsidiaries that were 100 percent owned and to charge a fee for this service. For highly diversified companies, this permissible intercorporate hauling meant increased fleet utilization and lower total transportation costs. Now, the DOT allows registration of fleets to operate for-hire, for a $200 fee and legal costs, in every state that the fleet will operate.[5] On average, fleets that have **for-hire authority** get 10 percent lower costs

Figure 13-2	Backhaul Cost Analysis Form

Total trip miles including backhaul	=	_____ miles (A)
Normal deliver round-trip miles	=	_____ miles (B)
Difference (excess miles)	=	_____ miles (C)
Multiplied by cost per mile	=	$ _____ (D)
Additional labor expended		
____ (hr) × $____ (avg wage + benefits)	=	$ _____ (E)
Total cost (D + E)	=	$ _____ (F)
Gross backhaul revenue	=	$ _____
Less total cost (Line F)	=	$ _____
Profit (or loss)	=	$ _____

Source: National Private Truck Council, "Filling Backhaul Miles for Private Fleets," 2006.

per mile. Fleets with for-hire authority must publish rates and charges with the government, which is a shift from the lack of reporting requirements under exclusive private transportation.[6]

One option that eliminates the requirement for for-hire authority is **trip leasing**. The lease agreement is between a private carrier and another firm, for a single trip, and cannot last more than 30 days. The private carrier is responsible for licensing and record-keeping, and a copy of the trip lease agreement must be carried in the vehicle during the trip.[7] The private carrier also may trip lease to another private carrier and charge a fee for the service provided.

Another solution to eliminating empty backhaul is the transportation of exempt commodities. Exempt commodities may be hauled without ICC authority or other economic regulations. Some examples of exempt commodities are ordinary livestock, agricultural products (grain, fruits, vegetables), horticultural goods (Christmas trees), newspapers, freight incidental air transportation (to and from airports), used shipping containers, and fish.

Private trucking is subjected to all federal safety requirements in the areas of:

- driver qualifications
- driving practices
- vehicle parts and accessories
- accident reporting
- driver hours of service
- vehicle inspection and maintenance
- hazardous materials transportation
- vehicle weight and dimensions

These safety regulations are enforced by the U.S. Department of Transportation (DOT), Bureau of Motor Carrier Safety, and the private carrier must register with the U.S. DOT.

In addition, the private fleet must comply with the state safety regulations governing speed, weight, and vehicle length, height, and width. Such state regulations fall within the purview of the constitutionally granted police powers that permit states to enact laws to protect the health and welfare of their citizens. Because the safety regulations are not uniform among the states, the fleet management must be aware of specific regulations in each of the states in which the fleet operates.

Driver hours-of-service regulations establish the maximum number of hours (minimum safety level) a driver may operate a vehicle in interstate commerce, and consequently they affect the utilization of drivers. Basically, a driver operating interstate is permitted to drive a maximum of 10 hours following 8 consecutive hours off duty. Following regulations amended in 2005, a driver may drive a maximum of 11 hours after 10 consecutive hours off duty. Further, on a weekly basis, no driver can be on duty more than 60 hours in 7 consecutive days or 70 hours in 8 consecutive days. The Bush Administration advocated increasing the maximum driving hours in 2007, loosening the restrictions, but the changes were rejected by a U.S. Court of Appeals later that year.[8]

Entries of driving activities are recorded on a driver's daily log, as shown in Figure 13-3. The driver's daily log entries must be kept current to the time of the last change of duty, and the driver and carrier (private) can be held liable to legal

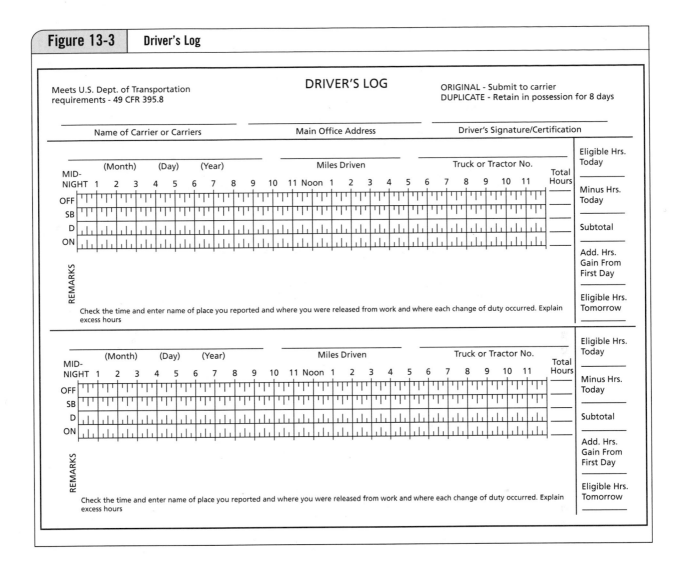

Figure 13-3   Driver's Log

prosecution for failure to maintain logs. The logbook is also an excellent source of performance data if the entries are accurate. The driver, vehicle, hours operated, miles driven, and trip origin and destination are found in the log entries. As the fleet management reviews the log to ensure driver availability, performance data can be compiled for each driver and vehicle.

Electronic Logs Electronic logbooks can alert drivers when they have reached the maximum allowable hours of driving time, reduce errors in recording information, and reduce the time it takes to capture and transmit data.[9] These electronic logs have been supported to prevent driver fatigue by reducing hours of service violations, and the Federal Motor Carrier Safety Administration has issued a proposed rule that would require motor carriers that have a certain level of hours of service (HOS) violations to install electronic logbooks.

SUMMARY

- Private transportation is an important component of the transportation system in most countries of the world, including the United States where it plays a significant and complimentary role to the for-hire sector of the total transportation system for all five modes of transportation.

- Private transportation is defined in the Interstate Commerce Act, and it essentially involves the movement of goods owned by a firm that also owns or leases and operates the equipment for the furtherance of its primary business.

- While private transportation is most prevalent in the trucking sector of the transportation system, it is also important in the rail, air, water and pipeline sectors. Private transportation in each of these five modes has some unique characteristics.

- Private rail transportation is special in that it usually takes the form of privately owned or leased rail cars of other businesses that are moved by a for-hire railroad company over their tracks. There are, however, some large manufacturing companies that operate on their own lines within the limits of their plant properties.

- Private air transportation, unlike the other modes of transportation, is used primarily for the movement of passengers. While usually more expensive than commercial airline service, private air service is usually rationalized on the basis of the time saved for valuable employees, especially currently with all the security controls at airports. Also, such service may be justified as the only alternative for getting to remote points by air.

- Private water transportation is very common in the movement of bulk, large volume, low-value products such as coal, ore, mining products, oil and agricultural products. Most private, domestic water service is provided by barge movements on the inland waterways, such as the Great Lakes or coastal waterway systems.

- Private pipeline service has been a major part of the oil industry since the nineteenth century where it was initially implemented for industry control purposes. However, the oil company pipelines were subsequently required by federal law to also operate as common carriers to ensure that other oil companies had adequate service at a reasonable cost.

- Private trucking is the most frequently used and most pervasive form of private transportation. About half of the ton-miles of commodities shipped domestically are moved by private truck transportation.

- Private trucking is typically justified on the basis of cost (efficiency) or service (effectiveness). Some private fleet operators maintain that both objectives are achieved, which obviously enhances overall profitability of the company.

- The decision to provide private transportation service requires careful analysis of all the costs involved as well as the value of the benefits. The cost analysis requires estimating both fixed and variable/operating costs and is frequently very challenging to ensure accuracy.

- Leasing of equipment is an attractive alternative to outright ownership for a growing number of companies that do not want to make the capital outlay for some reason. Leasing companies provide a variety of leasing arrangements that may benefit private fleet operations.

- Private truck transportation for some companies can be a complex undertaking because of the daily operation of a fleet of equipment, which requires knowledge of state and federal regulations about equipment and service; different taxes; driver management and utilization; equipment control and maintenance; and controlling empty back hauls.

STUDY QUESTIONS

1. What is private transportation? Discuss the legal constraints imposed on the operation of a private carrier.

2. The nature of private carriage varies among the modes. Describe the private carriage differences among the modes.

3. Private trucking is the most pervasive form of private carriage. Comment on the reasons why private trucking is so widely used in the United States.

4. Service and cost are the two areas most often cited as reasons for establishing a private trucking operation. Discuss the service and cost advantages afforded by private trucking.

5. What are the disadvantages of private trucking?

6. Using the data in Table 17-3, determine the managerial impact of (a) an increase in the annual miles operated per tractor/trailer from 100,000 to 125,000; (b) a decrease in the average load per trip from 40,000 pounds to 34,000 pounds; and (c) a 20 percent increase in the price of fuel from $1.10 to $1.32 per gallon.

7. If you were going to select trucks to operate over-the-road from Denver to Los Angeles, what type of equipment would you specify? Why? Would you specify the same type of equipment for a delivery operation within the county of Los Angeles? Why?

8. Why would a private fleet be organized on the basis of a cost center? A profit center?

9. Describe the methods available to a private carrier to operate as a for-hire carrier.

10. Discuss the economic and safety regulations imposed on private trucking by the federal government.

NOTES

1. Schulz, John D. 2008. "Silent Success." Logistics Management (April): p. 29.

2. National Private Truck Council. 2007. *America's Private Fleets.* 8.

3. Farris, M. Theodore. 2008. "Evaluating the Private Fleet." *Transportation Journal* (Fall).

4. Ibid.

5. National Private Truck Council. 2006. "Filling Backhaul Miles for Private Fleets." 1.

6. Ibid.

7. Ibid.

8. Farris, M. Theodore. 2008. "Evaluating the Private Fleet." *Transportation Journal.* (Fall).

9. Cantor, David, Thomas M. Corsi and Curtis M. Grimm. 2009. "Do Electronic Log Book Contribute to Motor Carrier Safety Performance?" *Journal of Business Logistics* 30(1): 203.

CASE 13-1

Nittany Products

Tracie Shannon, fleet manager for Nittany Products in Pleasant Gap, Pennsylvania, can recall the time when they could dispatch 20 units for delivery, have the equipment return empty, and still be profitable. However, that was 30 years ago and much had changed in the interim. In those days, fuel was inexpensive, even cheap; driver wages were relatively low; and the motor carrier industry was much less competitive because of regulation.

Nittany Products produces a variety of outdoor grills for private household as well as commercial use. The business was started by Tracie's father as almost a hobby. Nick Shannon liked to cook and particularly liked to do outdoor cooking on a grill. The size of the groups that he entertained kept growing as his barbeques became almost legendary. During this period, Nick became very dissatisfied with his standard K-mart grill. Being a metal fabricator by trade, he decided to build his own grill, which he did, and it was followed closely by 15 to 20 additional models with different features including fuel sources. Then his neighbors asked to buy grills, and he could not produce them fast enough in his garage. So, Nick borrowed some money for working capital, rented an abandoned gas station, and expanded from there. The rest is history.

Tracie took over their private fleet five years ago. Her older brother, Pete, managed the plant and her father, Nick, was the reigning CEO but expected to retire soon. Nick, Pete, and Tracie were concerned about their private fleet. They considered it a value-added feature of their business because the drivers would help commercial customers set up the larger customized grills and would even help noncommercial customers who purchased the larger, more elaborate grills. However, with escalating fuel costs, higher driver wages, and other challenges, they wondered whether they could continue providing private carrier delivery.

Nittany Products still had its empty backhaul problem, but they believed that current federal legislation regarding private fleets provided enough flexibility for Nittany Products to solicit backhaul traffic. If they could develop for-hire backhaul business, they believed that they could sustain their private fleet.

CASE QUESTION

1. You have been hired by Nittany Products to write a report presenting them with their options for developing backhaul traffic. Their fleet contains standard 40-foot trailers pulled by Volvo tractors.

CASE 13-2

Naperville Hardware Distribution

Matt Weber and Zach Heuer, CEO and COO respectively of Naperville Hardware Distributors, were frustrated with their fourth quarter financial results. At the beginning of the quarter they had been enthusiastic about the profit picture for the company. The economy had been in an economic slump last year, but the first quarter results of this year had shown a positive upturn in shipments. The second and third quarter results were even better. Matt and Zach had been almost exuberant even though profits had not shown much improvement. They both felt the profits in the fourth quarter would improve significantly because they had carryover expenses from the previous year, which they covered with revenue generated during the second and third quarters. While their net profits had again improved in the fourth quarter, the results were not what they expected.

They had their CFO, Carl Weber, do a "deep dive" on their costs for the year. Carl also did some benchmarking for them. Carl came to the conclusion that they were spending too much money on transportation and related distribution service. They were currently utilizing a third party logistics services company, LMZ. In addition to delivering the hardware products to wholesalers and large retailers, LMZ also received, processed, and filled the orders for delivery. Carl recommended that they "in-source" these services, including the transportation.

Matt and Zach were surprised by Carl's conclusion about the outsourcing of their transportation and related logistics services because they had been dealing with LMZ for about 10 years. But they were even more surprised by the recommendation to in-source. Private transportation service and order fulfillment was not one of their core competencies. They had some reservations.

CASE QUESTION

1. Matt and Zach had requested you to write a short white paper (2 to 3 pages) presenting the opportunities and challenges in going private.

Chapter 14

ISSUES AND CHALLENGES OF GLOBAL SUPPLY CHAINS

Learning Objectives

After reading this chapter, you should be able to do the following:

- Discuss the growing concern about U.S. transport capacity and the transport infrastructure needed to support global trade

- Understand what conditions or factors fostered prosperity during the 1980s and 1990s

- Appreciate the impact and challenges associated with congestion and the transport infrastructure in the overall economy

- Understand the challenges and issues related to congestion and infrastructure among the major modes of transportation in the United States

- Discuss why sustainability has become a major objective for businesses in general and especially for transportation

- Appreciate the impact that shipment consolidation and eliminating water from some finished products can have upon sustainability and supply chain costs

- Discuss the role and objectives of the SmartWay Transport Program sponsored by the U.S. Environmental Protection Agency

- Develop insights into the special challenges that transport companies will face in the 21st century with respect to energy

- Appreciate the opportunities that transport carriers will have to improve supply chain performance through proactive collaboration and technology

- Understand how supply chain visibility can help transport carriers to improve their efficiency and effectiveness

Transportation Profile

Emerging Conditions in Transport

Concerns over the state of the U.S. transportation infrastructure and capacity constraints have increased. Demand for transportation services has grown at a rapid rate, particularly those associated with global trade. Total freight volume moved on the U.S. transportation system, including both domestic and international freight, grew 13 percent during 2002–2006. The total freight volume is estimated to nearly triple by 2035, with particularly strong growth in imports and domestic freight.

The rapid growth in international trade is also placing great pressure on both U.S. **gateways**, particularly **water gateways**—through which nearly 80 percent of U.S. global freight by weight is moved—and inland transportation. Congestion was already an issue, particularly at West Coast ports due to growing trade between the United States and Asia and the Pacific. The luxury of inland transport excess capacity, primarily truck and rail transport, has become rarer in the total U.S. transport system. Congestion is also an issue on the nation's highways and at major freight rail gateways and corridors, most of which are critically important for traffic between West Coast port gateways and inland locations. While this issue has abated somewhat with the cyclical/short run downturn in the global economy during the 2008–2009 time period, the problem is essentially a long run/secular problem that will return as the global economy recovers from the economic downturn.

Capability to invest in the transportation infrastructure is also limited. The railroads' budget shortfall for expansion needed over the next 20 years is estimated to be up to $53 billion. Similarly, the end-of-year balance of the Highway Trust Fund (HTF), which indicates whether the expected revenues will be sufficient to cover the anticipated spending, is declining. The HTF is largely financed by the federal fuel tax, which is 18.4 cents per gallon for gasoline and 24.4 cents for diesel; the rates have not changed since 1993. There is great reluctance to increase these taxes because of the burden on the general public and the potential impact on the prices of consumer goods.

With the rising fuel prices, vehicle miles traveled in the United States has been on a decline, reducing funding for highways and transportation infrastructure initiatives even further. The HTF is currently projected to be facing a deficit of $3.2 billion or more by 2010, according to the White House. Driver shortages add further to the trucking service capacity concerns, especially in the long-haul truckload sector. In fact, with a high number of drivers near retirement age and higher levels of driver turnover, the long-haul truck driver shortage is estimated to reach 111,000 by 2014. The driver shortage also lessened during the 2008–2009 downturn in the global economy, but as indicated above, this shortage is a long-run/secular problem because of the average age of the long-haul drivers and the higher turnover rate. Consequently, it is not an issue that is going to go away and will need to be addressed more aggressively. It should be noted that some trucking companies have been proactive in working with their long-haul drivers to mitigate the problems associated with their home life. Some authors propose a rather simplistic solution, that is, raising wages. This tactic may be successful when there are limited employment opportunities, but it is not a long-run solution.

In addition, the volatile nature of fuel prices, which have escalated to levels exceeding $4 per gallon in recent years, has plagued the transport industry for some time. World crude oil prices have increased as high as 113 percent above their 2005 level during the last several years. Oil reached an all-time high of almost $118 per barrel in the second quarter of 2008. Despite recent drops in oil prices, they remain high compared to those before 2005 and especially since 1990. It is indeed a long-run global challenge and a problem that requires a multifaceted, multi-country approach for resolution.

Source: Kusumal Ruamsook and Dawn Russell, White Paper, Center for Supply Chain Research, Penn State University, January 2009.

Introduction

Chapters 1 and 2 discussed the role and importance of transportation in the firm and in the economy. The economic, political, and social contributions and significance of transportation were examined. Transportation was described as the "glue" that holds supply chains together and the "life blood" of economies, regions, and cities. Our modern civilization and the developments, which have occurred in many countries, would not have been possible without an efficient and effective transportation system. It was also noted that transportation has been a critical part of economic, political, and social development for hundreds of years. In fact, transportation may be the most important business for a developed economy.

During the 1980s, 1990s, and the early part of the 21st century, transportation became relatively less expensive for a given level of service, which contributed significantly to enhanced productivity and economic growth. This phenomenon was attributable to two major factors, namely, relatively inexpensive fuel and competition, particularly in the motor carrier sector of the transportation industry. In fact, one could argue that we were "spoiled" by these two conditions that fostered economic prosperity. However, times have changed, with increased fuel prices and a reduction in available capacity in the motor carrier sector, due to driver hour restrictions and other factors discussed in Chapter 5. The other modes of transportation, especially air carriers, have faced similar challenges. This change has occurred at a crucial time in worldwide global development. The concern is that the rising fuel changes, competitive market forces, and other factors could cause the cost of moving goods to increase in the years ahead. There are a number of factors, including congestion, the environment, and the transport infrastructure, that may affect the long, global, and frequently vulnerable supply chains with their movements of high-value, time-sensitive commodities. If these challenges are not mitigated, the cost of moving freight will thwart economic progress in developed as well as underdeveloped economies. Figure 14-1 clearly indicates the long-run potential for the

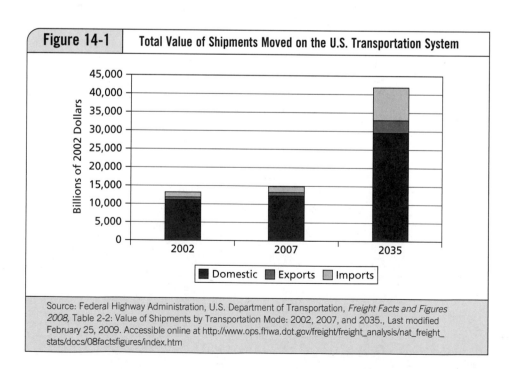

Figure 14-1 | **Total Value of Shipments Moved on the U.S. Transportation System**

Source: Federal Highway Administration, U.S. Department of Transportation, *Freight Facts and Figures 2008,* Table 2-2: Value of Shipments by Transportation Mode: 2002, 2007, and 2035., Last modified February 25, 2009. Accessible online at http://www.ops.fhwa.dot.gov/freight/freight_analysis/nat_freight_stats/docs/08factsfigures/index.htm

U.S. transportation system when all three flows for the system are considered. The flows associated with imports into the country are particularly noteworthy. It is imperative to the economic health of the United States and its citizens that the challenges indicated above and discussed in this chapter be addressed in an objective manner.

Since the transportation industry will have to address these challenges and issues in the future, we will discuss major issues in some detail and examine their impact on the important sectors of the transportation industry. The initial issue will be congestion and the transportation infrastructure, followed by sustainability, fuel prices, and technology.

Congestion and Transportation Infrastructure

All of us have experienced the frustration associated with congestion, usually while we were riding in an automobile. Some individuals experience congestion on a regular, daily basis if they live in or near a city and have to commute to and from work. However, we seldom consider the total or real **cost of congestion**. For individuals, the cost of extra fuel is the most obvious cost of congestion, but there is also the cost of the personal time lost, which could reduce personal earnings. If the congestion does not cause an obvious economic loss, it usually has an impact in the area of what an economist would call a *social cost*—reduced opportunity for leisure, reduced time with family, inconvenience for friends and family, and so on. The social cost is difficult to calibrate, but nevertheless it is a societal cost that needs to be included in the analytical equation for congestion.

For many businesses, however, the cost of congestion is real and important. Consider the fact that Nike estimates that they have to spend an additional $4 million per week to carry an extra 7–14 days of inventory to compensate for congestion delays. One day of delay requires American President Line's eastbound trans-Pacific services to increase its use of containers and chassis by 1300 units, which adds $4 million of additional cost per year. The bottleneck delays of trucks on U.S. highways cause over 250 million hours of delay to truckers throughout the United States. A conservative estimate of the cost of these delays is about $7 billion per year. When fuel costs and/or labor costs increase, the costs are compounded.[1]

Increased costs to carriers are eventually reflected in higher transportation rates for shippers. Between 2003 and 2006, rates increased 13 percent for truck transportation, 25 percent for rail transportation, 11 percent for scheduled air freight, 11 percent for water transportation, 9 percent for port and harbor operations, 5 percent for marine cargo handling, 22 percent for pipeline transportation of crude oil, and 8 percent for refined oil products.[2] Obviously, these increases reflect a combination of cost and demand factors, but the cost factors are the most important.

Highway Congestion and Infrastructure

It is estimated that congestion on highways will spread from large urban areas and some intercity routes to large stretches of intercity highways in both urban and rural areas. Without operational improvements, it is estimated that by 2035 recurring peak-period congestion will slow traffic on 20,000 miles of the National Highway System and create stop-and-go conditions on an additional 45,000 miles. The top ten highway interchange bottlenecks cause an average of 1.5 million annual truck hours of delay. The (conservative) estimated delay costs are about $30/hour to the trucking companies, but the cost to the shippers would usually be higher.[3]

Figure 14-2 indicates the funding challenges faced by our highway system. The revenue inflow is below the "need to maintain" level required to keep the current highway

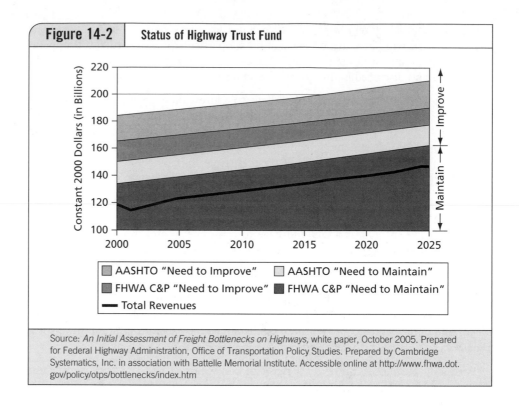

Figure 14-2 | **Status of Highway Trust Fund**

Legend:
- AASHTO "Need to Improve"
- AASHTO "Need to Maintain"
- FHWA C&P "Need to Improve"
- FHWA C&P "Need to Maintain"
- ▬ Total Revenues

Source: *An Initial Assessment of Freight Bottlenecks on Highways,* white paper, October 2005. Prepared for Federal Highway Administration, Office of Transportation Policy Studies. Prepared by Cambridge Systematics, Inc. in association with Battelle Memorial Institute. Accessible online at http://www.fhwa.dot. gov/policy/otps/bottlenecks/index.htm

system operating effectively. The delay costs indicated above will also need funds to improve the current system. The graph shows the projections for the 50 states and federal-level needs for what are considered to be required improvements. The combined total shows a staggering gap for the future. Revenues will have to be increased or the demand for highway usage decreased.

Railroad Congestion and Infrastructure[4]

The large interregional freight railroads have experienced a significant increase in demand, especially for **trailer-on-flatcar (TOFC)** and **container-on-flatcar (COFC)** movements. TOFC and COFC, once a relatively small market segment, is now a major source of revenue and traffic. These relatively high-speed intermodal trains compete for network space with the bulk traffic trains. The congestion is frequently exacerbated by seasonal surges in freight demand and disruptions that add to the congestion as volumes reach capacity on the reduced mainline rail network (reduced 50 percent between 1960 and 1980).

Congestion on the mainline railroad network is forecast to spread significantly by 2035. The American Association of Railroads reports that congestion will increase to almost 16,000 miles on the main lines of the railroads (30 percent of the network) if current capacity is not increased. Rail routes that have moderate to very limited capacity to accommodate maintenance without servicing delays and disruption will almost double by 2035, which will affect about 25 percent of the network. A potential solution to the rail congestion problem is the construction and return of double tracks to accommodate two-way traffic simultaneously, which was common on the main lines of most large railroads prior to World War II. The Union Pacific railroad has already initiated a double-track program in some areas. The addition of another track can be

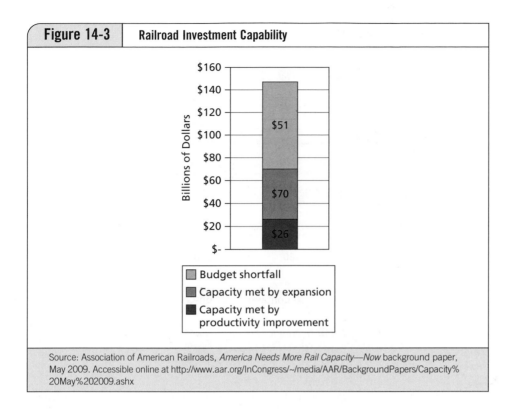

Figure 14-3 | **Railroad Investment Capability**

Source: Association of American Railroads, *America Needs More Rail Capacity—Now* background paper, May 2009. Accessible online at http://www.aar.org/InCongress/~/media/AAR/BackgroundPapers/Capacity% 20May%202009.ashx

accomplished more quickly and usually at less cost than adding lanes to an Interstate highway, but there is still a major investment cost that railroads are reluctant to accommodate on a private basis; that is, they want a government subsidy to underwrite the cost in whole or in part, similar to the other modes of transportation. Figure 14-3 clearly indicates the magnitude of the budget funding gap.

Waterway Congestion and Infrastructure[5]

On inland waterways, aging infrastructure and locks frequently cause bottlenecks. For example, of the 510,000 commercial vessel passages through federal and state locks, 31 percent experienced delays. Average delays for barge tows were one hour and 32 minutes. The average processing time was about 30 minutes. The challenge is that inland waterways are especially susceptible to weather delays, including problems caused by flooding, draughts, ice- and other storm-related disruptions.

Deep-draft ports on the three major coastlines have capacity challenges, which will be explored in the next section. The inland ports have capacity issues also, but most of them are not as problematic as the ocean ports. As indicated previously, the congestion problem at the ports is a real challenge, especially since these ports are the gateways for imports and exports, and the long-run projection for growth in global trade (imports and exports based upon weight) in the United States is 77 percent. The West Coast ports are particularly vulnerable because of the growth in trade with Asian countries. The concentration of vessels bringing freight through the West Coast ports is evident in Figure 14-4.

The port congestion problems are manifested in several areas. A growing share of waterborne commerce, especially imports, moves in very large container ships, the

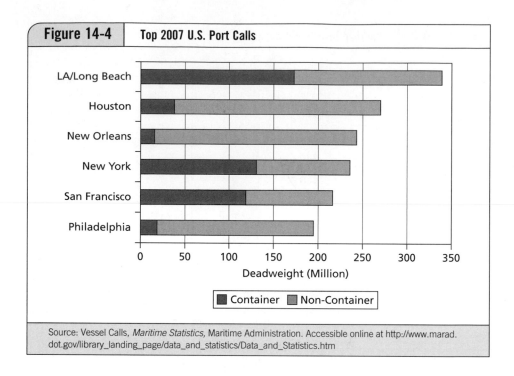

Figure 14-4 | Top 2007 U.S. Port Calls

Deadweight (Million)

■ Container ■ Non-Container

Source: Vessel Calls, *Maritime Statistics,* Maritime Administration. Accessible online at http://www.marad. dot.gov/library_landing_page/data_and_statistics/Data_and_Statistics.htm

largest of which can carry more than 8,000 containers, and the capacity of containers increased by over 26 percent between 2002 and 2007. As shown in Figure 14-5, the growing containerized imports and the large container ship sizes had led to container-ship capacity growth that was much stronger than that of non-container vessels. These large ships can take five to seven days to unload, compared to two to three days for

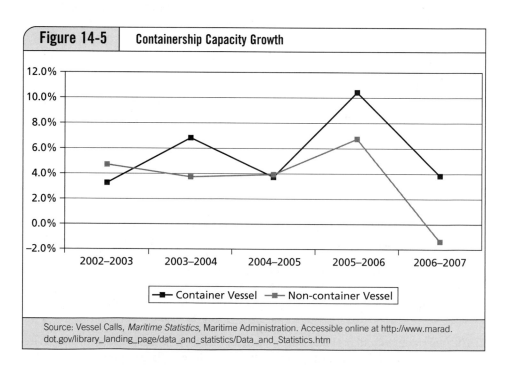

Figure 14-5 | Containership Capacity Growth

—■— Container Vessel   —■— Non-container Vessel

Source: Vessel Calls, *Maritime Statistics,* Maritime Administration. Accessible online at http://www.marad. dot.gov/library_landing_page/data_and_statistics/Data_and_Statistics.htm

many container ships. Only a few ports can accommodate these ships because of the draft requirements in the channels leading into the port areas. They also require more berths for unloading, special cranes for unloading and loading, and more dock space and transportation-related equipment for moving the containers from the dock area to local terminals or distribution centers. In addition, the congestion problem is exacerbated by the fact that transloading of the containers is frequently required since domestic containers can usually hold 50 to 60 percent more freight than the ISO international containers. In fact, this has caused an imbalance and shortage of the international ISO containers. Another related problem is that many port areas are constrained by the scarcity of land nearby and/or the high cost of such land for the development of marine terminals and related facilities.

Currently, the port congestion challenges are being addressed by improved port access (for example, with dredging); investment in technology and equipment by carriers and port operators; and longer operating hours. These strategies are aimed at reducing the dwell time of ships and containers in port areas and relieving some of the pressure for expansion. The trade-off costs associated with improving access routes and round-the-clock operations, which often include overtime payments, need to be evaluated. The situation is also exacerbated by the public's hue and cry about the disruption around the port areas when vessels are loading and unloading. There are also environmental challenges in the port area with the discharge of various fluids (intentionally or unintentionally); the garbage, trash, and other debris that may be thrown overboard; and other ecological damage. Some port areas are notorious for their insensitivity to the ecology of the marine environment. Major efforts are underway to improve the environmental impact of port area.

On a related note, the larger container ships have also caused some capacity and congestion problems on certain key waterways. A case in point is the Panama Canal, with locks that were built almost a hundred years ago when ships were much smaller. Most of these larger ships have had to take the longer route around South America, which adds about 9000 miles to the journey. Cognizant of this problem, the Panama Canal Authority has undertaken a $5.25 billion construction project to add a third lane to the ocean-linking canal waterway, add two new locks (one on the east side of the canal and the other on the west side), and to dredge the existing waterway, which will double the canal's capacity and allow the canal to accommodate the super-size container ships. The third lane is scheduled to open in 2014 and is likely to have a major impact on global trade routes as the large container ships begin to use the canal.

Global Perspectives   *Ships and Ports Explore Many Ways to Go Green*

Success usually carries some trade-offs. For container shipping lines and U.S. deep-sea global ports, the increase in the volume of global trade has raised the general public's awareness of their actions. This is especially true with respect to the impact of shipping lines and port traffic activity on the environment. Now, ships and ports have joined industrial factories, automobiles, and trucks as a symbol of pollution. In fact, commercial port areas are among the major contributors to poor air and water quality. In an effort to improve their public image and their operations, the carriers and ports are going green with a major push in that direction.

The approach to the issue of ports' environmental impact has several dimensions and is being spearheaded by important international organizations, including the **World Shipping Council**, the **International Maritime Organization**, **the Clean Cargo Working Group**, and the **Container Shipping Information Service**. Carriers are undertaking programs to reduce emissions of carbon dioxide (CO_2), nitrogen oxide, sulfur oxide, and other vessel pollutants. Other concerns include oil chemicals, ballast water, sewage, and garbage on the maritime side.

The easiest measure to initiate is slowing down the speed of ships to lower fuel consumption, but this raises costs in other areas such as inventory holding costs, as well as customer service. New technology can help, such as special valves to reduce nitrous oxide, low-sulphur fuel, improvements in propeller efficiency, and the use of environmentally safe silicon paints. On the port side, industry executives are pushing for global standards that would discourage local jurisdictions from formulating a host of conflicting rules.

Source: Adapted from R. J. Bowman, "Ships and Ports Explore Many Ways to Go Green," *Global Logistics and Supply Chain Strategies,* September 10, 2008

Sustainability: The Green Supply Chain

Going green is a slogan or objective that was given lip service for many years by individuals and organizations. Advocates were often labeled as "tree huggers" and ridiculed in private. There was an assumption that going green would mean increased cost to the enterprise, which was viewed as unacceptable. Pressure began to build in a number of quarters for green supply chains, which meant that both shippers and carriers would have to initiate efforts to eliminate pollutants, reduce carbon footprints, and so forth. The local, state, and federal governments also began to exert pressure on carriers and shippers to improve. Interestingly enough, some organizations found that they could actually reduce their carbon footprint and still lower their costs, along with their efforts to lower their negative impact on the environment.

Some discussion of the term **carbon footprint** is appropriate at this point. It is widely used by the various media (print, radio, and TV), academics, politicians, and others and has become a part of our vernacular. However, in spite of its ubiquitous use, definitions vary and are frequently not very specific. The common interpretation is that a carbon footprint is equated with a certain amount of gaseous emissions that are relevant to climate change and are associated with human production and consumption activities. However, there does not appear to be any consensus on how to measure or quantify the carbon footprint. The spectrum of definitions range from direct CO_2 definitions to full-lifecycle greenhouse gas emissions. There is an emphasis, however, on measuring CO_2 emissions directly and indirectly caused by an activity, which is the preference of the authors.

There is no doubt that the higher fuel prices in 2008 helped to spur interest among carriers and shippers to reduce fuel consumption. This effort to improve fuel efficiency also reduced the carbon footprint of commercial transportation, but it is only one of six reasons that is motivating business to drive their sustainability agenda. In fact, it has been documented that the rising energy costs was number five on the list of six market pressures. The others included corporate responsibility, a desire to increase or maintain brand reputation, competitive pressures, and internal and external stakeholder pressure or expectations. The last item was regulatory pressure—current and potential.[6]

It should be noted that in addition to fuel efficiency there are a number of other sustainability areas that are impacted by supply chains. These areas include packaging, facilities, and waste disposal. The important point is that there are many opportunities for transportation and logistics service companies to improve in areas related to sustainability and to reduce their negative impact on the environment. The internal and external stakeholder pressures have provided impetus for such change, but in the long run, the recognition that going green has economic advantages impacting profitability will be the most important driving force.

It is important to understand that there is an interrelationship or systems impact in play among logistics-related factors impacting the green supply chain. There are several time-proven axioms from transportation economics that are important to consider, such as "don't ship air" and "don't ship water." The first one recognizes that empty space in a motor carrier trailer or railcar from empty backhauls or less-than-capacity dispatches is wasted and never recovered. Transportation companies do not have the luxury of accumulating inventory. As noted in Chapter 1 and 2, they provide capacity to transport between two or more points, which is instantly perishable if not used.

Transportation companies and shippers can put an emphasis on consolidation to fill equipment to capacity or near capacity. Such a strategy has the potential to significantly reduce network miles, especially in the motor carrier sector. The reduction in network miles will improve fuel efficiency and reduce the carbon footprint. During the era of low-cost fuel and with pressure to have lean, demand-driven supply chains, transportation equipment was frequently dispatched without enough consideration for capacity utilization in an effort to improve customer service and lower inventory costs. Higher fuel charges along with sustainability-related costs have changed the system dynamics, and more emphasis is being given to "don't ship air," for the reasons cited above. While consolidation efforts may have an impact on shipment time, the reductions in fuel and carbon levels mitigate it. Also, when necessary, shipments can be expedited.

It should be noted that in addition to consolidation, packaging has an impact on wasted transportation capacity. Marketers have often followed one of their axioms from the theory of consumer behavior, namely, "perception is reality." Consequently, if consumers perceive that they are getting more for their money, it is "reality." One approach to influencing value perception is through packaging—using larger packages. For example, the paper-based rolls inside plastic wrap and aluminum foil were larger than they needed to be, but it resulted in an overall larger package. The larger package filled transportation equipment, warehouse space, and retailer shelves more quickly than necessary. The net result was a lot of "air" and wasted space. The trade-off was more sales revenue (hopefully). The current economic and social environment has led companies like Walmart to request change, and it has happened. The smaller rolls have led to smaller packages and improved capacity utilization in transport equipment, warehouses, and retail stores. This is only one example of many possibilities. Hopefully, the impetus for improving sustainability will lead to other packaging changes. Excess packaging is prevalent in our economy, and it usually ends up in landfills and, of course, increases logistics cost. The caveat on packaging is that it is also used to reduce damage, which can be a big issue for carriers. Obviously, this issue requires consideration, but there are many instances of too much packaging and wasted space inside packages—there is room for improvement.

The other old axiom noted above was "don't ship water," and it has a relationship to the "don't ship air" axiom. This maxim is based upon the premise that water is ubiquitous; that is, it is found almost everywhere. Early location theory and transport economics concluded that water should be added as close as possible to the point of consumption to reduce cost and especially to reduce transportation cost. The classic examples are beer and soda, which are about 90 percent water in terms of finished product weight. The conventional wisdom was that breweries and soda bottling plants should have market-oriented locations, where the water was added, to reduce total transportation costs by moving the water relatively short distances. With higher fuel prices, we may see some return to this network location strategy or a variant thereof.

Over the course of the last several decades, an increasing number of consumer products that were sold in a liquid form had water added, which gave the appearance of "getting more for your money." This was especially true of liquid detergents. Recently, Walmart put pressure upon their suppliers, such as P&G, to eliminate about half the water. The result was a smaller plastic bottle which had the same washing power. However, the total supply chain (manufacturer, warehouse, transporter, and retailer) benefited because the final product weighed less and occupied about 50 percent of the original space. It was an important outcome for sustainability. The cost of transportation and warehousing was significantly reduced while improving the shelf space challenge of retailers—a classic win-win-win! It also reduced the cost of packaging and improved capacity utilization. It was clearly a "home run" in spite of some initial resistance by consumers. There are many other possibilities for removing water and/or reducing the size of consumer packages. Consider, for example, the possibility of manufacturing a detergent tablet, and all the water being added in the washing machine (this concept is not new, but it received consumer resistance when previously tried).

The examples of green initiatives discussed are cascading through supply chains and encouraging initiatives by other suppliers and transportation companies. The transport sector is being pushed in this direction by customers, the government, and increased operating costs. As indicated above, most of the steps taken by the trucking industry to become greener are focused upon cost reductions related to fuel efficiency. However, fleet managers are investigating "clean" fuels and **hybrid tractors** and joining with shippers to examine reducing network miles, consolidating loads, and even changing the type of light bulbs used in terminals. Some of these changes, such as load consolidation and network mileage optimization, can be made in the short run for immediate impact, while others, such as alternative fuels and hybrid tractors, are longer-run changes that need evaluation.

These sustainability initatives are being enhanced by government programs such as the **SmartWay Transport Partnership**. This is a federal program initiated by the Environmental Protection Agency (EPA) in 2004 to target selected carriers to reach out to shippers. The goals of the program are a cleaner environment, more efficiency, and less costly transportation options through collaborative efforts. The program has doubled in size each year since 2004 and topped 1,100 members in 2008. The EPA expects the program to double again in a year or two. The members include motor carriers, railroads, ocean carriers, logistics service providers, and large shippers including Best Buy, Target, Coca Cola, Johnson & Johnson, Procter and Gamble, and Walmart. Even nonprofit groups such as the American Trucking Association are participating in these programs. SmartWay offers several tools and recommends several fuel-saving strategies. According to the EPA, carriers can save an average of $4,000 per truck per year by implementing some or all of the recommended measures. Collectively, SmartWay parents are saving close to 620 million gallons of diesel fuel per year and lowering fuel costs by about $2.5 billion. Furthermore, they are reducing carbon dioxide emissions by 6.8 million tons.[7]

Sustainability and an emphasis upon "Green Supply Chains" have gained momentum among major shippers and the various transportation modes. The recognition of the environmental and economic benefits for carriers and shippers along with government policy and public pressure has given these efforts much momentum. However, transportation companies still have many opportunities to improve. For example, have any trucks passed you lately on the highway when you were driving at the maximum posted speed (hopefully)?

An excellent example of what is possible was outlined recently in an article about the Subway restaurant chain. Their goal is to become the greenest quick-serve restaurant by eliminating waste and inefficiency in four areas: energy, resource utilization, waste materials, and food safety. Some recently reported results indicate that they are having success. Over the last several years, they have reduced carbon emissions by 120,000 metric tons, reduced oil consumption by 277,000 barrels on an annual basis, reduced truck miles by 9.3 million miles, and reduced the number of shipments by 16,653. Interestingly, their store locations increased by 12 percent to 24,262.[8] They have increased revenue and reduced operating cost while reducing their carbon footprint.

Transportation Technology   *Truck Navigation*

Navigational devices in personal automobiles have become very popular with many drivers. They are relatively inexpensive and very convenient for navigating in new locations and sometimes in familiar ones too. This technology has replaced maps for many individuals, particularly for short hauls. If you want to get specific directions, some of the equipment has the capacity to provide voice directions.

Recently, Rand McNally, which is best known for its road maps and truck navigation software, has joined with a digital map company to create new software that will literally provide dock-to-dock directional information to drivers. The software is designed to use GPS-accurate data developed specifically for trucking, including highway and street restrictions on truck driving, to help carriers and shippers navigate more efficiently.

The software allows class 8 and longer combination vehicles to route from origin to destination. It will provide comprehensive coverage for 6.5 million miles of road used by trucks in the United States, with more than 23 million links that contain unique truck attributes. The map data, combined with the truck attributes, will provide a level of routing accuracy and quality unparalled by other systems. The complete identification of truck attributes for height and weight restrictions will also serve to route more competent and complex truck combination. The program will also be able to integrate other logistics software packages.

The developers indicate that this dock-to-dock software program will fill an important need for carriers, enabling them to route and deliver effectively as well as efficiently from the first to the last mile. Given the growing concern over fuel prices and sustainability, the ability to manage the truck to save miles can cut time and reduce the carbon footprint. Furthermore, the program can minimize road delay, reduce the risk of accidents, and mitigate the probability of fines. The reduction in the level of uncertainty about road conditions and restrictions can be an enormous benefit to the drivers. Customers will also benefit because of on-time deliveries. Equipment utilization should also improve dramatically.

The visibility provided by this software application, plus perhaps RFID tags on the trailer, will provide carrier management a powerful tool to improve efficiency and effectiveness.

Source: Adapted from SCMR reports, Reed Business Information, May 22, 2009, p. 1

Fuel Cost and Consumption

Fuel price volatility along with overall price increases has been an issue with transportation carriers and shippers since the mid-1970s. Overall, it can be argued that this is a manifestation of world demand and the supply of crude oil. The demand for oil as a source of energy to power transport equipment and for private use has been growing steady, but crude oil is a limited natural resource. New oil fields have been discovered since World War II, but the known available supply of oil has not kept pace with the increased demand. Consequently, the general trend for fuel prices has been upward. This trend in price has been exacerbated by the location of the best oil fields in distant countries and the disproportionate share of oil consumption in the United States.

As Illustrated in Figure 14-6, the pattern of price increases and volatility have been a special challenge and issue in the first decade of the 21st century. World crude oil prices increased 113 percent between 2005 and mid-2008, when they reached a peak of $137.11 per barrel in July of 2008. The prices abated significantly in 2009, but there is an expectation that as the global economy recovers from the recession, the price of oil will be driven upwards by the growth in demand. Two factors not mentioned above have impacted the price of oil in this century, namely, the growth in demand from other countries (especially China) and the speculation that occurs in the futures market. An additional factor is the disruption that can occur with terrorist actions and political upheaval in certain parts of the world.

The challenge, then, for carriers and shippers will be to deal with the uncertainty and volatility of fuel prices and the expectation that the price will be increasing over time. However, the impact will vary among the modes of transportation because some are more fuel efficient than others, as noted in Chapters 5 through 8. Also, there is interest in low-sulfur diesel fuel, which is cleaner for the environment, hydrogen

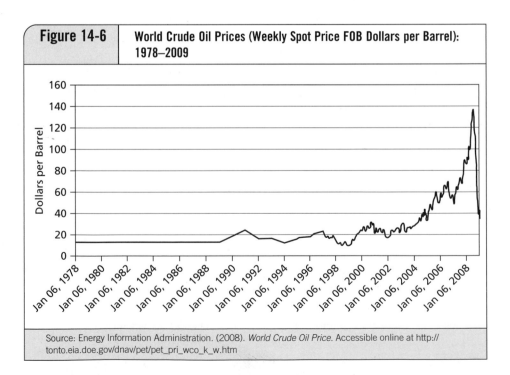

Figure 14-6 | World Crude Oil Prices (Weekly Spot Price FOB Dollars per Barrel): 1978–2009

Source: Energy Information Administration. (2008). *World Crude Oil Price*. Accessible online at http://tonto.eia.doe.gov/dnav/pet/pet_pri_wco_k_w.htm

fuel cells, and biofuels, as mentioned previously. These fuel alternatives are being tested as to their economic and operational viability and are longer-run solutions to the fuel issue.

Some discussion of the future impact of fuel prices on the various modes of transportation is appropriate at this point. As one would expect, the impact of fuel price increases and volatility will differ among the modes because of their different operating and market conditions.

Motor Carriers

As previously noted, the motor carrier industry is highly fuel intensive and therefore very sensitive to price increases and associated volatility. Motor carriers consume about 54 billion gallons of fuel per year and about 73 gallons of diesel fuel. The annual cost for fuel escalated over 70 percent over the course of 2004–2008.[9] To put this in perspective, the 2008 diesel expenses for the motor carrier industry were more than three times higher than the annual fuel bill for airlines, which is the most fuel-intensive mode of transportation. Fuel is approaching annual labor cost as the largest expense for this industry. Fuel surcharges helped the industry to cope during this period, but it was still challenging and some companies did not survive. In fact, almost 3000 motor carrier companies went bankrupt in 2008. reducing truck capacity by about 130,000 trucks. This was the largest number of carrier failures since 2001[10] The truckload carriers have had the biggest challenges in passing off the increased fuel charges.

Air Carriers

As indicated previously, airlines are the most intensive users of fuel. Similar to motor carriers, fuel costs have grown to be the largest expense for airlines. Fuel was normally 12 to 15 percent of the operating costs of airlines, but it grew to about 30 percent by 2007. The airlines have also used fuel surcharges for freight movements, but with limited success, and the surcharges became an inhibiter to air cargo growth. The increased gap between air cargo rates and ground transportation rates has shifted traffic away from airlines for distances up to 1500 miles.

The higher fuel charges have also been challenging for passenger movements. Competition among the airlines is a deterrent to significant price increases between major hubs. They have responded instead by decreasing aircraft size and eliminating some flights, which had a negative impact on air freight. Bankruptcy filings among some of the largest airlines have been an outcome of the higher fuel prices. The fuel price reductions of 2009 provided some relief, but passengers have been slow in returning. Intercity bus companies, however, have experienced growth. The airlines are the most sensitive mode to increased fuel charges. A return to oil prices above $130 a barrel would deal a very negative blow to the airline industry and their future economic viability.

Water Carriers

While water carriers are very fuel efficient, they are not insensitive to significant fuel price increases. This is particularly true for the global container shipping lines. Annual marine bunker fuel costs nearly doubled between 2005 and mid-2008. Fuel cost became the biggest challenge, reaching 50–60 percent of ship operating costs, depending on the type of ship. In addition, the marine carriers pay surcharges to the motor carriers and railroads that provide their intermodal moves for through service to and from inland points. To the extent that these surcharges cannot be passed on to shippers, they are additional cost pressures on the carriers. Consequently, the shipping lines have become more aggressive about collecting bunker fuel surcharges, but they have not been as successful as trucking companies in implementing an explicit set of charges related to the price of bunker fuel.[11]

Rail Carriers

With the advantages of fuel efficiency and constrained capacity, the railroad sector has not experienced the same level of cost pressure as the other modes of transportation. In fact, railroad profits increased by double digits in 2008 even with some decrease in traffic levels. The improved profit levels were attributable to a number of factors, including rate increases, fuel surcharges, and added efficiency. The latter was the result of faster line-haul time, faster terminal turnarounds, and some workforce ration allegation.

Domestic rail service has actually benefited from the higher fuel costs, since more shippers were interested in switching to rail intermodal service for long-haul freight. This is true for both trailers (TOFC) and containers (COFC) moving on an intermodal basis. Even with the decline in fuel prices in 2009, the demand for rail intermodal service has remained high. The later phenomenon is probably attributable to a belief that the fuel price reduction will be a short-run event; that even with lower fuel prices, rail intermodal service is more economical; and to the improved service times of the rail carriers.

Pipeline Carriers

As indicated previously in this chapter, during the period 2003–2006 (the most recent data available), pipeline rates for moving crude oil increased 22 percent, and for refined oil products, they increased 8 percent, which is an indication of higher operating costs. Some of this cost increase was attributable to the increase in pipelines' energy cost, but it is also a reflection of other cost increases related to security along the pipelines. As noted, pipelines operate very efficiently compared to other modes, which allowed them to price their services competitively as fuel prices escalated between 2006 and 2008. Also, some shippers are "tied" to the pipelines because of their location and limited alternatives for service. The net result was that pipeline traffic did not vary much in volume.

Carriers' Responses

Fuel surcharges have become the major component of the strategy of carriers to increase revenues for fuel cost recovery measures. Carrier contracts have become more sophisticated, with new surcharge formulas and new contract clauses to be more transparent and to correlate more closely with the fuel fluctuations. Surcharges have become a common practice for all modes in recent years and have become a centerpiece for carrier-shipper negotiations. However, there is no standard surcharge policy or formula for the transportation industry. The biggest challenge appears to be in the ocean shipping area because of the multiplicity of fuels, indexes, and carriers.

A second response, suggested above, has been service capacity and network rationalization. Some TL carriers have focused upon shorter routes or traffic lanes. One relatively simple response that impacts service capacity is to reduce cruise speed. Both the trucking companies and the ocean liners have implemented this approach with mixed results. There are definite fuel savings, but the reduced speed impacts customer service, which has been a contentious point with some shippers. Network rationalization usually means cutting or reducing service on unprofitable routes.

The important point for the future is that fuel prices will continue to have a major impact on transport carriers in terms of cost and service, which in turn will impact shippers. Some shippers are responding by implementing regionalized distribution centers with the expectation that with fuel price volatility and price increases, change will continue.

A third response to the fuel issues is to improve the operational efficiency of carriers. This can be done through fleet replacement and equipment modernization in terminal areas. As part of the fleet replacement program, carriers—especially motor carrier companies—can consider the option to buy equipment that utilizes alternate fuels.

The future will bring technology improvements that hopefully will make feasible alternatives available, such as electric hybrids. Also, lighter-weight equipment can be utilized. Again, there will be continuing pressure, because of fuel costs and the environment, to investigate opportunities to improve operating efficiency through equipment change and network change.

A fourth response both to the fuel issue and sustainability is the use of technology to manage and control equipment effectively. With large and/or widely dispersed fleets, this usually requires technology to provide **visibility** of the assets and related information to improve operations. Large motor carrier companies in particular are investing in relatively expensive technology that allows them to track and trace equipment on a real-time basis. It is useful for security purposes but is also enabling them to reduce their fleet size, because it does not get "lost." Also, the improved visibility can provide exception reporting when there is a problem, such as a breakdown, and corrective action can be taken.

The visibility feature can also allow carriers to share information with their shippers/customers. This can lead to shared information about shipment needs to help carriers plan in advance to meet demand. Such collaborative efforts offer much promise for a win-win environment for improving equipment efficiency. The topic of visibility and collaboration deserve additional consideration.

On the Line   *Transportation Report Card*

It is estimated that U.S. residents spend about 4.2 billion hours a year stuck in traffic, which costs the economy $78.2 billion or $710 per motorist. One-third of the major highways are in mediocre to poor condition, and 45 percent of urban highways are congested. We spend only about a third of what is really needed to maintain the road system adequately. Automobile vehicle miles increased 94 percent, and truck vehicle miles increased 105 percent during the last 25 years, while highway lane miles only grew by 3.5 percent for the same period. Furthermore, freight truck traffic increased by 33 percent and is forecasted to double over the course of the next 20 years with the increase in global trade.

It appears clear that the highway funding model currently in use is not adequate to maintain and improve the roads, since the federal highway trust fund (HTF) needs an estimated $5 to 7 billion to maintain existing construction projects this year. The highways are funded primarily with user charges added to gasoline and diesel fuel; there is a contradiction between user charges and the effort to reduce the carbon footprint of autos and trucks by reducing fuel consumption. In the future, there needs to be a national policy developed to address the shortfall and related issues. Innovative thinking from public, private, and academic sources will be required to address this issue. A special but related issue is the nation's bridges, because 25 percent of our bridges are either structurally deficient or functionally obsolete.

As has been stated previously, railroads are very fuel efficient, but growth in demand has constrained traffic in critical areas. An estimated $148 billion in improvements will be needed to accommodate the freight in 2035. The class I railroad share of the capital expense is about $135 billion, and they have embarked on an ambitious capital campaign to raise the money. They are making a great effort to fund their capital needs.

The inland waterway system contains over 12,000 miles of navigable waterways in four systems—the Mississippi River, the Ohio Basin, the Gulf intercoastal waterway, and the Pacific Coast system—that connect many of the states in the U.S. Since the average tow barge can carry the equivalent of 870 tractor-trailer loads, the inland waterways are a strategic resource, especially for the future with the need to reduce overall fuel consumption. However, the system has 257 locks, and at least 90 of them are 60 to 100 years old, well past their designed life span of 50 years. It would cost a $ 125 billion to replace them now.

As noted in Chapter 8, ports and harbors are a problem, and the American Association of Port Authorities (AAPS) stated in 2007 that public ports needed to invest $1.7 billion annually to update and modernize their facilities. The United States has fallen behind Europe and Asia in its ports, which will impact our global competitiveness during the 21st century. There is a major opportunity for the new secretary of transportation to lead change by providing vision or insight into the needs of the transport system and a strategic direction for the future.

Looking to the future and considering the challenges associated with volatility in fuel prices and the environment, much effort will be directed at the concept of the green supply chain. There is every indication that it is not just a concept but rather a growing commitment that has economic as well as environmental benefits to shippers and carriers. Whether it be consolidation of shipments, network optimization, lighter equipment, collaboration, or others, there are strategies that can produce win-win results. Remember that a gallon of fuel consumed produces 22 pounds of carbon dioxide. Reducing speeds and idling time have big benefits. We need to address highway congestion with renewed vigor from all quarters.

Source: Adapted from CSCMP, *20th Annual State of Logistics Report: Riding Out the Recession* June 17, 2009

Collaboration and Visibility: Art and Science

Some definitions of supply chain management refer to it as an art *and* a science. Used in this context, the authors indicate that there are many scientific and/or mathematics-based software applications that can help managers to improve efficiency, effectiveness, and execution in their supply chains. Examples include warehouse management systems (WMS), transportation management systems (TMS), scheduling models, inventory control models, and so on. This area also includes technology such as RFID tags, Global Positioning Systems (GPS), and other technologies that provide information to improve efficiency, effectiveness, and execution.

The "art" dimension of the supply chain definition refers to the person-to-person or company-to-company joint tactics, operations, and/or strategies that can improve supply chains. This is frequently referred to as the "softer side" of the supply chain business, which requires people, groups, and/or organizations to work together and trust each other in addressing challenges and issues that are obstacles to improvements for success. Collaboration gives companies the opportunity to leverage each other to perform better than they would acting alone, or as the old axiom from athletics states, "a team can be better than the sum of its individual parts."

There are many initiatives underway in the area of tactical or operational collaboration, including cooperative efforts to reduce loading and unloading times at consignor and consignee shipping and receiving facilities; increase hours of operation for drop yards and warehouse facilities; allow faster payment for carriers; reduce driver-assist times; and share capacity forecasts with carriers.[12] "This type of collaboration has had direct benefits for supply chains in the form of lower costs for shippers and carriers and improved customer service."[13]

The most important potential of collaboration is at the strategic level, and it involves the sharing of information to improve results for all members of the supply chain. For example, many consumer products companies offer a vendor-managed inventory (VMI) program for their largest customers. Under this program, they manage or co-manage their customer's DC inventory replenishment. They take full accountability for customer's key performance indicators (KPIs) such as DC in-stock inventory, inventory turns, and on-time delivery. The expected KPIs are incorporated into the performance objectives of the VMI analyst. On a daily basis, key information is provided from the key customers via electronic data interchange (EDI) transactions, such as on-hand inventory, SKUs on order, sales, and stockouts by SKU. In addition, the customers provide turn and promotional forecasts for 26–52 weeks. This information is also shared with the logistics service providers (asset-based) who provide transportation and some related services. The benefits include a reduction of DC out-of-stocks by 30–50 percent, increased inventory turns by 10–20 percent, fewer emergency orders, smoother flow of products through the supply chain, improved scheduling of pickups and deliveries, consolidated shipment dispatches, and a reduction in empty trailer miles. This is a win-win-win scenario for the buyer, seller, and logistics service provider. It is an example of collaboration at its best—organizations working together and sharing information to improve the efficiency, effectiveness, and execution of the supply chain.

The example discussed above to illustrate the benefits of collaboration also has elements of visibility built in via an old technology, namely, EDI. Visibility has become a popular buzzword in transportation, logistics, and supply chain circles. Benefits and advantages are touted by an increasing number of individuals. Interestingly, there is no universal definition of visibility. Initially, visibility was used mostly in conjunction with assets, for example, the level of inventory in a warehouse by SKU on a daily basis, the number and location of equipment, the level of chemicals or other liquids in a storage tank, and so forth.

The visibility applications introduced during the last decade expanded to include insight into the status of orders, inventory turns, and shipments across the supply chain, as indicated in the previous example of the VMI programs of consumer products companies. In other words, they became more practical tools to capture and analyze supply chain data for decision making, risk mitigation, and process improvement. Also, visibility applications could be used to alert analysts of supply chain disruptions such as shipment delays, unusual stockouts, and so on.

From an overview perspective, the applications can be summarized as follows:[14]

- Enhanced customer experience
  - Improved on-time delivery
  - Proactively alerts shippers of shipment delays
- Improved operations efficiency and agility
  - Reduced lead times and lead time unreliability
  - Shorter delivery windows
  - Ability to respond to need for midcourse changes
- Eased regulatory compliance and oversight
  - Improved monitoring of customer activities
  - Increased response to regulatory and security issues

A good example of the benefits and opportunities associated with a comprehensive visibility program is the fully automated track-and-trace program of Dole, Inc. Faced with the many challenges associated with producing and distributing fresh produce, and with increased government regulations, Dole created full visibility of its supply chain by leveraging technology to develop a fully automated track-and-trace process. The process uses RFID, GPS, and cell phone technologies, starting at the harvest field and running throughout their supply chains. Included are stops through cooling center warehouses, carrier terminals, and sorting plants. Dole is tracking time and quantities and will add temperature to the mix soon.

The key to the Dole example is tagging products as they leave the field. This visibility has allowed Dole to understand how product moved through the system and to be alerted to possible time and temperature abuse. As we look ahead, the direction of visibility programs usually starts with shipment and inventory tracking. The next phase is usually mitigation of risk associated with disruptions. The final phase is supply chain improvement.

As stated at the outset of this section, collaboration and visibility offer enhanced and growing opportunities for transportation and logistics service companies to combine to drive improvements in supply. They need to be more proactive in developing visibility applications and promoting collaboration within their supply chains and not depending upon shippers to initiate best practices.

SUMMARY

- Demand for transportation service has increased significantly during the last ten years with the expansion of global trade, giving rise to concerns about the transportation infrastructure and the capacity of the system to move the freight.

- During the 1980s and 1990s, transportation became relatively less expensive for users or shippers because fuel costs were relatively low and because the excess capacity that existed among the various carriers fostered a level of competition, which kept rates in check.

- Congestion has become a major issue for the U.S. transportation system, causing delays and inconvenience to ordinary citizens and increased cost in operations for carriers and shippers. Shippers may also experience increased inventory cost with the delays, and carriers may require additional equipment.

- Highway congestion has some significant costs attached to it for carriers. It is estimated that the top interchange bottlenecks cause an average of 1.5 million annual truck hours of delay.

- Rail and water carriers also are challenged by congestion and infrastructure problems. The projected growth in demand by 2035 will strain an already busy system of highways, railways, and waterways.

- Sustainability will become even more important in the future, and transportation and related supply chain services will continue to be a focus for reducing carbon footprints to improve the environment, but there are opportunities to also reduce cost.

- The green supply chain focus of many companies has led them back to some old axioms for transportation efficiency, namely, "don't ship air" and "don't ship water." The former refers to unused space or capacity in transportation equipment. The latter refers to the extra weight of water in products, which could be added in near the point of sale. Both axioms have an impact on sustainability and also on cost.

- The federal government's SmartWay Transport Partnership, initiated by the EPA, has solicited carriers to reach out to their customers in an effort to collaborate and to develop less-costly transport options that are more environmentally friendly. Smart-Way offers strategies to save fuel and help reduce carbon footprints.

- The volatility and general escalation in fuel prices has been a challenge for carriers in terms of their costs and profits. This situation has led carriers to insert fuel surcharges into their price structure to protect their financial viability when fuel prices increase. The surcharges have become a bargaining issue when carriers are negotiating a new contract or renegotiating an existing contract. The motor carriers have been the most successful in implementing fuel surcharges.

- Fuel cost has become the first or second highest cost for motor carriers, airlines, and even some water carriers and is a continuing challenge to their financial viability, causing some carriers to file for bankruptcy.

- Rail carriers have fared well during this era of higher fuel changes since they are very fuel efficient; their intermodal service has become more attractive to shippers and other carriers, especially motor carriers.

- Transportation and logistics organizations have an opportunity to provide leadership and promote more efficient and effective supply chains through collaborative strategies and visibility applications.

STUDY QUESTIONS

1. There have been an increasing number of editorials in newspapers and magazines about concerns over transport capacity and infrastructure. What is the nature of this issue? Why is it such a problem? How can it be resolved?

2. While we have concerns about transportation service currently, there did not appear to be any special challenges or big problems during the 1980s and 1990s. Why were these two decades so different as far as transportation is concerned?

3. We have all experienced highway congestion and "bumper-to-bumper" traffic, but congestion is a bigger issue for supply chains and transport service providers. Why?

4. Sustainability and the environment have captured the attention of ordinary citizens and also of shippers and carriers. What is the nature of the concern? How can shippers and carriers mitigate their impact on the environment?

5. "Don't ship air" and "don't ship water" are the bases of some important supply chain strategies. What do these statements really mean? What are the related strategies? How do these strategies help?

6. The U.S. Environmental Protection Agency has implemented the SmartWay Transport Partnership. Discuss the nature and role of the program. Do you think it will be effective? Why or why not?

7. Fuel prices have been very volatile during the last five years. What factors have contributed to this volatility? Why is it such a special challenge to supply chains? How can it be fixed?

8. What is collaboration? How can supply chains use collaboration to their advantage?

9. What is meant by the term *supply chain visibility*? How can it be used to advantage by shippers and carriers?

10. Are you optimistic or pessimistic about transportation in the 21st century? Why?

NOTES

1. FHWA, *The Economic Cost of Freight Transportation,* (Washington, DC: Freight Management and Operations, U.S. Department of Transportation May 2009), 1–3.

2. Ibid.

3. Ibid.

4. Ibid., p. 5.

5. Ibid., p. 6.

6. Jhana Senxian, "Sustainability Matters," (The Aberdeen Group, 2009), 67.

7. Evelyn Thomchick and Kusumal Ruamsook, "The Impact of Fuel Prices on the U.S. Transportation Industry" white paper, (Center for Supply Chain Research: Penn State University, December 2008), 8–12.

8. Tina Fitzgerald, "Subway's Journey to Green" *Logistics Management* (April 2009), pp. 22–26.

9. E. Thomchick and K. Ruamsook, *op. cit.*, pp. 4–8.

10. Ibid.

11. J. J. Coyle et.al. *Supply Chain Management: A Logistics Perspective* Mason, OH: Southwestern-Cengage, 2008), 5–7.

12. Beth Enslow, *The Transportation Benchmark Report,* Aberdeen Group, (September 2006).

13. Ibid.

14. Victoriya Sadlovska, "Beyond Visibility: Driving Supply Chain Responsiveness," Aberdeen Group, (September 2008).

CASE 14-1

Green and Lean

George Harry and Jeff Pilof, friends and former classmates in college, had not seen each other face-to-face for about 15 years when they had one of these chance meetings in the Atlanta Airport. They both just received the news that their flights to their respective destinations, Philadelphia and Boston, had been canceled. As they walked into an airport restaurant to get a sandwich and wait for their new flights, they spotted and immediately recognized each other. After the customary greetings and questions about family and mutual friends, they started discussing their current jobs and responsibilities. George had spent the last 20 years with two pharmaceutical companies, while Jeff had worked for a chemical company and a large retailer and had established his own package-delivery company. They were both now vice presidents of transportation for their latest companies—a very large retailer and a large consumer products company.

Surprisingly, George and Jeff found that they were both concerned about the same general area in their respective companies—how to survive in a "down" economy while initiating a program based upon being part of a green supply chain. They were concerned about having to cut costs while pushing sustainability.

CASE QUESTIONS

1. George and Jeff need some help in trying to understand how it would be possible to be green and lean at the same time. They need some help from you to understand how these two objectives can be achieved simultaneously. Give them some pointers on how it can be done.

CASE 14-2
Bald Eagle Valley Trucking

SCOR is a local nonprofit organization that provides advice and direction to new and/or small companies. The volunteers for the SCOR organization are all retired executives and/or entrepreneurs. At their weekly meeting, Herb Graves and Ned Book were discussing a proposal that they had received from a local trucking company that had been founded about two years ago. The company, Bald Eagle Valley Trucking (BEV), had enjoyed some success and had been able to secure a loan enabling them to expand to ten tractor and trailer units. Their success had been based largely upon a water bottling plant, owned by the Coca Cola Company, that had been increasing the volume they shipped. BEV felt that there was an opportunity to expand their business with Coca Cola into the Philadelphia, New York, and Washington, DC areas, but they needed additional capital to buy more equipment. BEV had requested help from SCOR to assist them with developing a strategic plan and supporting their request for a loan from a Pittsburgh-based bank.

Herb and Ned were very experienced executives but they had no direct experience in the transportation and supply chain business. So they contacted a nearby state university with a large and well-known Supply Chain and Logistics department. The department had a program whereby their students could be assigned a business-related project for course credit, and it would be supervised by a faculty member.

CASE QUESTIONS

1. You have been chosen to work on the BEV project, which will require you to answer the following questions:
   a. What are the major challenges and issues trucking companies face presently?
   b. What insights can you provide to help BEV mitigate some or all of the issues?
   c. What advice can you provide to help them with their request for funding?

Suggested Readings

Chapter 9 Transportation Risk Management

Manuj, Ila, and John T. Mentzer, "Global Supply Chain Risk Management," *Journal of Business Logistics,* Vol. 29, No. 1 (2008): 133–156.

Murphy, Sean, "Stepping Up Security: An Interview with James Williams," *Supply Chain Management Review,* Vol. 12 (November 2008): 40.

"Ocean Supply Chain Security," *United State Government Accountability Office* (April 2008): GAO-08-240.

Sarathy, Ravi, "Security and the Global Supply Chain," *Transportation Journal,* Vol. 45, No. 4 (Fall 2006): 28–51.

Voss, M. Douglas, Judith M. Whipple, and David J. Closs, "The Role of Strategic Security: Internal and External Security Measures with Security Performance Implications," *Transportation Journal,* Vol. 48, No. 2 (Spring 2009): 5–23.

Chapter 10 Global Transportation Planning

Bichou, Khalid, Kee-Hung Lai, Y. H. Venus Lun, and T. C. E. Cheng, "A Quality Management Framework for Liner Shipping Companies to Implement the 24-Hour Advance Vessel manifest Rule," *Transportation Journal,* Vol 46, No. 1 (Winter 2007): 5–21.

Burnson, Patrick, "Ocean Shipping Strategies: Risk Versus Reward," *Logistics Management* (September 2007): 35.

Miller, Tan, and Renato de Matta, "A Global Supply Chain Profit Maximization and Transfer Pricing Model," *Journal of Business Logistics,* Vol. 29, No. 1 (2008): 175–200.

Schulz, John D., "Global Transportation: The Big Picture," *Supply Chain Management Review,* Vol. 11 (March 2007): 20.

Wagner, Stephan M., "Innovation Management in the German Transportation Industry," *Journal of Business Logistics,* Vol. 29, No. 2 (2008): 215–232.

Chapter 11 Global Transportation Execution

"America's Container Ports: Delivering the Goods," *Bureau of Transportation Statistics* (2007).

Burnson, Patrick, "Ocean Shipping Strategies," *Logistics Management* (November 2008): 33–36.

Burson, Patrick, "U.S. Seaport Update: Location Matters," *Logistics Management* (September 2008).

Burson, Patrick, "Top U.S. Seaports; Slower Trade Means Time to Rebuild," *Logistics Management* (February 2009).

Carmichael, Gil, "Intermodal a "No Brainer' for Energy Efficiency," *Logistics Management* (May 2007): 16.

Paul Bergant, Interview, "Soaring Fuel Prices Are Driving Shippers to Embrace the Intermodal Option," *Global Logistics & Supply Chain Strategies* (August 2008).

Quinn, John Paul, "U.S. Ports Expand Keeping Pace with Import Growth," *Supply Chain Management Review,* Vol. 11 (April 2007): 57.

Theurmer, Karen E., "Intermodal Grows Up," *World Trade* (January 2009): 36.

Chapter 12 Third Party Logistics

Bolumole, yemisi A., Robert Frankel, and Dag Naslund, "Developing a Theoretical Model for Logistics Outsourcing," *Transportation Journal,* Vol. 46, No. 2 (Spring 2007): 35–54.

Burnson, Patrick, "Improving 3PL Management: Parting Is Such Sweet Sorrow," *Logistics Management* (April 2009): 29–32.

Kerr, John, "Burton Catches Air in New Markets," *Logistics Management* (January 2009): 37–41.

Lieb, Robert, and Karen Butner, "The North American Third-Party Logistics Industry in 2006: The Provider CEO Perspective," *Transportation Journal,* Vol. 46, No. 3 (Summer 2007): 40–52.

Maloni, Michael J., and Craig R. Carter, "Opportunities for Research in Third-Party Logistics," *Transportation Journal,* Vol. 45, No. 2 (Spring 2006): 23–38.

Terreri, April, "Creating a Winning Team," *Food Logistics* (May 2009): 18–23.

Chapter 13   Private Transportation and Fleet Management

"America's Private Fleets," *National Private Truck Council* (2008).

Burnson, Patrick, "Green Transportation Planning: Private Fleets Lead the Way," *Logistics Management* (August 2008): 52.

Dutton, Gail, "A Common Sense Approach to Transportation Fleet Management," *World Trade* (March 2009): 32.

Dutton, Gail, "Managing Fleets in Turbulent Times," *World trade* (February 2009): 28.

Hunter, Olen, "Full-Service Leasing Often Costs Less than Ownership," *Food Logistics* (May 2009): 34.

"Legislative and Policy Positions," *National Private Truck Council* (2009).

Petty, Gary, "The Evolution of the Private Fleet," *Fleet Owner* (June 2008): 38.

Schulz, John D., "Private Fleet Management: Silent Success," *Logistics Management* (April 2008): 28.

Chapter 14   Issues and Challenges of Global Supply Chains

Berman, Jeff, "Shippers Say Wall Street Crisis to Hinder Transportation Operations," *Logistics Management* (November 2008): 21.

Bowen, Douglas John, "Pacific Harbor Line Goes Green," *Railway Age* (April 2009): 23.

Bowman, Robert J., "Ships and Ports Find Many Ways to Go Green," *Global Logistics & Supply Chain Strategies* (September 2008).

Burnson, Patrick, and Jeff Berman, "Panama Canal Development Project on Pace for Completion," *Logistics Management* (January 2009): 20–21.

Burnson, Patrick, "Update on Vietnam and India Logistics: Strained," *Logistics Management* (May 2009): 36–38.

Hong, Junjie, and Binglian Liu, "Logistics Development in China: A Provider Perspective," *Transportation Journal*, Vol. 46, No. 2 (Spring 2007): 55–65.

Lu, Chin-Shan, and Ching-Chiao Yang, "Comparison of Investment Preferences for International Logistics Zones in Kaohsiung, Hong Kong, and Shanghai Ports from a Taiwanese Manufacturer's Perspective," *Transportation Journal*, Vol. 45, No. 1 (Winter 2006): 30–51.

Quinn, Paul John, "The Greening of America's Ports," *Logistics Management* (September 2007): 62S.

Glossary

absolute or comparative advantage   An area will specialize in the production of goods or services for which it has the greatest advantage or the least comparative disadvantage.

accessibility   The ability of the carrier to provide service between the origin and destination. It also refers to the carrier's ability to serve the shipper or consignee's place of business. For example, in order to ship and receive a railcar, both the origin and destination must have a side track.

accessorial service   Steps taken in relation to the acquisition of an item.

acid rain   Air pollution produced when acid chemicals are incorporated into rain, snow, fog, or mist. The acid in acid rain comes from sulfur oxides and nitrogen oxides, products of burning coal and other fuels and of certain industrial processes.

activity-based costing (ABC)   Costs specifically generated by performing a service or producing a product.

Advance Manifest Rules   Regulations governing shipment notification, which must be given ahead of time to Customs and Border Protection prior to arrival or departure.

advanced shipment notices (ASNs)   Electronic notification of pending deliveries; an electronic packing list.

advertising   The public promotion of some product or service.

agency tariff   A publication by a rate bureau that contains rates for many carriers. This publication is also called a "bureau tariff."

aggregate demand   The total effective demand for the nation's output of goods and services. This can also refer to the sum of individual demands for a mode's or carrier's services.

air cargo   Freight that is moved by air transportation.

air carrier   A transportation firm that operates aircraft for the transportation of passengers or freight as a "common carrier."

air freighters   Aircraft dedicated solely to the movement of freight.

air taxi   An exempt for-hire air carrier that will fly anywhere on demand; air taxis are restricted to a maximum payload and passenger capacity per plane.

air traffic control system   The method by which aircraft traffic is controlled in the air so that planes are separated by altitude and distance for safety. This system is administered by the Federal Aviation Agency.

air waybill   A contract for transportation between a shipper and an air carrier, which also evidences receipt of the cargo by the carrier.

airline safety   The theory, investigation, and categorization of flight failures and the prevention of such failures through regulation, education, and training.

Airport and Airway Trust Fund   A federal fund that collects passenger ticket taxes and disburses those funds for airport facilities.

all-cargo carrier   An air carrier that transports cargo only.

Amtrak   A quasi-governmental agency that provides interstate rail passenger service.

any-quantity (AQ) rate   A rate that applies to any size shipment tendered to a carrier; no discount rate is available for large shipments.

Army Corps of Engineers   A federal agency and major military command whose mission is to provide military and public works services to the United States by providing vital engineering services and capabilities, as a public service, across the full spectrum of operations—from peace to war—in support of national interests.

asset based providers   3PLs that fulfill customer requirements via tangible equipment and facilities they own.

auditing   A methodical examination of carrier freight bills to determine correct charges.

Automated Manifest System   A module of the Automated Commercial System of U. S. Customs designed to control imported merchandise from the time a carrier's cargo manifest is electronically transmitted to U.S. Customs until the cargo is properly entered, released by customs, and delivered.

average cost   Production cost per unit of output, computed by dividing the total of fixed costs and variable costs by the number of total units produced (total output); also known as "unit cost".

backhaul   The return trip made, as by a truck or cargo ship, after delivering a load to a specified destination.

balance load   This occurs when the shipper provides the carrier with round-trip loads to avoid an empty backhaul.

bareboat charter   A long-term lease or charter where the lessee provides the crew, fuel, and supplies and operates the ship. The lessor provides only the ship.

barge   The cargo-carrying vehicle that inland water carriers primarily use. Basic barges have open tops, but there are covered barges for both dry and liquid cargoes.

benefit/cost ratio   An analysis of the cost effectiveness of different alternatives in order to see whether the benefits outweigh the costs.

bilateral trade agreements   Treaty negotiated between two countries regarding trade.

Bill of Lading   A transportation document that is the contract of carriage between the shipper and the carrier; it provides a receipt for the goods tendered to the carrier, the "terms and conditions of sale" between the carrier and shipper, and the evidence of who has title to the goods while in transit.

blanket rate   A rate that does not increase according to the distance a commodity is shipped.

bonded warehouse   Building in which goods, on which the duties are unpaid, are stored under bond and in the joint custody of the importer or his agent and the customs officers.

boxcar   An enclosed railcar, typically 40- to 50-feet long, used for packaged freight and some bulk commodities.

bracing   Supports used to secure a shipment inside a carrier's vehicle to prevent damage.

brainstorming   An informal group problem-solving technique in which members spontaneously share ideas and solutions.

break-bulk   Ocean cargo that is not containerized but must be handled manually into and out of a ship.

broker   An intermediary or "third party" who represents either the shipper or the carrier and seeks to match freight with empty trucks. The broker's fee can be included in the freight charges or collected separately. A broker is not considered a carrier for legal purposes.

buffering strategy   Method of reducing risk related to capacity shortages or performance problems by providing additional resources.

bulk carriers   Catch-all category for ships that are dedicated to the transport of a specific bulk commodity on a voyage basis.

bull whip effect   Businesses that must forecast demand to properly position inventory will often carry an inventory buffer to anticipate spikes in demand, which varies in size depending on the participant's place in the supply chain. It has been observed that variations are amplified as one moves upstream in the supply chain, not unlike the cracking of a whip.

bundle of services   A grouping of services offered by a carrier that may be integrated into a total package. An example would be a carrier that offers line-haul, sorting, and segregating with local delivery to specific customers.

business logistics   The process of planning, implementing, and controlling the efficient, effective flow and storage of goods, services, and related information from the point of origin to the point of consumption for the purpose of conforming to customer requirements. Note that this definition includes inbound, outbound, internal, and external movements.

cabotage A federal law that requires coastal and intercoastal traffic to be carried in U.S.-built and -registered ships.

capability The ability of a carrier to provide service or multiple services to the shipper to meet the specific requirements of that customer.

car-supply charge In a rail contract rate, a fee imposed that depends on the specific type of car supplied for loading and shipment.

carbon footprint The total set of greenhouse gas emissions caused by an organization, event, or product, often expressed as an amount of carbon dioxide.

cargo airports Airports that, in addition to any other air transportation services that may be available, are served by aircraft providing air transportation of cargo only.

cargo inspection Critical appraisal involving examination, measurement, testing, gauging, and comparison of materials or items to determine if the material or item is in proper quantity and condition.

cargo preference A federal law requiring that at least 50 percent of certain U.S. government-owned or -sponsored cargo move on U.S. flag–registered vessels.

carload A full weight or size shipment placed into or on a railcar. This term also refers to rates that apply to a specific minimum weight for railcar shipments.

Carmack Act A law that defines the carrier's legal obligations to the owner of goods if they are lost or damaged while in the possession of a carrier. Recovery under the Carmack Act is subject to the terms contained in the bill of lading contract.

carriage and insurance paid to This term of sale defines the seller's obligations to pay transportation and insurance for a shipment to a specific location. At that location, the responsibility passes to the buyer.

carriage paid to This term of sale defines the seller's obligations to pay transportation for a shipment to a specific location. At that location, the responsibility passes to the buyer.

carrier A firm that transports goods or people.

carrier liability A common carrier is liable for all shipment loss, damage, and delay with the exception of that caused by act of God, act of a public enemy, act of a public authority, act of the shipper, and the goods' inherent nature.

carrying capacity The capability of a transport vehicle to carry or transport shipments of a particular weight or size in relation to the shipper's

requirements. As an example, a 53-foot trailer could carry 48,000 pounds or a shipment of 3,392 cubic feet.

cash flow Funds or money as it passes from buyer to seller during a commercial transaction and is sometimes measured in a time relationship.

certificate of analysis Document that attests to the composition and purity level of products.

certificate of certification Document usually provided by an independent inspector that confirms that goods conform to the manufacturing standards of the importing country.

Certificate of End Use Document that attests that the product will be used for legitimate or approved purposes.

Certificate of Manufacture Document that attests to the location at which the product has been produced or manufactured.

certificate of origin A legal document that verifies the country where a particular product originated. This certificate must often accompany the shipment so the importing country can determine if it complies with that country's laws.

certificate of public convenience and necessity The grant of operating authority that common carriers receive. A carrier must prove that a public need exists and that the carrier is fit, willing, and able to provide the needed service. The certificate may specify the commodities the carrier may haul, the area it may serve, and the routes it may use.

Champlin Oil case U.S. Supreme Court decision holding that oil pipelines were required to operate as common carriers.

chandlers Dealers in sails and ropes and other supplies for sailing ships; retail dealers in provisions and supplies.

channel members Other parts of a transportation system delivering similar services or utilizing similar or different modes.

charging what the traffic will bear Setting the highest price you can sell your goods at in the market you are in.

charter party Standard charter contract used to record the exact rate, duration, and terms agreed between the ship owner and the charterer.

charter service In ocean shipping, ships that are hired for a specific voyage or amount of time.

charterer The customer who hires a ship for charter service.

chock A wedge, usually made of hard rubber or steel, that is firmly placed under the wheel of a trailer, truck, or boxcar to stop it from rolling.

city driver A motor carrier driver who drives a local route as opposed to a long-distance, intercity route.

Civil Aeronautics Board Federal agency, created in 1940, that focused on safety rulemaking,

accident investigation, and economic regulation of the airlines.

CL Carload rail service requiring shippers to meet minimum weight.

claim A demand for payment made to a carrier for loss or damage to a shipment or the refund of alleged overpayment of freight charges.

class I carrier A railroad with an annual income over $256 million or a motor carrier with an annual income over $10 million.

class II carrier A railroad with an annual income less than $256 million but more than $20.5 million, or a motor carrier with an annual income less than $10 million but more than $3 million.

class III carrier A motor carrier with an annual income less than $3 million.

class rate A rate constructed from a classification and a uniform distance system. A class rate is available for any product between any two points.

classification An alphabetical listing of commodities, the class or rating into which the commodity is placed, and the minimum weight necessary for the rate discount; used in the class rate structure.

classification yard A railroad terminal area where railcars are grouped together to form train units.

Clayton Act A law that strengthened the Sherman Anti-Trust Act and specifically described some business practices as violations of the law. This was done to counter some practices that were used to avoid the Sherman Anti-Trust Act.

Clean Cargo Working Group A business-to-business collaboration dedicated to integrating environmentally and socially responsible business principles into transportation management.

Coast Guard A military unit attached to the Department of Transportation. The Coast Guard is charged with certain law enforcement tasks related to protecting the shores of the United States and the usage of waters both domestically and along the coasts. The Coast Guard is also tasked with safety standards for commercial users, search and rescue missions on inland and coastal waters, and small boat safety programs.

coastal carriers Water carriers that provide service along coasts serving ports on the Atlantic or Pacific Oceans or on the Gulf of Mexico.

COFC (container on flatcar) A type of rail shipment where only the container or "box" is loaded on the flatcar. The chassis with the wheels and landing gear is only used to carry the container to and from the railroad.

cold chain A temperature-controlled supply chain used to help extend and ensure the shelf life of products being shipped.

combi airplane Hybrid type of aircraft with the flexibility to move passengers and/or cargo on the main deck of the aircraft, depending on temporary configuration via movable partitions.

combination ships   Multipurpose vessels that can handle different types of commodities and load types.

commercial invoice   A specifically prepared invoice for the merchandise contained in a shipment. The document is often required for international shipments.

commercial zone   The area surrounding a city or town to which rate carriers quote for the city or town also apply; the ICC defines the area.

commodities clause   A clause that prohibits railroads from hauling commodities that they produced, mined, owned, or had an interest in.

commodities   Some good for which there is demand but which is supplied without qualitative differentiation across a market; that is, it is the same no matter who produces it.

commodity code   A code describing a commodity or group of commodities pertaining to goods classification. This code can be a carrier tariff or regulating in nature.

commodity rate   A rate for a specific commodity and its origin–destination.

common carrier   A transportation company that provides freight and/or passenger service to any who seek its services.

common carriers' duties   Common carriers must serve, deliver, charge reasonable rates, and not discriminate.

common cost   A cost that a company cannot directly assign to particular segments of the business; a cost that the company incurs for the business as a whole.

common law   A legal system based on court decisions and precedents that recognizes past decisions when deciding current legal questions. The legal system of the United States is based on common law along with civil or statuary law.

communication network   Infrastructure and devices linked together so that messages may be passed from one part of the network to another over multiple links and through various nodes.

commuter air carrier   An exempt for-hire air carrier that publishes a time schedule on specific routes; a special type of air taxi.

conferences   Groups of carriers that serve specific trade routes and ports and cooperate as legal cartels when setting prices for certain routs, agreeing not to compete on price and publishing standardized rate tariffs.

congestion   Result of an excessive accumulation; clogged.

consignee   The receiver of a freight shipment, usually the buyer.

consignment   Goods shipped to an agent/ customer when an actual purchase has not

transpired until the consignee agrees to release the consigned goods for production and payment.

consignor   The sender of a freight shipment, usually the seller.

consolidation   Collecting smaller shipments to form a larger quantity in order to realize lower transportation rates.

consular invoice   A specifically prepared invoice that is prescribed by the importing country for the merchandise contained in a shipment. The invoice will be written in the language of the importing country and may be required to be signed by an employee of the government of the nation to which the shipment is destined.

container   A specific type of "box" into which freight is loaded before the shipment is given to the carrier. The container can be rectangular such as those used for rail and ocean shipments or can be shaped to fit the transport vehicle, such as an aircraft. The container avoids the need for the carrier to handle individual parts of the shipment.

container rate   A rate that applies only when the shipment is placed into a container prior to tendering the shipment to the carrier. This rate recognizes that the shipment is much more easily handled by the carrier.

Container Security Initiative   Program launched in 2002 by the U.S. Bureau of Customs and Border Protection to increase security for container cargo shipped to the United States.

Container Shipping Information Service   An industry trade group formed in 2007, comprising 24 of the largest container shipping companies.

containerized freight   Freight that is loaded into or onto storage equipment (a container or pallet) at the origin and delivered to the destination in or on that same piece of equipment without additional handling.

containerships   Ships built for the specific purpose of moving standardized 20-foot and 40-foot oceangoing containers.

continuous improvements   The seeking of small improvements in processes and products with the objective of increasing quality and reducing waste.

contract carrier   A for-hire carrier that does not serve the general public but serves shippers with whom the carrier has a continuing contract.

contract logistics   Third-party logistics relationship where a contract exists between a provider of third-party logistics service and client.

cooperative association   A group of individuals or companies who band together to purchase goods or services jointly and achieve price incentives based on the combined purchasing power of the members. Typically, cooperatives are chartered as not-for-profit and require that the participant be members.

core competency   The set of skills, technologies, and processes that provide the basics for what a company does well.

cost and freight   A term of sale indicating that the price includes both the cost of the goods and the freight expense necessary to transport it to the buyer.

cost of congestion   Economic loss caused by incremental delay, driver stress, vehicle costs, crash risk, and pollution resulting from interference between vehicles in the traffic stream, particularly as a road system approaches its capacity.

cost of lost sales   The income that is lost when a customer chooses to purchase a product or service from another firm. This could be due to the product not being available when and where needed or the service did not meet the requirements of the buyer.

cost, insurance, and freight   A term of sale indicating that the price includes the cost of the goods, insurance premiums necessary to protect the cargo, and the freight expense necessary to transport it to the buyer.

cost-of-service pricing   A method used by carriers when they seek to only cover the actual expense of providing that specific service. Such pricing does not usually cover shared or overhead costs.

courier service   A fast, door-to-door service for high-valued goods and documents; firms usually limit service to shipments weighing 50 pounds or less.

cross-docking   The movement of goods directly from receiving dock to shipping dock to eliminate storage expense.

crude carriers   Ships that move petroleum products (crude oil, gasoline, diesel fuel, and so forth) in massive quantities.

currency adjustment factor (CAF)   An added charge assessed by water carriers for currency value changes.

customer attitude   The customer's perception of the service or product provider.

customer filter   The perception of the customer of the quality of the service that is "filtered" or influenced by more factors than just the quality of the specific offering.

customer perception   The way in which the customer views or perceives the service offering that will influence their decision to buy or use the service. This view could be based on judgment or past experience.

customs broker   A firm that represents importers/ exporters in dealings with customs. Normally responsible for obtaining and submitting all documents for clearing merchandise through customs, arranging inland transport, and paying all charges related to these functions.

Customs brokerage   Company that clears goods through customs barriers for importers and exporters (usually businesses).

Customs-Trade Partnership Against Terrorism A voluntary supply chain security program led by U. S. Customs and Border Protection and focused on improving the security of private companies' supply chains with respect to terrorism.

decreasing cost industries The relation between market price and the quantity supplied by all firms in a perfectly competitive industry after the industry has completed its long-run adjustment; an increase in the quantity produced leads to a decrease in the price per unit.

dedicated contract carriage A third-party service that dictates equipment (vehicles) and drivers to a single customer for its exclusive use on a contractual basis.

delivered at frontier A term of sale that indicates the title will pass from the buyer and seller. It also indicates to what extent freight and other expenses will be paid by the seller.

delivered duty paid A term of sale that indicates that the seller will pay any import duties or taxes levied by the importer's home country.

delivered duty unpaid A term of sale that indicates that the seller will not pay any import duties or taxes.

delivered ex quay A term of sale that indicates shipment will be delivered to the buyer at the seller's expense on the "quay" or pier alongside the ship. The seller will pay all expenses to that point including any cost associated with unloading the consignment from the ship.

delivered ex ship A term of sale that indicates shipment will be delivered to the buyer at the seller's expense alongside the ship. The seller will pay all expenses to that point, including any cost associated with unloading the consignment from the ship.

delivery delay Failure to make a scheduled delivery.

demand elasticity The amount that the demand for a product or service will change by the changes in price and the availability of substitutes.

demise charter The hiring of a ship and crew that shifts the control and possession of the vessel; the charterer takes full control of the vessel along with the legal and financial responsibility for it.

demurrage The charge a railroad assesses for a shipper or receiver holding a car beyond the free time the railroad allows for loading (24 hours) or unloading (48 hours).

density A physical characteristic measuring a commodity's mass per unit volume or pounds per cubic foot; it is an important factor in rate making because density affects the utilization of a carrier's vehicle.

density rate A rate based upon the density and shipment weight.

Department of Homeland Security Federal agency charged with the primary responsibilities of protecting the territory of the United States from terrorist attacks and responding to natural disasters.

Department of Transportation The cabinet-level branch of the U.S. government responsible for various aspects of transportation policy, safety, and, in some cases, economic regulation for all carriers and modes.

deregulation The removal or simplification of government rules and regulations that control or limit a company's ability to act.

derived demand The demand for a product's transportation is derived from the product's demand at some location.

detention The charge a motor carrier assesses when a shipper or receiver holds a truck or trailer beyond the free time the carrier allows for loading or unloading.

differential A distinction between individuals or classes.

dimensional weight Unit of measurement used by air carriers to calculate rates for carrying cargo, based on measuring volume taken as well as cargo weight.

direct service Movement of a shipment straight from its origin to its destination without transshipment.

discounts Reductions made from the gross amount or value of something.

dispatching The carrier activities involved with controlling equipment; it involves arranging for fuel, drivers, crews, equipment, and terminal space.

diversion A carrier service that permits a shipper to change the consignee and/or destination while the shipment is en route and to still pay the through rate from origin to final destination.

dock receipt A receipt that indicates a domestic carrier has delivered an export shipment to a steamship company.

domestic trunk line carrier A classification for air carriers that operate between major population centers. These carriers are now classified as major carriers.

double bottoms A motor carrier operation that involves one tractor pulling two trailers.

draft A type of bank transaction that insures payment for goods. It is a written order for a sum of money to be paid by the buyer to the seller upon presentation of the document to the buyer's bank.

drayage A motor carrier that operates locally, providing pickup and delivery service.

drivers In the context of forming a partnership, compelling reasons to partner.

driving time regulations U.S. Department of Transportation rules that limit the maximum time a driver may drive in interstate commerce; the rules prescribe both daily and weekly maximums.

dry-bulk carriers Ships with several holds in their hulls in which loose cargo such as grains, coal, ore, and other commodities are loaded.

duty A tax on imports.

economic deregulation The removal of governmentally enforced price and entry controls in the transportation industry. The "free market" will provide the necessary competition to ensure competitive prices and services.

economies of density Savings realized wherein unit costs are lower in relation to population density. The higher the population density, the lower the likely costs of infrastructure required to provide a service.

economies of scale As production of a good increases, the cost of producing each additional unit falls.

electronic data interchange The structured transmission of data between organizations by electronic means; used to transfer electronic documents from one computer system to another, such as from one trading partner to another.

emergency shipment Expedited, as-soon-as-possible delivery of items.

eminent domain The right of the state to take private property for public use.

employee assistance programs (EAPs) Employer-sponsored programs provided to their employees suffering from substance-abuse problems.

end-of-the-line terminal Terminal that serves a local area, providing direct contact with both shippers and receivers; The basic transportation service provided at this terminal is the pickup and/or delivery of freight.

end-to-end mergers Type of railroad company merger that aims to result in more effective intermodal and intramodal competition, usually by combining firms from different but complementary territories.

enlightened consumer Empowered by education, income, access to distant supply sources, and information from the Internet and the media, these resourceful consumers are knowledgeable and demanding.

enterprise asset management A company-wide system employing software and hardware to manage the plant maintenance processes to ensure equipment and inventory availability and to reduce asset downtime.

equipment substitution Advantageous replacement of a carrier's mode of transportation in order to maximize return; for example, changing a flight to a smaller plane in response to a shortfall in reservations.

Erie Canal Man-made waterway extending 363 miles from Albany to Buffalo, New York linking the Atlantic seacoast to the Great Lakes; in the years after its completion in 1825, the cost of transporting goods between the Midwest and New York City fell precipitously, in some cases by 95 percent.

event management   An aspect of shipment visibility that incorporates when things happen into its reporting system.

evergreen contract   A contract that does not have a specified expiration date.

ex works   The price that the seller quotes applies only at the point of origin. The buyer takes possession of the shipment at the point of origin and bears all costs and risks associated with transporting the goods to the final destination.

exception rate   A deviation from the class rate; changes (exceptions) made to the classification.

excess capacity   Underused or unused facilities and/or infrastructure; for example, an empty seat on an air carrier's flight.

exchange   Electronic marketplace that facilitates buying and selling of products and services.

exclusive patronage agreements   A shipper agrees to use only a conference member's liner firm in return for a 10- to 15-percent rate reduction.

exclusive use   Vehicles that a carrier assigns to a specific shipper for its exclusive use.

exempt carrier   A for-hire carrier that is exempt from economic regulations.

existence charge   A shipping charge related to the existence of some tangible item that is made against the person or unit regardless of the extent of use made of the services.

expediting   Determining where an in-transit shipment is and attempting to speed up its delivery.

export license   A document indicating that a government has granted a licensee the right to export specified goods to specified countries.

exporter   One who sells to merchants or industrial consumers in foreign countries.

extended enterprise   A way of looking at a process that extends beyond the bounds of a single firm to span the related activities of several participating or affected firms; a supply chain is an example of an extended enterprise that crosses the boundaries of the individual firms.

extent of market   This relates to the extent of the size of a market that a firm may serve on a competitive basis. Cost of the product and freight will determine how far from its base a firm may compete effectively.

F.O.B. Destination   Short for "Free On Board"; indicates that the geographical point at which title for the shipment passes from the seller to the buyer is at the shipment's destination point. After this point, the buyer is responsible for all risks and delivery costs.

F.O.B. Origin   Short for "Free On Board"; indicates that the geographical point at which title for the shipment passes from the seller to the buyer is at the shipment's origination point.

After this point, the buyer is responsible for all risks and delivery costs.

facilitators   In the context of forming a partnership, supportive corporate environmental factors that enhance partnership growth and development.

fair wage   A wage fairly and reasonably commensurate with the value of a particular service or class of service rendered.

Federal Aviation Administration   The federal agency within the Department of Transportation that is responsible for regulating air safety, promoting development of air commerce, and controlling navigable air space.

Federal Energy Regulatory Commission   The federal agency that oversees rates and practices of pipeline operators and is part of the Department of Energy.

Federal Highway Administration   The federal agency that oversees motor carrier safety including hours of services, driver qualifications, and vehicle size and weight, as well as overall operation and development of the national highway system. This agency is part of the Department of Transportation.

Federal Highway Trust Fund   A fund that receives federally collected fuel taxes used for highway construction and upkeep.

Federal Maritime Commission   The federal agency that regulates international rates, practices, agreements, and services of common carrier water carriers.

Federal Motor Carrier Safety Administration   Federal agency, created in 2000, whose primary mission is to reduce crashes, injuries, fatalities, and property loss involving large trucks and buses by regulating the workers involved.

Federal Railroad Administration   The federal agency that oversees railroad safety by establishing and enforcing rules and regulations. This agency is part of the Department of Transportation.

Federal Trade Commission   The federal agency that administers the Sherman Anti-Trust Act and the Clayton Act. This agency does not have direct control over transportation.

feu   Forty-foot equivalent unit, a standard-size intermodal container.

fixed costs   Costs that do not fluctuate with the business volume in the short run.

fixed costs per unit   Total fixed costs divided by the number of units produced.

flag of convenience   A ship registered in a foreign country for purposes of reducing operating costs or avoiding government regulations or taxes.

flatbed   A trailer without sides used for hauling machinery or other bulky items.

flatcar   A railcar without sides, used for hauling machinery.

FOB   A term of sale defining who is to incur transportation charges for the shipment, who is to control the shipment movement, or where title to the goods passes to the buyer; it originally meant "free on board ship."

for-hire authority   Licensing necessary for a person or company that provides transportation of cargo or passengers for compensation.

for-hire carrier   A carrier that provides transportation service to the public on a fee basis.

for-hire water carriers   Carriers operating on waterways that provide transportation service to the public on a fee basis.

foreign trade zone (FTZ)   An area or zone set aside at or near a port or airport, under the control of the U.S. Customs Service, for the holding of goods duty-free, pending customs clearance.

fourth party logistics (4PL)   Consulting firms specialized in logistics, transportation, and supply chain management.

free alongside ship   A term of sale that indicates that the buyer will pay all freight and insurance charges necessary to bring the consignment to the side of ship but will not cover the cost of loading.

Free and Secure Trade Program   A joint United States–Canadian program that offers pre-authorized importers, carriers, and drivers expedited clearance for eligible goods.

Free Carrier (FCA)   A trade term requiring the seller to deliver goods to a named airport, terminal, or other place where the carrier operates.

"free" cash flow   In corporate finance, describes the fiscal condition of companies with negative working capital who must collect from their customers before they can pay their vendors or suppliers.

free trade agreements   Treaties between nations that agree to eliminate tariffs, quotas, and preferences on many goods and services traded between them.

freight   Goods to be shipped; cargo.

freight all kinds   A pricing method where the carrier establishes a rate that will apply on any cargo loaded in the carrier's vehicle regardless of the nature of the freight.

freight bill   The carrier's invoice for a freight shipment's transportation charges.

freight contamination   To make goods unfit for use by the introduction of unwholesome or undesirable elements.

freight damage   Injury or destruction of cargo.

freight flows   The geographic direction in which freight "flows" or moves from producing locations to areas of consumption.

freight forwarder   A carrier that collects small shipments from shippers, consolidates the small shipments, and uses a basic mode to transport these consolidated shipments to a consignee destination.

freight management   A strategic system to optimize the efficiency of freight and commercial transport.

freight rating   Performing the calculations appropriate to calculate freight costs based on contract and tariff terms.

freight transportation   The movement of goods or products from the producer or manufacturer to the user or customer.

frequency and timing   How often and at what time a group of scheduled events occurs.

fronthaul   The first half of a round-trip move from origin to destination. The opposite is "backhaul," which is the return of the equipment to its origin point.

fuel costs   Amounts paid for materials used to power the engines driving a carrier's machines.

fuel surcharges   An additional tax or fee imposed due to the cost of fuel.

fuel-efficient   Operable using comparatively less fuel.

fully allocated cost   The variable cost associated with a particular output unit plus a common cost allocation.

gas carriers   Ships that transport compressed gases such as liquefied natural gas and liquefied petroleum gas in specialized tanks.

gateway   An opening, passage, or structure framing an opening that may be closed by a gate; an area, mechanism, or agency that provides access to another area, agency, or system; any passage by or point at which a region may be entered.

gathering lines   Oil pipelines that bring oil from the oil well to storage areas.

general average   The legal principle of maritime law according to which all parties in a sea venture proportionally share any losses resulting from a voluntary sacrifice of part of the ship or cargo to save the whole in an emergency.

general cargo rate   A pricing method where the carrier establishes a rate that will apply on any cargo loaded in the carrier's ship, regardless of the nature of the freight.

general-commodities carrier   A common motor carrier that has operating authority to transport general commodities, or all commodities not listed as special commodities.

geographic specialization   A nation, region, state, or city may produce those products and services for which it is best suited in terms of its capital, labor, raw materials, and other resources and talents when adequate transportation makes such specialization possible.

globalization   Recognition that commercial activity now spans the world and that many firms buy and sell throughout the world.

gondola   A railcar with a flat platform and sides 3- to 5-feet high, used for top-loading long, heavy items.

government policy and regulation   Laws passed on the state and federal level, as well as rules issued by their agencies that possess the force of law, which restrict a company's prices or business practices.

granger laws   A series of laws passed in the western United States after the Civil War to regulate grain elevator and railroad freight rates and rebates and to address long- and short-haul discrimination and other railroad abuses against farmers.

green supply chains   Supply chain management with an emphasis on energy efficiency and environmental friendliness.

gross weight   The total weight of the vehicle and the payload of freight or passengers.

harmonized commodity description and coding system (Harmonized Code)   An international classification system that assigns identification numbers to specific products. The coding system ensures that all parties in international trade use a consistent classification for the purposes of documentation, statistical control, and duty assessment.

hazardous materials   Materials that the Department of Transportation has determined to be a risk to health, safety, and property; includes items such as explosives, flammable liquids, poisons, corrosive liquids, and radioactive material.

headhaul   The first half of a round-trip move from origin to destination. The opposite is "backhaul," which is the return of the equipment to its origin point.

hedging strategy   Method of reducing risk by diversifying the risks presented by a single option.

high-density route   Transportation route with the greatest number of users or carrying the highest amount of cargo.

highway development   Planning and construction of high-speed roadways.

Highway Trust Fund   A fund into which highway users (carriers and automobile operators) pay; the fund pays for federal government's highway construction share.

highway use taxes   Taxes that federal and state governments assess against highway users (the fuel tax is an example). The government uses the use tax money to pay for the construction, maintenance, and policing of highways.

hold   The interior of a ship below decks; the cargo compartment of a plane.

home-flag airline   An airline owned or sponsored by the government of the country in which the carrier is based. Typically, only home-flag airlines are allowed to operate between airports within that country. This prevents foreign carriers from serving domestic locations.

hopper cars   Railcars that permit top-loading and bottom-unloading of bulk commodities; some hopper cars have permanent tops with hatches to provide protection against the elements.

hub   A central location to which traffic from many cities is directed and from which traffic is fed to other areas.

hub airport   An airport that serves as the focal point for the origin and termination of long-distance flights; flights from outlying areas meet connecting flights at the hub airport.

hull insurance   Insurance that covers damage to the hull and machinery of a boat.

hump yard   A railroad yard that uses an artificial hill or "hump" to assist in switching and classifying railcars. The cars are pushed up the hill by a switch engine, and at the top of the hill the railcar or group of railcars is uncoupled and rolls down hill to the correct track.

hundredweight (cwt)   The pricing unit used in transportation; a hundredweight is equal to 100 pounds.

hybrid tractor   Industrial or farm vehicle utilizing both traditional internal combustion engine with an electric motor powered by batteries.

ICC Termination Act of 1995   Federal statute that eliminated the Interstate Commerce Commission and transferred economic rail regulation to the Surface Transportation Board.

igloos   Pallets and containers used in air transportation; the igloo shape fits the internal wall contours of a narrow-body airplane.

importer   One who brings goods or merchandise from other countries into this one.

in-bond goods   Goods held or transported in-bond under Customs control either until import duties or other charges are paid, or to avoid paying the duties or charges until a later date.

incentive rate   A rate that induces the shipper to ship heavier volumes per shipment.

INCOTERMS   International terms of sale developed by the International Chamber of Commerce to define sellers' and buyers' responsibilities.

independent action   A carrier that is a rate bureau member may publish a rate that differs from the rate published by the rate bureau.

indirect forms of promotion   Subsidies and incentives intended to preserve the domestic shipbuilding industry.

indirect service   Movement of a shipment from its origin to its destination, making interim stops and/or transfer of freight between equipment.

inelastic   In the context of economic supply and demand, elasticity refers to the sensitivity of customers to changes in price; if customers are not sensitive to price, then demand is considered inelastic.

information flow   The flow or movement of information or data between trading partners or companies that facilitates commerce or business.

inherent advantage   The cost and service benefits of one mode compared with other modes.

inland ports   A specialized facility that executes some functions traditionally carried out at a seaport, made possible by the use of container shipping.

insurable interest   A financial interest in an individual or a thing such that you are in a position to suffer an assessable financial loss if that person should die or that thing be damaged, destroyed, or lost.

insurance   Coverage by contract whereby one party promises to guarantee another against loss by a specified contingency or peril.

integrated carriers   Air carrier companies that have the capability to provide door-to-door service because they own ground delivery equipment as well as aircraft.

integrated logistics management   The management of all activities involved in physically acquiring, moving and storing raw materials, in-process inventory, and finished goods inventory from the point of origin to the point of consumption.

integrated service providers   For-hire firms that perform a variety of logistics service activities such as warehousing, transportation, and other functional activities as a package service.

integration   The act of mixing various elements into a single group. An example would to combine transportation and warehousing to allow trade-offs between the two functions for the maximum benefit.

intercoastal carriers   Water carriers that transport freight between East and West Coast ports, usually by way of the Panama Canal.

interline   Two or more motor carriers working together to haul a shipment to a destination. Carriers may interchange equipment, but usually they re-handle the shipment without transferring the equipment.

intermediaries   Those being or occurring at the middle place or stage, such as brokers between ocean shippers and rail carriers.

intermodal   The combination of various modes to form a transportation movement. An example would be a truck picking up a trailer and taking it to a rail yard for movement by train to the destination city where another truck would take the trailer to the receiver's location. This term may also refer to competition between modes such as truck and rail.

intermodal bill of lading   Like a through bill of lading, except that the principal carrier or the freight forwarder assumes full liability for the cargo's entire journey over all modes of transportation.

intermodal marketing company (IMC)   An intermediary that sells intermodal services to shippers.

intermodal transportation   Transportation of freight in an intermodal container or vehicle, using multiple modes of transportation (rail, ship, and truck), without any handling of the freight itself when changing modes.

internal water carriers   Water carriers that operate over internal, navigable rivers such as the Mississippi, Ohio, and Missouri.

International Air Transport Association (IATA) An international industry trade group of airlines that represents the airline industry.

International Maritime Organization   A specialized agency of the United Nations tasked with developing and maintaining a comprehensive regulatory framework for shipping, including safety, environmental concerns, legal matters, technical co-operation, and maritime security.

Interstate Commerce Commission (ICC)   A former independent federal agency that supervised and set rates for carriers that transported goods and people between states.

interstate commerce   The transportation of persons or property between states; in the course of the movement, the shipment crosses a state boundary.

Interstate System   The National System of Interstate and Defense Highways; limited-access roads connecting major population centers.

intramodal   Movement within a modal- or carrier-type category. This could refer to shipments moved with more than one truck line. This term may also refer to competition within a mode, such as between trucking firms.

intrastate commerce   The transportation of persons or property between points within a state. A shipment between two points within a state may be interstate if the shipment had a prior or subsequent move outside of the state and the shipper intended an interstate shipment at the time of shipment.

jettison   A voluntary sacrifice of cargo to lighten a ship's load in time of distress.

joint cost   A common cost in cases where a company produces products in fixed proportions and the cost the company incurs to produce one product entails producing another; the backhaul is an example.

joint rate   A rate over a route that requires two or more carriers to transport the shipment.

just-in-time delivery   Component of an inventory strategy that strives to improve a business's return on investment by reducing in-process inventory and associated carrying costs.

just-in-time (JIT) inventory system   An inventory control system that attempts to reduce inventory levels by coordinating demand and supply to the point where the desired item arrives just in time for use.

Kanban system   A just-in-time inventory system used by Japanese manufacturers.

key performance indicators   Measures that are commonly used to help an organization define and evaluate how successful it is, typically in terms of making progress towards its long-term organizational goals.

Known Shipper Program   A security system put in place following the attacks of 9/11 that essentially eliminates the anonymous shipment of all documents, parcels, counter-to-counter packages, and freight on both passenger and cargo-only flights originating within the United States.

lading   The cargo carried in a transportation vehicle.

land bridge   The movement of containers by ship-rail-ship on Japan-to-Europe moves; ships move containers to the U.S. Pacific Coast, rails move containers to an East Coast port, and ships deliver containers to Europe.

land grants   Grants of land given to railroads to build tracks during their development stage.

landed cost   The cost of the product at the source combined with the cost of transportation to the destination.

landed cost advantage   The advantage one supplier has over another based on the lower transportation cost due to favorable proximity to the market.

Lardner's Law   A finding by transportation economist Dionysius Lardner that when transportation cost is reduced, the area where the producer can compete is increased in a directly proportional basis.

Law of Squares   An increase in the distance over which a given amount will cover the transport of goods will increase the market area of the product in an even greater ratio; also known as Lardner's Law.

LCL   Less than carload rail service; less than container load.

letter of credit   A document issued by the buyer's bank that guarantees payment to the seller if certain terms and conditions are met.

liability   Any legal responsibility, duty, or obligation.

lighter-aboard ship   A type of vessel that is capable of carrying barges or "lighters" onboard. This method of transportation allows a barge to be loaded on an inland waterway, transported to shipside, and taken to a harbor nearest destination, and the barge can then be taken to the destination by an inland waterway without having to rehandle any of the cargo.

line-haul shipment   A shipment that moves between cities and over distances more than 100 to 150 miles in length.

liner service   International water carriers that ply fixed routes on published schedules.

load factor   A measure of operating efficiency used by air carriers to determine a plane's utilized capacity percentage or the number of passengers divided by the total number of seats.

loading allowance   A reduced rate that carriers offer to shippers and/or consignees who load and/or unload LTL or AQ shipments.

local rate   A rate published between two points served by one carrier.

local service carriers   A classification of air carriers that operate between less-populated areas and major population centers. These carriers feed passengers into the major cities to connect with trunk (major) carriers. Local service carriers are now classified as national carriers.

logbook   A daily record of the hours an interstate driver spends driving, off duty, sleeping in the berth, or on duty but not driving.

logistics service providers   Companies that offer basic transportation services.

long ton   2,240 pounds.

longshoremen   Persons employed loading or unloading cargo from ships.

loss and damage   The risk to which goods are subjected during the transportation cycle. The shipment may be separated from its documentation and misdirected. Handling by the carrier as well as in-transit incidents can cause damage to or destruction of the shipment. This is a factor in mode and carrier selection as well as packaging and handling techniques. This risk factor also enters into the carrier's pricing decisions.

LTL shipment   A less-than-truckload shipment, one weighing less than the minimum weight a company needs to use the lower truckload rate.

lumping   The act of assisting a motor carrier owner–operator in the loading and unloading of property; quite commonly used in the food industry.

major carriers   For-hire air carriers with annual revenues of more than $1 billion.

manifest   A list of all cargoes that pertain to a specific shipment, grouping of shipments, or piece of equipment. Ocean carriers will prepare a manifest for each container.

maquiladora   The name for a manufacturing facility established inside Mexico within close distance of the U.S. border. Materials are shipped from the United States, processed in the maquiladora plant, and returned to the United States. No customs duties or fees are accessed.

marginal cost   The cost to produce one additional unit of output; the change in total variable cost resulting from a one-unit change in output.

marine insurance   Insurance to protect against cargo loss and damage when shipping by water transportation.

market share pricing   In an industry whose revenues are stagnant or declining, a firm will try to take market share from competitors through the use of lower prices.

marketing mix   This consists of the four basic elements of marketing: product, price, place, and promotion. This is also known as the "four P's" of marketing.

measurement ton   Forty cubic feet; used in water transportation rate making.

merger   The combination of two or more carriers into one company that will own, manage, and operate the properties that previously operated separately.

micro-bridge   A technique where ocean containers are transported to an interior destination, such as Chicago or St. Louis, on a through bill of lading and the cost of the inland move is included in the total price.

mileage allowance   An allowance, based upon distance, that railroads give to shippers using private railcars.

mileage rate   A rate or price based on the total mileage between the origin and destination including stop-offs, if any.

mini-bridge   A technique where rail transportation is substituted for a portion of ocean transportation. As an example, a shipment from Japan to New York could move via the Panama Canal. The mini-bridge substitutes rail from a West Coast port to New York for the Panama Canal portion.

minimum level of safety   A base requirement for all aspects of safe operation by a transportation firm, as prescribed by a government agency.

minimum weight   The shipment weight the carrier's tariff specifies as the minimum weight required to use the TL or CL rate; the rate discount volume.

mobility   The ease or difficulty with which people or goods are moved by the transportation network.

modal demand   The request or demand made by users for service provided by a particular type of carrier or method of transport.

modal split   The relative use that companies make of transportation modes; the statistics include ton-miles, passenger-miles, and revenue.

monopolistic   The ability of very few suppliers to set a price well above cost by restricting supply or by limiting competition.

monopoly   A market segment where there is only one supplier, such as public utilities.

multiple-car rate   A railroad rate that is lower for shipping more than one carload at a time.

national carrier   A for-hire certificated air carrier that has annual operating revenues of $75 million to $1 billion; the carrier usually operates between major population centers and areas of lesser population.

national defense   A primary function of a sovereign state is its ability to defend its territory, national waters, and air space against internal and external threats.

National Highway Traffic Safety Administration (NHTSA)   This branch of the U.S. Department of Transportation is responsible for motor vehicle safety. In this role, NHTSA oversees design features, sets performance-related safety standards, and oversees governmental fuel economy standards.

National Motor Freight Classification (NMFC)   A tariff that contains descriptions and classifications of commodities and rules for domestic movement by motor carriers in the United States.

National Private Truck Council   A U.S. national trade association that represents private motor carrier fleets.

National Transportation Safety Board   This agency is responsible for investigating transportation-related accidents, regardless of whether or not the incident involved the private sector or a public carrier. They are responsible for recommending preventative measures to avoid future accidents.

nationalization   Public ownership, financing, and operation of a business entity.

negotiations   A set of discussions between two or more enterprises to determine the business relationship.

net present cost   The sum of the present values of the individual cash flows, both incoming and outgoing.

net weight   The weight of the merchandise, unpacked, exclusive of any containers.

no-frills service   Any service or product for which the nonessential features have been removed to keep the price low.

non-asset based providers   3PLs that fulfill customer requirements via the resources of other companies.

noncertificated carrier   A for-hire air carrier that is exempt from economic regulation.

nonintegrated carriers   Air carrier companies that only provide service from airport to airport.

nonvessel-owning common carrier (NVOCC)   A firm that consolidates and disperses international containers that originate at or are bound for inland ports.

North American Free Trade Agreement (NAFTA)   An agreement signed by the United States, Canada, and Mexico to establish free trade between the three countries.

not-for-hire   A carrier who does not hold itself to the general public to provide transportation service but rather transports for the owner firm exclusively.

ocean bill of lading   A contract for transportation between a shipper and an ocean carrier, which also evidences receipt of the cargo by the carrier.

Ocean Shipping Reform Act   Federal law passed in 1998 that effected significant deregulation of the ocean carrier industry.

oligopoly   A shared monopoly where there are few suppliers and, in the case of transportation, entry barriers and cost are significant. Examples would be railroads and airlines.

open account   A credit account extended by a business to a customer or another business.

operating costs   The costs arising from the day-to-day activities of running a company.

operating expense   The cost of providing a service by a carrier. This can include such factors as taxes, interest, and depreciation but not necessarily profit.

operating ratio   A measure of operating efficiency defined as operating expenses/operating revenues $\times 100$.

order cycle time   Period between placing of one set of orders and the next.

out-of-pocket cost   The cost directly assignable to a particular unit of traffic, which a company would not have incurred if it had not performed the movement.

outsourcing   Purchasing a logistics service from an outside firm, as opposed to performing it in-house.

over-the-road   A motor carrier operation that reflects long-distance, intercity moves; the opposite of local operations.

owner–operator   A trucking operation in which the truck's owner is also the driver.

ozone reduction   Destruction of the stratospheric ozone layer which shields the earth from ultraviolet radiation harmful to life.

packing list   A detailed inventory of the contents of a shipment.

pallet   A platform device (about 4-feet square) used for moving and storing goods. A forklift truck is used to lift and move the loaded pallet.

Panamax ships   Large ships designed to be just under the maximum size that can pass through the Panama Canal.

passenger airplanes   Aircraft designed to carry people.

passenger revenue   Fares paid by passengers for traveling on transportation routes.

passenger transportation   The means and equipment necessary for the movement of persons, as opposed to freight.

passenger-mile   A measure of output for passenger transportation that reflects the number of passengers transported and the distance traveled; a multiplication of passengers hauled and distance traveled.

peak demand   The time period during which customers demand the greatest quantity.

peddle run   A truck operation where many pickups or deliveries are made while the vehicle travels over a preset route.

peddle time   This is the time that the driver is actively involved in either pickup or delivery.

penetration price   A pricing strategy that sets a price designed to allow the supplier to enter a market where there is already established competition by slightly underpricing the existing firms.

per diem   A payment rate one railroad makes to use another's cars.

per se violations   A violation of the law that is, on its own, deemed to be harmful, regardless of its effect on the market or competitors.

physical distribution management   The management and control of the activities involved in the storage, handling, and movement of goods within an organization and in their shipment to customers.

phyto-sanitary certificate   Document that confirms that plants being imported meet regulations regarding pests, plant diseases, chemical treatments, and weeds.

pickup and delivery (PUD)   The act of collecting freight from shippers or delivering freight to consignees.

piggyback   A rail-truck service. A shipper loads a highway trailer, and a carrier drives it to a rail terminal and loads it on a rail flatcar; the railroad moves the trailer-on-flatcar combination to the destination terminal, where the carrier offloads the trailer and delivers it to the consignee.

Pipeline and Hazardous Material Safety Administration   Federal agency, created in 2004, whose primary focus is pipeline safety and hazardous materials transportation safety operations.

place utility or place value   The usefulness or value of a good or service as a function of the location at which it is made available; For example, snow shovels have greater place utility in Boston than in El Paso.

police powers   The United States' constitutionally granted right for the states to establish regulations to protect their citizens' health and welfare; truck weight and speed, length, and height laws are examples.

pork barrel projects   Government spending for localized projects secured solely or primarily to bring money to a representative's district.

port authority   A state or local government that owns, operates, or otherwise provides wharf, dock, and other terminal investments at ports.

post-Panamax ship   Ships larger than a Panamax ship and which cannot pass through the Panama Canal.

postponement strategy   Method of reducing risk by delaying a commitment of resources.

prepaid   A freight term that indicates that charges are to be paid by the shipper.

price elasticity   The measurement factor by which the change in demand for a product or service is affected by the price.

price inelasticity   An economic condition where the change or increase in the price of a product or service does not produce a proportional change in demand.

price-sensitive   The relationship between prices and the demand for products or services.

primary trip markets   The geographic area of interest where a carrier focuses its sales and operational effort.

private air carrier   Air carrier that only transports company personnel or freight for the company that owns or leases the planes in support of the company's primary business.

private carrier   A carrier that provides transportation service to the firm that owns or leases the vehicles and does not charge a fee. Private motor carriers may haul at a fee for wholly owned subsidiaries.

private fleet   Group of vehicles operating together under the same non-governmental ownership.

private service   Charter service where the ships are owned or leased on a long-term basis by the company moving the goods.

private transportation   The movement of goods owned by a firm that also owns or leases and operates the transportation equipment for the furtherance of its primary business.

procurement   Another term for purchasing that represents more than just the buying of a product or service.

product flows   The course where goods move between the point of origin to the point of consumption.

pro-forma   A document issued by the seller to acquaint the importer/buyer and the importing country's government authorities with the details of the shipment.

profit maximization   The process by which a firm determines the price and output level that returns the greatest profit.

profit ratio   The percentage of profit to sales—that is, profit divided by sales.

proof of delivery (POD)   Information supplied by the carrier containing the name of the person who signed for the shipment, the time and date of delivery, and other shipment delivery-related information.

public aid   Government assistance to an enterprise or industry deemed advantageous to the public.

pure competition   A condition in which there is a large number of sellers, the product or service is standardized and interchangeable, and no one seller can control the price or output. An example would be the LTL sector.

qualitative risk analysis   A baseline evaluation of risks.

quality gap   The difference in perception of a product or service between the buyer and seller.

quantity utility   The usefulness or value of a good or service as a function of timely delivery and undamaged condition.

Railroad Revitalization and Regulatory Reform Act of 1976   Federal statute that provided federal funding for the startup of Conrail.

rate base point   The major shipping point in a local area; carriers consider all points in the local area to be the rate basis point.

rate basis number   This number is an expression of the relative distance between an origin and destination. The number may be given in miles or another factor and will form one of the required inputs to develop a rate between the two points.

rate bureau   A carrier group that assembles to establish joint rates, to divide joint revenues and claim liabilities, and to publish tariffs. Rate bureaus have published single line rates, which were prohibited in 1984.

reasonable rate   A rate that is high enough to cover the carrier's cost but not high enough to enable the carrier to realize monopolistic profits.

Reed-Bulwinkle Act of 1948   Federal law permitting motor carriers to fix rates in concert with each other, thus exempting such carriers from antitrust laws.

reefer   A refrigerated vehicle.

regional carrier   A for-hire air carrier, usually certificated, that has annual operating revenues of less than $75 million; the carrier usually operates within a particular region of the country.

Regional Rail Reorganization Act of 1973   A law passed by Congress in response to the bankruptcies of the Penn Central and other railroads. Conrail, which has since been purchased by the Norfolk Southern Railroad and CSX, was created from this law to operate the lines of six northeastern U.S. railroads.

regional trade agreements   Treaty negotiated by a group of nations within a broad geographic area regarding trade.

regular-route carrier   A motor carrier that is authorized to provide service over designated routes.

regulated water carriers   Water carriers that operate under the control of government or agency rules.

relative use   A fee placed on the users of a service or facility to cover the cost of providing that service or facility.

relay terminal   A motor carrier terminal that facilitates the substitution of one driver for another who has driven the maximum hours permitted.

released-value rates   Rates based upon the shipment's value. The maximum carrier liability for damage is less than the full value, and in return the carrier offers a lower rate.

reliability   A carrier selection criterion that considers the carrier transit time variation; the consistency of the transit time the carrier provides.

reliable   Suitable or fit to be relied upon; dependable.

resiliency   The ability to recover from or adjust easily to misfortune or change.

return on investment   The amount of money realized or generated on an investment that flows back to the lenders. This is often used to gauge the worthiness of an investment by measuring the potential profits and the source of the capital.

revenue   Amount generated from sale of goods or services, or any other use of capital or assets, associated with the main operations of firm before any costs or expenses are deducted.

reverse logistics systems   Logistical systems for the return of products that were unacceptable to the buyer for some reason (damage, maintenance, obsolescence, etc.); employed by an increasing number of organizations.

rights-of-way   The privilege of someone to pass over land belonging to someone else; the right of one vehicle or vessel to take precedence over another; the passage consisting of a path or strip of land over which someone has the legal right to pass.

risk identification   The effort to discover, define, describe, document, and communicate hazards before they become realized.

risk management process   Systematic approach to identifying risk, its causes and effects, and its ownership with a goal of reducing or eliminating hazards.

risk mitigation   Reduction of the chance of a hazard occurring.

risk proximity   Assessment of the time element in risk analysis.

risk retention   Self-insurance; a company may determine that it is more economical to forego cargo insurance for the anticipated risks and bear the loss itself.

risk transfer   Purchasing insurance to cover anticipated risks.

Robinson-Patman Act of 1936   Federal law that prohibits sales that discriminate in price on the sale of goods to equally-situated distributors when the effect of such sales is to reduce competition.

roll-on roll-off ship   A type of vessel that has ramps upon which vehicles can be driven directly into the hold of the ship. This type of vessel is often used to transport buses, trucks, construction machinery on wheels, and other types of wheeled shipments.

roller deck   The main deck of an air freighter equipped with rollers on the floor, which allows palletized or containerized cargo to be pushed into position.

routing   Directing to a specific direction or destination.

routing and scheduling   Directing to a specific direction or destination by a predetermined time.

Rule of Efficiency   The "Rule" refers to the fact that the most efficient transportation is in a continuous, straight line. There should be little circuitry or out-of-route operations with as few stops and starts as possible.

Rule of Reason   An alleged violation of an anti-trust law where economic harm to competitors must be proved.

seating capacity   The maximum number of passengers that can be accommodated.

security   The actions of a carrier to protect the goods entrusted to their care from loss or damage.

separable costs   In the context of cost structure, costs necessarily produced in fixed proportions; the production or generation of one product or service necessarily entails the production or generation of another product.

service   The furnishing of an operation that fulfills the needs of the customer. This could be transporting a product or person to the desired location.

service contract   A contract between a shipper and an ocean carrier or conference, in which the shipper makes a commitment to provide a minimum quantity of cargo over a fixed time period. The ocean carrier or conference also commits to a rate or rate schedule as well as a defined service level, such as space, transit item, port rotation, or other features.

service elasticity   Assuming no significant price differential, the mode or carrier providing the best level of service as perceived by the user will be the first choice.

service inelasticity   Price, rather than service, is the controlling factor. The customer's choice of supplier will be made on price, assuming the service offered also meets the requirements as perceived by the user.

service reliability   Dependability in the performance of any duties or work for another.

Sherman Anti-Trust Act   A body of law that restricts businesses' ability to dominate a market by engaging in certain practices. This includes price fixing and other free-market-constricting activities.

ship agent   A liner company or tramp ship operator representative who facilitates ship arrival, clearance, loading and unloading, and fee payment while at a specific port.

shipbroker   A firm that serves as a go-between for the tramp ship owner and the chartering consignor or consignee.

shipment consolidation   A logistics strategy that combines two or more orders or shipments so that a larger quantity can be dispatched on the same vehicle.

shipper   The party that tenders goods for transportation.

shipper terminals   Port facilities.

shipper's agent   A firm that primarily matches up small shipments, especially single-traffic piggyback loads, to permit shippers to use twin-trailer piggyback rates.

shipper's export declaration   A document filed by the shipper/exporter or its agent with the government of the country in which the shipper/exporter resides. This form supplies the government with information about the shipment for statistical and control purposes.

shipper's letter of instructions   Document that spells out the requirements for handling in-transit goods; important when the cargo is susceptible to damage or requires special attention, such as live animals and plants.

shippers association   A nonprofit, cooperative consolidator and distributor of shipments that member firms own or ship; acts in much the same way as a for-profit freight forwarder.

Shipping Act of 1984   A body of law that governs the pricing and services of ocean carriers operating between the United States and foreign countries.

shipping instructions   A document detailing the cargo and the requirements of its physical movement.

short ton   Two thousand pounds.

short-haul discrimination   Charging more for a shorter haul than for a longer haul over the same route, in the same direction, and for the same commodity.

side-by-side merger   A merger of railroads whose lines operate in proximity of each other, rather than end to end.

sight draft   A customer's order to a financial institution holding the customer's funds to pay all or part of them to another institution in which the customer has another account.

skimming price   A price set by a provider who seeks to attract a market that is more interested in quality, uniqueness, or status and is relatively unconcerned with price.

sleeper team   Two drivers who operate a truck equipped with a sleeper berth; while one driver sleeps in the berth to accumulate mandatory off-duty time, the other driver operates the vehicle.

slip seat operation   A motor carrier relay terminal operation in which a carrier substitutes one driver for another who has accumulated the maximum driving time hours.

slurry lines   Pipelines through which coal is moved in a pulverized form suspended in water; once the slurry has reached its destination, the water is removed and the coal is ready for use.

SmartWay Transport Partnership   A voluntary program administered by the Environmental Protection Agency to encourage the reduction of transportation-related emissions by shippers and their customers.

social responsibility pricing   Lowering prices in pursuit of advancing ethical or social values apart from maximizing profitability.

special commodities carrier   A common carrier trucking company that has authority to haul a special commodity; the 16 special commodities include household goods, petroleum products, and hazardous materials.

spot   To move a trailer or boxcar into place for loading or unloading.

spur track   A railroad track that connects a company's plant or warehouse with the railroad's track; the user bears the cost of the spur track and its maintenance.

Staggers Rail Act of 1980   Federal statute that provided major deregulation of the railroad industry.

standards   Accepted or approved examples of something against which others are judged or measured.

state regulation   Laws passed on the state and federal level that restrict a company's freedom of action.

statutory law   This is based on the Roman legal system and refers to a body of law passed by legislative bodies.

steamship conferences   Collective rate-making bodies for liner water carriers.

stem time   The time consumed by a truck to reach its first delivery after leaving the terminal and the time consumed by the truck to return to the terminal after making its last pickup.

stevedore services   Services provided by persons employed loading or unloading cargo from ships.

stevedores   Persons employed loading or unloading cargo from ships.

stockout   A situation in which the items a customer orders are currently unavailable.

stockout cost   The opportunity cost that companies associate with not having supply sufficient to meet demand.

stowability and handling   The ease or difficulty experienced in loading, handling, and unloading freight. This factor influences the carrier's cost of providing a service and will be reflected in the price charged for the shipment. This is also two of the four factors considered when classifying freight.

strategic alliance   Relationship in which two or more business organizations cooperate and willingly modify their business objectives and practices to achieve long-term objectives.

strategic services   Services provided when an organization uses a 3PL service provider for fully managing their supply chains.

strategy   A course of action, a scheme, or a principal idea through which an organization or individual hopes to accomplish a specific objective or goal. In other words, a strategy is designed to determine how someone is going to achieve something that has been identified as being important to future success.

subsidies   Grants by a government to a private person or company to assist an enterprise or industry deemed advantageous to the public.

sunk costs   Costs that cannot be easily retrieved or may not be retrieved at all when liquidating a business. This includes investments in specific machinery or buildings.

supertankers   The largest of the ships designed for the bulk transport of oil.

supplemental carrier   A for-hire air carrier having no time schedule or designated route; the carrier provides service under a charter or contract per plane per trip.

supply chain interruptions   Problems with a transportation channel that fall outside the control of the company.

supply chain management   The integration of the flows of products, information, and financials through the entire supply pipeline from the supplier's supplier to the customer's customer.

surcharge   An add-on charge to the applicable charges; motor carriers have a fuel surcharge, and railroads can apply a surcharge to any joint rate that does not yield 110 percent of variable cost.

Surface Transportation Board   The agency created under the Interstate Commerce Commission Termination (ICC) to replace the ICC and exercise economic jurisdiction of the modes of transportation.

survival-based pricing   The use of low prices to increase cash flow and volume and to encourage the higher utilization of equipment.

switch engine   A railroad engine that is used to move railcars short distances within a terminal and plant.

switching company   A railroad that moves railcars short distances; switching companies connect two mainline railroads to facilitate through movement of a shipment's rail car for longhaul movement.

systems concept   An approach to business management that views the organization as a system, that is, a collection of parts (or subsystems) integrated to accomplish an overall goal; systems have input, processes, outputs, and outcomes, with ongoing feedback among these various parts.

tactic Refers to an operational aspect that is necessary to support strategy. Tactics are more likely to involve daily short-run operations that help achieve the strategy that has been identified or agreed upon in the organization.

tactical services Services provided when an organization uses a 3PL service provider for executing specific services rather than for fully managing their supply chains.

tandem A truck that has two drive axles or a trailer that has two axles.

tank cars Railcars designed to haul bulk liquid or gas commodities.

tank farm A large group of storage tanks, usually at the end of a pipeline, where liquid products are stored pending transfer to a tank truck or tankcars for further shipment.

tanker A cargo ship fitted with tanks for carrying liquid in bulk.

tapering rate A rate that increases with distance but not in direct proportion to the distance the commodity is shipped.

tare weight The weight of the vehicle when it is empty.

tariff A publication that contains a carrier's rates, accessorial charges, and rules.

technology The systematic knowledge of a particular discipline or science.

tenders An offer to provide a minimum shipment size or volume in exchange for a price proposal from the carrier. This may also represent the minimum volume a carrier will accept or the least amount of money the carrier will accept for transportation of a specific shipment.

Tennessee Tombigbee project A 234-mile artificial waterway that provides a connecting link between the Tennessee and Tombigbee rivers, thus linking the Tennessee River and inland Mississippi and Alabama with the Gulf of Mexico.

terminal delivery allowance A reduced rate that a carrier offers in return for the shipper or consignee tendering or picking up the freight at the carrier's terminal.

terminal Either end of a carrier line having facilities for the handling of freight and passengers.

terms of payment Contractual terms governing what will be given in exchange for the object of the transaction and the method of its delivery.

terms of sale The details or conditions of a transaction including details of the payment method, timing, legal obligations, freight terms, required documentation, insurance, responsibilities of the buyer and the seller, and when the buyer assumes risk for the shipment.

terms of trade In an international transaction, terms specified in the contract that determine which shipping responsibilities are handled by the exporter (the international supplier) and which are managed by the importer (the company making the purchase).

TEU Twenty-foot equivalent unit, a standard-size intermodal container.

third-degree price discrimination A situation where a seller sets two or more different prices for separate groups of buyers of essentially the same commodity.

third-party logistics provider (3PL) An external supplier that performs all or part of a company's logistics functions.

through bill of lading A single bill of lading covering receipt of the cargo at the point of origin for delivery to the ultimate consignee, using two or more modes of transportation both domestically and internationally.

time charter A rental or long-term lease that includes both the vessel and crew and is for a specific length of time.

time draft A customer's order to a financial institution holding the customer's funds that is payable at a specified point in the future or under certain circumstances.

time-definite services Delivery is guaranteed on a specific day or at a certain time of day.

time/service rate A rail rate that is based upon transit time.

time utility The usefulness or value of a good or service as a function of its timeliness in meeting seasonal demand; the demand for a particular commodity may exist only during certain periods of time.

time value of money This relates to the value of money over the lifetime of a project. As inflation reduces the value or purchasing capability of a dollar over the life of a project, this must be taken into consideration when establishing an interest or discount rate for the borrowed funds.

TL (truckload) A shipment weighing the minimum weight or more. Carriers give a rate reduction for shipping a TL-size shipment.

TOFC (trailer on flatcar) A method where a highway trailer complete with wheels and chassis is loaded on a flatcar.

ton-mile A unit of measurement utilizing the distance that freight is hauled, measured in miles, and the weight of the cargo being hauled, measured in tons, expressed as a product (that is, multiplied by each other); thus moving one ton for one mile generates one ton-mile.

total fixed costs Sum of costs that do not fluctuate with the business volume in the short run.

total landed cost Total cost of a product once it has arrived at the buyer's door, including the original cost of the item, all brokerage and logistics fees, complete shipping costs, customs duties, tariffs, taxes, insurance, currency conversion, crating costs, and handling fees.

tracing Determining a shipment's location during the course of a move.

tracking Observing, plotting, and reporting the location of cargo or a cargo item throughout the transportation channel.

trade lane The combination of the origin and destination points.

traffic management The buying and controlling of transportation services for a shipper or consignee, or both.

tramp An international water carrier that has no fixed route or published schedule; a shipper charters a tramp ship for a particular voyage or a given time period.

transfer of ownership Act of conveying possession along with its benefits and responsibilities.

transit privilege A carrier service that permits the shipper to stop the shipment in transit to perform a function that changes the commodity's physical characteristics, but to still pay the through rate.

transit time The total time that elapses between a shipment's pickup and its delivery.

transload freight Freight that must be handled individually and transferred between transportation equipment multiple times.

transloading facility A facility where shipments can be transferred from one mode to another or within the same mode between carriers. This may be a rail-to-truck transfer or a situation where larger shipments are broken down for delivery to individual stores or consignees.

transportation The act of moving goods or people from an origin to a required destination. It also includes the creation of time and place utilities.

transportation infrastructure The roads, highways, bridges, rail lines, seaways, and similar public works that are required for an industrial economy, or a portion of it, to function.

transportation interaction The relationship and business exchanges between the three primary groups involved in this area: the users, the providers, and the government.

transportation management system (TMS) Logistics tool used to improve management of a firm's transportation processes, both inbound and outbound. A TMS can help optimize the movements of freight into multiple facilities, assist in tracking the freight through the supply chain, and then manage the freight payment process to the user's carrier base.

travel agent A firm that provides passenger travel information; air, rail, and steamship ticketing; and hotel reservations. The carrier and hotel pay the travel agent a commission.

trip leasing A lease agreement between a private carrier and another firm for a single trip, most often utilized when for-hire authority is not available or desired.

trunk lines Oil pipelines used for the long-distance movements of crude oil, refined oil, or other liquid products.

U.S. Coast Guard   A branch of the U.S. military (but operating under the Department of Homeland Security during peacetime) whose mission is maritime law enforcement.

U.S. Customs and Border Protection (CBP)   The federal law enforcement agency charged with regulating and facilitating international trade, collecting import duties, and enforcing U.S. regulations, including trade, drug, and immigration laws.

U.S. Department of Transportation   A federal Cabinet department of the U.S. government, established in 1966, that is concerned with transportation.

U.S. Post Office   Federal agency responsible for the posting, receipt, sorting, handling, transmission, or delivery of mail.

unit charge   A shipping charge assessed for use of a facility or resource; variable according to use, but does not distinguish between passengers or freight within each unit.

unit load devices   Specialized containers used in air freighters that fit properly within the rounded fuselage of an aircraft.

unit train   An entire, uninterrupted locomotive, car, and caboose movement between an origin and destination.

unit volume pricing   This is a technique whereby the carrier sets its prices to utilize its capacity to the fullest. Multiple pickup discounts in the LTL area and multiple car rates in the railroad sector would be two examples.

user charges   Costs or fees that the user of a service or facility must pay to the party furnishing this service or facility. An example would be the landing fee an airline pays to an airport when one of its aircraft lands or takes off.

utility creation   This refers to a form utility that results from production, time, and place utilities created by logistics.

Valdez   Infamous oil tanker that in 1989 hit a reef and spilled an estimated 11 million gallons of crude oil in one of the largest oil spills in history.

value added   The value added to the product or service through the utility created by the logistics function.

value creation   Value is created when the performance quality meets or exceeds customer perceptions of logistics service.

value of service   The rates charged for a transportation service or a particular level of service influence the demand for the product and thus the demand to transport the product; this impact on demand can be assessed as the value of service provided to the user of the product.

value-of-service pricing   Pricing according to the value of the product the company is transporting; third-degree price discrimination; demand-oriented pricing; charging what the traffic will bear.

variable cost   A cost that fluctuates with the volume of business.

vehicle standards   The requirements imposed by the National Highway Transportation Safety Administration for the design and manufacture of motor vehicles.

visibility   In the context of cargo shipping, the capability to track the whereabouts of items throughout their journey through the channel.

voyage charter   A rental or term lease that includes both the vessel and crew and is for a specific trip.

water gateway   A port, canal, or harbor linking one body of water to another.

waterway use tax   A per-gallon tax assessed for barge carriers for waterway use.

weight break   The shipment volume at which the LTL charges equal the TL charges at the minimum weight.

weight-losing raw material   A raw material that loses weight in processing.

working conditions   The physical environment in which an employee works, including the actual space, the quality of ventilation, heat, and light, and the degree of safety.

World Shipping Council   An industry trade group representing general cargo and container shipping lines, including the world's ten largest container shipping companies.

zone price   The constant price of a product at all geographic locations within a zone.

Name Index

Subject Index